THE PUZZLE OF
LATIN AMERICAN
ECONOMIC DEVELOPMENT

THE PUZZLE OF LATIN AMERICAN ECONOMIC DEVELOPMENT

Patrice M. Franko

ROWMAN & LITTLEFIELD PUBLISHERS, INC.
Lanham • New York • London • Oxford

ROWMAN & LITTLEFIELD PUBLISHERS, INC.

Published in the United States of America
by Rowman & Littlefield Publishers, Inc.
4720 Boston Way, Lanham, Maryland 20706
http://www.rowmanlittlefield.com

12 Hid's Copse Road
Cumnor Hill, Oxford OX2 9JJ, England

British Library Cataloguing in Publication Information Available

Library of Congress Cataloging-in-Publication Data

Franko, Patrice M., 1958–
The puzzle of Latin American economic development / Patrice M.
Franko.
p.   cm.
Includes bibliographical references.
ISBN 0-8476-9524-7 (cloth : alk. paper).—ISBN 0-8476-9525-5
(paper : alk. paper)
1. Latin America—Economic conditions—1982–   2. Latin America—
Economic policy.   I. Title.
HC125.F682   1999
338.98.—dc21   99–23761   CIP

Printed in the United States of America

♾ ™ The paper used in this publication meets the minimum requirements of American
National Standard for Information Sciences—Permanence of Paper for Printed Library
Materials, ANSI/NISO Z39.48–1992.

FOR SANDY—
STILL, AND ALWAYS

CONTENTS

List of Tables and Figures   ix

Preface   xiii

Maps   xvii

  1 Development in Latin America: Conceptualizing Economic Change in
     the Region   1

  2 Historical Legacies: Patterns of Unequal and Unstable Growth   29

  3 Import Substitution Industrialization: Looking Inward for the Source
     of Economic Growth   51

  4 Latin America's Debt Crisis: The Limits of External Financing   79

  5 Price Stabilization: A Critical Ingredient for Sustained Growth   111

  6 The Role of the State: Defining a Desirable and Sustainable Level of
     State Activity   141

  7 New International Capital Flows: The Benefits (and Hidden Costs) of
     Latin America's Return to Markets   173

  8 Contemporary Trade Policy: Engine or Brakes for Growth?   211

  9 International Industrial Competitiveness: Improving the Quality of
     Labor, Technology, and Infrastructure   251

 10 Agricultural Policy: Sowing the Seeds of Equitable, Sustainable
     Growth in Latin America   283

 11 Poverty and Inequality: Addressing the Social Deficit in Latin America   311

 12 Health Policy: Investing in People's Future   351

 13 Education Policy: The Source of Equitable, Sustainable Growth   373

 14 Environmental Challenges: Internalizing the Costs of Development   401

 15 Lessons Learned: Cycles in Latin American Development   433

Appendix A   Summit of the Americas, Declaration of Principles   447

Appendix B   A Sampling of Institutional Actors in Latin American
             Economic Policy   455

Glossary   461

Bibliography   477

Index   501

About the Author   529

Tables and Figures

TABLES

Table 1.1	Quality of Life Indicators, circa 1996	7
Table 1.2	Communications Indicators	9
Table 1.3	Comparative Indicators of Economic Development	20
Table 2.1	Historical Per Capita Growth Rates	31
Table 2.2	Performance of Major Regions	31
Table 2.3	Factors Shaping Patterns of Growth	33
Table 2.4	Racial Composition in New World Economies	36
Table 2.5	Single Commodity Exports	38
Table 2.6	Geographic Distribution of Latin American Exports, 1929	40
Table 2.7	Foreign Investment in Latin America, circa 1913	42
Table 2.8	Per Capita Net Foreign Capital Position, 1938	43
Table 2.9	Foreign Investment/GDP	43
Table 2.10	Stylized Characteristics of Early Growth Patterns in Latin America	47
Table 3.1	State Enterprise Share in the Brazilian Economy, 1973	59
Table 3.2	Foreign Shares of Selected Industries, circa 1970	62
Table 3.3	Percentage Growth in GDP per Capita	66
Table 4.1	The Debt Trap: Long-Term Project Lending	82
Table 4.2	Real Interest Rates, 1974–1984	84
Table 4.3	Debt and Distinct Patterns of Development	85
Table 4.A	Real Exchange Rate Indexes	87
Table 4.4	Capital Flight from Selected Latin American Countries	89
Table 4.5	Debt Indicators for Latin America and the Caribbean, 1980–1990	90
Table 4.6	Exposure of Nine Major U.S. Banks to Six Highly Indebted Countries, 1984	92
Table 4.7	Secondary Market Price Spreads on Latin American Debt	96
Table 4.8	Brady Deals to Date in Latin America	104
Table 4.9	Debt Indicators for Latin America and the Caribbean	105
Table 5.1	Inflation in Latin America, 1990	112
Table 5.2	Overall Fiscal Surplus or Deficit in Latin America, 1982–1990	114
Table 5.3	Average Annual Rates of Growth of Money Supply in Latin America, 1982–1990	115
Table 5.4	National Interest Rates in Latin America	116
Table 5.5	Macroeconomic Indicators for Brazil, 1982–1998	125
Table 5.6	Bolivia: Various Indicators, 1982–1996	127
Table 5.7	Selected Latin American Indicators	135

Table 6.1   Privatization Statistics of Latin American Countries,
             1990–1995   158
Table 7.1   Market Capitalization   179
Table 7.2   Top Multinationals in Latin America   184
Table 8.1   Current Account Balance for Latin America, 1980–1985   215
Table 8.2   Average Tariff in Latin America: Selected Years, 1985–1998   217
Table 8.3   Rates of Growth of Exports and Imports   218
Table 8.4   Latin America: Exports and Imports, 1995   219
Table 8.5   Trade Performance in Three Different Periods   220
Table 8.6   Latin America and the Caribbean: Exports of Goods Traded
             According to Categories, 1965–1995   222
Table 8.7   Exports of Basic Products from Latin America and the
             Caribbean   223
Table 8.8   Latin America and the Caribbean: Index of Real Effective
             Exchange Rate of Exports   224
Table 8.9   Regional Balance of Payments   226
Table 8.10   U.S.-Mexican Trade   231
Table 8.11   Regional Integration Agreements in the Americas after 1990   234
Table 8.12   Exports from Trade Areas by Destination, 1996   238
Table 8.13   Exports, Imports, and Balance of Goods by Selected
             Countries and Geographic Areas, 1998   242
Table 8.14   U.S. Trade with Latin America and Other Regions   243
Table 8.15   U.S. Oil Imports from Latin America, 1995   243
Table 8.16   Ministerials, Vice Ministerials, and Business Forums   245
Table 9.1   Employment and Wage Data for Latin America   258
Table 9.2   Latin America: Urban Unemployment   259
Table 9.3   Average Incomes and Labor Income Disparities   262
Table 9.4   Science and Technology Indicators circa 1990   267
Table 9.5   Infrastructure Deficit   271
Table 10.1   Key Agricultural Inputs   289
Table 10.2   Labor Force Employment in Agriculture   290
Table 10.3   Agricultural Production Index   291
Table 10.4   Gross Domestic Product of Agriculture at Constant Market
             Prices   292
Table 11.1   Changes in the Extent of Poverty, 1970–1990   313
Table 11.2   Poverty Gap, 1989   314
Table 11.3   Indicators of Living Standards in Latin America, 1994   316
Table 11.4   Houses and Available Housing   317
Table 11.5   Communication Profiles   321
Table 11.6   Poverty and Ethnicity   323
Table 11.7   Latin America and the Caribbean: Estimates of Landless or
             Nearly Landless Peasant Families   324
Table 11.8   Social Indicators: Bottom and Top 20% of the Population   324
Table 11.9   Income Distribution: Percentage Share of Income or
             Consumption   327

Table 11.10   Gaps in Human Development for Latin America and the
               Caribbean, 1995   328
Table 11.A   Income Distribution in Brazil   329
Table 11.11   Average Annual Percentage Growth Rate of Spending on
               Education and Health   332
Table 11.12   Informal Sector Size   337
Table 11.13   Social Expenditures in Latin American Countries   345
Table 12.1   Mortality by General Causes in Latin America, 1960–2020 355
Table 12.2   Health Statistics by Country   356
Table 12.3   Diseases of the Americas: The Epidemiological Transition 357
Table 12.A   Health Care Spending   368
Table 13.1   Adult Literacy Rate   375
Table 13.2   Net Enrollment Rates by Level of Education   376
Table 13.3   Educational Performance Index   377
Table 13.4   Repeaters   378
Table 14.1   Energy Consumption per Capita   410
Table 14.2   Estimates of Petroleum Reserves and Crude Oil Production 411
Table 14.3   Percentage Change of Forests in Latin America   415
Table 14.4   Consumption of Fertilizers   417
Table 14.5   Examples of Policy Linkages   418
Table 14.6   Table of Actors   425
Table 14.7   Bolivia: Rural Electrification Program   427

FIGURES

Figure 2.1   Merchandise Exports to GDP, 1929   39
Figure 4.1   Total Disbursed External Debt of Latin America   81
Figure 4.2   Aggregate Net Resource Flows and Net Transfers: Latin
               America and the Caribbean   99
Figure 4.3   Gross National Product of Latin America and the Caribbean 100
Figure 4.4   Urban Unemployment in Latin America   101
Figure 4.5   Evolution of Real Wages   102
Figure 5.1   Brazilian Inflation   123
Figure 5.2   Argentine Inflation, 1970–1997   130
Figure 5.3   Mexican Inflation, 1988–1998   130
Figure 6.1   Central Government Expenditures   152
Figure 7.1   Net Resource Flows   175
Figure 7.2   Net Private Capital Flows   177
Figure 7.3   Net Foreign Direct Investment   182
Figure 7.4   Mexico's Current Account Deficit, 1985–1994   194
Figure 7.5   Current Account Deficit and the Real Exchange Rate   195
Figure 8.1   U.S. Trade by Region (late 1990s)   240
Figure 9.1   Brazilian Labor Productivity versus Select Countries   266
Figure 11.1   Latin America: Income Distribution, 1995   326

Figure 12.1   Intersectoral Cooperation: The Health-Development
             Framework   353
Figure 12.2   Bolivian Health Care Coverage, 1992   364
Figure 13.1   Percentage of Population with Some High School   390
Figure 13.2   Average Years of Schooling in Brazil, 1970 versus 1990 391
Figure 14.1   The Complexity of Environmental Decision Making   404

PREFACE

This book explores the puzzle of economic development in Latin America. Despite a similar starting point in the late 1800s, why didn't Latin America continue to grow at the pace of North America? How can we understand the economic path it took? What are the contemporary opportunities and constraints? This is not a general textbook on development, but it tries to provide the tools from development, trade, and finance for students to evaluate policy outcomes in Latin America. Without ignoring the historical antecedents, the central task of the text is an analysis of contemporary problems in Latin America. It is essentially the story of the character and contradictions of the new economic model in Latin America.

The text begins with the conceptual and historical foundations of development in Latin America. After briefly raising questions about the meaning of development and issues on the Latin America economic agenda in chapter 1, chapter 2 sets a broad historical context with a focus on inputs and outputs to characterize the period leading up to World War II. The question of primary product exports as an engine for growth is a central theme. Chapter 3 takes up import substitution industrialization, providing a theoretical and applied context for state-led development policy in the region. A case study of the auto industry is provided. The debt crisis and macroeconomic stabilization attempts are treated in Chapters 4 and 5. Questions of credibility and confidence return as constraints on flexible adjustment in the 1990s.

The challenge of the first part of the text was compressing into five chapters readings that used to constitute the bulk of a course on Latin American development. Beloved material is missing. But if a course on Latin America is to be one semester, we no longer have the luxury of spending two weeks on dependency theory, and then another two unraveling structuralism and import substitution industrialization. Where I used to spend nearly a month debating the debt problem and hyperinflation, if we do so there is less room for capital markets, trade integration, social policy, and the environment. Yet students need to understand the historical antecedents to appreciate the difficulties of contemporary policy. This book provides the background in a condensed approach, then moves on to the neoliberal model and contemporary challenges.

The second part of *The Puzzle of Latin American Economic Development* begins with an exploration of the role of the state in chapter 6. After discussing the downsizing of the state and efforts to enhance revenues, it takes up the question of the appropriate role of the state in Latin America, setting up a debate between the neoliberal view of a reduced state, the neoinstitutionalist prescription for institutional deepening, and a neostructuralist perspective of selective state action. This question of how much state intervention is appropriate in the economic arena arises in subsequent chapters. After discussing new capital flows to the region in chapter 7, we debate interventions by states to reduce vulnerability. In chapter 8, after a review of trends in trade liberalization, cooperative state action in integration efforts is discussed and the potential for a free trade area of the Americas is evaluated. Chapter 9 looks at the way in which globalization and marketization have affected competitiveness of industry and associated input markets for labor and technology, while chapter 10 takes up the contemporary challenges of agriculture. The unifying theme of these chapters is the optimal degree of policy intervention in the face of opportunities and constraints presented by globalization of finance and production.

The final group of chapters addresses the social and environmental challenges the region faces. After analysis of the problem of persistent poverty and inequality in the region in chapter 11, chapters 12 and 13 grapple with the problem and promise of health reform and education. The chapter on the environment in Latin America reinforces the environmental dimension that has run through the text. Social, gender, and environmental issues pervade the text because they are intimately connected with problems of stabilization, liberalization, and competitiveness in the global arena. The chapters on poverty, education, health, and the environment focus the student on these issues not as the effects of other policies but as profound challenges that must be addressed for Latin America to meet the goals of sustainable, equitable development.

This book is written for students with varying economics competencies. My students often ask whether they should take this course before or after taking trade, finance, and development. My experience is that the benefits accrue either way. If the student has strong theoretical tools, the depth of understanding of the problem of development in Latin America is more nuanced. However, engaging the difficult choices facing Latin American economic policy makers provides an applied context to acquire conceptual tools to solve the puzzle of strong, sustainable, and equitable growth in the region. For many students the luxury of how to sequence economics courses is a moot point. They come to a course on the economics of Latin America after realizing through a study abroad program or through interdisciplinary coursework that an understanding of economic trends in the region is critical to a comprehension of contemporary politics and society. For them, this will be their only course in Latin American economic development. This book therefore has no prerequisites other than an introductory sequence of economic principles. Throughout the text terms are explained, and box presentations provide illustrations and real-world examples. Highlighted words are defined in the glossary at the end of the book. This is designed to minimize the distraction to the better-equipped student eager to cut to the heart of the development issue.

Unlike many of the fine edited collections that provide a rich array of reading material, this text presents the fundamentals alongside the issues. An instructor may want to use a reader or create a personalized reader from some of the terrific pieces cited in the footnotes of each chapter. Writing this book has been a gratifying and humbling experience. There was so much engaging work on the problem of economic development in Latin America from which to draw. It was of course always daunting to condense a thoughtful, provocative, and well-researched book into a two- or three-line summary. Ideas for new cases examples and additional readings will be posted on the Rowman & Littlefield website associated with this text. Notes have been left in throughout the text to indicate to even the beginning student that the theory of economic development in Latin America is the product of a mosaic of ideas and policies. The more advanced student should aggressively track down these readings, to provide the nuanced texture of the debate in the field that a single text could never hope to convey. My thanks to all upon whose work I drew, and my apologies for any errors or omissions. I look forward to hearing from readers of this book, to clarify pieces that I may have misrepresented or point out works that I neglected to consult. A web site for this book may be found at http://rowmanlittlefield.com/puzzle/index.html.

This book is the legacy of years of teaching bright and engaged students in my course on contemporary economic policy in Latin America at Colby College, Maine. My students pushed me with their insightful questions (some of which I hope are answered herein) and motivated me with their enthusiasm for understanding Latin American economic development. My research assistants over the past few years have been active collaborators in this book effort. Justin Ackerman, Jeana Flahive, Justin Harvey, Joanna Meronk, and Mary Beth Thomson became data sleuths and Internet wizards. In addition to work during the semester, Erwin Godoy, Luisa Godoy, Gillian Morejon, and Jill Macaferri each spent a summer helping to develop this manuscript; each has left an indelible imprint on the text. Former assistants now with professional degrees of their own in the field—M. Holly Peirce, Marina Neto Grande, and David Edelstein—were valuable sources of information. I am very grateful for all of my students' hard work and dedication. Of course all the mistakes are mine alone. The enthusiastic and patient guidance of my editor, Susan McEachern, transformed what could have been an unpleasant struggle into a productive and energizing process. Copyeditor A. J. Sobczak and Assistant Managing Editor Lynn Weber's helpful suggestions considerably improved the manuscript. My family has supported my efforts not only on this text but throughout my academic endeavors. My stepchildren Dana and Josh were more than understanding when summer visits at the lake were structured around my work schedule. But my greatest debt of gratitude is to my husband, Sandy Maisel, who believed in my ability to see this project through even when I wasn't sure myself. He provided the pragmatic advice, personal inspiration, untiring encouragement, and steaming coffee every morning to take this project from conception to reality. I dedicate this book to him with all my love.

North and South America

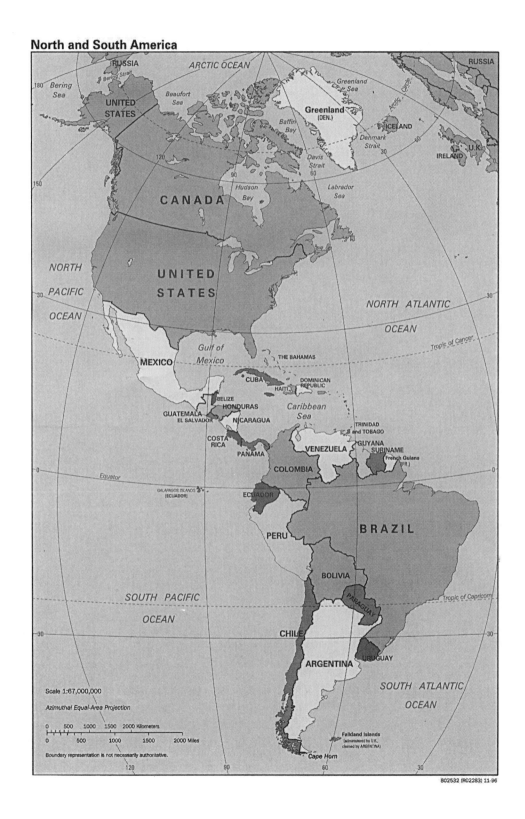

RUSSIA
ARCTIC OCEAN
Bering
Sea
Bering Strait
Beaufort
Sea
UNITED
STATES
180
Greenland
Sea
Greenland
(DEN.)
ICELAND
Arctic Circle
RUSSIA
60
IRELAND
U.K.
30
Baffin
Bay
Denmark
Strait
Davis
Strait
150
90
120
Hudson
Bay
60
Labrador
Sea

CANADA

NORTH
PACIFIC
OCEAN
30
UNITED
STATES
NORTH ATLANTIC
OCEAN
30

Tropic of Cancer
Gulf of
Mexico
THE BAHAMAS
MEXICO
CUBA
HAITI
DOMINICAN
REPUBLIC
BELIZE
GUATEMALA
EL SALVADOR
HONDURAS
NICARAGUA
Caribbean
Sea
TRINIDAD
and TOBAGO
COSTA
RICA
PANAMA
VENEZUELA
GUYANA
SURINAME
French Guiana
(FR.)
COLOMBIA
0
Equator
GALAPAGOS ISLANDS
[ECUADOR]
ECUADOR
0

PERU
BRAZIL

BOLIVIA

SOUTH PACIFIC
OCEAN
PARAGUAY
Tropic of Capricorn

30
CHILE
URUGUAY
ARGENTINA
SOUTH ATLANTIC
OCEAN
30

Scale 1:67,000,000

Azimuthal Equal-Area Projection

0   500   1000   1500   2000 Kilometers

0   500   1000   1500   2000 Miles

Boundary representation is not necessarily authoritative.

120
90
60
Cape Horn

Falkland Islands
(administered by U.K.,
claimed by ARGENTINA)

30

802532 (R02283) 11-96

South America

Central America and the Caribbean

Gulf of Mexico

North Atlantic Ocean

UNITED STATES

THE BAHAMAS

Grand Bahama

Tropic of Cancer

Yucatan Channel

MEXICO

Bahía de Campeche

Ciudad del Carmen

CUBA

Havana

Isla de la Juventud

JAMAICA

George Town   Cayman Islands (U.K.)

Montego Bay

U.S. Naval Base Guantanamo Bay

HAITI

Port-au-Prince

DOMINICAN REPUBLIC

Santo Domingo

Santiago

Puerto Rico (U.S.)

San Juan

Turks and Caicos Islands (U.K.)

Grand Turk

ANTIGUA AND BARBUDA

ST. KITTS AND NEVIS

Guadeloupe (FRANCE)

DOMINICA (FRANCE)

Martinique (FRANCE)

Fort-de-France

ST. LUCIA

Castries

BARBADOS

Bridgetown

ST. VINCENT AND THE GRENADINES

Kingstown

GRENADA

St. George's

TRINIDAD AND TOBAGO

Port-of-Spain

BELIZE

GUATEMALA

HONDURAS

Tegucigalpa

EL SALVADOR

NICARAGUA

SWAN ISLANDS (HONDURAS)

Isla de Providencia (COLOMBIA)

Isla de San Andrés (COLOMBIA)

Caribbean Sea

Aruba (NETH.)

Oranjestad

Netherlands Antilles

Curaçao (NETH.)

Willemstad

Bonaire

COSTA RICA

PANAMA

North Pacific Ocean

Isla del Coco (COSTA RICA)

VENEZUELA

COLOMBIA

Bogotá

GUYANA

BRAZIL

Scale 1:12,500,000
Lambert Conformal Conic Projection,
standard parallels 9°N and 17°N

0   100   200   300 Kilometers
0   100   200   300 Miles

Boundary representation is not necessarily authoritative.

CHAPTER ONE

DEVELOPMENT IN LATIN AMERICA

Conceptualizing Economic Change in the Region

Latin America contains cities of splendor . . . *(Courtesy of David Mangurian and the Inter-American Development Bank.)*

Latin Americans live in a complex economic system, simultaneously inhabiting the frontiers of finance and technology while also appearing hopelessly mired in a vicious circle of poverty. Consider the following stories.

> Uruguayan born financier Juan Navarro has become the buyout king of Latin America. From his modern, elegant offices in Buenos Aires, Argentina, Navarro has built his **equity** buyout company, Exxel Group, into one of the country's largest privately owned holdings, with 38 companies with over $3 billion in sales and $500 million in profits. Identifying undervalued firms in emerging markets, particularly the Mercosur countries of Brazil, Paraguay, Uruguay and Argentina, Navarro has convinced global investors such as GE, Travelers Insurance, Brown and Princeton Universities, Bankers Trust and General Motors to invest in supermarkets, the privatization of postal services and duty free shops, a Mastercard franchise and a music and electronics chain. With plans to expand these companies throughout the region, Navarro is positioning himself to go up against global giants such as the US Wal Mart and France's Carrefour. But for this aggressive Latin businessman, beating the odds, transforming underperforming companies into success stories, has become part of his game.[1]

> Brazilian soccer superstar Ronaldo has become the highest paid player in soccer history. A striker for the Italian team Inter Milan, he has signed deals with Nike and the Italian milk company Parmalat, as well as the number one beer maker, Brahma. Born in a poor favela or slum in Rio de Janeiro, Ronaldo had to quit soccer as a young boy because he didn't have the bus fare. Sixteen of Ronaldo's

. . . and pockets of poverty. *(Courtesy of David Mangurian and the Inter-American Development Bank.)*

Peruvians sign onto the World Wide Web. *(Courtesy of David Mangurian and the Inter-American Development Bank.)*

relatives live at the home where he grew up sleeping on the sofa with his older brother. The home is simply furnished—no telephone but a freezer and a television. Ronaldo is currently involved with a program in Brazil that takes poor kids out of the favelas and puts them in soccer camps to ensure that others have a chance for a future.[2]

Jessy Contreras, a cosmetology student, has long dreamed of logging on the Internet to study the latest Parisian trends. But saving enough money for a computer and access in a poor country like Peru where average income is less than $300 per month and few have private phones lines seemed too far a stretch. Fortunately, Peruvians are signing on in droves through the Peruvian Scientific Fund, a network begun with $7,000 in seed money from the U.N. development fund and other cooperative arrangements with universities, hospitals and nongovernmental organizations. Manuel Molla Madueno, a psychologist making somewhere in the range of $400–500 a month, is able to access the international journals and participate in bulletin boards. Local teachers are able to monitor Spanish culture from around the world. Unfortunately, expansion is limited by the slowness of Telefonica, the telephone company, in installing telephone circuits.[3]

Judith Yanira Viera, from El Salvador, is 18 years old. For over a year she worked in the Taiwanese-owned Mandarin International maquiladora factory in the San Marcos Free Trade Zone where she made shirts for the Gap, Eddie Bauer and J.C. Penney. From Monday to Thursday her shift went from seven in the morning until nine at night. On Fridays she would work straight through the night, starting at 7

A.M. and working until 4 A.M. She and her co-workers would sleep overnight on the factory floor. The following day, they would work from 7 A.M. until 5 P.M. Despite these very long hours, the most she ever earned was 750 colones, about $43 per month.[4]

Blasio and Claire Lehman struggle with the help of their two teenage sons to make approximately $900 a year as tobacco farmers in Brazil. With a simple home on a small piece of land, their dream when they married 22 years ago was a future in tobacco. But competition in the global tobacco market has soured their dream. Small farmers are forced, in a feudal-like arrangement, to take bank loans to buy kits comprised of seeds, pesticides, herbicides, fertilizers, a plastic sheet to cover the soil and protective gear for applying chemicals. When purchasing the kits they must pledge to sell their harvest to the companies. Fifteen percent of the payment for the first harvest is withheld to ensure complete delivery. If growers try to hold back crops because they disagree with the companies' valuation of the product, police assist the companies in seizing the crops. Illiteracy prevents farmers from mobilizing. Some farmers work in the tobacco processing plants to supplement crop income. The Lehmans' son Ismail has offered to quit school to make his family's ends meet—to save the $35 a month in bus fare. His future would brighten if the family could switch to another crop—but that would take money for start up costs. Too bad that the fiscal incentives provided to the big tobacco companies—including Philip Morris—couldn't find their way into more affordable transportation.[5]

Economically, Latin Americans range from the very wealthy Juan Navarro to the desperately poor Judith Yanira Viera. Resources available to create working lives may be the tobacco plant or on the complex strands of the Internet. International markets—for clothing, fruit, or sports—may propel some to relative affluence, but there are always the masses left behind in Ronaldo's favela. Economic life in Latin America is multilayered, from traditional rural life to dirty assembly factories to ultramodern skyscrapers in cosmopolitan cities. Latin American economic **development** is a puzzle. This text invites you to make some sense of this complex problem. Questions that we will explore in trying to unravel this puzzle include the following:

- How do so many fragments of different levels of economic life join to form a coherent whole?
- With a far wider range in income than industrial countries, with available technologies running from a simple shovel to a sophisticated financial machine, what kind of macroeconomic policies can address the complex microeconomic structure of Latin America?
- How does this multilayered economy interface with the world market?
- How have the pressures of globalization and the international market transformed the varied lives of Latin Americans?

As an introduction to the puzzle of Latin American economic development, this book attempts to clarify the complexity of economic life in Latin America. We will try to understand the potential that Juan Navarro has been able to tap, as well as the constraints keeping many farmers and factory workers in poverty.

A CONCEPTUAL MAP:
WHAT IS ECONOMIC DEVELOPMENT?

To understand the multilayered economic home of Jessy Contreras and Juan Navarro, we first need to contextualize it within a theory of economic development. The objectives of this chapter are to explore briefly the meaning of development and to highlight selected characteristics of economic policy and performance in Latin America. In an ideal world, readers of this text would have taken a course in economic development, international trade, and international finance before embarking on a study of Latin American economics. However, many students come to understand the economic importance of Latin America late in their academic career and simply don't have the

> **QUESTION FOR THOUGHT**
>
> Using the Internet site www.latinolink.com, identify stories of the economic lives of Latin Americans. (In the search feature you might try keywords such as agriculture, environment, indigenous people, maquilas, poverty, and women to bring up stories of interest to you.) What contrasts can you identify in the lives of people in the region?

time (or may even lack the interest) to backtrack through this important theoretical framework. The economic component may be only a small part of your broader interest in the region. For you, this section raises some of the questions that would be grappled with over a longer period of time in a course on development theory. Students with a background in development theory are invited to draw on their broader conceptual framework and apply it to the case of Latin America to answer a fundamental question of this book: How can we understand the process of economic development in the Latin American region? How can we reconcile the different lives of Ronaldo and the Lehmans within a single economic system?

Characteristics of Development

What characteristics do we normally associate with developed and less developed countries? Try ranking the United States, Mexico, Brazil, Ecuador, Canada, and France on the following measures:

- Which countries have the highest rates of urbanization?
- Which country has the highest per capita rate of **growth**?
- Which countries have the highest weight of international trade in the economy as measured by net exports/GDP?
- Which countries have the highest per capita carbon dioxide emissions?

Clean, potable water is a step forward for the community—but its collection is part of the double duty of work that women perform in the developing world. *(Courtesy of the Inter-American Development Bank.)*

The answers might surprise you. In Brazil, 78 percent live in urban areas; this is followed by 77 percent in Canada, 76 percent in the United States, 75 percent in Mexico, 73 percent in France, and 58 percent in Ecuador. Average growth of GNP from 1985 to 1995 per capita ranged from -0.08 percent in Brazil and 0.1 percent in Mexico to 0.4 percent in Canada, 0.8 percent in Ecuador, 1.3 percent in the United States, and 1.5 percent in France. Trade plays the greatest role in Canada at 71 percent of GDP in 1995, followed by Ecuador at 56 percent, Mexico at 48 percent, France at 43 percent, the United States at 24 percent, and Brazil at 15 percent. The United States has the dubious honor of leading the list of per capita carbon dioxide emissions at 19.1 metric tons in 1992, followed by Canada at 14.4, France at 6.3, Mexico at 3.8, Ecuador at 1.8, and Brazil at 1.4.

This short exercise raises a few questions. What do we mean by a developed (versus an underdeveloped) country? Are countries neatly classifiable? What is the diversity of economic experience within Latin America itself? How can we begin to think about a development strategy with relatively divergent conditions? You might want to open the most recent *World Development Report* or log on to the World Bank homepage at www.worldbank.org to look at some of the other data within the Latin America region and comparisons between Latin America and the rest of the world. Tables 1.1 and 1.2 summarize some of these statistics. You may be surprised at the diversity you find.

Table 1.1.   Quality of Life Indicators, circa 1996

Country	Child Malnutrition (% of children under 5)	Under 5 Mortality (rate per 1,000)	Female Life Expectancy at Birth	Access to Sanitation (% of urban population)	Growth of Private Consumption 1980–1996 (adjusted for inequality)
Guatemala	33	56	69	78	-0.1
Nicaragua	24	57	70	34	-1.3
Honduras	18	50	69	89	-0.1
Ecuador	17	40	73	87	-0.1
Bolivia	16	102	63	64	-0.4
Mexico	14	36	75	81	-0.1
El Salvador	11	40	72	78	1.4
Peru	11	58	71	62	-0.5
Colombia	8	31	73	76	0.6
Brazil	7	42	71	55	0
Panama	7	25	76	—	0.8
Venezuela	5	28	76	64	-0.4
Paraguay	4	45	74	—	0.8
Argentina	2	25	77	100	—
Costa Rica	2	15	79	—	0.4
Chile	1	13	78	100	1.4
United States	—	8	80	—	1.1

Source: World Bank, *World Development Report 1998/9* (New York: Oxford University Press/World Bank, 1999), 192–193.

Lack of access to adequate housing leaves millions in misery. *(Courtesy of David Mangurian and the Inter-American Development Bank.)*

Table I.2.   Communications Indicators

Country	Television Sets (per 1,000 people) 1996	Daily Newspapers (per 1,000 people) 1994	Telephone Main Lines 1996	Mobile Phones (per 1,000 people) 1996	Personal Computers (per 1,000 people) 1996	Internet Hosts (per 10,000 people) 1997
Panama	24	62	18	0	1.2	0.07
Honduras	80	44	31	0	—	0.94
Guatemala	122	23	31	4	2.8	0.79
Peru	142	86	60	8	5.9	2.63
Paraguay	144	42	36	7	—	0.47
Ecuador	148	72	73	5	3.9	0.9
Nicaragua	170	30	26	1	—	1.6
Venezuela	180	215	117	35	21.1	2.06
Colombia	188	64	118	13	23.3	1.81
Mexico	193	113	95	11	29.0	3.72
Bolivia	202	69	47	4	—	0.69
Costa Rica	220	99	155	14	—	12.14
El Salvador	250	50	56	3	—	0.34
Chile	280	100	156	23	45.1	13.12
Brazil	289	45	96	16	18.4	4.2
Argentina	347	138	174	16	24.6	5.32
Latin America average	217	83	185	5	17.1	6.53
East Asia and Pacific	228	28	41	7	4.5	0.57
Canada	709	189	602	114	192.5	228.05
United States	806	228	640	165	362.4	442.11

Source: World Bank, *World Development Report 1998/9* (New York: Oxford University Press/World Bank, 1999), 226–227.

In table 1.1, we can see that although some countries in Latin America exhibit poor performance on indicators of child malnutrition and child mortality, others perform extremely well. Guatemala, for example, is the worst performer with nearly one in three children malnourished, but in Costa Rica only 2 percent of children suffer from hunger. Similarly, Guatemala, Nicaragua, and Bolivia demonstrate tragic rates of infant mortality, whereas Chile, Argentina, and Costa Rica demonstrate strong records. In Brazil only 55 percent of the population has access to in-house sanitation as measured by connections to public sewers or household systems such as flush latrines, septic systems, or communal toilets. Honduras, Ecuador, Mexico, Argentina, and Chile all have rates higher than 80 percent. Throughout the region the growth of private consumption has been slow or negative. This number measures the change in consumption per capita, adjusted for the degree of inequality in the country. It is a measure of whether the population, on average, is materially better off. As we will see in this text, the long hard road of economic adjustment to the debt shocks and the tough macroeconomic stabilization packages of the 1980s and 1990s have left most Latin Americans with little more in their homes than they had when they started the decade.

Table 1.2 gives a few measures of what you might expect to find in homes in the Americas. There are about 10 times as many TVs in the United States (per 1,000 people) than there are in Honduras and about three times as many mobile phones in Canada than in Venezuela. Chileans have access to about twice as many computers per person as do Brazilians, and Costa Ricans lead Latin America with the most Internet hosts per person. Of course we want to be careful with these data; cross-country data are always difficult to collect, especially when you are estimating houses with access to sanitation or computers. Furthermore, we don't want to suggest that televisions or mobile phones are the bellwethers of what it means to be developed. We need to be aware of data difficulties even as we develop more sophisticated measures to evaluate progress and poverty in the region in later chapters.

What do we mean by development?

When we think about the challenges of development and underdevelopment in Latin America, what do we really mean? Are TVs and toilets the goal of development? How does "promoting development" translate into something concrete for the policy maker to target? U.S. President Harry S Truman, in his inauguration speech in January 1949, envisioned a bold new program, based on "the concepts of democratic fair-dealing," to make the "benefits of our scientific and industrial progress available for the improvement and growth of underdeveloped areas."[6] Although the word "underdeveloped" had been introduced in 1942 by Wilfred Benson, a member of the secretariat of the International Labor Organization, development economists such as Paul Rosenstein-Rodan spoke of "economically backward areas," and Arthur Lewis characterized the emerging challenge as the gap between rich and poor countries throughout the 1940s. Truman popularized the term "underdevelopment" but did not clearly define it. Since Truman, the goal of development has been to undo the hardships of underdevelopment—without a clear statement of the positive objective. What does it mean to be developed? With the advent of the Cold War, the world was divided into industrial market economies, the communist or "second" world, and finally the rest of the globe or the "third" world. These nations were once again the residual—what was left over when the rest of the counting was done. Since the collapse of the Berlin Wall, the second world has euphemistically been referred to as "transitional economies."

> **QUESTION FOR THOUGHT**
>
> How do you define development? List elements that you believe are important in defining a policy objective of promoting economic development.

What exactly are they transitioning toward? What is a usable definition of the goal of "development"?

In common language, development describes a process in which the potential of an organism is released to achieve its mature form. Dictionary definitions point to growth or expansion to bring about a more advanced state. When we think of the development of a tree or an animal, we have a clear idea of the appearance of the mature, advanced form. In economics we find ourselves in a bit of trouble. We can measure degrees of industrialization or access to a wider array of consumer products, but things become murky when we try to associate the terms "modern," "mature," and "developed" with societies having well-articulated economic infrastructures. Given the long list of ills associated with modern society, we should be clear in our understanding that more sophisticated production techniques and a wider range of electronic toys do not necessarily imply a better or happier society. In addition, we don't know which members of society have access to the gains of economic growth. More industrialization—particularly with the associated environmental costs—does not necessarily mean an increase in the well-being of citizens.

How then should we think about development? Is a developed country simply the opposite of a poor country? Is a developing country a rich country in the making? Box 1.1 presents the thoughts of development economists and practitioners on defining the term. Generally, they find it easier to agree on what constitutes the alleviation of poverty and meeting the basic needs of a population than on what represents the achievement of wealth or the satisfaction of material wants. This text looks at development as a process of meeting the basic human

> **QUESTION FOR THOUGHT**
>
> Which definitions of development do you find most compelling? Is there anything missing as compared to your own view of development? Can you identify ways in which the definition of development has changed over time?

needs of the population and enhancing options for the allocation of economic resources both today and in the future to increase the choices citizens have in their daily lives. It pays particular attention to how much is produced and for whom, and it addresses the environmental sustainability of production for future generations.

Growth versus Development

From the definitions in box 1.1, we can see that most economists agree: development is far more than economic growth. It is useful, however, to clarify the difference between the two terms. Joseph Schumpeter distinguishes growth as a process of gradual change, with all quantities, such as wealth, savings, and population, increasing slowly and continuously; development is characterized as rapidly propelled by innovations.[24] Robert Lucas defines growth as the increase of income proportional to the increase of population, and development as the process whereby income increases more rapidly than population. In other words, growth does not presuppose technical change; development does.[25] For both Schumpeter and Lucas—economists of very different dispositions—development centrally engages the question of how **technological change** takes place in an economy. A key element in development is the management of technological change or how technology is used to transform the economic structure. This of course presupposes that technology is in scarce supply and its use has a price. In this sense, policy matters very much. Economic development is not simply driven by factor endowments or the quantity of resources but by how land, labor, and capital are combined in new ways to increase productivity and the choices available to a population.

Box 1.1.   Development, Underdevelopment, and Growth: An Evolution of Definitions

WEBSTER'S DICTIONARY

"The act, process, or result of developing; the state of being developed; a gradual unfolding by which something is developed, a gradual advance or growth through progressive changes."

W. ARTHUR LEWIS (1954)

"The central fact of economic development is rapid capital accumulation, including knowledge and skills with capital."[7]

CELSO FURTADO (1964)

"Economic development, being fundamentally a process of incorporating and diffusing new techniques, implies changes of a structural nature in both the systems of production and distribution of income. The way in which these changes take place depends, to a large extent, on the degree of flexibility of the institutional framework within which the economy operates."[8]

P. BAUER AND B. YAMEY (1967)

"The widening of the range of alternatives open to people as consumers and producers."[9]

B. HIGGINS (1968)

"A discernible rise in total and in per capita income, widely diffused throughout occupational and income groups, continuing for at least two generations and becoming cumulative."[10]

THEOTONIO DOS SANTOS (1968)

"Development means advancement towards a certain well-defined general objective which corresponds to the specific condition of man and society or can be found in the most advanced societies of the modern world. The model is variously known as modern society, mass society and so on."[11]

DENIS GOULET (1971)

"Underdevelopment is shocking: the squalor, disease, unnecessary deaths, and hopelessness of it all! No man understands if underdevelopment remains for him a mere statistic reflecting low income, poor housing, premature mortality, or underdevelopment. The most empathetic observer can speak objectively about underdevelopment only after undergoing, personally or vicariously, the 'shock of underdevelopment.' "[12]

CHARLES K. WILBER (1973)

"Development itself is simply a means to the human ascent."[13]

DUDLEY SEERS (1972)

"The questions to ask about a country's development are therefore: what has been happening to poverty? What has been happening to unemployment? What has been happening to inequality? If all three of these have declined from high levels, then beyond doubt this has been a period of development for the country concerned."[14]

SIMON KUZNETS (1973)

"A country's economic growth may be defined as a long-term rise in capacity to supply increasingly diverse economic goods to its population, this growing capacity based on advancing technology and the institutional and ideological adjustments that it demands."[15]

JAMES J. LAMB (1973)

"If there is to be a possibility of choosing a human path so that all human beings may become the active subjects of their own history, it must begin at the level of new analysis. Development should be a struggle to create criteria, goals, and means for self-liberation from misery, inequity, and dependency in all forms. Crucially, it should be the process a people choose which heals them from historical trauma, and enables them to achieve a newness on their own terms."[16]

PAUL STREETEN (1979)

"A basic-needs approach to development starts with the objective of providing the opportunities for the full physical, mental, and social development of the human personality and then derives ways of achieving this objective."[17]

PETER J. A. HENRIOT (1981)

" 'Underdevelopment' is seen as the flip side of the coin of 'development.' It refers to the process whereby a country, characterized by subsistence agriculture and domestic production, progressively becomes integrated as a dependency into the world market through patterns of trade and/or investment."[18]

ORTHODOX PARADIGM (1980s)

"The view of the historical process contained in the orthodox paradigm is clear from this characterization: it is one in which developing societies move toward ever greater availability of goods and services for their citizens."[19]

WORLD COMMISSION ON ENVIRONMENT AND DEVELOPMENT (1987)

"Humanity has the ability to make development sustainable—to ensure that it meets the needs of the present without compromising the ability of future generations to meet their own needs. . . . **sustainable development** is not a fixed state of harmony, but rather a process of change in which the exploitation of resources, the directions of investment, the orientation of technological development, and institutional change are made consistent with future as well as present needs."[20]

GERALD M. MEIER (1995)

"Although requiring careful interpretation, perhaps the definition that would now gain widest approval is one that defines economic development as the process whereby the real per capita income of a country increases over a long period of time—subject to the stipulations that the number of people below an 'absolute poverty line' does not increase, and that the distribution of income does not become more equal."[21]

(continued)

(continued)

AMARTYA SEN (1998)

"It is not hard to see why the concept of development is so essential in general. Economic problems do, of course, involve logistics issues, and a lot of it is undoubtedly 'engineering' of one kind or another. On the other hand, the success of all this has to be judged ultimately in terms of what it does to lives of human beings. The enhancement of living conditions must clearly be an essential—if not the essential—object of the entire economic exercise and that enhancement is an integral part of the concept of development."[22]

JOSEPH E. STIGLITZ (1998)

"It used to be that development was seen as simply increasing GDP. Today we have a broader set of objectives, including democratic development, egalitarian development, sustainable development, and higher living standards."[23]

New technologies require new ways of doing things. The leap from feudalism to early capitalism was propelled by technological changes—the introduction of the horse and plow as well as the three-field crop rotation system—that made an agricultural surplus possible. But like the transition into early capitalism, the contemporary process can be politically and socially tumultuous. Development policy can be viewed as the implementation of economic tools when political and social structures as well as economic institutions are rapidly changing. In contrast to the thrust of standard economic theory, where in principle we begin with the ceteris paribus conditions, or "all else held constant," development policy is harder to carry out consistently due to simultaneous changes in a number of arenas. An economic policy maker in an industrialized country may be able to rely on a bit of automatic pilot under stable conditions; in the developing world, navigation is far more demanding with a variety of new challenges at each turn.

This text chronicles the development journey of Latin America. We begin by trying to understand the attempts of Latin American policy makers to promote growth and development in the region. Chapter 2 focuses on the engine of trade and Latin America's export performance in the late colonial and early independence periods. Chapter 3 looks at a growth strategy widely adopted in the region from roughly the 1950s through the 1980s: import substitution industrialization. We can see, in both cases, that the strategy centered largely on the problem of growth and made less progress in the arena of social and environmental change. In chapters 4 and 5 we discuss two unintended results of the development strategies adopted: high rates of inflation and increased vulnerability to macroeconomic shocks. The policy response to economic disequilibrium was to step back and rely more on markets and less on state intervention in the economy. Chapter 6 takes up this changed role of the state under the neoliberal model; chapters 7 and 8 look at its implications for international capital flows and trade. How industry and agriculture have fared under a more open, internationalized economic model is taken up in chapters 9 and 10. Although policies that transformed the structure of Latin American economies from closed to open markets have been largely successful in macroeconomic terms, the rest of our book explores some of the deficits in human and social development hindering sustainable growth.

Basic Human Needs versus Growth as Measures of Development

In addition to thinking about how economies change, we must raise the question of growth: who benefits from new economic opportunities? Technological change—new combinations of capital and labor to produce a surplus—does not address the general well-being of society. Does the process of economic development help the rich or the poor? A modest goal of development might be for a developed nation to meet the basic human needs of its population. Paul Streeten defines enhancing basic human needs as improving income earning opportunities for the poor, reforming public services that reach the poor, augmenting the flow of goods and services to meet the needs of all members of the household, and increasing the participation of the poor in the policy-making arena.[26] Streeten goes on to suggest why growth itself is not a good measure of economic development. Rather than generating the predicted theoretical results that growth would trickle down to the poor or that governments would extend benefits through progressive taxation or social services, Streeten argues that growth has been accompanied by increasing **dualism.** That is, when countries grow as measured by annual GDP growth rates, the rich often become richer and the poor more destitute in the process of change. We see the expansion of the modern, capitalist sector alongside a traditional, backward sector—two distinctly different worlds growing side by side. Dualism—the simultaneous existence of modern and traditional economies—complicates the policy maker's task. More important, if an economy magnetized by growth neglects the plight of the poor, people without assets are marginalized by the growth process and made even worse off. Those without land, capital, or education, like the poor peasant in feudal times who lost access to the agricultural commons, can be pushed into the margins of society. Without access to resources, the poor can become poorer. Their attempts to scrape together a subsistence existence often pressure the environment as desperation drives people to use up land or forests or dump open sewage or waste today without thought of tomorrow—for tomorrow holds little promise when they struggle with hunger or sickness.

For development economists such as Todaro, growth must be accompanied by a change in the economic and social rules of the game. Todaro defines development, in addition to raising people's living levels, as "creating conditions conducive to the growth of people's self-esteem through the establishment of social, political, and economic systems and institutions that promote human dignity and respect and increasing people's freedom by enlarging the range of their choice variables."[27] But this is a difficult task. As we will see in chapters 10 and 11, the social deficit in Latin America must be addressed to promote an equitable and sustainable development policy. As we investigate poverty in chapter 10, we will analyze ways of measuring human development including the **HDI** (human development index), which is a composite index comprising three indicators: life expectancy (representing a long and healthy life), educational attainment (representing knowledge), and real, inflation-adjusted GDP (representing a decent standard of living). Poverty and the associated social challenges of promoting education and growth are discussed in chapters 11 and 12.

The United Nations, in its *Human Development Report*, suggests that a human development paradigm incorporates four elements—productivity, equity, sustainability, and **empowerment**. People must be enabled to increase their own productivity and participate as fully in the economy as their own talents allow. Economic growth is therefore a subset of human development models. To encourage fair outcomes, people must have access to equal opportunities. Economic and environmental sustainability is enhanced when all forms of capital—physical, human, and environmental—are replenished to promote access to opportunity, which must be for future generations as well as the present. Finally, development must be by people, not for them. People must participate fully in the decisions and processes that shape their lives for the benefits of genuine development.

Is There a Development Theory?

If the goal is to imitate industrial countries, is the road to a modern economy well marked by stages? Or are there different pathways to modernization? If countries are to progress economically and improve the quality of life for their inhabitants, what is the best way to do it? Is there a theory of economic development that is distinct from the economic theory we apply to our understanding of industrially advanced countries?

These are questions that economists have been grappling with for centuries. Adam Smith in *The Wealth of Nations* puzzled over how nations can best mobilize resources to produce the greatest wealth for their citizens. Box 1.2 highlights some of the conceptual guides that pioneers of development theory have offered in response to these questions. In contemporary times economists have struggled with the problem of understanding why some countries grow and others do not. This text does not assume that countries undergoing rapid economic change will necessarily follow the same pathway to achieve improvements in the quality of life. There may be different strategies to achieve the goal of raising the well-being of their citizens. The new global context for growth that Latin American economies face as we begin the twenty-first century requires a different set of policies from the ones used by the United States and Europe during the industrial revolution. A country's place in the region, its size, and its natural endowments may also condition its development strategy. Development theory and practice is dynamic, evolving over time.

If development is more than growth, development theory must explain not only how nations grow but also how their economic structures adapt to meet new challenges over time. If the modest goal is to meet basic needs, is growth in the developing world different from growth in industrialized countries? Are poor countries intrinsically different from rich ones? How? What are some of the defining characteristics? Can the same combination of economic tools be used to address the problems confronted by policy makers in less industrialized as compared

Box 1.2. Pioneers in Economic Development

WALT W. ROSTOW (NEW YORK CITY 1916–)

Walt W. Rostow, an American economic historian, is known for his theory of the stages of economic growth. For Rostow, development was a linear process that began with traditional society, which then moved into the stage of "preconditions for take-off into self sustaining growth." The economy would then "take off," follow "the road to maturity," and finally hit "the age of high mass consumption." Rostow believed that the "takeoff" would be caused by an increase in investment, leading manufacturing sectors, and the existence of an institutional framework consistent with expansion.

PAUL ROSENSTEIN-RODAN (AUSTRIA-HUNGARY 1902–1985)

Development economist Paul Rosenstein-Rodan advanced the concept of balanced growth. He believed that in order to achieve sustained growth, an economy must develop various industries simultaneously, requiring a coordination of investment or a "big push." He was one of the first economists to emphasize market failure and the need for state intervention.

RAGNAR NURSKE (ESTONIA 1907–1959)

Ragnar Nurske, like Rosenstein-Rodan, advocated balanced growth and further elaborated upon his colleague's work. For Nurske, small market economies were victims of a vicious cycle hindering growth. The small size of the market was responsible for the limited amount of production and income, and for the perpetual poverty and stagnation. To break the cycle, an economy needed a "big push" coordinated by a government properly allocating domestic and foreign resources.

ALBERT OTTO HIRSCHMAN (GERMANY 1915–)

Economist Albert O. Hirschman provided a contrary thesis: the idea of unbalanced growth as the principal strategy for development. Building on the concept of development as a state of disequilibrium, Hirschman identified and attacked bottlenecks to growth. Like Nurske and Rosenstein-Rodan, he called for government intervention to achieve sustained growth. Yet Hirschman believed that decision making and entrepreneurial skills were scarce in underdeveloped economies. Governments should therefore concentrate this scarce resource in a few sectors rather than on the entire economy. Planners and policy makers would need to use "forward and backward linkages" between industries to attack the bottlenecks within an economy.

W. ARTHUR LEWIS (WEST INDIES 1915–1991)

W. Arthur Lewis, a Nobel Prize winner in economics in 1979, formulated a model in the 1950s known as "economic development with unlimited supplies of labor." Lewis's structure of the economy has a dualistic nature, with divisions into the subsistence sector and the capitalist sector. According to Lewis, underdeveloped economies are characterized by a large subsistence sector with surplus labor and a small capitalist sector, which contributes directly to a low savings rate. Economic growth occurs when there is an increase in the savings rate, which is made possible only when the capitalist sector expands and absorbs the surplus labor from the agricultural sector.

RAÚL PREBISCH (ARGENTINA 1901–1986)

Raúl Prebisch was an Argentine economist and former chairman of the U.N. Economic Commission for Latin America (ECLA). Prebisch is well known for the "Prebisch-

(continued)

(continued)

Singer thesis," which claims that the export of primary products prevalent in developing countries results in a decline of terms of trade—the price of exports compared to the price of imports. There are two important implications of the thesis: first, that a decline in terms of trade results in the transfer of income from the periphery (the developing countries) to the center (the developed countries), and second, the periphery then needs to export more and more to be able to import the same quantities as before. Prebisch's pessimism on terms of trade was used to support import-substitution industrialization policies in Latin America.

PAUL ALEXANDER BARAN (UKRAINE 1910–1964)

Paul Baran is known for his neo-Marxist view of development and for his contributions to the dependency school of thought. Although not completely agreeing with Marx, Baran used Marxist principles to locate the causes of underdevelopment. Countries suffer from low per capita income because the ruling classes fail to productively use the surplus extracted from peasants and wage laborers. Instead, they hold monopoly power over production and the political system. To break this monopoly power and achieve growth, a revolution must take place to replace the dominant classes with one committed to social and economic development.

GUSTAV RANIS (GERMANY 1929–) AND JOHN FEI (1923–1996)

Gustav Ranis's early work focused on the economic development of Japan in the post-Meiji period and used it as a successful case of transition to modern growth. From there he began to focus on balanced growth and teamed up with another economist, John Fei, to further develop concepts used by Rostow and Lewis. For both Ranis and Fei, the process of "takeoff," as introduced by Rostow, would occur when the industrial sector absorbed both redundant labor and the disguised unemployed, using Lewis's process of absorption of surplus labor.

IRMA ADELMAN (ROMANIA 1930–)

Irma Adelman is well known for a forty-three-nation cross-country study done with Cynthia T. Morris. The results of the study show an increase in income inequality as poorer nations grow. Both women also provided a quantitative analysis of the effects of social and political factors on economic conditions. Prior to their work, social and political factors had been ignored. Adelman also worked with Sherman Robinson in the area of policy analysis and economic planning for developing countries and the application of computable general equilibrium models. Her current interests include land reform, trends in income distribution and poverty, agriculture-development-led industrialization, and the modeling of institutional change.

ANNE KRUEGER (NEW YORK 1934–)

Anne Krueger's work on foreign trade controls creating windfall gains, known as rent-seeking behavior, and its relationship to corruption in developing countries influenced a new theory in development—the new political economy. Her early work concentrated on international trade and payments theory. She is currently researching policy reform in developing countries, the political economy of policy formation, and U.S. economic policy toward developing countries.

REFERENCES

Blaug, Mark. *Who's Who in Economics.* Cambridge, Mass.: MIT Press, 1986.
———. *Great Economists since Keynes: An Introduction to the Lives of One Hundred Modern Economists.* Totowa, N.J.: Barnes and Noble, 1985.

Blomstrom, Magnus, and Bjorn Hettne. *Development Theory in Transition: The Dependency Debate and Beyond, Third World Responses.* London: Zed, 1984.

Hunt, Diana. *Economic Theories of Development: An Analysis of Competing Paradigms.* Savage, Md.: Barnes and Noble Books, 1989.

Lewis, John P., and Valeriana Kallab, eds. *Development Strategies Reconsidered.* U.S.-Third World Policy Perspective, no. 5. Washington, D.C.: Overseas Development Council, 1986.

Meier, Gerald M. "From Colonial Economics to Development Economics." In *From Classical Economics to Development Economics.* New York: St. Martin's, 1994.

Meier, Gerald M., and Dudley Seers. *Pioneers in Development.* Oxford: Oxford University Press, 1984.

Toye, John. *Dilemmas of Development.* 2d ed. Oxford: Blackwell, 1987.

to more industrialized countries? Should it be? Before we answer these questions, it will be useful to compare statistics of a Central American nation, Mexico, with the United States and a European nation, Spain, as a way of thinking about economic contrasts.

From table 1.3 we note certain differences between a large industrial nation, the United States; a smaller industrial economy, Spain; and a largely developing economy, Mexico. On the macroeconomic front, Mexico delivered relatively strong growth rates for 1996, in part as a turnaround from a financial crisis in 1994–1995. Inflation, a sign of underlying instability, is higher in Mexico than in the two industrial countries. Mexico, like Spain, has found growth in the agricultural sector problematic, as low productivity has intervened with competitiveness. Cheaper labor in the manufacturing sector has, however, contributed to growth in industrial production. As smaller economies, Mexico and Spain are more open to international trade, with imports and exports together accounting for up to 50 percent of GDP. In financial terms, we can see Mexico's greater vulnerability to international capital. Although U.S. financial markets can provide up to 132 percent of domestic credit, in Mexico domestic intermediation is limited to just over 50 percent. Mexico also lags considerably in indicators of scientific as well as basic infrastructure. The number of scientists and engineers per million inhabitants is 5 percent that of the United States; it has only 15 percent as many telephone lines to carry personal and commercial traffic. Health expenditures as a percentage of GDP are nearly one third lower than in the United States, a problem particularly for Mexico's poor. The highly unequal distribution of income in Mexico is one of the largest impediments to a sustainable development policy.

> **DATA EXTENSION**
>
> Consulting the sources for table 1.3, locate data for other Latin American countries. Select different country types (large and small) from different subregions. For example, consider the performance of Brazil, Ecuador, Guatemala, and Chile. How are they alike? Different?

Although there is considerable diversity in terms of the performance of Latin American nations on each of these indicators, comparing Mexico with Spain and the United States provides insight into some of the characteristics of economies in

Table 1.3. Comparative Indicators of Economic Development

	United States	Spain	Mexico
Macroeconomic indicators			
Real GDP (annual % change for 1996)	2.40	2.20	5.10
Inflation (GDP deflator for 1993–1995)	2.3	4.3	20.7
Unemployment (1996 est.)	5.40%	22%	10%
Gross domestic saving (as % of GDP for 1995)	15	22	19
Growth of output by sector			
Agriculture (annual % growth for 1990–1995)	3.60	−1.70	0.40
Industrial production growth rate (% for 1996)	3.10	5	11
International sector			
Exports of goods and services (as % of GDP for 1995)	11	24	25
Imports of goods and services (as % of GDP for 1995)	13	23	22
Financial sector			
Domestic credit provided by banking sector (as % of GDP for 1995)	132.10	105.70	53.10
Stock market (value traded as % of GDP for 1995)	10.70	73.50	13.70
Technology			
Scientists and engineers in R&D (per million people for 1981–1992)	3,873	956	226
Communication, transportation, and pollution			
Telephone mainlines (per 1,000 people for 1995)	627	385	96
Television sets (per 1,000 people for 1995)	776	490	192
Vehicles (per 1,000 people for 1995)	748	454	131
Carbon dioxide emissions (per capita metric tons for 1992)	19.1	5.7	3.8
Human development indicators			
Income distribution	(for 1985)	(for 1988)	(for 1992)
• Lowest 20%	4.7	18.1	4.1
• Second 20%	11	23.4	7.8
• Third 20%	17.4	36.6	12.5
• Fourth 20%	25	21.8	20.2
• Highest 20%	41.9	—	55.3
Literacy (% of age 15 and older who read and write)	97 (1979 est.)	96 (1986 est.)	89.6 (1996 est.)
Health (expenditures, private and public, as % of GDP for 1990–1995)	14.30	17.40	5.30
Access to sanitation (% of population for 1994–95)	85	97	70

Sources: International Monetary Fund, *World Economic Outlook, 1997;* Central Intelligence Agency, *The World Fact Book,* available on the World Wide Web at www.odci.gov/cia; and World Bank, *World Development Indicators, 1997* (Washington, D.C.: World Bank, 1997).

Latin America. As we proceed, we will see questions of macroeconomic stability, depth of markets, distributional issues, and the role of the state generating considerable controversy.

Challenges for Development Policy in Latin America

Developing countries must contend with a set of economic issues that make economic policy more difficult—and for a student perhaps more interesting—than traditional theory. Throughout this text we will analyze how these issues have been addressed in Latin America from its earliest economic history through contemporary times. It is useful to raise some of these challenges here, to help you begin to think about the dilemmas of economic policy making in the region. It is important to remember, however, that each of these challenges plays out differently in each country in Latin America: the diversity of experience is probably as great as the set of common problems.

INTERNAL VERSUS EXTERNAL MACROECONOMIC BALANCE

Developing countries, in large part because by definition they are capital poor, find themselves reliant on international capital to fuel the growth process. Unlike the United States (which until recently focused little on domestic economic policy effects on the international sector because they were relatively small), Latin American countries have had to weigh carefully the effects of changes in domestic macropolicy—traditional money supply and fiscal tools—against their effects on the external sector. There is a constant tension between internal and external balance. Lessons from economic history in Latin America will show that a one-sided focus on either the internal or the external sector results in imbalances and the deterioration of the economic plan. Integrating a nation into international capital markets raises important complexities. This may be done in the form of debt (as in the 1890s and 1970s) or through foreign direct investment in the economy, raising questions of multinational presence (such as in the control of United Fruit Company in Guatemala in the 1950s) or contemporary questions of international labor standards. Countries that orient themselves toward the international export economy—as in Chile through copper or in Ecuador through oil—may have to sacrifice domestic goals to maintain an exchange rate that is compatible with international market conditions. One response to the trade conundrum has been to pursue alternate trade regimes in the form of integration efforts such as the Central American Common Market (CACM) or the South American Common Market (Mercosur). We will be grappling with the need to achieve internal and external balance throughout this text.

Internationalization creates a wide range of opportunities, but it also introduces constraints in domestic policy making. For new entrepreneurs like Juan Navarro, it creates profit, but it may limit the relative well-being of the Lehman family. For now, remember that developing economies are especially sensitive to the internal versus external balance.

Stability versus Change: The Question of Timing

The process of development involves rapid structural change, yet economic agents like certainty. In traditional economic models we assume perfect information held by all agents. We know that divergence from the assumption of perfect information leads to inefficiencies in the market. How to handle economic agents' need for greater certainty and good information in an environment that is almost by definition (when it is working best) characterized by change is a challenge of policy makers in the developing world. Officials in Latin America must at once be agents of change, flexibly adapting to the dynamic needs of the economic transformation, while also acting as strict guardians of confidence and stability. The ability to walk this policy tightrope as both motivators and moderators of change often defines policy success. When governments fail to navigate and anchor the economy, they suffer a loss of confidence. Given rapid rates of change, past policy responses have often been volatile and unpredictable, creating uncertainty. Latin American governments have a smaller store of institutional credibility than, for example, the German Bundesbank or the U.S. Fed—where the big news might be a 0.25 percent increase in the interest rate and not the freezing of all bank accounts, the 30 percent devaluation of a currency, or the implementation of a currency peg. During Ismail Lehman's young life, for example, the Brazilian currency has changed names five times. Confidence building in economic policy making is a long and slow process—one not easily achieved when the economic waters are rough and choppy. Students of Latin American economic policy always need to ask how the policy proposed is going to affect the confidence and long-run credibility of economic agents.

Policy for Whom?

Economic policy affects different groups within an economy differently. One of the fundamental challenges facing policy makers in Latin America is the deep divisions that exist in its socioeconomic structure. Latin America is characterized by high degrees of income inequality. There is a huge gap between the lives of Juan Navarro and Judith Yanira Viera. The goal becomes promoting not only growth but some form of equitable growth—quite a tall order. Income inequality introduces complications in the measurement of growth. If equality is important, the change in a poor person's income should carry roughly the same weight as that of a rich person. But given inequality, if a rich person earns twenty times more than a poor person, changes in the income of the wealthy receive twenty times the weight of changes in income of the poor in the national growth calculation.[28] If growth is supposed to measure economic performance, even the measures are far from the mark.

In many cases inequality is exacerbated by an ethnic and cultural mosaic of cultural approaches to economic life. Traditional forms of social organization in indigenous communities may clash with the marketization of economic life. Gender also plays a key role in the assessment of policy outcomes. In a society often conditioned by traditional gender roles, policy makers sensitive to the gender divide must ask, for example, how accessible terms of credit or access to technology are to the widest range of citizens. Although these problems are not unimportant in policy making in more industrialized countries, the range of difference confronts the policy maker with hard choices. Women in Santiago, for example, may be well-educated, active economic contributors, whereas their sisters in the Altiplano live a far more traditional life. In assessing policy in Latin America, do not neglect to ask: policy for whom? Whose needs should policy be designed to meet? The Lehmans'? Or Juan Navarro's?

PRESENT VERSUS FUTURE VALUE: THE ENVIRONMENTAL DIMENSION

Promoting not only development but also sustainable development—or a strategy that leaves future generations as well-off as the present—may be unrealistic when more than half of a population lives on the verge of starvation or when inflation eats away at the meager earnings of the working poor. Policy makers in the developing world—like those anywhere—are constrained by political and financial capital. There are only so many things that can be done with limited energy and finances. Daily crises take precedence over long-term planning. This becomes quite evident in the environmental arena. The challenge becomes how not to forfeit future growth while confronting present dilemmas. Even in industrial market economies, characterized by less sensational economic twists and turns, it is hard enough to promote incentives for sustainable use of resources. Imagine the difficulties in a developing country. Enforcement of environmental laws in industrial economies, with stronger institutional and financial resources, is often lax or ineffective. Yet without an environmental sensitivity to the future, policy will not be sustainable over time. Bad choices today have costs tomorrow. Policy to promote rational environmental decision making in Latin America must be carefully crafted—and perhaps supplemented with external capital—for long-term investment in the future. Macro- and microeconomic policies must be assessed through environmental lenses to protect resources for future generations.

THE STATE AND THE MARKET: PROMOTING PARTNERSHIP

Who should be the primary development actor in the region? What should be the relative balance between the state and the market in promoting development in

Latin America? This question has framed much of the twentieth-century policy debate in the region. We will see that the pendulum has swung from a market-led to a state-dominated economy, and in the 1990s has recently returned to the market. Whether or not you support a stronger role for the state in economic decision making may be conditioned by your view of the relative sophistication of economic institutions in the region. Irma Adelman and Cynthia Taft Morris, two highly respected development economists, suggest that the crucial factor affecting development is the effectiveness of economic institutions and how economic institutions mediate the way in which gains from growth are distributed.[29] Are the economic institutions—central banks, capital, land and labor markets, redistributive agents, and laws governing property rights—sufficiently strong to promote equitable and sustainable growth without much day-to-day state interference? If independent market institutions or the property code is weak, is policy intervention warranted? Defining where the state can and should supplement the activity of the market is an important element in crafting effective policy for development in Latin America.

Three broad schools of thought can be identified with respect to the role of the state in development policy.[30] During the 1950s and 1960s, the success of the socialist model in jump-starting industrialization in the Soviet Union led to a **planning model** that accorded a strong role to the state in promoting development. The economists within Latin America who broadly believed that state intervention was critical to promoting development were called **dependency** theorists. Since markets were viewed as incomplete and unable to send strong and accurate price signals to economic agents, the state was viewed as an essential vehicle to orchestrate the growth process. Without an interventionist state, markets alone would not spontaneously generate growth. State-run activity was seen as necessary in providing infrastructure such as roads and railways, and public services in education and health. In addition, state activity was encouraged in the direct production of goods and services in which private initiative had failed. The state was also supposed to help to counterbalance the power of domestic and international elites. We will consider the extension of this model to Latin America in chapter 3 on import substitution industrialization. Today, the potential gains from globalization and international trade, the benefits of entrepreneurship and the profit motive, and the difficulties introduced by problems of accountability and enforcement have created a shift away from the planning model.

The second broad approach falls within the **institutionalist tradition.** Institutionalists accord a strong role to nonmarket institutions. In particular, institutionalists suggest that rather than relying solely on price signals, other forms of organization—judges, chieftains, priests, or community councils—may intervene to settle disputes arising from the conflict over scarce economic resources.[31] Economic problems must therefore be treated within the context of legal, social, and political systems. Economic outcomes were often determined as much by power as by price signals. As the wealthy would be better able to command resources, high degrees of inequality would bias development against the poor. For institutionalists, with a variety of factors influencing outcomes, development does not tend toward equilibrium but may be a bumpy and discontinuous process. As we will see in chapter 3, the planning model and dependency theorists as well as institutionalist thought informed the position of some of the structuralist thinkers and policy makers in Latin America. Structuralists—economists who believed that the particular structure of developing economies warranted a different policy approach—dominated regional policy from the 1940s through the 1970s.

A third school of thought in development economics is the neoclassical tradition. Linked in part to the **Chicago school** of orthodox economic policies, it places the market at the center of the development equation. Their key to development policy is in ensuring that economic agents face accurate price incentives without interference to make the best of all possible economic decisions. State-led activity in infrastructure and public services is seen to have a poor performance record. Well-intended short-term market interventions are argued to perpetrate unintended long-run misallocations of resources.[32] Strict neoclassical theorists therefore see a minimalist role for the state as a guarantor of rules and property rights and a provider of a limited array of public goods such as defense. The private sector, through the profit motive and Adam Smith's invisible hand, will generate the greatest good for all. Foreign trade and international prices should become the engine for growth. Under the leadership of Milton Friedman, the Chicago school was the principal articulator of the Pinochet model in Chile, and it broadly informs the neoliberal policies that have dominated development strategies in Latin America in the 1990s.

All development approaches do not necessarily fall into one of these three policy boxes. However, the three tend to define answers to the critical question: is the market the best of all possible mechanisms to organize economic activity and promote growth, or is state intervention a necessary ingredient to development policy in Latin America? The planner would argue for the hand of the state to guide development policy, the institutionalist would suggest that mechanisms beyond the market are critical in determining economic outcomes, and the subscriber to the Chicago school would staunchly support market-based policies. As we proceed through the puzzle of development in Latin America, you will need to resolve for yourself the most beneficial mix of market, state, and complementary institutions to promote development in the region. We will address this question in chapter 6 as we take an in-depth look at the contemporary role of the state in development.

These five issues—external balance, credibility, distribution, environmental sustainability, and the role of the state—pervade our examination of the backdrop to development policy in the region and our treatment of contemporary issues. In chapters 2 and 3 we will see how they played out in early development theories in the region. Chapters 4 and 5 address two of the dramatic legacies of imbalances of past mistakes—hyperinflation and debt. Chapter 6 introduces the new economic model in the region and chapter 7 chronicles the return of Latin America to international capital markets. In chapter 8 we consider contemporary trade performance, and then we go on to analyze sources of industrial competitiveness as well as the potential of the agricultural sector in chapters 9 and 10, respectively. We will see the radical economic changes adopted by the region in the 1990s and evaluate their significant gains. But challenges remain. In chapter 11 we take up the problem of poverty, and in chapters 12 and 13 we assess educational and health systems in the region. Finally, although we pay attention to the environment throughout this text, in chapter 14 we look at environmental priorities in Latin America and suggest an agenda for action. We conclude in chapter 15 with an evaluation of the relative weight of the state and the market in addressing the challenges to a sustainable and equitable development strategy in Latin America.

Key Concepts

Chicago school	Growth	Planning model
Dependency	Empowerment	Sustainable
Development	Equity	development
Dualism	Institutionalist tradition	Technological change

Chapter Summary

Development: Definitions and Theory

- Development is a word not easily definable in the context of economic advancement. Questions arise as to what kinds of characteristics "developed" countries have or should have.
- A distinction exists between development and economic growth. Development usually presupposes technological change, and economic growth considers political and social factors.
- The goals of development are more than just economic growth. These goals may include meeting the basic human needs of the population, increasing the economic opportunities of the poor, empowerment, and ensuring economic benefits for future generations.
- Economists have not been able to agree on a theory of development with a well-defined pathway to modernization. The development process for developing nations will be different from the one taken by nations that are currently industrialized. Furthermore, less industrialized countries are likely to require different approaches to development depending upon their location, size, and natural endowments.
- There are three schools of thought for development policy: the planning model, the institutionalist tradition, and the Chicago school. Each of these defines a degree to which the state should intervene in the development process and the extent to which the process should be left in the hands of the market.

Challenges in Development Policy in Latin America

Latin America faces five major challenges when implementing development policy. First, there is a delicate balance between the external sector and domestic macropolicy. Second, policy needs to be adaptive to the changing nature of the economic environment of developing countries, but, at the same time, policy makers must preserve confidence and stability within their respective countries. Third, if equitable growth is one of the goals of development, then policy must be fashioned in a way to target different economic, ethnic, and gender groups. Fourth, a careful balance between meeting the needs of the present generation and securing resources for future generations must be sought for development to be sustainable. Fifth, policy makers need to decide the extent to which the state should supplement the activity of the market in facilitating equitable, sustainable development.

Notes

1. Monica Larner and Ian Katz, "It's Ronaldo's World," *Business Week,* 22 June 1998, p. 204; and Alex Bellos, "Ronaldo's Fame Hasn't Hit Home," *Minneapolis Star Tribune,* 10 July 1998, 6c.

2. Excerpted from Monica Larner and Ian Katz, "It's Ronaldo's World," *Business Week*, 22 June 1998: 204; and Alex Bellos, "Ronaldo's Fame Hasn't Hit Home," *Minneapolis Star Tribune*, 10 July 1998: 6c.

3. Calvin Sims, "A Web Entree for Peruvians without PCs," *New York Times,* 27 May 1996, sec. 1, p. 29. (Accessed via LEXIS-NEXIS database.)

4. "In the Gap and Sweatshop Labor in El Salvador," *NACLA Report on the Americas* 29, no. 4 (January–February 1996): 37.

5. Diana Jean Schemo, "Brazil Farmers Feel Squeezed by Tobacco Companies," *New York Times,* 6 April 1998. On-line edition.

6. Harry S Truman, inaugural address, January 20, 1949, in *Documents on American Foreign Relations* (Connecticut University Press, 1967), as quoted in Wolfgang Sachs, ed., *The Development Dictionary: A Guide to Knowledge as Power* (London: Zed, 1992), 2.

7. W. Arthur Lewis, "Economic Development with Unlimited Supplies of Labour," *Manchester School* 22, no. 2 (1954). Reprinted in A. N. Agarwala and S. P. Singh, eds., *The Economics of Underdevelopment* (New York: Oxford University Press, 1963).

8. C. Furtado, *Development and Underdevelopment,* trans. Ricardo W. de Agruar and Eric Charles Drysdale (Berkeley: University of California Press, 1965), 47. (Originally published as *Dialectica do desenvolvimento, Rio de Janeiro* [Berkeley: University of California Press, 1964].)

9. P. Bauer and B. Yamey, *The Economics of Underdeveloped Countries* (New York: Cambridge University Press, 1967), 151.

10. B. Higgins, *Economic Development: Problems, Principles, and Policies* (New York: W. W. Norton, 1968), 148.

11. T. Dos Santos, "La crisis de la teoría del desarollo y las relaciones de dependencia en América Latina," *Boletin de CESO* 3 (1968). This article appeared in English as "The Crisis of Development Theory and the Problem of Dependence in Latin America," in *Underdevelopment and Development,* ed. H. Bernstein (Harmondsworth, U.K.: Penguin, 1973).

12. Denis Goulet, *The Cruel Choice: A New Concept in the Theory of Development* (New York: Atheneum, 1971), 23.

13. Charles K. Wilber, *The Political Economy of Development and Underdevelopment* (New York: Random House, 1973), 355.

14. Dudley Seers, "What Are We Trying to Measure?" *Journal of Development Studies* (April 1972).

15. Simon Kuznets, "Modern Economic Growth: Findings and Reflections," *American Economic Review* 63, no. 3 (June 1973): 247.

16. Kenneth P. Jameson and Charles K. Wilber, *Directions in Economic Development* (Notre Dame, Ind.: University of Notre Dame Press, 1979), 38. Originally in James J. Lamb, "The Third World and the Development Debate," *IDOC-North America,* January–February 1973, p. 20.

17. Paul Streeten, "A Basic Needs Approach to Economic Development," in Jameson and Wilber, *Directions,* 73.

18. Peter J. Henriot, "Development Alternatives: Problems, Strategies, Values," in *The Political Economy of Development and Underdevelopment,* ed. Charles K. Wilber, 2d ed. (New York: Random House, 1979), 11.

19. Jameson and Wilber, *Directions,* 7.

20. World Commission on Environment and Development, *Our Common Future* (Oxford: Oxford University Press, 1987), 8–9.

21. Gerald M. Meier, *Leading Issues in Economic Development,* 6th ed. (Oxford: Oxford University Press, 1995), 7.

22. Amartya Sen, "The Concept of Development," in *Handbook of Development Economics,* vol. 1 (Netherlands: North-Holland, 1988).

23. Boris Pleskovic and Joseph E. Stiglitz, eds., *Annual World Bank Conference on Development Economics, 1997* (Washington, D.C.: World Bank, 1998), 19.

24. Schumpeter (1939), as presented in Paolo Sylos Labini, "The Classical Roots of Development Theory," in *Economic Development: Handbook of Comparative Economic Policies,* ed. Enzo Grilli and Dominick Salvatore (Westport, Conn.: Greenwood, 1994), 3.

25. Lucas (1988), as presented in Sylos Labini, "The Classical Roots of Development Theory," 3.

26. Paul Streeten, "From Growth to Basic Needs," in *Latin America's Economic Development: Institutionalist and Structuralist Perspectives,* ed. James L. Dietz and James H. Street (Boulder, Colo.: Lynne Rienner, 1987). Originally appeared in *Finance and Development* 16 (September 1979).

27. Michael P. Todaro, *Economic Development,* 5th ed. (White Plains, N.Y.: Longman, 1994), 670.

28. Gerald K. Helleiner, "Toward a New Development Strategy," in *The Legacy of Raúl Prebisch,* ed. Enrique V. Iglesias (Washington, D.C.: Inter-American Development Bank, 1994), 178.

29. Irma Adelman and Cynthia Taft Morris, "Development History and Its Implications for Development Theory," *World Development* 25, no. 6 (1997): 831–840.

30. Karla Hoff, Avishay Braverman, and Joseph Stiglitz, "Introduction," in *The Economics of Rural Organization,* ed. Karla Hoff, Avishay Braverman, and Joseph Stiglitz (New York: Oxford University Press/World Bank, 1993).

31. Ibid.

32. John Martinussen, *Society, State, and Market: A Guide to Competing Theories of Development* (London: Zed, 1997), 260.

CHAPTER TWO

HISTORICAL LEGACIES

Patterns of Unequal and Unstable Growth

Historical patterns of land distribution have left a legacy of high inequality in the region. *(Courtesy of the Inter-American Development Bank.)*

In *One Hundred Years of Solitude,* Colombian novelist Gabriel García Marquez warns us that Latin America recycles its past. To evaluate contemporary policy we must understand the historical legacies of the region. The economic history of Latin America, a continent with diverse national stories and richly textured social histories, is far more complicated and nuanced than this short chapter on historical legacies can ever hope to convey. It can only abstract some of the patterns shaping development in the region. Perhaps some of the questions raised in our study of contemporary policy in the region will motivate the serious student of Latin America to revisit the historical pattern of growth at another time.[1] Some questions we will consider include the following:

- What factors shape the growth patterns of countries?
- Why, despite relatively similar starting points, did Latin America fall behind the United States and Canada in terms of growth?
- What are the characteristics of primary product-led growth?
- What were the social forms of economic organization conditioning development patterns?
- What were the environmental implications of the early pattern of development in Latin America?

This chapter assumes the overwhelming challenge of putting contemporary development into a simplified historical framework. It explains how the colonial and early independence periods shaped later development problems by focusing on the inputs and outputs of production. This brief foray is designed to provide a context for policy making today. Like the Buendía family in the García Márquez novel, this chapter highlights the opportunities and the cyclical constraints in the development experience in Latin America.

The Puzzle of Comparative Growth Patterns

What early patterns of economic organization in Latin America shaped later growth? Rather than a conventional time line, our discussion is organized around the inputs to development: availability of labor, capital, and technology to promote agricultural and industrial growth at home and abroad. How did available resources constrain and shape development? In table 2.1 we can see that in 1700, per capita GDPs in Mexico and the United States were roughly equal. As late as 1850, Argentina and Brazil enjoyed per capita GDPs higher than Canada's. Why did Latin America stagnate in the twentieth century while the United States and Canada surged ahead?

Thinking about Inputs, Outputs, and Economic Change

Economic development may be thought of as a process whereby the structure of the economy evolves to adapt to the changing needs of a growing population. As

Table 2.1. Historical Per Capita Growth Rates (GDP per capita in 1985 U.S. dollars)

	1700	1800	1850	1913	1989
Argentina	n/a	n/a	874	2,377	3,880
Brazil	n/a	738	901	700	4,241
Chile	n/a	n/a	484	1,685	5,355
Mexico	450	450	317	1,104	3,521
Peru	n/a	n/a	526	985	3,142
Canada	n/a	n/a	850	3,560	17,576
United States	490	807	1,394	4,854	18,317
% of US per capita GDP					
Argentina	n/a	n/a	62.70	48.97	21.18
Brazil	n/a	91.45	64.63	14.42	23.15
Chile	n/a	n/a	34.72	34.71	29.24
Mexico	91.84	55.76	22.74	22.74	19.22
Peru	n/a	n/a	37.73	20.29	17.15
Canada	n/a	n/a	60.98	73.34	95.95
United States	100.00	100.00	100.00	100.00	100.00

Source: Stanley Engerman and Kenneth Sokoloff, *Factor Endowments, Institutions, and Differential Paths of Growth among New World Economies: A View from Economic Historians of the United States,* National Bureau of Economic Research Historical Paper no. 66 (Cambridge, Mass.: National Bureau of Economic Research, 1994).

evidenced in the data extension that follows, growth of output must outstrip population growth to improve the resources available to people. Population, or labor, constitutes one of the inputs of production. How is it organized and combined with other inputs to produce output? It is useful to think about the fundamentals shaping the structure of an economy. These in turn condition the economy's performance in meeting the requirements of society. Why do economies begin to produce cer-

Table 2.2. Performance of Major Regions

	Population (millions)		GDP (millions of 1990 U.S. dollars)	
	1820	1992	1820	1992
Western Europe	103	303	133	5,255,000
Western offshoots (U.S. & Canada)	11	305	13,255	6,359,000
Southern Europe	34	123	27,000	1,016,000
Eastern Europe	90	431	69,000	2,011,000
Latin America	20	462	13,580	2,225,000
Asia and Oceania	736	3,163	405,000	10,287,000
Africa	73	656	33,000	842,000
World Total	1,068	5,441	695,000	27,995,000

Source: Angus Maddison, *Monitoring the World Economy, 1820–1992* (Washington, D.C.: OECD Publications and Information Center, 1995), table 1.2, p. 20.

DATA EXTENSION
COMPARATIVE GROWTH RATES

It is interesting to take a comparative look at regional performance over the 1820–1992 period. Table 2.2 presents a slightly different set of comparative data from that presented in table 2.1. What patterns emerge?

A few calculations will underscore different growth patterns in the region. You may want to copy table 2.2 into an electronic spreadsheet for quick calculations.

First, to measure Latin America's performance compared to that of the western offshoots, divide the totals for population and GDP of the offshoots by the data for the same year for Latin America. If you did your calculations right, you will see that GDP in the offshoots in 1820 is roughly equal to that of Latin America. (In fact, with a ratio of 0.97, it is slightly higher.) By 1992 the offshoots' GDP was 2.85 times that of the South.

Second, GDP alone doesn't tell us much about the standard of living. If population growth rates outstrip the increase in national output, people are worse off. To get a better approximation of the relative standard of living, divide GDP by population for each respective year. When you then take the ratio of the offshoots to Latin America, you can see that GDP per capita was roughly 1.75 times more in the offshoots in 1820, and the ratio rose to 4.32 by 1992.

Third, another way we can highlight the different rates of change is to look at how quickly GDP and GDP per capita grew from 1820 to 1990 in Latin America as compared to the rest of the world. If you divide Latin America's GDP in 1992 by that of 1820, you will see that GDP multiplied roughly 160 times over the period. This is second in terms of regional performance, following that of the western offshoots at around 450. Western and southern Europe's GDP multiplied about forty times, and Africa and Asia lagged at twenty-five. However, when you perform the same calculation for GDP per capita, you will note that the faster population growth in Latin America divided the GDP gains among a larger number of people. Where population only multiplied about three times in western Europe, the per capita change in GDP from 1820 to 1992 was about 13.5. In Latin America, as the population increased twenty-three times during the period, the share per capita only grew a bit more than seven times in the region.

What conclusions can you derive about population growth and GDP from these data?

tain goods? How do specializations evolve and change over time? One way to answer this is to consider the inputs available for production and the characteristics of the output market that define product demand. What inputs are available to be made into desired output? What technology is available—and who controls it—to facilitate the process? Whose tastes and desires—local, international, rich, poor—are the target market? Looking at the factors affecting supply and demand will allow us to say something about the structure of an economy and to evaluate how policy was used historically to improve the responsiveness of an economy to the needs of its citizens. Table 2.3 summarizes some of these factors shaping patterns of growth.

What factors condition the menu of goods and services a country produces? Resources, raw materials, and the physical characteristics of land affect production possibilities. Is a country rich in natural resources? Is there a diversity of available resources? Or does the country rely on a limited number of natural commodities?

Table 2.3. Factors Shaping Patterns of Growth

Natural resources	Is the country resource abundant?
	Who owns resources?
Land	How is land distributed? Who decides who owns land?
	Are landholdings concentrated or spread out among small stakeholders?
	Are the claims or titles to landholdings clear?
	What is the quality of available land?
Labor resources	How abundant is labor?
	What is the skill level of workers?
Financial capital	Is there a domestic surplus available for reinvestment?
	Do domestic investors find better returns at home or abroad?
	Is growth dependent on an external infusion of funds?
Technology	What is the technological base of the nation?
	Who controls the access to technology?
	Do international patents restrict the free flow of technology?
Policy environment	Is the driving force behind growth the market or the state?
	Is the policy inwardly oriented or open to the international economy?

Who owns resources and how they are distributed throughout the population both matter enormously. Asset ownership confers the ability to make a profit on the sale or use of that factor of production. Is the ownership of key resources concentrated in a small, powerful group, or it is evenly spread around the population? Do these assets—land or mines or timber or fish—generate a profit for the owners above and beyond subsistence needs? The development of a group of people with a profit or surplus above and beyond personal subsistence requirements creates an elite class of potential capitalists or investors. These capitalists can then reinvest the surplus to create new growth opportunities—or can send it out of the country to earn money elsewhere. If this pool of national capital falls short of domestic investment demand, the country finds itself dependent on international sources of funds for growth. The choices domestic elites make about where to invest their money also shape the available stock of technology employed in the production process. Investments in technological inputs may enhance the productivity of the labor force, or resources may be directed toward producing sophisticated products outside the reach of the common consumer. As we can see, land, capital, and labor—the primary inputs to production—help define the productive structure.

But this structure does not operate in a vacuum. Public policies fashion the productive environment. The legal structure defines property rights and social responsibilities. The policy environment may be shaped by a market philosophy limiting the sphere of government activity, or there may be a demand for the government to address collective needs or redress some of the imbalances created by economic growth. Furthermore, what a country produces, as well as how and by whom, is conditioned by what the rest of the world is doing. Borders are generally permeable to ideas, goods, services, and prices; countries view productive capabilities relative to the endowments and technological achievements of other nations.

Relative advantage matters. A country's position in the international economic order also defines possible pathways to growth. A late-developing country may find that others have already cornered the market in a particular product or process.

These supply characteristics of inputs and production rules interact with demand. The most efficient producer of an undesired good goes broke. The characteristics of a product—how responsive people are to price changes, the number of substitutes, the frequency and size of purchase—as well as the internal and external market size for a country's tradable goods create the opportunity for profit.

Fundamental supply and demand conditions affect and are affected by macroeconomic variables. Supply constraints or excess demand may give rise to inflation; failure to capture a surplus for reinvestment may result in anemic or slow growth. Attempts to jump-start an economy may simply fuel inflation; policies to manipulate the exchange rate to gain competitive advantage may have unintended domestic effects. The macroeconomic environment therefore shapes the activity of producer and consumer in the market.

> **QUESTION FOR THOUGHT**
>
> Given this list of factors influencing growth, can you construct a story of the important factors shaping the pattern of growth in the country of your birth?

How have the supply conditions— land, labor, capital, and technological availability—interacted with the demand factors and the macroeconomic environment to condition historical growth in Latin America? What were the available resources? Who controlled them? What technology was available to the owners of resources? What were the rules of the market? How did demand for products from Latin America affect growth patterns? How and where were profits reinvested? Finding answers to these questions gives us a sense of the historical factors shaping growth in the region.

NATURAL ABUNDANCE: THE REWARDS OF THE EXTRACTIVE ECONOMY

In analyzing the importance of different factors of production in Latin American growth, we can see that exploitation of natural resources was at the heart of the colonial period of Latin American development. Latin America was resource rich. Exploration of the region was driven by the Spanish mercantilist search for silver and gold. The New World provided new opportunities for wealth in Europe. Monopoly control over mines and land in the New World was accorded through the **encomienda** system, with a share of the output, or **repartida**, owed in return. Under the encomienda system, rights to land were parceled out by the monarchy, with an associated portion of the profits to be shipped back to Europe. Labor, however, was scarce. In 1503 Queen Isabella of Spain "entrusted" the Indians to the landlords, requiring the heads of the estates, or **caciques**, to provide payment, protection, and instruction in the Christian faith in exchange for their services. Extractive activities also laid a toll on the local labor force to bring the silver and gold to Spain. Indigenous peoples were obliged to provide the labor for mining, and Indian populations were decimated by European diseases—smallpox, yellow fever, malaria, and bubonic plague. As indigenous communities were broken up in support of an emerging agricultural sector, the "biological holocaust," as some have called it,[2] claimed the lives of the large majority of the continent's indigenous population.

The Portuguese, given claim to Brazil by the treaty of Tordesillas in 1494, were initially less driven by the search for precious metals. When the Portuguese arrived, they did not find and conquer the highly organized indigenous civilization of the Incas or the Mayans to lead them to a fabulous pot of silver or gold. Furthermore, with the indigenous population scattered throughout the vast Amazon, labor was a problem. Agriculture took hold before mining. The early import of African slaves solved labor shortages in the emerging sugar industry. The gold rush began in Minas Gerais, Brazil, in the late 1600s and continued through the middle 1700s, increasing Portuguese interest in the colony. But the relatively early development of Brazilian agriculture exerted a stabilizing influence on the early development pattern. As in the United States, importing slaves relieved the labor constraint in production.

LABOR AND SOCIAL RELATIONS

The exploitation of indigenous labor supplies, the import of Africans, and European immigration radically changed the racial composition in the region. Around 1900, there were approximately 20 million Latin Americans, a regional population about equal to that of Great Britain and double that of the United States. The small national populations were seen as a constraint on development. Argentina and Brazil were the second and third most popular intercontinental destinations for European immigrants in the late 1800s and early 1900s, but they attracted only 20 percent of the immigration flow, compared to 60 percent for the United States.[3] As we can see in table 2.4, limited immigration flows set up different racial patterns in the region. In Spanish America, by 1935 blacks accounted for 13.3 percent of the population and Indians 50 percent; in Brazil, African Brazilians made up 35 percent of the population, surpassing the Indian population. Interestingly, slavery in Latin America was abolished soon after independence in most Latin American nations, with little of the turmoil that accompanied the transition in the United States. Even in Brazil, where slavery lasted until 1888, racial integration has been far more harmonious than in North America.

Differing racial patterns in Spanish America and Brazil as compared to the United States and Canada had a clear economic dimension. The production of export crops such as sugar and mining activities relied on imported slave labor and forced Indian labor. Although the U.S. South also solved its labor constraint through slavery, 80 percent of the population in the United States and Canada was white in 1825, whereas whites composed only between 20 and 25 percent of the population in Spanish America and Brazil. The small number of white Europeans in Latin America were granted property from the monarchies, whereas the bulk of the population were slaves or manual laborers without assets.[4] Income—derived from the ownership of assets—was highly unequal and tied to race from the start

Table 2.4. Racial Composition in New World Economies (percentages)

		White	Black	Indian
Spanish America	1570	1.3	2.5	96.3
	1650	6.3	9.3	84.4
	1825	18	22.5	59.5
	1935	35.5	13.3	50.4
Brazil	1570	2.4	3.5	94.1
	1650	7.4	13.7	78.9
	1825	23.4	55.6	21
	1935	41	35.5	23
U.S. and Canada	1570	0.2	0.2	99.6
	1650	12	2.2	85.8
	1825	79.6	16.7	3.7
	1935	89.4	8.9	1.4

Source: Stanley Engerman and Kenneth Sokoloff, *Factor Endowments, Institutions, and Differential Paths of Growth among New World Economies: A View from Economic Historians of the United States,* National Bureau of Economic Research Historical Paper no. 66 (Cambridge, Mass.: National Bureau of Economic Research, 1994), table 3.

in Latin America. When the data on per capita GDP in table 2.1 are combined with our information about the small share of the white population, since the per capita estimates are an average of the population, we can imagine how well the white European elite must have lived compared with the rest of the population.

Despite differences in the emphasis on mining and agricultural activity between Brazil and the rest of the region, early social relations in both the Spanish and the Portuguese colonies tended to be feudal. The traditional authority of the Catholic Church reinforced these social patterns. The encomienda system accorded property rights to a small number of landholders, concentrating ownership and crowding the indigenous and mestizo, or those of mixed heritage, onto less productive land. This system of the **latifundia,** the feudal estates in Spanish Latin America, and the **fazenda** system in Brazil set up a highly unequal socioeconomic system. Furthermore, since internal markets were relatively small, the latifundia largely fostered an agricultural sector directed toward Europe. Profits were repatriated, leaving little at home for reinvestment. Those eking out a subsistence existence on the **minifundia**, the small parcels of land the peasants farmed, could do little more than feed themselves with their meager earnings. Compared to the United States, greater inequality in wealth, human capital, and political power likely promoted the evolution of weaker internal markets in Latin America.[5] The poor didn't have much money to buy goods. Elites retained positions of political power, blocking forces of economic change.

INDEPENDENCE: POLITICAL CHANGE WITHOUT ECONOMIC TRANSFORMATION

National independence, achieved regionally by 1822 (with the exception of Cuba and Puerto Rico), allowed for a change in rules regarding property rights and trade. However, the violence, lawlessness, and political turmoil of the period of independence reinforced the legitimacy of latifundia as a form of political and economic organization. Lawlessness and revolt were common. People wanted security. The growing pains of nations—the difficulty in raising taxes and providing public services—highlighted the stability of the semifeudal system of social, political, and economic protection that the coronel, or the head of the latifundia, provided. The preservation of elite political interests, rather than institutional modernization favoring equal legal rights for citizens, may have had the effect of slowing growth in Latin America as compared to the North.[6]

The pattern of land tenure was perhaps unnecessarily concentrated. Although we can trace the roots of unequal land holdings to the colonial land tenure system, it is important to point out that after independence, new national governments missed opportunities to redistribute land from conquest, held by the former crowns, or further appropriated from indigenous communities. If political elites tied to this system had not been so powerful, fundamental land reforms would have created greater competition in the agricultural sector. With a larger number of small holdings, competitive pressure may have fostered activity in other sectors. Infrastructure, including transportation and energy, was also weak, making it difficult to set up local manufacturing. Thin domestic capital markets made it tough to raise money. In addition, local market demand was too small and product quality was too low for manufacturing to exploit the international sector. Political and economic structures did not help create a climate conducive to institutional change.

Contributing to the desire to maintain a political oligarchy was the fact that people were relatively well-off. By the end of the 1800s, the per capita income in Latin America was $245 at a time when it only reached $239 in North America.[7] Unfortunately for national growth, income was concentrated, and reinvestment of profits in entrepreneurial activity was limited. The lack of political change hindered economic transformation. Given the control of the political system by elites, it made little sense to venture into risky investments. The security of the latifundia system mitigated against economic risk taking. With political and economic gains consolidated, why embark on an investment likely to fail? As shown in table 2.5, nations tended to hitch their economic star to a dominant commodity. Coffee, sugar, bananas, and their associated feudal structures of production dominated the export profile. Exports were seen as the engine of economic growth.

But there are winners and losers in the global export game. Despite the similarities in socioeconomic systems, there was a great deal of diversity in economic performance throughout the region, largely connected to the so-called **commodity lottery**.[8] The luck of natural endowment and agricultural advantage—copper and silver in Chile; sugar in Cuba; coffee in Brazil, Colombia, and Costa Rica; cattle in Argentina; bananas from Central America; guano in Peru—defined the winnings in the international export market. International demand had expanded with the opening of the British agricultural market and industrialization in Europe and the United States. In the late 1800s through the early 1900s, a broad consensus for agriculture-led export growth prevailed. This **golden age of primary product exports** in Latin America was facilitated by political stability, expansion of transportation systems encouraging geographic integration, improvements in capital markets promoting capital investment, and secondary industrialization taking place

Table 2.5.   Single Commodity Exports

Country	Commodity	% of Total Exports, 1938
El Salvador	Coffee	92
Venezuela	Petroleum	92
Cuba	Sugar	78
Panama	Bananas	77
Bolivia	Tin	68
Guatemala	Coffee	66
Honduras	Bananas	64
Colombia	Coffee	61
Dominican Republic	Sugar	60
Chile	Copper	52
Haiti	Coffee	51
Costa Rica	Coffee	49
Nicaragua	Coffee	47
Brazil	Coffee	45

Source: Simon Hanson, *Economic Development in Latin America* (Washington, D.C.: Inter-American Affairs Press, 1951), 107.

in textiles, food packing, and transportation in support of the agricultural sector. Latin America responded to new demands from the industrializing international system by providing raw materials, including key minerals and food.[9] In figure 2.1 we can see, especially for Chile, Peru, Argentina, and Colombia, the strong external orientation of the economy. During this period Central America began the export of bananas, and Brazil entered the rubber boom.

Single commodity exports, however, were an unstable basis for balanced, sustainable economic growth. Development policy was preoccupied with the needs of the export sector, with little attention to the links with domestic production and demand. In bananas, much of the production was dominated by U.S. multinationals functioning as an export **enclave** contributing little to the social development of the country. The powerful United Fruit Company, for example, did not pay a cent of tax to the Costa Rican government, and its workers bought goods imported duty-free in the company store.[10] Central American economies became inextricably linked to an international political economy beyond domestic control. As table 2.6 shows, the problems of single commodity exports were exacerbated by a high concentration in market destination. Demand for the product was essentially determined abroad. The old saying that when the United States sneezes, Latin America gets pneumonia began in this period.

THE GIANT SUCKING SOUND OF SINGLE COMMODITY EXPORTS

Placing bets in the commodity casino leaves a country vulnerable to the vagaries of the international market. Commodity wealth—gold, silver, tin, coffee, rubber,

Figure 2.1.   Merchandise Exports to GDP, 1929

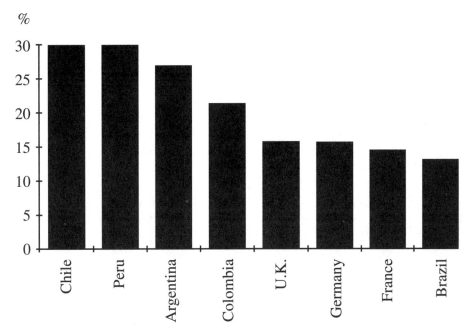

Source: Angus Maddison, "Economic and Social Conditions in Latin America, 1913–1950," in *Long Term Trends in Latin American Economic Development,* ed. Miguel Urrutia (Washington, D.C.: Inter-American Development Bank/Johns Hopkins University Press, 1991), table 1.13.

sugar, oil—can exert negative effects on the process of development. With strong international demand for a particular product, national resources are sucked into the production or extraction of a single commodity. As international prices boom, so do profits at home. Given comparative advantage, it makes great sense to concentrate production on addressing international demand. Resources move to the hot sector, pressuring input prices throughout the economy. Dubbed the **Dutch disease** because of Holland's experience with natural gas, this produces a distorted pattern of development precariously predicated on the hot commodity. International resources are drawn in, overvaluing the exchange rate. When a commodity is booming, why should investors place their money in a less lucrative outlet? If tin mining is returning high rates of profit, why invest in a dress factory? Furthermore, if profits from the boom are unequally distributed, a broader multiplier effect of the windfall income in industrial development is even less likely. Investors have monopoly or oligopoly control on the industry, and their continued access to profits or monopoly rents appears assured.

But booms have their busts. When commodity prices in the international market fall, they drag the whole economy down with them—because the commodity has essentially become the economy. For example, in 1920, sugar—a key crop for several Latin American nations—sold at 22.5 cents in May but fell to 3.625 cents

**Table 2.6.   Geographic Distribution of Latin American Exports, 1929
(% of total exports)**

	U.S.	U.K.	France	Germany
Cuba	76.6	12.6	2.1	0.8
Colombia	75.2	4.7	0.5	2.1
Mexico	60.7	10.3	3.9	7.6
Brazil	42.2	6.5	11.1	8.8
Peru	33.3	18.3	1.3	6.1
Venezuela	28.2	1.9	2.9	4.7
Chile	25.4	13.3	6.1	8.6
Uruguay	11.9	23.0	11.9	14.5
Argentina	9.8	32.3	7.1	10.0
Average	40.4	13.6	4.2	7.0

Source: Angus Maddison, "Economic and Social Conditions in Latin America, 1913–1950," in *Long Term Trends in Latin American Economic Development,* ed. Miguel Urrutia (Washington, D.C.: Inter-American Development Bank/Johns Hopkins University Press, 1991).

by the end of that same year.[11] By the end of the decade it reached an all-time low of 1.471 cents—quite a fall for an economy revolving around "king sugar." Coffee prices dropped 40 percent from 1929 to 1930—a tough shock to national coffers.[12] Another dramatic example was the guano economy in Peru. Between 1840 and 1880, Peru's economy revolved around guano deposits left by birds on the island coasts off Peru, where it barely rains. When substitutes were found for this valued fertilizer, Peru's economy crashed. Because most governmental receipts came from taxes on foreign trade, the effect of a commodity bust was magnified.

ENGEL'S LAW AND DECLINING TERMS OF TRADE

In addition to price volatility, concentration in primary product exports is also complicated by the nature of primary product demand. Primary products, particularly agricultural goods, are relatively price and income inelastic. If prices go up for coffee or sugar, as in a boom period, people cut back only slightly on their consumption of these perceived necessities. But on the downslope, with prices falling, people don't buy much more at a lower price. There is a limit to how much coffee or sugar people want. Furthermore, we observe a statistical relationship called **Engel's law,** that as income increases there is a weak increase in the demand for primary products. As world income grows and people become wealthier, the demand for agricultural products does not keep pace, unlike that for most manufactured products. If your country is an agricultural producer, compared to the rest of the world getting richer through manufactured goods, you stagnate. The net result of declining terms of trade is that high rates of growth in the primary product sector may not be enough to act as a catalyst for development. **Export pessimism**—the belief that exports would not be the engine of growth—began to characterize the policy maker's mind-set by the early 1900s.

Mining projects such as this one in Venezuela have been a source of export revenues but also introduce questions of export price instability and declining terms of trade. *(Courtesy of the Inter-American Development Bank.)*

THE EFFECTS OF WEAK INDUSTRIAL LINKAGES AND ABUNDANT FOREIGN CAPITAL

Despite declining terms of trade and export pessimism, primary product export growth is not necessarily a bad thing. Indeed, export growth can provide the opportunity for a country to capture a surplus, reinvest this profit, and reduce dependency on the agricultural product. In Latin America, however, weak links between export industries and the rest of the economy, labor shortages in the manufacturing sector, and foreign competition in industry depressed relative returns. Some export production exhibits characteristics of enclaves isolated from the rest of the economy. Linkages between commodity production and other products were relatively low. For example, coffee does not send signals back down the production chain for much in the way of capital necessary for production—a kind of **backward linkage**—nor does it generate the demand for new industries or products—a **forward linkage.** (The Starbucks coffee bar had yet to be developed!) Cattle ranching is an example of an industry that did contribute to forward linkages in leather processing and the shoe industry, but for the most part, commodity-led industrialization did not stimulate production in other sectors of the economy. In addition, with the notable exception of Argentina, immigration policies limited the labor market, creating shortages in the industrial sector. Ironically, compared to today, high-priced labor in Latin America made manufacturing costly. Domestic markets for financial capital were relatively weak, and foreign investment flowed to areas in which technological or capital constraints restricted entry of local firms.

Foreign capital was able to dominate large sectors of some economies. Tables 2.7–2.9 present data on foreign investment. Great Britain led the capital surge in Latin American in 1913 with 43.5 percent of the inflows. In Argentina about half of the capital was foreign owned, the bulk of it being British.[13] As a result of the strong inflow, we can see in table 2.8 that per capita foreign investment was much higher in Latin America than in Asian economies, tightening the link between Latin America and the rest of the world. The combination of high levels of foreign investment with commodity export economies tended to generate low returned value or a small part of export revenues that the host economy retained.[14]

One notable exception to the weakness of domestic capital markets was the case of Brazil. It has been suggested that Brazilian coffee barons were able to underwrite the industrial base of São Paulo while continuing to expand coffee production. It is theorized that this took place because the coffee land was not suitable for agricultural diversification, and fazendeiros found themselves in the manufacturing sector in search of new profits.[15] Furthermore, coffee production itself needed so little in the way of reinvestment of surplus that profits were best placed outside the sector.[16] In another case of national ownership, a Bolivian entrepreneur in the tin sector was thwarted from expanding into other sectors by weak linkages in input markets and underdeveloped national institutions to promote infrastructure investment, forcing him to import supplies from Chile and Europe.[17]

Table 2.9 illustrates the high rate of foreign investment as a percentage of GDP in the beginning of the century compared to later periods. Having been dominated by foreign investment, when this capital was withdrawn during World War I, local financial systems were not sufficiently developed to intermediate capital needs. Reflecting the importance of external finance and trade, Argentina, for example, did not have a central bank until 1935. Instead, its monetary authority, the Caja de Conversión, was responsible for guaranteeing the external value of the currency, with no domestic lender of last resort in the system.[18] The role of foreign and domestic commercial lenders was also differentiated. Because international bank-

Table 2.7.   Foreign Investment in Latin America, circa 1913

Creditor	Capital (in U.S.$)	Percentage
Great Britain	3,700	43.5
France	1,200	14.1
Germany	900	10.6
USA	1,700	20.0
Others	1,000	11.8

Source: W. Baer, "Leteinamerica und Westeuropa. Die Wirtschaftsbeziehungen bis zum Ende des Zweiten Weltkriegs," in *Lateinamerica-Westeuropa-Vereinigte Staaten Ein atlantisches Dreieck,* ed. W. Grabendorff and R. Roett (Baden-Baden, 1985); cited in Walther L. Bernecker and Hans Werner Tobler, eds., *Development and Underdevelopment in America: Contrasts of Economic Growth in North and Latin America in Historical Perspective* (Berlin: Walter de Gruyter, 1993).

Table 2.8.   Per Capita Net Foreign Capital Position, 1938

	Foreign Obligations (per capita)	Total Foreign Obligations (U.S.$ millions)
Chile	258	1,267
Argentina	230	3,154
Cuba	176	781
Uruguay	136	248
Venezuela	97	354
Mexico	93	1,759
Brazil	51	2,025
Peru	51	324
Colombia	37	320
China (including Manchuria)	3	1,787
India	11	3,441
Indochina	17	391
Indonesia	35	2,371
Korea (1941)	73	1,718
Malaya	164	695

Source: Angus Maddison, "Economic and Social Conditions in Latin America, 1913–1950," in *Long Term Trends in Latin American Economic Development,* ed. Miguel Urrutia (Washington, D.C.: Inter-American Development Bank/Johns Hopkins University Press, 1991), table 1.5.

ers dominated short-term, less risky portfolios, domestic institutions were left with longer-term loans in firms and real estate. When foreign banks pulled out, domestic institutions were not able to liquidate their assets quickly enough to respond to the capital shortage, and they could not respond to the needs of the local economy to finance the accumulation of physical capital.[19] Dependence on foreign capital has decreased over the course of the century, but vulnerability to the whims of the international capital market has remained a constant challenge for policy makers

Table 2.9.   Foreign Investment/GDP (percent)

	1900	1914	1929	1938	1950	1980	1990
Argentina	4.15	2.6	1.12	0.87	0.12	0.23	0.64
Brazil	2.55	2.96	0.92	0.7	0.18	0.32	0.36
Chile	1.88	2.11	1.56	1.63	0.49	0.27	0.4
Colombia	0.74	0.27	0.34	0.35	0.24	0.13	0.21
Mexico	1.55	1.83	1.28	0.79	0.17	0.23	0.32
Peru	1.78	1.21	0.64	0.46	0.22	0.32	0.48
Uruguay	3.14	1.62	0.67	0.59	0.18	n/a	0.31
Venezuela	2.52	0.98	1.05	0.73	0.55	0.32	0.47
Average	2.29	1.7	0.95	0.77	0.27	0.26	0.4

Source: Alan Taylor, *Argentina and the World Capital Market: Saving, Investment and International Capital Mobility in the Twentieth Century,* National Bureau of Economic Research Working Paper no. 6302 (Cambridge, Mass.: National Bureau of Economic Research, 1997).

in the region. International crises created local reverberations as money was withdrawn from Latin America to supplement European war chests.[20]

Increased flows of foreign capital also meant heightened exposure to financial collapse. Foreshadowing the debt crisis we will study in chapter 4, lending at the turn of the century was rapid, volatile, and heedless of institutional safeguards or appropriate accounting or monitoring procedures.[21] As high interest rates prior to the stock market crash of 1929 drew capital back to New York, Latin American projects were left underfunded. When markets crashed, commodity prices plunged worldwide, and protectionist barriers were erected, bringing the export engine to a grinding halt.

THE ENVIRONMENTAL DIMENSION

The environmental costs of an agricultural and extractive economy geared to export markets were substantial. Ecologically sustainable systems of communal agriculture had been practiced in Mesoamerica since at least 1500 B.C. The Spanish conquest succeeded in its goal of extracting natural riches and also destroyed ancient communal villages and practices.[22] After the mines were stripped, colonists cleared the land for agricultural crops. The introduction of sugar and coffee prompted vast ecological change, transforming the Central American region from subtropical forest to an agricultural export economy by clearing and planting, pushing the frontier, and exhausting the soil. Cattle were introduced, making further claims on land. Land held by the Catholic Church or publicly held Indian lands called **ejidos** came to be seen by liberal free market reformers as constraints on further development of the export economy. By 1880, every Central American country had titling laws granting coffee growers rights to land formerly held by Indian communities. Exports surged, but so did the devastation of indigenous groups. The confiscation of traditional lands led Indians to the ecologically more fragile mountains or lowlands, compounding environmental problems. When coffee estate owners faced labor shortages, the government forced communities to provide workers for the labor-intensive harvest through the **mandamiento** program, often under brutal working conditions. The expansion of banana production in the 1920s and 1930s increased pressure on the land and local food crops as firms dominated by multinationals competed with less powerful campesinos for the best high-nutrient soils.

Devastation was not limited to Central America. Brazilian B. F. Brandão provided one of the earliest accounts of this destruction in 1865 in this description of his youth on a Brazilian fazenda:

> At six o'clock in the morning the overseer forces the poor slave, still exhausted from the evening's labor, to rise from his rude bed and proceed to his work. The first assignment of the season is the chopping down of the forests for the next year's planting. . . . The next step is destruction of the large trees. . . . They set fire to the devastated jungle, and then they cut and stack the branches and smaller tree trunks which have escaped the fire . . . and could hinder development of the crop. . . . Centuries-old tree trunks which two months before had produced a cool, crisp

atmosphere over a broad stretch of land, lie on the surface of a field ravaged by fire and covered with ashes, where the slaves are compelled to spend twelve hours under the hot sun of the equator, without a single tree to give them shelter.[23]

Initially trees were burned in a short-term effort to increase soil fertility; they were also felled because they were thought to compete with coffee for limited moisture.[24]

In mining, industry, and some agricultural activities, local governments allowed control by foreign multinational firms. As characterized by Eduardo Galeano, Latin America's open veins of tin and copper poured into multinational coffers with little commitment to sustainable environmental policy. For example, a New York firm was granted a concession to mine in the Cerro de Pasco region of Peru's Central Andes. It constructed a network of roads, railroads, smelters, mining camps, hydroelectric plants, and haciendas to serve the mines; in 1922 it opened a smelter-refinery using timber, promoting deforestation, and polluting air and rivers with sulfuric acid and iron-zinc residues. Products were sold globally, but the devastation was local.

But foreign capital was not entirely to blame. In the 1940s Brazil's president expressed the following philosophy: "To conquer the land, tame the waters and subjugate the jungle, these have been our tasks. And in this centuries-old battle, we have won victory upon victory."[25] Resource-based growth was premised on taking advantage of the riches the land had to offer—at a clear cost to the environment. Even where an early consciousness of environmental protection existed, institutional resources for implementation were weak. The Brazilian government implemented a forest code in the 1930s, prohibiting deforestation along watercourses, limiting cutting on property, and protecting rare species. With limited financing, however, it was unenforceable.[26]

THE ISOLATION OF THE WAR YEARS: A BLESSING IN DISGUISE?

World War I had a profoundly dislocating effect on Latin America. World War I took countries off the gold standard, introducing financial instability. Oil-producing countries such as Venezuela benefited, but the confusion surrounding world war masked fundamental structural changes taking place in the global economy. As advanced industrial products were developed, the value of agricultural trade declined. New products such as

> **QUESTION FOR THOUGHT**
>
> Despite the costs, why was the primary product export model so enduring?

synthetics displaced traditional raw materials. The Great Depression exacerbated global commodity market instability, leaving the externally oriented development strategy without robust markets for products. Growing protectionism abroad further limited export potential. The terms of trade—what a country receives for its exports relative to what it pays for its imports—fell between 21 and 45 percent when international markets collapsed. International capital inflows to fuel industrial development virtually dried up by 1929.[27] But there was a silver lining to this cloud. As a result of these external shocks to the trade-driven model, Latin America was forced to adjust. It turned inward, adopting a set of economic policies called import substitution industrialization, the subject of chapter 3, to address the cycle of instability and vulnerability it faced under the externally oriented commodity export model. Although import substitution industrialization was not the solution to the puzzle of Latin American development, new strategies to meet

QUESTION FOR THOUGHT

Given the political constraints of colonial control, could Latin American economies have taken a different shape? Were policy mistakes made?

growing internal and external economic challenges were introduced. Unfortunately, as we will see in the following chapters, a changed focus toward internal growth did little to change the fundamental pattern of asset ownership, reinforcing the highly unequal pattern of growth in the region.[28]

HISTORICAL LESSONS

To conclude our rapid tour of Latin American history, we have summarized some of the factors influencing growth in the region in table 2.10. Natural resource dependence, unequal distribution of land, and labor, capital, and technological constraints shaped early development outcomes. What kind of lessons can we draw about these historical factors affecting Latin American development? We need to be very careful about concluding too much about historical causality, especially given the diverse set of circumstances in the region, but we can point to several legacies.

First, the colonial pattern of asset distribution in the region was unequal and tied to privilege. The political and economic power of the elites was replicated in the postindependence period and set the stage for contemporary policy. Persistent and rising inequality is the defining characteristic of the region's growth. Because capital was relatively abundant, it did not have to turn to enhancing labor productivity as a source of growth. The poor in Latin America were rarely invested in.

Second, as a region rich in resources and blessed with agricultural abundance, Latin America first pursued a strategy of export promotion. Financial resources were drawn to the dynamic export sectors, to the neglect of balanced development strategies. Colonial inequality was reinforced by the region's successful integration into the global economy and its access to relatively cheap external capital and technology. Government efforts were focused not on improving the local human capital of the peasants, but on attracting external capital as the source of growth.[29] The encomienda system established the pattern of depleting and not replenishing the region's human capital.[30]

Third, given the openness to world trade, Latin America was unable to protect itself from external shocks in the global economy. When the booms turned to busts and prices fell, entire economies suffered. The Great Depression and the war years

Table 2.10.   Stylized Characteristics of Early Growth Patterns in Latin America

Natural resources	Resource abundant but often dependent on a single commodity Ownership was concentrated
Land	Land was initially distributed by the Crown Landholdings were concentrated in large latifundia or fazendas Peasants did not hold clear title to the land they worked Land quality varied; lack of title for peasants decreased incentive for investment
Labor resources	Labor in agriculture and mining was scarce; slavery and Indian labor in addition to immigration relieved the labor constraint Low skill level; little investment in education
Financial capital	Part of the surplus was returned to Europe Concentrated ownership protected high returns in agriculture and resources, creating little incentive for domestic investment in industry During periods of commodity booms, high returns in agriculture made investment in industry risky A domestic savings gap create international financial dependency
Technology	Weak science and technology infrastructure Domestic technological gaps began to emerge between industrial north and Latin America Technological control by the North began
Policy environment	The golden age of exports gave way to import substitution in the post–World War II period International protection through trading companies limited export options

produced dramatic structural changes in Latin America that forced a reconsideration of the externally oriented primary product model.

Finally, the commodity export model exacted a high environmental and social price. The dislocation of indigenous communities and devastation of the land had enduring consequences. Pristine forest lands and diverse wildlife fell under the reign of sugar, coffee, and banana exporting economies. Contemporary patterns of social conflict in the region—for example, the recently ended civil war in Guatemala or the movements of the landless people in Brazil—certainly find their roots in the historical pattern of unequal land distribution.

The dissatisfaction arising from the externally oriented commodity export model gave rise to a new model of development in Latin America—import substitution industrialization. Import substitution industrialization located the answer to the question of why Latin America stagnated after the war period while Europe and the United States took off in the vulnerability of external orientation and dependency on international primary product markets. As we will see in the next chapter, the focus on substituting imports with a wider array of domestically produced goods was envisioned as means of diversifying the source of growth and harnessing the emerging locomotive for growth: technological change.

Key Concepts

Backward linkage	Encomienda	Golden age of primary
Caciques	Engel's law	product exports
Commodity lottery	Export pessimism	Latifundia
Dutch disease	Fazenda	Mandamiento
Ejidos	Forward linkage	Minifundia
Enclaves		Repartida

Chapter Summary

Growth Patterns

- Growth patterns of the industrialized nations and of Latin America show that disparities existing between the two did not become apparent until the twentieth century.
- Factors such as natural endowments, choices made by the owners of factors of production, the policy framework, the macroeconomic environment, and the interactions of supply and demand in a historical context help us understand the pattern of growth and contemporary economic issues in Latin America.

An Extractive Economy

- During the colonial period, Spaniards and Portuguese used exploitative techniques to extract the riches and abundant resources of Latin America. These techniques included the establishment of the encomienda system, the latifundia, and the use of indigenous populations and imported slaves from Africa to maximize the extraction of resources. These methods left a small elite in control of capital and political power, a weak internal market, and the majority of the population characterized by poverty.
- During the period of Latin American independence, despite the opportunity to change the rules of property rights and trade, the political elite maintained the system of the encomienda for purposes of stability. Yet the lack of political change hindered economic development. During the late 1800s and early 1900s, Latin America benefited from an agricultural export boom, but the boom was short lived for two main reasons: development policy was preoccupied with the needs of the export sector, ignoring domestic production, and demand for exports was determined abroad.
- Single commodity exports were characterized by various problems. First, as

exemplified by the Dutch disease, single commodity exports tend to absorb a country's resources and give way to unbalanced development. The dependence on that one export is fatal for the country when the price of the export drops, greatly decreasing revenues.

• When the single commodity export is a primary product, as was the case in most Latin American countries, the commodity suffers from being price and income inelastic; regardless of the price of the good or of people's income, people buy only so much of the good. Growth potential is limited.

• Single commodity export growth can be positive if the country reinvests its profits to expand its economy. In Latin America, however, the characteristics of the export commodity did not stimulate production in other sectors of the economy through forward or backward linkages. Furthermore, the influx of foreign capital did not foster the development of domestic financial institutions. The needs of the local economy depended on foreign capital.

• Environmental costs of the extractive economy were high. Colonists interrupted traditional agricultural practices, substituting environmentally unsustainable methods through extractive techniques. Environmental degradation continued with foreign penetration as well as neglect by Latin Americans themselves.

• The negative effects of World War I and the Great Depression (e.g., financial instability and the displacement of traditional raw materials) forced Latin America to adjust and become less dependent on single commodity exports.

Notes

1. Bradford E. Burns, ed., *Latin America: Conflict and Creation: A Historical Reader* (Englewood Cliffs, N.J.: Prentice-Hall, 1992); and Benjamin Keen, *Latin American Civilization*, 3d ed. (Boston: Houghton Mifflin, 1974) are suggested starting points. Even a few hours dabbling in these readers will help capture the rich and complex regional history.

2. See, for example, Bill Weinberg, *War on the Land: Ecology and Politics in Central America* (Atlantic Highlands, N.J.: Zed, 1991).

3. Colin M. Lewis, "Industry in Latin America," in *Dependency and Development in Latin America*, ed. Fernando Enrique Cardoso and Enzo Faletto (Berkeley and Los Angeles: University of California Press, 1979).

4. Stanley Engerman and Kenneth Sokoloff, *Factor Endowments, Institutions, and Differential Paths of Growth among New World Economies: A View from Economic Historians of the United States*, National Bureau of Economic Research Historical Paper no. 66 (Cambridge, Mass.: NBER, 1994).

5. Ibid., 30.

6. John Coatsworth, "Notes on the Comparative Economic History of Latin America and the United States," in *Development and Underdevelopment in America*, ed. Walther Bernecker and Hans Werner Tobler (New York: Walter de Gruyter, 1993).

7. There is some inconsistency in the historical data. Although estimates of Latin American income at the time were almost certainly biased upward, as Bulmer-Thomas notes, "Latin America's relatively privileged status within what is now the third world at

the end of the 18th century is difficult to dispute." Victor Bulmer-Thomas, *The Economic History of Latin America since Independence* (New York: Cambridge University Press, 1994), 27.

8. Victor Bulmer-Thomas uses the term "commodity lottery" to describe the effects of export orientation in the 1800s. Much of the discussion of economic history in this chapter relies on Bulmer-Thomas's illuminating text.

9. Rosemary Thorp, *Progress, Poverty, and Exclusion: An Economic History of Latin America in the 20th Century* (Baltimore: Johns Hopkins University Press/Inter-American Development Bank, 1998), 49.

10. Daniel Farber, *Environment under Fire* (New York: Monthly Review Press, 1993), 34.

11. Simon Hanson, *Economic Development in Latin America* (Washington, D.C.: Inter-American Affairs Press, 1951), 107.

12. Ibid., 106.

13. Gerardo della Paolera and Alan Taylor, *Finance and Development in an Emerging Market: Argentina in the Interwar Period*, National Bureau of Economic Research Working Paper no. 6236 (Cambridge, Mass.: National Bureau of Economic Research, 1997), 8.

14. Thorp, *Progress*, 69.

15. Fernando Henrique Cardoso and Ernesto Faletto, in Lewis, "Industry in Latin America," 295.

16. Thorp, *Progress*, 56.

17. Ibid., 72.

18. Della Paolera and Taylor, *Finance*, 12.

19. Ibid., 18.

20. Thorp, *Progress*, 64.

21. Ibid., 104.

22. Farber, *Environment under Fire*, 15.

23. Burns, *Latin America*, 40.

24. Thorp, *Progress*, 57.

25. John Ryan, "The Shrinking Forest," *NACLA Report on the Americas* 25, no. 2 (September 1991): 19.

26. Thorp, *Progress*, 21.

27. Vittorio Corbo, "Economic Policies and Performance in Latin America," in *Economic Development*, ed. Enzo Grilli and Dominick Salvatore (Westport, Conn.: Greenwood, 1994), 299.

28. Thorp, *Progress*, 6.

29. Coatsworth, "Comparative Economic History," 24.

30. Timothy Yeager, "Encomienda or Slavery? The Spanish Crown's Choice of Labor Organization in Sixteenth Century Spanish America," *Journal of Economic History* 55, no. 4 (December 1995).

CHAPTER THREE

IMPORT SUBSTITUTION INDUSTRIALIZATION

Looking Inward for the Source of Economic Growth

Many of the state-led investments under import substitution industrialization were in large-scale industries such as petrochemicals. *(Courtesy of the Inter-American Development Bank.)*

At the beginning of the twentieth century Argentina was one of the world's wealthiest nations. Why did Buenos Aires's elegant and luxurious buildings begin to seem locked in time as other nations modernized? Why did much of Latin America, despite its rich natural resources, experience slow growth? The export-led model discussed in chapter 2 did not deliver the anticipated growth. Distribution also had not improved. Why were the peasant campesinos stuck in a cycle of poverty? Emerging from the Depression and the world wars, Latin America lagged behind its northern hemispheric neighbors. Once behind international competitors, how could Latin American nations ever hope to catch up?

Hoping to answer these questions, Latin American policy makers compared the performance of the region with that of North America and Europe; they also looked with interest at the takeoff of the Soviet Union. Two answers to the puzzle of slow growth emerged: first, an explanation for Latin America's falling behind and, second, a prescription for what to do about it. Political economists such as Paul Baran and Andre Gundar Frank suggested that Latin America was not falling behind but was being *pushed* back by the exploitative development process in the powerful industrial countries. Raúl Prebisch and those at the Economic Commission for Latin America and the Caribbean (ECLAC) defined the development problem as the need to promote growth in the face of an international system controlled by the center countries. This chapter explores these tools of inward-looking development in the policy of **import substitution industrialization**. It treats the role of the state as a developmental actor and introduces the exchange rate and trade tools used to promote industrialization. It concludes by evaluating the performance of import substitution industrialization as an answer to the puzzle of how to promote development in Latin America. The following questions form the core of our investigation:

- How did theorists make sense of Latin America's declining position in the world economy?
- How did the theory of import substitution industrialization (ISI) propose to overcome the constraints on Latin American economic development?
- What were the key elements in the ISI toolbox?
- Was the approach successful in practice?

Understanding import substitution industrialization is an important step in unraveling the puzzle of Latin American development. It gives us a sense of the historical backdrop to contemporary policy and also locates one end of the policy spectrum with respect to the role of the state in development against which we can evaluate current practices.

DEPENDENCY THEORY:
AN EXPLANATION FOR BACKWARDNESS

For some analysts, answering the question of why some nations were growing and others were stagnating required looking not at countries in isolation, as individual plants in a garden, but rather at how countries interacted with each other in the international system. Proponents of **dependency theory** postulated that a country did not thrive or falter simply because of its own national endowments. Rather, progress could be attributed to the power it had to set the rules of the international economic game. Center countries, or the industrialized countries, defined the rules; the periphery, or developing countries, were pawns in the international pursuit of profit. As dependency theorist Andre Gundar Frank postulated, underdeveloped countries were not developed countries in the making; rather, industrial countries had caused underdevelopment in other nations in the process of economic expansion. For Frank, underdevelopment was generated by the same historical process that produced economic development: the march of capitalism.[1] Industrialized countries had access to cheap inputs for growth through the extraction of resources, the export of minerals, and the exploitation of cheap labor in the underdeveloped world. Rich countries became rich by making other countries poor.

The owners of the resources—the wealthy in the underdeveloped region— benefited from the international market. According to dependency theorist Paul Baran, local elites formed alliances with international capitalists, hindering long-term, dynamic growth in favor of short-term profits. Baran pointed to the feudal coherence of the latifundia system and the monopolistic market structure as impediments to vigorous long-run growth.[2] A social glue bonding local and international elites cemented economic privilege for the upper class. Those with power had no interest in sharing it. Relatively concentrated markets weakened competitive pressures. For Baran and for Frank, while the periphery was tied to the center, there was no possibility of sustainable growth. As long as traditional elites remained in power, periphery countries would be shackled to center country interests. Revolution, therefore, was in order.

Other theorists, such as Fernando Henrique Cardoso and Enzo Faletto, disagreed with the revolutionary prescription. Although concurring with the assessment that the center countries controlled the dynamic of growth, Cardoso and Faletto argued that autonomous development was indeed possible within the periphery. It would, however, involve an active state policy to counterbalance the greedy hand of the international market. A powerful state acting in the national interest could counteract the strength of local and international economic elites to promote genuine development in the periphery.

FROM DEPENDENCY THEORY TO DEVELOPMENT POLICY: ECLA AND THE STRUCTURALIST SCHOOL

The dependency theorists' critique of the international economic system informed but did not completely define the position of the **structuralists** at the United Nations Economic Commission for Latin America (ECLA).[3] Under the leadership of Raúl Prebisch, ECLA analysts looked at the disappointing economic performance of Latin America in the first half of the century, focusing on the volatility of primary product exports, and the progressive difficulty of paying for more technologically sophisticated (and expensive) products with the limited agricultural returns.[4] Technological progress was controlled by the powerful center-industrialized countries and spread slowly into the periphery. ECLA researchers in the 1950s were also fascinated by a seeming correlation between the interruption of normal trade patterns with the industrialized countries during the war periods and accompanying

---

BOX 3.1. BIOGRAPHY OF RAÚL PREBISCH (1901–1986)

Raúl Prebisch was an Argentine economist born in the town of Tucuman in 1901.[5] His contributions to development economics broke with the neoclassical tradition and greatly influenced Latin American economic policy in the 1950s. Though his theories were later criticized, his views and ideas questioned the extent to which the free market and free trade could solve the problem of underdevelopment.

Prebisch was educated in the University of Buenos Aires,[6] and during the 1920s he worked as a statistician for the Sociedad Rural, a stockbreeder's association.[7] Toward the beginning of his career, Prebisch was a believer in neoclassical economics, but the Great Depression and the writings of economist John Maynard Keynes shattered his faith in the free trade model.[8] Prebisch began to formulate different theoretical views in the early 1940s. This shift was first manifested in *The Economic Development of Latin America and Its Principal Problem,* written by Prebisch in 1949.[9] By this time Prebisch had served as director general of the Argentine Central Bank (1935–1943). He had also witnessed the devastating effects of the Depression on Argentina, which suffered from falling prices and debt payment difficulties. His 1949 manifesto reflected the effect of these external influences on economic development.

In the document, Prebisch divided the world in two, labeling one part the center and the other, the periphery. The center referred to advanced economies, which produced primarily industrial goods; the periphery referred to developing countries, which produced primary products. Behind this division, Prebisch saw a skewed relationship between the two, with the center gaining at the expense of the periphery. For Prebisch, productivity gains in the North (the center) were translated into rising wages, not falling prices, due to the market power of business and unions. In the South (the periphery), surplus labor kept wages low, and slow productivity growth in agriculture and mining acted as a drag on the economy.[10] The unequal distribution of economic gains was due primarily to **declining terms of trade,** as developing countries would have to export more and more to be able to import the same quantities as before. It is clear that by this point Prebisch rejected the idea that comparative advantage was the answer to growth for developing countries and opted for other policy prescriptions.

In 1948, the U.N. Economic Commission for Latin America was created; Prebisch became its chairman in 1949.[11] Prebisch's diagnosis for the causes of underdevelopment led him to advocate what is known as import substitution industrialization (ISI). Prebisch's thesis and policy prescriptions were adopted by ECLA, which, with Prebisch's leadership, strongly influenced Latin American economic policies in the 1950s.

From 1964 to 1969, Prebisch was the secretary-general of the U.N. Conference on Trade and Development (UNCTAD).[12] During this time period, Prebisch put aside his theoretical thinking and formulated policies that were later ignored by both the developed and developing world. When Prebisch returned to his theoretical endeavors after the UNCTAD years, he suggested that a post-ISI policy was required, including removing protection from certain industries and encouraging nontraditional exports. He pointed to the need to develop internal savings to decrease reliance on external debt, suggested institutional changes in the labor market and financial sector, and advised budgetary reforms to consolidate change in Latin America.[13]

robust internal growth in the Latin America region. Isolation from the international system apparently helped growth at home.

In part the disadvantaged position of periphery countries in the international system derived from the kind of goods they offered. Developing countries principally traded primary products, such as raw materials and agricultural goods, for more technologically advanced products in the international arena. Within this unequal framework, they faced what was seen as declining terms of trade for their products. There are only so many bananas that people want to eat or so much coffee that they can drink. Given the low income elasticity for agricultural products, as the global economy grows, the relative demand for primary products declines. Instead, rewards tend to accrue to those engaged in technological entrepreneurship. Technological sophistication adds value to a good, increasing its market price well beyond the cost of basic inputs. Declining terms of trade for primary products reflected the argument that as the prices of sophisticated goods rose, developing countries would need to export more and more oranges or wheat to pay for the more expensive technological machinery. Without mastering technology, countries had little hope of advancement.

In addition to the position that all goods do not generate equal rewards, structuralists also offered a view contrary to that of traditional economists on how economies functioned. Challenging the tenets of neoclassical economic theory, which assumes that rational, self-interested profit maximizers operating in open and competitive international markets will produce the greatest good for all, structuralists argued that the economy was shaped by power and politics. For the structuralists, economic activity is conditioned by interest group politics. Markets in Latin America are controlled by concentrated oligopolies in which firms are price makers and elites establish patterns of consumption. Because fashions in modern consumption are determined by New York's Madison Avenue, elites tend to demand sophisticated goods produced by industrial economies. Importing these items would do little to spur local growth. The promises of trickle-down economics hold no magic for the masses of the poor in the developing world. In the structuralist's eyes, the development process is not a movement toward equilibrium but rather is driven by imbalances and tension. Although the neoclassical model predicts benefits for poor countries from international trade, structuralists contend that international trade exacerbates inequality between and within nations because those countries and companies with control set the rules of the game in their favor. For the structuralist, the neoclassical model does not conform with the hard, cold facts of the international economy.

From Structuralism to Import Substitution Industrialization

The arguments of the dependency theorists and the structuralists shaped a policy package widely adopted in Latin America and known as import substitution industrialization. Perceiving the international game as stacked against them and with multiple external shocks repeatedly destabilizing the economy, Latin American policy makers turned inward to promote internal sources of economic growth. Instead of relying on the international economy as the engine of growth, ISI poli-

cies sought to develop industries in a protected environment. The goal was to create industries capable of producing substitutes for expensive imports while simultaneously promoting industrial growth and the expansion of internal economies. The notion was that import substitution industrialization would induce a process of learning driven by exposure to new ideas and processes that would dynami-

QUESTION FOR THOUGHT

Are the characteristics of Latin American economies as described by the dependency theorists and the structuralists consistent with the historical view of development portrayed in chapter 2? Are there pieces missing or overstated?

cally spill over into the whole economy.[14] Rául Prebisch and ECLA structuralists placed the role of technological change at the center of the development process and identified a strong role for the state in promoting national technological capabilities.[15] Without mastering technological processes, developing countries had no chance to catch up. The only economic actor strong enough to counterbalance the weight of multinational corporations was the state.

The strategy of import substitution industrialization was informed by Albert Hirschman's concepts of bottlenecks and linkages. For Hirschman, imbalances in the system, such as supply shocks and bottlenecks, were central to development as signals for investment.[16] Hirschman characterized the development process as a bottle with a thin neck. Inputs—land, labor, capital—were constrained from freely flowing from the bottle by the constricting neck of scarce complementary factors such as technology, infrastructure, or entrepreneurial capital. If the state could break the bottlenecks in crucial industries, resources would flow back up the production chain, stimulating the demand for intermediate inputs, or they would flow forward in the consumption pattern to create the demand for new products. Therefore, by promoting a steel sector, for example, **backward linkages** such as those to the iron ore and smelters would stimulate the growth of these supplier industries while **forward linkages** would stimulate the auto or machine industries. If the state could target those industries with the largest backward and forward linkages, it could act as an engine of development.

A strong state was critical to the structuralist program. ISI theorists pointed to a simple fact: if the market could work on its own, why had it not been successful in promoting growth in Latin America? **Market failure** to produce sustainable growth provided the rationale for state intervention. Given the weak private sector and the large economies of scale attached to industrial endeavors, an active state was viewed as a necessary complement to the market economy.[17] The ability of the state to deliver on public project investments contributed to the perceived need of governments to also meet the demand for social projects. This emanated from the highly unequal income distribution in Latin America.

The political demands of populism, of attending to the broad needs of the domestic population in the name of social peace, were consistent with the economic theory of import substitution industrialization. Populism drew on the charismatic power of leaders such as Juan Perón of Argentina or Getulio Vargas of Brazil to mobilize support within labor and industrial elites in the service of a nationalist development strategy. Traditional populist strategies encouraged support for a developmentalist model to meet the changing needs of society without explosive class conflict. By co-opting key labor and industrial groups into the quest for change, support for interventionist policies could be maintained. **Economic populism**, a term applied to the developmental strategies of the 1950s, 1960s, and 1970s, emphasized growth and redistribution of income to the neglect of internal and external constraints. That is, as long as financing was available, the state kept attempting to buy off each group in the conflictual process of development. Labor, politically powerful, was given strong protection under the law. Industrialists were favored with development schemes. State-led strategies to reduce poverty and promote infrastructure were pursued to keep local political leaders happy. But constraints on development—inflation, fiscal deficits, external imbalances—were often ignored until it was too late and crisis erupted.[18] Political demands to moderate the distributional tensions of development were consistent with the state-led ISI model.

THE ISI TOOLBOX

Import substitution industrialization relied on a variety of economic tools to achieve its aim. The toolbox can be broken down into three categories: active industrial policy, protective international instruments, and accommodationist fiscal and monetary policy complemented by a careful program of transnational participation. It is important to note that although these tools were at the disposal of all policy makers in the region, they were applied in varying degrees in each country. We will discuss these three broad tools in turn.

Active Industrial Policy: The Role of SOEs

Industrial policy was anchored in the formation of state-owned enterprises (SOEs) throughout the region. Under the assumption that the state was the only able domestic actor with the resources to produce in relatively underdeveloped markets, state firms were formed in a wide range of heavy industries, including oil, petrochemicals, telecommunications, steel, and aircraft. In some cases these enterprises were wholly owned by the state, and in others they operated as mixed enterprises, incorporating state and private capital. State firms had access to public funds for investment, research, and development. Backed by sovereign guarantees, they also had easier access to international financial markets to borrow for large development projects. State ministries could assist in the negotiation of international technology transfer packages to jump-start production. They had the resources to hire some of the brightest national scientists, engineers, and managers to run operations. Additionally, the pressures of producing initial annual profits were relieved as state firms were able to extend their time horizon for investment returns.

Although the public enterprise status held many advantages, there were also restrictions. Hiring and pay scales were subject to national standards, sometimes placing a ceiling on the pay for skilled labor. State firms were subject to the whims of politicians and often became agencies for employing large numbers of constituents. Furthermore, the services of industries in basic infrastructure, such as the electrical or telecommunications sectors, were often underpriced to provide cheap inputs to stimulate the growth of the private sector. Cheap inputs allowed for a local manufacturing boom; however, underpricing electricity or phone service led to losses that were absorbed by the SOEs. As resources became increasingly constrained, underpricing also resulted in underinvestment over time. Because firms were carrying losses, they couldn't afford to expand to meet the demand.

Despite the difficulties that state-owned enterprises confronted, they proliferated rapidly from the 1950s to the 1970s in Latin America. In table 3.1 we see what types of industries were most subject to state ownership and ISI policies in the case of Brazil. We see that high rates of state ownership existed particularly in industries that required significant investment, such as public goods enjoyed by all citizens and critical industries, including national security enterprises.

In an analysis of the cause for state intervention, Tom Trebat identifies six reasons for state enterprises: a weak private sector, economies of scale, public externalities, dynamic public managers, natural resource rents, and public historical factors. In steel, electrical energy, and telecommunications, state-owned firms were formed after private sector failures. Particularly in Brazil, developmental nationalists believed state intervention was the pragmatic response to the failure of the free market. Economies of scale and the need for large investments to lower costs provided further grounds for state activity. In industries with clear public value, such as railroads, energy, and ports, it was argued that there were benefits to state provision of these services, especially when private providers had not emerged in the market. For some firms, because of public visibility and prestige, state enterprises were able to attract the most dynamic managers. Finally, where industrialization was resource based, such as in oil and mining, it was argued that these resources belonged to the nation and should therefore be managed on the public's behalf.[19] Thus there was an economic rationale (although perhaps not always a compelling one) for state activity in the industrial sector.

The High Tariff Walls of ISI: Protectionism as a Tool of ISI

International economic tools facilitated the industrialization process. If your grasp of international economics is rusty, box 3.2 provides a quick review of terms. The growth of state and private enterprises was encouraged under the protection of high tariff and trade restrictions. These protective walls were designed to give less-competitive national industries, conceived of as infant industries, the chance to develop without the competition of large multinational firms. There was a perceived need for protection while an economy developed the necessary conditions to promote learning and innovation within the firm.[20] The policy objective wasn't to ignore exports; rather, the hope was that temporary protection would lead to the development of new products.[21]

We can measure the degree of protectionism by looking at tariff rates. Average nominal protection over consumer and manufactured goods was 131 percent in Argentina, 168 percent in Brazil, 138 percent in Chile, 112 percent in Colombia, 61 percent in Mexico, and 21 percent in Uruguay in 1960.[22] In the case of Mexico in 1970, the effective rate of protection—the nominal tariff rate adjusted for the protection also present in the purchase of intermediate goods used to produce the final good—was as high as 671 percent for fertilizer and insecticides, 226 percent for synthetic fertilizers, 206 percent for pharmaceuticals, 102 percent for automo-

Table 3.1.   State Enterprise Share in the Brazilian Economy, 1973

	Proportion of Assets in State-Owned Firms
High Degree of State Participation ($\geq$ 50%)	
Railways	100
Port services	100
Water, gas, and sewers	99
Telegraph and telephone	97
Electricity	79
Mining	63
Developmental services	51
Chemicals	50
Medium Degree of State Participation (20–49%)	
Water transport	45
Banking and finance	38
Metal fabrication	37
Services	36
Air transport	22
Low Degree of State Participation (<20%)	
Construction and engineering	8
Rubber	6
Road transport and passengers	6
Agriculture and forestry	4
Nonmetallic minerals	2
Transport equipment	2
Food and beverages	1
Machinery	0
Electrical machinery	0
Wood products and furniture	0
Textiles	0
Tobacco	0
Printing and publishing	0
Leather products	0
Radio and television	0
Commerce	0

Source: Peter Evans, *Dependent Development* (Princeton, N.J.: Princeton University Press, 1979), adapted from table 5.1, p. 221.

BOX 3.2.   A REVIEW OF THE TOOLS OF PROTECTIONISM

Tariff   A tariff, the most common type of protectionism, is a tax on imports. A tariff works best when the demand for the good in question is elastic or price sensitive. If buyers do not respond to the higher price, a tariff will not limit imports. With a tariff, the central government collects revenues. Nominal tariff protection is measured by looking at the tariff rate on the final manufactured good. Effective rates of protection adjust this rate for tariffs on intermediate inputs.

Quota   A quota is a quantitative limit on imports. A quota presents a fixed limit on the quantity of goods that may be imported. Quotas may be assigned to suppliers or they may be auctioned, creating revenue for the central government.

Import licensing   The legal requirement to obtain a license to import a certain kind of good. Import licensing boards evaluate national availability of goods to assess whether the import is critical or whether the need can be met by national production.

Foreign exchange controls   To restrict the quantity of imports or to direct imports to certain sectors, the government may ration foreign exchange. This generally involves compelling exporters to sell foreign exchange to the government at a fixed price. Selective importers of key goods are offered preferential prices for foreign exchange, whereas importers of luxury items or those wanting to travel pay more local currency for their dollars, yen, or deutschmarks. Foreign exchange controls are therefore linked to a system of multiple exchange rates. Not surprisingly, as there are therefore different prices for the same commodity—money—a black or a parallel market often develops. The black market price can sometimes be used as an indicator of how far the exchange rate has been taken off course by policy distortions.

Industrial incentives   Direct payments or tax breaks to a firm engaging in a particular line of production. These credits act as a protectionist device if an international competitor cannot meet the lower, subsidized price in the local market.

Export subsidy   A fiscal incentive, sometimes in the form of a tax break, for reaching export targets. Export subsidies promote the development of export industries at home, arguably to unfair advantage compared to the international firms.

biles, and 67 percent for electrical equipment. Across the board, for durable consumption and capital goods in Mexico in 1970, effective protection rates averaged 35 percent.[23] High import tariffs often induced multinational firms to set up factories within the country. In 1970 in Mexico, 62 percent of the machinery sector, 49.1 percent of transport vehicles, and 79.3 percent of electric equipment were dominated by foreign enterprises.[24] Although ownership was not national, labor learned new production techniques, and the technological level of production was raised.

Somewhat ironically, in the first stages of import substitution industrialization, national imports usually rose. Steel, for example, could be produced only with huge furnaces, and they had to be bought somewhere. To promote the import of these critical inputs, states tended to maintain **overvalued exchange rates**, making imports relatively cheaper to purchase. Imports and access to this underpriced foreign exchange were often then licensed to control the demand for imported goods to those critical to the industrialization process. As reviewed in box 3.2, import licensing boards evaluated the quality and availability of national substitutes, their prices, and their importance in the production process.[25] International trade and foreign exchange tools insulated the economy from rival foreign firms

dominating the market. Box 3.3 contrasts the effects of various exchange rate regimes in development strategies.

Additional Tools of Industrial Policy: Targeted Lending, Multinational Activity, and Passive Monetary Policy

Ownership was not the only tool of industrial policy in Latin America. Industrial
policy was accommodated by monetary and fiscal measures. The state provided
subsidies to domestic firms, and it granted tax credits and soft credit to jump-start
the national industrial motor. National development banks were formed, such as
Chile's Corporación de Fomento de la Producción (CORFO) and Brazil's State
National Development Bank (BNDE), to target investments in the economy. A
national development bank has an advantage over commercial lenders in planning

---

BOX 3.3.   EXCHANGE RATE POLICY AND DEVELOPMENT

An exchange rate is simply the price of one currency in terms of another. Ideally, exchange rates should equate the value of one nation's goods with those of another.[26]
    There are basically three types of exchange rate regimes that countries chose among:
fixed, flexible, and crawling pegs. Under the gold standard (1870–1914) and the Bretton
Woods systems (1945–1973), countries fixed their currencies to an anchor—gold or the
U.S. dollar. A fixed exchange rate has the advantage of promoting stability. A critical
price—the price of domestic goods in terms of international goods—is fixed. If a country
is running a balance of payments deficit at that rate, it must clear its accounts by exporting gold or defend its rates by selling dollars or reserves. Because money supplies are
tied to reserves such as dollars and gold, the economy contracts and over time, payments
imbalances should adjust. The economy should therefore expand only at the rate of its
accumulation of real reserves. The best way to understand the concept is to visualize the
old terms of trade: if France imported more from Great Britain, it had to send or "export" gold to pay for it, thus lowering the national money supply.
    Today many countries pursue a floating exchange regime. Under a floating system,
if a country is running a balance of payments deficit, the price of foreign exchange
adjusts or depreciates. Rather than a country exporting gold, the market changes the
value of national money. As imports become more expensive and exports appear cheaper
in international markets, if consumers are responsive to price change, flows should begin
to balance. A large stock of reserves is not needed to defend the rate. Nevertheless,
whereas the fixed exchange rate promotes price stability, as a floating exchange rate
depreciates, making crucial imports more expensive, floating rates may exert an upward
pressure on domestic prices and may be inflationary.
    Finally, some countries attempt to have both the stability of a fixed anchor and the
flexibility of floating rates with the use of a crawling peg. Under this exchange rate
system the currency is set to a central value but is allowed to fluctuate around that target
in the short run.
    What is the "right" exchange rate in the long run? Essentially, the same good should
sell for the same price in two different markets. If it does not, and transportation costs
are minimal and trade is free, some enterprising person will buy goods in the cheaper
market and sell them where they are dear. Not surprisingly, using the exchange rate as a
tool of industrial promotion interferes with arriving at the "right rate." Imbalances
emerge that become difficult to sustain over time.

strategic investment projects. As a state bank, it has a longer return horizon and is able to be active in more risky sectors because bottom-line profits are not the objective. Key industries such as machinery, automobiles, shipbuilding, and telephones were targeted as central to industrial growth. In Mexico, the Law of New and Necessary Industries provided select tax exemptions to promote growth in a limited number of unrepresented but critical sectors in the economy.

In "strategic" sectors such as autos or steel, **transnational corporations** were welcomed as providers of needed technology and capital within the import substitution industrialization model. In table 3.2 we can see the significant role played by multinational corporations in manufacturing. In or about 1970, 24 percent of manufacturing in Argentina, 50 percent in Brazil, 30 percent in Chile, 43 percent in Colombia, 35 percent in Mexico, 44 percent in Peru, and 14 percent in Venezuela was under foreign control. Some of this participation predates the ISI period, but the strong involvement of transnationals, particularly in industrial production, was seen throughout the postwar ISI period.[27]

The entry of transnational corporations was somewhat paradoxical. ISI, after all, was attempting to reduce dependency on the international structure of production. However, there was also a degree of pragmatism at work. Transnationals provided critical financial capital and technology. The goal became to utilize these assets selectively, employing bargaining power to transform the rules of the game. ISI policies set new rules: to produce and sell in the domestic market, transnational companies had to commit to technology transfer and the training of labor. Under the threat of market closure to the sale of their products, transnational firms agreed to joint ownership arrangements and the use of local inputs. In the automobile industry in Brazil, for example, GM do Brasil was a joint venture between Brazilian capital and General Motors (GM). Ford, Volkswagen, Fiat, and GM sparked the development of an industrial park. With high tariff rates, local production would be the only viable solution to selling cars nationally. Multinational firms defended market shares against the possibility of being shut out through local manufacture. If they did not participate according to local rules, their international competitors would. Development of local parts suppliers was promoted by requiring 99 percent local content by weight for passenger cars produced locally.[28] Mexico was able to

Table 3.2.   Foreign Shares of Selected Industries, circa 1970 (percentage)

	Argentina	Brazil	Chile	Colombia	Mexico	Peru	Venezuela
Food	15.3	42.1	23.2	22.0	21.5	33.1	10.0
Textiles	14.2	34.2	22.9	61.9	15.3	39.7	12.9
Chemicals	34.9	49.0	61.9	66.9	50.7	66.7	16.5
Transport equipment	44.4	88.2	64.5	79.7	64.0	72.9	31.1
Electrical machinery	27.6	83.7	48.6	67.2	50.1	60.7	23.2
Paper	25.7	22.3	7.9	79.3	32.9	64.8	20.1
All manufacturing	23.8	50.1	29.9	43.4	34.9	44.0	13.8

Source: Rhys Jenkins, *Transnational Corporations and Industrial Transformation in Latin America* (New York: St. Martin's, 1984), excerpted from table 2.4.

ISI contributed to the development of light manufacturing such as this Mexican knife producer. *(Courtesy of the Inter-American Development Bank.)*

prod concessions in creating national joint ventures in the electrical industry by playing one multinational against another.[29] In addition to local content laws, contracts often stipulated the number of local managers to improve national managerial capacity, an assurance of technology transfer of technological processes (not simply sending the more sophisticated parts preassembled in the United States or Europe), and limits on the repatriation of profits to promote local reinvestment of revenues. Our case study of the auto industry in the appendix to this chapter further illustrates these concepts.

A large domestic market enhanced national bargaining power in establishing contract terms with the multinationals. Clearly Brazil and Mexico had greater bargaining power than Ecuador or Paraguay, as there were many more likely Brazilian or Mexican buyers of locally produced cars. Yet, even in the Mexican and Brazilian cases, exports of locally manufactured multinational products were necessary to take advantage of economies of scale. Nonetheless, even where bargaining power was strong, nationalist sentiments reserved strategic industries, such as oil in Mexico, to wholly local ownership.

For the most part, a loose monetary policy greased the fiscal wheels of development. Particularly from the mid-1960s on, the dominant political system in Latin America was an authoritarian government. Developmental nationalists saw it as their mission to promote development as a critical element of security. Rules were changed to decrease the autonomy of central banks, forcing them to accommodate fiscal spending programs. In areas of monetary, fiscal, or international affairs, reliable data about developing nations were sorely lacking, and many decisions were made by guesswork and intuition.[30]

> **QUESTION FOR THOUGHT**
>
> Given the characteristics of Latin American economies in the postwar period, would you have recommended the use of import substitution industrialization tools at the time? Would you have made any adjustments in the toolbox?

THE PERFORMANCE OF IMPORT SUBSTITUTION INDUSTRIALIZATION

How well did import substitution industrialization work? By the barometer of average annual growth rates of 5.5% over the period 1950–1980, one could call import substitution a successful strategy. Throughout the 1950s, Latin American economies were growing comparatively faster than the Western economies, and between 1950 and 1970 Latin American GDP tripled.

As illustrated in Table 3.3, performance varied by country, with Brazil, Ecuador, and Mexico exhibiting the strongest growth rates over the ISI years of roughly 1950–1980. The production of basic consumption goods was widespread throughout the region, and some countries successfully initiated heavy machine goods industries as well.[31] Production outstripped population growth—a problem identified in our data in chapter 2. While the population of the region roughly doubled over the period 1945–1980, gross domestic product in real terms quintupled.[32]

Import performance was variable. Most countries did not see a decline in imports as a ratio of GDP. Brazil was more successful. Comparing 1964 with 1949,

---

Box 3.4.   ISI Tool Box: A Summary

Industrial policy

Form state-owned firms
Form mixed economic enterprises—part state, part private   STATE
Require government purchases from national firms   CAPITALISM
Require foreign firms to establish joint ventures
Pressure foreign firms to increase local content

International instruments

Tariffs on final goods
Quotas on imports
Exchange rate overvaluation
Exchange rationing
Import licenses

Fiscal and monetary policy

Subsidies for cheap inputs such as electricity
Subsidies for public transportation
Tax breaks in production
Preferential interest rates
Accommodating monetary policy

---

imports in the Brazilian economy decreased substantially as a percentage of total national supply, ranging from 19.0% in 1949 to 4.2% in 1964. Predictably, during the first stages of ISI in Brazil, the import of capital producer goods doubled from 1949 (15.8 b Cr) to 1959 (29.2 b Cr) as machines were needed to produce other goods. However, by 1964, imports of capital producer goods had fallen to nearly half the rate of the 1949 levels. Over the same period domestic production of consumer and producer goods rose substantially, with national production of all manufactured products increasing 266% from 1949 through 1964.[33]

    Less tangible gains also accrued.[34] Import substitution created forces for the development of an urban middle class, which demanded infrastructure entitlements in public utilities such as water and sewage systems. A national business class and a parallel labor union movement emerged, changing the agrarian balance of power. This coalition supporting the model, however, often intervened in policy making to thwart changes such as exchange rate valuations that might have prevented the accumulation of large fiscal imbalances.

The Crisis of Import Substitution Industrialization

Despite the apparent gains, import substitution industrialization was both unsustainable over time and produced high economic and social costs. In theory, ISI should have developed an internal momentum, expanding industrialization through

Table 3.3.   Percentage Growth in GDP Per Capita

Country	1941–1949	1950–1959	1960–1969	1970–1979	1980–1989
Brazil	1.6	3.6	2.8	6.1	0.8
Ecuador	4.1	2.4	1.8	7.0	−0.1
Mexico	3.7	3.1	3.5	3.2	−0.3
Dominican Republic	3.0	3.4	1.4	4.6	0.7
Panama	−2.2	1.8	4.8	1.9	−0.6
Costa Rica	4.7	2.8	2.2	3.3	−0.8
Colombia	1.6	1.8	2.1	3.2	1.6
Peru	2.5	3.0	2.5	1.2	−2.1
El Salvador	9.3	1.8	2.2	1.8	−2.6
Guatemala	0.3	0.5	1.9	3.1	−2.1
Paraguay	0.6	−0.7	1.1	5.0	0.9
Argentina	2.3	0.8	2.8	1.3	−2.3
Honduras	1.5	−0.1	1.8	2.4	−1.0
Chile	1.5	1.3	1.9	0.6	1.9
Uruguay	2.5	1.0	0.3	2.5	0.1
Nicaragua	4.2	2.4	3.6	−2.5	−3.8
Bolivia	0.6	−1.7	3.2	1.9	−3.0
Venezuela	6.7	2.9	0.0	−0.1	−3.4

Source: ECLA data as found in Vitorio Corbo, "Economic Policies and Performance in Latin America," in *Economic Development: Handbook of Comparative Economic Policies,* ed. Enzo Grilli and Dominick Salvatore (Westport, Conn.: Greenwood, 1994), 308.

interindustry linkages. Using his concept of linkages, Hirschman predicted that industrial growth should have occurred based on targeted investments. However, some contend that, given the limited size of the internal market in Latin America, ISI became "exhausted." It was postulated that as one moves to ever more sophisticated production, especially heavy machinery, the minimum plant size increases. Successful substitution would therefore be limited to sectors in which the internal demand for the good exceeded plant size—or where exports could make up the difference. The export vent, however, was largely closed due to the unfavorable exchange rates for sales abroad and less competitive industries. One study suggested that with such a high degree of income inequality, a massive devaluation to make Latin American exports globally competitive would have been politically and socially explosive.[35] Some programs were successful, such as the Brazilian BEFIEX (Special Fiscal Benefits for Exports) scheme, which provided incentives for exports. The benefits, however, were limited to countries and sectors with internationally competitive products. In many cases nationally manufactured goods did not meet international quality standards after growing up under protective tariffs, and firms were not forced by competition to become efficient. ECLA economists advocated economic integration within the region to expand the economies of scale, but the integration process was also limited in its achievements. Economic performance was too varied across the region, and political differences made subregional integration difficult at times.

Others explained the crisis of import substitution industrialization in political and sociological terms. Because the industrial process was largely in the hands of elites, it failed to create a new entrepreneurial class that would have given the process greater dynamism. Given elite power, import substitution industrialization may have provided more support to industrialists than to industry.[36] Many of the tools used to manage ISI—import licenses, investment permits, and government contracts—created the possibility of profitable personal rents for those able to control them.[37] Corruption became economically expedient under the ISI model. This led to the views of the new political economists, which will be discussed in chapter 5, suggesting a minimalist role for government.

ISI exacerbated inequality in the region. With more than a third of the region's population living in poverty, internal demand was severely limited. Consumption patterns imitated those of the center elite instead of attending to the needs of the masses. Import substitution industrialization may also have been a more reactive and a less coherently implemented strategy than is often supposed. That is, the policy-making process frequently may have been responding to balance of payments crises in erecting tariffs rather than proactive protection.[38] Finally, rather than promote risk-taking behavior, the comfort of state ownership and international protection coddled the business culture. ISI fostered the creation of inefficient economic institutions that have persisted into the contemporary period.[39]

With resources focused on industrialization, agriculture was neglected. Necessary investments in agricultural infrastructure were not made as capital was directed to the industrial sector. Labor also gravitated toward urban industrial regions, pressuring cities. In some cases the decline in agricultural production meant an increase in the quantity of food imports, further pressuring the balance of payments. The neglect of agriculture weakened not only a source of profits but also the food security of nations. The urban, industrial bias was unsustainable. ISI was an imbalanced strategy.

Inefficiencies and inconsistencies abound under import substitution industrialization. Even Raúl Prebisch, founder of the ECLAC school, was not blind to the emerging challenges in the region in the late 1960s and early 1970s.[40] Prebisch noted that overvalued exchange rates biased growth against the export sector. Where exports are a source of international or hard currency, this introduces a foreign exchange gap to finance development. Differences in domestic expenditures and revenue in state-owned firms lead either to persistent deficits or to monetary expansion that results in inflation. We will consider these inflationary biases in chapter 5. Internal and external resource gaps were met through external borrowing, adding annually to debt obligations (chapter 4). As long as international financial markets were willing to extend financing, the model could be sustained; however, once the spigots of international finance were turned off, internally driven industrialization ground to a halt.

LESSONS FOR DEVELOPMENT: WAS ISI INHERENTLY FLAWED?

Does the failure of import substitution industrialization in the 1980s mean that it was a misguided policy from the start? Some contend that the triumphant adoption of the neoliberal model throughout the region testifies to the inherent flaws of ISI.

Others such as economist Werner Baer suggest that import substitution industrialization was the appropriate policy for the period but that times changed.[41] Indeed, it could be argued that the development of the industrial sector under import substitution industrialization made the dynamic private sector model possible in the 1990s. The international environment also changed substantially, with expanding globalization. After we look more closely at the neoliberal model in chapters 6–9, consider the counterfactual question for the case study of the automobile industry in Latin America: would the industry have been so successful without import substitution industrialization? Although we will come to no definitive conclusion, entertaining this question may foreshadow some of the future needs in Latin America with respect to the role of the state. Remember Gabriel García Márquez's warning (chapter 2) about the repetitious cycles in Latin American history. Before we discard the goals and tools of import substitution industrialization forever, we might do well to consider that in the future, the past may reappear, with a stronger need for the state in addressing some of the problems of market failure.

> **QUESTION FOR THOUGHT**
>
> Do you believe that ISI was inherently flawed or simply outlived its usefulness as domestic and international conditions changed?

But this is getting well ahead of our story. In the next two chapters we will look more carefully at some of the problems associated with the later ISI period: the problems of macroeconomic instability and the debt crisis. This will then position us for a careful look at the neoliberal model, with a strong role for the private as opposed to the public sector.

APPENDIX: THE AUTOMOBILE INDUSTRY IN LATIN AMERICA—A CASE OF SUCCESSFUL IMPORT SUBSTITUTION INDUSTRIALIZATION?[42]

Introduction

The automobile industry is one of the most important sectors in many Latin American economies. In Argentina, the industry and its linkages account for 22 percent of employment. After oil, automobiles and automobile components are the second most important export in Mexico. Brazil and Argentina combined are expected to surpass Germany in automobile sales by the first decade of the twenty-first century. You may be surprised to learn that the automobile industry in Latin America is not merely an assembly operation. Full-fledged production has been in place since the early 1950s; Brazil and Mexico have become centers of innovative production. As in the developed countries, the automobile industry occupies a central role in many Latin American economies, although it has not brought the same level of development. Unlike highly industrialized economies, the Latin American automobile industry is foreign owned. Since its beginnings, like the region, it has experienced a tendency toward stagnation. Therefore, a look at the development of the automobile industry can enhance our understanding of Latin America's economic development in the twentieth century.

The Automobile Industry and Its Role in Industrialization

As a leading sector in the development strategies of underdeveloped and developed countries, the automobile industry is credited with innovation in a number of production processes that have changed labor relations and international trade. Two such processes are Fordism and Toyotaism. Fordism—named after Ford Motor Company's production strategy—introduced the assembly line, innovated the five dollar workday, and separated geographically the managerial aspect of production—white-collar jobs—from industrial activities—blue-collar jobs. Toyotaism or "just in time" production (named after Toyota's manufacturing strategy) has replaced Fordism's concept of an assembly line with "flexible manufacturing," using technology, robotics, and skilled labor to cut down inventory costs. Furthermore, Toyotaism integrates manufacturer and supplier to create more quality control and meet more varied consumer tastes. Both Fordism's and Toyotaism's innovations have been so successful they quickly spilled over to other industries. It is therefore no wonder why developing countries would seek to establish an automobile industry.

Why Promote an Automobile Industry in Latin America?

The many forward and backward linkages of automobile manufacturing prompted Latin American governments to give it a central role in their development strategies. As Hirschman suggested, a large number of forward and backward linkages will stimulate development. The automobile industry creates backward linkages because it needs suppliers of steel, iron, glass, paint, rubber, and textiles. This stimulates the growth of steel mills, glass producers, rubber producers, and paint manufacturers. It creates forward linkages because automobiles need gas, oil, replacement parts, service shops, and better roads. This demand leads to private investment in oil refineries, gas stations, automobile parts, and construction companies. The result is an increase in economic growth, employment, and aggregate demand. In the mid-1950s a Brazilian admiral who was very closely involved with the promotion of the automobile industry stated, "As in the highly industrialized countries, the automotive industry will be without doubt the leading sector of the entire economy, by force of its magnitude, complexity, and dynamism."[43]

The Early Automobile Industry in Latin America

The growth potential of the automobile market led multinationals to the region. In 1916 Ford opened its first assembly plant in Argentina. In the following years operations by other automobile firms were established in Brazil, Mexico, and Chile. The market was too limited to support full production but was profitable for assembly operations. To promote expansion of locally based multinational corporations (MNCs), governments, at the request of the established foreign firms, set tariffs on fully assembled vehicles of nonresident producers to increase the profit margin of firms with local plants.

The importance of the Latin American market grew as a result of the expansion of road networks in the early 1920s. American manufacturers moved quickly at the opportunity to extend their U.S. production run of parts and components to these markets, since the European market was highly protected. By the late 1920s Argentina represented a market twice as large as Italy and a third the size of France and the United Kingdom.

The Role of the State in the Automobile Industry

A drop in commodity prices during the Great Depression debilitated the import capacity of Latin America. As available imports declined during World War II, a local parts supply sector owned by private national capital developed to service the aging stock of vehicles. The strong demand for raw materials for war efforts boosted Latin American exports, creating huge reserves of foreign exchange.

The immediate postwar period witnessed a flood of automobile imports in response to the backlog in demand, but the availability of foreign exchange was short-lived. By 1947 vehicle imports to Argentina reached 80,000; in Brazil they peaked at 110,000 in 1951.[44] This surge of imports led to a balance of payments deficit and endangered the existence of local parts producers. In response, the governments of Brazil, Mexico, and Argentina—the countries with the largest automobile operations—raised trade barriers to limit the number of finished automobile imports and protected local producers by setting local manufacturing content requirements for domestic assembly operations. These state actions were crucial for the transition to manufacturing operations and reflected the beginning of a government commitment to an ISI policy. In 1956 the Brazilian government banned all imports of cars, requiring any international producers wishing to sell in the Brazilian market to establish local operations. It also required that 90 percent of parts be procured from national producers within five years, stimulating the development of a supplier industry.[45]

Foreign capital, as a source of technology and know-how, was crucial to this strategy. Since automobile corporations were among the largest and most technologically sophisticated in the world, governments had a particular interest in ensuring that they continued to invest locally. Therefore, import barriers and local content requirement were matched with high fiscal incentives. Between 1956 and 1969, the Brazilian government

> **QUESTION FOR THOUGHT**
>
> Given your understanding of the automobile industry and economic policy, were appropriate strategies followed throughout the course of the development of the automobile industry?

offered 89 cents worth of subsidies for every dollar in investment. Mexico offered 50–60 percent of the value of investment.[46] In addition, to make the market even more attractive, governments created policies to control wages. Government subsidies were important in moving from assembly to manufacturing because the small elite market limited economies of scale. Therefore, fiscal incentives made the transition to manufacturing profitable for the foreign automobile firms. As a result, by 1962 Brazil produced 191,194 vehicles per year; Mexico produced 193,000 by 1970, whereas ten years before it assembled only 50,000 with low domestic content.[47]

Export Promotion and Debt-Led Growth

State intervention was also critical in moving from production exclusively for the domestic market to exports. Balance of payments shocks driven by the oil crisis of the 1970s prompted export promotion to relieve current account pressures. Brazil developed the Special Fiscal Benefits for Exports (BEFIEX) program in the early 1970s. Manufacturers wishing to qualify for continued fiscal benefits and reduced tariffs had to meet a dollar value export target. Otherwise, they were subject to exorbitant import taxes for capital goods, parts, components, and raw materials. In 1977 the Mexican government issued an automotive decree that mandated automobile firms to eliminate their trade imbalances by 1982. Established firms complied to fend off increased competition by Japanese firms eager to enter the market. Instead of undertaking austerity measures, the government followed a debt-led growth strategy that provided subsidies and credits for those firms that would begin exporting automobiles with a high domestic content. Given the high production costs, it was very unlikely that the Latin American industry would have generated exports without government intervention.[48]

The majority of established firms complied with the export requirements. During the second half of the 1970s and the 1980s exports from Brazil and Mexico shot up. By 1981 the proportion of vehicles being produced for export in Brazil had increased to 27.3 percent, up from 2.2 percent in 1972.[49] The Mexican automobile industry by 1986 had reached a trade surplus of U.S.$1,117.7 million, over the 1977 industry deficit of U.S.$385.3 million.[50] Argentina, the third major automobile producer in Latin America, had a short-lived boom in exports during the mid-1970s. However, the coup of 1976 brought a military government with liberalization policies that led to an increase in imports, dominating 25 percent of the domestic market. Although government fiscal policies in the 1970s led to the debt crisis, the automobile industry's new capacity to export helped reduce losses from a contracted domestic market.

The Debt Crisis and a Contracting Market

During the "lost decade" of adjustment to the debt crisis, the domestic automobile market shrank. Increasing income inequality and erratic price changes made automobiles a luxury reserved for the rich. Governments eliminated many of the industry's preferential subsidies and the depressed domestic market provided little incentive for firms to add capacity. Firms shifted their exports to the United States and Europe because their traditional LDC export markets contracted. In Mexico, the market was so depressed that in 1986 the industry was producing 43 percent less than in 1981, most of which was for export.[51] Firms with minimal investments like Renault pulled out, but the largest firms—GM, Ford, Chrysler, Volkswagen, and Fiat—had invested too much to dismiss their Latin American operations as a loss.

Austerity, Market Forces, and a Domestic Boom

During the 1990s the automobile industry has experienced a complete turnaround from the previous decades. Demand in Brazil and Argentina is so high that automobile firms need to build more plants to accommodate the booming market. Plants in Brazil operate twenty-three hours a day and cannot meet domestic demand. Mexico's market, although it suffered a setback during the 1994–1995 peso crisis, grew by 33 percent in the first quarter of 1997.[52] In Argentina, automobile sales have been running at an annual rate of 400,000 units, while in Brazil the yearly rate is 2.2 million vehicles.[53] Brazil and Mexico have surpassed Italy, becoming the tenth and eleventh leading automobile producers in the world. In 1987, Ford and Volkswagen entered a partnership called AutoLatina to save their investments in the depressed market of the 1980s. In 1994 the partnership was dissolved because the market was once again big enough to handle the two competitors. The turn in market conditions is attributed to the sustained growth experienced by most Latin American countries. Price stability and available credit are making automobile ownership a reality for many Latin American families. A study by Honda shows that more than 2.7 million households in Brazil have an annual income of $48,000 and an additional 8.6 million earn at least $24,000.[54] Argentina, which has always boasted of the largest middle class in the region, has an antiquated automobile fleet, with an average age of fifteen years, that is rapidly being replaced.

Alongside growth and an expanding market have been neoliberal policies of maintaining price stability and a self-regulating market. In the 1990s these policies, instead of fiscal subsidies, enticed automobile manufacturers to invest in the region. From 1995 to 2000, automobile manufacturers are expected to pour $23 billion into new automobile factories, more than half of which will be in Brazil.[55] Chrysler Corporation, which had not invested in developing countries since 1965, opened a plant in Argentina in 1997. The Japanese view Argentina and Brazil as the most lucrative markets in the world, and Toyota has invested $200 million in a factory outside of São Paulo to serve Mercosur. Furthermore, technological spillover is finally coming to fruition. In the second half of the 1990s, Latin America has become a locus of technological innovations in production and labor relations. Most plants are using automation and robotics, requiring skilled labor. In 1996 Volkswagen opened a factory in Brazil that it claims is the most advanced in the world. This factory binds VW and seven suppliers in the manufacturing and assembly process. VW supplies only two hundred workers while the bulk of labor belongs to the suppliers. This has reduced costs by 50 percent and has increased worker productivity by 12 percent.[56] GM is following suit by renovating the bulk of its plants from assembly line operations to more flexible manufacturing.

Economic Integration Allows for Economies of Scale

Aside from economic growth, economic integration and liberalization in the 1990s have been responsible for the heavy investment by the automobile firms. In the 1950s and the 1960s, automobile manufacturers were reluctant to begin manufacturing operations without government incentives because the markets were too small to reap the benefits from economies of scale. Today, the markets of Mercosur, NAFTA, and the Andean Pact have made it possible for companies like VW, GM, and Ford to take advantage of economies of scale. Mercosur member countries have lowered tariffs for producers within the customs union to 35 percent. This has made it possible for companies to integrate their operations to serve the entire customs union. Mexico has for a long time produced GM engines for Detroit. During the peso crisis, automobile production in Mexico did not fall as much as it could have because NAFTA provided an escape valve through which producers could switch from production for the domestic market to U.S. and Canadian markets. Venezuela, with its very limited automobile industry, is now enjoying investment from the American "big three" automobile producers, who use it as an export platform to markets in Ecuador and Colombia.

Economies of scale allow for cost savings. GM is scheduled to begin production of a new small car that will be the cheapest car in the Brazilian market. Another reason for falling prices and rising investment is the significant decrease in common external tariffs on imports from outside the integrated area. Imports have significantly increased, forcing the traditional producers in the Latin American economies to cut costs and prices. In Mercosur, external tariffs on automobiles are supposed to drop to only 20 percent by the year 2000.[57] Competition appears to be working to spur improvements in productivity.

Reconsidering ISI and Neoliberalism

The contemporary success of the automobile industry is forcing some economists to reconsider their judgments on ISI. Many contend that the industry's success today dates to the ISI policies of the 1950s and 1960s and the export policies of the 1970s. Producers were forced to consider the region as a profitable long-term production site. Once their investments were made, they complied with government decrees to protect their privileged access into the region. In the 1980s firms had invested too much to pull out from the region. As a result, today GM, Ford, VW, and Fiat hold 99 percent of the South American market and are among the top investors.

However, the technological spillover that state officials foresaw did not bear fruit during the years of ISI. Instead, neoliberals contend that it wasn't until governments began to focus on getting prices right, downsizing the state, and liberalizing the economy that Latin America has become fertile ground for technological breakthroughs in automobile production. Furthermore, neoliberal policies have reinstated growth and market forces that have driven automobile MNCs to cut costs through technological innovations.

Key Concepts

Backward linkages
Declining terms of trade
Dependency theory
Economic populism
Forward linkages

Import substitution
  industrialization (ISI)
Market failure
Overvalued exchange
  rates

Structuralists
Transnational
  corporations

Chapter Summary

The Dependency and Structuralist School

- The core of dependency theory states that the center—industrialized nations—expanded at the expense of the periphery—the developing nations.
- The structuralist school, as defined by the U.N. Commission for Latin America, had two main characteristics. The first saw declining terms of trade as hindering economic development for Latin America, since countries would need to export more to import the same amount. The second was the role of concentrated oligopolies and elites in the economic system, who determined prices and consumption patterns incompatible with growth for the region.

Import Substitution Industrialization (ISI)

- Import substitution industrialization was the policy pursued by Latin America in response to dependency theory and the structuralist school. ISI sought to promote and protect domestic industries through an interventionist state that would attack bottlenecks and market failure.
- ISI relied on various tools to promote industrialization: active industrial policy through the use of state-owned enterprises; protective international instruments such as tariffs, quotas, import licenses, foreign exchange controls,

industrial incentives, and export subsidies in order to protect infant industries; targeted lending to industries such as machinery and automobiles; subsidies and tax exemptions for particular industries, including transnational corporations that provided critical financial capital and technology, but with strict rules such as local content laws; and passive monetary policy to finance projects under ISI.

- Although data show that ISI had a positive effect on growth until the 1980s, there were also negative consequences. Nationally manufactured goods in many cases failed to meet international quality standards, making them uncompetitive in the global market. ISI exacerbated inequality by failing to create an entrepreneurial class and preserving the power of the elite. The agricultural sector was neglected, which weakened a source of profit and food security. There was a bias against export growth through overvalued exchange rates. This led to differences in domestic expenditures and revenue that would contribute either to persistent deficits or inflation.

Notes

1. Andre Gundar Frank, *Capitalism and Underdevelopment in Latin America* (New York: Monthly Review Press, 1967).

2. Paul A. Baran, "On the Political Economy of Backwardness," *Manchester School* 20, no. 1 (1952); reprinted in A. N. Agarwala and S. P. Singh, eds., *The Economics of Underdevelopment* (New York: Oxford University Press, 1963), and in Charles K. Wilber, ed., *Political Economy of Development* (New York: Random House, 1973). Also see the classic piece written by Gabriel Palma, "Dependency: A Formal Theory of Underdevelopment or a Methodology for the Analysis of Concrete Situations of Underdevelopment?" *World Development* 6, no. 7–8 (July-August 1979): 881–924.

3. The Spanish acronym for ECLA is CEPAL, the Comisión Económica Para América Latina. ECLA later became ECLAC, with the C reflecting the incorporation of the Caribbean.

4. Enrique V. Iglesias, ed., *The Legacy of Raúl Prebisch* (Washington, D.C.: Inter-American Development Bank, 1994).

5. Gerald M. Meier and Dudley Seers, *Pioneers in Development* (Oxford: Oxford University Press, 1984), 173.

6. Ibid., 173.

7. Ronald V. A. Sprout, "The Ideas of Prebisch," *CEPAL Review* 46 (April 1992): 178.

8. James L. Dietz and James H. Street, eds., *Latin America's Economic Development: Institutionalist and Structuralist Perspectives* (Boulder: Lynne Rienner, 1987), 81.

9. Meier and Seers, *Pioneers*, 176.

10. Henry Bruton, "A Reconsideration of Import Substitution," *Journal of Economic Literature* 36 (June 1998): 905.

11. Meier and Seers, *Pioneers*, 176.

12. Sprout, "Ideas of Prebisch," 179.

13. Ibid., 182; and Nancy Birdsall and Carlos Lozada, "Recurring Themes in Latin

American Economic Thought: From Prebisch to the Market and Back," in *Securing Stability and Growth in Latin America*, ed. Ricardo Hausman and Helmut Reisen (Paris: OECD Publications, 1996).

14. Henry Bruton, "Import Substitution," in *Handbook of Development Economics*, ed. Hollis Chenery and T. N. Srivivasan, 3d ed., vol. 2 (New York: Elsevier, 1996), 1609.

15. Victorio Corbo, "Economic Policies and Performance in Latin America," in *Economic Development: Handbook of Comparative Economic Policies*, ed. Enzo Grilli and Dominick Salvatore (Westport, Conn.: Greenwood, 1994).

16. Charles K. Wilber and Steven Francis, "The Methodological Basis of Hirschman's Development Economics: Pattern Modeling vs. General Laws," *World Development* 14, no. 2, special issue (February 1986): 181–191.

17. For a discussion of the role of the state in economic development, see Thomas Trebat, *Brazil's State-Owned Enterprises: A Case Study of the State as Entrepreneur* (New York: Cambridge University Press, 1983).

18. Rudiger Dornbusch and Sebastian Edwards, "The Political Economy of Latin America," in *The Macroeconomics of Populism in Latin America,* National Bureau of Economic Research Conference Report, ed. Rudiger Dornbusch and Sebastian Edwards (Chicago: University of Chicago Press, 1991), 9. Also see Alan Knight, "Populism and Neo-Populism in Latin America, Especially Mexico," *Journal of Latin American Studies* 30 (1998): 223–248.

19. Trebat, *Brazil's State-Owned Enterprises*.

20. Bruton, "Import Substitution," 1607.

21. Rosemary Thorp, "Import Substitution: A Good Idea in Principle," in *Latin America and the World Economy: Dependency and Beyond*, ed. Richard J. Salvucci (Lexington, Mass.: Heath, 1996), 140–146. The Salvucci book is a good reader to accompany chapters 2–3 of this text.

22. Victor Bulmer-Thomas, *The Economic History of Latin American since Independence* (New York: Cambridge University Press, 1994), 280. "Nominal" refers to the tariff rate on the final good without adjusting for tariffs on intermediate inputs.

23. Adriaan ten Kate and Robert Bruce Wallace, "Nominal and Effective Protection by Sector," in *Protection and Economic Development in Mexico*, ed. Adriaan ten Kate and Robert Bruce Wallace (Hampshire, U.K.: Gower, 1980), 122, 151.

24. Tom Warts, "Protection and Private Foreign Investment," in *Protection and Economic Development in Mexico*, ed. Adriaan ten Kate and Robert Bruce Wallace (Hampshire, U.K.: Gower, 1980), 198.

25. Robert Bruce Wallace, "Policies of Protection in Mexico," in *Protection and Economic Development in Mexico*, ed. Adriaan ten Kate and Robert Bruce Wallace (Hampshire, U.K.: Gower, 1980).

26. This is based on the theory of purchasing power parity and the law of one price. Two sweaters should sell for the same price in two markets (adjusted for transportation costs). If they didn't, some enterprising person would buy sweaters where they are cheap and sell them where they are dear.

27. Rhys Jenkins, *Transnational Corporations and Industrial Transformation in Latin America* (New York: St. Martin's, 1984), 40.

28. Gary Gereffi and Peter Evans, "Transnational Corporations, Dependent Development, and State Policy in the Semiperiphery," *Latin American Research Review* 16, no. 3 (1981): 31–64.

29. Richard S. Newfarmer, "International Oligopoly in the Electrical Industry," in *Profits, Progress, and Poverty* (Notre Dame, Ind.: University of Notre Dame Press, 1984), 147.

30. Bruton, "A Reconsideration," 910.

31. Robert J. Alexander, "Import Substitution in Latin America in Retrospect," in Progress Toward Development in Latin America: From Prebisch to Technological Autonomy, ed. James L. Dietz and Dilmus James (Boulder and London: Lynne Rienner, 1990).

32. Albert O. Hirschman, A Propensity to Self Subversion (Cambridge, MA: Harvard University Press, 1995): 156.

33. Bela Belassa, "Brazil," in The Structure of Protection in Developing Countries (Baltimore: The Johns Hopkins Press, 1971): Table 6.2, p. 107.

34. This paragraph draws from Rosemary Thorp, Progress, Poverty and Exclusion: An Economic History of Latin America in the 20th Century, Johns Hopkins Press for the Inter-American Development Bank, 1998: 197.

35. James E. Mahon Jr., "Was Latin America Too Rich to Prosper? Structural and Political Obstacles to Export-Led Industrial Growth," Journal of Development Studies 28, no. 2 (1992): 242.

36. Alan M. Taylor, "On the Costs of Inward-Looking Development: Price Distortions, Growth, and Divergence in Latin America," Journal of Economic History 58, no. 1 (March 1998): 20.

37. Bruton, "A Reconsideration," 923.

38. Bruton, "Import Substitution," 1616.

39. Taylor, "On the Costs of Inward-Looking Development," 21.

40. Enrique V. Iglesias, "The Search for a New Economic Consensus in Latin America," in The Legacy of Raúl Prebisch, ed. Enrique V. Iglesias (Washington, D.C.: Inter-American Development Bank, 1994).

41. Werner Baer, "Changing Paradigms: Changing Interpretations of the Public Sector in Latin America's Economies," Public Choice 88 (1996): 365–379.

42. This case was written by Erwin Godoy, Colby College graduating class of 1997.

43. Lúcio Meira, "A propagação dos efeitos promocionais da indústria automobilística," Economia Brasileira 4 (1958): 67, as quoted in Helen Shapiro, Engines of Growth: The State and Transnational Auto Companies in Brazil (Cambridge: Cambridge University Press, 1994), 39.

44. Jenkins, Transnational Corporations, 21.

45. Auto case study in McKinsey Global Institute, Productivity: The Key to Accelerated Development Path for Brazil 1998 (São Paulo: McKinsey and Company, 1998), 2.

46. Jenkins, Transnational Corporations, 59.

47. Shapiro, Engines of Growth, 193.

48. Jenkins, Transnational Corporations, 191.

49. Ibid., 211.

50. Shapiro, Engines of Growth, 229.

51. Ibid., 228.

52. "Mexico Domestic Sales Rise Sharply," Reuters Financial Service (LEXIS-NEXIS database), 4 June 1997.

53. Laurence Zucherman, "In South America Car Makers See One Big Showroom," New York Times, 25 April 1997 (on-line edition).

54. Ibid.

55. Economic Commission for Latin America and the Caribbean, Foreign Investment and the Caribbean: 1997 Report (English summary). Available at www.eclac.cl/english/Publications/invest/summary.html SUMMARY AND CONCLUSIONS.

56. David Woodruff, Ian Katz, and Keith Naughton, "VW's Factory of the Future," Business Week, 7 October 1996.

57. "Mercosur Survey," The Economist, 12 October 1996.

CHAPTER FOUR

LATIN AMERICA'S DEBT CRISIS

The Limits of External Financing

The macroeconomic crisis threatened the meager savings and social security of Latin America's poor. *(Courtesy of David Mangurian and the Inter-American Development Bank.)*

The debt crisis in Latin America was a development crisis. It called into question the viability of the import substitution industrialization model of development and shaped the economic future of the region.

How did the crisis come about? Borrowing to finance development is not in itself a bad thing. Developing countries are by definition capital poor. Funding is needed for investment and growth. If a country, like a person, wants to grow or expand, borrowing provides necessary capital for change. As a student, you might be borrowing money to finance educational expenses in anticipation of a better future. This is rational behavior. Borrowing becomes a crisis when an individual or a country fails to make payments on the outstanding value of the loan. If the investment you make in your education doesn't generate a decent salary by the time your first loan payment is due, you will have a personal financial crisis. For a nation, if the returns on the investments don't match the debt obligations when they come due, a crisis also ensues. Unfortunately, the development model in Latin America was dependent on a continuous infusion of capital, with new lending required to finance the development of long-term projects. When conditions in the international market changed dramatically in the early 1980s, Latin American economies, one after another, collapsed under the mountain of external debt. The debt crisis transformed economic policy in the region—at a very high price.

In this chapter we begin by analyzing how borrowing to support import substitution industrialization became an unstable foundation for growth. We then consider the problem of debt-led growth and why a change in external conditions brought inward-looking development to a halt. Finally, we turn to the changes in development policy that enabled economies to survive the crisis and we analyze the economic and social costs to the region. Questions that will shape our analysis include the following:

- What fueled the accumulation of external debt?
- What role did internal and external factors play in precipitating a crisis?
- How did countries and the international financial community respond to the crisis?
- What are the legacies of the debt crisis?
- Is the Latin American debt crisis over?

THE MOUNTAIN OF DEBT: AN UNSTABLE FOUNDATION FOR DEVELOPMENT

Economic growth under the import substitution model of development was fueled by external savings. With thin domestic financial markets, by 1982 Latin America had borrowed more than $300 billion from the rest of the world. Figure 4.1 shows this accumulation of Latin American total disbursed external debt in 1970–1993. Under the import substitution model, the first stage of industrialization is driven by the import of capital goods—particularly machinery—to be used to produce goods domestically. In many cases, the capital was also used to finance large infra-

Figure 4.1.   Total Disbursed External Debt of Latin America

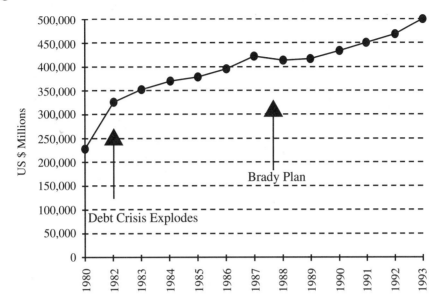

Source: World Bank, *World Debt Tables* (Washington, D.C.: World Bank, various years).

structure projects such as roads, electricity, telecommunications, or water supply, all of which are vital to a nation's advancing growth. Borrowing in itself is not a bad thing. Problems arise, however, when the borrowing requirements for long-term projects outpace the ability to repay past loans. Crises may erupt due to the mechanics of borrowing or the **debt trap** (unproductive investments or investments with very long time horizons that do not generate returns in time to help service loans), internally inconsistent economic policies that impede the success of projects, or external shocks that derail the domestic economy. Let's consider these causes in turn.

It is easy to fall into a debt trap when lending is for long-term projects but obligations to repay begin in the short term. This problem is made clear with a simple mathematical example. Assume the following (rather lenient) borrowing conditions. You contract to borrow $1,000 dollars a year for a project that is going to take ten years. You agree to pay $50 a year back in principal for each $1,000 borrowed over twenty years at an interest rate of 10 percent per year on the outstanding balance of the debt. As can be seen in table 4.1, in the first year you receive $1,000 and repay $50, leaving a balance of $950. At 10 percent interest your net outflow, the interest plus the principal, is $95 plus $50 or $145. In the second year you again receive $1,000 of new money to continue your project, pay $100 in principal (the first and second $50 principal payments), leaving $185 of interest to be paid on the balance of $1,850. Your principal plus interest therefore totaled $285. Your annual net transfer, the $1,000 coming in minus the $285 going out, is $715.

Table 4.1.   The Debt Trap: Long-Term Project Lending

Year	New Lending	Total Debt Incurred	Principal ($50/year for 20 years)	Outstanding Debt	Interest Payment (10%)	Total Outflow = Interest + Principal	Net Transfer = Disbursement/ Outflow
1	1,000	1,000	50	950	95	145	855
2	1,000	2,000	100	1,850	185	285	715
3	1,000	3,000	150	2,700	270	420	580
4	1,000	4,000	200	3,500	350	550	450
5	1,000	5,000	250	4,250	425	675	325
6	1,000	6,000	300	4,950	495	795	205
7	1,000	7,000	350	5,600	560	910	90
8	1,000	8,000	400	6,200	620	1,020	− 20
9	1,000	9,000	450	6,750	675	1,125	− 125
10	1,000	10,000	500	7,250	725	1,225	− 225

This formula of new money minus principal and interest payments goes on for several years. Notice that each year, because of the obligation to pay the principal on past loans and the increasing interest burden, the net transfer—the amount of money coming in after payments have been made—substantially dwindles. Indeed, by the eighth year the $1,000 of new money doesn't even cover your payments on past obligations, much less fund new investment. If your multiyear project is incomplete or if it is not yet generating significant returns, you would need to borrow even more just to make payments. You have landed flat in the debt trap.

Mismatched Projects and Returns

Import substitution was fueled by regular infusions of capital not unlike our example above. In part, the import substitution industrialization model was driven by the failure of the private sector to provide critical goods and services in the economy. We remember that this took place most frequently in industries with large economies of scale and in sectors in which the complementary infrastructure was not available. This led to state investment in sectors with high capital requirements for entry as well as in large-scale projects to develop needed infrastructure in energy, telecommunications, and transportation. Unfortunately, the payback period for these multiyear investments was not always consistent with the terms of commercial lending. Furthermore, the returns to social investments by the state are not easily captured in state tax coffers for repayment.

Even when lending for large-scale infrastructure projects was efficient and well managed, multiyear development projects were not easily financed. If a road, for example, is constructed over a ten-year period and then it takes another ten years for businesses to move into the area and pay taxes, the project itself may not generate returns—and repayment of debt—until well into the future. Debt-generated investment should create the ability to service that debt in the future. Investments must have a sufficient rate of return within a compatible term structure. When this is not possible in huge undertakings, the government often steps in with public lending. Although it is a function of government to sequence projects and manage these flows, the magnitude of large-scale investments under import substitution industrialization left Latin American governments vulnerable to the willingness of capital markets to finance the gap between the period of investment and the long-term returns on the project. Given sovereign guarantees and the low likelihood of countries defaulting (as opposed to companies), markets were willing to lend. Debt was accumulated to service past debt.

Unsustainable Domestic Policies

Despite the simple mathematical lesson of the debt trap, the intersection of politics and economics promoted debt-led development. Latin America has a long history of populism, or the use of political rhetoric to mobilize the masses. Old-style populists, such as Juan and Eva Perón of Argentina, charismatically co-opted labor and middle-class groups as well as domestic industrial elites to maintain power. But buying off the masses costs money. As we saw in chapter 3, **economic populism** in the 1970s emphasized growth and income redistribution and deemphasized the risks of inflation and deficit finance, external constraints, and the reaction of economic agents to aggressive nonmarket policies.[1] The populist political culture encouraged spending, which was made possible by favorable conditions in the international financial markets.

Unfortunately, the large state-run development model also lent itself well to inefficiency and corruption in lending. In some instances, lending was for pharaonic megaprojects with limited utility for social development. The history of Latin America contains numerous stories of a state firm's payrolls padded with dead people, construction taking place only on paper, and misguided attempts at development such as the Transamazonian highway. Debt was incurred for projects that would never generate the ability to repay.

External Shocks

Of course, at some level, politicians understood that one day the piper would have to be paid. However, extraordinarily attractive international prices for capital played into the short-term political incentive to borrow. Real international interest rates—that is, interest rates adjusted for global inflation—were negative from 1974 until 1977. As shown in table 4.2, the U.S. prime rate adjusted for inflation (the real prime rate) ranged between −2.9 and −1.4 percent. If someone asked you whether you would like to borrow money today, have the use of that money for some period of time, and repay less than what was borrowed, how would you

Table 4.2.   Real Interest Rates, 1974–1984

Year	U.S. Nominal Prime Rate (%)	U.S. Inflation Rate (%)	U.S. Real Prime Rate (%)
1974	10.81	13.1	−2.2
1975	7.86	11.1	−2.9
1976	6.84	8.3	−1.3
1977	6.83	8.5	−1.4
1978	9.06	7.2	1.7
1979	12.67	9.2	3.2
1980	15.27	11.9	3.0
1981	18.85	10.1	8.1
1982	14.77	7.5	6.8
1983	10.81	5.1	5.5
1984	12.04	4.8	6.9

Source: Economic Commission for Latin America and the Caribbean, *Economy Survey of Latin America and the Caribbean* (Santiago, Chile: Economic Commission for Latin America and the Caribbean, various years); International Monetary Fund, *International Financial Statistics, 1987* (Washington, D.C.: International Monetary Fund, 1987), 113.

respond? Although much of the lending was on a floating rate basis—that is, each year your interest rate would change to reflect market conditions—after several years of negative real rates and the possibility that you wouldn't even be in office when repayment time came around, the decision to borrow could be seen as a rational response to price. It would be as if the interest rates in the debt trap example presented earlier were −2 percent rather than +10 percent. At that rate it would take twenty-one years, perhaps five different government administrations for net flows to become negative. Within that time, the project may be bearing returns. Given those conditions, it would be hard for a politician to do anything but incur the loan!

Although the demand for finance was driven by developmental needs as defined by the import substitution model and the populist politics of its implementation, lending would never have taken place on such a broad scale without an ample supply of global cash. During the 1970s banks needed to recycle the proceeds from the quadrupling of oil prices, called petrodollars. Unless banks lent these petrodollar deposits, they would be unable to pay interest to the OPEC creditor nations. Many lender simply saw it as easier and more lucrative to advance megaloans to state-owned enterprises (backed by sovereign governments) than to package small business or agricultural loans in the United States. The competition to lend was ferocious.

Distinct Patterns, Same Result: Crisis

It is important to note that Latin American countries pursued a variety of economic strategies during this time period—yet all were strongly hit by crisis. Table 4.3 compares three cases: Mexico, Brazil, and Argentina. The Mexican debt crisis was

Table 4.3. Debt and Distinct Patterns of Development

Policy Instruments	Mexico	Brazil	Argentina
Long- and short-term external debt (billions of 1985 U.S. dollars)	96.8	106.1	50.9
Fiscal policy	Overexpansion of fiscal policy driven by investments in the oil sector. New oil discoveries led to expanded investments by Pemex. Fiscal deficit exploded to 17% of GDP.	Responded to global recession with growth of domestic demand. Maintained high protective tariffs. Wages increased.	Inconsistent fiscal policy; 1976 military regime adopted orthodox model.
Monetary policy	Loose monetary policy with low interest rates led to massive capital flight. Outflows reached $8.4b in 1981 and $6.6b in 1982. Inflation soared.	Economy indexed to respond to inflation. Money supply passively accommodated expansionary fiscal policy.	High peso interest rates initially generated strong capital inflow; when confidence was lost, capital flight ensued.
Exchange rate policy	Maintained fixed exchange rate policy despite inflation. Overvaluation resulted.	Limited devaluation of cruzeiro to 50% despite inflation rates twice as high. Overvaluation resulted.	Overvalued exchange rate depressed exports and accelerated imports. Acute reserve loss led to borrowing just to maintain the exchange rate.
Exogenous shocks	Tightening U.S. monetary policy raised real interest rates; oil prices plunged.	Oil crisis pressured balance of payments; high interest rates; commodity price shock; contagion effects from Mexico.	Tight U.S. policy raised cost of capital.
Comments	As an oil exporter, Mexico had access to capital. Its problem derived from its attempts to limit social conflict through state spending while simultaneously expanding the oil sector.	Brazil attempted to maintain state-led development model despite changes in the international economy. Its large size allowed it to pursue this strategy too long.	Argentina pursued an aggressive liberalization policy with the exchange rate priced to restrain inflation—not to promote exports.

Source: Derived from information presented in (fax newsletter) Warburg Dillon Read, *The Latin American Adviser* (February 1998).

driven by an attempt to expand the oil sector while maintaining social peace at home through domestic spending programs. International bankers were only too happy to lend to Mexico because the loans were collateralized by the black gold of new oil discoveries. Domestic expansion exploded into inflation, which the government attempted to restrain through a fixed exchange rate. This exchange rate became overvalued, compromising the ability of the nonoil export sector to perform. As described below, Mexico sounded the first alert to the international community of the debt crisis in August 1982 when it announced its inability to meet its financial obligations.

Brazil also enjoyed easy access to international finance. Because it was one of the ten largest economies in the world, lenders believed that investments in this emerging powerhouse were well placed. Loans to state enterprises were seen as backed by the sovereign guarantee of the government of Brazil. The government would not default on obligations. As international financial conditions changed in the 1980s, Brazil's size also slowed the incentive for its adjustment. It was able to maintain its inward-looking model of development and turn to domestic money creation to service external debt. Inflation soared, but a sophisticated system of indexing interest rates, wages, and prices minimized the pain for economic agents. We will consider these macroeconomic responses in chapter 5. A rate of devaluation of the exchange rate slower than the rate of inflation was designed as a brake on rising prices but had the unfortunate effect of reducing export performance.

Whereas debt accumulation in Brazil and Mexico was driven by investments through state firms, Argentina's inward-looking development model ran out of steam under the populist Peronist regime. The military took over in 1976 and radically opened the economy. Unfortunately for Argentina, borrowing was used for financial purposes and did not result in an increase in the productive capabilities of the nation. Instead, a misguided attempt to maintain an overvalued exchange rate led to borrowing to defend the fixed currency price. Money flowed into the country in the form of short-term loans used to support the exchange rate, but those same dollars quickly exited in private portfolios betting against the ability of the Argentine government to restrain inflation and jump-start growth. At the crux of the Argentine problem was the fact that the overvalued exchange rate, used as an anchor for inflation, could not simultaneously promote exports. (Please see box 4.1 for a review of overvalued exchange rates.) Despite these differences in internal development models, Mexico (an oil exporter), Brazil (a nation inwardly focused on its large domestic market), and Argentina (an economy open to the international economy) were all rocked by changes in the international economy that transformed a heavy debt profile into an insupportable burden.

The Crisis Builds: External Shocks and Capital Flight

The accumulation of external liabilities to finance development is not a crisis. However, external conditions changed radically and evidence began to mount that called into question the ability of governments to service their debt. In 1979 U.S. President Jimmy Carter appointed Paul Volcker as Chairman of the Federal Re-

Box 4.1. Overvaluation of Exchange Rates and the Debt Crisis

An overvalued exchange rate can be seen as both a cause of the accumulation of debt and an effect of the macroeconomic instability perpetuated by the debt crisis.

Before explaining the economic cause and effect of an overvalued rate, we should clarify what is meant by an overvalued exchange rate. An overvalued exchange rate exists when the currency is "too strong," making imports a bargain. A currency's rate is too strong when it artificially allows the purchase of more foreign currency than the trade patterns might indicate. That is, one peso might buy one dollar's worth of currency (and therefore goods) when it is really only worth fifty cents. With a strong currency, people buy more from abroad. An undervalued rate is "too weak," favoring exports. Imports become prohibitively expensive, and exports cheap, in world markets. The Goldilocks question of figuring out which rate is "just right" goes back to a theory of exchange rate determination called purchasing power parity, or PPP. In its simplest form, PPP argues that a good should sell for the same price in two countries when prices are adjusted for the exchange rate. Holding transportation costs constant, if Costa Rican coffee does not sell for the same price in San Jose, Costa Rica, and San Jose, California, people would buy it where it is cheap (Costa Rica) and sell it where it was dear (California), driving the price up in Costa Rica and down in California. Because one would need colones to purchase the coffee in Costa Rica, this would drive up the value of the colon until the value of the two goods was identical in the two markets. If the exchange rate were set by the government (rather than being a floating market rate) the "right" price for the currency should generate one price for coffee. However, if tastes changed, and people drank less coffee and demanded fewer colones to buy it, an unadjusted exchange rate would become overvalued.

Alternatively, if the Costa Rican government increased the money supply, the colon should be worth less than the dollar. For example, if prices in Costa Rica were rising at 20 percent per year but in the United States they were only rising by 5 percent a year, this means that Costa Ricans could purchase 15 percent $(20 - 5)$ less a year with the same income as those in the United States. Again, under a floating system, this should be reflected in a 15 percent fall in the value of the currency, or the exchange rate. Once again, if the exchange market isn't functioning smoothly or if the government intervenes to fix a currency price and does not allow the devaluation to take place, we would say that this currency is overvalued.

A look at table 4.A shows that from 1979 through 1981, currencies became significantly overvalued in Latin America. The numbers presented are indexes that set 1980–1982 as a base year. By 1981, for example, Argentina's currency was 7 percent too

(continued)

Table 4.A. Real Exchange Rate Indexes

(1980–82 = 100)	Argentina	Brazil	Chile	Mexico	Venezuela
1976–78	73	116	75	98	95
1979	101	96	79	98	94
1980	116	85	95	104	93
1981	107	103	108	114	100
1982	76	112	97	82	110
1983–85	74	85	86	86	98

Source: Selected from Rudiger Dornbusch, *Stabilization, Debt, and Reform: Policy Analysis for Developing Countries* (Englewood Cliffs, N.J.: Prentice-Hall, 1993); Original source Morgan Guarantee, *World Financial Markets.*

(continued)

strong, Brazil's 3 percent, Chile's 8 percent, and Mexico's 14 percent; only Venezuela's was "just right." (We see, however, not for long.)

Why would a country allow overvaluation to take place? First, if the country is pursuing import substitution, the strong currency value allows companies to purchase intermediate inputs at a lower cost. Because the policy was often to discourage the importation of final consumer goods, import licenses at these preferential rates were sometimes required. Second, countries may choose to link their currency to a vehicle currency such as the dollar as an inflation fighting anchor. Just as global currencies were set to the dollar under the Bretton Woods system following World War II or under the gold standard, developing countries have at times viewed the link as a stabilizing force. Currency boards have also been used (as in Argentina today) to establish a one for one link, constraining the growth of the domestic money supply to the number of dollars held in reserve. Whether the link is firm or whether the government uses the dollar value as a guide to monetary policy, under a fixed exchange rate regime this should be anti-inflationary. Nonetheless, if all inflation is not immediately squeezed out of the economy, and a rate is fixed, when the local currency should be losing value to reflect inflation but it isn't, overvaluation is taking place.

Finally, even when a country knows that a devaluation is indicated, at times it is reticent to do so. In addition to incurring a political cost (citizens concluding that the government was unable to control inflation), the devaluation can serve as an additional inflationary shock because imports now become more costly. The vicious circle between inflation causing the need for devaluation and then a devaluation increasing prices in the economy pressuring for a further devaluation is the economic minister's nightmare.

Capital flight makes the pressure toward devaluation worse. If indications point to the possibility of a devaluation, investors will move their assets out of the country. The rationale is clear. Say you have 1,000 pesos in the bank and that initially they can buy you 1,000 dollars worth of goods at a 1:1 exchange rate. Now assume that you have a 20 percent devaluation of the peso. This means that to buy the same U.S.$1,000 worth of goods, you will have to come up with 1,200 pesos. Therefore, if you think there will be a devaluation, you will sell pesos and hold dollars (perhaps in a Miami bank account or perhaps under your bed). Selling pesos, not surprisingly, weakens the peso. Under a fixed exchange rate, the government must intervene in the market, selling dollars and buying pesos to maintain the value. It is forced to sell the dollars that it holds in reserves for such foreign exchange transactions. However, a fall in reserves in the balance of payments numbers erodes confidence. Everyone knows that reserves are dwindling and that a devaluation is inevitable because the central bank does not have infinite resources to defend the currency. Capital flight accelerates in the face of a possible devaluation, making that change in the currency value inevitable.

serve Board. Volcker's inflation-taming efforts drove the U.S. prime rate to 18.8 percent in 1981. Floating rate obligations skyrocketed to a real, or inflation-adjusted, positive 12 percent. In addition to facing escalating interest payments, countries found it difficult to generate the hard currency—usually dollars—to pay the debt. Debt in Latin America was generally dollar denominated, since no international bank would issue a loan in pesos when the peso was likely to be devalued. To repay the loan, the country therefore had to earn or buy dollars. The most direct means of augmenting dollar holdings was to sell Latin American goods in the United States. Unfortunately, Volcker's inflation-fighting tools also generated recession, shrinking the United States as a market for Latin American goods. The slowdown became global, and the region found itself with increasingly burdensome obligations and a limited ability to earn the money owed.

Evidence of the unsustainability of the debt began to mount. Table 4.4 shows the capital flight from unsustainable policies in Argentina, Mexico, and Venezuela from 1980 through 1982. Capital flight as a percentage of total external debt reached 76.9 percent in Argentina, 73.3 percent in Mexico, and 131.5 percent in Venezuela. Capital flight takes place when a national makes a deposit or investment outside the home country. On one hand, capital flight is simply good international investing. A Brazilian economist once commented, "Why is it that when an American puts money abroad it is called 'foreign investment' and when an Argentinean does the same it is called 'capital flight'? Why is it that when an American company puts 30 percent of its equity abroad it is called 'strategic diversification' and when a Bolivian businessman puts only 4 percent abroad it is called 'lack of confidence'?"[2] On the other hand, if one's portfolio preference is decidedly against domestic investment or if investors or savers actively circumvent laws to prevent scarce capital from leaving the country, capital flight has taken place. Capital votes with its feet. Many Latin American families, for example, have savings accounts in Miami to guard against the possibility that the value of all of their savings would be decimated by poor economic management, followed by a devaluation. As shown in box 4.1, overvaluation of a currency contributes to capital flight because agents do not want to be caught holding assets denominated in a currency that is likely to be devalued. In some cases corruption exacerbated capital flight. Dollars coming in as loans to state-owned enterprises found their way out of the countries in the coffers of corrupt public agents.

Capital flight further destabilizes macroeconomic management. In an attempt to bribe capital to stay at home, interest rates may be set too high. When capital leaves the tax base, the government's ability to raise revenues is weakened. There is stronger incentive for seignorage, the process of printing money to cover the deficit. Because people want to sell the local currency and trade it in for dollars, the excess supply of the local currency is inflationary. We will come back to this problem in chapter 5.

Other measures of indebtedness fueled uncertainty, aggravating capital flight and the loss of confidence in economic management in the region. Since export

Table 4.4. Capital Flight from Selected Latin American Countries (U.S.$ billions)

	1979	1980	1981	1982	1983	1984
Argentina	2.2	3.5	4.5	7.6	1.3	−3.4
Brazil	1.3	2.0	−1.4	1.8	0.5	4.0
Mexico	−1.1	2.2	2.6	4.7	9.3	2.6
Venezuela	3.0	4.8	5.4	3.2	3.1	4.0

Source: Robert Cumby and Richard Levich, "On the Definition and Magnitude of Recent Capital Flight," Working Paper 2275 (Cambridge, Mass.: National Bureau of Economic Research, 1987); cited in Sebastian Edwards, *Crisis and Reform in Latin America: From Despair to Hope* (New York: Oxford University Press/World Bank, 1995), 23.

Table 4.5.   Debt Indicators for Latin America and the Caribbean, 1980–1990

Year	Total Debt/ Exports of Goods and Services	Total Debt/GNP	Total Debt Service/Exports of Goods and Services	Interest/ Export of Goods and Services	Interest/ GNP
1980	206.0	36.2	36.9	19.6	3.4
1981	210.9	37.8	21.6	11.1	2.0
1982	269.1	46.9	47.6	30.3	5.3
1983	309.1	58.6	43.0	29.8	5.6
1984	291.4	59.3	39.9	27.2	5.5
1985	312.9	61.3	38.2	27.9	5.5
1986	376.6	63.2	43.6	27.5	4.6
1987	377.6	66.1	37.4	23.0	4.0
1988	332.6	56.7	39.6	24.1	4.1
1989	293.3	50.1	32.1	16.6	2.8
1990	277.4	45.0	26.3	13.0	2.1

Source: World Bank, *World Debt Tables* (Washington, D.C.: World Bank, various years).

earnings finance debt payments, it is important to look at the weight of debt to exports as well as debt service—the interest and principal that must be paid for by exports. A measure greater than 200 percent in the level of total external debt to exports or a debt service to export ratio over 40 percent is unhealthy, pointing to great pressure on exports for debt payments and leaving little capital for other investment. We can see in table 4.5 that by 1982 total debt over exports had reached 269 percent and that total debt service over the exports of goods and services was edging toward 50 percent. Interest payments alone ballooned to 30 percent of exports, without reducing future liabilities. Latin America was in trouble.

Can't Pay, Won't Pay

In August 1982, Mexico announced to the international financial community that it could no longer service its debt. When the financial community saw that the sovereign government of Mexico would not or could not make good on its obligations, confidence in all developing countries eroded. It was a crisis for Mexico that quickly spread through the region and all developing countries, and threatened the international finance system. At the time that Mexico signaled the international financial community of the severity of the crisis, exposure to debt was a problem not only for the countries but also for the banks. As can be seen in table 4.6, the exposure of the nine major banks to six highly indebted countries exceeded an average of 174 percent of shareholders' equity in the banks. Exposure to either

> **QUESTION FOR THOUGHT**
>
> Were internal or external causes more to blame in the Latin American debt crisis?

Box 4.2.   Key Debt Terms

Arrears   The amount of past-due payments (interest and principal) on outstanding debt owed by any given debtor.

Bilateral loans   Loans from governments and their agencies, from autonomous bodies, and from official export credit agencies. These differ from private creditors (commercial banks and bonds) who did the bulk of the lending leading to the debt crisis.

Concerted lending   **Involuntary lending** by a bank. When the Mexican crisis began in 1982, large banks formed bank advisory committees to represent all banks and to keep them informed of debt negotiations. These committees, along with industrialized countries and the IMF, pressured smaller banks to continue lending to prevent defaults.

Debt service   The sum of principal repayments and interest payments actually made.

Disbursements   Earnings on loan commitments during the year specified.

LIBOR (London Interbank Offer Rate)   Traditional benchmark interest rate for international lending by private European banks.

Loan default   A bank declaration that a borrower is not expected ever to repay its debt, usually following an extended cessation of principal and payments by the debtor.

Long-term external debt   Debts with a maturity of more than one year owed to nonresidents, payable in foreign currency, goods, or services.

Moratorium   A declaration by a debtor country of its intent to stop principal and interest payments to its creditors.

Net flows   Disbursements minus principal repayments.

Net transfers   Net flows minus interest payments during the year.

Sovereign default   A government's decision to default on its external debt obligations.

REFERENCES

Biersteker, Thomas J. *Dealing with Debt.* Boulder: Westview, 1993.
Krugman, Paul R., and Maurice Obstfeld. *International Economics: Theory and Policy.* 3d ed. New York: HarperCollins, 1994.
World Bank. *World Debt Tables, 1995–1996.* Washington, D.C.: World Bank, 1996.

Mexico or Brazil alone would have been approximately half of shareholders' capital.

The IMF Approach

When Mexico rang the alarm bell on the mountain of external debt accumulated by developing countries, the depth of the problem was poorly understood. The international financial community diagnosed the difficulty primarily as a liquidity crisis. The *World Development Report* of 1983 noted, "Debt problems of most major developing countries are caused by illiquidity, not by insolvency."[3] Returning to the analogy of personal finances, **illiquidity** might mean that because you were laid off from your job or because you went wild with your credit cards, you can not make your payments when due. However, with time and budgeting, you could honor your commitments and not be forced into bankruptcy or insolvency. In

Table 4.6.   Exposure of Nine Major U.S. Banks to Six Highly Indebted Countries, 1984

	% of Shareholders' Equity (common and preferred)
Manufacturers Hanover	268.5
Chase Manhattan	212.7
Citicorp	206.7
Chemical	196.7
Bankers Trust	177.6
Bank of America	150.9
Morgan Guarantee	143.5
Continental Illinois	129.9
Wells Fargo	129.8
First Chicago	126.9
Average	174.32

Source: John Charles Pool, Stephen C. Stamos, and Patrice Franko, *The ABCs of International Finance,* 2d ed. (Lexington, Mass.: Lexington Books, 1991), 113.

the banking world, the assumption was that debtors would regain creditworthiness through a combination of internal adjustments and more favorable global economic conditions.

The internal adjustments were, for most countries, tough medicine to swallow. The presumption was that countries were living beyond their means and therefore had to reduce domestic **absorption** of resources. If fewer goods were consumed at home, more could be exported to service the debt. If we allow Y to represent national income and A to stand for the domestic consumption of goods and services (including imports), we can see in the simple formula $Y - A = B$ that B (the balance) is the residual. A trade surplus, then, would help restore financial health by decreasing the need to finance imports, leaving the balance to pay off the debt.

The Absorption Approach: $Y - A = B$

How should domestic absorption be decreased? The IMF prescription for achieving balance revolved around decreasing government and personal absorption of resources and increasing the attention to the international sector. In contrast to the state-centered import substitution strategy, the IMF recommended that states decrease spending on public works, privatize state-owned enterprises, and eliminate subsidies on goods and services. To combat inflation, monetary policy should be contractionary. If wages were indexed to a public minimum wage, it was generally suggested that wage increases be minimal. Devaluation was indicated to adjust overvalued exchange rates, and liberalization of markets through the reduction of tariffs and quotas was favored. The devaluation was designed to change the relative price of goods, making imports more expensive and exports cheaper. This creates incentives for expenditure switching by raising the opportunity cost of tradable goods. Fewer tradables will be consumed at home, and more will be released for sale abroad. Rather than borrowing, foreign investment was seen as the vehicle for the capital necessary for growth. The overriding principle was to get prices right. Resources should be directed to their most productive use through accurate price signals.

QUESTION FOR THOUGHT

At this juncture, what do you believe should have been the policy response to the debt crisis?

The IMF package was inherently contractionary, premised on decreasing fiscal spending and monetary emission. The hope was that the infusion of capital from abroad and initiative from the local private sector would fuel growth. The program generated a good deal of economic dislocation. Workers in bloated state-owned enterprises were laid off. Recipients of state-subsidized milk or tortillas faced dramatic price increases. The price of public transportation rose, and spending on infrastructure fell. Companies that had grown up behind the protection of high tariff walls found it difficult to compete with international firms. Tight money meant high interest rates, which retarded investment. Devalued exchange rates sent price shocks through imported consumer goods. Agricultural exports were rapidly promoted, often at high environmental cost.

But the bitter IMF pill was necessary if countries were to maintain access to finance. When a country found itself unable to make payments on its external obligations, banks would lend no more until the country had signed a letter of intent with the IMF to implement the tough economic policies. Targets for macroeconomic performance would be set, and if countries adopted the conditions specified to achieve these goals, IMF funding would be released. **Conditionality**—the adoption of strict fiscal, monetary, and trade policies in exchange for the release of funds—was designed to alert the private sector that substantial change in the spending habits of the country was under way. This signaled a green light for further lending.

The lending, however, was not fresh money for new projects. Instead, given the severity of the financial crisis, the loans were intended to provide the capital to make payments on past liabilities coming due. For a price—and at a higher interest rate—old loans were rolled over into new loans with maturity dates further in the future. The presumption was that when these repackaged loans came due again, the benefits of the tough economic medicine would be available to service the obligations. Called **involuntary lending**, this rolling over of obligations was designed to provide financial breathing room until payments could be made from more productive economies.

Unfortunately, international macroeconomic conditions did not cooperate. Real interest rates did not decline rapidly, and the prices that countries received for their exports—primarily agricultural commodities—were depressed. By 1985 Latin American countries had not returned to good standing in the international market. The problem was clearly more than a short-term liquidity issue. But was the IMF approach wrong?

Criticism of IMF conditionality packages centered on the IMF's diagnosis of the problem as well as the policy measures to bring about change. In Latin America, the theoretical debate was led by the structuralist school. It faulted the IMF approach as too standardized. The same IMF recipe, based upon the assessment of the need to reduce excess demand, was applied in all cases. The structuralists focused instead on the particular economic characteristics of each country. They puzzled at how a country with an unemployment rate of 15 percent and a capacity utilization rate of 75 percent could have excess demand. Furthermore, they challenged the IMF proponents to explain how a crisis triggered by the external shock of high global interest rates and expensive oil imports could be solved by domestically reducing aggregate demand. The structuralists argued that IMF programs were unnecessarily recessionary and increased inequality. They contended that the restrictive short-run targets set by the IMF exacerbated the negative impacts. Finally, the structuralists argued that the international financial community played a significant role in the accumulation of debt and should therefore bear some of the adjustment burden.[4]

Despite the standardized prescriptions, this first stage of the debt crisis was defined by a case-by-case approach to the resolution of the problem. That is, a region-wide approach was rejected by creditors. The politics of the case-by-case strategy on the part of the IMF, the World Bank, and the debtor countries may explain in part why Latin America did not default on the debt. Despite the fact that at the outset the debtor countries had some bargaining power given the exposure of money center banks, collective action was not effective. As shown in Box 4.3, in the Declaration of Quito (1984), Latin American countries called for an immediate response from the creditor countries to ameliorate the dramatic fall in living standards. In June 1984 the Cartagena Consensus Group of debtors argued that the burden of Latin American foreign debt threatened both the very stability of the international monetary system and the emergence of democracy in the region. But the Declaration of Quito was all talk and no action. Although some countries such as Peru declared a partial moratorium, stating that it would devote no more than 10 percent of exports to debt, and Brazil announced in 1987 a unilateral moratorium on the payment of interest of $68 billion of medium- and long-term money, the carrots for good behavior—the flow of new money into countries—were sufficiently enticing to keep countries largely in line.[5]

The Market Reacts to the Continuing Crisis

While countries were engaged in difficult adjustment measures, the financial sector quietly found ways to reduce its exposure to debt. Through the process of **provisioning**, or setting aside profits before dividend payments against risky loans, banks set aside the capital to guarantee their positions in the event of a default. Banks also found means to reduce their exposure to unwanted debt through innovative new market instruments. A **secondary market** for debt developed. Because loans were assets, they could be resold to other, more risk-inclined, buyers for a dis-

BOX 4.3. THE 1984 QUITO DECLARATION AND ACTION PLAN FOR LATIN AMERICAN RECOVERY

On January 9–13, 1984, governmental representatives of twenty-six Latin American and Caribbean countries met at the Latin American Economic Conference at Quito, Ecuador, to discuss renegotiations of the external debts, reformation of the international monetary and financial system, and an expansion of intraregional trade.

QUITO DECLARATION

All the countries in the region experienced deterioration of the terms of trade, diminishing trade, inordinate increases in interest rates, the sharp contraction of the capital flows, and widening external indebtedness. Adjustments that caused prolonged declines in production, employment, and living conditions were not compatible with the policy objectives. The declaration acknowledged the need for monetary and fiscal reforms and the dismantling of existing protectionist trade barriers in the industrialized countries to promote an increase in exports from the region.

ACTION PLAN PROPOSALS

- Export earnings should be consistent with the maintenance of adequate and sustainable levels of internal economic activity and output.
- Debt service payments should be reduced, and the debt servicing of each country should be stabilized in accordance with its payments profile.
- Debt renegotiation should be accompanied by an improvement in the terms of trade, especially in the access of the Latin American and Caribbean exports to world markets and the elimination of increasing protectionism in developed countries.
- The possibility of converting part of the accumulated debt into long-term obligations should be explored.
- An essential component of external debt renegotiations should be increasing flows of new public and private financial resources for all the countries in the region.
- Finance ministers and central bankers should carry out confidential exchanges of information on terms of debt refinancing and rescheduling.
- An expansion of intraregional trade should be pursued via a commitment not to increase trade barriers, along with measures to increase an exchange of goods and services among the Latin American countries, that is, establishment of a regional tariff preference that will create trade flows toward Latin America and the Caribbean. An expansion of the present system for reciprocal payments and credits in the region was suggested as a support mechanism to improve financial cooperation among the countries.

The external economic debt of Latin America passed from being a purely economic matter to being a serious political problem. Moreover, Latin American and Caribbean countries have already made extraordinary adjustments in their economies to meet international obligations, incurring high social, political, and economic costs. In contrast, the adjustment process should operate via an increase in the volume and price of exports and a decrease in real interest rates, but not by additional restrictions of imports vital to internal economic recovery.

"People who are malnourished or sick, who lack education, employment, housing and, above all, faith, hope and confidence in the future, will not heed to the call to build an integrated and democratic Latin America," warned Assembly President Jorge E. Allueca.[6]

Source: "Declaration and Action Plan for Latin American Economic Recovery," *UN Chronicle* 21, no. 3 (March 1984): 13–17.

count. The new holder of a million-dollar loan to Mexico might have paid only $510,000 for this asset if it were purchased in August of 1987. The value of the discount would be steeper the lower the likelihood the country would ever repay the full amount. As we can see in table 4.7, by 1987 expectations were so low that Peru would ever make good on its external obligations that its debt could be purchased for between 2 and 7 cents on the dollar.

> ## QUESTION FOR THOUGHT
>
> Given the causes, did the international financial community bear a responsibility to shoulder more of the burden of adjustment to the debt crisis?

Beyond allowing those who were more risk averse—particularly the medium-sized regional banks—to exit, the secondary market produced another innovation, **debt-for-equity swaps**. For example, a firm wishing to build a factory in a Latin American country could use the secondary market to purchase the debt note. In August 1987 a firm wanting to invest in Chile could purchase $100,000 worth of debt for about $64,000. The country then owed the firm instead of the bank. However, the firm could turn to the government and say "I don't need to be paid in dollars (hard earned through exports). In fact, in setting up this factory, I need pesos to buy supplies and pay my workers locally." In this way the debt purchased at a discount could be presented at the central bank for payment in local currencies. If the country had a strong bargaining position, such as good firm location, it too could negotiate a deal and agree to pay only $90,000 worth of pesos to the firm. Firms were satisfied because the secondary market gave them access to discounted funds, and governments could pay in local currency, not scarce foreign exchange.

On the surface, debt-for-equity swaps are a win-win proposal. The banks sell their poorly performing loans, the company makes a profit on the difference between the discount and the local payment, and the country, in addition to reducing its debt in hard currency, gains in jobs through the foreign direct investment. Indeed, Chile reduced 10 percent of its external obligations in this way. However, it was not the perfect scheme. It is important to identify how the local currency was

Table 4.7. Secondary Market Price Spreads on Latin American Debt (% of face value)

Country	July 1985	January 1986	January 1987	August 1987	October 1987
Argentina	60–65	62–66	62–65	45–47	34–38
Brazil	75–81	75–81	74–77	52–54	35–40
Chile	56–69	65–69	65–68	64–66	52–56
Colombia	81–83	82–84	86–89	80–82	75–80
Ecuador	65–70	68–71	63–66	41–43	31–34
Mexico	80–82	69–73	64–57	51–53	46–49
Peru	45–50	25–30	16–19	7–10	2–7
Venezuela	81–83	80–82	72–74	72–74	50–54

Source: George Anayiotos and Jaime de Piniés, "The Secondary Market and the International Debt Problem," *World Development* 18, no. 2 (1990): 1655–1660.

raised. If the central printing presses were simply run a little longer, there could be inflationary impacts. If the government borrowed internally to finance the pesos, indebtedness hadn't really changed—the holders just switched from international to domestic lenders. It was also questionable whether the investments by firms would have taken place anyhow—perhaps bringing hard currency into the country. Some critics raised concerns over sovereignty, charging that foreign firms were using cheap money to compete against local entrepreneurs. Finally, use of debt-for-equity swaps was a strategy suited for only the best performers. Logically, it would work only if multinational corporations wanted to operate in the host country. If economic adjustment had not been substantial, it was unlikely that foreign capital was going to be banging down the doors.

Despite these drawbacks, the appeal was strong. The secondary market was also used to facilitate **debt-for-nature swaps**. In this instance, rather than purchase materials, international organizations purchased the discounted notes and offered cancellation or partial payment in exchange for the country's promise to establish a nature preserve. As discussed in box 4.4, Costa Rica, in particular, pursued this alternative.

Beyond Muddling Through: The Baker Plan

"Muddling through" (as some called the first period of adjustment to the debt crisis) did not work to restore creditworthiness and growth to the region. Adjustment under IMF programs was largely unsuccessful. The burden of debt service had become painfully obvious. As seen in figure 4.2, high debt service costs resulted in a persistent outflow of resources from Latin America from 1982 through 1990. This loss of capital resulted in the flat growth in gross national product seen over the same period in figure 4.3. As growth slowed, unemployment rose in the 1980s, and real wages did not increase to improve the standard of living for the masses. In figure 4.4 we see urban unemployment rising to over 8 percent in 1984, and in figure 4.5 we see wages flat or falling in all countries except Brazil.

The costs of adjustment were enormously painful. As will be discussed in later chapters, poverty increased and environmental damage was exacerbated. Political and social dislocation led to labor strikes, supermarket looting, and bus burning in response to depressed wages and higher prices. Fragile democratic regimes were threatened as people began to idealize the stability and prosperity of military rule. To promote prosperity and stability, in 1985 U.S. Treasury Secretary Baker announced a plan designed to jump-start growth. The premise of the Baker plan was that countries could not continue to service their debt through contractionary policies. Growth and adjustment became linked. The Baker plan targeted fifteen less developed countries for $29 billion of new money, $20 billion from commercial banks and $9 billion from the IMF and the World Bank.

The Baker plan was important in shifting policy from austerity to growth. It also identified a new role for the World Bank in promoting institutional change. The failure of traditional IMF measures to resolve the debt crisis changed the understanding of the debt crisis from a short-term liquidity problem (with primary

Box 4.4.   Debt-for-Nature Swaps

Although the debt crisis was catastrophic for Latin America, in an ironic way it was turned into a blessing for international environmental nongovernmental organizations (NGOs) trying to persuade Latin American governments to adopt sustainable development policies. Third world debt, in the form of debt-for-nature swaps, gave NGOs a bargaining tool to influence the creation of environmental measures in Latin America. Some countries were persuaded to implement environmentally sound projects and policies in exchange for a reduction in their outstanding debt.

Debt-for-nature swaps were first proposed in 1984 by the then vice-president of the World Wildlife Fund, Thomas Lovejoy. Yet, it was not until 1987 that Bolivia, Costa Rica, and Ecuador engaged in this form of debt reduction. Pointing to the negative environmental effects of debt service through natural resource exploitation to earn dollars, Lovejoy and others argued for a pro-environmental policy. Debt-for-nature swaps could reduce hard currency indebtedness while making investments critical to the environment.

To carry out a debt-for-nature swap, three requirements must be met. There must be a donor, usually an NGO, who funds the initiative by purchasing a portion of a developing country's debt from the secondary market. In addition, the country's central bank must be willing to accept the debt note and able to finance the negotiated environmental programs. Finally, a private or governmental agency must carry out the environmental programs. Two types of debt-for-nature swaps have taken place: bond-based programs, where the interest on government bonds is used to pay for environmental and conservation activities, and policy programs where the government commits to implementing a series of environmental policies. The process for both types is similar. The donor negotiates with the debtor government on the terms and then purchases debt from the secondary market at a price lower than the face value of the outstanding debt. The debtor country now owes the donor instead of the creditor. If a bond-based program was negotiated, the purchased debt is converted to government bonds issued in the name of a local NGO that receives the interest over the life span of the bond. On the other hand, if a policy program is negotiated, in exchange for the debt note, the government agrees to implement environmental policies such as creating environmental reserves or ensuring that forests are managed sustainably. Finally, the funds are transferred to a local private or government agency for the implementation of negotiated projects.

Although debt-for-nature swaps sound like fabulous deals that benefit every party involved, they have limitations. They reduce little debt. In fact, the maximum debt reduction took place in Costa Rica, where less than 5 percent of external debt was reduced. There is a fear the central bank will engage in money creation, triggering inflation. Further, conservation projects may take precedence where other, more critical sustainable development projects are more drastically needed. This also raises the question of sovereignty among nationalists who see foreign NGOs dictating the national environmental agenda.

Despite these restrictions, Costa Rica has been able to make good use of debt-for-nature swaps by making them an extension of government policy. The major reason for Costa Rica's success is the high level of government participation. To safeguard against inflationary tendencies, officials set a ceiling on the number of swaps allowed yearly. Costa Rica has demonstrated that used properly, debt-for-nature swaps can help reduce some of its external debt. More important, debt becomes an instrument to achieve another policy goal: promoting environmental sustainability.

REFERENCES

Caldwell, Laura. "Swapping Debt to Preserve Nature." *Christian Science Monitor*. 11 September 1990.
Patterson, Allen. "Debt for Nature Swaps and the Need for Alternatives." *Environment* 21 (December 1990): 5–32.
World Bank. "Other Financial Mechanisms: Debt-for-Nature Swaps and Social Funds." Available on the World Wide Web at www-esd.worldbank.org/html/esd/env/publicat/edp/edp1116.htm

**Figure 4.2.   Aggregate Net Resource Flows and Net Transfers:
Latin America and the Caribbean**

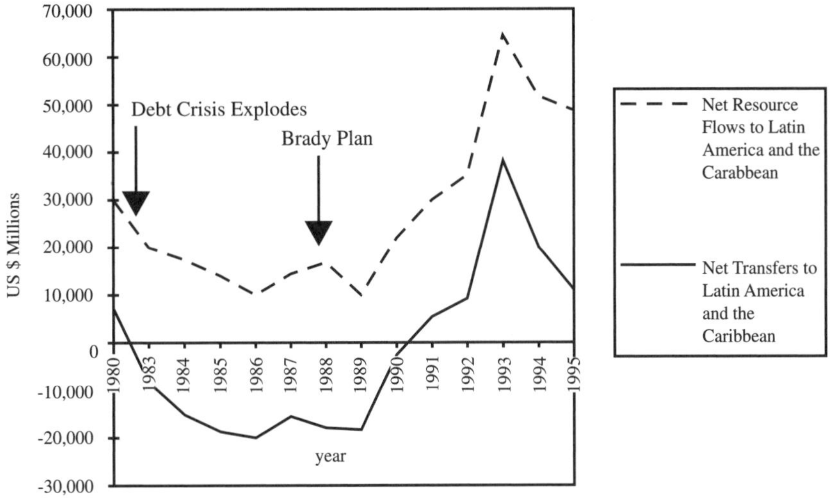

Source: World Bank, *World Debt Tables* (Washington, D.C.: World Bank, various years).

responsibility lodged in the IMF) to a long-term problem of **structural adjustment**. Debt came to be understood as a development problem, and the World Bank was charged with assisting in the management of the adjustment process. As a result, the World Bank began to engage in macroeconomic policy, formerly the purview of the IMF, and the IMF was forced to design lending facilities to support long-term structural change. There was general agreement that adjustment with growth would be led by the export engine, but there was a greater appreciation for the fact that severely contractionary monetary policy would not favor investment, the deepening of markets, or democracy.

This conceptual shift was important, but the Baker plan itself was too little, too late. Twenty-nine billion dollars may have made a difference if it were targeted toward one or two countries, but given the almost trillion dollars in external obligations on the part of developing countries at the time, it was inconsequential. Furthermore, commercial banks were unconvinced that new lending to debtor countries made any sense. In their view, why throw good money after bad?

Registering its "no confidence" vote for the success of the Baker plan, in 1987 Citicorp announced that it would allocate $3 billion from the loan loss reserves it had been setting aside against its developing country debt portfolio. Some had feared that such a move would lower Citicorp's stock value (since its assets are its loans, which were now worth less); instead, the stock market greeted the news with applause. The consensus was that the banks were prepared to take a realistic position on developing country debt: it would never be repaid in full. Accompanied by a $200 million dollar write-off in the same year by the Bank of Boston, this

Figure 4.3.   Gross National Product of Latin America and the Caribbean

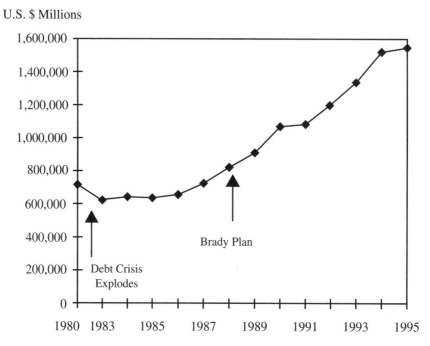

U.S. $ Millions

Source: World Bank, *World Debt Tables* (Washington, D.C.: World Bank, various years).

was seen as the death of the Baker plan. Jump-starting growth would not work until the debt burden was reduced two years later under the Brady plan.

The Social and Environmental Costs of Debt Adjustment

The burden of adjustment to the debt crisis may have fallen disproportionately on women. Several studies showed that in poor households, women were responsible for changes in work, child care, and consumption patterns. Household incomes were maintained by increasing the number of workers per home. Unlike the effects of the Great Depression in the United States, where women tended to withdraw from the work force in favor of men, in Latin America women entered the work force during austerity to help meet family needs; their entrance appears permanent.[7] Skilled men were eligible for unemployment compensation; their wives sometimes went into the informal sector to compensate for income loss. The entrance of men into the informal sector of unregulated, poorly compensated jobs tended to be inversely related to skill level.[8] Girls often assumed more domestic tasks, including child care of younger siblings, sometimes leaving school to do so. People cut back on food expenditure, eating fewer meals and consuming less protein and fresh vegetables. Health care was also postponed, often until a medical

Figure 4.4.   Urban Unemployment in Latin America (Average Annual Rates)

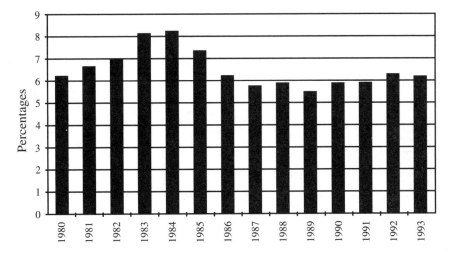

Source: United Nations Economic Commission for Latin America and the Caribbean, *Economic Survey of Latin America and the Caribbean* (Santiago, Chile: Economic Commission for Latin America and the Caribbean, various years).

condition became severe. Households were forced to dig into savings, pawn their possessions, and borrow from relatives or loan sharks. Pressures to make ends meet took an emotional toll on families as they struggled to survive the adjustment to the debt crisis.[9]

From Adjustment through Growth to Debt Reduction: The 1989 Brady Plan

The 1989 Brady plan addressed the need for debt reduction as a necessary step toward stable growth in developing countries. The Brady plan offered three options: decreasing the face value of debt, extending the time period of obligations, or infusion of new money. Countries were officially able to decrease the face value through buybacks in the secondary market. Whereas earlier buybacks were considered cheating and not sanctioned as indicating good performance in servicing loans, countries such as Costa Rica were able to reduce official debt by $1.1 billion.[10] Alternatively, countries were able to swap old loans for 30-year bonds with a 30–35 percent discount on the face value at a variable interest rate, or swap loans without the discount but at a fixed interest rate of 6.25 percent. The longer time period of the Brady bonds made them consistent with the long-term strategies needed for growth. A novel feature of Brady deals were the guarantees to the lender. The United States, Japan (a primary financier), and the developing country put up guarantees (usually in the form of U.S. Treasury bonds) to safeguard payment in the event of default, encouraging investor confidence. Finally, new money

Figure 4.5.   Evolution of Real Wages

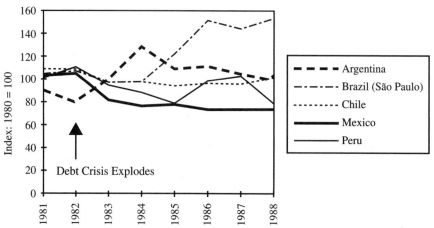

Source: James E. Wilkie, ed., *Statistical Abstract of Latin America,* vol. 29, pt. 1 (Los Angeles: UCLA Latin American Center Publications, 1992), 406.

could be extended to cover interest in the early years and smooth the transition to the market economy. To be eligible for any of the three options, countries had to show credible political will and a strong track record in economic reform.

The Mexican Brady deal in 1989 restructured $48 billion of its liabilities by floating $20.8 billion in bonds that had been discounted from the face value at 35 percent and $22.4 billion in par value bonds at 6.25 fixed interest. In addition, Mexico received $4.4 billion in new money at the rate of LIBOR plus 13–16 percent.[11] The World Bank estimated that this debt relief reduced net transfers by $4 billion per year, nearly 2 percent of GDP, from 1989 through 1994.[12] Box 4.5 recalls the tough economic road Mexico faced up to the debt relief of the Brady plan, underscoring how crisis drove policy throughout the decade.

Unlike the Baker plan, the commercial sector responded enthusiastically to the Brady options. Its realistic appraisal of the need to reduce the debt overhang, as well as its insurance guarantees, made the plan appealing. Investors found the plan pragmatic and less risky than the traditional short-term financial commitments. Table 4.8 lists the Brady deals. It is also important to note that by 1989, Latin America had already undertaken substantial reforms and was emerging as an intriguing investment arena. Brady bonds arrived as a vehicle for investment in a region that, after much painful adjustment, was beginning to be viewed as ripe for growth.

Is the Debt Crisis Over in Latin America?

Tough adjustments in Latin America appear to have paid off in the region. Table 4.9 shows the decline in the ratio of external debt to exports of goods and services, as well as interest as a percentage of exports of goods and services. By 1996 total

Box 4.5.   Mileposts in Mexican Debt

Date	Event	Total External Debt (percentage)	Debt to U.S. Banks (in U.S.$ billions)
1978–1981	3-month London Interbank Offer Rate (LIBOR) jumps from 8.8 percent to 16.8 percent	23.3–56.9	45.49–37.79
February 1982	President Lopez Portillo vows to "defend the currency like a dog" but is forced to devalue	64.4	38.66
12 August 1982	Moratorium placed on dollar-denominated deposits held in Mexican banks		
15 August 1982	Mexico announces it can no longer meet interest payments on foreign debt	77.1	38.23
Fall 1982	Mexico signs stand-by agreement with IMF	91	
1986	Peso devalued	99.3	31.62
October 1987	Mexican stock market collapses, losing 74 percent of its value in less than 40 days; inflation at annual rate of 159 percent		
December 1987	Unsuccessful Baker plan provides only $1.1 billion in debt relief for Mexico	101.7	28.83
April 1989	Mexico signs three-year, $3.64 billion loan agreement with IMF	100.9	23.15
July 1989	U.S. Treasury Secretary Brady introduces collateralized Brady bonds, reducing Mexican debt to foreign banks by U.S.$48.5 billion and cutting annual debt payments by U.S.$3 billion for next four years		

Source: Helen Shapiro, *Mexico: Escaping the Debt Crisis,* Harvard Business School case (Boston: Harvard Business School, 1991).

Table 4.8.   Brady Deals to Date in Latin America

Country	Date of Agreement	Terms of Brady Deal
Argentina	April 1993	$19.3 billion in debt swapped for 30-year bonds
Bolivia	July 1992	Collateralized interest-free 30-year bullet-maturity par bonds
Brazil	April 1994	$48 billion in debt swapped for (1) 30-year discount bonds, (2) 30-year fixed interest par bonds, (3) 15-year variable interest bonds
Costa Rica	May 1990	$579 million in debt-for-bond exchange
Dominican Republic	August 1994	$107.01 billion in (1) debt buybacks, (2) discount exchange bonds, (3) past-due interest bonds
Ecuador	February 1995	$7.8 billion in debt exchanged for discount and reduced-rate bonds
Mexico	March 1990	$20.5 billion in debt exchanged for 35% discount bonds, $22.4 billion for reduced-interest bonds, and $5.3 billion in conversion bonds
Mexico	May 1996	May 7—$2.4 billion in Brady bonds swapped for $1.8 billion fixed rate bond
Mexico	September 1996	September 24—buyback of $1.2 billion in Brady bonds
Panama	April 1996	$3.9 billion public external debt exchanged for (1) discount bonds, (2) par bonds, (2) 18-year front-loaded interest-reduction bonds (FLIRBs)
Peru	November 1996	$8 billion in public external debt exchanged for (1) discount bonds, (2) reduced-interest par bonds, (3) FLIRBs, (4) discounted buyback
Uruguay	February 1991	$628 million in discounted cash buyback, $535 million in collateralized debt reduction bonds, $447 million in debt conversion notes, $89 million in new money
Venezuela	December 1990	$19.7 billion in debt exchanged for (1) 91-day short-term notes, (2) discount bonds, (3) reduced at fixed-rate-interest bonds, (4) temporary stepdown interest rate bonds

Source: World Bank, *Global Development Finance* (Washington, D.C.: World Bank, 1997), 94–98. For updates on Brady bonds, consult www.emgmkts.com.

Table 4.9.   Debt Indicators for Latin America and the Caribbean

Year	Total Debt/ Exports of Goods and Services	Total Debt/GNP	Total Debt Service/Exports of Goods and Services	Interest/ Exports of Goods and Services	Interest/ GNP
1989	293.3	50.1	32.1	16.6	2.8
1990	277.4	45.0	26.3	13.0	2.1
1991	282.0	45.5	26.2	13.7	2.2
1992	276.2	42.7	28.9	12.5	1.9
1993	274.6	40.0	30.0	11.8	1.7
1994	258.6	37.2	27.5	12.4	1.8
1995	254.2	39.6	30.3	14.7	2.3

Source: World Bank, *World Debt Tables* (Washington, D.C.: World Bank, various years).

external debt had reached the manageable level of 41.4 percent of gross national product, and exports, or the ability to earn hard currency, had expanded while interest rates had fallen, bringing the drain of interest payments on the export bill down to 11.8 percent. As we will see in chapter 7, international capital has returned to the region. Net capital inflows reached U.S.$69.2 billion in 1996 as foreign direction investment, portfolio investments, and bonds captured the attention of global investors.[13]

Latin America's recovery from the debt crisis has been a long and painful process. The turnaround in the region is quite dramatic. Many nations are emerging as major players in the world's debt and equity markets. Some countries have initiated their own stabilization and emergency funds to circumvent the need for a future return to the IMF.

These funds have been developed in response to international lenders' reluctance to deal directly with Latin American governments. Since the 1980s, financing has been restricted mostly to the corporate sector. Some of this is changing as confidence grows regarding the sustainability of stabilization programs. A 1999 agreement with the IMF shored up investor confidence that the Argentine reforms were permanent changes, able to weather the storms of the Asian and the Brazilian crises. Labor market, social security, and tax reforms will be accelerated, restoring investor faith in Argentina's ability to honor its debts.[14]

A second important sign of the maturity of Latin American markets is the shift in focus of Latin American firms to domestic markets for investment capital. Many Latin American firms are turning to the region's healthy private pension and mutual funds for financing. This explosion in private pension funds, which currently manage about $130 billion and grow about $1 billion per month, has provided Latin American markets with ample domestic funding for investment. Bankers point to the increase in privatizations in the region as another reason for the increase in loanable funds.[15] The rescheduling of Panama's private debt through the use of Brady bonds in 1996 allowed the state telecommunications company, INTEL, to return to the market with a $28 million package underwritten by Citi-

bank.[16] The increase in domestic lending has also spurred a rise in foreign investment banks setting up and buying local brokerage houses within Latin America.

Finally, an important sign of the
strength of Latin America markets is that
these issues (both debt and equity) are
being denominated in local currencies
rather than U.S. dollars. Investors have
placed an increasing degree of trust in
Latin American currencies as countries
have been able to maintain economic
credibility. Internal debt, however, is also
cause for serious concern. In the Brazilian case, for example, the total net public
debt has reached 42 percent of GDP; 36
percent of this is domestically held debt. Domestic debt in Brazil exploded from
1994 to 1998, when inflation fighting precluded printing money to finance deficits.
Because a tough fiscal adjustment hadn't taken place, the government issued debt
as the alternative. An unhealthy social security system increased pressure on government accounts, and high interest rates to sustain an overvalued currency increased the burden. The key to predicting the stability of Brazilian debt is
estimating the tolerance of domestic institutional investors. The debt to GDP ratio
in Italy and Belgium has exceeded 100 percent. Do Brazilians have this kind of
confidence in their government to honor its obligations?[17]

These changes in the Latin American markets point to an overall increase in
confidence for these developing nations. Although there is still much progress to
be made, recent trends suggest that Latin America may be ready to take on a
more influential position in the world market. However, underneath the shiny new
exterior, the mountain of external debt still remains to be paid in full.

LESSONS OF THE DEBT CRISIS

What are the lessons of the crisis? The most salient and the most painful lesson is
that strong fundamentals matter. Unlike the populist policies of the past, countries
must attend to price stability and budget constraints. Responsible fiscal policy—
keeping the domestic house in order—has clear effects on a country's external
balance. This is perhaps more important today in highly integrated capital markets.
Information travels quickly, and negative performance on critical indicators carries
a high price. Maintaining the confidence of the market is a vital ingredient for
success. Without credible and predictable policies, capital will quickly respond to
uncertainty by fleeing to less risky instruments. Politics and market psychology
are intertwined with sound economic policy.

But generating the necessary macroeconomic stability in the region was no
easy task. Several countries in the region had annual inflation rates exceeding
1,000 percent. In the next chapter we will consider how governments in Latin
America took on the inflation problem. Tied to the ability to restrain inflation has

been a reengineering of the role of government. In contrast to the central role of the state under ISI, Latin American governments had to redefine the boundaries between the public and the private sectors. We will consider this revolution in political and economic space in chapter 6. The transformation of the inward-oriented model to an export-driven growth strategy has engendered strategic changes in the behavior of firms and states in the region. This will be discussed in chapter 8, "Contemporary Trade Policy." These radical changes in the rules and goals of the economy in Latin America have not been without cost. Poverty rose throughout the region, and the environment suffered from the natural resource export drives— the subject of chapters 10 and 14. As we explore these issues, we will see that the resolution of the debt crisis has fundamentally transformed the development model in the region.

Key Concepts

Absorption	Debt trap	Secondary market
Capital flight	Economic populism	Structural adjustment
Conditionality	Illiquidity	
Debt-for-equity swaps	Involuntary lending	
Debt-for-nature swaps	Provisioning	

Chapter Summary

The Accumulation of Debt

- The debt crisis was a natural consequence of spending practices in the 1950s, 1960s, and 1970s. Careless borrowing for sectors with high capital requirements and large-scale projects, when returns would not be generated until well into the future, was partly responsible for the accumulation of debt in Latin America. The immediate effects of many of these multiyear investments to support ISI and borrowing in order to finance the projects was the need to borrow more in order to pay past debts, leading to a debt trap. Economic populism, inefficiency, and corruption led to unnecessary or extravagant fiscal spending financed through more loans.
- Part of what made borrowing so attractive and easy during the 1970s was negative real interest rates and the influx of petrodollars into the banking system. In other words, in real terms, countries would have to pay back less than what they borrowed and had an almost unlimited amount of funds available.
- Not every Latin American country pursued the same policies, as can be

seen through the cases of Mexico, Brazil, and Argentina. However, the end result—accumulated debts that would eventually lead to a crisis—was the same.

On the Road to a Crisis

- In 1979 the Federal Reserve Bank of the United States raised interest rates. The effects were detrimental for Latin America because this action increased their interest payments on past loans and shrank the U.S. market for Latin American exports, the principal way of earning foreign exchange to pay the loans.
- Capital flight weakened governments' ability to raise revenues, and the excess supply of local currency fueled inflation as locals sent their money abroad.
- Mexico's inability and unwillingness to pay its debt signaled to the international community that the Latin American debt was on the verge of crisis.

Responses to the Debt Crisis

- Under the assumption that Latin American countries needed to reduce domestic absorption, the IMF prescribed a decrease in fiscal spending, tight monetary policy, and strict trade policies in return for finance. What has become known as IMF conditionality spurred criticism from various circles, including the structuralist school, for unnecessarily contracting the economy without changing the structural problems within the economy.
- The response of the market to the crisis was to reduce their exposure to unwanted debt through the sale of debts in the secondary market, debt-for-equity swaps, and debt-for-nature swaps.
- The Baker plan, though it was too little, too late, represented a shift away from IMF conditionality. A new role was given to the World Bank, focusing on structural adjustment.
- More successful than Baker, the Brady plan decreased the face value of debt, extended the time period of obligations, or infused new money.

After the Crisis

- The return of international capital to Latin America, the shift toward domestic markets for financing, and an increase in the degree of trust in domestic currencies are signs of an increase in the maturity of Latin American markets.

Notes

1. Federico A. Sturzenegger, "Description of a Populist Experience: Argentina, 1973–1976," in *The Macroeconomics of Populism in Latin America*, ed. Rudiger Dornbusch and Sebastian Edwards (Chicago: University of Chicago Press, 1991), 79.

2. John T. Cuddington, *Capital Flight: Estimates, Issues, and Explanations*, Princeton Studies in International Finance, no. 58 (Princeton, N.J.: Princeton University Press, 1986), 10.

3. Sebastian Edwards, ed., *Crisis and Reform in Latin America: From Despair to Hope* (New York: Oxford University Press, 1995), 17.

4. Patricio Meller, "IMF and World Bank Roles in the Latin American Foreign Debt Problem," in *The Latin American Development Debate: Neostructuralism, Neomonetarism, and Adjustment Processes*, ed. Patricio Meller (Boulder: Westview, 1991).

5. "Til Debt Do Us Part," *The Economist*, 28 February 1987, p. 85.

6. "Declaration and Action Plan for Latin American Economic Recovery," *UN Chronicle* 21, no. 3 (March 1984): 15.

7. Irma Arriagada, "Unequal Participation by Women in the Working World," *CEPAL Review* 40 (April 1990): 83–98.

8. Helena Hirata and John Humphrey, "Workers' Response to Job Loss: Female and Male Industrial Workers in Brazil," *World Development* 19, no. 6 (1991): 671–682.

9. Frances Stewart, *Adjustment and Poverty: Options and Choices* (London: Routledge, 1995), 189. Stewart summarizes results of studies published in the late 1980s.

10. U.S. Department of State, *1996 Country Reports on Economic Policy and Trade Practices*, a report submitted to the Senate Committee on Foreign Relations, the Senate Committee on Finance, the House Committee on Foreign Affairs, and the House Committee on Ways and Means, January 1997. (Available at www.state.gov/www/issues/tradereports/latinamerica99/costarica96.html)

11. Edwards, *Crisis and Reform*, table 4.3.

12. Ibid., 81.

13. World Bank, *Global Development Finance* (Washington, D.C.: World Bank, 1997), 89–90.

14. Bloomberg Latin America, "Argentine Markets Climb after IMF, Banks Move to Shore up Confidence." (Retrieved from the World Wide Web 14 July 1999 at www.quote.bloomberg.com)

15. CANTV was partially privatized in 1991, sold to VenWorld, a consortium led by GTE Corp.

16. U.S. Department of State, *1996 Country Reports on Economic Policy and Trade Practices*, a report submitted to the Senate Committee on Foreign Relations, the Senate Committee on Finance, the House Committee on Foreign Affairs, and the House Committee on Ways and Means, January 1997. (Available at www.state.gov/www/issues/economic/tradereports/latinamerica96/panama96.html)

17. "Brazil: Domestic Debt Dynamics and Implications," *ING Barings Emerging Markets Weekly Report*, 5 March 1999, p. 1–3.

CHAPTER FIVE

PRICE STABILIZATION

A Critical Ingredient for Sustained Growth

The debt crisis contributed to the lost decade of development in Latin America. *(Courtesy of the Inter-American Development Bank.)*

Inflation plagued Latin American economies from the 1980s through the first part of the 1990s. Imagine the difficulty—as was experienced in Argentina, Brazil, Nicaragua, and Peru—of living with inflation rates exceeding 2,000 percent per year! These were not isolated exceptions; as we can see in table 5.1, only Costa Rica, Panama, and Bollivia had rates under 20 percent in 1990.

Inflation exacts a high cost. Real wages—earnings after the inflationary bite—fall, thus reducing purchasing power. Inflation hits the poor particularly hard; the wealthy can insulate themselves through financial mechanisms indexed to the inflation rate. Macroeconomic instability creates uncertainty and undermines the investment climate. Inflation compromises the business environment, making long-run decision making impossible. It erodes tax earnings and reduces the ability of the government to provide public services. It promotes consumption today, reduces savings, and creates environmental pressure. Inflation hurts nearly all economic actors.

Despite these costs, excessive inflation persisted in Latin America for nearly fifteen years. Our discussion in this chapter revolves around several questions:

- Why was Latin America so inflation prone?
- What caused inflationary pressures in the region?
- Why was inflation so intractable?

Table 5.1.   Inflation in Latin America, 1990

Country	Hyper (> 2,000%)	High (> 30%)	Medium (> 20%)	Low (< 20%)
Nicaragua	7,485			
Peru	7,481.5			
Brazil	2,937			
Argentina	2,313.7			
Uruguay		112.5		
Guyana		63.6		
Ecuador		48.5		
Guatemala		41.2		
Venezuela		40.6		
Paraguay		38.2		
Colombia			29.1	
Mexico			26.6	
Chile			26	
El Salvador			24	
Honduras			23.3	
Suriname			21.7	
Costa Rica				19
Bolivia				17.1
Panama				0.8

Source: Inter-American Development Bank, Economic and Social Progress in Latin America (Washington, D.C.: Johns Hopkins University Press, various years); and International Monetary Fund, World Economic Outlook, 1997 (Washington, D.C.: International Monetary Fund, 1997), 148.

- What mechanisms were used to bring inflation under control in the region?
- What worked?
- Is inflation in Latin America now gone for good?

Latin America has been a virtual laboratory for macroeconomic experiments in the 1980s. This chapter will address these issues of macroeconomic stabilization, underscoring the causes and costs of inflation and highlighting the measures used to address it. It will look at the range of policies introduced to provide some insight on the difficult problem of maintaining stable prices while an economy is going through the complex and sometimes tumultuous process of economic growth.

THEORIES OF INFLATION: MONETARISTS VERSUS STRUCTURALISTS

Policies to attack inflation rest on an understanding of inflation's causes. Two broad schools of thought address the problem: the monetarists and the structuralists. For monetarists, or orthodox theorists, the cause of inflation is rather simple: too much money chasing too few goods. Monetarists such as Milton Friedman and the Chicago School look to the equation of exchange as a key to the cause of inflation. With M representing the quantity of money, V equal to the velocity or the number of times per year a unit of currency is used to purchase final goods and services, P as the price level, and Q standing for national output or GDP in real terms, monetarists argue that

$$M \times V = P \times Q.$$

If the rate of growth of output and velocity are assumed to be constant in the short run, prices are determined by the quantity of money in circulation. A rising level of money in circulation causes price acceleration. Although in the short run resource price shocks or shortages may accelerate prices temporarily, monetarists perceive that inflation over time is caused by excess liquidity in the system. Understanding persistent inflation for the monetarist involves highlighting why monetary authorities would continue to make policy errors by increasing the money supply in the face of rising prices. Monetarist explanations for such excess in Latin America include irresponsible deficit financing, erosion of the tax base, and mismanagement of the debt crisis. Let's consider these in turn.

Deficit Financing

If a government is spending more than it is taking in, the deficit must be financed. This can be done in three ways: print money, issue domestic debt, or borrow from foreign sources. As John Maynard Keynes pointed out in 1923, a government can live for a long time by printing money.[1] A government's ability to buy goods and services by printing money is called **seignorage**. Indeed, if the economy is growing at a strong pace, the quantity of goods and services available increases and the price effect may be moderate. However, once growth slows down, there is too much money chasing too few goods.

The alternative to printing money is issuing debt to finance government spending. Governments are often precluded from issuing domestic debt—the equivalent of a U.S. Treasury bond—by underdeveloped local capital markets. If the public cannot be induced to hold bonds, a government must borrow externally or print money. When the debt crisis hit in the early 1980s in Latin America, the external borrowing option dried up and the simplest response to deficits was to monetize them.

We can observe the pattern of macroeconomic instability in Latin America up to the 1990s in tables 5.2, 5.3, and 5.4. In table 5.2, we note the trend of strong and persistent deficits throughout the region from 1982 to 1990. Only two countries—Chile and Paraguay—had surpluses nearly as often as deficits. Brazil's consistent deficit averaged 10 percent of GDP over the period. Although we should be careful not to overinfer about the cause of the growth of the money supply, indeed we can see that in the countries with strong and persistent deficits, the average annual rates of growth of the money supply are startling. In Brazil, Argentina, Nicaragua, and Peru, the rate of growth of the money supply exceeded 1,000 percent in 1990. In an attempt to raise money internally to finance deficits as well

Table 5.2.   Overall Fiscal Surplus or Deficit in Latin America, 1982–1990 (as a percentage of GDP)

Country	1982	1983	1984	1985	1986	1987	1988	1989	1990
Argentina	−3.7	−10.1	−5.7	−2.9	−3.2	−4.4	−3.8	−2.6	−1.7
Bolivia	−13.7	−17.0	−18.3	−9.3	−1.7	−3.7	−5.0	−2.0	−1.3
Brazil	−3.1	−4.3	−5.0	−11.1	−14.0	−12.6	−16.3	−17.5	−6.2
Chile	−2.6	−3.7	−3.0	−1.9	−0.5	2.3	3.6	5.0	1.4
Colombia	−2.0	−1.0	−4.3	−2.7	−1.3	−0.5	−1.4	−1.7	−0.1
Costa Rica	−3.2	−3.4	−3.1	−2.0	−3.3	−2.0	−2.5	−4.1	−4.4
Ecuador	−4.4	−3.0	−0.6	1.9	−2.2	−6.2	−2.0	0.4	3.5
El Salvador	−5.9	−4.1	−3.2	−2.0	−3.6	−0.9	−3.0	−3.7	−1.5
Guatemala	−4.7	−3.6	−3.7	−1.8	−1.5	−1.3	−1.7	−2.9	−1.8
Guyana	−34.3	−40.1	−44.5	−56.1	−58.8	−42.4	−31.6	−6.6	−22.9
Honduras	−9.7	−9.0	−9.8	−7.2	−6.0	−5.8	−4.1	−6.0	−4.1
Mexico	−11.9	−8.2	−7.2	−7.6	−13.1	−14.2	−9.7	−5.0	−2.8
Nicaragua	−13.3	−30.0	−22.5	−21.3	−14.5	−16.0	−25.1	−3.5	−18.7
Panama	−11.4	−6.2	−7.4	−3.4	−4.5	−4.2	−5.2	−6.9	−6.8
Paraguay	−1.5	−4.7	−3.5	−2.3	0.0	0.4	0.6	2.4	3.2
Peru	−3.1	−7.3	−4.4	−3.0	−4.3	−6.9	−3.9	−6.3	−3.5
Suriname	−1.7	−17.6	−18.4	−21.4	−26.0	−24.8	−21.3	−14.0	−6.3
Uruguay	—	−4.2	−5.8	−3.1	−1.3	−1.3	−2.0	−3.4	−0.1
Venezuela	−2.1	−0.6	2.8	2.0	−0.4	−1.6	−7.4	−1.0	−2.1

Source: Inter-American Development Bank, *Economic and Social Progress in Latin America* (Washington, D.C.: Johns Hopkins University Press, various years).

Table 5.3.   Average Annual Rates of Growth of Money Supply in Latin America, 1982–1990

Country	1982	1983	1984	1985	1986	1987	1988	1989	1990
Argentina	154.2	362.0	582.3	584.3	89.7	113.5	351.4	4,168.2	1,023.2
Bolivia	228.8	207.0	1,798.3	5,784.6	86.1	36.6	35.3	2.4	39.5
Brazil	68.5	102.7	204.1	334.3	330.1	215.4	426.9	1,337.0	2,333.6
Chile	2.8	15.6	22.8	24.2	43.3	21.0	46.5	17.2	23.3
Colombia	25.4	23.4	24.1	10.7	—	—	25.7	—	—
Costa Rica	70.3	38.9	17.6	7.7	31.0	0.3	53.2	-2.0	3.9
Ecuador	14.0	31.9	39.6	25.6	20.1	34.7	52.7	43.8	59.0
El Salvador	3.7	-1.3	13.8	27.0	19.1	-0.4	8.1	13.5	22.3
Guatemala	1.4	6.0	4.3	54.9	19.5	9.8	14.4	20.7	33.0
Guyana	25.3	17.4	20.2	20.3	19.4	51.4	54.8	34.0	54.5
Honduras	13.5	13.6	2.5	-3.2	8.2	26.6	11.9	20.0	23.6
Mexico	62.6	40.3	60.0	49.5	67.2	118.1	67.8	37.3	63.1
Nicaragua	25.7	67.1	83.5	162.8	252.2	637.0	11,673.4	2,368.3	6,286.7
Panama	5.4	-1.8	2.2	7.5	9.8	-1.6	-31.3	1.0	41.0
Paraguay	-3.6	25.6	29.4	28.0	26.7	53.6	34.8	31.7	28.3
Peru	40.4	96.5	104.4	281.2	88.0	122.0	515.0	1,654.9	6,710.0
Suriname	17.7	8.0	26.9	52.5	39.6	27.1	24.5	11.3	4.0
Uruguay	19.8	9.0	48.4	107.6	86.1	58.1	63.7	72.9	101.0
Venezuela	4.5	25.0	27.0	8.9	5.3	40.8	22.7	22.2	54.6

Source: International Monetary Fund, *International Financial Statistics, 1996* (Washington, D.C.: International Monetary Fund, 1996), 81.

as to stem capital flight, national interest rates in 1990 exceeded 1,000 percent in Brazil and were above 30 percent in eight countries. But this was something of a losing battle. Although these interest rates were necessary to attract money for debt servicing, they also made borrowing for investment problematic. The result was simultaneous inflation and recession.

Deficit financing creates a vicious circle. Persistent inflation lowers the cash balances that people want to hold, because the value of the currency is declining quickly. People prefer to purchase goods to retain the value of their earnings, driving up prices in the market. Inflation therefore begets inflation. A second perverse effect has also been identified. Whereas deficit spending in most industrial countries is countercyclical, in Latin America it has largely been procyclical. That is, instead of spending to stimulate the economy during a recession, Latin American governments tend to contract during recession. This is tied to access to funds. As recession erodes the government's ability to raise money in international markets, it must reign in spending. Unfortunately, such procyclical policies, by their very nature, exacerbate macroeconomic volatility.[2]

The Tax Connection

If a government has lost credibility or if its population is very poor, tax collection as a percentage of government expenses is very low. Furthermore, as inflation

Table 5.4.   National Interest Rates in Latin America (central bank discount rates, end of period in percent per annum)

Country	1982	1983	1984	1985	1986	1987	1988	1989	1990
Brazil	174	194	272	380	89	401	2,282	38,341	1,083
Colombia	27	27	27	27	33.83	34.82	34.25	36.94	46.45
Costa Rica	30	30	28	28	27.5	31.38	31.5	31.61	37.8
Ecuador	15	19	23	23	23	23	23	32	35
Guatemala	9	9	9	9	9	9	9	13	18.5
Guyana	14	14	14	14	14	14	14	35	30
Honduras	24	24	24	24	24	24	24	24	28.15
Nicaragua	—	—	—	—	—	—	12,874.63	310.99	10
Paraguay	—	—	—	—	—	—	10	21	30
Peru	44.5	60	60	42.58	36.07	29.84	748.04	865.61	289.6
Uruguay	83.7	112.7	133.2	145.1	138.4	143.4	154.5	219.6	251.6
Venezuela	13	11	11	8	8	8	8	45	43

Source: International Monetary Fund, *International Financial Statistics, 1996* (Washington, D.C.: International Monetary Fund, 1996), 96.

rises, the real value of tax collection falls. Taxes for 1986 are due in 1987; because they are paid in 1987 dollars, they are worth less after inflation. The phenomenon by which inflation eats away at the value of tax receipts is called the **Olivera-Tanzi effect.** An extreme case was Bolivia, where by 1984 only 2 percent of Bolivia's government expenditure was covered by taxes.[3] More printed money was therefore needed to cover the deficits. Inflation, as a result, exceeded 8,000 percent. We will return to the problem of taxation in the region in chapter 6.

Effects of the Debt Crisis

As access to foreign loans dried up, there was more pressure to raise money domestically to service existing debt. This left printing money as the most popular action to purchase the foreign exchange to make the interest payments on debt. This was the case in Argentina after 1982.[4] Furthermore, the devaluation often required in IMF stabilization packages increased the value of the external debt in domestic terms. That is, as the currency became worth less, it took more of it to buy the dollars to service the external debt. This increased the temptation to print money to service the debt. Running up a down escalator may be a good metaphor for this type of policy.

At the center of the monetarist explanations for inflationary financing were profligate governments running budget deficits. The monetarist solution to restrain inflation in the region was therefore quite straightforward: decrease government spending. If the monetarists are right and inflation is tied to excessive government spending, the solution is clear: eliminate deficit-driven policies. Yet this was easier said than done. Deficit reduction proved politically tough.

Why do governments run large fiscal deficits despite the inflationary risks associated with them? The research in this area indicates that countries with less stable political systems are more likely to engage in deficit financing. As political instability increases, politicians see it in their own interest to buy political favor and to avoid making hard choices.[5] Politically threatened governments find it difficult to carry through on promises of fiscal responsibility. Political change can therefore make economic stabilization more problematic. Clearly this plays out in cases such as Peru or Nicaragua. Political change from an authoritarian government to a democracy was taking place over this period for countries such as Brazil and Argentina. Instability likely played a role in the capacity of states to follow sound economic programs.

In contrast to these monetarist explanations, for the **structuralists** the explanation of deficit-led instability was too simple. Structuralists do not deny that excess liquidity or budget deficits can cause inflation, but they do not believe that these are the sole or even central causes of inflation in Latin America. Attention to monetary variables is complemented by the study of a host of other factors. Because structuralists add other factors to the orthodox focus on the money supply, their policy is sometimes called **heterodox.** Structuralist or heterodox explanations focus on the structure of the underdeveloped economy as the propagating mechanism for inflation. Instead of making the equilibrium assumptions of the classical model upon which the monetarist theory is based, structuralists contend that economies in Latin America can best be understood as incomplete markets that do not automatically tend toward full employment equilibrium. For the structuralists, bottlenecks in both the agricultural and the industrial sectors create price pressures. If input markets cannot quickly adjust to price signals to meet supply requirements, inflation will result. External price shocks from the international economy can also introduce or exacerbate instability in the domestic market.

Cost-push elements were therefore central to the structuralist explanation. Internal shortages and external price shocks such as the oil crisis interact with the structure of industry and labor organization to fuel an inflationary struggle. In contrast to the perfect competition assumption in neoclassical models, both output and labor markets in Latin America are highly concentrated. Under oligopolistic conditions, prices are sticky downward. Shortages ratchet up prices, but during periods of slack demand or recession, prices rarely fall. Furthermore, firms may engage in markup pricing to maintain profit margins. Large firms often have internal sources of capital as well, circumventing the need to pay high interest rates for capital. When prices increase, powerful labor unions demand wage increases—which firms are able to cover because they pass the cost on to the consumer. Inflation then reflects the distributive conflict between capital and labor. If all agents assume inflation, each side wants to build predicted price increases into its share of the pie.

Monetary authorities may passively accommodate the demand for money. Central banks in the region were often not independent of the executive branch and were therefore subject to political pressure. In Brazil the central bank was ordered by the military government to finance the public deficit automatically from 1971 to 1974; from 1974 until 1994, the minister of finance had overwhelming control of the central bank. In 1994 Brazil finally formed a National Monetary

Servicing the debt encouraged unsustainable exports of forest products in the region.
(Courtesy of the Inter-American Development Bank.)

Council as a supervisory and coordination organ for money policy, accountable not only to the presidency but also to the Congress.[6] For the structuralists, underdeveloped political systems, the lack of accountability of military governments, and later nascent democracies unable to handle competing demands contributed to inflationary tendencies.

In the structuralist model, inflation becomes embedded in the economy. People begin to anticipate inflation. Such **inertial inflation** results when economic agents come to expect inflation and automatically adjust for it in their wage demands and pricing patterns. Not surprisingly, expected inflation is a self-fulfilling prophecy as people adjust behaviors accordingly. However, for the structuralist, inflation was an unwelcome but not unexpected result of the conflicts inherent in the process of economic development. Since markets in developing countries had unique characteristics that did not favor equilibrium, the recessionary costs of forcing austerity under these circumstances were just too high. Structuralists were willing to live with inflation as a price associated with growth in the developing world. The policy challenge became reducing the costs of living in an inflationary society.

INDEXATION, INFLATIONARY EXPECTATIONS, AND VELOCITY

In the 1980s structuralist thought dominated much policy making in the Latin American region. Measures were introduced to minimize the costs of inflation.

Most wages were indexed to a public minimum salary that was adjusted monthly to accommodate inflation. A teacher's contract might, for example, be written for seven times the national minimum wage. As the minimum wage rose each month, salaries tracked inflation. Some prices were also indexed to inflation. If you got into a taxi in Rio de Janeiro, you would not pay the price on the meter. Rather, the meter reflected a price on a tabela, or list of prices, that could be adjusted by decree. In stores, clothing was tagged with letters of the alphabet. Although K might mean a Cr$50 dress one day, a week later a buyer might have to come up with Cr$65. Interest on bank accounts was also indexed. Checking accounts were interest bearing (similar to U.S. NOW accounts), and borrowers had to pay the real rate of interest plus inflation. Rents were likewise increased alongside interest and bond rates through this inflation adjustment, sometimes euphemistically called the "monetary correction."

In some periods the official rate of **indexation** was set at less than the rate of inflation to act as a brake against future inflation. But people quickly figured this out, and they took it into account in setting wage demands and prices. Ironically, although indexation was introduced as a defense against inflation, it made the transfer of inflation from the present to the future automatic, even when the government tried to manipulate expectations by lowering the percentage adjustment for inflation. Because it was built into the system, people came to expect it. Indexing made inflation easier to live with while inadvertently reinforcing its place in the economy.

Vicious Circles

Although indexation was designed to mitigate the costs of inflation, it created unintended inflationary side effects. **Inflationary expectations** became ingrained in the culture. People expected inflation, the government accommodated inflation, and the public got inflation. Inflation today was equal to inflation in the past period plus additional demand pressures and the effects of any supply shocks. As inflation accelerated, it made tax collection less efficient, pressuring fiscal balances and often leading to a further increase in the money supply. Inflation complicated exchange rate management. If the exchange rate was fixed, the erosion of the value of domestic money made it worth less relative to international or "hard" currencies. If the fixed rate was not adjusted, the currency was posted at an overvalued rate, creating a bias against exports. If the rate was devalued or if the currency was allowed to float freely, the higher prices of imported goods introduced additional inflationary pressures in the economy. To account for inflation and risk, nominal interest rates were high, often retarding investment.

The **velocity of money** changed in response to economic agents learning to live with inflation. A review of velocity will help illuminate this problem. Velocity is the number of times money turns over in a system each year. If the payment for a dinner to a restaurant owner is quickly used to purchase linens for a beach house, and those receipts are rapidly used (in concert with other receipts) by the curtain maker to buy a new sewing machine, and that revenue in turn is immediately used to pay workers, a given physical quantity of money is supporting the purchase of many goods. Velocity is a measure of how much output is supported by the stock of money, or gross domestic product (GDP) divided by the money supply (M). If velocity is increasing—that is, if a decreasing stock of money supports a given amount of output—increasing that stock of money without changing the productive capability of the economy will result in inflationary pressures.

In an inflationary economy, people have the incentive to transform their rapidly worthless currency into goods. If a worker in Brazil waited until the end of the month to buy groceries or other goods from a monthly paycheck, in 1990 prices would have risen by approximately 70 percent by the month's end, leaving 70 percent less in the grocery basket. It made good sense to buy quickly. Of course the shortages that the "buy now" behavior created further increased prices.

The banking system may respond to the pressure to turn money over quickly, further increasing velocity. If you deposit a check and it takes three days to clear, you may not use that money for three days without bouncing another check. However, if your checks clear instantaneously, it is time to go shopping again! A higher velocity will support the purchase of more goods and services per dollar. Once a system has adapted to a higher velocity rate, modest increases in the money supply will have a stronger expansionary effect. If supply constraints prevent the rapid provision of goods and services in response to the increase in the money base, inflation will be ignited.

The velocity numbers are dramatic in the Brazilian case. During an inflationary period the velocity of money in Brazil was an astounding 125, compared to 16 in the United States. The highly efficient system of interest-bearing transactions balances allowed money holders to escape from the direct use of currency through something similar to checkable money market funds. The Brazilian money supply therefore supported a higher volume of goods and services per dollar than in the United States. Changes in the money supply would be magnified in inflation rates.

TIMING AND ADJUSTMENT

The monetarist versus structuralist policy debate in part boils down to a decision as to how much macroeconomic imbalance is tolerable in the medium term. Monetarists argue that imbalances should be swiftly redressed. Excesses in external accounts or in fiscal deficits should not be tolerated because they will quickly aggravate inflation. Structuralists contend that it is not that simple. Given the underdeveloped nature of markets in the developing world, they expect imbalances in domestic accounts or in external spending. Harsh and rapid adjustment, for the structuralist, is too high a price. Rapid reductions in the money supply to reduce domestic absorption might also have the effect of strangling long-term growth.

Monetarists and structuralists also had different views of the degrees of freedom of countries in their ability to isolate themselves from the effects of the "inconsistent trinity" or the "trilemma." Policy makers face inevitable tensions in balancing goals of domestic monetary policy, fixed exchange rates, and capital mobility.[7] A country cannot have all three. Under a fixed exchange rate regime, if international capital is mobile, and governments accept the rules of the game—that is, that a current account deficit will result in a decrease in money supply—autonomy in domestic monetary policy is forfeited. If a fixed exchange rate is maintained to preserve an international price anchor, capital controls and sterilization may give temporary relief, but exchange rate crises will certainly erupt if adjustment is incomplete. Governments might be tempted to pump up the money supply, but this will result in ballooning trade deficits. If nations want to pursue monetary autonomy they can certainly abandon the fixed rate and let the exchange price float, but without high credibility in international markets this is likely to introduce an inflationary bias into the economy. Unless markets believe that the government is pursuing a deflationary price policy, the expected depreciation of the currency will raise import prices and foment inflation. Facing this "trilemma," monetarists largely counseled abandoning domestic monetary policy and linking to a "hard" international currency; structuralists suggested exchange controls to preserve domestic autonomy. Rather than forfeit autonomous monetary policy or the exchange anchor, structuralists preferred to restrain capital mobility. Box 5.1 summarizes this trilemma of open economies. It is worth recalling that such capital controls were before the days when globalization and liberalized markets were the trademarks of sound policy.

How did these policies play out in practice in Latin America? Drawing in elements of both schools, Latin American nations adopted a variety of approaches

BOX 5.1.   THE MACROECONOMIC POLICY TRILEMMA

Tool	Objective	Conflict
Domestic monetary autonomy	Activist monetary policy to shorten recessions and restrain inflation	Under fixed exchange rate, adhering to "rules of the game" (a deficit renders a decrease in the money supply) renders independent monetary policy impotent. If domestic capital is not also mobile, the central bank can perform offsetting domestic interventions (sterilization).
Fixed exchange rate	Price anchor—tie exchange rate to a firm anchor and force real adjustment	Lose monetary independence; could float exchange rate but lose price anchor. If capital is immobile, can create different domestic prices for money.
Capital mobility	Encourage international investment; buoy confidence	Interest rates must be equal to international rates plus inflation; lose interest rate wedge in monetary policy. Could float, but lose inflation anchor.

to macroeconomic stabilization. The fixed versus floating rate constraint was softened somewhat in practice by using intermediate exchange rate solutions such as crawling pegs or exchange rate target zones and other forms of managed exchange rate regimes. In these cases a target is set—either pegged to a hard currency such as the dollar or set within a range, with a ceiling and a floor between which it can fluctuate. Depending on pressures on the currency, the monetary authority intervened by buying or selling to stabilize the currency but was not bound to defend a fixed price. This kind of flexibility accounted for the fact that inflation in developing countries is generally higher than in the industrial world. A crawling peg or target zone can allow for small, regular devaluations to take inflation differentials into account and prevent an overvaluation of a currency. There are rich lessons in the experience of macroeconomic stability in Latin America. Here we consider four cases: structuralist policies in Brazil, a monetarist approach in Bolivia, a change from a structuralist to a monetarist stance in Argentina, and a social compact to soften the adjustment costs to Mexico.

> **QUESTION FOR THOUGHT**
>
> Does the structuralist or the monetarist approach to inflation appear most consistent with your own sense of economic theory and with the Latin American reality? Who had it right?

HETERODOX APPROACHES TO INFLATION STABILIZATION IN THE 1980S: BRAZIL

Brazilian policy makers diagnosed inflation in the 1980s as structural. The external oil price shocks of 1973 and 1978–1979 in conjunction with the interest rate shocks of the early 1980s intersected with a highly concentrated industrial sector able to pass on cost increases to the public. Maxi devaluations of the currency in 1979 and 1983 took place because of current account pressures, fueling price increases. Orthodox policies to reduce inflation had been tried under the military governments with painful social results. Sectoral conflicts between industry and agriculture as well as social conflicts between powerful labor and industrial organizations were thereafter resolved through spending. The state itself played an active role in the economy through state-owned enterprises, especially in the provision of infrastructure such as electricity and key inputs such as steel. In these sectors prices were held down to spur development of industry, but the difference was made up in deficit spending. As inflation accelerated, bonds, credit, and wages were indexed with increasingly frequent intervals. The lack of independence of the Bank of Brazil from the Treasury left it in a role to passively accommodate expansion.

When monthly inflation hit 459.1 percent in January 1986,[8] a radically different stabilization plan was called for. The **Cruzado plan** included a general price freeze and a partial freeze on wages following an 8 percent readjustment. If the consumer price index increased more than 20 percent, wage increases would be permitted. Indexation of contracts with less than one year's duration was prohib-

Figure 5.1.   Brazilian Inflation

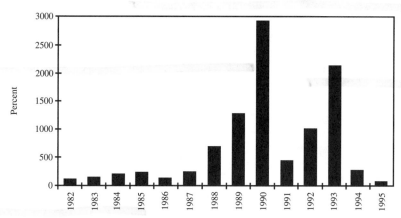

Source: Inter-American Development Bank, *Economic and Social Progress in Latin America* (Washington, D.C.: Johns Hopkins University Press, various years).

ited. A new currency was created called the cruzado, set equal to 1,000 cruzeiros. After a devaluation, the cruzado was fixed at 13.84 cruzados to the dollar. Popular favor was cultivated as Brazilian President Sarney deputized all Brazilians as "fiscais," or price inspectors, to police the price freeze in supermarkets and shopping malls. Citizens could arrest store managers for raising prices. People felt empowered by the fight against inflation. The goal was to eliminate the inertial aspect of inflation, creating expectations for price stability rather than inflation.

The preliminary results were dramatic. By April prices actually fell 4.5 percent, and in May they rose only 1 percent. Because inflation was not eating away at paychecks, Brazilians enjoyed a real wage increase for the first time in years, and economic growth was led by the strong demand for consumer durables. However, Brazilian industry was not able to meet the surge in consumer demand, and the economy began to overheat. Shortages emerged. The sustainability of the plan was called into question. As businesses lost faith in the plan, they withheld goods from the market, anticipating that the price freeze could not last indefinitely. Fiscal reform was limited, and monetary policy accommodated the deficit pressures. With state and gubernatorial elections in the fall of 1986, politics would not permit austerity. By December 1986 monthly inflation was back in triple digits. Following the elections, adjustments were made to the price framework, and a crawling peg for the exchange rate temporarily relieved the pressure for devaluation. Contracts were once again indexed to ease the costs of inflation. But credibility was destroyed, and a year and a half after the introduction of the plan, inflation topped 1,000 percent. Although the plan worked initially to reduce inflation dramatically, when the economy was unable to respond to the increased demand, credibility eroded in the government's ability to manage the economy.

Brazil continued its heterodox experiment with the **Bresser plan** in mid-1987. The Bresser plan also froze wages, although the caps were designed to be readjusted every ninety days to minimize misallocation and shortages. The exchange rate was managed through a series of minidevaluations. Interest rates were targeted above inflation to keep the lid on the consumer boom that overheated the economy under the Cruzado plan. Finance Minister Bresser placed heavy emphasis on controlling the public deficit in theory but was unable to realign the political priorities of the Sarney administration. A follow-on "summer plan" included another revaluation of the currency, lopping off three zeros once again and calling it the Novo Cruzado. However, it did little to change the underlying politics of the Brazilian situation. Fiscal pressures continued, inflation accelerated, and confidence was low.

Pres. Collor

In 1990 a new president—the first directly elected by the people in nearly thirty years—came into office with a strong mandate to "kill inflation with a single bullet." President Collor engineered the most dramatic of stabilization plans, with both heterodox and orthodox elements. With annual inflation nearing 3,000 percent, and consistent with prior stabilization plans, Collor froze wages and prices, and once again readjusted the monetary unit, renaming it the cruzeiro. Agreeing with the monetarists that inflation indeed had a strong monetary component, Collor implemented a radical liquidity freeze, immediately reducing the money stock by 80 percent. All bank accounts in excess of $1,000 were frozen. Brazilians were shocked. People who had, for example, sold one house but were in the process of buying another could not go ahead with their purchases. By law, they were not allowed access to their own money. The economy—including prices—was essentially at a standstill. These drastic measures were accompanied by planned reductions in the shape of government, including privatizations and layoffs of government employees.

The plan backfired. Rather than change expectations toward a low inflation economy, it eroded confidence in the government as a guarantor of the rules governing the economic game. If the government could step in and freeze a family's life savings, what would it not do? The powerful business lobby, represented by FIESP, the federation of industries of São Paulo, was not consulted in the plan, leaving an angry and alienated industrial sector. The plan collapsed with a loss of legitimacy. Tragically, Collor later fell to charges of corruption and was impeached. Changing the shape of government had not addressed some of the personalistic privileges government officials had usurped. Nonetheless, this early test of Brazilian democracy led, after an interim presidency of Itamar Franco, to the election of Fernando Henrique Cardoso on the platform of price stabilization.

Cardoso's Real Plan

As Franco's economics minister, Cardoso introduced the **Real plan**. The Real plan was a pragmatic mix of orthodox and heterodox elements. Its premise was heterodox in spirit: eliminate the inertial elements of inflation to break out of a cycle of indexed price increases that adjusted for past inflation. The preliminary stage of the plan lasted three months. It began in December 1993 by identifying disequilibria, eliminating price distortions, and introducing emergency fiscal adjustments. In March monetary reform was introduced. All wages, prices, and taxes, and the exchange rate, were redenominated in a new accounting unit called the urv, or the real unit of value, roughly set at par to the U.S. dollar. The urv was a kind of superindex as an intermediate step on the path back to using money as the measure of value. Indexation to other rates was prohibited, and the money supply was tightened, indicating a monetarist bent. By July a new currency, the real, was introduced; it was tied initially one to one to the urv accounting unit. Once again this new currency was designed to erase the inflationary memory associated with the old unit. What was different in the case of the real was that the policy changes implemented in association with the real plan were credible to the public. The gradual, preannounced nature of each step served to calm expectations. Furthermore, after more than two decades of unsuccessfully battling inflation, the public was simply ready to bite the bullet. Expectations of inflation were changed. As President Cardoso said on the second anniversary of the real plan, "Brazil used to be like a casino. Everyone, not only banks, speculated here. This is coming to an end."[9] By 1996 the inflation rate, at 13–14 percent, was the lowest in Brazil in 39 years. As we can see from the data in table 5.5, growth resumed, buoyed by consumer confidence, and unemployment did not rise.

The real was a stable anchor against inflation through mid-1998, but imbalances began to emerge in the Brazilian economy. Government deficits, fueled by a lack of fundamental restructuring in fiscal outlays, became alarming. Strong spending—led by workers finally able to save enough to buy consumer durables—led to trade balance problems. The real was becoming overvalued relative to economic fundamentals. As we will discuss in chapter 7, when currency crises shook Asia and Russia, the unstable Brazilian economy was unable to withstand the capital outflows. The government abandoned the fixed exchange rate, allowing the

Table 5.5. Macroeconomic Indicators for Brazil, 1982–1998

Year	Inflation	Growth	Unemployment
1982	98.1	0.6	6.3
1983	142.0	−3.4	6.7
1984	196.7	5.1	7.1
1985	226.9	8.0	5.3
1986	125.0	7.5	3.6
1987	233.3	3.4	3.7
1988	690.0	0.3	3.8
1989	1289	3.2	3.4
1990	2,937.7	−4.2	4.3
1991	440.9	0.3	4.8
1992	1,008.7	−0.8	5.8
1993	2,148.6	4.2	5.4
1994	2,668.6	6.0	5.1
1995	84.4	4.2	4.6
1996	18.2	3.0	5.7
1997	7.5	3.0	5.7
1998	3.0	0.5	7.6

Sources: Inter-American Development Bank, Economic and Social Progress in Latin America (Washington, D.C.: Johns Hopkins University Press, various years); International Monetary Fund, World Economic Outlook (Washington, D.C.: International Monetary Fund, various years); Economic Commission for Latin America and the Caribbean, Statistical Yearbook for Latin America and the Caribbean (Santiago, Chile: Economic Commission for Latin America and the Caribbean, various years).

currency to float on international markets. The associated 30–40 percent depreciation raised fears of igniting another inflationary round in Brazil.[10] Restraining the resurgence of inflation will be a function of the government's ability to put its fiscal house in order. Under pressure of financial turmoil and the loss of an IMF rescue package, President Cardoso was able to extract important fiscal reforms from Congress and restrain inflation to about 10 percent, a significant achievement given the country's hyperinflationary past. This is no small task in Brazil, where the 1988 constitution hampers the president's ability to change a complex system of taxes and entitlements controlled by a powerful Congress.

What lessons for inflation stabilization can we take from the Brazilian case? Clearly, heterodox policy alone is not enough. Simply focusing on expectations and taming the inertial component does not eliminate the imbalances creating the expectations. Fiscal and monetary fundamentals also need to be adjusted. Without reshaping the fundamentals, it is not possible to generate confidence that the imbalance in the domestic economy has been corrected. By the same token, a pure orthodox approach was not dramatic enough to generate confidence and support. In the Brazilian case, simply restraining the money supply had perverse effects. When the money supply was cut and interest rates rose as a result, economic agents perceived this as a rise in the nominal interest rate—or a signal that inflation was heating up again. They therefore increased their demands for higher wages or prices to adjust for expected future inflation. Without a change in expectations of inflation, without a clear sense of a change in the rules of the game, inertial aspects of inflation will plague the orthodox strategy. Finally, the fight for shares, the struggle to adjust to inflation by stepping on the back of other economic agents, was indeed prevalent in the Brazilian case. In an economy characterized by a high degree of inequality and structural constraints on the road to equilibrium, this battle between capital and labor cannot be ignored. With Brazil's relatively closed economy, agents did not have to look to the external sector for competitive price setting. By the same token, resolving the problem of conflict over social shares cannot be passed around like a hot potato by ineffective government. Confidence in the ability of government to mediate this conflict, to stabilize the playing field, is crucial to a compact on the part of all agents in restraining inflation. Not surprisingly, this confidence begins at home, with a transparent and credible plan for managing fiscal accounts. Solving chronic budgetary problems is the key to sustainable prices over time.

EARLY MONETARIST APPLICATIONS: BOLIVIA

The Bolivian stabilization experience provides an interesting orthodox contrast to the Brazilian case. Bolivia had also embarked on a period of hyperinflation by 1985. External factors such as the crash of international tin prices from $6 to $3.5 from 1982 to 1985 severely contracted tax revenues. Tin export earnings fell from $234.8 million to $75.1 million. At the same time foreign debt service requirements increased from 0.4 percent of GDP in 1979 to 10.8 percent in 1983. As in other developing countries, due to the debt crisis, there was virtually no access to new funding in international markets. In addition to the fall in revenues, inflation was eating away at the value of tax receipts. Because the government was pursuing an expansionary policy, financing the internal and external deficits required monetary emissions, or increases in the money supply. By 1984 the government deficit had risen to nearly one-fifth of gross national product. The jump in the money supply, or seignorage to finance government spending, mirrored the decline in resource flows from abroad. In interesting contrast to the Brazilian case, wage and price indexation was not widespread. In a futile attempt to provide a monetary anchor, the exchange rate was fixed. Rather than price stability, the result was an overvalued exchange rate. When an exchange rate is fixed and exchange controls are imposed to restrict the amount of hard currency in the system, international currencies are strongly demanded in black—or, as they sometimes were called to reflect the openness of the transactions, parallel—markets. In Bolivia by 1985 the controlled rate was at 67,000 pesos per dollar while the free black market rate was running at 1,143,548. This 1,600 percent overvaluation made legal exports unprofitable. Underground transactions therefore emerged as evidenced by oddities in international data. Peru, for example, despite its lack of tin mines, became a tin exporter (of illegal Bolivian exports) during this period. Of course illegal exports are not taxed, further eroding the ability of the Bolivian state to finance its affairs. Speculation in foreign exchange became quite profitable. If a person could buy the overvalued official peso (sometimes illegally), money could be made in selling cheaply acquired dollars on the black market. Politically, Bolivia had a weak government trying to adjudicate increasing claims on the state to address

Table 5.6. Bolivia: Various Indicators, 1982–1996

Year	Inflation (in percent)	GDP (U.S.$ millions)	GDP/Capita (U.S.$ millions)	Public Deficit as % of GDP
1982	185.7	6,280	1,069	−13.7
1983	200	5,684	943	−17
1984	1,300	5,886	1,001	−18.3
1985	11,804.80	5,830	969	−9.3
1986	276.3	4,646	772	−1.7
1987	14.6	4,766	775	−3.7
1988	16	4,907	781	−5
1989	15.2	5,093	793	−2
1990	17.1	5,330	811	−1.3
1991	21.4	3,610	834	0.7
1992	12.1	5,703	827	−1
1993	8.5	5,969	845	−3.7
1994	7.9	6,267	866	−3.4
1995	10.2	6,692	903	—
1996	10.4	6,956	916	—

Sources: International Monetary Fund, World Economic Outlook, 1997 (Washington, D.C.: International Monetary Fund, 1997), 148; Inter-American Development Bank, Economic and Social Progress in Latin America (Washington, D.C.: Johns Hopkins University Press, various years).

problems of poverty and inequality. A powerful military and labor movement pressured the spending arm of the state. Falling external prices made these constraints all that much more acute.

In 1985, Victor Paz Estenssoro came to power and announced the New Economic Policy. A devaluation of the exchange rate followed by managed floating addressed the priority of getting international prices right.[11] The state-led development strategy was abandoned. Enterprises were privatized or scaled down, resulting in a reduction of the public sector wage bill. In particular, COMIBOL, the powerful state tin producer, reduced its employment from 30,000 in 1985 to 7,000 in 1987. Public sector revenues were increased through tax reform. Greater confidence in the government also resulted in higher compliance with tax obligations. Debt was rescheduled, and funding from multilateral institutions and foreign governments was secured in exchange for the adoption of these orthodox economic policies. Widespread liberalization of trade and capital accounts was implemented to attract private capital inflows. An amnesty was declared for the return of dollars that had fled abroad. Dollar deposits were also legalized without proof of origin, permitting the entry of coca dollars into the economy.[12]

The immediate result of this austere package was a call for a general strike. However, after three years of hyperinflation, the public chose to support the government rather than the workers and the tough package was upheld. To minimize the social costs of adjustment, an emergency social fund (ESF), financed by the Inter-American Development Bank and the World Bank, was implemented. It provided funds for small-scale, labor-intensive projects proposed and implemented by local NGOs. The projects financed were mostly in infrastructure; they are estimated to have created nearly 41,000 jobs and added 2 percent to the GNP over the period.[13] We will return to the use of social funds in chapter 11, which discusses poverty.

Despite the innovations of the ESF, the costs of inflation stabilization in Bolivia were enormous. While inflation was dramatically controlled, the price was a long period of recession. Over the period 1985–1996, the rate of growth of GDP per capita ranged from −20.33 percent to +2.86 percent in 1991. If the goal of development is to improve the well-being of its population, falling or stagnant rates of growth of GDP do not present opportunities for economic advancement. By 1994 GDP finally climbed back to the 1982 level—a lost decade of development for Bolivians. GDP per capita in 1996 did not reach 1982 levels. The Bolivian orthodox strategy eradicated inflation, but at a high price for growth.

THE CASE OF ARGENTINA: FROM THE AUSTRAL PLAN TO THE CONVERTIBILITY PLAN

Stabilization in Argentina was conceptually path breaking with its heterodox attempt in the 1980s and its orthodox plan in the 1990s. The Argentine Austral plan of 1985 provided many of the elements followed by Brazil. Inflation was diagnosed as having a strong inertial component. A decade of failed stabilization attempts had taught economic agents to expect inflation and adjust for it in wage and price setting. The Austral plan therefore froze wages and prices (including the exchange rate), and introduced a new currency with a promise not to print money. Fiscal adjustment was the third element of the plan. There was a close relationship between fiscal deficits and money creation in Argentina. Eliminating deficits would stem the need for seignorage, or money printing, as the last resort for financing. Initially the plan succeeded as inflation decreased from 350 percent in the first half of 1985 to 20 percent in the second.

Nonetheless, the Austral plan collapsed as signs of disequilibrium emerged. The exchange rate became overvalued and external accounts deteriorated. The government made adjustments for price flexibility, but the credibility of the plan was undermined. Argentines needed to have their expectations grounded in a firm and credible long-run strategy. They found this in the 1991 **convertibility plan** introduced by Minister Cavallo in the Menem administration. President Menem succeeded President Alfonsín as the second democratically elected president after years of military rule. International markets held their breath because Menem was a renowned populist of the Peronist party. However, the old style of populist spending to appease conflicts between industry, labor, and the military was surprisingly transformed into a personal populism that allowed Menem to introduce one of the toughest austerity programs in the region. The convertibility plan locked the Argentine peso to the U.S. dollar. Through a currency board independent of the Treasury, by law the money supply could be increased only if the U.S. dollars held in reserve were to rise. This took the central bank out of the position of being the lender of last resort and removed the temptation to finance domestic deficits with new money creation. Monetary policy was nondiscretionary, fixed to the long-run performance of the external sector. Liberalization of the economy promoted exports and the inflow of foreign investment to increase the stock of dollars in Argentina. The peso, which formerly lost value daily, became indistinguishable from the U.S. dollar. Indeed, in bank machines in Buenos Aires one can select whether to receive cash in dollars or pesos. As we will study in chapters 6 and 7, fiscal adjustment was dramatic. The government embarked on a large-scale privatization program, putting fifty-one firms on the auction block between 1989 and 1992 and generating approximately U.S.$18 billion.[14] Tax reform increased revenues to balance government books. Smaller government demanded less inflationary financing.

As we can see in figure 5.2, inflation tumbled in Argentina from the peak of more than 3,000 percent to an astoundingly low rate of 0.1 percent in 1996. Domestic and international capital believed in the long-run commitment of the plan. International capital flowed to Argentina, convinced of the sustainability of the program and lured by the values of the privatized firms on the stock exchange. What has been most remarkable about the plan has been its durability. Despite high social costs of 17 percent unemployment, Cavallo was tough and held firm on the convertibility plan. When the Mexican peso crisis of 1994–1995 rocked the international financial community's faith in Latin America, Argentina stuck to the plan even as capital temporarily fled the region. Cavallo left the administration in July 1996 with the economy contracting at a rate of 4.6 percent in 1995; nonetheless, the new economics minister, Roque Fernandez, continued to ground the Ar-

Figure 5.2.   Argentine Inflation, 1970–1997

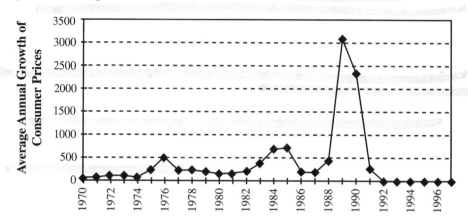

Source: Inter-American Development Bank, *Economic and Social Progress in Latin America* (Washington, D.C.: Johns Hopkins University Press, various years).

gentine peso firmly in the value of the dollar. Despite the recession, Fernandez attacked the budget deficit, increasing taxes and cutting spending. The costs of not erasing the inflationary memory in Argentina were simply much greater than the pain of recession. Although unemployment remains high nationally, the strategy seems to have paid off. GDP growth registered 8.4 percent for 1997, and the rate of growth of productivity is one of the highest in the region. When its trading partner, Brazil, let the real float in 1999, Argentina reinforced its commitment to the dollar-peso lock with a dramatic proposition: a monetary association treaty with the United States, allowing it to adopt the U.S. dollar as its national currency.

Figure 5.3.   Mexican Inflation, 1988–1998

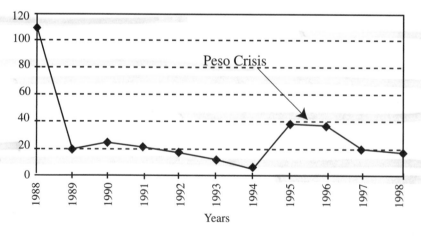

Source: Data from the Inter-American Development Bank and Economic Commission for Latin America and the Caribbean.

Efforts to stabilize the Argentine currency took a heavy toll on growth, with GDP growth falling by half to 4 percent for 1998.[15] Whether dollarization moves forward is subject to debate; its short-run importance was a signal to markets of Argentina's firm commitment to keep the peso-dollar lock as its inflation anchor.

THE MEXICAN SOCIAL COMPACT

The case of price stabilization in Mexico is an interesting lesson in how social conflict tied to rising prices of goods and labor might be resolved. In December 1987 the Salinas government placed at the centerpiece of its reform a liberalization package to open Mexico to the international economy. Liberalization was seen as especially important in taming the power of highly oligopolistic markets. Competition from abroad would challenge domestic oligopolies. The exchange rate became a primary inflation fighting tool to provide an anchor for the economy. Privatizations and budget cutting helped to improve the fiscal stance. The innovative feature of the Mexican plan, however, was the **Pact for Economic Solidarity** (Pacto), explicit price agreements between business, labor, and the state to cooperate to limit price increases. Business agreed not to raise prices, and labor agreed not to push for wage increases. Wage increases became tied to productivity gains rather than past inflation. It was government's role to pursue a responsible fiscal policy and continue structural adjustment. The benefit of the Pacto was the ability to generate a social consensus on the hard choices in economic stabilization. It provided a framework for policy negotiations among key economic actors to maintain the long road toward stabilization.

As shown in figure 5.3, Mexican inflation was low and stable for the first half of the 1990s. The downfall of the plan was its very success. International capital found Mexico enticing, and the inflow generated an overvalued exchange rate. The strength of the currency undermined the export drive and led to expectations of a devaluation. As the Mexican government tried to hold firm on the nominal anchor, speculators bet in the opposite direction. When political crises, including the assassination of a presidential candidate and the social uprising in Chiapas, called the effectiveness of government into question, the peso crisis of 1994 ensued. We will return to this crisis in chapter 7, which concerns international capital flows.

> **QUESTION FOR THOUGHT**
>
> Argentina's and Bolivia's plans were far more contractionary than those in Mexico and Brazil. Was this necessary? Why? What are the costs?

LESSONS FOR STABILIZATION

Box 5.2 summarizes the variation of the stabilization experiences we have just studied. What lessons can we draw from these cases of stabilization in Latin America? As Jeffrey Sachs notes, there are three components to inflation reduction: (1) finding a solution to chronic budgetary problems at the core of high inflation; (2) identifying a means of eliminating inertial inflation, principally wage and price indexation; and (3) introducing one or more nominal anchors to the price level at the start of stabilization to ground expectations and the behavior of central bank authorities.[16] In all the cases, without out clear and credible attention to the fiscal crisis, inflation will resurge in the economy. Fiscal imbalances will prevent stabilization and the government will likely respond by monetizing the difference.

> **DATA EXERCISE**
>
> Update data for inflation, deficits, and GDP growth for our four case countries. Which countries appear to be performing best over time? Why? Try the following sites on the World Wide Web:
>   World Bank: www.worldbank.org/wdi/cd_rom/cdets.pdf
>   ECLAC: www.eclac.cl/english/statistics/statistics.htm
>   IMF: dsbb.imf.org/category.htm

Restructuring the role of government in the economy has an additional benefit: creating the perception that business as usual has changed. Generating the confidence that the government is serious about reform and will—and can—remain committed to a stable policy is critical to success. This involves erasing the inflationary memory, the backward-looking behavior of agents that reflexively drives price increases. Tying the currency to an anchor—either firmly as in the case of Argentina or loosely in terms of a crawling peg to the dollar—provides monetary restraint. Beyond these tools, the population needs to believe in the benefits of inflation fighting. In Argentina the public was so tired of struggling to live with inflation that it was willing to quit cold turkey. Much like an alcoholic, the public understood that one little ounce of price inflation would tip the economy into an inflationary binge. Bolivians, also subject to ravaging hyperinflation, were willing to swallow the tough contractionary pill. In Mexico the support was negotiated through the Pacto, providing a framework for sharing the burden of stabilization. Brazilians have been able to stave off some of the more dramatic social conflicts, perhaps in part due to the size of their economy and the ability to insulate it to some degree from the shock of international competitiveness. Whether this will prove to be a good thing in the long run remains to be seen.

Sustained stabilization may also involve the development of new financial markets. One of the defining features of underdeveloped economies is the lack of a long-term capital market. In part this is a self-fulfilling prophecy—instability decreases the incentive for long-term investments. But this makes macroeconomic stabilization in the short term problematic. Without long-term confidence, bond markets cannot be used as an effective instrument of open market operations to smooth cyclical variations in the economy. This lack of monetary instruments places increasing pressure on governments to use the blunt tools of decreasing fiscal expenditures to stabilize growth.[17]

FROM STABILIZATION TO GROWTH

The dramatic change in price stabilization is evidenced in table 5.7 with a fall in the increase in consumer prices from an annual rate of 662 percent in 1990 to

Box 5.2. Variations on the Stabilization Experience

	Brazil's Cruzado Plan 1986	Brazil's Real Plan 1994	Argentina's Convertibility 1991	Bolivia's New Economic Policy 1985	Mexico's Economic Solidarity Pact December 1987
Diagnosis of inflation	Structural; inflation is a fight over social shares; address inertial inflation	Provide nominal anchor tied to exchange rate, de-index economy and correct fiscal imbalances	Erase inflationary memory and control expectations; provide firm price anchor	Monetary emissions to accommodate government spending; fall in tax revenue forces seignorage; exchange rate overvalued	Restrain fight for social shares to allow the effects of liberalization to work
Fiscal policy	Reform unsuccessful	Short-run emergency adjustment; long-run change stalled in Congress	Restrictive; cut expenditures; strong privatization; tax increase	Tax reform, increase public sector prices; cut state-owned enterprises (SOEs)	Austerity
Monetary policy	Increases in money supply due to fear of raising nominal interest rate giving inflation signal	Contractionary	Nondiscretionary; tied to U.S. dollar reserves	Tight	
Exchange rate policy	Fixed at 13.84Cr = US$1	Crawling peg set to dollar	Fixed on par with U.S. dollar; money supply tied to reserves	Establish stable, unified rate; devalue then dirty float	Consolidate exchange rate, which then becomes anchor
Wages and prices	Freeze	Flexible	Flexible	No controls	Wage indexation
Currency	1 CZ = 1,000 CR	New currency real tied to urv, loosely set to dollar	Peso interchangeable with dollar		
Political	Price inspectors			Restrain influence of labor unions	Business agrees not to raise prices; labor agrees not to push up wages
Trade	Continued internal orientation	Temporary erection of tariffs	Aggressive liberalization	Liberalization	Acceleration of trade reform

(continued)

(continued)

Indexation	Prohibit con-tracts of less than one year with index-ation clauses	All index-ation except to new urv prohibited	None		
Initial results	Inflation falls from 22 per-cent monthly in February to 0.3 in May; growth surges led by strong con-sumer dura-bles	Inflation low-est in nearly 40 years; consumption exploded with increase in real in-come; some tightening	Dramatically low inflation	Drove hyper-inflation out	Monthly in-flation dropped from 15 percent in January to 1 percent in December
Persistent im-balances	Shortages, withholding of goods; plan col-lapses as in-flationary expectations escalate	Fiscal imbal-ance; real structural change awaits Con-gressional approval	Unemployment at 17 percent	High social costs; anemic growth rates	
Balance of payments	Trade surplus shrinks; re-serves fall; exchange rate held fixed too long to main-tain internal external bal-ance	Loss of ex-port dyna-mism due to overvalued currency			

approximately 8.7 percent in 1998. Imagine what that price stability means to agents trying to plan for the future. Real GDP growth accelerated to a high of 5.4 percent before falling as a result of the global slowdown. Growth in per capita GDP is lower, however, reflecting the mismatch between the rate of growth of the economy and the needs of growing populations in the region. The process has not been smooth. The Inter-American Development Bank's 1996 report characterizes the pattern of reform in five phases: stabilization and implementation of reforms, economic recovery or boom, stress, correction or crisis, and postreform growth.[18] As in Brazil's or Argentina's first packages, successful stabilization measures dis-cussed above created consumer and investor confidence that leads to economic recovery or boom. Growth increases at a rate 4 percent higher than normal, and the resulting increase in income tax revenues improves fiscal balances. The boom, usually lasting about three years, creates imbalances. Credit tightens and interest rates rise. Higher domestic spending leads to an appreciation of the currency, squeezing exports. The economy slows, and fiscal deficits emerge. Investors, in-cluding foreign capital, become wary. Confidence erodes, and the economy enters into a period of stress. Pressures are often exacerbated by political factors, and, as happened in Mexico in December 1994, economies can spiral into crisis. The re-

Table 5.7. Selected Latin American Indicators

	1990	1995	1996	1997	1998	1999*	2000*	2001*
Increase in consumer prices (%)	662	44.1	21.7	12.3	8.7	14.6	9.9	
Increase in real GDP per capita (%)	−1.9	−1.0	2.0	3.7	0.5	−2.3	1.0	2.4
Increase in real GDP (%)	−0.1	0.6	3.7	5.4	2	−0.8	2.5	3.9

Source: For 1990–1997, www.iadb.org; for projections of 1999–2001 and 1998 data, World Bank, *Global Development Finance 1999* (Washington, D.C.: World Bank, 1999), 161.
*Forecast.

form process can be temporarily derailed by the crisis. However, if corrections are swift and credible, while slower growth can be expected, the downturn need not be traumatic. Chile provides an example of a country that, after more than twenty years of reform, has entered into the final stage of postreform. This is not to say that the economy is perfectly functioning. Challenges, particularly the social challenges of poverty and inequality, require response. But policy making has achieved a level of continuity and normalcy that encourages measured, long-run responses.

THE PRICE OF PRICE STABILITY: THE CHALLENGE OF RESOLVING THE SOCIAL DEFICIT IN LATIN AMERICA

Despite stabilization, the magic of the market has not completely fulfilled the promise of development in Latin America. It is important to recall the huge human cost of austerity measures designed to stabilize inflationary economies. Like adjustment to the debt crisis, policies to reduce inflation come at the expense of current consumption—and for the poor, reducing a thin margin means human suffering. The fragility of this model was clearly demonstrated as the repercussions of the crash of the Mexican peso were felt around the region. Domestic difficulties call into question the ability of governments to continue to apply tough austerity measures at home in the hopes of maintaining investor confidence abroad.[19] Large portions of the populations are left out of the process of growth. The social deficit—the enormous unmet need in the region for education, housing, medical services, transportation, and other public services—may not be resolved by the market. Women have borne the brunt of macroeconomic stabilization. As the guardians of the family, they are left with the task of designing strategies of survival. They must do more with less. Often forced outside the home for long hours to make up lost income, their daughters must fill motherly roles with younger siblings. Macrocrisis can be considered a social "tax" on women's time.[20]

The road to economic reform in Latin America has been rocky. In all cases the social costs of stabilization have been the daily reality of Latin Americans. Poverty rates in the region have risen, and human capital investments have suffered from the cuts in government programs in education, health, and social services. Macroeconomic equilibrium is seen as a necessary but not sufficient condition for development. Development, as we remember from chapter 1, revolves around the question of structural change. Several problems must be addressed to move from stability to growth. Sufficient savings must be generated and channeled into productive investment, resources must be allocated efficiently, and a setting must be developed that is conducive to generating the incentives to find new, potentially better ways of doing things.[21] The broad framework should move beyond macro-economic policy reform to address trade liberalization, private sector development, innovative policies for technological change, and reform of the state, focused on greater equity, efficiency, participation, and environmental sustainability.[22] We will take up these issues in the following chapters.

Key Concepts

Austral plan
Bresser plan
Convertibility plan
Cost-push elements
Cruzado plan
Heterodox

Indexation
Inertial inflation
Inflationary
    expectations
Olivera-Tanzi effect

Pact for Economic
    Solidarity
Real plan
Seignorage
Velocity of money

Chapter Summary

Monetarist Theory of Inflation

- Monetarists believe that persistent inflation in Latin America was caused by irresponsible deficit financing, the erosion of the tax base, and the debt crisis. With weak capital markets, and with foreign sources of capital drying up after the debt crisis, Latin American governments financed their deficit through seignorage, or the printing of money, inducing inflation. Unable to generate revenue with a deteriorating tax base, governments again looked at seignorage as a form of financing deficits. The debt crisis only exacerbated the conditions, making it difficult to finance the deficit through other means. The monetarist solution was to decrease government spending—although this was politically difficult.

The Structuralist Theory of Inflation

- The structuralists focused on cost-push elements as the main factors inducing inflation. Bottlenecks causing shortages, oligopolies, external shocks, and labor interacted to push prices up and prevented them from falling under normal market conditions. The political power of business and labor made it difficult to resist accommodating money demands. Inflation then became imbedded in the system and, for the structuralists, a necessary price for growth in the developing world.

- With ingrained expectations of inflation, some countries adopted indexation to adjust to the increase in prices. At the same time, indexation propelled inflation as price increases were automatically passed around the economy. Inflationary expectations also increased the velocity of money. With higher velocity, an increase in the money supply has a stronger expansionary and inflationary effect.

- Latin America is a laboratory of inflation-fighting policies. Brazil, characterized by a culture of inflation, began its fight against inflation with the Cruzado plan, which initially was successful. It failed due to a loss of credibility and political pressures. The next attempt was the Bresser plan in 1987, which fell to shortages and balance of payments pressure. President Collor tried to bring the economy to a standstill by eliminating inflationary expectations but succeeded only in eroding credibility. Using a mix of heterodox and orthodox measures, Finance Minister (later President) Cardoso introduced the Real plan, which managed to bring down inflation. The fixed exchange rate aspect of the plan was abandoned, however, as international capital was wary of the lack of fundamental reform in the wake of the Asian crisis. Inflation appears to have stabilized.

- The decrease in foreign capital in the mid-1980s induced Bolivia to finance government spending through seignorage. To reduce the inflationary effects of its policies, Bolivia adopted a monetarist approach by devaluing the currency, privatizing, tax reform, liberalizing trade and capital accounts, and rescheduling the debt. The austerity package brought about a general strike, but the government was able to uphold its package. The effects were further felt as the economy contracted tremendously throughout the 1980s and into the 1990s.

- The 1985 Austral plan to bring down inflation in Argentina initially succeeded but, like the Cruzado plan in Brazil, ultimately collapsed as inflationary expectations resurged. Populist President Carlos Menem surprised the country by introducing an austerity program to fight inflation in 1991. Menem tied the Argentine peso to the dollar to limit any increases in money supply and liberalized the economy. Though inflation came down from 3,000 percent to 0.1 percent, Argentina continues to suffer social costs of high unemployment.

- Mexico's approach to inflation differed from that of Bolivia, Argentina, and Brazil in its emphasis on social consensus. Under the Mexican Pact for Economic Solidarity, business, labor, and the state agreed to share the costs of economic stabilization. The economy was opened, encouraging competition, and the size of the state was reduced.

- Lessons for stabilization include the need for fiscal sustainability, generating confidence in the ability to tackle tough choices, and the development of new sources of finance. The human and environmental costs of stabilization have been high, resulting in a huge social deficit and environmental degradation.

Notes

1. Rudiger Dornbusch, *Stabilization, Debt, and Reform: Policy Analysis for Developing Countries* (Englewood Cliffs, N.J.: Prentice-Hall, 1993), 19.

2. Michael Gavin, Ricardo Hausman, Roberto Perotti, and Ernesto Talvi, *Managing Fiscal Policy in Latin America and the Caribbean: Volatility, Procyclicality, and Limited Creditworthiness*, Inter-American Development Bank, Office of the Chief Economist Working Paper no. 326 (Washington, D.C.: Inter-American Development Bank, 1996), 4.

3. Victor Bulmer-Thomas, *The Economic History of Latin America since Independence* (New York: Cambridge University Press, 1994), 393.

4. Dornbusch, *Stabilization*, 20.

5. Sebastian Edwards, "The Political Economy of Inflation and Stabilization in Developing Countries," *Economic Development and Cultural Change* 42, no. 2 (January 1994): 235–266.

6. G. Tullio and M. Ronci, "Brazilian Inflation from 1980 to 1993: Causes, Consequences and Dynamics," *Journal of Latin American Studies* 28 (October 1996): 635–666.

7. Obstfeld and Taylor refer to these as the macroeconomic policy trilemma for open economies. As cited in Alan M. Taylor, "On the Costs of Inward-Looking Development: Price Distortions, Growth, and Divergence in Latin America," *Journal of Economic History* 58, no. 1 (March 1998): 22.

8. Inflation series from Donald V. Coes, *Macroeconomic Crises, Policies, and Growth in Brazil, 1964–90* (Washington, D.C.: World Bank, 1995), table A.10.

9. Interview with President Fernando Henrique Cardoso on the occasion of the second anniversary of the Real plan, as reported by the Foreign Broadcast Information Services, Latin America (FBIS-LAT-96-129, 3 July 1996), first appearing on Rede Globo (the Brazilian television station) at 10:30 Greenwich Mean Time, 1 July 1996.

10. The range for the depreciation depends on the day it is measured. On 30 January 1998, for example, it had depreciated 37 percent from its initial value.

11. "Managed floating" refers to an exchange rate policy in which the price is largely market determined; the government may intervene in the market by buying and selling currency to stabilize the value.

12. Adapted from Juan Antonio Morales and Jeffrey Sachs, "Bolivia's Economic Crisis," in *Developing Country Debt and the World Economy*, ed. Jeffrey Sachs (Chicago: University of Chicago Press, 1989).

13. Diana Tussie, *The Inter-American Development Bank*, vol. 4 of *The Multilateral Development Banks* (Ottawa: North-South Institute, 1995), 112.

14. Sebastian Edwards, *Crisis and Reform in Latin America: From Despair to Hope* (New York: Oxford University Press, 1995), 196.

15. Economic Commission for Latin America and the Caribbean, *Preliminary Overview of the Economies of Latin America and the Caribbean* (Santiago, Chile: Economic Commission for Latin America and the Caribbean, 1998), 26.

16. Jeffrey Sachs and Alvaro Zini, "Brazilian Inflation and the Plano Real," *World Economy* 19, no. 1 (January 1996).

17. José María Fanelli and Roberto Frenkel, "Macropolicies for the Transition from Stabilization to Growth," in *New Directions in Development Economics: Growth, Environmental Concerns and Government in the 1990s*, ed. Mats Lundahl and Benno J. Ndulu (London: Routledge, 1996), 46.

18. As characterized by Michael Gavin, "Surviving Economic Surgery," *The IDB*, December 1996, pp. 4–5.

19. "A New Risk of Default," *Euromoney*, September 1996, p. 283.

20. Lance Taylor and Ute Piper, *Reconciling Economic Reform and Sustainable Human Development: Social Consequences of Neo-Liberalism*, United Nations Development Programme Discussion Paper Series (New York: UNDP, 1996).

21. Fanelli and Frenkel, "Macropolicies," 41.

22. Colin Bradford Jr., "Future Policy Directions and Relevance," in *The Legacy of Raúl Prebisch*, ed. Enrique V. Iglesias (Washington, D.C.: Inter-American Development Bank, 1994), 164.

THE ROLE OF THE STATE

Defining a Desirable and Sustainable Level of State Activity

CHAPTER SIX

Privatization of public utilities created huge investment opportunities.
(Courtesy of the Inter-American Development Bank.)

The shape and the function of the state in Latin America changed dramatically in the 1990s. We saw the state as the engine of growth under import substitution industrialization. It is truly remarkable that coincident with a political transformation to democracy throughout the region, an economic transformation producing a smaller state sector also took place. We recall that debt crises and macroeconomic instability forced a reconsideration of the capabilities of the state. From chapter 5, we remember the pattern of deficit financing that emerged in Latin America in the 1980s. These deficits were compounded by interest rate and commodity price shocks. Capital flight contributed to the erosion of the tax base. Government spending was a source of macroeconomic instability. Fiscal reform, in terms of both decreasing expenditures and increasing revenues, was essential to macroeconomic stabilization in the region.

With greater vulnerability to international capital markets, Latin American policy makers must be able to exercise more fiscal discipline more rapidly and strictly than counterparts in industrial countries.[1] Given the fiscal crisis of the state, one aspect of reform has been the downsizing of the public sector. Another element of this reform is the privatization of state enterprises, changing the shape of state activity in the region. Decreasing the financial liabilities of the state included decreasing state provision of public services. As we analyze these dramatic changes in the region, key questions emerge with respect to the new, streamlined Latin American state:

- How have decreases in the quantity of resources controlled by the state changed the role of government in the region?
- What were the mechanics of the massive transfer of resources from state-owned enterprises to the private sector? Just how are enterprises privatized without creating a garage sale, give-it-all-away atmosphere?
- What has been the record to date on privatization in the region? What remains to be done?

Driven by crisis, the first stage of downsizing—cutting aggregate public expenditure and privatizing firms—was relatively straightforward. Deficits had to be reduced to sustainable levels. The next stage is more problematic.

- What size and roles should the new, streamlined government assume?
- How should state efforts be directed in terms of social and environmental programs?
- What is the best use of public funds to promote competitiveness in the global arena?
- What should be the balance between the state and the market in Latin America?

In a sense, the first stages of stabilization were easier—by decree governments lowered tariffs, reducing gross inefficiencies and improving macrodisequilibria. What lies ahead includes the tougher steps for Latin American states: an era of institution building.[2] Institutional arrangements, particularly how policy makers are elected to office and the rules of the game in allocating budgets among competing priorities, affect levels and efficiency of spending.[3]

THE NEW ROLE FOR THE STATE IN LATIN AMERICA

Privatization and fiscal stabilization revolutionized the traditional role of the strong state in Latin America. Altering levels of expenditures and mechanisms for raising revenue should be undertaken in the light of a clear vision of the appropriate role of the state in Latin America. The traditional state in Latin America was subject to a paradox; it was both omnipresent and extremely weak. Large and unwieldy, it was unable to accomplish its functions efficiently. A source of political favors and populist responses, it was also captured by numerous interest groups that competed to extract rents from the state.[4] Macroeconomic crisis brought with it unintended benefits. Internal and external shocks shook up interest group politics. Ruling coalitions broke down in many countries as exogenous shocks led to the fiscal crises of the state. What should be the new shape of the state in the region?

According to Dani Rodrick, the huge capacity gap between what the state promised and what it was actually able to deliver prompted an era of excessive pessimism with respect to state intervention in the economy. State effectiveness in delivering public goods changed the shape of the Latin American state. Rodrick suggests further that, having overcome "excessive pessimism," we are on the threshold of a serious reconsideration of the role of the state in development.[5] The question remains, however, of the character and scope of efficient and effective government intervention in Latin American economies. How should the state behave to promote economic development in the region?

Two broad forces suggest a possible increase in state intervention: globalization and the social challenges in the region. According to Evans, international trade is increasingly organized as a flow of goods within productive networks that are structured globally rather than nationally.[6] Goods are produced transnationally, not within a single country's borders. Decisions taken in multinational headquarters are as important to workers as policy choices of the national central bank. Globalization has also increased the power of global capital markets in relation to governments. Should governments intervene to ameliorate the effects of globalization?

Rodrick finds a correlation between exposure to such global trade networks and government expenditures. More open states appear to employ greater intervention. He concludes that globalization may require larger states to insulate their citizens from the uncertainty of globalized markets.[7] In addition to the external forces of globalization, the legacy of the debt crisis and macroeconomic instability has been a huge social deficit. As we will see in later chapters, while the market may contribute to solutions, effective state leadership is critical in investing in health and education systems.

But developing countries find it difficult to decrease vulnerability to external shocks and promote human capital development at home. First of all, unless they solve the puzzle of how to raise tax revenues, they do not have the fiscal capacity to protect citizens from the costs of globalization or prepare them as healthy, educated global citizens. Second, international lending practices constrain activity by developing states. Although they are beginning to change their position on this, multilateral development institutions frown upon intervention in the national interest, favoring free market outcomes. Intervention in the domestic interest may have an international financial cost. Given conditionalities by multilateral institutions, a question arises as to where the main accountability of the state lies—with the voters in a fragile democratic system or with the external aid organizations who hold significant purse strings? As the state in Latin America shapes new roles, questions of internal and external accountability will have to be resolved.

THE MARKET FOR GOVERNMENT SERVICES

Within a restricted market for state activity, how should governments respond to different demands for services? One can think of the state as the arbiter of demands by competing interest groups. As Weingast notes, "A well functioning and stable state in which all interest groups are represented and can interact freely must exist before efficiency-enhancing policies can emerge."[8] Consolidation of democratic procedures and deepening of institutional reform is critical. Without a state apparatus that can fairly mediate competing concerns, policy will be driven by the interests of the powerful—whether or not these happen to be the majority's interest. As Evans argues, "Civic engagement flourishes more easily among private citizens and organized groups when they have a competent public sector as an interlocutor."[9] If development policy is to respond to the needs of the people, there must be some sort of political "market" where these demands can be expressed. Moves toward decentralization of power are designed to allow for bottom-up, demand-driven policies. A system of fiscal federalism can limit arbitrary behavior of the central government by introducing accountable institutions at lower levels and restricting the ability of central governments to overtax.[10] However, if local institutions are dominated by local elites, this effect can be overrun. Accountability and transparency are critical ingredients of good governance. Given the history we considered in chapter 2, this, of course, is a tall order for Latin America.

THE SHAPE OF THE STATE

What should be the responsibilities of the public sector? ECLAC suggests a **fiscal covenant** or a basic sociopolitical agreement that establishes terms of interaction with civil society.[11] Defining the fiscal covenant as the "basic socio-political agreement that legitimizes the role of the State and establishes the areas and scope of government in the economic and social spheres,"[12] it suggests five dimensions to the compact: consolidating the ongoing fiscal adjustment, raising the productivity of public management, making fiscal activity more transparent, promoting social equity, and encouraging development of democratic institutions. Consolidation of the fiscal adjustment is a critical signal to markets that irresponsible deficits are a thing of the past and fiscal policy is on a sustainable trajectory. After the size of bureaucracies has been reduced, remaining employees need to be made more efficient through adoption of better information systems and management practices. Transparency allows constituents to follow the decision-making process, conferring greater legitimacy on outcomes that are seen as procedurally fair. The state has a role in ameliorating the high degree of economic inequality that is increasingly giving rise to social tension in the region. Finally, ECLAC suggests that states must be ever conscious of how policies affect the consolidation of democracy over time.

The 1997 *World Development Report* also takes up the question of the changing nature of the state. It revalidates the importance of the state in economic development. This is a dramatic change from the position of minimizing the state in favor of market activity. The bank suggests a principle of matching the activities of the state with its capability to carry out these roles effectively. The principle is simple: don't take on more than you can handle. Governments should first address core activities before expanding into new arenas. The report isolates five fundamental tasks: establishing a foundation of law; maintaining a nondistortionary policy environment, including macroeconomic stability; investing in basic social services and infrastructure; protecting the vulnerable; and protecting the environment. A foundation of law creates stable, predictable outcomes for economic actors. A strong system of guaranteeing property rights encourages investment today in anticipation of safe returns in the future. Macroeconomic stability enhances predictability as agents do not have to contend with wild gyrations in price. The bank suggested that the provision of basic social services and infrastructure is a central function of the state and that the state has a responsibility for improving the lives of the poor and attending to environmental concerns. Without progress in these areas, shared, sustainable poverty-reducing development is seen as impossible.

Listing areas of state intervention skirts the issue of how change should be engineered given the difficulties of raising revenue. One approach is to pursue innovations to encourage markets to do more in the public arena. The key question becomes the appropriate mix of market and government to achieve progress in these areas. The *World Development Report 1997* posits that the state and the market are complementary: state activity is essential to ensure a strong institutional foundation for markets. Back in 1944 Karl Polanyi observed that "the road to the free market was opened and kept open by an enormous increase in continuous, centrally organized and con-

> ## QUESTION FOR THOUGHT
>
> In his address to the annual World Bank Conference on Development Economics (1996), Joseph Stiglitz, then chair of the U.S. Council of Economic Advisers and now senior vice president, Development Economics, and chief economist at the World Bank, suggests that governments must work to build infrastructure in the broadest sense by promoting education, advocating technological development, supporting the financial sector, investing in infrastructure, preventing environmental degradation, and creating and maintaining a social safety net. In the following chapters we will be considering policy options in these areas. Prior to this investigation, what do you believe is the appropriate role of Latin American governments in each of these areas? How much can and should governments do?

Decentralization has encouraged local participation. *(Courtesy of the Inter-American Development Bank.)*

trolled interventionism."[14] Through the innovative use of market-based initiatives, private sector energies can be harnessed to achieve positive social and environmental goals. Enhancing the capability of the state to undertake and promote efficient collective actions in law and order, public health, and basic infrastructure through more efficient delivery systems will facilitate market confidence and growth. States can enhance capability to meet society's demand for public and social goods by strengthening rules and restraints, including judicial independence and watchdog bodies; increasing the competitive pressures for service delivery; promoting voice and partnership at the local level through deliberative councils; and local cost sharing.[15] States can facilitate the institutional framework and promote incentives for projects to encourage greater productivity in the public sector.

The absolute size of the state may not matter as much as how the state intervenes in the economy to support private sector activity. As Enrique Iglesias of the Inter-American Development Bank suggests, "What really matters is not the exact size of the government but how well government performs its legitimate functions (without stepping into functions that properly belong in private hands) and how well government handles its relationship to the market and to the various actors of society."[16] Some contend the state should do as little as possible; others suggest that taking the state out of development policy only works when markets are well functioning. World Bank economists indicate that states should do less in areas where markets can be relied upon, working with market forces and not against them.[17] Two criteria should be met: government actions should address serious marketplace imperfections and they should be designed such that their benefits outweigh their costs.[18] In other words, governments should intervene when markets break down, but only if government action in this arena is preferable to other uses of scarce government funds. Intervention should be selectively targeted in areas of greatest possible returns.

Enhancing the effectiveness of markets often involves strengthening the role of non-market, non-state actors: nongovernmental organizations or NGOs. This broader definition of the market actors includes local economic and social organizations and institutions. A concept of civil-state synergy in which civic engagement may strengthen state institutions and effective state institutions may foster civic engagement has been proposed to strengthen market outcomes.[19] Examples of such organizations include community health cooperatives, soup kitchens, and farmers' extension groups. A key aspect of the synergy includes complementary or mutually supportive relations with a clear division of labor between public and private actors. States can provide private citizens with inputs such as health care or agricultural extension that they could not have access to on their own. However, states should allow private actors to work with these inputs and not interfere where the private sector, including nonprofit community action groups, work best. A second ingredient of the synergy thrives on bridging the state-private divide to build relationships of trust and collaboration at the community level. Embedded relations between state and society built on reciprocal trust between, for example, health extension agents and their clients, making the state agencies a part of the communities where they work.[20]

THEORETICAL APPROACHES TO STATE ACTIVITY IN DEVELOPMENT

Despite the significant statement on the part of the World Bank that the state and the market are complementary institutions, a formulaic mix of just how much state versus how much market is not provided. This echoes Adam Smith's seminal question: just how much should states do to promote the wealth of nations? In part, the answer to this policy question has to do with the assumptions about states and markets you bring in approaching the problem of economic development in Latin America. Box 6.1 outlines some of the conditions under which market solutions are optimal. As we consider the specific circumstances of state participation in the areas of international trade, finance, social policy, and the environment in the following chapters, we can look to three broad theoretical perspectives to pattern policy responses: the **new political economy**, the new institutionalist theory, and the neostructuralists.

The first model is loosely based on the new political economy, or NPE. NPE grounds its assumptions in the material self-interest and rational calculus of economic actors. A position long espoused by economist Milton Friedman and the Chicago school, NPE suggests that people make their own best individual economic choices. Intervention by the state distorts the necessary market signals for accurate decision making. Interfering with market signals by providing a soft social cushion, for example, will only prolong the long-run process of adjustment.[21]

BOX 6.1.   WHEN DO MARKETS WORK BEST?

- Markets are most effective for goods that can be consumed by one person at a time, or when the characteristic of subtractability is present. For example, with a finite supply, one person's use of scarce water subtracts from that available to a community, but one person's use of a road does not significantly diminish its future availability for others.
- Individuals must face the threat of being easily prevented from consuming the good, or excludability, to be willing to pay. For example, people cannot be easily excluded from breathing air.
- Common pool goods such as common pastures and irrigation water are difficult because there is high subtractability but low excludability. The use of water that threads through many farms takes away from that available downstream, but it is hard to prevent one farmer from taking more than a fair share. Incentives for cooperation and persuasion through local participatory institutions work best with common pool problems. Community involvement can promote local resource management.
- When subtractability is missing, or when the use by one person does not reduce the availability to others while excludability is also low, as in the case of public goods, powerful incentives exist to free ride and not pay for resources. It is hard to get individuals to pay to clean the air because if some individuals choose not to pay, you can't say "don't breathe." A mix of hierarchy to enforce payment and local community involvement can help solve the public good problem.
- Toll goods with characteristics of low subtractability and high excludability such as piped water not in scarce supply can be managed through a combination of market and hierarchy. Regulated private water companies, private concessions, or autonomous public corporations may be used depending on local conditions. Fair and transparent administration of private contracts to manage public resources are a key ingredient to success.
- Private markets work best when both excludability and subtractability are present. For smooth functioning of markets, a strong institutional framework ensuring private property rights is key.
- To decrease some of the conflicts generated by unfettered free markets such as pollution externalities or overuse of natural resources, the private voluntary sector or nongovernmental organizations can be effective in mobilizing grassroots energies to counter negative market effects. Lester Salamon notes that "we are in the midst of a global associational revolution that may prove to be as significant to the latter twentieth century as the rise of the nation-state was to the latter nineteenth." New institutional capital created by the voluntary sector may be a critical ingredient in holding market-based strategies together.

Source: Adapted from Robert Picciotto, *Putting Institutional Economics to Work: From Participation to Governance*, World Bank Discussion Papers, no. 304 (Washington, D.C.: World Bank, 1995).

New political economists assume that self-promoting politicians and bureaucratic elites will form coalitions to control resource allocation in accord with their own narrow interests. Corruption on the part of public officials is seen as systemic because it is in their self-interest.[22] For new political economists, sometimes broadly called neoliberals, markets save on scarce administrative capacities. These decentralized institutions oriented by profit signals avoid the pitfalls of big bureaucracies and are more responsive to consumer needs.

New political economists do agree that outcomes in developing countries may have an internal logic inconsistent with long-run efficiency. For example, a peasant farmer may continually divide the family fields into small plots that make cultivation difficult. Although there is an associated loss of efficiency and output, the peasant rationale is simple: diversification of risks among the local community.[23] Nonetheless, the presumption of the model is that the same assumptions about individual maximization of utility adhere in the developing world as in industrial market economies. Rolling back the size of the state will facilitate the reach of the market and the ability of economies to get price signals right. Foreign trade will introduce competitive price pressure and create incentives for external orientation and transparency in public policy. For neoliberals, the free market is the best of all possible worlds.

NPE is transformed by the NIE—the **new institutional economics** associated with economists Coase, North, and Williamson—to include the importance of institutions. They support the tenets of individual choice within neoclassical economics but conclude that mainstream economics has ignored transaction costs, particularly those associated with market failure. Institutions have developed to minimize transaction costs—although they may not always be efficient actors. Institutions are defined as the rules of the game of the society and are composed of formal rules such as statute laws, common laws, and regulations as well as informal constraints including conventions, norms of behavior, and self-imposed codes of conduct. Organizational players include political bodies such as parties, city councils, or regulatory agencies; economic bodies including firms, unions, and cooperatives; and social bodies such as churches or clubs and educational bodies.[24] New institutionalists suggest that neither the state nor the market may be the best way to organize the provision of goods and services.[25] This belief is driven in part by a different view of the market. For the new institutionalists the market is not the "impersonal economic exchange of homogeneous goods by means of voluntary transactions on an equal basis between large numbers of autonomous, fully informed entities with profit-maximizing behavioral motivations able to enter and leave freely" on which neoclassical theorists build their models.[26] Instead, NIE assumes that information is rarely complete and that there are transaction costs in finding out relevant prices, negotiating contracts, and monitoring and enforcing them.[27] Economic performance depends crucially on the setting in which market transactions occur. NIE emphasizes the economic benefits of institutional arrangements that help bring down transaction costs, including transparent, effective, and accessible legal and judicial arrangements. It allows that cultural norms and values may create institutional outcomes distinctly different from those in industrial market economies, where traditional norms might mediate questions of allocation and income.

Economic modernization for the new institutionalist depends on a favorable institutional environment. A core concept is that strong market institutions make for market friendliness. North lays out four essential conditions for successful industrial development: secure property rights, effective and impartial judicial systems, transparent regulatory frameworks, and healthy institutional arrangements to promote complex interpersonal exchange, including enforcement of contracts, establishment of limited liability corporations, and easy entry and exit of firms.[28]

For the new institutionalists, capacity building in state institutions will facilitate market outcomes. Markets left alone will be inefficient; developing states need to foster the development of strong market institutions. New institutionalists do not believe that markets develop spontaneously; they must must be nurtured by careful state policy.

In contrast, neostructuralists see a broader scope for state activity. Building upon the assumptions of the structuralists studied in chapter 3 that the facts describing developing economies do not conform to those of industrial market economies, they suggest a case for effective selectivity in state intervention in the economy. Calling for a modernization strategy that would respond to socioeconomic backwardness and excessive vulnerability, neostructuralists recognize a vital role for the state in making up for market failures. They specifically suggest intervention to promote or simulate missing markets (such as long-term capital markets), strengthen incomplete markets (including technology), eliminate or correct structural distortions (heterogeneous production structures, concentration of property), and eradicate or compensate for the most significant market imperfections arising from economies of scale, externalities, and learning.[29] They part with their intellectual fathers in the dependency school in placing greater emphasis on outward-looking export development as opposed to inward-directed import substitution and place less faith than the new institutionalists (and certainly than the new political economists) in the ability of markets to meet the difficult challenges of development without significant state activity. The neostructuralists believe that markets alone—even relatively efficient ones—will not solve intractable problems such as poverty or the environment or meet the challenge of promoting dynamic technological change in a globally integrated world, for the markets are a necessary but not sufficient condition for economic development. Instead, an effective state is key to sustainable development.

This is not to say that neostructuralists naively believe that all state intervention is positive. In a typology of states, one can distinguish between states that are captured by elite constituencies and those able to maintain policy independence. The first type has been called a factional state; it may be either democratic or authoritarian. The second has been characterized as autonomous. The autonomous state may be seen as either guardian or predatory. A guardian state may attempt to maximize the welfare of its subjects or despotically create its own rules under the assumption that it is more enlightened than its constituency. The predatory state focuses on the extraction of resources from the population for its own benefit. Gains may accrue to a single ruler or to enhance the power of state bureaucracy.[30] Clearly the goal is to establish parameters for public policy that would encourage the development of an autonomous guardian state responding to the will of the people.

Some have suggested a non-Washington consensus in counterpoint to the policies of recent years.[31] Such a package would include an appreciation for fiscal equilibrium but add an additional focus on the links between the fiscal, foreign, and savings gaps with a particular eye to the distributional and political aspects of fiscal equilibrium. The non-Washington consensus advances the position that getting prices right is neither easy nor without cost and that wage reductions resulting from economic reforms adversely affect human capital development. The orthodox interpretation of sound macroeconomic policy backfires into an anemic state and economic stagnation, and privatization in itself is not desirable. Investment in a better-educated, better-paid, and healthier labor force is a long-term process with limited payoffs in short-run economic expansion. Finally, preset blueprints for macroeconomic policy do not apply to all cases. Each country has its own set of historical circumstances and institutional norms that need to be taken into consideration when designing policy. State economic policy must be carefully crafted to local conditions.

Not surprisingly, new political economists disagree with many of the neostructuralist prescriptions. New political economists might agree that markets will not generate perfect outcomes, but in their eyes government, even when acting in a benevolent fashion, does not know more than markets in terms of the "right" intervention schemes. Government does not have enough information or sharp enough tools to minimize the costs of intervention and maximize the benefits. Market prices—the quintessential magnification of disaggregated decision making—are a better guide to resource allocation.[32] New political economists contend that markets will move the economy toward the best of all possible levels of economic growth. New political economists, consistent with their orthodox roots, suggest that intervention in the market will only divert the economy from its long-run efficient equilibrium. Under the guise of making things better in the short run, intervention will only leave the economy worse off over time. Furthermore, when policy interventions are possible, agents are encouraged to engage in rent-seeking behavior to influence outcomes. Nonmarket activities such as lobbying or offering bribes become a mechanism for securing preferences by the state.[33]

As we continue in our text to investigate development challenges in Latin America, the broad framework of the new political economists, the new institutionalists, or the neostructuralists may guide your policy perspective. Do you believe that the market alone will generate the best of all possible outcomes? Do you support the proposition that transaction costs might interfere with the efficient workings of the market, warranting different institutional arrangements? Or do you subscribe to the view that the state has a legitimate role as an actor in economic development in the region? Clarifying your position on the appropriate mix of market and government activity will facilitate your ability to formulate coherent policy positions.

THE SIZE AND STRUCTURE OF THE LATIN AMERICAN STATE

As you consider the conceptual framework for the role of the state, it is important to understand the realities and contemporary trends of state activity in Latin America. The public sector in Latin America is roughly half the size of the typical industrial country government. Accounting for approximately 25 percent of GDP, the Latin American state spends less on social security, defense, health, and education than OECD counterparts. The only area where the Latin American state, on average, is more active is public investment, spending 6 percent as opposed to 2 percent of GDP as compared to industrial economies.[34] Interest payments on debt constitute 3.5 percent of GDP for both Latin American and industrial countries, but because the size of government is smaller, Latin American nations spend nearly twice the industrial average of 8 percent of central government expenditure on interest payments.[35] Although there is considerable diversity of performance, as evidenced in figure 6.1, state spending in Latin America is lower than in both industrial states (OECD) and Southeast Asia. Furthermore, unlike industrial country counterparts, spending has declined in recent years, placing it ten percentage points below the peak attained in the early 1980s.[36]

Why are Latin American states relatively small? The small size of the Latin American state is in part driven by its more limited capacity to raise revenues as compared to an industrial country government. This limited capacity stems from the region's large informal markets, which largely escape taxation, and from a weak bureaucratic structure for tax collection. Tax evasion is high, imposing higher costs on those complying with tax obligations. The administration of tax collection is weak, on average relying on one tax official per 6,649 inhabitants versus an average for industrial countries of 1,835.[37] Without an increased capacity to raise revenue, and lacking the financial capacity to run persistent deficits, Latin American governments must limit the functions of the state. The tough lessons of overblown state sectors without the financial capacity to sustain them were made clear to Latin American governments in the high costs of debt service and macroeconomic instability.

Progress on reducing the fiscal deficit in Latin America has been far more dramatic than changes in the fiscal stance of industrial countries. Both began the

Figure 6.1. Central Government Expenditures (% of GDP)

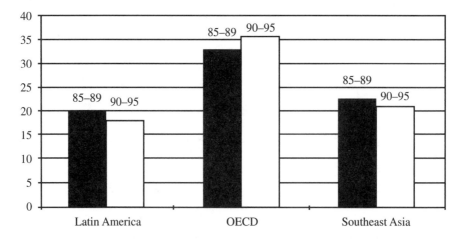

Source: Economic Commission for Latin America and the Caribbean, *The Fiscal Covenant: Strengths, Weaknesses, Challenges* (Santiago, Chile: Economic Commission for Latin America and the Caribbean, 1998).

1970–1995 period with deficits of nearly 4 percent of GDP; isolating 1990–1995, Latin America had slashed its deficits to 2 percent with little change in industrial country deficits. Debt, the accumulated deficits of past years, was lower than the OECD average for six Latin American countries and higher for eleven. Nonetheless, because domestic credit markets are more shallow in Latin America, governments are more vulnerable and exposed than in industrial countries. Relative to the size of the domestic financial system, Latin American deficits were three times the OECD average for the 1970–1994 period.[38] Furthermore, the public is less interested in holding government debt when more secure international investment vehicles are available. The difficulty in raising money domestically pressures local interest rates and introduces macroeconomic disequilibrium. The downsizing of the Latin American state has left little room for further decreases in expenditures. Sustained macroeconomic stabilization is contingent on the ability of the state to increase revenues.[39]

INCREASING REVENUES: THE TAX PROBLEM

The challenge in Latin America is generating a sustainable increase in fiscal resources, permitting the provision of needed services. Increasing spending on social services such as health, education, or environmental protection without provoking macroeconomic instability is contingent upon increasing government revenue. How might this be done? Tax revenue derives from a number of different sources. Liberalization has made reliance on international trade taxes problematic and forced a shift toward domestic taxes. Tax reform in Latin America has been oriented toward the reduction of rates and the simplification of the individual income tax system as well as the widespread use of withholding.[40] With respect to direct income and property taxes, the threshold limit for income taxes has been raised and the maximum lowered for individuals (from 47 to 28 percent) as well as for corporations (from 43.3 to 35.5 percent).[41]

The dismantling of import substitution industrialization prompted a dramatic revision of the source of tax revenue. Where international trade taxes—tariffs on imports or taxes on exports—constituted 27.7 percent of total tax revenue in 1980, this ratio fell to 20.5 percent for the 1991–1995 period.[42] Most dramatic was the case of Argentina, where in 1980 international trade taxes accounted for 45.8 percent of total tax revenue; by the first half of the 1990s this had fallen to 5.6 percent.

There is an apparent preference in the region for indirect taxation such as the VAT, or **value added tax**. Advantages of the VAT include its domestic, international, and intertemporal neutrality and its self-monitoring nature.[43] The VAT is seen as improving the likelihood of tax compliance. By 1995, twenty-one countries in Latin America used the VAT. The VAT is a consumption tax. It is assessed at various levels of the production process, with each buyer of an input paying a percentage. It is therefore self-policing in that it is in the interest of the buyer to ensure that the tax at the previous level has been fairly paid to receive credit on the already taxed input. A large number of goods, including foodstuffs and most services, are excluded from the VAT. Goods with negative externalities—such as alcoholic beverages, tobacco, and fuels—are generally taxed at a higher rate. VAT rates can also be used as an instrument to promote gender equality because men and women tend to purchase different items. Those services that might decrease the burden of the double day that women face in the home and the marketplace might, for example, be taxed at a lower rate.[44]

In contrast, an income tax is difficult to administer because it is spread among a variety of activities, the number of potential taxpayers is large (but compliance low), and the administrative tax collection process does not generate a self-policing paper trail. The average income tax revenue for Latin America and the Caribbean is 4.3 percent of GDP, compared to 7 percent in Asia. Given difficulties in income tax collection, the VAT, which encourages the next agent in the chain to certify that the tax was paid at the stage before, is often seen as preferable.

Throughout Latin America the concept of decentralization—of redirecting state functions from centralized bureaucracies in state capitals to the local level—has taken hold. However, this is problematic in that decentralization has weakened the capacity to promote fiscal balance. The absence of accountability on borrowing at lower levels of government and the incentives for subregions to generate their own funds suggest that a decentralization of administration of tax services must accompany the political process of devolution of authority to the local level. Local politicians may be more prone to corruption. In Colombia, for example, many local governments are controlled by guerrilla groups or drug cartels.[45] Decentralization can also exacerbate inequalities by enhancing regional disparities in income. Wealthier regions can raise revenues while poor areas fall further behind in the provision of health care and education to a needy population. Increasing regional inequality may be a long-run constraint on sustained national development.

Despite advances in deficit reduction, fiscal reform in the region is incomplete. Policy alternatives include combating tax evasion, increasing direct taxation (especially the income tax), introducing green taxes to promote environmental compliance, and readjusting central versus local revenue raising capabilities.[46] Mexico provides an example of decreasing the rate of evasion. In 1989 it introduced a tax on assets. Many firms did not pay income taxes, declaring a loss or no profits for the taxable period. In this case, if the firm had not paid taxes equal to 2 percent of its assets, it would be liable to that limit; credit would be given against the asset taxes for tax paid on profit.[47] Only by generating a stable and predictable level of revenue will the state be able to execute an active, developmental role.

THE PROMISE OF PRIVATIZATION

Beyond fiscal balance, privatization in Latin America has become a dramatic and visible symbol to the international community of the depth of the commitment to a new economic model. Selling state-owned enterprises to the private sector signals a long-term commitment to the market model. But simply privatizing might not resolve some of the market inefficiencies that gave rise to the perceived need for state ownership in the first place. As Douglas North noted in his Nobel Prize acceptance speech, "Transferring the formal political and economic rules of successful Western market economies to third world economies is not a sufficient condition for good economic performance. Privatization is not a panacea for solving poor economic performance."[48] Changes in rules must accompany changes in ownership. Key questions must be resolved. Is a private monopoly any better than a state monopoly? Can the provision of important public services be guaranteed by market magic? What are the distributional implications of privatization? Will workers or consumers be hurt? Some of the concerns surrounding privatization can be addressed if the privatization process is carefully planned. How should that be done? This section will discuss the privatization record in Latin America with an eye to key complementary policies—particularly competition—that will reduce the costs and enhance the gains of privatization.

THE MECHANICS OF PRIVATIZATION

Privatization can be achieved in a variety of ways. An enterprise might be sold to the private sector by issuing stock in the corporation, a concession for the provision of public services can be auctioned off, or the regulations grounding economic activity might be changed. These three types of privatization—sale of assets, contracting for services, and deregulation—are very much conditioned by the type of good or service produced and the existing market structure. If the market is relatively competitive, the outright sale of assets is most likely. Sometimes deregulating the market can enhance competitiveness. If the newly private firm will enjoy considerable market power, the state might choose to retain ownership and contract private services or introduce public regulations to make the private monopoly accountable to the public good. This may be appropriate in the case of natural monopolies. It is important to note, however, that privatization does not take place in a vacuum, but is integrated as part of a comprehensive package of reforms. The success or failure of the privatization is intertwined with the overall progress of reforms.

The first wave of privatizations in Latin America in the 1980s generated significant resistance. At the time, state firms accounted for approximately 12 percent of GDP in Latin America.[49] Not surprisingly, managers and workers in state firms were threatened by the potential loss of jobs. Nationalist sentiments ran strong, contending that foreign capital would purchase the country's patrimony at bargain basement prices. The military was concerned about the vulnerability of strategic industries, and the state itself did not want to lose the political power that control of jobs and production conferred.

Nonetheless, the potential gains from privatization were compelling. Many state-owned enterprises were inefficient and operating at a loss. Privatization, it was argued, would increase efficiency and decrease the pressure on state coffers. Whether the productivity gains and the desired macroeconomic effects were achieved was very much influenced by how the privatization was conducted. Privatization is a process involving a range of complementary measures. Simply selling shares in a corporation does not guarantee competitiveness. Furthermore, particularly if a state-owned company was already relatively efficient, the revenue gains from the sale have only a one-time fiscal effect. That is, it is much like selling grandmother's silver to finance a vacation. The deficit may be helped temporarily, but once the heirloom is gone it carries no asset value.

The success of privatization is shaped by the measures taken before the sale as well as the broader economic environment. Efforts to improve the efficiency of enterprises prior to the sale increase the value of the firm on the market. Conglomerate restructuring, administrative reorganizations, personnel cutbacks, debt rescheduling, and liquidation of nonviable operations contribute to the firm's attractiveness. To prevent shares from being sold at below their worth, valuations of the firm (usually using a net present value calculation) provide a minimum reference price below which shares are not sold. How shares are offered on the market can have distributional and efficiency consequences. If the firm had been owned by the public, should the citizenry continue to have an interest in the corporation through widely distributed shares, or does a tightly held corporation make more sense? Several methods can be employed: sale of stock to workers, private individuals, and corporate entities; sales of stock on an exchange; and competitive bidding through public auctions.[50] The selection of which method to use depends in part on the sophistication of markets and their ability to distribute shares in a fair, efficient, and transparent manner.

The speed of privatization matters. Rapid, comprehensive privatization signals strong political will to adhere to the market. However, if complementary measures such as market deregulation to promote competition cannot be implemented at the same pace, privatization efforts are likely to falter. Market structure may indeed be more important than ownership in explaining the comparative performance of companies. Where privatized firms become natural monopolies without regulatory reforms, consumers may be no better off. Large private powerhouses can extract monopoly rents and provide low quality services to consumers. Trade liberalization encouraging international competition may help mitigate monopolistic abuses.

To promote successful, sustainable service to the population, privatization may need to be accompanied by measures to promote competition. In the privatization of utilities, telecommunications, water, and sewage, for example, state monopolies may become private monopolies without appropriate rules to govern behavior. In the Chilean case, it was found that although privatization of these sectors led to improvements in the quality and quantity of services, without an enforceable regulatory structure, prices did not fall with the privatization of services.[51] In the energy sector, energy losses were cut from 23 percent to 7 percent, and the number of clients per worker doubled. The number of phone lines tripled, and the phone line per worker ratio rose from 74 to 235 from 1987 to 1995. As monopolists, firms were able to charge the highest price the market would bear. The only areas experiencing falling prices were those where competition emerged. Long-distance telephone rates, for example, fell 50 percent as new competitors entered the market; monopolized local rates rose by 35 percent. In a noncompetitive setting, efficiency gains have not been passed on to the consumer in the form of lower prices. An alternative to competition policies is a strong regulatory role for the government. Regulation of utilities tends to be problematic given the classic problem of public regulation: asymmetry of information. Only the firm knows the true cost of services; there is an incentive to inflate costs if the regulator's price formula is based on costs. Increasing competition between firms acts as a natural brake on price increases and avoids the problems of regulation.

The rules for both national and international actors must be perceived as fair to build public support. The transition from state-owned enterprises to a competitive private market may be facilitated by multilateral support in preparing bids for sale, developing new management plans, or downsizing the work force. International participation—either through a public agency such as the World Bank or a private concern such as an international consulting firm—is important in safeguarding transparency and generating credibility in the fairness of the process. In the absence of transparency, the perception that private firms are "stealing" from what had been the national patrimony is fostered. Domestic political commitment at the highest level is critical to sustain privatization;[52] otherwise, the losers from the process will stonewall progress.

Privatization may include measures to reduce short-term labor costs. Measures may be introduced as part of the package to delay employment reduction or spread it over a longer period of time. Often the deal includes temporary protection of the labor force for a specified period after privatization. Fair severance packages and early warnings for mass layoffs can help cushion the blow to workers when jobs are not protected. Bonuses can induce voluntary layoffs to secure political support and the cooperation of unions in the privatization process. The state may also facilitate the movement of laid-off workers into other forms of employment through job search and mobility assistance, retraining, or vocational education programs. Political support for privatization can be expanded if it is construed as part of a wider process of increasing democratic participation in public decision making on issues such as whether to spend more on loss-making public enterprises or instead increase spending on health and public education. Consultation by government and the incoming private management with workers is critical in minimizing the social costs of adjustment in privatization efforts.[53] The privatization of CANTV, the Venezuelan telecommunication company, highlights these important institutional elements for a successful experience, as shown later in the chapter in box 6.2.

WHO HAS PARTICIPATED?

Generating sufficient investor interest in a wide array of newly private activities may be problematic when capital markets are thin. Foreign capital has been a significant source of privatization revenues, accounting for 39.7 percent region-wide for the 1990–1995 period. In 1994 and 1995 foreign revenue jumped to 71.4 and 76.7 percent respectively. Nevertheless, there is a good deal of cross-country diversity. As can be seen in table 6.1, in Bolivia, Peru, and Uruguay, more than 80 percent of the privatization revenues flowed from abroad. A new trend has been intraregional foreign direct investment through privatization. Latin Americans are now investing in other countries in the region. The Argentine steel producer SOMISA, for example, was acquired by a consortium composed of the Argentine group

Table 6.1. Privatization Statistics of Latin American Countries, 1990–1995

	Privatization Revenues	Number of Privatization Transactions	Privatization Revenue as % of GDP	Privatization Revenue as % of Central Government Expenditure	Privatization Revenue from Abroad as % of Total Privatization Revenue	Foreign Direct Investment Privatization as % of Privatization Revenue from Abroad	Foreign Direct Investment from Privatization as % of Total Foreign Direct Investment
Mexico	24,271.0	174.0	2.0	11.5	28.7	27.2	7.9
Argentina	18,446.0	123.0	1.2	6.9	47.9	67.3	30.4
Brazil	9,136.0	45.0	0.3	0.8	14.5	31.5	5.2
Peru	4,358.0	72.0	1.6	11.5	82.4	97.6	76.7
Venezuela	2,510.0	29.0	0.6	2.8	66.6	93.4	66.0
Chile	1,259.0	14.0	0.5	2.1	51.9	100.0	25.3
Colombia	735.0	16.0	0.2	1.7	64.4	11.8	1.4
Bolivia	637.0	28.0	2.0	11.4	96.6	100.0	103.6
Trinidad and Tobago	448.0	17.0	1.6	5.8	96.5	100.0	26.4
Jamaica	316.0	26.0	1.5	5.2	32.2	100.0	16.7
Nicaragua	126.0	75.0	1.5	5.2	3.7	100.0	5.0
Panama	100.0	9.0	0.3	1.6	62.9	100.0	−0.9
Ecuador	96.0	9.0	0.1	0.8	55.9	0.0	0.0
Honduras	74.0	32.0	0.5	1.9	1.1	100.0	0.3
Belize	59.0	4.0	2.5	8.1	0.0	n/a	0.0
Barbados	51.0	6.0	0.7	2.0	99.7	100.0	110.5
Guyana	50.0	19.0	1.7	3.3	n/a	n/a	n/a
Costa Rica	46.0	4.0	0.1	0.7	0.0	n/a	0.0
Bahamas	25.0	6.0	0.1	0.7	0.0	n/a	n/a
Paraguay	22.0	1.0	0.1	0.5	50.0	100.0	1.9
Uruguay	17.0	7.0	0.0	0.1	94.1	100.0	0.4
Dominican Republic	0.0	0.0	0.0	0.0	n/a	n/a	n/a
Guatemala	0.0	0.0	0.0	0.0	n/a	n/a	n/a
Haiti	0.0	0.0	0.0	0.0	n/a	n/a	n/a
Surinam	0.0	0.0	0.0	0.0	n/a	n/a	n/a
Latin America	62,780.0	716.0	0.8	4.8	39.7	n/a	n/a

Source: Inter-American Development Bank, *Economic and Social Progress in Latin America, 1996* (Washington, D.C.: Johns Hopkins University Press, 1996).

Technit, Chilean CAP (Compaña de Acero), Brazilian USIMAS, and CVRD. Investment is coming not only from industrial countries but also from within the region.

For most countries, privatization revenues come in the form of **foreign direct investment** (FDI). Notable exceptions are Mexico, Argentina, Brazil, and Colombia, where more sophisticated capital markets allow for portfolio investors. Although portfolio investors such as mutual funds and insurance companies have invested in these markets heavily, they have no significant day-to-day control. In contrast, foreign direct investors acquire sufficient shares to control the strategic direction of the firm. Additionally, foreign direct investment generates additional FDI flows to modernize plants and equipment. There may also be spillover effects beyond the particular company as the privatized firm improves the provision of key services and raises the profitability of investments in other sectors. One study found that worldwide, each dollar of FDI privatization revenue generates an additional 88 cents of FDI transactions outside the privatization.[54] Privatization therefore has the potential to generate future capital flows as the business climate improves in a country. We will return to the role of foreign investment in chapter 7, as we evaluate its effects on economic performance.

THE PRIVATIZATION RECORD

Privatization generated much excitement in Latin America in the 1990s. Fifty-six percent of all privatizations in developing countries from 1990 to 1994 took place in Latin America.[55] Ambitious programs of privatization in Latin America were undertaken in Chile, Argentina, and Mexico. Chile has the longest regional track record in privatizations. In 1973 state-owned enterprises accounted for nearly 40 percent of Chilean GDP.[56] From 1974 to 1992, more than 500 firms were privatized, primarily under the supervision of the state holding company CORFO. The first stage of the privatization, from 1974 to 1982, was largely debt led, with workers and other buyers taking advantage of relatively cheap credit to finance purchases. The Chilean crisis in 1982 resulted in the failure of many of these vulnerable firms, and the second stage involved more equity than debt and was accompanied by sweeping regulatory reform. Public enterprises not privatized in the first wave were given a mandate to behave "as if" private and were forced to face competition in liberalized markets. Many of these firms were privatized in a later stage, reducing state ownership to 16 percent of GDP by 1989, or 6.6 percent if Codelco, the copper giant, is excluded from the count. In the case of the Chilean electric firms CHILGENER and ENERSIS, privatization contributed to higher profitability, improved productivity, and increased investment. The loser was the Chilean government, which was no longer able to appropriate the quasi-rents from electrical sales. The sale of CTC, the Chilean telecommunications monopoly, resulted in increased foreign investment, expansion of services, and improved labor productivity with a net gain to state coffers. A comparison of the two sectors underscores that the positive fiscal effect is a function of whether the firms were profitable or not in the first place. Furthermore, Chile was able to enhance the gains from privatization by requiring that foreign investors commit to investments to improve services. Workers gained in both sectors through participation in the ownership and appreciation of the shares they acquired. On balance, privatization improved the well-being of society.[57]

Privatization in Argentina has been extensive, including television, petroleum, trucking, gas and electric, water and sewage, railroads, ports, the postal service, manufacturing enterprises, telecommunications, and the airlines. International participants in Argentine privatizations included Chile (6 percent), Spain (15 percent), the United States (12 percent), Italy (9 percent), and France (7 percent).[58] One of the largest privatizations to take place in emerging markets was of the Argentine oil company YPF. Prior to privatization YPF had been a huge conglomerate including hospitals and schools in addition to an array of energy-related businesses. Not only was it poorly run, but it was also bled by other state agencies benefiting from underpriced energy and unpaid bills. Before the IPO, or initial public offering, YPF was downsized, trimming the firm to its core activities where it had competitive advantage. It was then restructured, with a focus on upstream exploration and production, downstream refining and marketing, and well-defined business units for information processing and personnel. The capital was distributed such that the federal government retained 20 percent of the shares, provincial governments were accorded 11 percent, workers were given 10 percent, and the balance was offered in national, U.S., and international tranches. Despite a relatively weak oil market, the launching of the stock exceeded expectations, in large part due to enhanced efficiency prior to the sale. YPF has gone on not only to become a regional player, building upon a strong understanding of the South American business environment and the growth of trade in Mercosur, but also to acquire a U.S.-based subsidiary, Maxus Energy Corporation. Despite adverse economic conditions in Argentina from the 1995 Mexican peso crisis, YPF was able to turn itself and Maxus around to post historically high profits in 1997.

Nonetheless, beyond the YPF success story, nationwide measures to promote competition were sacrificed in the name of speed. This was perceived as necessary because President Menem used the privatizations as a bold signal to the global market of the transformation of the Argentine economy. Deregulation of markets is following at a slower pace. The opening up of Argentina's phone monopoly was slated for 1999. Although the privatization of the national phone company created two geographically divided companies that have increased the number of lines from 3 to 7 million, calling rates remain high by international standards due to the lack of competitiveness. The introduction of up to eight competing international companies should not only increase service but also lower prices in the local, long-distance, and cellular markets.[59]

Mexico has recently privatized between 2.1 and 3.2 percent of GDP, reserving strategic industries such as petroleum for national control. The state sector had grown to 1,155 enterprises accounting for 12.6 percent of GDP and 38 percent of investment.[60] By 1994 the number of state firms in Mexico was reduced to eighty.[61] Privatization in Mexico enjoyed more political support than in other Latin American countries, in large part because it was tied to a tripartite agreement between labor, business, and the government. Labor ownership came to play a large role in the privatization effort. Foreign participation played only a minor role in the Mexican case. The success of the Mexican privatization effort can be attributed to strong commitment at the highest levels of Mexican government and transparency in the rules governing the process such that all parties could fairly evaluate conditions of sale. A big success story was the privatization of Teléfonos de México, the monopolistic provider of local and long-distance service, whose stock value soared from 25 cents a share to U.S.$7 a share after privatization. The negotiations governing the sale included commitments to expand the number of lines in service, increase coverage of small towns, add significantly to the number of public telephones, and improve the speed of repairs. Service and access dramatically improved along with profitability. Aeroméxico, a big money loser, was made profitable through privatization, in contrast to the privatization of another state airline, Mexicana, where productivity gains were not realized in the divestiture. Overall, divestiture in the Mexican case met its most important goal: cutting the budget deficit to facilitate macroeconomic stabilization.

Brazil came late to the privatization game with legal changes in 1990. Before the process began, the state held 100 percent of sales in public utilities, 67 percent of steel, 67 percent of chemicals and petrochemicals, 60 percent of mining, 35 percent of transportation services, 32 percent of gasoline distribution, 26 percent of fertilizers, and 21 percent of transportation equipment.[62] Raising approximately $3 billion in 1996 and $5.5 billion in 1997, progress has been substantial. Privatization in Brazil is very much tied to the increase in capital inflows that we will study in the next chapter. Initial efforts were in the steel, petrochemical, and fertilizer industries. Privatization has been extended to transportation, including railways and the energy sector.

CVRD, Compania Vale do Rio Doce—the world's largest iron ore exporter, Latin America's biggest producer of gold, Brazil's largest exporter, and the biggest foreign exchange earner in Brazil—was placed on the auction block in 1997. The privatization took place in three stages. In the first, the government released 45 percent of voting shares, out of its holdings of 51 percent, to enable a small group of strategic investors to gain control. Employees were allowed to buy 10 percent of the firm, facilitated by BNDES loans to acquire stock, with the rest sold through a global stock offering.[63]

Merrill Lynch did the valuation, with a minimum price set at $9.8 billion. The government held a golden share for the first five years, to be able to veto decisions. No single investor may hold more than 45 percent of equity, with no one firm holding more than 10 percent to prevent monopoly control. The CVRD privatization was the biggest privatization deal since the $3 billion offering of Argentine oil conglomerate YPF. Following the sale costs were reduced by 30 percent, 4,500 people were let go, and new management systems contributed to profitable performance.[64]

In the federal railway privatization, the government leased federal railroad concessions, reducing the public rail workforce from 45,000 to 400 (to collect rents from the concessions and provide oversight).[65] The government retained Coopers and Lybrand to help set up regulatory measures to govern the private utilities. The Brazilian BNDES, the national development bank, is promoting privatization at the state level with funding for investment and debt reduction prior to privatization. Rio is privatizing its state bank and several utilities; other states have followed suit.[66]

Telebrás, Brazil's national telecommunications network, was auctioned off in twelve restructured pieces for $19.1 billion, topping London's privatization of British Telecom in the early 1990s. Despite protests from labor unions, the historically poor service of the company created public support for the sale. With just eleven phones and three mobiles per 100 inhabitants and a two-year waiting list for phones in some areas, the telecom sale in the world's eighth largest economy was characterized as a sale of "repressed demand" of the huge unanswered market of Brazilian talkers. The Spanish firm Telefónica won the crown jewel, São Paulo's Telesp, and MCI picked up another key piece, EMBRATEL, Brazil's long-distance and international carrier.[67] We will return to the implications of improvements in the efficiency of the privatized Telebrás when we consider infrastructure deficits in chapter 9.

THE SPECIAL CASE OF THE BANKING SECTOR

Privatization has also extended to the banking sector. Under ISI, state banks were used to finance activities that were not attractive to the private sector but had developmental promise.[68] The Brazilian BNDES, for example, was instrumental in financing both state enterprises and private activity. Bank privatization presents a special case because of links with the international financial sector and domestic financial intermediation. States still have a strong incentive to maintain control. The experience of bank privatization in the region is mixed. Privatization has led to systemic financial instability in cases where new forms of regulation did not accompany the privatization. The nature of banking also results in a relatively concentrated market structure after privatization.[69] Early privatizations in Chile and Argentina suffered from coincident macroeconomic crises, leading to liquidity problems and bank rescues.

In part this has to do with the problems of adverse selection and moral hazard in lending that are exacerbated in a newly liberalized environment. Adverse selection is an asymmetric information problem, that is, a situation when one side of a deal has more information than another, leading to the selection of an undesirable outcome. For example, people who are conservative and risk averse are less likely to gamble on a chancy venture. Therefore, loan applicants are, as a group, likely to be risk takers. This results, over time, in banks lending less money because there is a smaller chance of getting a good loan candidate in the borrowers' pool. Moral hazards also stem from asymmetric information. Borrowers have more information than lenders about their own likely behavior after the sale. If sufficient collateral is not secured prior to the loan, the borrower has an incentive to pursue high-risk behavior because the gains will be high if the project succeeds but will be shared by the lender if it fails.[70]

Good information gathering on the part of the bank or predictable borrowing on the part of state-run firms can mitigate banking risks. With deregulation and

Box 6.2. The Privatization of CANTV

In 1989, Venezuela embraced a new economic model under President Carlos Andrés Pérez. Pérez inherited a nation on the verge of disaster, resulting from a program of state-led development and import substitution. The president's goal was to move forward with reforms that would make Venezuela more efficient, more competitive, and less reliant on government forces. One of his key reforms was the privatization of state-owned enterprises, including CANTV (Compania Anonima Nacional Teléfonos de Venezuela), the telecommunications giant of Venezuela.

Under government control, the company was notorious for poor service and corrupt management. Under private sector control, the administration hoped for the modernization of Venezuelan telecommunications, improved services, and a revenue windfall from the sale. CANTV had represented a yearly loss for the government, requiring constant injections of capital. Oil revenues had made this possible, and declining oil prices in the 1980s made it unsustainable. Not all of CANTV was to be privatized, however; only 40 percent of shares were put on the market, while the government retained 49 percent. The other 11 percent were put in trusteeship for employees to allay their concerns stemming from the privatization.

The privatization process began with preliminary measures under the control of the Venezuelan Investment Fund (FIV) to improve the company's operating performance and to obtain appropriate valuations. Bidders were asked to meet certain requirements and were given a copy of the regulations under the concession contracts. The highest bidder would have a right to a nine-year monopoly that would expire in the year 2000, but it would also have to meet yearly investment requirements. Hence, the government found it necessary to create a regulatory system, Conatel, to control the actions of the resulting monopoly. The concession was finally granted to the GTE consortium consisting of AT&T, Electricidad de Caracas, Compania Nacional de Espanola, and Banco Mercantil on December 6, 1991.

After privatization, services dramatically improved. Overall customer satisfaction soared from below 30 percent before privatization to 80 percent by mid-1994.[71] The new CANTV also managed to raise real wages, improve working conditions, and increase the number employed. Even so, CANTV faced opposition from the unions, which opposed the merit-based management system. Strongly supporting the unions was Causa R, a Venezuelan political party that played on resentment of foreigners to increase opposition. CANTV soon lost all political support when Pérez, facing public opposition to his reforms, left office in May 1993.

The new administration under Rafael Caldera used an interventionist approach to deal with the country's economic woes. By imposing exchange rate controls, the administration managed to drive the partially privatized CANTV to the verge of default as it was unable to obtain enough foreign exchange to pay its dollar-denominated debt. Only after almost a year of renegotiating its debt with forty banks did the government provide CANTV with almost free access to dollars. While CANTV faced political opposition from the unions, Causa R, and the administration, privatization as a whole had come to a halt. This proved to be unfortunate scenario for CANTV. FIV had been planning to sell the remaining 49 percent of shares that were still under government control, but with economic difficulties and political instability, foreign investors lost interest.

The privatization program came back to life in April 1996, when Caldera initiated a new reform program, Agenda Venezuela. It was aimed at restoring growth, reducing inflation, and easing poverty. A key element of the program was the $1.4 billion IMF credit to support the program.[72] Multilateral support proved favorable for CANTV because it improved foreign confidence. With Agenda Venezuela, the government was able to resume its plans to sell the remaining shares. The government's commitment to a sale

(continued)

(continued)

date informed the international community that it was ready to resume the privatization of CANTV that had started in December 1991.

CANTV itself also had been through several changes that helped improved investor confidence. One of these was the appointment of Gustavo Roosen, a Venezuelan with strong government connections, as the CEO of CANTV in June of 1995. He had served as the president of Petroleos of Venezuela and had been the minister of education. Furthermore, on June 17, 1996, the International Finance Corporation announced a financing package for CANTV of $250 million to assist it in its ongoing modernization and expansion program for 1996 and 1997. This would include the installation of 658,600 new digital telephone lines and 12,700 public phones, along with expansion of cellular phone networks in order to meet negotiated investment goals.

The success of the final stage of privatization would very much depend on how the shares traded on the market. On November 22, 1996, all waited anxiously to see how CANTV would fare on the New York Stock Exchange. Fortunately for the government and CANTV, the share price had remained in and above the anticipated range, making it a successful day of trading. CANTV's success was not limited to the first day; first quarter results for 1997 were above market expectations. A new economic program with signs of political commitment had managed to restore foreign confidence in the privatization process in Venezuela.

REFERENCES

"Cia Anonima Nacional Telefonos de Venezuela (CANTV)." *UBS Securities Equity Research*. 18 December 1996.
"Compania Anonima Nacional de Teléfonos de Venezuela (CANTV)." *CS First Boston Equity Research-Americas*. 18 December 1996.
Goering, Laurie. "A Push for Privatization." *Chicago Tribune*. 23 November 1996.
Sedelnik, Lisa. "CANTV: Inside the IPO." *Latin Finance* 83 (1997): 43–46.
Stopford, Michael. "IFC Announces Investment in Venezuelan Telecom Company." World Bank, press release no. 96/114.

privatization, however, the informational advantage further shifts from the bank to the private sector. Mexican banks that were nationalized in 1982 had directed roughly 50 percent of their lending to the government. Privatization in the early 1990s left the banks without formal credit bureaus to monitor and assess risk on household and small business loans. As the demands of the now burgeoning private sector intensified, bank lending escalated from 10 percent of GDP in 1988 to more than 40 percent in 1994, quickly exceeding monitoring capabilities. An interest rate spike in January 1995 exacerbated the adverse selection problem, leaving only the most venturesome in the market for loans. With the peso crisis, increased uncertainty in stock markets and in firm balance sheets skewed the fundamental values upon which the loans were originally based. With the peso halved in value from December 1994 to March 1995, inflationary pressures escalated. Interest rates were ratcheted up to 100 percent to stem the bleeding, and the Mexican stock market fell 60 percent in dollar terms. International investors fled—particularly those with limited knowledge of the Mexican market—exacerbating the financial crisis. Many firms and households could not meet bank debt obligations, and a banking crisis ensued as their balance sheets deteriorated.

The collapse of the banking system was forestalled by government intervention to provide funds to protect depositors. (Remember that it was the depositors' money lent out to the now failed firms.) However, unlike an industrial country government, which can reflate the economy in a crisis, developing economies must guard against the perception of resumed inflation eroding confidence. Reflating the economy may also precipitate depreciation of the currency, and with many loans denominated in dollars, the debt burden on the firm in the developing country is extended. When the U.S. government injected liquidity into the economy following the 1987 stock market crash, there was little fear of inflation. However, recovery in a fragile and internationally dependent developing country is more complicated and fraught with pitfalls. Although bank privatization was not the root cause of financial instability in Mexico, the lack of a strong bank supervisory system coupled with rapid changes throughout the economy left the economy more vulnerable to a free fall. Independent, transparent, well-funded agencies need to be able to enforce adequate accounting and disclosure practices on the part of borrowers and the banking community to safeguard against banking crises. If an appropriate regulatory institution is not in place prior to privatization and deregulation, failure is likely.[73]

THE GAINS FROM PRIVATIZATION

What have been the welfare consequences of privatization? A fair evaluation of the consequences of privatization for society involves an analysis of the particular market structure, the variables used to measure performance, and a control group of contrasting cases. The degree of competitiveness in input and output markets will determine whether gains accrue to society or are appropriated as monopoly rents to large, now private, firms. The employment effects of privatization are ambiguous. It is difficult to separate the effects of privatization from other changes in the economy. Some argue that privatization will increase the capacity of the economy to create jobs through a more efficient use of capital and labor.[74] Others, however, suggest that privatizing existing industries will reduce the number employed in state agencies, which, as a political goal, had inflated employment. Profitability as a measure of performance may not always be consistent with long-run productivity gains or the social and environmental externalities generated through production. That is, state firms may have served other social objectives such as employment generation. An evaluation of the divestiture process must take into account the trade-off that private firms might perform more efficiently, but that the private means and ends might not be in the social good. Finally, because a controlled experiment with both public and private enterprises operating in the same market under the same macroeconomic conditions cannot be run, it is difficult to attribute gains to privatization as opposed to liberalization or lower inflation.[75]

CONCLUSION

Redefining the role of the state in Latin America has included elements of fiscal austerity, tax reform, and privatization to reduce the drag of deficits and the restructuring of the ownership role of the state. Reform of the state sector is a balancing act between a desirable and a sustainable level of state activity. We began our

chapter with a discussion of the three schools of thought: the new political economists, the new institutionalists, and the neostructuralists. Because the new political economists believe that a small state is the most efficient outcome, reducing deficits and eliminating state responsibilities for production and provision of services should free the public sector from the need to raise additional money through taxes. Trimming the size of the state and improving its efficient delivery of a limited array of services is the focus of reform. Financing expenditures is more problematic for the new institutionalist and the neostructuralist. At least until market institutions mature and transactions costs are lowered, new institutionalists would call for a stronger mediating role for government in the marketization of the economy. They are concerned about the regulatory capabilities of states to oversee privatized monopolies. Regulation and supervision are not free, necessitating some new finance for public activity. Neostructuralists must match an active role for government as it supplements the activity in the market with an enhanced capacity to pay and to deliver needed services more efficiently. Committed to the notion that the state is an important actor in promoting equitable development, especially where markets are imperfect, neostructuralists face the challenge of convincing constituencies of the necessity to pay for public goods. For the neostructuralists, however, the long-run payoff of decreased poverty and improved education and health is worth the long-run investment.

Key Concepts

Fiscal covenant
Foreign direct
  investment

New institutional
  economics
New political economy

Value added tax

Chapter Summary

The New Role of the Latin American State

- What should be the new role of the Latin American state? The state must balance accountability to multilateral organizations and accountability to voters. One possibility for the role of the state is the social covenant as suggested by ECLAC, in which the state establishes a socioeconomic agreement on its interaction with civil society. The World Bank in 1997 suggested that states should only engage in those activities in which they have the capacity to be effective, such as investing in basic social services. Given revenue constraints, there needs to be the right mix of state and market to achieve progress. The state must interfere only when and where there is market failure and to strengthen the role of nonstate actors.

The Theoretical Framework for State Intervention

- The theoretical framework for state intervention is divided into three main schools of thought: new political economy, new institutionalist economics, and neostructuralism. New political economists believe that state intervention will interfere with market signals; therefore, the role of the state should be minimal. New institutionalists claim that neoclassical economics ignores transaction costs. The principal tenet behind new institutionalist economics is that market actors rarely receive perfect information. There is a need for institutional norms such as transparent, effective, and accessible legal and judicial arrangements to reduce transaction costs. Unlike the new institutionalists and new political economists, neostructuralists are not optimistic about the market's ability to enhance development. Neostructuralists call for effective state intervention when the market fails.

A Weak Public Sector

- The Latin American public sector is on average half the size of that of industrialized countries. Its small size stems primarily from a weak tax bureaucracy and a large informal sector that is difficult to tax.
- There has been a shift in the source of tax revenue from custom duties to domestic taxes. The most popular tax instrument has been the value added tax (VAT) over the income tax because of its self-regulating mechanism. The next steps for Latin America are to combat tax evasion and increase revenue from direct taxes and green taxes.

Privatization

- Privatization of generally inefficient state-owned enterprises requires a complementary set of policies and their swift implementation to maximize the benefits. During privatization, governments should avoid creating a natural monopoly. They also need to maximize the value of the sale by improving the efficiency of the firms prior to the sale. Foreign financing has played a major role in privatization in Latin America.

- Leading the wave of privatization was Chile in the late 1970s and early 1980s. Although these initial attempts encountered difficulties, subsequent privatization efforts proved more successful because complementary policies were introduced to increase efficiency.
- Privatization of the banking sector presented a different kind of problem, one of asymmetric information where the borrower has the advantage, that became visible during the Mexican peso crisis. Successful banking sector privatization must be accompanied by an appropriate regulatory institution.

Notes

1. Ricardo Hausmann and Ernesto Stein, "Searching for the Right Budgetary Institutions for a Volatile Region," in *Securing Stability and Growth in Latin America*, ed. Ricardo Hausmann and Helmut Reisen (Paris: Organization for Economic Cooperation and Development, 1996), 247.

2. Shahid Javed Burki and Sebastian Edwards, *Latin America after Mexico: Quickening the Pace* (Washington, D.C.: World Bank, 1996).

3. Ernesto Stein, Ernesto Talvi, and Alejandro Grisanti, *Institutional Arrangements and Fiscal Performance: The Latin American Experience*, National Bureau of Economic Research Working Paper no. 6358 (Cambridge, Mass.: National Bureau of Economic Research, 1998).

4. Shahid Javed Burki and Sebastian Edwards, *Dismantling the Populist State* (Washington, D.C.: World Bank, 1996), 23.

5. Dani Rodrick, in Peter Evans, "The Eclipse of the State?: Reflections on Stateness in an Era of Globalization," *World Politics* 50 (October 1997): 83.

6. Evans, "Eclipse," 66.

7. Dani Rodrick, "Why Do More Open Economies Have Bigger Governments?" *Journal of Political Economy* 16, no. 5 (1998).

8. Barry Weingast, in Hans P. Binswanger and Klaus Deininger, "Explaining Agricultural and Agrarian Policies in Developing Countries," *Journal of Economic Literature* 35 (December 1997): 1978.

9. Evans, "Eclipse," 80.

10. Binswanger and Deininger, "Explaining Agricultural and Agrarian Policies," 1987.

11. Economic Commission for Latin America and the Caribbean, *The Fiscal Covenant: Strengths, Weaknesses, Challenges* (Santiago, Chile: Economic Commission for Latin America and the Caribbean, 1998), 1.

12. Ibid., 9.

13. Joseph E. Stiglitz, "The Role of Government in Economic Development," in *Annual World Bank Conference on Development Economics 1996* (Washington, D.C.: World Bank, 1997), 12–14.

14. Takashi Hikino and Alice Amsden, "Staying Behind, Stumbling Back, Sneaking Up, Soaring Ahead: Late Industrialization in Historical Perspective," in *Convergence of Productivity: Cross-National Studies and Historical Evidence*, ed. William Baumol, Richard R. Nelson, and Edward N. Wolff (New York: Oxford University Press, 1994), 290.

15. World Bank, "Overview," in *World Development Report 1997* (New York: Oxford University Press for the World Bank, 1997).

16. Enrique V. Iglesias, "The Search for a New Economic Consensus in Latin America," in *The Legacy of Raúl Prebisch*, ed. Enrique V. Iglesias (Washington, D.C.: Inter-American Development Bank, 1994), 93.

17. John Martinussen, *Society, State, and Market: A Guide to Competing Theories of Development* (London: Zed, 1997), 266.

18. Stiglitz, "The Role of Government," 12.

19. Peter Evans, ed., "State-Society Synergy: Government and Social Capital in Development," *World Development* 24, no. 6, special edition (June 1996).

20. Ibid., 185.

21. Mick Moore, "Toward a Useful Consensus," in "The Bank, the State, and Development: Dissecting the World Development Report, 1997," *IDS Bulletin* 29, no. 2, special edition (1998): 41.

22. Martinussen, *Society, State, and Market*, 262.

23. Popkin, as cited by Martinussen, *Society, State, and Market*, 244.

24. Douglas C. North, "The New Institutional Economics and Third World Development," in *The New Institutional Economics and Third World Development*, ed. John Harriss, Janet Hunter, and Colin M. Lewis (London: Routledge, 1995), 23.

25. John Harriss, Janet Hunter, and Colin M. Lewis, "Introduction: Development and Significance of the NIE," in *The New Institutional Economics and Third World Development*, ed. John Harriss, Janet Hunter, and Colin M. Lewis (London: Routledge, 1995), 1.

26. Barbara Harriss-White, "Maps and Landscapes of Grain Markets in South Asia," in *The New Institutional Economics and Third World Development*, ed. John Harriss, Janet Hunter, and Colin M. Lewis (London: Routledge, 1995), 87.

27. Harriss, Hunter, and Lewis, "Introduction," 3.

28. North, as cited by Martinussen, *Society, State, and Market*, 254.

29. Osvaldo Sunkel, *Development from Within: Toward a Neostructuralist Approach for Latin America* (Boulder, Colo.: Lynne Rienner, 1993), 7.

30. C. Gunnarsson and M. Lundahl, "The Good, the Bad, and the Wobbly," in *New Directions in Development Economics: Growth, Environmental Concerns, and Government in the 1990s*, ed. Mats Lundahl and Benno J. Ndulu (London: Routledge, 1996), 256–257.

31. As synthesized by Nader Nazmi, *Economic Policy and Stabilization in Latin America* (New York: M. E. Sharpe, 1996), 7–8.

32. Anne Krueger uses the term "benevolent social guardian" to characterize a well-intended but inefficient state. As described in Gunnarsson and Lundahl, "Good, Bad, and Wobbly," 256.

33. Ibid., 260.

34. Inter-American Development Bank, *Latin America after a Decade of Reforms: Economic and Social Progress 1997 Report* (Washington, D.C.: Johns Hopkins University Press/Inter-American Development Bank, 1997), 104.

35. Ibid., 109.

36. Ibid., 105.

37. Ibid., 84.

38. Michael Gavin, Ricardo Hausman, Roberto Perotti, and Ernesto Talvi, *Managing Fiscal Policy in Latin America and the Caribbean: Volatility, Procyclicality, and Limited Creditworthiness*, Inter-American Development Bank, Office of the Chief Economist Working Paper, no. 326 (Washington, D.C.: Inter-American Development Bank, 1996), 4.

39. José María Fanelli and Roberto Frenkel, "Macropolicies for the Transition from Stabilization to Growth," in *New Directions in Development Economics: Growth, Environmental Concerns, and Government in the 1990s*, ed. Mats Lundahl and Benno J. Ndulu (London: Routledge, 1996), 41.

40. Guillermo Perry and Ana Maria Herrera, *Public Finances, Stabilization, and Structural Reform in Latin America* (Washington, D.C.: Johns Hopkins University Press/Inter-American Development Bank, 1994).

41. ECLAC, *Fiscal Covenant*, 13.

42. Inter-American Development Bank, *Economic and Social Progress in Latin America, 1995 Report: Overcoming Volatility* (Washington, D.C.: Johns Hopkins University Press, 1995), table 3.1, p. 126.

43. Inter-American Development Bank, *Latin America after a Decade of Reforms*, 72.

44. Ingrid Palmer, "Public Finance from a Gender Perspective," *World Development* 23, no. 11 (1995): 1984.

45. Vito Tanzi, *Fiscal Federalism and Decentralization: A Review of Some Efficiency and Macroeconomic Aspects*, presented at the World Bank Conference on Development Economics, World Bank, May 1995. (As summarized by *The Economist*, 3 June 1995, p. 74.)

46. ECLAC, *Fiscal Covenant*, 14.

47. Carlos Elizondo Mayer-Serra, "Tax Reform under the Salinas Administration," in *The Changing Structure of Mexico*, ed. Laura Randall (Armonk, N.Y.: M. E. Sharpe, 1996).

48. Douglas C. North, "Economic Performance through Time," acceptance lecture, 1993 Alfred Nobel Memorial Prize in Economic Sciences, published in *American Economic Review* 84, no. 3 (1994).

49. Rolph Van der Hoeven and Gyorgy Sziraczi, *Lessons from Privatization* (Geneva: International Labour Office, 1997), 4.

50. M. Sánchez, R. Corona, L. F. Herrera, and O. Ochoa, "A Comparison of Privatization Experiences: Chile, Mexico, Colombia, and Argentina," in *Privatization in Latin America*, ed. M. Sánchez and R. Corona (Baltimore: Johns Hopkins University Press, 1993).

51. Eduardo Bitran and Pablo Serra, "Regulation of Privatized Utilities: The Chilean Experience," *World Development* 26, no. 6 (1998): 945–962.

52. Emanuel Delovitch and Klas Ringskog, *Private Sector Participation in Water Supply and Sanitation in Latin America* (Washington, D.C.: World Bank, 1995), 3.

53. Van der Hoeven and Sziraczi, *Lessons from Privatization*, 12–17.

54. Sader (1993) as cited in chapter 5, "Privatization," in *Economic and Social Progress in Latin America 1996 Report* (Washington, D.C.: Inter-American Development Bank), 179.

55. Developing countries located in Latin America received $56.1 billion, East Asia and the Pacific $20.2 billion, Europe and Central Asia $15.3 billion, the Middle East and Africa $1.4 billion, South Asia $6.2 billion, and sub-Saharan Africa $1.7 billion over the 1990–1994 period for a total of more than $100 billion. "Privatization," *Economic and Social Progress in Latin America 1996 Report*, table 5.1a, 169.

56. Ahmed Galal, Leroy Jones, Pankaj Tandon, and Ingo Vogelsang, "Divestiture: Questions and Answers," in *Welfare Consequences of Selling Public Enterprises* (Washington, D.C.: World Bank, 1994), 184.

57. Galal et al., "Divestiture," 288.

58. This is in 1992. *World Investment Report 1994* (New York: United Nations, 1994), 93.

59. Clifford Kraus, "Argentina to Hasten End of Phone Monopoly," *New York Times*, 11 March 1998, p. D4.

60. Galal et al., "Divestiture," 407.

61. Sebastian Edwards, ed., *Crisis and Reform in Latin America: From Despair to Hope* (New York: Oxford University Press, 1995).

62. Werner Baer and Annibal V. Villela, "Privatization and the Changing Role of the

State in Brazil," in *Privatization in Latin America*, ed. Werner Baer and Melissa Birch (Westport, Conn.: Praeger, 1994).

63. "Privatization," *Euromoney*, September 1996, p. 294.

64. "Brazil's Iron King," *Financial Times*, 29 June 1998, p. 13.

65. "It's Time to Bite the Bullet," *Euromoney*, September 1996, p. 300.

66. "Cost-Cutting Takes a Private Road," *Euromoney*, September 1996.

67. "Telebras Sold for US$19.1b," *Latin American Weekly Report*, 4 August 1998, p. 352; and Seth Schiesel, "Brazil Sells Most of State Phone Utility," *New York Times*, 30 July 1998, p. D1.

68. Baer and Villela, "Privatization," 2.

69. Kenneth P. Jameson, "The Financial Sector in Latin American Restructuring," in *Privatization in Latin America*, ed. Werner Baer and Melissa Birch (Westport, Conn.: Praeger, 1994), 120.

70. This section draws extensively on Frederick Mishkin, "Understanding Financial Crises: A Developing Country Perspective," in *Annual World Bank Conference on Development Economics 1996* (Washington, D.C.: World Bank, 1997), 28–30.

71. "CANTV in 1994," *Harvard Business School Case Studies*, 28 February 1996, p. 6.

72. Thomas T. Vogel Jr., "Venezuela Privatization Proves Paltry," *The Wall Street Journal*, 17 July 1996.

73. Ibid., 28.

74. Van der Hoeven and Sziraczi, *Lessons from Privatization*, 11.

75. Galal et al., "Divestiture," 13–14.

NEW INTERNATIONAL CAPITAL FLOWS

The Benefits (and Hidden Costs) of Latin America's Return to Markets

Foreign capital has flooded regional stock markets. *(Courtesy of David Mangurian and the Inter-American Development Bank.)*

After the long period of painful structural adjustment to the debt crisis, the adoption of the neoliberal model in Latin America led to a surge in new capital flows to the region in the mid-1990s. Macroeconomic stability, opening of closed economies to international markets, lucrative privatizations, and subregional integration made potential returns in Latin America enticing to foreign capital. Capital flows to the region for 1996 were twice 1995 levels. Inflows in 1997 maintained a healthy rate, despite the Asian financial crisis. After a decade of isolation, Latin America was again a darling of international investors.

Although new capital is of course a welcome way to spur growth, rapid inflows raise questions about the ability of economies to absorb international funds productively. Are funds being channeled to improve the productive capacity of the region or are they fueling asset bubbles or consumption booms? A lesson of the debt crisis was the vulnerability of regional economies to changes in international liquidity. The Mexican peso crisis of 1994–1995, the Asian currency crises of 1997–1998, and the Brazilian crisis of 1998–1999 underscore the fragility of developing economies in highly integrated international capital markets. What if Latin America is once again cut off from capital inflows? Policy must carefully appraise not only the huge growth potential but also the possible pitfalls of the new capital flows to Latin America.

The following questions will guide our discussion of new capital flows to the region:

- Why has capital returned with such intensity to the region?
- How do the different kinds of capital—short- and long-term portfolio investments as well as long-term **foreign direct investment** through multinational corporations—affect development prospects in the region?
- Does this new reliance on international capital make Latin America vulnerable once again to swings in international markets?
- Are there ways of minimizing vulnerability while maintaining the confidence of international capital?

Understanding the changing nature of capital flows to the region will enhance our understanding of the promise and the limitations of liberalization as a strategy for Latin American economic development. Like trade, which we will study in the next chapter, the free flow of capital brings opportunities for growth but may be accompanied by an increase in uncertainty and volatility. Unlike the inward-looking model of import substitution industrialization, financial and trade liberalization make a nation more sensitive to changes in the global economy—the good *and* the bad.

AN INTRODUCTION TO THE BEHAVIOR OF CAPITAL FLOWS

The neoliberal model places private capital flows at the center of development finance. Capital, it is argued, will flow to its most productive uses. Tough austerity measures that transform the productivity of an economy should therefore be rewarded by improved access to international capital markets. This has, to some extent, taken place in the Latin American region. We can see in figure 7.1 that capital flows in the 1990s are dramatically higher than in earlier periods. This is an extraordinary vote of confidence on the part of international markets in Latin American economic reform.

It should be pointed out that foreign capital inflows are not a solution for all countries. Although private capital flows to developing countries have risen dramatically, they are relatively concentrated in a few countries. In 1995 private flows to developing countries exceeded $170 billion, three times official flows and four times levels five years ago. However, 75 percent of the flows went to twelve countries, and fifty countries received virtually no private flows.[1] At the same time, official aid flows to poor countries are diminishing quickly—at $59 billion they were at their lowest point in twenty-three years.[2]

Although the trickle of capital to poorer countries is problematic, ironically the rapid infusion of international capital to hot countries may also have economic costs. International capital is an undependable friend. It can flow out as quickly as it comes in, following the highest rate of return. How permanent are capital flows to Latin America? How predictable? Rapid inflows may be too much of a good thing, distorting asset and foreign exchange prices.

To understand the implications of rapid capital flows it is useful to analyze what drives the demand for foreign assets. As we have noted, the restructuring of Latin American economies created new growth potential. Remember that investors buy today in anticipation of returns in the future. Unlike buying a car or a stereo, where you can pretty well predict what the asset will be worth next year, financial investments carry an uncertain future value. Purchases are made based on *expected*

Figure 7.1. Net Resource Flows

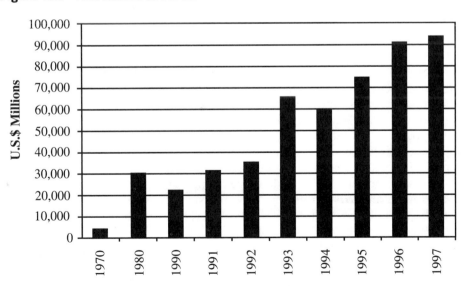

Source: World Bank, *Global Development Finance* (Washington, D.C.: World Bank, 1998), 26.

value. Do you think the value of the asset will rise or fall over the term of the investment? This applies to investments in stocks, bonds, or commodities such as copper or tin. If there is a high degree of uncertainty as to the future performance of an asset, investors must be compensated for additional risk. If the asset is denominated in a foreign currency, the possibility that the currency may lose value over the term of the investment must also be taken into account. Stability, confidence, and predictability are key to promoting sound financial investments.

Because international investment decisions are made one versus another—that is, investors evaluate *relative* returns—the policy or performance in Latin America may not be the sole factor. Relative returns on other assets—perhaps the dollar or maybe investments in Europe or Asia—could become more lucrative. Latin America may be interesting because returns in other regions are low. But a country can't control what is happening in the rest of the world. Capital flows must therefore be looked at not only for their investment potential today, but also for their sustainability in promoting long-term development. This chapter will analyze these flows and address policies Latin American governments have introduced to tame their volatility in the region. It will also look at interactions with other macroeconomic variables, especially the exchange rate. If capital—say, dollars—is flowing in, this will increase the supply and decrease the price of the dollar relative to the national currency. If the national currency as a result becomes stronger, this may compromise the ability of the country to pursue an aggressive export drive. As we will see, capital's helping hand may also choke off the growth of exports. The gains to financing in the internal market may not be consistent with the external requirements of the economy. We will explore whether policy instruments are needed to balance capital flows in emerging markets.

EXPLAINING CAPITAL FLOWS TO LATIN AMERICA

A variety of factors explain the increase in global private capital flows and the new interest in Latin America relative to other regions. Beginning with the supply side, international flows have responded to changes in international markets, following global integration. Technological changes facilitating the transfer of money and ideas have made the world a smaller place, reducing transaction costs for international investment. With better information and changes in the U.S. legal code, new groups of institutional investors such as pension and insurance funds have internationalized investment opportunities.[3] The aging of the baby boomers created a pool of capital in search of high returns. Low interest rates in the United States in the early and mid-1990s made domestic investments less attractive. There is simply more international money to be invested. These external supply factors, including developments in international financial markets, have been shown to be the primary determinant of capital flows to the region.[4] More investors are looking for productive opportunities around the globe.

Why invest in Latin America instead of other regions? In addition to the factors that have increased the global supply of capital, structural changes in Latin America have pulled financing into the region. Tough austerity measures have improved financial solvency. In most countries in the region changes in investment codes and macroeconomic policy are perceived to be permanent. National exchange rate regimes are less susceptible to megadevaluations. Investors have greater confidence in their ability to predict the long-term macroeconomic environment for business. Legislation has favored international investment, and privatization has created new investment opportunities. Simultaneous political reform and the deepening of democracy reduced the political risk associated with investment. We can summarize these factors by saying that the relative yield of countries' assets as well as financial solvency has improved, while political instability and potential losses due to devaluation or nationalization have declined. In short, Latin America has become a good investment risk.[5] Nonetheless, it is important to remember that no matter how well structured Latin America's reforms, international capital chooses a home based on *relative* appeal: opportunities for profit not only have to be good, but they must be better than expected returns, adjusted for uncertainty and risk, everywhere else.

Characteristics of Latin American Markets: What Is the Absorptive Capacity?

The fact that capital is flowing to Latin America doesn't mean that investments there are always productive. Can Latin America productively absorb the capital flowing into the region? Understanding the absorptive capacity involves an appreciation of the types of capital coming into the region. The flow of capital into the region takes four forms: foreign direct investment, bond purchases, portfolio equity flows, and lending directly to support trade.[6] Figure 7.2 shows the increase

Figure 7.2.   Net Private Capital Flows

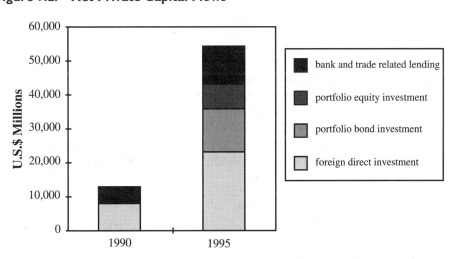

Source: World Bank, *World Development Indicators* (Washington, D.C.: World Bank, 1997), table 5.2.

Some multinationals contract with smaller local producers for piecework to export. *(Courtesy of David Mangurian and the Inter-American Development Bank.)*

in all types of capital flows to the region from 1990 to 1995. Foreign direct investment increased 2.8 times, portfolio equity 6.5 times, and **portfolio bonds** 129 times. Coping with the rapid influx of short-term or hot money is a source of policy concern. We will explain the role each type of capital plays in turn.

Portfolio bonds and **equity investments** can be transitory. Portfolio bond flows are bond issues purchased by foreign investors. These might be government bonds similar to U.S. Treasuries to finance public investments, or they might be corporate offerings. Remember that bonds are essentially a promise to pay in the future. Equity investments are the sum of country funds, depository receipts,[7] and direct purchases of shares by foreign investors. Short-term (less than one year) capital with the exception of loans to finance trade is broadly characterized as speculative or "hot" money. It is this stateless, agile capital that concerns policy makers. As we learned in the chapter on the debt crisis in the 1980s, financing long-term development on short-term capital is a risky venture. Portfolio flows create problems for long-term sustainability.

Equity investments, or the purchase of stocks, are also considered liquid, short-term capital, particularly if the holder maintains less than a 10 percent share. Nonetheless, equity or stock investments are less risky to a company than bonds. If an economy or a firm experiences a downturn and the stock value plummets, stockholders lose. When hard times hit a company that has financed expansion through bonds (or through commercial bank loans), the firm or nation must still make good on that obligation or face the ramifications of default. Stocks, therefore, spread risk from firms to investors. We can measure market capitalization or market value by taking the share price times the number of shares outstanding on an exchange. Market size is an important predictor of a country's ability to mobilize capital and diversify risk. The level of stock market development closely tracks a country's overall development level. Finance in less developed economies tends to be dominated by commercial banks, rather than stock exchanges. The growth of stock markets may increase liquidity and diversify risk.[8] As shown in table 7.1, stock markets in Latin America, as measured by the ratio of capitalization to GDP, are small compared with those in developed countries.[9] The outlier is certainly Chile, where the sophisticated market was 120 percent of GDP in 1995. The markets are modest; only Brazil's market value comes close to the European country of Spain. With fewer shares traded and fewer participants, small stock markets can be overwhelmed by foreign participation. Furthermore, Latin American equity markets are relatively concentrated. Ownership is highly entrenched among a small number of participants in closed and family-owned corporations such that markets are not easily contestable.[10] Nonetheless, they have exhibited substantial growth in the past five years. As box 7.1 shows, some believe there is greater potential for smaller investors. While market size is small, growth has been rapid. Of countries in the region where market capitalization is at least 10 percent of GDP, the slowest growth from 1990 to 1995 has been Mexico at 177 percent and the fastest Ecuador at 5,157 percent—both significantly faster than the robust growth of the U.S. market at 124 percent.

Table 7.1.   Market Capitalization

Country	1990 Value (U.S.$ millions)	1995 Value (US $ millions)	% Rate of Growth 1990–1995	% of GDP 1995
Argentina	3,268	37,783	1,056	13.5
Brazil	16,354	147,636	803	21.8
Chile	13,645	73,860	441	120.8
Colombia	1,416	17,893	1,164	23.5
Ecuador	69	3,627	5,157	14.6
Mexico	32,725	90,694	177	36.3
Panama	226	831	268	11.2
Peru	812	11,795	1,353	20.5
France	314,384	522,053	66	34
Spain	111,404	197,788	78	35.4
United Kingdom	848,866	1,407,737	66	87
United States	3,059,434	6,857,622	124	55.7

Source: World Bank, *World Development Indicators, 1997* (Washington, D.C.: World Bank, 1997), table 5.3.

Box 7.1.   The New Entrepreneurs—Not Just for Big Players: Stock Markets Could Open the Door to Entrepreneurs

Latin America's stock markets are still dominated by a relatively small number of large corporations. But according to Jorge Roldán, chief economist for the Inter-American Investment Corporation (IIC), medium-sized and even small companies could soon tap this rich source of low-cost, long-term capital. Roldán spoke to *IDB EXTRA* about the future of financing for Latin American entrepreneurs.

Q. Have small companies benefited from the billions of dollars in foreign investment that have flowed into the region in recent years?

A. Yes, but to a very limited degree. Most of the money has gone to established corporations listed on the stock exchanges of countries with larger economies, such as Mexico, Brazil, Argentina, Chile, Colombia, Peru, and Venezuela.

Traditional private venture capital funds make equity investments in established companies and help them to upgrade technology and management expertise in order to become internationally competitive. The typical investment is between $20 million and $80 million in a company worth from $50 million to $300 million. Once the company reaches the desired volume of business, the venture fund typically cashes out. Unfortunately, in some cases, the fund may pull out at the first hint of a downturn, either in the company itself or in the economy of the country.

Q. How does the IIC fit into this picture?

A. We have a development-oriented investment strategy. We specialize in much smaller companies and allocate a large part of our portfolio to the countries that private investors tend to overlook. Our typical loan or equity investment ranges between $2 million and $10 million, and we're willing to make a longer commitment, usually in the 10-year range.

We work very closely with the managers of the companies we invest in to help them adopt new technologies that improve productivity and competitiveness. We also have a very strict commitment to environmental protection. We won't invest in companies that don't have a viable plan for ameliorating the environmental consequences of their activities.

Q. Small companies in Latin America have traditionally depended on debt financing to expand. Should they be looking to local stock markets as an alternative way to raise funds?

A. Absolutely. Interest rates on bank loans remain prohibitively high in many of the region's countries. Issuing stock or bonds on a local securities market can be a much cheaper way to obtain long-term financing, even for a relatively small firm. We have a project in Guatemala, for instance, where a developer placed $2 million in bonds on the local stock exchange to help finance a new hotel.

The problem is that most smaller companies are not used to the rigorous financial reporting requirements that investors demand before they are willing to buy stocks or bonds. So one of our principal goals is to help companies put their house in order and get to the point where they can be listed on an exchange.

Along with the Multilateral Investment Fund, the IIC has been working to help regional governments modernize their stock markets and harmonize reporting requirements. This is especially important in the smaller countries, where there isn't enough of a critical mass to sustain individual markets. In Central America and the Caribbean, for example, we are helping to coordinate regulatory and reporting standards in order to create regional exchanges. That way an investor in Honduras could easily buy stock in a Costa Rican company, for instance.

Our board has just approved a very innovative line of credit to a Brazilian bank, Credibanco, that is going to assist medium-sized companies to go through the process of preparing to go public. Our credit facility will be used to purchase dollar-denominated bonds issued by medium-sized enterprises. This will give a number of companies access to longer-term financing for much less than they could hope to get by borrowing. Beneficiary companies will be required to register with the local securities and exchange commission. In Brazil, this is the first step in the process of becoming publicly listed.

Ultimately, we think local stock markets will be the best way to channel domestic savings towards entrepreneurs and small companies. There are several countries where public pension reforms based on individual retirement accounts are quickly creating a huge pool of savings that needs to be invested. We have already seen the benefits of that approach in Chile. Now we want to extend it to other countries.

Source: IDB EXTRA, June 14, 1998. On-line edition.

LONG-TERM INVESTMENT: THE ROLE OF MULTINATIONAL CORPORATIONS

In contrast to short-term bond and equity flows, foreign direct investment largely represents a long-term capital flow with a commitment to local manufacturing. It is generally measured by acquiring a lasting management interest or 10 percent of the voting stock or by establishing a subsidiary or production branch. On average, foreign direct investment in Latin America accounts for approximately 2.2 percent of a country's GDP.[11] We can see in figure 7.3 that foreign direct investment grew enormously throughout the 1990s, with an increasing diversity of recipients. Flows for 1998 were 386 percent greater than for 1991, even adjusting for a slight downturn due to the Asian crisis. Multinationals from Spain, the Netherlands, Switzerland, and the United States snatched up cheaply priced Latin American firms in the telecommunications, banking, electric utility, and consumer finance sectors to strengthen their stakes in key markets in Brazil, Argentina, and Chile.[12] Inflows to Mexico and Argentina in the beginning of the decade have been supplemented by investment in Brazil, Venezuela, and other Latin American countries. Nevertheless, we can see that all the investment in the smaller countries of the region is about half that of Mexico or a quarter of Brazil's. Although the importance of single firms such as Chiquita Brands or General Motors in the economies of the subregion is not inconsequential, foreign direct investment is not the solution for all countries that want to spur development. That is, multinationals do not necessarily want to produce where conditions are unstable or the infrastructure is incomplete. Foreign direct investment can be seen as preferable to short-term capital flows in that it reflects a long-term commitment to the nation. It should in fact translate into an increase in a country's productive potential. Of course it raises other questions with respect to balanced development and domestic entrepreneurship.

Multinational corporations are extraordinarily powerful, accounting for one-third of world production and with total sales exceeding the value of world trade. Table 7.2 shows the activity of the top twenty MNCs in the region. Worldwide, ranked by output, fifty-one of the top "countries" are multinational corporations. In addition, more than half of world trade consists of transnational firm trading activity, largely of an intrafirm nature.[13] That is, half of world trade is associated with firms like Coca-Cola or Nike sending subassembly materials and final prod-

Figure 7.3.   Net Foreign Direct Investment

U.S.$ Millions

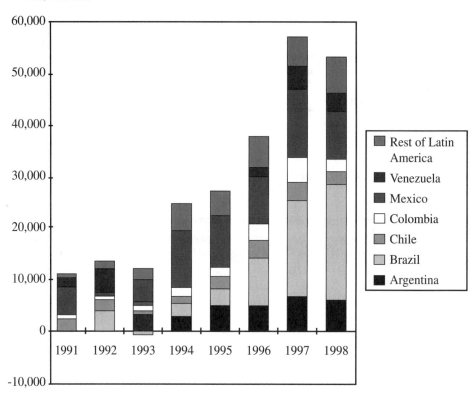

Source: Data from the Economic Commission for Latin America and the Caribbean and the International Monetary Fund, available on the World Wide Web at www.eclac.org/espanol/Publicaciones/bal98/cuadros/cua12.gif. *Balance preliminar de las economías de América Latina y el Caribe 1998* (Santiago: Cepal, 1998).

ucts among their own subsidiaries. Box 7.2 summarizes the debate on the pros and cons of multinational production. Multinationals may provide technology, improve efficiency, and create jobs. Some charge that multinationals invest abroad to take advantage of cheaper labor or less stringent environmental standards. Producers of textiles, for example, have long moved to where unskilled workers, often women, can be paid a tenth of the going wage in the United States. Environmentalists worry that companies set up shop in countries with lax pollution laws, a phenomenon called environmental dumping.

The good news is that globalization of information systems has decreased the ability of multinationals to get away with social and environmental abuse. As the Internet and CNN bring corporate activities into stockholders' living rooms, firms have been forced to comply with new standards. For example, after celebrity Kathy Lee Gifford was charged with exploitation of female workers in Central America

BOX 7.2. IS MULTINATIONAL PRODUCTION GOOD FOR DEVELOPING COUNTRIES?

Pros	Cons
• With a technology gap, the farther behind you are the faster you can pick up the leader's innovations to catch up. MNCs provide a positive contagion effect.[14]	• Traditional dependency arguments— powerful international capital exploits workers, maintains control of technology, and preempts local development of production.
• Spillover efficiency—even if the MNC does not directly share technology with local firms, it may have positive productivity effects through competition, as domestic firms are given an incentive to catch up; through training of labor and management; and through effects on local suppliers including higher standards of quality and delivery.[15]	• MNC production is culturally inappropriate, introducing products unsuited for local conditions.
• Source of capital for investment (if not squeezing local capital out of domestic markets).	• MNCs engage in human rights abuse, unfairly taking advantage of female and child labor.
• Employment source of jobs that generally pay higher wages than local firms.[18]	• MNCs circumvent international law in the environmental arena.
• Provides needed management skills to the economy.	• Global production causes job loss in home economy—although one study shows that U.S. multinationals compete only at margins with affiliates.[16]
	• MNCs are production enclaves—there is a low level of linkages with local suppliers; evidence on this is mixed, depending on the type of MNC.[17]
	• Net capital outflow—after initial injection of capital, MNC may remit more in profits than it put in.
	• Use of technology inappropriate for local conditions—more capital intensive than appropriate. Big gap between local and MNC forestalls spillovers.
	• Reliance on foreign technology retards local development, causing negative effects on productivity.[19]

in the production of her clothing line for K-mart, the negative publicity generated a fall in the stock price. The firm was forced to adopt codes of corporate conduct that improve the lives of workers. As dismal conditions and low wages have become well documented, college students across America have pressured for changes in sweatshop practices and adoption of a fair labor code by boycotting bookstore apparel.[20] Globalization of production has increased the multinational's reach but has made its activities more transparent.

Does the surge in multinational investment improve the productive capabilities of Latin American economies? As Latin America has moved away from protected state-run industries to allow greater multinational participation, how has productivity changed? One study of foreign production in Mexico shows that a high multinational presence is correlated with an increase in productivity in locally owned firms and that the rate of catch-up with international productivity standards

Table 7.2. Top Multinationals in Latin America

Corporation	Country	Sectors	Sales (U.S.$ millions)	Operations in
General Motors	USA	Automotive	5,381	Brazil, Mexico, Argentina, Chile, Colombia, and Venezuela
Volkswagen	Germany	Automotive	1,302	Brazil, Mexico and Argentina
Ford Motor Company	USA	Automotive	1,200	Brazil, Mexico, Argentina, and Colombia
Royal Dutch Shell	UK/Netherlands	Petroleum	9,825	Brazil, Mexico, Argentina, and Venezuela
Fiat Spa	Italy	Automotive	9,188	Brazil, Argentina, and Venezuela
Coca-Cola	USA	Beverages	8,659	Brazil, Mexico, Argentina, and Chile
Exxon	USA	Mining/petroleum	7,260	Brazil, Argentina, Chile, and Colombia
Carrefour Super-markets	France	Commerce	6,835	Brazil and Argentina
PepsiCo.	USA	Food	6,766	Brazil, Mexico, and Argentina
Telefónica de España	Spain	Telecommunications	6,756	Brazil, Argentina, Chile, and Peru
Chrysler	USA	Automotive	6,672	Mexico and Argentina
Nestlé	Switzerland	Food	6,452	Brazil, Mexico, Argentina, Chile, Colombia, Peru, and Venezuela
IBM	USA	Electronics	5,899	Brazil, Mexico, Argentina, Chile, and Peru
Unilever	UK/Netherlands	Food	5,569	Brazil, Mexico, and Argentina
Philips Morris Companies	USA	Tobacco	4,924	Brazil and Argentina
Endesa Spain	Spain	Electricity	4,507	Brazil, Argentina, Chile, and Colombia
Wal-Mart	USA	Commerce	4,481	Mexico and Argentina
Bunge & Born	Argentina	Food	4,311	Brazil and Peru
British American Tobacco	UK	Food	4,166	Brazil, Mexico, Argentina, Chile, and Venezuela
Cargill	USA	Food	3,347	Brazil, Argentina, Chile, and Colombia

Source: Unit on Investment and Corporate Strategies, Economic Commission for Latin America and the Caribbean, available at www.eclac.org/english/Publications/invest98/generaleng/sld012.htm.

is positively associated with the degree of foreign concentration in the industry. This suggests spillovers from multinational production to less efficient local firms. Multinational firms may act as a catalyst to productivity growth, speeding up the convergence in productivity levels between developing and industrialized countries.[21] The authors warn, nonetheless, of extrapolating too much from the Mexican case because there is extensive movement of labor and capital between Mexico and the United States, especially in border production. Furthermore, multinational investment in Mexico is problematic as a model because all countries are not as attractive to significant amounts of foreign investment.[22] Box 7.3 summarizes Mexico's long love–hate affair with foreign capital, and box 7.4 gives an example of multinational activity that has minimized the costs and maximized the benefits of foreign direct investment in Peru.

BOX 7.3.   MEXICO'S LOVE-HATE AFFAIR WITH FOREIGN DIRECT INVESTMENT

Mexico has progressed through a variety of positions in terms of the role of foreign direct investment in its economy, reflecting different views—sometimes simultaneously—of foreign investment in Mexico. Opposition to foreign intervention was a hallmark of early Mexican history since the days of the Spanish conquest. Nonetheless Porfirio Díaz and his científico advisers espoused liberalization policies and encouraged foreign investment during the Porfiriato, 1876–1911.

The Revolution to 1944 was marked by the establishment of state ownership, particularly in the mining sector and the 1938 nationalization of petroleum companies. The formation of the Banco de Mexico took the role of financing from foreign commercial banks. Ownership rules were defined by sector in the 1930s: strategic industries, including primary product exports and utilities, were dominated by state ownership. Manufacturing, under import substitution industrialization, drew on FDI, and the early maquilas used cheap labor to re-export goods to international markets.

Fears of foreign takeover of the Mexican economy led to the 1944 law requiring majority Mexican ownership except with permission of the Secretariat of Foreign Relations. "Mexicanization" extended to radio, cinema, domestic airlines, buses, soft drink bottlers, publishing, and tires. Paradoxically, at the same time efforts were made to recruit foreign investment to fill the capital needs of industrialization. National ownership in banking, finance, and extractive industries was secured while foreign investment boomed in areas of manufacturing.

The Maquila program was introduced in 1965, allowing firms to import inputs tax free if they were to be transformed into exports. Mexico benefited through employment and foreign exchange, while the transnationals found high profit margins with cheap labor. In contrast, the 1973 Law to Promote Mexican Investment and Regulate Foreign Investment diverted policy inward, regulating foreign entry and enforcing Mexicanization and local majority ownership.

Capital constraints with the debt crisis again prompted a change of policy, including a 1989 liberalization law to encourage investment. Mexico acceded to the General Agreement on Tariffs and Trade (GATT) in 1985, lowering tariffs and reducing import controls. Signature of the North American Free Trade Agreement (NAFTA) formalizes this open investment regime and symbolizes Mexico's firm commitment through an international treaty to encourage international investment.

Source: Michael J. Twomey, *Multinational Corporations and the North American Free Trade Agreement* (Westport, Conn.: Praeger, 1993), 27–34.

Box 7.4.   Best Practices: A Positive Case of Multinational Involvement

"Against the Odds: How a Seemingly Hopeless Energy Project Became a Model for Investors," by David Mangurian

(IDB América, March 1998; available on-line at www.iadb.org)

The plan that Maple Gas Corp. of Dallas, Texas, took to prospective investors seemed a long shot at best.

It was 1993, and the company was proposing to drill gas wells in a remote section of the Peruvian jungle that was controlled by anti-government subversives. The gas would fuel an electric power plant to be built next to a town controlled by cocaine drug traffickers. And all of this would happen in a country that was just getting its yearly inflation rate below three digits and was still an outcast to the world's financial community.

Furthermore, the proposed facilities would be built east of the Andes mountains, meaning that thousands of tons of equipment and material would have to be shipped 3,200 km up the Amazon River by freighter, then off-loaded onto barges and hauled another 800 km up the smaller Ucayali River during the four-month rainy season when the river was deep enough for barges to reach their destination. Then the equipment would be trucked to the project sites on washboard-surfaced, potholed dirt roads that turned to mud when it rained.

The price tag? A quarter of a billion dollars. Not an easy sell. The idea might have seemed far fetched, except that the economic case for the project was overwhelmingly strong. Peru's electricity demands were growing 9 percent a year. The country desperately needed more low-cost power, and the gas was just 2,500 meters under the jungle floor. The project's payback period was calculated at less than eight years and the profit potential was excellent.

It looked like a perfect opportunity for Maple Gas. The company had just sold off most of its assets in the United States to concentrate on developing a more lucrative foreign venture. At the same time, Peru had started privatizing its energy sector and was preparing to award concessions to commercialize existing hydrocarbon reserves. Among the properties the government was putting up for bid was the Aguaytía gas field, which had been discovered by Mobil Oil in 1961 in the jungle west of Pucallpa. The field had never been developed because of the high cost of building a pipeline to transport the gas over the Andes to Peru's coastal cities.

Maple executives saw a different way to tackle the problem of getting the energy from the wellhead to the consumer. They proposed building a gas-powered electricity generating plant at Aguaytía and running transmission lines across the Andes, figuring that this alternative would cost much less than a pipeline.

In 1993, Maple outbid other companies in a public auction to win a 30-year concession to develop and commercialize the Aguaytía gas field. As soon as the concession papers were signed in early 1994, and long before Maple had any guarantee of financing, the company began planning for construction. In fact, Maple became so confident of success that it began putting most of its money into the Aguaytía project.

The first thing Maple did after it won the concession was to run tests on the wells drilled in the Aguaytía field 33 years earlier to confirm the results. Maple hired a burly, retired Peruvian special forces commander, Jorge Meza, to assemble a security team to protect people working in the project area. Although the Peruvian government had by then made substantial progress in controlling guerrillas and drug trafficking, security was still a very real problem.

"It was still an area of high risk from subversives," recalls César Valderrama, area operations manager for Maple Gas. "We practically had a regiment of marines at the well site. It looked like a battlefield. We were surrounded by soldiers."

Meza and others also recommended a community action program to develop long-term relationships with residents near the project's multiple sites, and thereby help avoid local opposition that might delay construction. Maple sent medical teams into villages to immunize children and teach basic hygiene, and the company sponsored programs with local schools.

SEARCH FOR INVESTORS

The well tests proved positive: there was enough gas to fuel a new 155,000 kW power plant as well as Pucallpa's existing 20,000 kW power plant for at least 28 years. In addition, gas liquids could be processed into bottled gas for cooking and gasoline to generate further income. Maple now had a viable "integrated" gas and electricity project to sell potential investors.

But investors were skeptical, particularly when they saw the local conditions. Meza recalls one instance: "I drove a group of Americans across the route of the [planned] transmission lines. No car had been there for 30 years. We had to spend the night in a very poor hotel high in the Andes. These were investors used to five star hotels. So I told them: 'Tonight you'll be staying at a hotel with more than five stars. You'll be at a hotel with all the stars of the heavens.' "

But as the months passed, the strengths of Maple's proposal became increasingly apparent. By 1996 the company had put together a group of equity investors and banks willing to commit a total of $254 million to the project, including a $60 million loan from the IDB. The financing arrangement broke new ground and drew accolades from international project finance experts.

In Peru, the project was seen as a resounding vindication of the government's privatization program. "Aguaytía is the first private sector 'Test' of Peru's economic reforms," stated the IDB loan document.

Construction began in August, 1996, and was to be completed in just 18 months. Contractors would be charged substantial penalties for each day of delay. The company hired some 2,200 construction workers. Conditions in the jungle were tough: high humidity, temperatures up to 45 degrees (C), tarantulas and poisonous snakes, and frequent, thundering downpours that mired trucks and equipment in mud.

Planning had to be meticulous because of the extremely complicated logistics. If the giant generators, transformers and other pieces of heavy equipment and machinery were not built and shipped on time, they would not make it the 4,000 km up the Amazon and Ucayali rivers to Pucallpa before the river level dropped to unnavigable levels.

The equipment started arriving in January 1997. "We unloaded the last shipment on the last day Pucallpa's port was open," recalls Valderrama. Now the 122-ton generators, 86-ton transformers and other equipment had to be hoisted off the barges and onto the trucks for their arduous trip overland to Aguaytía. This would be the job of a 140-ton crane, which was trucked in from Lima in six pieces, a 785-km trip that took four days.

"If you had a heavy load on a truck and it rained, you had to wait for hours after the rain stopped for the road to dry before you could move on," says Naef. The 300 km of pipelines for natural gas and natural gas liquids, and 400 km of electricity transmission lines were routed alongside existing roads in order to minimize the impact on the environment. Maple employed a team of archeologists to ensure that important sites were not disturbed by construction of the transmission lines across the Andes. These and other environmental measures added $10 million to the project's cost.

This March, gas operations are to begin and one of the two gas turbines at the Aguaytía electric power plant is to begin operations. Full commercial operations are expected by April 1.

"The officers of Maple Gas had to have a lot of tenacity to sell this project to investors," says Valderrama. "Most were afraid. Aguaytía was one of the first large private investments in Peru."

(continued)

(continued)

Much has changed in Peru since Maple Gas arrived on the scene. The country has consolidated sweeping economic reforms and is becoming a magnet for investors. In 1997 the inflation rate dropped to 7 percent and private foreign direct investment hit $7 billion, four times the 1993 level.

The Aguaytía project now looks like a superb investment, not the risky venture of five years ago. "It has become an example for other companies to follow," said Valderrama.

The gains and the costs of multinational production should be evaluated on a case by case basis. One study showed that the positive effects of multinational transfer of technology were strong only when there was already a well-developed human capital base.[23] Some of the issues we consider in later chapters on social development and education may therefore play a key role in shaping costs and benefits. Government policy in establishing the rules of the game for multinationals is important in evaluating outcomes. The size and number of other firms in a market also condition multinational behavior. If a multinational company is the only employer in a small town, it is less likely to treat workers well. If, however, it is in competition with a large number of firms, it is more likely to provide good working conditions. An ethical dilemmas arises in considering labor standards for multinational production. Should home country or host country labor codes be employed? Labor standards in poor countries may approximate conditions in industrial countries fifty years ago. Should U.S. multinationals meet U.S. safety and health standards in a Guatemalan plant? Some contend that best practices should apply worldwide; others suggest local standards as a baseline while developing countries catch up.

> **QUESTION FOR THOUGHT**
>
> Can you think of ways to minimize the costs and maximize the benefits of multinational production in developing countries?

REWARDS AND RISKS OF NEW CAPITAL FLOWS TO LATIN AMERICA

In addition to rewards, multinational activity has its drawbacks, including questions with respect to sovereignty and to labor and environmental standards. Nevertheless, although plant closings are possible, the commitment to production is generally of a long-term nature. This stands in contrast to hot money flows, or short-term capital investments, which, while used to finance investments and spur growth, introduce questions of volatility. What are the implications of short-term capital flows to Latin America? New capital flows to the region can be seen as financial rewards for the painful process of structural adjustment. Greater global integration can be seen as a movement toward the more efficient worldwide utilization of capital. For advocates of new capital flows, maintaining access to international financial markets is simply the result of sound domestic economic management. They see international inflows as complementary to national capital. The infusion of funds will spur growth which will then encourage savings.

Is money moving to the region because it is most efficiently employed in Latin America as compared to other investment alternatives? To evaluate the arguments of proponents of capital inflows, it is important to situate the theoretical argument in the context of the reality of Latin American markets. Latin American markets are not exactly like the Wall Street variety. If markets are relatively thin and uncompetitive, efficiency gains will be limited. Furthermore, the price signals driving capital to certain markets may be flawed. Informational bottlenecks and the institutional peculiarities of investors may interfere with market efficiency. Many new investment instruments are complex and not completely understood by participants, increasing the underlying risk. Transactions in many markets are unregulated, accounting standards are lax, balance sheets are inscrutable, and financial disclosure is not as strictly enforced as in the United States. With incomplete information, the globalization of capital may not generate as much efficiency as claimed.[24] Capital may be more fickle and less efficient than is sometimes assumed.

Because ultimately it is the stockholders who take the risk, the question of efficiency of investments is of less concern to countries themselves than some of the macroeconomic effects of capital flows. Some policy makers in Latin America are wary of long-run dependency on the new capital flows, particularly **short-term money**. Concerns revolve around both the volatility of flows and the interaction with other economic variables. Because the decision to invest is made on relative rates of return, a country continuing to pursue a sound policy course might find itself out of favor in the international market as another nation or region becomes the Wall Street flavor of the month. A long history of negative effects of external price changes—such as the oil price and interest rate shocks precipitating the debt crisis of the 1980s—make policy makers nervous concerning external vulnerability. Uncertainty is built into the structure of current financing. For example, a major source of capital supporting infrastructure expansion are bonds with an average maturity of four years. What if they are not renewed at expiration?[25] Can development planning be creatively financed with short-term inflows?

In addition to volatility, capital inflows may adversely affect other economic variables. In particular, some economists are concerned about the degree to which capital inflows are consistent with sustainable levels of the exchange rate and the interest rate. Because capital inflows change the supply of money available for investment, they also change the price of money—both nationally, as measured by the domestic interest rate, and relatively, measured by the exchange rate. If inflows are strong, finance becomes cheaper and the interest rate falls. International money is more abundant, and therefore the local currency, relatively scarcer than it was before, appreciates. Low interest rates could have a negative effect on national savings rates, discouraging local sources of financing. An appreciated exchange rate may stand in the way of pursuing an export orientation. In particular, if financial markets are shallow and uncompetitive, they may not be able to intermediate the capital surges effectively, exacerbating instability. If capital surges accelerate demand beyond the capacity of the economy, they may also create inflationary pressures. Box 7.5 discusses the exchange rate effects further. For some countries, the boom in capital flows is a high risk venture that threatens national control over key monetary variables. In Argentina, for example, in 1992 the country received about $12 billion in capital inflows—roughly half the stock of domestically generated financial assets. It is no wonder that the exchange rate became overvalued with this surge in demand for Argentine assets in the international market.[26]

Financial innovation and international capital flows have decreased the degrees of freedom available to Latin American policy makers.[27] The speed of international capital markets requires greater flexibility in economic instruments; paradoxically, it also demands stability. Instantaneous movement of capital implies that markets are overly responsive to small policy mistakes, increasing the tendency toward instability.[28] The policy makers' tightrope is more threatening in international markets. Capital inflows, while acting as a spur to development, can also have a high cost.

INTERNATIONAL CAPITAL FLOWS AND DOMESTIC BANKING

A strong banking system can serve to dampen domestic macroeconomic instability. Under a sound banking system, if domestic investors decide to sell long-term financial assets, they move into domestic bank deposits. That is, if in the United States you are uncertain about the performance of the stock market or long-term mutual funds, you might opt for the safety of a certificate of deposit or CD. As people move into CDs, the greater availability of funds makes it easier to lend to companies, and expansion is encouraged, counteracting the downward trend in the market. However, if there is a lack of confidence in the banking sector, the substitute is international instruments or **capital flight**.[29] When banks fail to provide domestic intermediation, the effects of crises are magnified. Furthermore, as has been demonstrated in the Asian financial crisis of 1997–1998, if domestic loans to large conglomerates—or, in the Latin case, *grupos*—sidestepped sound accounting procedures, a downturn may result in a resounding crash. The Chilean crisis in 1982–1993 and the Mexican crisis were exacerbated by loans made to huge conglomerates riding high on overinflated asset prices without corresponding real collateral to secure the megaloans. When the crisis hit in each country—and later in Asia—the high percentage of nonperforming loans magnified the contractionary effects on the economic system. Weak banks exacerbated rather than minimized the crisis.

The banking sector in Latin America was relatively fragile in the beginning of the 1990s. Years of high inflation and fiscal mismanagement had weakened the sector. **Capital controls** during the 1980s restricted competition, technological advances lagged, and most banking relationships were driven by personal or political ties.[30] The 1990s heralded a new era of openness, but institutional development is often slow. Privatization in Mexico, for example, led to a high degree of concentration, with fifty-eight institutions consolidated into eighteen commercial banks, of

Box 7.5. Exchange Rate Policy and New International Capital Flows

In the wake of the Asian currency crises, there has been much discussion about alternative exchange rate regimes in an era of highly mobile capital. Policy makers face a choice in terms of fixing the exchange rate to an international currency or basket of currencies, or allowing currencies to float to their market-determined value. Whereas a floating currency that loses value is called depreciated, devaluation refers to a government change in the value of a currency fixed in terms of another. We remember from chapter 3 that devaluation makes exports more competitive, can create new jobs, and may permit governments to offer lower interest rates because they no longer have to maintain an artificially high level to shore up the currency. The costs of devaluation include the fact that imports are more expensive and confidence in the currency is threatened.

Confidence is the key to avoiding speculative attacks on your currency. By fixing your currency in terms of another, you are promising international markets that you will maintain the currency's value. Devaluation breaks the trust that currency traders, exporters, and importers have placed in your government. In locking your currency, you have pledged to use other economic tools—such as a restrictive monetary policy—to promote equilibrium. With the integration of global capital markets, broken promises carry larger penalties: with the stroke of a key, footloose capital finds a more secure haven. Minor adjustments of the exchange rate—long a policy tool—may be met with massive capital outflows by fickle investors. Countries linked through regional trading blocs may also suffer contagion effects as nervous investors pull out. Governments are then forced to offer exorbitant interest rates to bribe financial capital to stay, while simultaneously putting at risk business borrowers in need of loans to expand productive activity. Stabilization becomes excessively recessionary. Direct currency intervention in foreign exchange markets through buying the national currency with scarce international reserves is also very costly.

Some governments have responded to the demand for global investor confidence by removing the devaluation tool from policy makers' hands. Argentina, for example, with its currency board, by law rules out the possibility of devaluation. Of course, laws could be changed, but they are far less likely to be modified than the monthly course of a central bank's policy.

The other response is to simply let your currency float. If the currency value falls—depreciation in this case—the government is not obliged to defend the value with counterproductive high interest rates or direct foreign exchange interventions. Mexico adopted floating rates following the peso crisis of 1994–1995, when it simply could not withstand currency market attacks. Brazil abandoned its inflation lock on the real when it devalued for one day before cracking under market pressure to institute a float in January 1999. The downside to this strategy is that without the exchange rate anchor, other tools must be employed in the fight against inflation.

Given the problems of exchange rate regimes with highly integrated global capital, critics have suggested a change in the international rules of the game. In part the problem of developing country currency crises derives from the fact that international capital is highly mobile in integrated markets operating under a global system of flexible exchange rates. The big players float (or, in the case of the European Union, link to one another) while less influential countries tie their fortunes to a central currency. Some believe that a return to a fixed exchange rate system like the one that operated under Bretton Woods would cut the flows of speculative capital. In this scheme, everyone's currency is fixed, decreasing the incentive for speculation against a weak regime member. Others suggest a tax on speculative capital flows to slow the wheels of short-term finance. Finally, there has been a call for strengthening the early warning and rescue capabilities of the IMF to assist with stabilization policies.

Source: Robert Kuttner, "What Sank Asia? Money Sloshing Around the World," *Business Week*, 27 July 1998, p. 16; and Sylvia Nasar, "The Cure That Can Sometimes Kill the Patient," *New York Times*, 19 July 1998, p. 16.

which six were considered national, with the balance regional. As noted in chapter 6, the speed of privatization—a bank was sold every three weeks—led to improper asset valuation, sloppy accounting, and a tendency toward political expediency in sales.[31] Few developing countries can muster the institutional resources necessary for a strong, functioning independent regulatory authority.[32] Paradoxically, liberalization of capital markets decreases the ability and increases the need for sound government oversight at the national and international levels of lending practices of banks.[33] Opening up too fast may overwhelm institutional capacities to behave as financial watchdogs.

To deepen capital markets, necessary ingredients include macroeconomic stability, a sound legal framework, an efficient and reliable clearing and settlement system, an adequate accounting system, an efficient microstructure for trading securities, and a proper regulatory and supervisory framework.[34] However, this kind of institution building may take time. Some have suggested that financial liberalization may have taken place too quickly, not giving markets enough time to develop appropriate institutions.[35] In the Mexican case, for example, reprivatization of banks was simultaneously accompanied by lifting constraints on credit expansion. Overzealous lending without adequate supervision may have contributed to the depth of the ensuing financial crisis. Time and timing of changes matter. In the interim, the policy question becomes how to decrease the vulnerability of domestic financial systems to crisis and instability while strengthening financial institutions.

The Mexican Peso Crisis

The Mexican peso crisis of 1994–1995 highlights the problematic effects of international capital flows for internal macroeconomic stability. It underscores the conflict between domestic stabilization and attending to the international concerns of international capital in policy making. How should authorities balance national domestic concerns such as inflation and unemployment against external constraints of exchange rate stability and current accounts when there are two different judges of success: voters and international capital?

Mexico had become a darling of the international community. A poster child for liberalization, the country had, since the 1982 debt crisis, undertaken tough reform measures including fiscal stabilization, privatization, and the opening of internal markets to international trade. Markets were eager to lend to this nation that had battled budget deficits and revamped the rules of doing business. Unlike conditions during the debt crisis of the 1980s, much of the lending was in the private sector. Between 1987 and 1994 commercial credit expanded by more than 100 percent, with credits for housing ballooning 100 percent and consumption credit growing by 450 percent. GDP growth was strong, and prices were steady. Two-thirds of the $91 billion inflows were portfolio investments, quickly attracted to high returns in the new Mexico. Implementation of NAFTA promised new gains in markets and productivity. Relatively low interest rates in the United States made the returns in Mexico particularly lucrative. Mexican markets were hot.

This optimism created an asset price boom in Mexico. As investors were attracted to high returns, others, afraid to miss out on the rising market, jumped on the bandwagon. Incentives in the investment industry tend to draw clients in on an upward trend. Brokers are more frequently fired for missing a great opportunity than for crashing when everyone else around them is also falling.[36] Upward trends tend to reinforce themselves, overshooting real values, creating a divergence between the true investment potential and the asset bubble. Of course, the further the investment gets from its fundamental value, the harder is the landing when the market corrects itself. Small events can lead to major speculative attacks as investors who jumped on the bandwagon knowing little about the investment overreact without taking the time to get better information. Unfortunately, those who pay the highest price for the crash—like the poor Mexicans who must bear the brunt of adjustment—are not necessarily those involved in creating the speculative bubble.

Oddly, in the midst of Mexico market euphoria, the true performance of the Mexican economy was below the glowing predictions. Although both multilateral agencies such as the IMF and private sector firms such as Bear Sterns painted a rosy picture, actual performance fell short of potential. While Mexico was being certified as low risk, investment-grade potential by J. P. Morgan and being heralded as a success story by the World Bank, real exchange rate appreciation caused by capital inflows was sending the wrong signal to the real sector, eroding competitiveness.[37] The same price for the exchange rate was not clearing both financial and tradable goods markets.

Warning signs of unsustainability of the Mexican situation and an impending crisis appeared on the horizon. The Mexican peso began to appreciate substantially as a result of capital inflow. Adjusted for inflation differences with the United States, some estimated it was overvalued by 30 percent. Others, including those within the Mexican government, contended that the appreciation was warranted by the improved productive potential of the Mexican economy. They argued that the currency was not overvalued but reflecting stronger GDP growth. Why, they reasoned, would private capital continue to flow in if the underlying fundamentals weren't sound?

Nonetheless, there was a clear cost to the external account imbalance. Figure 7.4 shows that by 1994 Mexico's ballooning current account deficit had nearly reached 8 percent of GDP. Was this sustainable? We remember that deficits on the current account, composed primarily of an excess of imports over exports, must be financed by surpluses on the capital account. Indeed, if imports are used to enhance productive potential (as opposed to luxury consumption), and if international capital is willing to finance these investments, trade deficits are not necessarily a bad thing. The question of sustainability revolves around the willingness of international markets to continue to supply funds to cover the deficits. If investors continued to believe that Mexico's future performance outpaced other alternatives, deficits could be sustained. Because inflows were largely private—albeit short-term—capital, Mexican authorities contended that they were a simple market reflection of Mexico's new growth potential.

Whether or not this argument was accurate, it was certainly politically expedient. The ruling party of Mexico, the PRI, was facing its first real electoral challenge

Figure 7.4.   Mexico's Current Account Deficit, 1985–1994

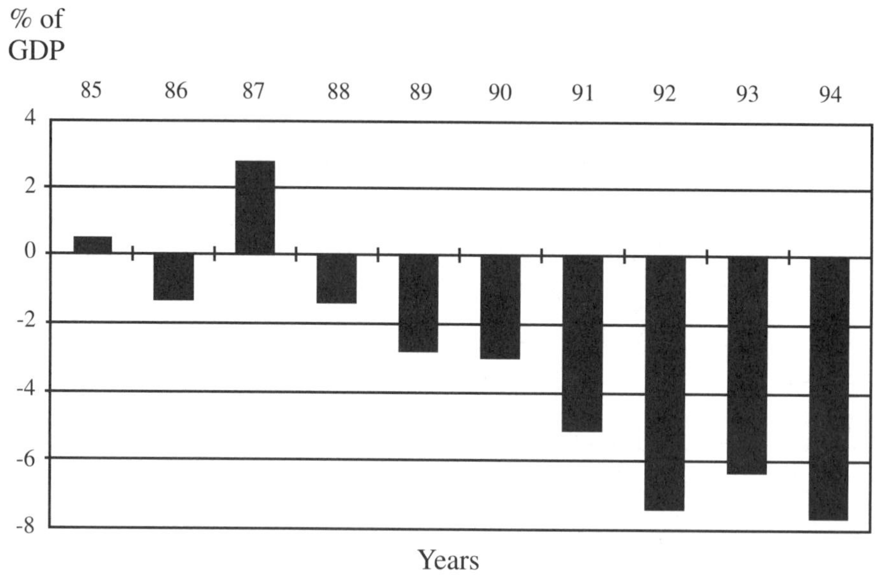

% of
GDP

Years

Source: Stephany Griffith-Jones, "The Mexican Peso Crisis," *CEPAL Review* 60 (December 1996): 155–175.

from both the right and the left since the Mexican Revolution. Selling economic stability and the success of the Mexican liberalization plan were central to reelection efforts.

In hindsight we can see the folly of this argument. We can analyze current account sustainability through a simple formula:

$$C/y = gk*$$

C, or the current account, as a percentage of y, gross domestic product, should be equal to the real growth rate of the economy, called g, times k*, or international investors' willingness to expose themselves to that nation's financial instruments, also as a percentage of GDP. The logic of this formula comes from the balance of payments rule that to be sustainable, a current account deficit must be financed by capital inflows. The allowable size of the deficit will vary with the growth rate of the country and foreigners' interest in holding that nation's liabilities. This willingness, as expressed here by k*, is largely determined by investors' assessment of the risk involved in holding the securities as well as the difference in expected returns between investments at home and abroad. A Mexican treasury bond is seen to be riskier than one issued by Uncle Sam; therefore, the Mexican government will have to offer higher interest rates to compensate investors for risk.

If we assume that initially a country is in a steady state, and we observe in this case that foreigners are interested in holding liabilities equal to 50 percent of GDP, and if the growth rate of GDP is 4 percent, a current account deficit of 2 percent of GDP is sustainable. (Fifty percent or one-half of 4 percent is 2 percent.) If, however, investors believe that risk has decreased or that expected returns have risen, say to 75 percent, the same rate of growth will sustain a 3 percent deficit. (Three-quarters or 75 percent of 4 percent is 3 percent.) Indeed, at their peak, foreign holdings of Mexican securities were in the 50 percent range, and growth was under 4 percent. By this formula, Mexico should have had a current account deficit of between 2 and 3 percent, not the nearly $50 billion, or 8 percent, shown in figure 7.5. Moreover, not only were deficits too high, but exchange rates overvalued by capital inflows indicated that they would continue to rise. Again in figure 7.5, we see a fall in the real exchange rate, indicating an overvaluation on the order of 30 percent.

Authorities ignored these signs and struggled to maintain market confidence, continually pointing to the soundness of the Mexican economy. Because disequilibrium in accounts was lodged in the private sector, they contended that private market price signals should eventually correct this distortion. We don't know whether this self-correction would have taken place in the long run. In the interim, political crises spooked markets. In January 1994, an armed uprising in the poor southern region of Chiapas by insurgent rebels panicked investors. Presidential candidate Luis Donaldo Colosio was then assassinated in the March before the August elections. The selection of lesser-known Ernesto Zedillo Ponce de Leon as candidate did little to quell suspicions of Mexico's instability. Pressing social and

Figure 7.5.   Current Account Deficit and the Real Exchange Rate

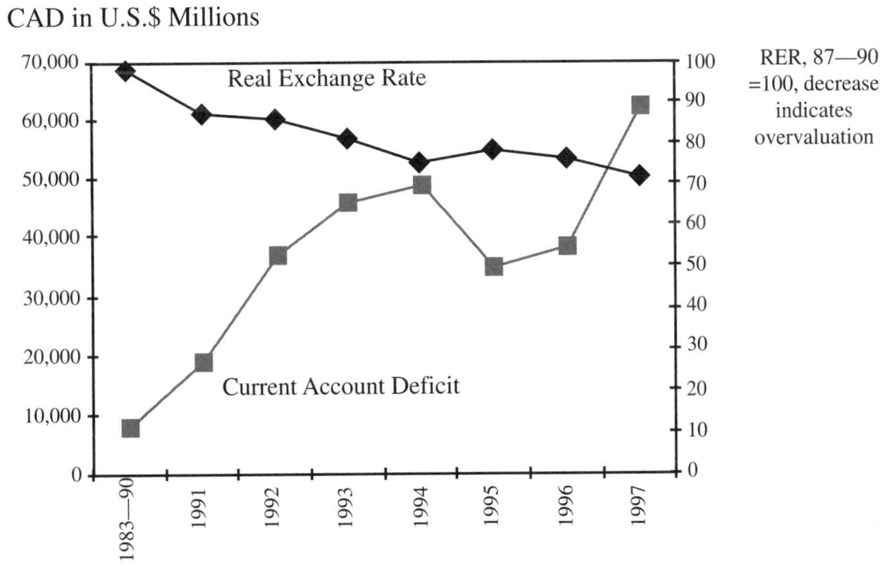

CAD in U.S.$ Millions

Source: Ricardo Ffrench-Davis, "Policy Implication of the Tequila Effect," *Challenge* (March–April 1998): 36.

political problems threatened economic gains. Investors began to wonder if Mexico was a political backwater or a strong emerging nation.

International capital began to vote with its feet. Because capital moves faster than trade patterns can adjust, Mexico's balance of payments deficits were being financed by dwindling international reserves. As importers went to the central bank to get dollars to pay suppliers, fewer dollars were available. To maintain the exchange rate, the central bank was forced to supply dollars from reserves. Mexico reportedly spent U.S.$10 billion from March through May attempting to defend the peso in the wake of the Colosio assassination, although lags in the release of data decreased the transparency of events to the international community. The exchange rate, set using a crawling band, was under severe pressure, yet the government did not want to fuel inflationary expectations with a devaluation.

Nonetheless, knowing that the Bank of Mexico did not have the capacity to stem the outflow, both domestic and international investors came to expect a large devaluation to correct the trade imbalance. At the same time, the government didn't want to raise interest rates to keep capital at home, because this would have a recessionary effect on the domestic economy. Because the risk premium for holding foreign securities includes foreign exchange rate risk, investors needed to be compensated for the fact that if the devaluation took place, their assets would be worth less. If you are holding a financial instrument denominated in pesos and the peso is worth less, your asset value falls by the same proportion. To entice capital to stay, the government began to offer dollar-denominated treasury bonds, called **tesobonos**, to replace the peso-denominated cetes. In creating this option, the Mexican government essentially internalized the currency devaluation risk, simultaneously trying to send a signal that it perceived that the crisis was caused by short-term political factors. These would soon blow over, it argued, rendering a megadevaluation unnecessary.

Ruling party PRI candidate Zedillo was elected president in August, and to the surprise of many in the international financial community, the government did not alter the exchange rate or the monetary or fiscal stance. With the support of business and labor under Mexico's Pacto, President Salinas and President-elect Zedillo forged ahead. The hope was that business as usual would reassure markets that the turbulence was temporary and Mexico was ready to resume course. Mexican officials declared that a devaluation was out of the question.

But markets were unconvinced. By the end of November, reserves of $12.5 billion were insufficient to cover even half of the $27 billion short-term public debt, 70 percent of it in dollar-denominated tesobonos. When reserves reached critically low levels of around $6 billion in December, the government had little choice but to devalue. It adjusted the band on the peso by 15 percent. However, this attempt to release a little steam exploded. Investors felt they had been deceived by Mexican authorities. Although instruments were dollar denominated, there was a lack of confidence that the government would be able to honor its obligations. The devaluation was not accompanied by any policy changes to assure markets that the disequilibrium would be addressed, and capital took a fast flight out of Mexico. After the Mexican government lost $4 billion in one day trying to defend the peso, it had no choice but to let it float—or, more appropriately, let it sink like lead—in international markets.

Emergency measures were taken to rescue the Mexican economy. An agreement with U.S., Canadian, and European banks allowed for $7 billion of financial guarantees to back the maturing short-term tesobonos coming due. Belated measures were taken to restructure the economy. The pace of privatization was quickened in railroads, satellites, and ports. The banking system was opened to foreign investment, labor unions agreed to hold down wages, and the government cut spending. Interest rates rose to 55 percent to hold investors at home, but this created a recessionary drag on the economy. Investor confidence further deteriorated, and uncertainty was extended to other Latin American economies. This so-called tequila effect created regional pressure, especially for Argentina with its currency board, to readjust internal accounts. Other Latin American countries were guilty by association.

Mexican adjustments were too little, too late. The initial devaluation had been announced in a policy vacuum, creating a panic disproportionate to the underlying fundamentals in the economy. As a result of consulting domestic business and labor prior to the devaluation, capital anticipated the devaluation, further depleting reserves. Timing was bad. The announcement of the devaluation took place on a Tuesday, prior to Christmas. Fridays are better bad news days, giving investors the weekend to calm down before markets reopen for the week. Furthermore, holiday markets were thin, so there were fewer engaged in fishing the bottom for great deals to counter the downward market trend. Finally, the new administration's finance minister had yet to solidify ties with the international financial community. When panic erupted, there were few calming voices of reason because hardly anyone had the inside scoop as to the government's intentions. Credibility and confidence were shaken.

After conditions deteriorated further, the United States proposed a rescue package in January to assist its southern neighbor. Isolationist forces in the U.S. Congress resisted, and President Clinton, not willing to see the positive gains Mexico had achieved through liberalization evaporate, used his own emergency authorities to provide loan relief. The IMF and the Bank for International Settlements (the banker's bank) came up with $17.8 billion and $10 billion in loans, respectively, all of which collateralized by Mexico's oil reserves. With a concerted international rescue, markets settled and Mexico began another long and painful climb to economic recovery.

Several lessons emerged from the crisis. First is the importance of maintaining sustainable current account performance. Given confidence and economic growth, a sustainable deficit should not exceed 3 percent of GDP.[38] The composition of capital inflows to sustain the deficit is critical. Short-term capital inflows are extremely sensitive to political events. Changes to rely less on short-term international capital and more on internal sources of savings will encourage longer-term stable growth. Finally, the inflexibility of the exchange rate as an inflation anchor can be dangerous as economic fundamentals move out of line. The anchor becomes something of an albatross weighing down the process of flexible adjustment.

THE CHILEAN CASE: REGULATING GLOBAL INFLOWS

The rise and fall of the Mexican economy in the mid-1990s prompted a search for alternatives to the volatility of hot capital flows. Portfolio investments are tied to stock prices, reflecting increases in the real value of firms, and short-term capital flows or hot money respond to interest rate differentials or the expected appreciation of the currency—in Chile's case, the peso.[39] Speculative portfolio inflows rose in the early 1990s, concerning policy makers. Much attention was paid to the Chilean case. In Chile, net capital inflows ranged from 11 percent to 18 percent of GDP from 1979 to 1981. Over the period 1990–1993, the low was 1.9 percent and the high was 7.6 percent.[40] The composition of flows changed markedly as well, moving from medium- and long-term loans in the earlier period to foreign direct investment and Chilean investment abroad as well as portfolio investments and hot money in the 1990s. Laws governing foreign direct investment in Chile are highly favorable to foreign capital. The bulk of FDI in Chile has been in the export sectors, with over half in mining alone. Laws governing the outflow of capital were liberalized in 1991, leading to significant investment abroad. In a new twist, Chilean companies poured billions into the rest of Latin America, the bulk of which flowed into just three countries: Argentina, Bolivia, and Peru. In Argentina, Chileans command a large share of the privatized electricity business as well as owning assets in ceramics, disposable diapers, bottled gas, welded products, caddies, cables, and industrial oils. They operate the railways in Bolivia. In Peru, Chileans direct the fast-expanding pension fund industry and make everything from copper wire to spaghetti.[41]

Although new capital flows may appear to be beneficial, the effects on the exchange rate are the dark side of the inflow of speculative money. The Chilean development model is driven by the export sector. Throughout Latin America, structural adjustment was led by the export sector, yet paradoxically, good performance was rewarded by capital inflows that appreciated the currency and retarded export performance. Accounting for more than one-third of GDP, the diversified export sector has been a source of dynamism in Chilean growth. To the degree that capital inflows appreciate the peso, these financial flows undermine efforts in the real economy.[42] Ironically, countries can be hurt by their own successful adjustment. As the international market sees the assets of a country as a good investment, inflows appreciate the exchange rate, choking off the export drive that made for the success in the first place. The real exchange rate appreciation caused by capital inflows works against international competitiveness.[43]

The policy dilemma becomes balancing external sector growth and internal stability. What should be done to offset these negative effects of financial flows? The Chilean central bank and ministry of finance utilized a combination of pragmatic measures designed to reduce short-term inflows. These included regulating short-term movements through reserve requirements, quotas, and fees; foreign exchange market intervention; and sterilizing the monetary effect of foreign exchange.[44] The goal of this policy has been to expand the leeway for domestic monetary policy by increasing domestic savings and decreasing the flow of international hot money.[45] Pragmatic management of the exchange rate has reduced

Chile's vulnerability to capital swings, allowing it to pursue a more stable path in a highly liberalized market regime. The Chilean government has employed a crawling band system pegged to three international currencies; the peso has performed at the bottom of the band, indicating that appreciation would have been larger without intervention.[46] This is a case of government policy augmenting the stability of markets—and not the kind of zealous free market wizardry often associated with the Chilean model. The Chilean government also promoted foreign direct investment, in both traditional and nontraditional exports. Four out of the five largest fruit companies (which together account for one-half of fruit exports) are transnational corporations. Several new mining projects involve TNCs. Capital continues to enter Chile, but it is on Chilean terms.

The downside to capital controls includes the fact that they are difficult to enforce, may signal risk and therefore drive up capital prices, and, if effective in the short term, may delay needed economic reforms. Furthermore, few countries have the long track record of adjustment demonstrated by Chile. Whereas the Chilean government has the accumulated credibility to apply brakes without coming to a screeching stop, other economies could be devastated by a chilly signal to international markets.

THE ASIAN ECONOMIC CRISIS AND THE CONTAGION EFFECT

The dilemma of how to slow capital inflows may be a moot point in the face of new apprehension about emerging market investments in the wake of the Asian crisis. In the summer of 1997, the currencies of Thailand, Malaysia, and Korea came under attack. The loss of confidence in the once heralded "Asian Tigers" quickly spread not only throughout Southeast Asia but to all emerging economies. Beset by the contagion effect, Latin America was confronted with a crisis not of its own making. Despite nearly two decades of adjustment since the eruption of the debt crisis in 1982, regional economies were challenged by a global loss of investor confidence in developing economies. The nosedive in stock and bond markets throughout the region had little to do with underlying economic fundamentals. Capital frightened of any emerging market risk indiscriminately pulled out of the region, leaving governments to sustain policies structured around open markets and the infusion of capital from abroad. Governments were forced to raise domestic interest rates as a means of bribing capital to stay at home. High domestic interest rates had contractionary effects on growth and increased unemployment. International commodity prices have also fallen as a result of global recessions. Sugar prices fell 21.14 percent, copper was down 22.7 percent, coffee declined 29.35 percent, and oil lost 32.6 percent with weakened Asian markets.[47] For commodity exporters such as Chile, this translates into balance of payments problems on the current account. The 30 percent devaluations of East Asian currencies have also made manufactured goods from Korea, Malaysia, Thailand, Indonesia, and the Philippines more competitive in world markets, where they may be competing against goods from the larger Latin American industrial producers in Brazil and

Mexico. Adjusting for the overvaluations throughout Latin America, the real cross-rate devaluations for South Korea, for example, range from 78.8 percent for Venezuela to 45.8 percent for Brazil. This is a hefty price difference for Brazilian or Venezuelan firms competing in international markets![48] Unfortunately, competitive devaluations by Latin American governments may lead to a feared resurgence in inflation.

When the Russian ruble collapsed in 1998, eyes turned to the last bulwark against total collapse in emerging markets: Brazil. In Brazil, the black market rate for dollars rose from the normal range of 2 cents over the official exchange rate to 30 cents, evidencing the stronger demand to convert into dollars, perhaps to send to bank accounts in Miami. Reserves fell by between $500 million and $1 billion a day in the wake of the uncertainty created by the Russian ruble.[49] The timing of the crisis was particularly unfortunate. President Fernando Henrique Cardoso, the architect of the Brazilian Real plan, was engaged in a contest for reelection with left-leaning "Lula," the nickname for contender Luis Inacio da Silva. Having already raised domestic interest rates, Cardoso was reluctant to further clamp down on the economy and irritate the vote of labor. Although he won the election, the margin was thin, reflecting national frustration with stabilization-induced high unemployment. After the election, Cardoso announced a fiscal austerity plan, including $20 billion in budget cuts. Devaluation, a key to increasing exports and jobs, was feared because of the possibility of reigniting inflation. The international community, perhaps belatedly, recognized the importance of Brazil, with an economy larger than those of South Korea, Thailand, and Malaysia combined.[50] It made ready a $41.5 billion dollar IMF standby package to avoid seeing Brazil and the $800 billion Brazilian economy join Indonesia and other Southeast Asian nations in the international intensive care ward.[51]

The Asian crisis highlights the fickle nature of international capital flows. Apart from the problem with commodity prices, the difficulties facing Latin America are in large measure stemming from a change in global risk aversion. Based on the fall of Asian markets, investors have become wary of emerging market investments, without making distinctions for country performance. Said Chilean Finance Minister Eduardo Aninat, "It's the packaging effect. Analysts don't differentiate between regions, countries, or sectors anymore."[52] The difficulties facing Asian economies—especially the closed nature of business dealings dominated by cronyism—had already been in large part addressed through the painful adjustment of the 1980s and 1990s. Yet the rewards for good market behavior were not forthcoming.

International investor uncertainty was intensified by the reluctance of Brazilian politicians to pass Cardoso's budget. The ballooning government deficit had reached 8 percent of GDP and pushed domestic short-term interest rates above 40 percent in October 1998. A preliminary rejection of a key component of the plan, an increase in private contributions to the generous state-supported pension fund, frightened already jittery investors in early December. Local political feuds exacerbated uncertainty as the governor of a powerful state (and former president of the country Itamar Franco) declared a unilateral moratorium on obligations owed to the federal treasury. Fearing that Brazil would not be able to meet its financial obligations, investors began pulling out. Capital outflows accelerated. As international reserves plummeted, the government found it impossible to defend the Brazilian real and engineered an 8 percent devaluation on January 13 to relieve the pressure. Investors, having been burned by Asian devaluations, interpreted this as a sign of weakness and fled even faster. The Brazilian government was forced to abandon the Real plan, which had anchored the economy from inflation since 1994, and simply floated the currency on world markets. The currency fell another 20 percent, although stock markets in Brazil rallied on the news that the government would not continue to be bled of reserves in an uphill battle to defend the currency.

The price shock to Brazilians was dramatic. Imagine a Brazilian family with a child in an American university. Within days, the cost of tuition increased 30–40 percent. Many Brazilians who traveled during the holidays returned home to credit card bills now inflated by one-third or more. Import prices for medicines and supplies rose.[53] As the new, higher costs work their way through the supply chain, the specter of inflation rose on the Brazilian horizon. Tough contractionary measures, however, resulted in recession. Congress passed painful tax increases and cut government workers, although much tough work remains on the fiscal front. Auto workers in Brazil's multinational factories were laid off. The ramifications may extend to the U.S. balance of payments as this fifteenth largest trading partner is poised for a tailspin. Argentina, linked to Brazil through the Mercosur common market, found its trade balance under pressure.[54] Fearing a run on its currency by guilt of geographical association, the Argentines proposed abandoning the peso and substituting the U.S. dollar as the unit of value. International capital mobility left those in South America reeling in 1999.

LESSONS FOR CAPITAL MOBILITY: QUESTIONS OF FINANCIAL SECTOR REFORM

The vulnerability of Latin America to the Asian and Russian crises has renewed questions with respect to the sustainability of the externally driven model versus the need to promote stable domestic growth. Maintaining strong capital inflows over time will require either higher interest rates for bonds or loans or improved profitability of equity investments. Higher interest rates have a clear domestic cost. If higher rates are offered to attract capital, the domestic cost to borrowers—the firms that want to use this capital to expand—is necessarily higher. This also increases the cost to the government of servicing publicly held domestic debt.[55] Higher interest rates therefore act as a drag on productive domestic investment. They may also create pressures to appreciate the currency, making it more difficult for exporting firms and pressuring the balance of payments. Once again the exchange rate paradox emerges, because one indicator of country risk is a trade deficit.

Playing with the price of money is therefore unlikely to work in the long run. For capital inflows to remain stable, financial investments must be translated into real gains in productivity. If a disproportionate share of investments is directed toward the stock market or consumption, asset bubbles and imbalances will emerge.[56] Firms can be made more profitable through productivity improvements, but this is tough work. The "easy" stage of reorganization driven by privatization efforts is coming to a close. Firms will be forced to focus on long-run efforts to improve productivity, including human capital investments in health and education. Unfortunately, these take time and are not costless.

To escape the vicious circle of external vulnerability and internal recession, two other domestic policy possibilities emerge. Decreasing consumption in favor of domestic savings may lower the reliance on capital inflows for growth. Savings rates in the region have remained flat, at rates incompatible with sustainable growth. One of the reasons Latin American countries have been so vulnerable to international capital flows is the underdeveloped nature of long-term capital markets. In 1995 Brazil's savings was 20.3 percent, Argentina's 18.8 percent, and Mexico's only 14 percent; savings rates in Asia range around 30 percent. Chile, at 27 percent, is the only Latin American country that comes close to the Asian average.[57] Coupled with a sound banking structure, Chile's high rate of saving, related to its private pension funds, may have softened the "tequila effect" of the Mexican peso crisis.[58] For other countries, increased reliance on domestic savings would reduce volatility, making them less vulnerable to the sudden withdrawal of foreign money. Changing savings rates, however, is a difficult long-term process. Rather than save, many Latin Americans have chosen to consume, particularly as overvalued exchange rates encouraged the purchase of imports. Weaning a country off capital flows requires substituting domestic for foreign savings to maintain growth. Encouraging savings may be accomplished by changing the relative opportunity cost of consuming today as compared to saving for tomorrow. Nevertheless, it is rarely popular with voters.

The second alternative is to promote tradable goods (exports) over nontradables, to strengthen the balance of payments. However, where the exchange rate is fixed in terms of the dollar, and thus represents a real and psychological anchor against inflation, changing relative prices between imports and exports becomes problematic.[59] Furthermore, primary product exports have their own source of instability. We will turn to the possibilities and limitations offered by the tradable goods sector in the next chapter.

In addition to changes that developing countries themselves might implement, others have suggested that the architecture of the global economy needs revision. Some contend that the IMF is too weak to grapple with the force and the ramifications of international capital flows, and that the lending authority of the IMF may be too limited to deal with the needs of large countries such as Brazil or Mexico. They argue for an effective lender of last resort, much like the U.S. Federal Reserve system for domestic banks. International financier George Soros, believing that "international capital movements need to be supervised and the allocation of credit regulated," has called for the establishment of an international credit insurance corporation.[60] Diagnosing financial instability as in part caused by a "great asymmetry between an increasingly sophisticated and dynamic international financial market and the existing institutional arrangements, which are inadequate to regulate it," ECLAC has called for a new institutional framework.[61] Arguing that the international community helps to create speculative crises, with risk-rating agencies drawing attention to "hot" countries, thus creating bubbles bound to burst, ECLAC urges negotiations to establish an institutional framework capable of providing accurate information in an increasingly sophisticated and dynamic international financial world.[62]

Others suggest, however, that an expansion of lending capabilities of the IMF or a new financial institution would create a moral hazard. That is, countries might act irresponsibly knowing that the IMF would be there to bail them out. This contention, however, is countered by those who say that governments would not risk paying the political price of austerity measures for some short-term emergency capital. The costs of adjustment are simply too high. At issue in policy circles is whether a new framework to provide enhanced international stewardship through improved early warning and data collection, as well as greater accountability to strengthened international regulations and accounting practices, might smooth the volatility—and its associated costs—in the international financial system.[63] The IMF itself is working to promote better transparency and dissemination of data, especially on short-term debt, but as Deputy Managing Director Stanley Fischer points out, change can be accomplished only with the full support of the IMF's 182 member countries.[64] The IMF has encouraged members to release public information notices, letters of interest, and policy framework papers that accompany IMF consultations; indeed, with member consent, some of these documents can be found posted on the IMF web page.[65] The IMF is also encouraging better dissemination of private banking data through expanded coverage of the Bank for International Settlements (BIS) data and addressing gaps in banking supervision and adoption of standards. These efforts can be seen on the BIS homepage at www.bis.org. As noted by managing director of the IMF, Michel Camdessus, in an era of intense integration of global capital markets, the most challenging aspect of reform has been the question of involving private sector actors in forestalling and resolving crises.[66]

What to do about the problems of the instability and crises associated with international capital flows may be thought of using our three policy perspectives. A pure neoliberal approach would suggest that interfering with the market allocation of private capital would promote inefficiency. Although the neoliberal might acknowledge the costs of volatility, intervention would only slow the path of adjustment. The best policy response would be to leave the market alone. The only warranted intervention might be to strengthen and clarify regulations and standards of reporting of reporting in domestic and international financial markets such that participants could make decisions on the best available data. A neoinstitutionalist would perhaps look to see if any of the transactions costs in global capital markets might be reduced. In particular, the neoinstitutionalist might suggest that while institutional deepening is pursued, countries should pursue countervailing measures to lessen the domestic costs of short-term capital. This may, for example, include a tax on short-term interna-

> **QUESTION FOR THOUGHT**
>
> Do you believe that capital controls should be used to manage short-term capital flows? Or should international capital flows be left alone? Look at recent financial data for Mexico and Chile to substantiate your point.

tional capital flows along the lines of a Tobin tax of 0.1 percent of the value of a transaction to slow the wheels of international finance until markets could be made more efficient. The neostructuralist would be more concerned with the distributional implications of the international financial casino. The state might be called upon as a financial intermediary to generate domestic sources of savings, leaving countries less exposed to international capital flows. For example, special investment funds could be set up by the government and incentives created to promote opportunities to invest in small and medium-sized firms, increasing both savings and income flowing to smaller businesses.[67] Your vision of the appropriate role of the state may guide you in outlining preferred policy options. The roles you assign to the state and the market may have something to do with the relative weight you place on each of three objectives of financial system reform: fostering efficiency and growth by allocating capital to areas of highest returns, reducing the risks of financial crises, and softening the impact and equitably sharing the burden of adjustment when crises hit.[68]

Key Concepts

Capital controls	Foreign direct	Short-term money
Capital flight	investment	Tesobono
Equity investments	Portfolio bonds	

Chapter Summary

Capital Flows and Latin America

- In the 1990s, after the debt crisis, there was an influx of foreign capital. The new interest stemmed from changes in international financial markets as well as structural changes within Latin America which have made it a good investment risk.
- Capital inflows into Latin America can be divided into short-term and long-term capital. Short-term capital includes portfolio bonds or equity investments, which are not as preferable as foreign direct investment. However, foreign direct investment has both its pros and cons. For example FDI can represent a source of technology, increase efficiency, and generate employment with higher wages. Yet multinational corporations have also been responsible for human rights abuses and production in enclaves with low levels of linkages to the local economy. Whether a multinational is helpful or harmful is best measured on a case by case basis.
- For advocates of capital inflows, these funds represent finance that is needed to spur growth and, subsequently, savings. However, imperfect information

and thin markets, as sometimes occur in Latin America, may lead to inefficiency in the market. An influx of short-term money, such as portfolio bonds, may lead to lower interest rates, discouraging domestic savings, as well as an appreciated exchange rate, discouraging exports. It may also create inflationary pressures.

- With the liberalization of financial markets, an appropriate institutional framework is needed to provide supervision and oversight. However, the banking sector in Latin America was fragile after liberalization.

The Mexican Peso Crisis

- After engaging in a fiscal stabilization, privatization, and the opening of internal markets to international trade, Mexico was perceived to be a safe haven for investors. The optimism in the Mexican economy induced high levels of capital inflows and an appreciation of the Mexican peso. The appreciation exacerbated the current account balance, which was already at unsustainable levels, financed mostly by volatile capital inflows. After the uprising in Chiapas and the assassination of presidential candidate Luis Donaldo Colosio, investors panicked. The Mexican government, in its attempt to defend the exchange rate, saw reserves rapidly dwindling. In response to the imminent crisis, the government began to offer tesobonos, dollar-denominated treasury bonds, refusing to raise interest rates or devalue the currency. The markets were unconvinced by the attempt, and the Mexican government was forced to let the currency float and, hence, devalue. To bail out Mexico from the crisis, the Clinton administration, along with the IMF and the Bank for International Settlements, provided loan relief. Three main lessons stemmed from the Mexican peso crisis: a sustainable current account balance is important, short-term capital is volatile, and the inflexibility of the exchange rate as an inflation anchor can be dangerous.

Regulating Capital Inflows: Chile

- A strong economy and one driven by export growth, like the Chilean economy, is generally rewarded with capital inflows. As capital flows increase, the currency appreciates, choking the export sector. As a response to this dilemma, Chile established reserve requirements, quotas, and fees, as well as engaging in foreign exchange market intervention and the sterilization of the monetary effect of foreign exchange. Its aim was to reduce portfolio inflows and increase domestic saving.

Effects of the Asian and Russian Crises on Latin America

- The Asian economic crisis and the collapse of the Russian ruble had negative repercussions on Latin American economies. The loss of confidence in the

Asian Tigers spread to the Latin American region, leading to significant capital outflows, an increase in interest rates, and a loss of competitiveness for Latin American goods against cheaper Asian goods. The hardest hit country has been Brazil. It was forced to float its currency, abandon the Real plan established in 1994 as an anchor for inflation, and subsequently experience a large devaluation.

Lessons for Capital Mobility

- It is clear that capital inflows incur a cost for the domestic economy. The higher interest rates needed to attract investors also represent a higher price for domestic borrowers and, hence, negatively affect investment. They also increase the cost of servicing the publicly held domestic debt and lead to pressure for an appreciation of the currency. Two possible solutions have been suggested to deal with this dilemma. The first is decreasing current consumption in favor of domestic saving, which may reduce the reliance on capital inflows. The second is promoting tradable goods over nontradable goods. On the global scale, a form of international credit insurance corporation has been suggested. All of these have their limitations.

Notes

1. James D. Wolfensohn, remarks to the Board of Governors of the World Bank Group, 1 October 1996. LEXIS-NEXIS database.

2. "Of Cranes, Aid, and Unintended Consequences," *The Economist,* 5 October 1996, p. 70.

3. As of October 1992 U.S. authorities approved increasing the number of institutional investors, including pension plans and insurance funds, allowed to invest in privately placed securities. Standardization of legal and accounting practices between the United States and Mexico has also helped.

4. Sebastian Edwards, *Capital Flows into Latin America: A Stop-Go Story?* National Bureau of Economic Research Working Paper no. 6441 (Cambridge, Mass.: National Bureau of Economic Research, 1998), available at www.nber.org/papers/w6441. Edwards cites a 1993 IMF staff paper by Calvo and a 1997 World Bank study on capital flows.

5. Adapted from José Angel Gurría, "Capital Flows: The Mexico Case," in *Coping with Capital Surges: The Return of Finance to Latin America,* ed. Ricardo Ffrench-Davis and Stephany Griffith-Jones (Boulder, Colo.: Lynne Rienner, 1995), 189.

6. Lending directly to support trade includes bank letters of credit that provide financing for exports in transit until the importer pays for the goods, as well as commercial bank lending.

7. Depository receipts represent purchases made through another exchange. A depository receipt is a security issued by a U.S. bank in place of the foreign shares held in trust by that bank. Essentially, it is a mechanism for listing on the U.S. exchange. For example, American depository receipts could represent shares of Brazilian Telebras bought on the U.S. stock exchange. Each Telebras ADR that is traded on the New York Stock exchange

represents 1,000 preferred shares held by the bank of New York. An advantage of the ADR is that the liquidity and visibility of the stock increase. Some American retail investors by their own rules are not permitted to buy emerging market shares but can purchase an ADR. In some countries, to control capital inflows and outflows, only qualified institutional buyers approved by the central bank can invest in local shares. To qualify for an ADR the foreign firm must file with the SEC (Security and Exchange Commission) and abide by SEC rules. The costs associated with filing (e.g., registration, lawyers, and investment bankers) are high, and the requirements for listing in terms of transparency and reporting are stringent. However, the gains in increasing market size are often worth the cost.

8. World Bank, *World Development Indicators, 1997* (Washington, D.C.: World Bank, 1997), table 5.3, "About the Data."

9. John Welch, "The New Face of Latin America: Financial Flows, Markets, and Institutions in the 1990s," *Journal of Latin American Studies* 25 (1993): 1–24.

10. Ibid., 18.

11. This is unweighted by the share of a country's GDP in regional GDP; it is a straight average of foreign direct investment taken as a percentage of 1995 GDP. World Bank, *World Development Indicators, 1997.*

12. Ian Katz, "Snapping up South America," *Business Week*, 18 January 1999, p. 60.

13. Alejandro C. Vera-Vassallo, "Foreign Investment and Competitive Development in Latin America and the Caribbean," *CEPAL Review* 60 (December 1996).

14. Richard E. Caves, *Multinational Enterprise and Economic Analysis*, 2d ed. (Cambridge: Cambridge University Press, 1996), 230.

15. Mangus Blomström and Edward N. Wolff, "Multinational Corporations and Productivity Convergence in Mexico," in *Convergence of Productivity: Cross-National Studies and Historical Evidence*, ed. William Baumol, Richard R. Nelson, and Edward N. Wolff (New York: Oxford University Press, 1994), 265.

16. S. Lael Brainard and David Riker, *Are U.S. Multinationals Exporting U.S. Jobs?* National Bureau of Economic Research Working Paper no. 5958 (Cambridge, Mass.: National Bureau of Economic Research, 1997).

17. Ibid.

18. Ibid., 228.

19. Blomström and Wolff, "Multinational Corporations," 265. For a general discussion of multinationals, consult Thomas J. Biersteker, *Distortion or Development? Contending Perspectives on the Multinational Corporation* (Cambridge, Mass.: MIT Press, 1978).

20. Aaron Berstein, "Sweatshop Reform: How to Solve the Standoff," *Business Week*, 3 May 1999, p. 186.

21. Blomström and Wolff, "Multinational Corporations," 276.

22. Takashi Hikino and Alice Amsden, "Staying Behind, Stumbling Back, Sneaking Up, Soaring Ahead: Late Industrialization in Historical Perspective," in *Convergence of Productivity: Cross-National Studies and Historical Evidence*, ed. William Baumol, Richard R. Nelson, and Edward N. Wolff (New York: Oxford University Press, 1994), 291.

23. E. Borenstein, J. De Gregorio, and J. W. Lee, "How Does Foreign Investment Affect Economic Growth?" *Journal of International Economics* 45 (1998): 115–135.

24. Robert Devlin, Ricardo Ffrench-Davis, and Stephany Griffith-Jones, "Surges in Capital Flows and Development: An Overview of Policy Issues," in *Coping with Capital Surges*, ed. Ricardo French-Davis and Stephany Griffith-Jones (Boulder: Lynne Rienner, 1995), 234, 243–244; and "Some Mutual Funds Go Back Full Throttle to Emerging Markets," *The Wall Street Journal*, 12 November 1996, p. A1.

25. Devlin, Ffrench-Davis, and Griffith-Jones, "Surges in Capital Flows and Development," 243–244.

26. José María Fanelli and Roberto Frenkel, "Macropolicies for the Transition from

Stabilization to Growth," in *New Directions in Development Economics: Growth, Environmental Concerns, and Government in the 1990s,* ed. Mats Lundahl and Benno J. Ndulu (London: Routledge, 1996), 47.

27. Comment by Agustín Carstens and Moises Schwartz in *Securing Stability and Growth in Latin America,* ed. Ricardo Hausmann and Helmut Reisen (Paris: Organization for Economic Cooperation and Development, 1996), 128.

28. Comment by Charles Wyplosz in Hausmann and Reisen, *Securing Stability,* 132.

29. Liliana Rojas-Suarez and Steven R. Weisbrod, "Building Stability in Latin American Financial Markets," in *Securing Stability and Growth in Latin America,* ed. Ricardo Hausmann and Helmut Reisen (Paris: Organization for Economic Cooperation and Development, 1996), 140.

30. Walter Molano, *Financial Reverberations: The Latin American Banking System During the Mid-1990s,* working paper, SBC Warburg, April 1997, 2.

31. Ibid., 27.

32. Ethan Kapstein, "Global Rules for Global Finance," *Current History,* November 1998, p. 358.

33. Robert Wade, "The Asian Crisis and the Global Economy: Causes, Consequences and Cure," *Current History,* November 1998, p. 362.

34. Comment by Jans Blommestein in Hausmann and Reisen, *Securing Stability,* 171.

35. Stephany Griffith-Jones, "The Mexican Peso Crisis," *CEPAL Review* 60 (December 1996): 156–157.

36. Ibid., 155–175.

37. Sebastian Edwards, "The Mexican Peso Crisis: How Much Did We Know? When Did We Know It?" *World Economy* 21, no. 1 (1998): 1–7. Much of this section follows the argument Edwards makes in this article. Also see James T. Peach and Richard Adkisson, "Enabling Myths and Mexico's Economic Crises (1976–1996)," *Journal of Economic Issues* 31, no. 2 (June 1997).

38. Shahid Javed Burki and Sebastian Edwards, *Latin America after Mexico: Quickening the Pace* (Washington, D.C.: World Bank, 1996), 5.

39. If the interest rate in Chile adjusted for risk is higher than in the rest of the world, capital will flow to that higher return. If people expect an appreciation, they will purchase the currency today when it is still cheaper, making money on the transaction when it strengthens. Of course, such expectations are self-fulfilling. If the market believes a currency will rise in value, it is purchased, and its price, or value, not surprisingly increases.

40. Ricardo Ffrench-Davis, Manuel Agosin, and Andras Uthoff, "Capital Movements, Export Strategy and Macroeconomic Stability in Chile," in *Coping with Capital Surges,* ed. Ricardo Ffrench-Davis and Stephany Griffith-Jones (Boulder, Colo.: Lynne Rienner, 1995), 104.

41. Jonathan Friedland, "Their Success Earns Chileans a New Title: Ugly Pan-Americans," *The Wall Street Journal,* 3 October 1996, p. A1; and Ffrench-Davis, Agosin, and Uthoff, "Capital Movements," 114.

42. The inflow of foreign capital increases the supply of, for example, dollars. The price of dollars falls, and that of pesos rises. Remember as well that dollars coming into Chile are also purchasing Chilean assets—which increases the demand for (and the price of) pesos.

43. Edwards, *Capital Flows into Latin America.*

44. Sterilization involves an offsetting action on the part of the central bank. If, under a fixed exchange rate, foreign capital flows in, thereby increasing the money supply, the central bank can draw money out of domestic circulation to offset the capital flow.

45. Eduardo Aninat and Christian Larraín, "Capital Flows: Lessons from the Chilean Experience," *CEPAL Review* 60 (December 1996).

46. Edwards, *Capital Flows into Latin America.*

47. Warburg Dillon Read, "The Impact of the Asian Crisis on Latin America," 14 July 1998, p. 2. Fax newsletter.

48. Ibid., 5.

49. Diana Jean Schemo, "Brazilians Fret as Economic Threat Moves Closer," *New York Times*, 20 September 1998. On-line edition.

50. Paul Lewis, "Latin Americans Say Russian Default Is Hurting Their Economies," *New York Times*, 6 October 1998. On-line edition.

51. Mac Margolis, "Hat in Hand," *Newsweek*, 12 October 1998, 32B.

52. Lewis, "Latin Americans," p. A13.

53. "Brazil's Affluent Are Hurt by Crisis," *Washington Post*, 25 January 1999, p. A18.

54. Larry Rohter, "Crisis Whipsaws Brazilian Workers," *New York Times*, 16 January 1999. On-line edition.

55. Remember that a Latin American government—just like the U.S. Fed or the Bank of England—issues domestic debt to finance fiscal expenditures. If the Fed raises the interest rate, the cost of financing the U.S. debt goes up; correspondingly, when a Latin American government raises interest rates, it increases the cost of financing domestically held debt.

56. Ricardo Ffrench-Davis, "Policy Implications of the Tequila Effect," *Challenge*, March–April 1998, p. 36.

57. "A New Risk of Default," *Euromoney*, September 1996, p. 288.

58. Felipe G. Morandé, "Savings in Chile: What Went Right?" *Journal of Development Economics* 57, no. 1 (1998): 201–228.

59. This problem is discussed in José María Fanelli and José Luis Machinea, "Capital Movements in Argentina," in *Coping with Capital Surges: The Return of Finance to Latin America*, ed. Ricardo Ffrench-Davis and Stephany Griffith-Jones (Boulder, Colo.: Lynne Rienner, 1995), 183.

60. In Richard N. Haass and Robert E. Litan, "Globalization and Its Discontents," *Foreign Affairs* 77, no. 3 (1998): 4.

61. José Antonio Ocampo, "Towards a Global Solution," *ECLAC Notes* no. 1 (November 1998): 2.

62. Communique of the Economic Commission for Latin American and the Caribbean on the international financial crisis, 15 September 1998. Available at www.cepal.org. english/coverpage/financialcrisis.htm.

63. *Current History*, November 1998, includes a set of accessible articles on the global financial crisis.

64. Stanley Fischer, "Reforming World Finance," *The Economist*, 3–9 October 1998. Reproduced at www.imf.org.

65. See, for example, the May 1999 Argentine letter of interest at www.imf.org/external/np/102/1999/051099.htm.

66. Michel Camdessus, "The Private Sector in a Strengthened Global Financial System," remarks at the International Monetary Conference, Philadelphia, 8 June 1999, as posted at www.imf.org/external/speeches.

67. Lucy Conger, "A Fourth Way? The Latin American Alternative to Neoliberalism," *Current History*, November 1998, p. 380–384.

68. Michael Mussa, as reported in "Involving the Private Sector and Preventing Financial Crises," *IMF Survey* 28, no. 12 (21 June 1999): 195.

CHAPTER EIGHT

CONTEMPORARY TRADE POLICY

Engine or Brakes for Growth?

Liberalization of trade has encouraged production and processing of nontraditional exports. *(Courtesy of the Inter-American Development Bank.)*

Trade liberalization has been at the center of economic reform in Latin America. In contrast to the period of import substitution industrialization during which development strategies were internally oriented, Latin America is looking to the global market as the source of dynamic growth. In part this change in orientation was motivated by the debt crisis. Without external financing, the internal orientation of ISI was not viable over time. International trade rather than the state has become the engine for growth. Yet even without the financing constraint, many analysts argued that an open trading regime is preferable to a closed model. As globalization of trade, finance, and production came to define the international agenda, an external orientation was adopted by a wide spectrum of economists in the region as the only strategy compatible with global trends. In particular, isolation from the rapid flow of information and technology in the global system highlighted the stagnant nature of the closed model.

This chapter provides the theoretical underpinnings for the free trade argument. But some of the concerns of the ISI period about the vulnerability of less powerful nations competing in a trading arena dominated by industrial giants remain. This chapter will consider these objections and analyze policies consistent with an open trading regime that may mitigate some of the costs. To enhance the gains from trade, some advocate economic integration with other regional partners. We will therefore consider the benefits of subregional integration as well as the progress toward a hemispheric free trade agreement. Different strategies have different risks and opportunities. Free trade with a large number of partners should be weighed against the possible trade diverting effects of integration. What is clear, however, is that the orientation of Latin America toward the international trading system is a permanent change in the policy stance of regional governments.

The following questions will orient this chapter:

- What are the theoretical benefits of free trade?
- What concerns do some analysts have with the free trade model?
- What has been the record of liberalization in the region?
- Who trades what and why?
- Why have countries entered into subregional trading arrangements?
- Is a hemispheric free trade agreement desirable and feasible?

THE THEORETICAL BENEFITS OF FREE TRADE

Economists have long been enamored with the gains from free trade. In 1776 Adam Smith posited trade as the answer to a central development question: How do nations become wealthy? In contrast to the mercantilist, state-centered policies of the seventeenth and eighteenth centuries in Europe, Smith countered that nations become wealthy through open trade with each other. For Smith, open markets encouraged individuals to pursue greedy self-interest—the surplus of which could be traded for overall gain.

David Ricardo, in the nineteenth century, provided the conceptual underpinnings for the theoretical argument for free trade: the **theory of comparative advan-**

tage. In a classical model, where all factors of production can be reduced to the labor required to produce them, Ricardo showed that if each country produces the good it is relatively best at producing, world output would increase. Even if a country is absolutely better in both growing wheat and producing engines, if in comparison to another country it is relatively better at engine production, it should build engines and leave wheat to be grown elsewhere. The gains derive from the benefits of specialization.

To understand the gains, first imagine there is no trade. Each country must produce both wheat and engines. Given scarce resources (a fixed supply of labor), a certain number of each good can be produced. Because there are only two goods in this hypothetical model, we can create an internal trading price of how much wheat it would take to buy an engine. For example, we might find that each engine costs 100 bales of wheat, or each engine's trading price is $1/100$ of a bale of wheat. Now drop our imaginary trade barriers. By specializing in the product you are relatively better in, you can produce that product more cheaply than the other country. In another country each engine might cost 200 bales of wheat or each wheat $1/200$ of an engine. An engine costs more here, but wheat costs less—$1/200$ rather than $1/100$ of an engine. Furthermore, if you are the country that produces both goods well, because you are not using scarce labor to produce the good that you are only second best at, your labor can focus on machinery, your star performer.

This is analogous to the often told story of the lawyer who can type faster than her secretary. Should the lawyer type her own briefs? The answer is no, because the secretary can't appear in court to try the cases. With each person doing what she is relatively best at, the law firm will make more money. The same logic is extended to countries. Even if the United States can produce textiles and cars more cheaply than Guatemala, if textiles can be produced relatively less expensively in Guatemala, there are gains from trade.

The **Heckscher-Ohlin theorem** extends the concept of comparative advantage to a two-factor model. In the H-O model, factor proportions determine the direction of trade. A country relatively well endowed with labor should produce and export labor-intensive goods; the country with a larger proportion of capital than labor should focus on capital-intensive products. Relative costs once again drive the two-factor model. In a country where labor is abundant relative to capital, the excess supply of labor will make for lower wages and the scarcity of capital will exact higher interest rates. Producing labor-intensive products will allow the labor-abundant country to bring the cost advantage of the cheaper labor to the international market.

Two corollaries to the H-O theorem extend its range to include distributional implications. The **Stolper-Samuelson effect** indicates that if a labor-abundant country produces cheap labor-intensive goods, over time the increased international demand for these goods will raise their price and by association the price of their key input, labor. The Stolper-Samuelson effect therefore predicts that trade will initially benefit the least well-off—the poor workers. As more people in the world demand Guatemalan textiles, workers should share in the rewards. A second corollary, the **factor price equalization** theorem, suggests that as wages increase in the labor-abundant country (and fall in the capital-rich country), international prices of labor and capital will each converge. Therefore, at least in theory, there should be greater equality of prices for each factor in the international economy: both wage rates and interest rates should be nearly equal in all markets.

THE CRITIQUE OF LIBERALIZATION

The theory of free trade therefore contends that by producing in accord with comparative advantage, global output and income distribution will improve. In May of 1978, Carlos Díaz Alejandro, a Colombian economist, wrote an article in the *American Economic Review* questioning the theory of free trade in practice.[1] Using the construct of a Martian landing on earth, he challenged readers to explain why, if the theory of free trade is so compelling, haven't the gains from trade been more apparent in developing countries? Why were countries still so poor? Why were the poor workers in these countries still suffering? Why hadn't the prices of capital and labor equalized?

Problems with applying the free trade model to the real economy motivated import substitution industrialization. The developing world believed that free market trade theory wasn't benefiting them in practice. Indeed, the theory itself doesn't predict necessarily *which* country will gain from the increased production in trade, but simply that there will be gains to global welfare. In practice, developing countries perceived that the gains were accruing to the powerful industrial countries, leaving the periphery further and further behind. In particular, we remember from the discussion in chapter 2 on dependency theory the problem of declining terms of trade; control of technology in the center made it more and more difficult for the periphery countries to export a sufficient quantity of goods to purchase the high tech products. For the South, trade was therefore impoverishing. Dependence on commodity exports left countries open to export price instability. Furthermore, rather than trade improving the lives of poor workers, the belief was that multinational corporations were exploiting the cheap labor in the periphery and keeping the additional profits for themselves. The critics' solution to the unequal terms of trade was to turn inward, developing domestic industrial sectors to attend to the needs of the population.

In addition to the dependency critique, two other negative assessments of the results of trade emerged: the environmental and the gender dimensions. Environmentalists fear that specialization in accord with comparative advantage will further encourage countries to base their economies on export crops such as timber or agricultural crops such as bananas or coffee that can be environmentally damaging. Environmentalists are also concerned that in an open global trading system, companies seeking to reduce production costs will flee to those countries in the developing world with the lowest environmental standards or lax enforcement. Those concerned about the gender impli-

QUESTION FOR THOUGHT

How would you explain the results of the contemporary trading system to Díaz Alejandro's Martian?

cations of free trade point to the cases of multinational production exploiting a cheap female labor force in the developing world. Because women, with double obligations in the home and in the factory, find it difficult to organize, low wages and poor working conditions result.

WHY LIBERALIZATION? GAINS FROM TRADE IN THE 1990S

Despite concerns with respect to the benefits of trade, liberalization is on the agenda of nearly every nation in the region. Why? Economic imbalances had built up under import substitution industrialization. The overvalued exchange rates typical of the period resulted in a bias against exports. As we can see in table 8.1, by 1981 regional current account deficits had reached $42 billion annually. In 1982, no country had a positive current account balance. If you import more than you export, someone has to pay for it. Current account deficits became unsustainable without external financing.

In contrast to deteriorating performance in Latin America stood the export-oriented growth model in Asia, the success of which captured the attention of multilateral agencies as well as governments. Although the Asian model also relied in good part on an active role for the state, the IMF, the World Bank, and the IDB

Table 8.1. Current Account Balance for Latin America, 1980–1985 (U.S.$ millions)

Country	1980	1981	1982	1983	1984	1985
Argentina	−4,784.40	−4,712	−2,353	−2,495	−2,495	−952
Bolivia	6.5	−465	−173	−138	−174	−282
Brazil	−12,792.70	−11,751	−16,312	−6,837	42	−273
Chile	−1,970.50	−4,733	−2,304	−1,117	−2,111	−1,413
Colombia	−204.3	−1,961	−3,054	−3,003	−1,401	−1,809
Costa Rica	−663.1	−409	−267	−280	−151	−126
Dominican Republic	−719.5	−389	−443	−418	−163	−108
Ecuador	−669.9	−988	−1,196	−115	−273	76
El Salvador	30.6	−251	−120	−28	−54	−29
Guatemala	−163.7	−573	−399	−224	−377	−246
Honduras	−316.7	−303	−228	−219	−316	−220
Mexico	−10,753.20	−16,061	−6,307	5,403	4,194	1,130
Nicaragua	−411.2	−592	−514	−507	−597	−726
Panama	−321.6	−360	−207	337	133	123
Paraguay	−276.4	−374	−375	−248	−317	−252
Peru	−104.1	−1,728	−1,609	−872	−233	92
Uruguay	−709.1	−461	−235	−60	−133	−99
Venezuela	4,731.10	4,000	−4,246	4,427	4,651	3,327
Latin America	30,175.70	−42,633	−41,784	−8,199	−939	−2,298

Source: Inter-American Development Bank, *Economic and Social Progress in Latin America* (Washington, D.C.: Inter-American Development Bank, various years).

came to promote trade liberalization as an engine of growth. It is also important to note the change in the global context. The process of globalization—the integration of production and trade structures, the expansion of international financial markets, the information revolution that knows no borders—had transformed the way states and firms participated in the international economy. The world had changed, and Latin America needed to change with it. The game was global.

In addition to the predicted gains in resource allocation from trade in accord with comparative advantage, new protrade arguments began to dominate the liberalization debate. Openness to the international market brings with it better access to technologies, inputs to production, and a wider array of intermediate and final goods. An economy producing for the international market is also better positioned to take advantage of economies of scale in production. Also very important is the fact that opening borders to the influx of new products as well as investment by multinational firms encourages competition in the domestic market. Oligopolistic power to set prices enjoyed by large firms in protected domestic markets gives way to the competition of international markets. Production under conditions of competition not only encourages lower prices but also provides incentives to produce goods more efficiently. The shake-up of domestic industries from the challenge of international competition may create a Schumpeterian effect as firms adapt to the new business environment.[2] Participation in the international market opens firms to new ideas and the transfer of knowledge that defines success in the global economy. Indeed, improvements in productivity rates have been correlated with periods of liberalization in Latin America.[3]

How Should Liberalization Be Implemented?

Despite the gains from liberalization over time, there are also short-run costs. Tearing down trade barriers can decimate inefficient firms, putting large numbers of employees out of work. The time path of liberalization is therefore important. How quickly should it proceed? Should industries gradually adapt to international price signals, giving them time to modernize or become more efficient? In contrast, does a gradualist approach prolong the agony of adjustment, suggesting that a quick, tough shock, although painful, might be preferable? Some research indicates that a staged process of reduction works best. In the first stage tariffs might be brought down to a uniform rate of, say, 50 percent. After industries adapt to this structure, tariffs could be lowered to an across the board 10 percent rate. However, others suggest that a quick and thorough opening of the external sector is an important element in establishing credibility in the seriousness of the reform process.

In addition to the question of the time path, liberalization should be seen in the context of a package of policies to maximize its benefits. Trade liberalization without an appropriate exchange rate is dangerous. If a currency is or becomes overvalued and trade barriers are low, the country will face an explosion of imports and exporters will find it difficult to sell goods internationally. Trade liberalization may also need to be accompanied by short-term incentives from the state (perhaps financed through multilateral agencies) for export promotion. The Asian model does not indicate a free market, but one in which the state selectively promoted the growth of the export sector. In particular, firms that have been producing for domestic consumption need to learn international marketing. They may also need state assistance in the form of trade missions and financing to establish themselves abroad. Finally, trade liberalization works best when it is preceded by fiscal reform. If internal consumption—either public or private—is too high, the surplus for export disappears. Relieving pressures on the internal balance facilitates the generation of an external equilibrium. Without fiscal reform, internal interest rates may become too high, attracting short-term financial capital, leading to an appreciation of the exchange rate and thwarting export efforts. It is clear that trade liberalization must be seen in the context of overall structural reform.

The Record of Liberalization in Latin America

Average tariff rates in Latin America declined significantly over the last decade. The average tariff for the region was nearly 50 percent in 1985, with rates as high as 80 percent in Brazil and Colombia. By 1995, average tariffs in the region had come down to just above 12 percent, a radical transformation in the structure of the economies. There is far less dispersion in rates, signaling the consensus view that open economies are more conducive to growth. In table 8.2 we can see the

Table 8.2. Average Tariff in Latin America: Selected Years, 1985–1998 (percentage)

Country	1985	1986–1987	1988	1989–1990	1992	1994	1995	1998
Argentina	28	39.54	43.72	21	14.8	19.3	13.95	13.9
Bolivia	20	21.9	18.6	13.38	9.78	9.68	9.68	9.7
Brazil	80	74.06	50.55	32.38	17.6	11.26	12.59	14.6
Chile	36	20.16	15.08	14.94	10.97	10.96	10.96	11
Colombia	83	46.44	47.63	23.24	11.64	11.42	11.42	11.6
Costa Rica	53	26	n/a	n/a	n/a	n/a	11.7	n/a
Ecuador	50	41.41	39.86	32.97	11.29	11.41	11.23	11.8
El Salvador	n/a	23	n/a	n/a	n/a	n/a	9.2	n/a
Guatemala	50	25	n/a	n/a	n/a	n/a	10.8	n/a
Honduras	n/a	n/a	n/a	41.9	n/a	n/a	17.9	n/a
Mexico	34	27.83	10.59	13.1	13.11	12.76	13.69	13.2
Nicaragua	54	21	n/a	n/a	n/a	n/a	17.4	n/a
Panama	n/a	n/a	n/a	n/a	n/a	n/a	n/a	n/a
Paraguay	71.7	19.29	19.28	16	9.18	7.99	9.4	9.5
Peru	64	62.97	67.77	68.05	17.63	16.31	16.31	13.5
Uruguay	32	35.74	26.98	27.65	18.28	14.75	9.63	12.2
Venezuela	30	30.62	33.81	18.95	11.77	11.77	11.79	12
Latin America	49.98	38.18	33.99	25.61	13.28	12.51	12.35	12.09

Source: Data from Inter-American Development Bank.

high rates and variability in the tariff structure in the prereform period. Although Honduras, Nicaragua, and Peru retain higher than average tariff rates, they are relatively close to the low tariff countries of Bolivia, Uruguay, Paraguay, and El Salvador. Most of the reductions were introduced gradually over the period to soften the adjustment effects on industries, but in cases such as Peru, the tariff surgery was radical and swift, with rates falling from 68.05 percent in 1990 to 17.63 percent in 1992.

Lower tariffs and free access of goods to the region without high taxes was accompanied by a surge in growth of exports of goods and services from the region. As we note in table 8.3, the average annual export growth rate has roughly doubled in the 1990s relative to either the 1970s or the 1980s. Latin American exports for 1996 had the highest growth rate in the world at 11 percent, tripling the world average.[4] As can be seen in table 8.4, exports as a percentage of GDP averaged nearly 30 percent in 1995, representing a significant change from the precrisis export to GDP ratio of 10.7 percent. With tariff liberalization it is not surprising that the average annual rate of growth of imports and the import to GDP ratios have also risen. Indeed, this can be seen as a positive effect if the goods coming into the country introduce new technologies or better production techniques. Imports were severely curtailed during the period of adjustment imposed

Table 8.3. Rates of Growth of Exports and Imports

	Exports of Goods and Services (%)			Imports of Goods and Services (%)		
	1970–80	1980–90	1990–97	1970–80	1980–90	1990–97
Argentina	5.0	4.1	8.3	9.0	−3.8	23.1
Bolivia	1.5	2.0	6.8	3.0	0.6	7.4
Brazil	10.3	8.4	3.7	9.2	−0.1	16.5
Chile	9.5	6.8	10.1	4.6	3.2	13.5
Colombia	5.2	5.1	8.4	7.4	2.1	16.0
Costa Rica	6.6	5.4	8.6	7.6	3.1	8.2
Ecuador	13.2	4.5	7.0	9.8	−1.1	3.9
El Salvador	n/a	−4.8	13.8	n/a	−1.6	14.9
Guatemala	5.7	−1.4	6.7	4.5	−3.0	8.4
Honduras	4.3	0.3	2.0	5.1	−0.5	2.9
Mexico	7.8	6.4	12.5	12.0	4.4	12.7
Nicaragua	1.4	−4.7	10.8	7.2	1.2	7.6
Panama	9.9	6.2	n/a	5.7	2.8	n/a
Paraguay	10.5	5.5	8.2	11.2	8.1	16.1
Peru	3.3	−2.6	5.9	4.3	−1.4	12.6
Uruguay	7.0	4.6	8.7	6.7	−0.2	12.8
Venezuela	−3.5	1.7	7.3	9.2	−7.1	7.2
Latin America	4.7	4.8	8.2	8.8	0.6	13.0

Source: Data available on the World Wide Web at www.iadb.org, Statistics and Quantitative Analysis Unit.

by the debt crisis to a rate of growth of 0.6 percent; this increased to 13 percent in the 1990s. A concern with liberalization is that import growth does not outpace export performance, leaving the country to struggle with a current account deficit.

Chile provides an interesting example of trade liberalization. From an average level of 105 percent at the time of the military coup in 1973—with some tariffs reaching more than 700 percent—Chile unilaterally implemented a 10 percent tariff rate within four years of the Pinochet government. How did such a radical and rapid restructuring of the economy take place?[5] Five stages distinguished the Chilean process. After a dramatic reduction of trade barriers as part of a comprehensive stabilization package including a real exchange rate devaluation in the first period (1974–1978), the second stage was characterized by exchange rate overvaluation when the peso became the anti-inflationary anchor. During the third stage (1983–1985) Chile suffered through a temporary reversal during a deep economic crisis, while in the fourth, from 1985 to 1990, liberalization accompanied recovery. With the transition to democracy in the fifth stage, Chile began its turn to preferential trading agreements to complement its unilateral liberalization.

Foreshadowing later reform efforts in the region, economic crisis drove the adoption of a new model. Views of economists trained at the University of Chicago—later called the Chicago boys—gained ascendancy in the Pinochet regime. Criticism of the distributional implications of the open trading model were carefully voiced by economists opposed to the authoritarian regime. Nevertheless,

Table 8.4.   Latin America: Exports and Imports, 1995 (percentage of GDP)

Country	Exports/GDP	Imports/GDP
Argentina	10.58	11.51
Bolivia	23.51	26.86
Brazil	11.02	14.27
Chile	33.61	36.49
Colombia	20.95	30.95
Costa Rica	43.80	49.31
Ecuador	30.94	21.55
El Salvador	25.85	50.54
Guatemala	20.67	33.62
Honduras	32.47	46.48
Mexico	26.39	24.80
Nicaragua	19.03	35.95
Panama	100.7	98.1
Paraguay	47.16	58.74
Peru	13.13	17.99
Uruguay	22.52	28.81
Venezuela	35.97	22.37
Average	29.83	36.20

Source: Inter-American Development Bank, *Economic and Social Progress in Latin America* (Washington, D.C.: Inter-American Development Bank, various years). Available on-line at www.iadb.org/int.

when these economists came to power in the democratic transition in 1990, it became clear that the open trading model would not be altered. The consistency of policy was made possible through a variety of compensation schemes designed to buy off the losers in the liberalization and stabilization process, including owners of import-competing industries, nontradable goods industries, and labor. Export promotion schemes and assistance in export diversification channeled private sector energies from import substitution toward the external economy. Accompanying financial sector reforms reduced the prices of credit for domestic entrepreneurs. Repression of labor unions made restructuring easier on firms, albeit at a high political price. Although organizing activity was repressed, however, maintenance of real wages in labor contracts was enforced by law. Subsidies were maintained to ease the transition in the agricultural sector. The Chilean example surprisingly contains some of the elements we discussed in chapter 6 with respect to the role

Table 8.5.   Trade Performance in Three Different Periods (percentage)

	Precrisis (1974–1979)	Transition (1984–1988)	Liberalization (1989–1995)
GDP average annual growth rate			
Latin America	4.9	2.3	2.3
World	3	3	2.6
Average annual growth rate of exports			
Latin America	4.1	5.2	6.1
World	4.7	6.9	6.5
Export/GDP ratio			
Latin America	10.7	13.4	16.7
World	16.7	20.2	24.6
Average annual rate of imports			
Latin America	7.5	5.7	10.3
World	4.7	6.9	6.5
Import/GDP ratio			
Latin America	14.3	10.6	16.6
World	16.7	20.2	24.6
Average export/import ratio			
Latin America	74.9	126.6	103.2
Trade balance/GDP			
Latin America	−3.6	2.8	0.1
Total trade/GDP			
Latin America	25	23.9	33.3
World	33.4	40.4	49.2
Real effective exchange rate (1990 = 100), annual average			
Latin America	86.9	110.1	98
Real effective exchange rate change			
Latin America	1.3	2.8	−2.6

Source: Inter-American Development Bank, *Economic and Social Progress in Latin America, 1996* (Washington, D.C.: Johns Hopkins University Press, 1996), 105.

of government in an internationalized economy. As Rodrick noted, there may be an enhanced role for the state.

COMPOSITION OF GOODS

The type of goods Latin America is exporting to the rest of the world has changed over recent decades. As can be seen in table 8.6, although primary products composed 59.9 percent of exports in 1965, by 1990 they accounted for 43.1 percent, and with liberalization they accounted only for 26.6 percent of exports. Although their total value did increase marginally over the period, the surge in both traditional and nontraditional industrial exports accounts for the changing composition of trade. Nonetheless, traditional primary products still play a large role in the export profile of the region. As can be seen in table 8.7, bananas account for 38 percent of Panama's exports, 25 percent of Costa Rica's, 18 percent of Honduras's, 18 percent of Ecuador's, 8 percent of Guatemala's, and 6 percent of Colombia's. Similarly, coffee accounts for 33 percent of exports in El Salvador, 31 percent in Honduras, 22 percent in Colombia and Nicaragua, 21 percent in Guatemala, 14 percent in Costa Rica, 10 percent in Ecuador, and 5 percent in Brazil and Peru. It is interesting to compare table 8.7 with table 2.5 to see how single-product dependency has changed over time. Among Central American nations, Costa Rica has had the most success with nontraditional exports, which make up 40 percent of exports and include products such as fresh shrimp, lobster, plantains, pineapple, and macadamia nuts.[6]

> ### DATA EXERCISE
>
> Prepare a report card for the later part of the 1990s on trade performance in Latin America. What has happened to current account balances? The export to GDP ratio? The import to GDP ratio? Can you explain these trends? For trade and current data, you might want to consult the following addresses on the World Wide Web:
> ECLAC: www.eclacl.cl/english/statistics/statistics.htm
> IMF: dsbb.imf.org/category.htm

The historical problem of export price instability discussed in chapter 2 continues to plague the region. Of the exports in 1995, nearly 20 percent went to the region and almost half to the United States, with Japan and Asia accounting for 9.8 percent and the European Union 15.8 percent. In part as a result of the Asian crisis and the global slowdown in growth, prices of coffee fell 29.35 percent, copper 22.77 percent, sugar 21.14 percent, soybeans 10.31 percent, and oil 32.62 percent, leaving primary product exporters particularly vulnerable.[7] There is, of course, considerable variation by country in the regional export numbers. For example, Chile, a Pacific Basin country, exports 18.3 percent of its goods to Japan, with another 16.5 percent going to other countries in Asia. The European Union is its next largest trading destination with 26.1 percent, with the United States lagging at 12.6 percent. Mexico, a **NAFTA** partner of the United States, sells 83.4 percent of its goods to its northern neighbor, with only 2.4 percent going to Asia and 4.2 percent to the European Union. In contrast, Brazil's largest export market is the European Union at 27.9 percent of exports.[8]

Table 8.6. Latin America and the Caribbean: Exports of Goods Traded According to Categories, 1965–1995

Exports	1965 Value	%	1970 Value	%	1980 Value	%	1990 Value	%	1995 Value	%
Primary goods	6,513	59.9	7,596	51.4	47,062	50.8	51,899	43.1	56,664	26.6
Agriculture	3,743	34.4	4,387	29.7	16,247	17.5	17,988	14.9	27,122	12.7
Minerals	715	6.6	1,084	7.3	4,457	4.8	5,752	4.8	7,144	3.3
Energy	2,055	18.9	2,126	14.4	26,358	28.5	28,158	23.4	22,398	10.5
Industrialized Goods	4,228	38.9	7,093	48	45,120	48.7	67,758	56.3	154,895	72.6
Traditional	1,743	16	2,980	20.2	16,318	17.6	23,264	19.3	45,964	21.5
Food and Tobacco	1,412	13	2,228	15.1	10,120	10.9	12,476	10.4	19,832	9.3
Other	331	3	752	5.1	6,198	6.7	10,789	9.0	26,132	12.2
Traditional with high economies of scale	2,369	21.8	3,647	24.7	23,178	25	29,502	24.5	26,132	23.6
Durable disseminators of technological progress	98	0.9	368	2.5	3,503	3.8	8,996	7.5	23,845	16.2
Other goods	133	1.2	97	0.7	415	0.4	788	0.7	1,847	0.9
Total	10,874	100	14,786	100	93,597	100	120,445	100	213,407	100

Source: Economic Commission for Latin America and the Caribbean, *Indicadores Economicos* (Santiago, Chile: Economic Commission for Latin America and the Caribbean, 1997), 60.

Table 8.7.   Exports of Basic Products from Latin America and the Caribbean

Product	% of Exports of Principal Exporter
Iron minerals and concentrates	Brazil (5%)
Bauxite and concentrates of aluminum	Jamaica (6%)
Copper	
Mineral	Chile (10%)
Not refined	Peru (5%)
Refined	Chile (23%), Peru (12%)
Zinc	
Mineral	Bolivia (9%), Peru (5%)
Estano	
Mineral	Bolivia (10%)
Gold	Bolivia (11%), Peru (8%)
Petroleum	
Crude	Venezuela (48%), Ecuador (31%), Trinidad and Tobago (18%), Colombia (11%), Mexico (11%), Argentina (7%)
Derivatives	Trinidad and Tobago (29%), Venezuela (27%)
Sugar	Belize (34%), Barbados (18%), Guatemala (11%), Jamaica (6%)
Bananas	Panama (38%), Costa Rica (25%), Honduras (18%), Ecuador (18%), Belize (12%), Guatemala (8%), Colombia (6%)
Shrimp	Ecuador (15%), Panama (15%), Honduras (12%), Nicaragua (12%), Belize (11%)
Soy	Paraguay (27%)
Soy flour	Argentina (8%), Brazil (5%)
Soy oil	Paraguay (5%), Argentina (5%)
Fish	Chile (5%)
Fish flour	Peru (17%)
Beef	Uruguay (11%), Nicaragua (8%), Paraguay (6%), Honduras (6%)
Coffee	El Salvador (33%), Honduras (31%), Colombia (22%), Nicaragua (22%), Guatemala (21%), Costa Rica (14%), Ecuador (10%), Brazil (5%), Peru (5%)
Wood	
Wooden boards	Bolivia (6%)
Pulp	Chile (5%)
Natural fibers	
Algodon	Paraguay (19%)
Wool	Uruguay (9%)

Source: Economic Commission for Latin America and the Caribbean, *Panorama de la Insercion Internacional de America Latina y El Caribe, 1996* (Santiago, Chile: Economic Commission for Latin America and the Caribbean, 1996), 57.

EXCHANGE RATE PERFORMANCE

A critical price in promoting trade is the exchange rate (see table 8.8). Two factors have limited the ability to use a competitive exchange rate as an export promotion tool: inflation fighting and the performance of the U.S. dollar. Several regional currencies have used an exchange rate fixed to the U.S. dollar as a means of introducing credibility and stemming inflationary fears. Argentina maintains a one to one parity, and the Brazilian real is loosely linked to the dollar. A devaluation of the currency would raise inflationary expectations and derail stabilization. Indeed, rather than devaluing vis-à-vis the rest of the world, as the dollar has gained strength, so have the linked currencies. For example, in 1997 the Brazilian real was up 7 percent against the German mark and 8.1 percent against the Japanese yen, pressuring the balance of payments. Nonetheless, concerns with respect to confidence on the inflation-fighting front have dominated trade, leaving many exchange rates in the region overvalued.

QUESTION FOR THOUGHT

Review the objections Latin American structuralists had to export-led growth prior to ISI. Do the new global conditions change their prescriptions? What do you recommend as a trade policy for the region?

Table 8.8. Latin America and the Caribbean: Index of Real Effective Exchange Rate of Exports

Country	1980	1985	1990	1991	1992	1993	1994	1995	1996
Argentina	58.7	94.7	100	83.3	77.5	74.0	78.4	87.0	89.0
Bolivia	72.8	50.4	100	108.3	116.3	117.6	125.1	126.5	120.5
Brazil	141.7	149.9	100	119.7	128.4	113.5	92.6	70.5	65.0
Chile	50.5	71.2	100	98.9	95.3	97.5	96.5	92.4	88.1
Colombia	52.2	59.6	100	101.0	90.0	85.6	74.8	74.5	71.6
Costa Rica	64.7	90.0	100	108.3	103.0	100.4	101.0	98.8	98.9
Ecuador	48.4	62.3	100	95.2	94.7	83.5	78.2	78.5	80.0
El Salvador	139.0	75.9	100	98.4	98.2	88.0	83.9	80.9	75.6
Guatemala	57.0	47.2	100	87.9	87.0	88.9	85.1	82.6	82.5
Honduras	66.4	53.4	100	107.9	102.4	112.5	125.3	112.3	114.7
Mexico	76.2	95.3	100	91.1	84.1	79.7	81.9	121.1	109.4
Nicaragua	243.4	70.1	100	104.6	105.2	108.3	113.3	118.8	117.1
Paraguay	50.4	80.8	100	86.9	90.6	93.9	97.4	106.8	104.3
Peru	220.2	232.6	100	82.1	80.9	89.1	84.6	85.6	82.4
Uruguay	59.5	78.0	100	88.1	84.1	786.8	76.6	79.4	80.4
Venezuela	45.9	52.2	100	93.9	88.5	88.9	92.5	70.6	90.0

Source: Economic Commission for Latin America and the Caribbean, *Indicadores Economicos* (Santiago, Chile: Economic Commission for Latin America and the Caribbean, 1997), 38.
    A rise in the index implies a depreciation.

Box 8.1.   The New Entrepreneurs: From Concept to Profit

Small Firms Need a Level Playing Field to Succeed

Shrimp production looked like a sure bet, at least to Nicaraguan businessman Emilio Baltodano. So he and a group of 14 investors formed Camarones del Pacífico (CAMPA), a company that would raise the esteemed Ecuadorian White shrimp on a stretch of salt flats on the Pacific coast.

First, however, Baltodano and his associates needed funding to construct the farm's impoundments, dikes, pumping systems, and buildings. But long-term financing for small firms is hard to come by in Nicaragua.

Fortunately, the Inter-American Investment Corporation (IIC) also saw a future in shrimp. In 1992 the IIC agreed to provide CAMPA with a $1 million loan and $400,000 as an equity investment. Today, the company is selling 470,000 tons of shrimp annually to France, Spain, and the United States for a total of $3.5 million.

CAMPA's story is far from unusual, judging from presentations at a seminar on small and medium-sized businesses held in March as part of the annual meetings of the boards of governors of the IDB and the IIC. The region's small firms, said Jorge J. Zablah of the Salvadoran Development Foundation, "have the ideas and the ability to export and to be real engines of development for their countries."

But before these ideas can turn into productive enterprises, entrepreneurs must first overcome several major hurdles, the greatest of which is financing. Here, CAMPA was fortunate. "IIC funding, with the right amount and terms, made it possible to carry out a pioneering, risky project," said Baltodano.

Another common problem examined at the seminar was the lack of a legal and regulatory framework to protect small firms from unscrupulous competitors or customers who break contractual agreements. "This is not something Ford or Bayer have to worry about," said Jordi Pujol, president of the Generalitat de Catalunya. "But it does concern a small-businessperson."

It also concerns the Multilateral Investment Fund. This IDB-administered fund is financing projects in seventeen countries to help change what its manager, Donald F. Terry, called the region's "intellectual infrastructure," in such sectors as energy, water, transport, and telecommunications.

Although small firms need help, they do not need special favors, Nancy Birdsall, IDB executive vice president, said at the seminar. But they do need the same access to financing, legal safeguards, and information sources as their larger counterparts. The payback for such help is substantial. Small businesses such as CAMPA are not only the backbone of their nations' economies but also a mainstay of the middle class, democratic institutions, and the social fabric. In particular, small firms are crucial to a country's ability to reduce unemployment. CAMPA is doing its share. The firm employs 134 permanent workers and hires 100 more during the shrimp harvest.

THE BOLÍVAR PROGRAM: CROSS-BORDER MATCHMAKER

Finding an international partner can be daunting for a small company with limited resources. But for the growing number of small and medium-sized Latin American businesses that are focusing on exports, foreign partnerships are essential.

Since 1992 the IDB-financed Bolívar Program has been building bridges between such companies and interested parties in the Northern Hemisphere. The program functions as a matchmaking service, accepting queries at offices in two Asian, eleven European, and twenty Western Hemisphere countries. Program officers then tap an extensive "network of networks" that includes companies, financial institutions, and government agencies interested in international trade.

After initial contacts have been established, the program offers a package of additional services to help bring a business venture to fruition.

Source: IDB América, March 1998, available at www.iadb.org.

TRADE IMBALANCES

Liberalization of trade does not, of course, imply that a country's trade accounts will be balanced. Improvement in exports, if outpaced by an increase in imports, will result in a deteriorating trade balance. Unless this trade deficit is matched by strong inflow of capital to finance them, the country may quickly find itself with balance of payments problems. As we can see in table 8.9, as export performance flattened out in 1998—in part due to the fall in exports attributed to the Asian crisis—imports continued to accelerate. Although the current account deficit in 1997 was more than covered by the strong capital inflows, a decrease in the capital account in 1998 driven by a loss of investor confidence in emerging markets pressured the balance of payments. Reserves and IMF credits were necessary to compensate for the shortfall. Promoting a sustainable global balance that does not draw down reserves or necessitate IMF interventions is a delicate process. External variables, including the performance of the global economy, play havoc with national accounts. One mechanism to attempt to decrease some of the extraregional effects of trade disturbance has been to pursue regional trade integration. However, as we will see below with the effects of the Brazilian currency crisis on **Mercosur**, there may be some unintended effects in the transmission of disturbances within the region.

REGIONAL TRADING ARRANGEMENTS: THE THEORY OF TRADE INTEGRATION

Beyond opening their borders to trade, countries may choose to negotiate trade agreements with other nations. There are four broad categories of trade integration: a **free trade area**, a **customs union**, a **common market**, and an **economic union**. In a free trade area, or FTA, trade restrictions are abolished between participating coun-

Table 8.9.   Regional Balance of Payments (U.S.$ millions)

	1996	1997	1998
Exports of goods and services	296,473	327,376	327,310
Imports of goods and services	304,432	359,026	377,715
Balance on goods	5,982	−12,295	−32,910
Balance on services	−13,941	−19,355	−17,495
Current account balance	−7,959	−31,650	−50,405
Balance on capital and financial accounts, including errors and omissions	62,432	80,431	62,320
Global balance	25,773	16,762	−21,585
Reserves	−25,617	−15,786	15,050
Lending and use of IMF credit	−156	−976	6,535

Source: Data available at www.eclac.org.
Note: An outflow of reserves is reflected by a positive number (export of capital) and an inflow by a negative number (import of capital).

tries, but each country maintains an independent trade policy and separate tariff rates with the rest of the world. In a bit of an ironic play on words, a free trade area is actually a step away from pure free trade. Economists define free trade as an open, multilateral system in which countries do not define preferences for partners but simply buy the cheapest goods available in the global market. A free trade area negotiates preferential status for member countries, diverging from pure unfettered trade. A customs union takes preferential arrangements a step further, establishing a common external tariff for the group, and a common market advances cooperation in other policy-making measures, such as agriculture and the social sector. Full economic integration, including a common monetary policy and a common currency, is an economic union. Because trade integration tends to occur on a regional basis to take advantage of geographic proximity, the different forms are sometimes lumped together under the term regional integration arrangements (RIAs) or preferential trade agreements (PTAs).

Why pursue economic integration? Economic integration may create special opportunities to take advantage of economies of scale, allowing them to promote export diversification by producing for a larger market. Absent trade restrictions and in the presence of a stable currency, trade might proceed as if it were between Massachusetts and Connecticut. This may be particularly useful in broadening the markets for nontraditional exports, where global markets themselves remain relatively protected. Where labor training, technology, and long-term capital are scarce in developing markets, economies of scale may offer new opportunities to strengthen these markets and create new sources of international competitiveness.[9] Regional trading arrangements may also be a means of moving beyond opening markets for goods to promote "deep integration" in trade in services, harmonization of regulatory regions, and the coordination of macroeconomic policies.[10]

A free trade agreement can work to open markets that had been protected, creating new sales opportunities. Countries with similar tastes and cultural predispositions as well as common language ties may find invigorating marketing opportunities. Opening to trade through regional integration may meet less political resistance than unilateral tariff reductions. The perception of neighborliness and reciprocity may serve to soften the price of sectoral reform. As new competitors emerge in the regional context and as the dislocation that always accompanies the change in the trading rules of the game dissipates, new players may be better positioned in the global economy. The learning curve in terms of international marketing and shipping infrastructure can be extended to the world marketplace.

Integration may also have an effect on the expectations of investors, promoting credibility in the permanence of reforms. This is due to the difficulty of rolling back trade liberalization after it has been locked in by a treaty with another country. For example, when Mexico suffered from the 1994–1995 peso crisis, it raised tariffs on 550 products—except for those exported to NAFTA partners. The political costs of abrogating a treaty may exceed the short-term pain of economic adjustment.

The gains or losses from economic integration may be assessed in light of the existing distance from a free trade ideal. If a free trade agreement opens a country further, it is said to have a trade creating effect. If a country trades more—and in the process makes more efficient use of its own resources—welfare will increase. If, however, the treaty serves to create an economic enclave, it is trade diverting, as purchases are now made from a partner, not the most efficient global producer. Some have suggested that trade integration in the region has diverted trade from its most efficient sources. Traditional suppliers of textiles from the Caribbean countries, for example, may have suffered from Mexico's improved access to the U.S. market under the NAFTA.[11]

The free trade ideal may not, however, be the most practical benchmark to assess efforts. One of the difficult parts of assessing the impact of regional trading arrangements is figuring out what would have happened in its absence. Would there have been more movement toward the pure trade model, or greater protectionism? Analysis of regional economic integration parallels the joke about the economist who is asked "How is your love life?" and replies "Relative to what?"[12] Evaluating integration involves a benchmark: should the benchmark be the free trade ideal or increasing global isolation?

In promoting integration in the area, ECLAC has embraced a concept called **open regionalism**. This concept refers to a coupling of regional integration with overall liberalization of trade barriers to nonmember countries. Countries accompany lower tariffs to integration partners with a general opening of the economy to world trade. In characterizing contemporary trade agreements, ECLAC's Enrique Iglesias notes that "One difference between our earlier integration experiences and those of today is that the latter, as a general rule, have a more limited scope in terms of the countries, sectors and interests involved in them, as well as greater flexibility, greater sensitivity to market signals and a less preprogrammed approach."[13] In this sense intraregional trade may be considered a complement to and not a substitute for an open global trading arena. Let us turn to consider the wide range of integration efforts in the region to evaluate this proposition.

THE NORTH AMERICAN FREE TRADE AGREEMENT

In 1991 the United States, Canada, and Mexico began negotiating the North American Free Trade Agreement, or NAFTA, which was then signed in 1994. NAFTA was the first formal regional trading agreement to involve both developed and developing countries. The centerpiece of the NAFTA is the gradual elimination of tariffs over a ten-year period, including the elimination of restrictions in textiles and apparel in the United States and Canada.[14] Intellectual property rights were also strengthened. To prevent the abuse of the free trade status by nontreaty countries, the legislation includes tough rules of origin specifying what proportion of the value of a product must be added locally and imposing strict domestic content rules for the purchase of inputs. Computers, for example, could not be assembled in Mexico with imported components from around the globe and qualify for NAFTA trade preferences.

Key elements of the NAFTA accord include changes in agriculture, manufacturing, and services. The accord provides for liberalization of the export of fresh fruits and vegetables from Mexico into the United States as well as that of corn

Trade is dependent on export infrastructure such as this port in Paraguay. *(Courtesy of the Inter-American Development Bank.)*

and other grains from the United States to Mexico. It promotes liberalization of tariffs and quotas on textiles and apparel. It removes tariffs on cars imported into Mexico over a five- to ten-year period, and it opens the Mexican telecommunications and government procurement markets. Finally, it speeds implementation of GATT intellectual property rights and provides national treatment to investors of other NAFTA countries.[15] Unlike the European Union, NAFTA makes no provision for the free movement of labor within the bloc. It is notable that the only sectors where the new regime explicitly benefits Mexico are concessions in the U.S. markets for fruit, textiles, and clothing. The more industrialized partners realized significant gains in lucrative telecommunications and government markets. In an effort to gain credibility with international investors, Mexico may have given up more than it got in the NAFTA negotiations. Liberalization with industrialized partners came at a relatively high price for the Mexicans.

The signing of NAFTA generated a great deal of controversy. In the United States and Canada, opponents were concerned about the potential loss of jobs as manufacturers moved south of the border to take advantage of cheaper labor. Environmental advocates were also fearful of the motives of big business in relocating to avoid tougher environmental regulations in the North. In Mexico there was the apprehension that the *yanquis* would invade again, taking advantage of Mexican labor and putting Mexican corporations out of business.

Some of these fears were unfounded. It is important to note that Mexico had already engaged in substantial liberalization, such that the decrease in tariff rates was not particularly dramatic, with the exception of changes in agriculture and government services. Those opposing NAFTA failed to point out that capital was already well dispersed throughout Mexico through the *maquiladora* program. Begun in 1965, for thirty years this twin-plant program has allowed foreign firms to import components without duty so long as the final product was reexported. Capital that wanted to be in Mexico because of the cheap labor platform largely was already there. In fact, foreign direct investment from the United States to Mexico did not increase much with NAFTA, and Mexico's share of total U.S. foreign direct investment declined.[16]

Furthermore, in assessing the effects of cheap labor, it must be remembered that low wages do not magically guarantee a profit. Low wages may be the result of low levels of productivity such that the cost per unit of product is not reduced. In fact, although wages in the United States are roughly eight times the wages paid in Mexico, U.S. workers produce 8.2 times as much as Mexicans in maquila plants. This is not to say that *if* cheaper Mexican workers can be made more productive with better education and equipment, Mexico wouldn't be more of a threat, but rather that the claims for the widespread job loss in the United States, given Mexican productivity levels, were exaggerated. Profit increases only when productive labor is paid less than it is worth.

In the United States, the AFL-CIO, an organization of affiliated labor unions, charged that NAFTA helped keep inflation-adjusted average hourly wages of U.S. workers flat, at approximately $12 per hour. What NAFTA may do is make the threat of plant relocation to Mexico more real to American workers, and therefore depress wage demands in collective bargaining. One study found that 60 percent of union organizing efforts after NAFTA were met by the threat of plant closings, compared to 29 percent before.[17] Nonetheless, NAFTA does not change the fact that multinationals could always threaten to move abroad. As we just noted, maquiladoras have been around for thirty years. If it wasn't Mexico, it would be Malaysia. Jobs may also be created through integration. Transportation sector jobs such as trucking have also benefited, as goods are moved over land between the NAFTA countries. In cases such as the U.S. Fisher-Price Corporation, a job-creating effect of NAFTA was relocating production from Hong Kong to Monterey, because firms such as Celadon Trucking, which move goods from Mexico into the U.S. market, must hire drivers.[18] There is the possibility that NAFTA created as many jobs as it may have lost.

Job creation or job loss is difficult to measure in part because you can't tell which workers are dedicated to "NAFTA production" and which are making goods sold elsewhere. We know that employment has fallen over the first five years of NAFTA, but this can hardly be attributable to the accord. We also know that when workers are laid off from jobs due to firms moving to Mexico, they may register for benefits under the NAFTA Transitional Adjustment Assistance. As of March 1997, a total of 177,000 workers (about 39,000 per year) qualified; this is a very small share of the annual job losses totaling about 1.5 million per year in the United States. So if NAFTA has had a role in job loss, it is unnoticeably small on a national level.[19] We might also expect that job loss would be concentrated the most in the areas where the greatest deficit exists in U.S.–Mexican trade. From table 8.10, we can see this deficit in the machine transport or automotive sector. Nevertheless, few auto workers have filed. In this case Mexican imports might be seen as a complement to U.S. production, boosting the competitiveness of U.S. firms as they market their goods around the world. For the most part, it is macroeconomic conditions and not trade agreements that determine the level of employ-

Table 8.10. U.S.-Mexican Trade (1998 U.S.$ millions)

	Exports to Mexico	Imports from Mexico
Food and live animals	3,840.17	4,322.94
Beverages and tobacco	82.86	844.59
Crude materials, inedible, except fuels	3,072.74	879.62
Mineral fuels, lubricants, and related materials	1,773.18	5,300.16
Animal and vegetable oils, fats and waxes	460.1	44.75
Chemicals and related products, N.E.S.	6,873.59	1,503.85
Manufactured goods classified chiefly by material	10,790.01	7,465.86
Machinery and transport equipment	38,839.44	54,558.77
Miscellaneous manufactured articles	9,639.12	15,799.42
Commodities and transactions, N.E.S.	3,638.88	3,988.72
Total	79,010.09	94,708.67

Source: U.S. Census Bureau, official statistics. Available on-line at www.census.gov/foreign-trade/sitc1/1998/.

ment in an economy.[20] National levels of income determine aggregate demand; changes in the sectoral distribution of which country is producing each item will not determine an overall job loss.

Another reason the job loss hasn't been as high as predicted is the domestic content regulations. Where firms, particularly those that had set up in the maquiladora zones before NAFTA, had imported components from Asia, now they must purchase from American suppliers. Exports to Mexico may have been higher had the peso crisis not sent the Mexican economy into a tailspin. Some forecast that Mexico will become the second largest U.S. export market after Canada, overtaking Japan.[21]

Environmental dumping was also a concern for both sides. U.S. firms in conformance with environmental regulations did not want to be put at a disadvantage with respect to firms located in Mexico, and Mexicans themselves did not want to breath dirtier air or drink more polluted water courtesy of multinational capital. As a result of tough lobbying, NAFTA also includes important side agreements concerning labor and the environment. Under the United States–Mexico Border XXI Program, five-year goals were set for achieving a cleaner environment. Nine binational groups were created to work on reducing vehicle emissions at border crossings, tracking transport of hazardous wastes, minimizing the risk of chemical spills, reducing solid waste, monitoring children's health risks from pesticide exposures, and reducing the impacts of growth on fish and wildlife resources. Two institutions were set up under NAFTA to promote sustainable environmental practices: the Border Environment Cooperation Commission and the trinational Commission for Environmental Cooperation (CEC). An interesting innovation in the international legislation makes it possible for citizens and NGOs to make direct complaints to the CEC.

Unfortunately, dissatisfaction remains as to the efficacy of the environmental agreements in practice. Some have argued that the institutions are underfunded and that the political attention in Mexico given to macroeconomic stabilization took away from progress on the environmental front. One critic noted that only 1 percent of the $2 billion in cleanup funds promised under NAFTA has been spent.[22] The NADBank, or North American Development Bank, which was set up to finance capital requirements of environmental projects, has been slow to review project proposals and has approved funding for only a handful of projects. Environmental conditions along the border are making people sick. Rates of hepatitis, diarrheal diseases, and gastroenteritis are two to six times the Texas state average— and things are worse on the Mexican side. With a doubling of the border population in the past decades, sanitary services are pressed beyond capacity.[23] New mechanisms may be needed to facilitate lending, as the bank's charter limits it to projects viable on commercial terms. It may need a special concessional window to attend to the needs of the poorest and most vulnerable communities, expanding projects to include some of the structural causes of environmental degradation such as housing and poor sanitation.[24]

The jury is still out on the effects of NAFTA. It is, in a certain sense, a work in progress. Compared to 1991, when NAFTA negotiations began, by 1998 total bilateral trade between the United States and Mexico has increased nearly 2.7

times. Table 8.10 shows U.S.–Mexican trade by commodity. You may recall figure 7.3, which documented capital flows; there was little increase in foreign direct investment in Mexico following the signing of the NAFTA accord. The increases were no larger than the increases in investment in other Latin American countries, and they hardly bore out Ross Perot's dramatic prediction of a "giant sucking sound" of foreign investment drawn south of the border should the accord be adopted. Given the commonality with other countries in the region, the trend likely had as much to do with overall restructuring as the signing of a piece of paper. It is difficult to separate out the direct effects of the trade agreement, the unrelated negative macroeconomic effects of the peso crisis and its aftermath, and the historically positive binational atmosphere NAFTA has generated. Isolating the effects of the trade agreement from a 45 percent devaluation of the peso, a 7 percent drop in Mexican output, and a 22 percent fall in Mexican real wages staggers even the economists' imagination.[25] At the same time, the spirit of NAFTA worked to encourage both business confidence and a willingness to work together on binational issues.

Perhaps the greatest gains in NAFTA have been the indirect effects of an improved climate of negotiations between the two countries. One example of this spillover from the economic realm to the policy plate has been in the area of immigration policy. As noted, NAFTA has no provisions for the free movement of labor. What it has created, however, is a better climate for negotiations concerning tough issues surrounding migration policy, particularly along the border area. Whereas these negotiations had always been contentious and crisis oriented, a binational U.S.-Mexican commission on immigration is an example of the spirit of cooperation NAFTA promoted.[26]

> **QUESTION FOR THOUGHT**
>
> NAFTA has been called an "iterative process." That is, it is a document flexible enough to allow for change. What priorities would you define to strengthen North American trade?

Beyond the NAFTA, numerous free trade agreements were signed in the 1990s. As is shown in table 8.11, a network of free trade agreements links the region, consistent with ECLAC's concept of "open regionalism." The web of bilateral agreements is loosely coordinated through the Asociación Latinoamericana de Integractión (ALADI), the successful organization established in 1980 to replace the Latin American Integration Association (LAIA). We will discuss three of the regional arrangements in depth: Mercosur, the **Andean Community**, and the **Central American Common Market**.

MERCOSUR

The second largest trading agreement in the region after NAFTA is Mercosur. The groundwork for Mercosur began with a bilateral program signed in July 1986 between Argentina and Brazil for industrial integration. Extending from Brazil's tropical jungles to the sub-Antarctic zone of Argentina in Tierra del Fuego, Mercosur countries account for approximately half the Latin American land mass and

Table 8.11.   Regional Integration Agreements in the Americas after 1990

Agreement, Date, and Membership	Objective	Current Status	Status/Comment
Andean Trade Preference Act, 1991 (Bolivia, Colombia, Ecuador, Peru, United States)	Duty-free status for $324 million in imports from Andean countries to the United States	Operational	
Chile-Mexico Free Trade Agreement, 1993	Establishment of a free trade area by January 1996	Present maximum reciprocal tariff of 7.5%	Aggregate GDP, $241.2 billion; population, 94.9 million; intraregional trade, 0.1% of total foreign trade
Chile-Venezuela Free Trade Agreement, 1993	Establishment of a free trade area by 1999	Maximum tariff to imports from Chile to be 20% in 1994; Chile's tariff rate remains at 11%; tariffs scheduled to reach 0% in 1999	Aggregate GDP, $76.7 billion; population, 32.5 million; total foreign trade, $38.9 billion; intraregional trade, 1.4% of total foreign trade
Colombia-Venezuela Free Trade Agreement, 1992	Establishment of a free trade area by 1992	Common tariff agreed in 1992; conversations initiated with Mexico (Group of Three) to establish free trade area	Aggregate GDP, $91.3 billion; population, 52 million; total foreign trade, $34.7 billion; intraregional trade, 1.4% of total foreign trade
El Salvador–Guatemala Free Trade Agreement, 1991	Establishment of a free trade area	Entered into operation in October 1991	
North American Free Trade Agreement, 1992 (Canada, Mexico, United States)	Establishment of a free trade area by 2009; elimination of tariffs in five, ten, or fifteen years depending on the product; exceptions to Canadian agriculture and Mexican petroleum products; contains precedent-setting rights, services, trade, and investment; U.S.-Canada dispute settlement system extended to Mexico	Agreement signed and ratified; in phase as of January 1994	Aggregate GDP, $6,204.6 billion; population, 362.7 million; total foreign trade, $1,223.8 billion; intraregional trade, 18.85% of total foreign trade

Agreement, Date, and Membership	Objective	Current Status	Status/Comment
Group of Three, April 1993; Venezuela Free Trade Agreement, 1993	Economic cooperation; in April 1993, the three countries agreed to establish a free trade area by 1994	Energy sector agreements signed; negotiations under way; draft accord of November 1993 provides for immediate 20% tariff for some items and a ten-year transition for others, except in automobiles and agricultural goods; Mexico will cut tariffs faster than Colombia and Venezuela; signing date of January 1994 postponed because of Chiapas rebellion; agreement ratified by new Venezuelan authorities in February 1994	Aggregate GDP, $305.8 billion; population, 138.2 million; total foreign trade, $94.4 billion; intraregional trade, 0.8% of total foreign trade
Costa Rica–Mexico Free Trade Agreement, 1994	Establishment of a free trade area	Negotiations in progress; removal of all tariff and nontariff barriers by both countries; Mexican exports of goods that Costa Rica does not produce will enter duty-free beginning in 1995; tariffs on remainder of Mexican exports to be reduced over five, ten, and fifteen years; most Costa Rican exports will enter Mexico duty-free in five years or less; rigid rule of origin requires goods to be made with inputs from the region	
Mexico–Central America Free Trade Agreement, 1992 (Costa Rica, El Salvador, Guatemala, Honduras, Mexico, Nicaragua)	Establishment of a free trade area by December 1996	Safeguard regime, technical rules, and dispute-resolution agreements under negotiation; framework agreement for trade cooperation signed August 1992; Costa Rica engaged in bilateral negotiations with Mexico	Aggregate GDP, $240.3 billion; population, 112.4 million; total foreign trade, $72.4 billion; intraregional trade, 1.6% of total foreign trade

(continued)

(continued)

Agreement, Date, and Membership	Objective	Current Status	Status/Comment
Venezuela–Central America Free Trade Agreement, 1992 (Costa Rica, El Salvador, Guatemala, Honduras, Nicaragua, Panama, Venezuela)	Provides for a nonreciprocal transition period in which unilateral tariff cuts will be made by Venezuela, with eventual goal of a free trade area	Negotiations gained impetus after Group of Three presidential summit in 1993 but have proceeded slowly since	
Nueva Ocotepeque Agreement, 1992 (El Salvador, Guatemala, Honduras)	Establishment of free trade area by 1993; long-run objective to create a customs union; includes recent complementary agreement signed among these countries	Not clear	Aggregate GDP, $17.1 billion; population, 19.7 million; intraregional trade, 11.8% of total foreign trade, $7.3 billion
CARICOM-Colombia Free Trade Agreement, 1991 (Antigua and Barbados, the Bahamas, Belize, Colombia, Dominican Republic, Grenada, Jamaica, Monserrat, St. Kitts and Nevis, St. Lucia, St. Vincent and the Grenadines, Trinidad and Tobago)	Provides for a nonreciprocal transition period in which unilateral tariff cuts will be made by Colombia, with the eventual goal of an FTA	Negotiations are proceeding slowly due to CARICOM's demands for unilateral tariff reductions	
CARICOM-Venezuela Free Trade Agreement, 1993 (Antigua and Barbados, Bahamas, Barbados, Belize, Dominica, Grenada, Jamaica, Monserrat, St. Kitts and Nevis, St. Lucia, St. Vincent and the Grenadines, Trinidad and Tobago, Venezuela)	Provides for duty-free imports from CARICOM into Venezuela to be phased in over a five-year period; after five years, negotiations are to begin to eliminate tariffs on Venezuelan exports to signatory countries	Negotiations are proceeding slowly due to CARICOM's demands for unilateral tariff deductions	
Colombia–Central America Free Trade Agreement, 1993 (Colombia, Costa Rica, El Salvador, Guatemala, Honduras, Nicaragua, Panama)	Provides for a nonreciprocal transition period in which unilateral tariff cuts will be made by Colombia, with the eventual goal of a free trade area	Negotiations gained impetus after the Group of Three presidential summit in 1993 but have proceeded slowly since	

Source: Sebastian Edwards, *Crisis and Reform in Latin America: From Despair to Hope* (New York: Oxford University Press, 1995), 143–147.
Note: FTA = Free Trade Agreement.

GDP, 43 percent of the population, and 33 percent of regional trade. Because Mercosur countries include some of the world's richest agricultural and mineral resources, there are ample opportunities for growth and production. The 1991 Treaty of Asunción, including Uruguay and Paraguay, expanded this bilateral agreement to include progressive, automatic tariff reduction; a CET (common external tariff) of 20 percent for 85 percent of goods; and harmonization of macroeconomic policies. Exceptions were made for four years to the free trade in textiles, steel, automobiles, and petrochemicals.

Chile initially did not join the agreement because it wanted to maintain a lower external tariff than the Mercosur countries, although in 1996 it signed a bilateral agreement with the union as an associate member. Bolivia became an associate member in 1997. Mercosur places fourth among the world's economic blocs, with more than $750 billion in GNP and more than 220 million inhabitants. By 1999, Mercosur and the EU are expected to begin talks that could lead to a free market agreement, perhaps edging the United States out. The EU's two-way trade with Mercosur totaled U.S.$23 billion in 1995 versus U.S.$29 billion with the United States. In particular, Europe is active in the infrastructure arena, buying telephone companies and utilities in Brazil, Chile, Peru, and Argentina. Seven of the ten largest private companies in Brazil are European owned; only two are dominated by Americans.[27]

Administratively, Mercosur is governed by six institutions. The council, a political leadership group, is composed of the foreign relations and economics ministers of the four member states and oversees all other Mercosur institutions, with decision-making authority over member state institutions. The Common Market Group, or the executive organization of the community, has both policy-making and administrative responsibilities. The Mercosur Commerce Commission (MCC) is divided into eleven working groups charged with monitoring the common commercial policy, including the common external tariff and competition policy. The joint Parliamentary Commission is an advisory commission representing national legislatures; the Forum, a consultative body, reflects the views of various sectors such as producers, consumers, workers, and merchants; and a small secretariat with a permanent staff of about thirty professionals headquartered in Montevideo, Uruguay, completes the list. In comparison to the autonomy built into EU institutions, political control in Mercosur resides in the hands of the member states. In the European Union, "European" delegates are elected; in Mercosur, institutions are staffed by national representatives.

Mercosur is not yet a true common market. Although members have achieved a customs union, full market status targeted for 2006 awaits progress in the coordination of economic, legislative, environmental, infrastructure, and technology policies. Member countries face the hard task of harmonizing standards and establishing a supranational bureaucracy beyond the national control of member states. Evaluated by the criteria of common market, Mercosur is still a bit thin. Nonetheless, the achievements of Mercosur are important, particularly in locking in progress toward free trade in the region.[28] It is also important to remember that economic unions such as the EU have been decades in the making; slow progress in negotiating tough international issues is rather predictable.

Trade within Mercosur tripled since 1990, growing from approximately U.S.$5 billion in 1990 to more than U.S.$16.9 billion in 1996. Argentina sells more than one-third of its exports—especially agricultural and natural resource products—to Brazil, making Brazil Argentina's largest trading partner after the United States. Brazilian multinationals have set up shop in Argentina. International auto makers have taken advantage of the new scale economies to expand auto production in the region. Investments in the auto sector are expected to be close to $20 billion for 1994–2000, a vote of confidence in the strength of the region's economies.[29] As shown in table 8.12, trade within the subregion accounts for more than 20 percent of the countries' total net trade. This is large compared to any of the other subregional arrangements, in part due to the large internal market presented by Brazil. Cost margins have come down, there has been some rationalization of production patterns to take advantage of larger scale, and there has been an increase in total factor productivity growth with increased trade. Once again, however, we are confronted with the problem of simultaneous changes. It is unclear how much of these improvements have been tied to Mercosur policies and how much to the concurrent process of trade liberalization and economic restructuring aggressively pursued by the countries.[30] Some have also questioned whether the cross-border production, particularly in heavy goods, is trade diverting and therefore lowering efficiency.[31] Others suggest that overall trade in Mercosur countries has increased productivity.[32]

Harmonization of monetary and tax policies has had less success, partly due to the late stabilization of Brazil under the Real plan. Imbalances in the Brazilian economy in 1997, in part driven by its policy of using a strong currency to control inflation, resulted in temporary import limits against Mercosur partners. Common industrial policies to direct resources toward new areas have also lagged. The asymmetrical nature of the economies make noncompliance difficult to address. Brazil's economy overwhelms that of Argentina. For example, the increase in output in one year of Brazil's beer giant Brahma was equal to Argentina's entire consumption of brew. Given its size, Brazil can act without much regard for the effects a policy may have on Mercosur partners. Relatively weak enforcement institutions make the unilateral actions on Brazil's part unpunishable. Argentina has

Table 8.12. Exports from Trade Areas by Destination, 1996 (as % of total exports)

| | | | Destination | | | | |
Exporter	Mercosur	Andean Group	Central American Common Market	CARICOM	NAFTA	Latin America	Hemisphere
Mercosur	21.51	4.23	0.29	0.26	17.27	31.86	47.82
Andean Group	3.53	10.84	1.67	3.00	46.72	21.40	69.83
CACM	0.20	1.97	19.92	0.59	38.12	28.43	64.22
NAFTA	2.24	1.61	0.78	0.47	47.31	12.26	53.53

Source: Inter-American Development Bank, *1996 Intra-Hemispheric Exports by Integration Group,* 12 July 1997. Available at www.iadb.org/statistics/notaest.htm.

become vulnerable to the performance of the Brazilian economy. Said Argentine Vice President Ruckauf, "If Brazil catches a cold, Argentina will sneeze."[33] Mercosur holds promise but also pitfalls for participant countries. In the wake of the Brazilian crisis of 1998–1999, Mercosur may be behaving slightly more like a free trade area than a common market, turning outward to European and U.S. markets as a source of dynamism. Mercosur countries, in light of the crisis, were pushing for reductions on tariffs in industrial countries on agricultural policies, with the hopes of easing recession through traditional export markets.[34] The durability and depth of Mercosur is being tested by the crisis in its largest economy.

OTHER REGIONAL TRADING AGREEMENTS

The **Andean Community** has a long but uneven history. A modern realization of independence hero Simón Bolívar's vision of unification, the treaty was signed in 1969. It provided for free commerce between Bolivia, Colombia, Ecuador, Venezuela, and Peru, with a common external tariff adopted.[35] The hope was that subregional production would overcome the limitation of economies of scale faced under import substitution industrialization. Problems in the early stages of the Andean Pact derived in large part from political disputes as well as very different domestic economic policies and goals. An ambitious emphasis on industrial planning and joint industrialization was more than the meager sums dedicated to the projects could support, particularly as disputes arose between the more powerful countries and the smaller nations.

With greater homogeneity in economic policies in the 1990s, there are improved prospects for the development of subregional trade. Exports among the Andean countries have increased at an average annual rate of 27 percent. Accomplishments in the 1990s include establishing a free trade area among four of its five member countries,[36] negotiating a common external tariff (CET), and the adoption of sectoral policies in foreign investment, intellectual property rights, and air transportation. **Trade creation** seems to dominate **trade diversion** in an assessment of the impacts of the union. The regional market appeared to play a key role in promoting export expansion. Scale economies in intraindustry trade between Andean partners are preparing firms for competition in the global marketplace.[37] Difficulties in further progress include the problem that with incomplete participation among member countries in free trade, the arrangement is part FTA and part customs union. Also, disagreement among the members on how to proceed with integration with the rest of the hemisphere as well tension surrounding the confrontation between Peru and Ecuador in 1995 stalled progress.[38]

The **Central American Common Market**, formed in 1960, has had a rocky history. Progress in the 1970s was set back by geopolitical struggles and civil war in the region. Although by 1970 intraregional trade had reached 26 percent,

> **QUESTION FOR THOUGHT**
>
> What have been the costs and benefits of subregional trade organizations? What measures should be considered to strengthen integration efforts?

small market size and social revolutions turned the clock back. The 1990s, however, saw new resolve to exploit the economies of scale offered by integration. Both business and civil society have taken leadership roles in propelling integration efforts forward. Given that most countries in the Central American region have already pursued trade liberalization, convergence at a low CET between 5 and 20 percent was arrived at. Countries have liberalized capital accounts, and investment is returning to the region. Nonetheless, progress by mid-decade was stalled by macroeconomic instability, weak infrastructure, and unskilled human capital. Priorities of the new regional economic integration (REI) program include strengthening the legal and institutional framework, joint actions to reduce debt, and promoting cooperation on sectoral issues such as upgrading infrastructure in transport, energy, and telecommunications. Trade is seen as the regional catalyst for growth.[39]

TOWARD A HEMISPHERIC FREE TRADE AGREEMENT?

Should subregional hemispheric efforts be linked in a regional free trade agreement? Would a hemispheric free trade agreement benefit the United States? Latin America is a growing market for U.S. exports. From the perspective of the United States, the answer in part depends on the economic importance of the hemisphere. Figure 8.1 shows U.S. trade broken down by trading region. The WHFTA member countries accounted for 41 percent of U.S. trade. The United States sells more to

Figure 8.1. U.S. Trade by Region (late 1990s)

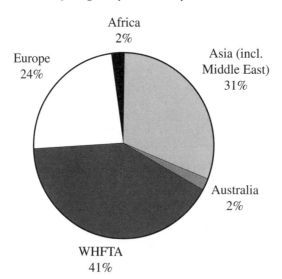

Source: Data available on the World Wide Web at the *Monthly Trade Update* of the U.S. Department of Commerce and International Trade Administration at www.ita.doc.gov.

Chile than to India and more to Central America than all of Eastern Europe.[40] Brazil, with its large population, is seen as a huge potential market; the United States currently sells more there than in China. Table 8.13 gives a more detailed breakdown of U.S. trade, and table 18.14 presents U.S. trade by region. South America is the only region in the world where the United States is currently running a trade surplus.

Of particular importance to the United States are oil imports from the region. A strong argument for improving relations in the hemisphere is protecting energy security. Over one-third of U.S. oil imports come from Latin America; as shown in table 8.15, Mexico and Venezuela in 1995 were among the largest suppliers. OLADE, the Latin American Energy Organization, was formed to promote cooperative efforts for conservation, sales, and development of oil resources in the region. Given the shorter distances to transport oil compared to the Middle East, Latin American oil sources are more secure, with shorter, less congested routes to travel. After the decontrol of many state-owned oil companies, there has been an increased trend in cross-border ventures, particularly with Venezuela. In 1997, for the second straight year, Venezuela was the leading source of foreign crude oil for the United States, with 1.32 million barrels per day, the highest single country volume since Saudi Arabia in 1992.[41] The oil sector gives the United States a strong incentive for enhanced integration in the Latin American region.

Many other factors contribute to making Latin America a natural market for U.S. business. These range from historical ties in the Andean region, where the United States holds 35 percent of the market share, to dominance of the U.S. media in Central America, where consumers have a preference for American products. The U.S. Department of Commerce is strongly encouraging U.S. business to invest in the region because it expects the real growth rate of the region to equal or exceed that of any other region by the year 2010.

At the Summit of the Americas, held in Miami in December 1994, regional presidents agreed to negotiate a Western Hemisphere Free Trade Agreement by the year 2005. It should be noted that negotiations are not implementation: the agreement may be phased in over a period of fifteen or twenty years. The idea behind the FTAA, the Free Trade Agreement of the Americas, is the consolidation of the nearly twenty-five free trade pacts already operating in a region of nearly 800 million inhabitants. Is this a feasible notion? Widely different levels of economic development as well as divergent interests make this process fraught with difficulty. For the FTAA to move forward, argues Enrique Iglesias, head of the Inter-American Development Bank, a second generation of structural reforms must take place, in areas such as education, pensions, health, modernization of the state, and financial regulation, to promote competitiveness on the part of Latin America. Hemispheric integration should drive structural reform.

Is an FTAA the best approach to deepening trade ties in the region? Some contend that subregional units should be the building blocks. Brazil has been a strong proponent of this approach. Iglesias rejects the either/or nature of this question. He argues that the process of subregional integration in the formation of subregional blocks is complementary to a hemispheric agreement.[42] Others think that trading blocs—hemispheric or subregional—are trade diverting. On the other

Table 8.13.   Exports, Imports, and Balance of Goods by Selected Countries and Geographic Areas, 1998 (not seasonally adjusted, U.S.$ millions)

	Balance	*Exports*	*Imports*
U.S. Total Balance of Payments Basis	−247,985	671,055	919,040
North America	−34,235	235,318	269,552
Canada	−18,536	156,308	174,844
Mexico	−15,699	79,010	94,709
South/Central America	13,029	63,435	50,406
Argentina	3,633	5,885	2,252
Brazil	5,035	15,157	10,122
Colombia	165	4,817	4,652
Other	4,196	37,576	33,380
Western Europe	−28,929	163,019	191,948
European Union	−26,896	149,470	176,367
Finland	−680	1,915	2,595
France	−6,349	17,728	24,077
Germany	−23,182	26,642	49,824
Italy	−11,986	9,027	21,013
United Kingdom	4,278	39,070	34,792
Eastern Europe/FSR	−3,416	7,474	10,890
Russia	−2,149	3,585	5,734
Pacific Rim Countries	−160,395	167,461	327,856
China	−56,898	14,258	71,156
Japan	−64,094	57,888	121,982
Hong Kong	2,385	12,923	10,538
Korea	−7,398	16,538	23,936
Singapore	−2,684	15,673	18,357
Taiwan	−14,966	18,157	33,123
OPEC	−9,023	25,115	34,138
Indonesia	−7,047	2,291	9,338
Nigeria	−3,375	820	4,195
Saudi Arabia	4,186	10,525	6,339
Venezuela	−2,763	6,520	9,282
Other OPEC	−24	4,960	4,984

Source: Report FT900 (CB-99-31), Bureau of the Census, Foreign Trade Division, December 1998.
Note: This exhibit is not additive. Selected countries are included in more than one area grouping. Indonesia is included in both OPEC and Other Pacific Rim; Venezuela is included in both OPEC and Other South/Central America.

hand, proponents of the FTAA suggest that the FTAA is "GATT-plus." That is, it moves beyond the issues on the worldwide trade agenda to push barriers in services, intellectual property, and government procurement.[43]

In a May 1997 meeting of trade ministers from thirty-four countries, little progress was made, in part due to divergent interests on the part of some Mercosur members. Their position has been that consolidation of Mercosur prior to a hemi-

Table 8.14.   U.S. Trade with Latin America and Other Regions (% of U.S. total trade)

Region	1991	1992	1993	1994	1995
Latin America					
Exports to the region	13.5	15	15.3	16.6	15
Imports from the region	11.7	12	11.8	12.3	13.1
Africa					
Exports to the region	2.1	2.2	2.0	1.8	1.7
Imports from the region	2.9	2.7	2.5	2.1	2.1
East Asian NICs					
Exports to the region	10.8	10.8	11.3	11.6	12.7
Imports from the region	12.1	11.7	11.1	10.8	11.0
ASEAN					
Exports to the region	4.9	5.4	6.1	6.3	6.8
Imports from the region	5.9	6.7	7.3	7.9	8.3
Eastern Europe					
Exports to the region	1.1	1.2	1.3	1.0	1
Imports from the region	0.4	0.4	0.6	0.9	0.9
Western Europe					
Exports to the region	28.1	26.1	24.4	23.1	23.1
Imports from the region	20	20.1	19.9	19.7	19.6

Sources: International Trade Administration, U.S. Department of Commerce, *U.S. Foreign Trade Highlights* (Washington, D.C.: U.S. Department of Commerce, 1995); and preliminary figures for 1996 available at www.ita.doc.gov/industry/otea/usfth/hili.html.

spheric agreement will strengthen Latin America's bargaining position vis-à-vis the United States. On the part of the United States, President Clinton was denied congressional authorization in November 1997 for fast track authority to negotiate the FTAA. Fast track authority would have permitted the president to negotiate a package to present to Congress for an up or down vote. Because trade agreements

Table 8.15.   U.S. Oil Imports from Latin America, 1995 (% of U.S. total oil imports)

Country	Amount
Argentina	0.8
Colombia	2.8
Ecuador	0.7
Guatemala	0.2
Mexico	14.1
Peru	0.2
Venezuela	15.5
Region	34.3
Saudi Arabia	18.3
Canada	15.9
Nigeria	9.4

Source: Energy Information Administration, *Petroleum Supply Annual, 1995* (Washington, D.C.: U.S. Department of Energy, 1995).

are complicated and different constituencies would like to pick them apart after they are constructed, fast track authority improves the likelihood of the final passage of an agreement. Nevertheless, some progress has been made. Table 8.16 lists the meetings held since the summit on trade issues. Interestingly, the initiatives of the April 1998 hemispheric summit in Santiago, Chile, had little trade content, focusing on issues of technology, education, gender, and the environment. Consider the following initiatives from the meeting, which can be found on the OAS homepage at www.oas.org.

- Strengthen the human rights systems by reinforcing institutional structures and support the Inter-American Commission on Human Rights with particular attention to the recently created Special Rapporteur for Freedom of Expression
- Train police and correctional officers, offer human rights education for judges, and promote education for democracy at all levels to teach individual ethical values, a spirit of cooperation, and integrity
- Support the Inter-American Program to combat corruption and strengthen national efforts in control of illicit drug consumption and trafficking
- Promote the development of civil society institutions such as National Councils for Sustainable Development or the Inter-American Strategy for Public Participation
- Use new technologies to mitigate the effects of El Niño; address questions of maritime transport of hazardous wastes
- Upgrade telecommunications plans and promote affordable access for phones and Internet
- Cooperate with PAHO, the Pan American Health Organization, to promote regional health policies
- Promote the equality of opportunity between men and women, following up on commitments made by the Inter-American Commission on Women
- Exchange information on labor legislation and observe internationally recognized core labor standards; support migrant workers
- Proceed with intergovernmental examination of the OAS framework of the Proposed American Declaration on the Rights of Indigenous Peoples

There is little in the plan of action that directly relates to trade. Consistent with the recommendation of the Inter-American Bank's Enrique Iglesias, advances first need to be made on the social and environmental agendas before meaningful integration can take place in the hemisphere. In appendix B, the Declaration of Principles of the Summit of the Americas is reproduced. Whether these goals will be realized will be a function of whether political will toward integration is strong enough to overcome regional, political, social, and economic differences.

From a business perspective, an FTAA with Latin America may bring di-

> **QUESTION FOR THOUGHT**
>
> Is a hemispheric free trade agreement good for Latin America? Which countries are likely to benefit most? Which countries are likely to have high costs?

Table 8.16.   Ministerials, Vice Ministerials, and Business Forums

9–11 December 1994	Summit of the Americas	Miami, United States
30 June 1995	First Western Hemisphere Trade Ministerial	Denver, United States
1–2 July 1996	First Business Forum of the Americas	Denver, United States
18–20 March 1996	Second Business Forum of the Americas	Cartagena, Colombia
21 March 1996	Second Western Hemisphere Trade Ministerial	Cartagena, Colombia
16–17 September 1996	Western Hemisphere Vice Ministerial	Florianopolis, Brazil
25–27 February 1997	Western Hemisphere Vice Ministerial	Recife, Brazil
April 1997	Western Hemisphere Vice Ministerial	Rio de Janeiro, Brazil
13–15 May 1997	Third Business Forum of the Americas	Belo Horizonte, Brazil
16 May 1997	Third Western Hemisphere Trade Ministerial	Belo Horizonte, Brazil
29–31 July 1997	Western Hemisphere Vice Ministerial	San Jose, Costa Rica
28–30 October 1997	Western Hemisphere Vice Ministerial	Costa Rica
10–12 February 1998	Western Hemisphere Vice Ministerial	Costa Rica
16–18 March 1998	Fourth Business Forum of the Americas	San Jose, Costa Rica
19 March 1998	Fourth Western Hemisphere Trade Ministerial	San Jose, Costa Rica
19 April 1998	Second Summit of the Americas	Santiago, Chile
1–3 November 1999	Fifth Business Forum of the Americas	Toronto, Canada
4 November 1999	Fifth Meeting of Ministers of Trade	Toronto, Canada
2001	Third Summit of the Americas	Quebec City, Canada

rect and indirect benefits. In addition to the elimination of tariffs and other restrictions on goods and services and changes in rules governing investment practices, the FTAA provides an opportunity to design mechanisms to ensure that governments do not divert from existing environmental, health, safety, or labor measures to gain competitive advantage in trade or investment. It also aims at increasing transparency in both government policies and practices in areas affecting business, particularly in establishing standards and regulatory requirements, improving intellectual property protection rights, and adhering to OAS and OECD accords to combat corrupt business practices.[44] In this way, the FTAA provides a negotiating forum for issues that are created by the process of globalization of trade and finance, but are outside pure market mechanisms for resolution.

FREE TRADE AND TRADE INTEGRATION REVISITED

Latin America has radically reoriented its trade approach in the past two decades. It has gone from a relatively inward-looking to an outwardly oriented development model. Much of this has taken place through unilateral changes in accord with global trading rules. A second wave of trade reform was prompted by the movement to subregional trading arrangements. These arrangements have encouraged countries to negotiate some of the tougher issues of market access and management of externalities. A spirit of neighborliness is evolving in the region, where collective goals figure prominently on the agenda of the hemisphere's leaders. Whether the countries of the hemisphere will be able to capitalize on this momentum to create a regional trading system is uncertain. Neighborliness is somewhat easier at the subregional level, where countries may share common economic characteristics or have a clear incentive to solve common border problems. In the spirit of cooperation, we should also not forget to ask again whether such a regional regime is desirable. Will a hemispheric agreement increase trade or divert trade from other, more efficient suppliers in the world? Nevertheless, in the end it may, like the NAFTA, be a story less of pure economic effects and more of the ways in which a genuine trade partnership may open the door to solutions on tough problems facing the region on the social and environmental agendas. The initiatives of the Santiago Summit indicate a willingness to pursue the social agenda. After we look at the effects of the new economic model on sources of competitiveness in the industrial and agricultural sectors in chapters 9 and 10, we will turn to these difficult issues of poverty, human capital formation, and environmental degradation that require remediation for the nations of the region to pursue genuinely sustainable and dynamic integrated development.

Key Concepts

Andean Community	Factor price equalization	Open regionalism
Central American	Free trade area	Stolper-Samuelson
Common Market	Heckscher-Ohlin	effect
Common market	theorem	Theory of comparative
Customs union	Mercosur	advantage
Economic union	NAFTA	Trade creation
		Trade diversion

Chapter Summary

The Theory of Free Trade

- The theoretical underpinning of free trade is the theory of comparative advantage, which states that countries should trade those goods they can most efficiently produce to maximize global output. Since its introduction by David Ricardo, different economists have further developed the theory to include a two-factor model of labor and capital and distribution implications.
- Critics of free trade contend that in practice, there are few gains from trade for developing countries. From dependency theory to gender and environmental dimensions, critics believe that free trade can actually be damaging to sustainable growth.
- During the 1980s, Latin America experienced deteriorating current account deficits, although Asia prospered from export-oriented growth. Using Asia as an example, trade liberalization was promoted by the international community as a way of improving growth conditions in Latin America.
- If free trade is to be implemented, then policy makers must consider several issues including an adequate time frame, appropriate exchange rates, state assistance in adapting to the transition, and fiscal reform.
- Current performance in Latin America shows that these countries in general have reduced tariffs and there has been an increase in the flow of goods, both exports and imports. The composition of goods has also changed, though primary products continue to play a dominant role.

Integration

- There are four ways a country can integrate its markets: a free trade area, a customs union, a common market, and an economic union. Integration can be beneficial because it takes advantage of economies of scale, opens markets, and promotes credibility for the region. Integration also has negative consequences if it diverts trade from the most efficient producers.
- NAFTA, a regional trade agreement among the United States, Canada, and Mexico, sought to decrease tariffs over a ten-year period and increase trade in the region. The controversy surrounding the agreement was based upon fears that NAFTA would lead to job loss in the North, contribute to environmental degradation, and tug at the nationalistic sentiments of the Mexican population.
- Mercosur is a regional trade agreement among Brazil, Argentina, Uruguay, and Paraguay, with associate members Chile and Bolivia. Since its inception, trade has increased not only among the member states but with the European Union as well, though harmonization of policies has proved more difficult.

Two other regional agreements include the those of the Andean Community and the Central American Common Market.

- The increased importance of Latin America as a trading partner for the United States has led many to lobby for a Free Trade Agreement of the Americas. Despite the increase in interest among many Latin American countries and the United States, an actual agreement could prove difficult in the near future for political, social, and economic reasons.

Notes

1. Carlos Díaz Alejandro, "International Markets for LCDs: The Old and the New," *American Economic Review*, May 1978, p. 254–269.

2. Schumpeter argued that shocks to an industry, like crises in the life of an individual, might force the sector to grow and adapt. Industries, like people, he suggested, sometimes need to be pushed to try something different.

3. Sebastian Edwards, "The Opening of Latin America," in *Crisis and Reform in Latin America: From Despair to Hope* (New York: Oxford University Press, 1995).

4. World Trade Organization, "World Merchandise Trade in 1996 by Region and Leading Trader," *International Trade*, 30 July 1997, available at www.wto/intltrad/iiworld.htm.

5. This section summarizes the findings of Sebastian Edwards and Daniel Lederman, *The Political Economy of Unilateral Trade Liberalization: The Case of Chile*, National Bureau of Economic Research Working Paper no. 6510 (Cambridge, Mass.: National Bureau of Economic Research, 1998). Available at www.nber.org/papers/w6510.

6. Andrew Zimbalist, "Costa Rica," in *Struggle Against Dependence: Nontraditional Export Growth in Central America and the Caribbean*, ed. Eva Paus (Boulder: Westview, 1988), 26.

7. Warburg Dillon Read, *The Latin American Adviser*, 9 July 1998, p. 16 (fax newsletter).

8. All data are from Commission Economica Para America Latina, *Indicadores Económicos* (Santiago, Chile: Commission Economica Para America Latina, 1997).

9. Ricardo Ffrench-Davis, comment on L. Allan Winters, "Assessing Regional Integration," in *Trade: Towards Open Regionalism*, proceedings of the 1997 World Bank Conference on Development in Latin America and the Caribbean (Washington, D.C.: World Bank, 1998), 73–74.

10. Sarath Rajapatirana, *Trade Policies in Latin America and the Caribbean: Priorities, Progress, and Prospects* (San Francisco: International Center for Economic Growth, 1997), 15.

11. Jagdish Bhagwati, "The FTAA Is *Not* Free Trade," in *Trade: Towards Open Regionalism*, proceedings of the 1997 World Bank Conference on Development in Latin America and the Caribbean (Washington, D.C.: World Bank, 1998).

12. L. Allan Winters, "Assessing Regional Integration," in *Trade: Towards Open Regionalism*, proceedings of the 1997 World Bank Conference on Development in Latin America and the Caribbean (Washington, D.C.: World Bank, 1998).

13. Enrique V. Iglesias, "The Search for a New Economic Consensus in Latin

America," in *The Legacy of Raúl Prebisch*, ed. Enrique V. Iglesias (Washington, D.C.: Inter-American Development Bank, 1994), 97.

14. Domestic lobbies in both countries kept the tariffs on textiles high.

15. Arvind Panagariya, "The Free Trade Area of the Americas: Good for Latin America?" *World Economy* 19, no. 5 (1996): 496.

16. Magnus Blomström and Ari Kokko, *Regional Integration and Foreign Direct Investment*, National Bureau of Economic Research Working Paper no. 6019 (Cambridge, Mass.: National Bureau of Economic Research, 1997). The U.S. FDI stock went from U.S.$13,370 million in 1992 to U.S.$14,037 million; this represents a decline from 2.73 percent of total U.S. foreign direct investment to 1.97 percent.

17. "NAFTA: Where's That Giant Sucking Sound?" *Business Week*, 7 July 1997, p. 45. Cites study by Kate Bronfenbrenner of Cornell University.

18. Ibid.

19. Ibid.; and Jeffrey J. Schott, "NAFTA: An Interim Report," in *Trade: Towards Open Regionalism*, proceedings of the 1997 World Bank Conference on Development in Latin America and the Caribbean (Washington, D.C.: World Bank, 1998).

20. Employment Policy Foundation, "Open Trade: The 'Fast Track' to Higher Living Standards," *Contemporary Issues in Employment and Workplace Policy* 111, no. 10 (October 1997). Internet publication available at http://epfnet.org.

21. Sidney Weintraub, "In the Debate about NAFTA, Just the Facts, Please," *The Wall Street Journal,* 20 June 1997, p. A19.

22. Congressman David Bonior, "I Told You So," editorial, *New York Times*, 13 July 1997.

23. Sam Howe Verhovek, "Pollution Problems Fester South of the Border," *New York Times*, 4 July 1998. On-line edition.

24. Data from Lustig's comment on Jeffrey J. Schott, "NAFTA: An Interim Report," in *Trade: Towards Open Regionalism*, proceedings of the 1997 World Bank Conference on Development in Latin America and the Caribbean (Washington, D.C.: World Bank, 1998), 127.

25. Ibid., 125.

26. Report on the Binational Commission, International Studies Association meetings, Washington, D.C., 20 February 1999.

27. John Templeman, "Is Europe Elbowing the U.S. Out of South America?" *Business Week*, 4 August 1997, p. 56.

28. *Argentina Business: The Portable Encyclopedia for Doing Business with Argentina* (San Rafael, Calif.: World Trade Press, 1995).

29. "Auto Industry Delivers Vote of Confidence in Brazil and Mercosur," *Latin American Weekly Report*, 3 February 1998, p. 49.

30. Danny Lepziger, Claudio Frischtak, Homi J. Kharas, and John F. Normand, "Mercosur: Integration and Industrial Policy," *World Economy* 20, no. 5 (1997): 596.

31. A study by Alexander Yeats at the World Bank caused an uproar when it argued that Mercosur lowered efficiency. Michael Phillip, "South American Trade Pact Is under Fire," *The Wall Street Journal*, 23 October 1996.

32. World Bank, *Towards Open Regionalism* (Washington, D.C.: World Bank, 1998).

33. "Brazil's Neighbors Are Very Nervous," *Business Week*, 17 November 1997.

34. Diana Jean Schemo, "A Latin Bloc Asks U.S. and Europe to Ease Trade Barriers," *New York Times*, 23 February 1999. On-line edition.

35. Venezuela joined in 1973; Chile was a member between 1969 and 1976.

36. Peru does not participate.

37. Juan José Echavarría, "Trade Flow in the Andean Countries: Unilateral Liberal-

ization or Regional Preferences," in *Trade: Towards Open Regionalism*, proceedings of the 1997 World Bank Conference on Development in Latin America and the Caribbean (Washington, D.C.: World Bank, 1998), 95.

38. Miguel Rodríguez-Mendoza, "The Andean Group's Integration Strategy," in *Integrating the Hemisphere, 1997: The Inter-American Dialogue*, ed. Ana Julia Jatar and Sidney Weintraub (Santafé de Bogotá, Colombia: Tercer Mundo, 1997).

39. Eduardo Lizano and José M. Salazar-Xirinach, "Central American Common Market and Hemispheric Free Trade," in *Integrating the Hemisphere, 1997: The Inter-American Dialogue*, ed. Ana Julia Jatar and Sidney Weintraub (Santa Fe de Bogotá, Colombia: Tercer Mundo, 1997).

40. Thomas F. McLarty, "Hemispheric Free Trade Is Still a National Priority," *The Wall Street Journal*, 26 May 1995, p. A11. Facts confirmed in *U.S. Total Exports to Individual Countries, 1991–1997*. Available at www.ita.doc.gov.

41. Andre Chipman, "U.S., Latin-American Oil Companies Build Alliances as Mideast Clout Fades," *The Wall Street Journal*, 9 March 1998.

42. As reported in "The Key Points of the FTAA Agenda," *Latin American Weekly Report*, WR-97-20 (1997), p. 230.

43. Paulo Wrobel, "A Free Trade Area of the Americas in 2005?" *International Affairs* 74, no. 3 (1998): 547–561.

44. Robert Mosbacher, chairman, Council of the Americas, "Trade Expansion within the Americas: A U.S. Business Perspective," remarks at the Chile–United States Issues Round Table, Crown Plaza Hotel, Santiago, Chile, 17 April 1998. Available at http://207.87.5.23/sr.html; accessed 12 July 1999.

CHAPTER NINE

INTERNATIONAL INDUSTRIAL COMPETITIVENESS

Improving the Quality of Labor, Technology, and Infrastructure

Better roads will facilitate bringing goods to market for peasant farmers.
(Courtesy of David Mangurian and the Inter-American Development Bank.)

Competitive participation in global markets demands radical structural changes in both input and output markets in Latin America. Labor markets have become more flexible to adapt to global production requirements. Technological change defines the production frontier, and complementary infrastructure is critical for rapid communication and transportation of goods. In chapter 8 we learned that trade theory indicated that labor-abundant countries should export labor-intensive goods. But not all labor is the same. Clearly the quality of the labor force will affect the efficiency and the relative cost of goods. Simply having abundant and cheap labor is not enough to win in the global trading game. Furthermore, it must be combined with effective and dynamic technological systems. To make the most of labor in a dynamic technological setting, firms must also have adequate transportation and telecommunications infrastructures to promote global competitiveness.

This chapter will survey some of the changes in input markets, with a focus on labor, technology, and infrastructure. We will explore both how policy changes have affected inputs and ways in which the improvement of input quality might enhance growth. Our questions for consideration include the following:

- How has internationalization affected labor markets?
- Has an external orientation improved the position of workers, or has it made them worse off?
- What are the technological requirements of global competitiveness?
- How can less technologically advanced economies compete in the international arena?
- With a decrease in the role of the state, who should be investing in technology and infrastructure?
- How have manufacturing and agriculture responded to international opening?
- Have new areas of comparative advantage been identified for Latin American firms?

The chapter will look at some of the changes that have already taken place in the 1990s but will also identify deficiencies in input quality and an agenda for further development of sources of competitiveness in the global arena.

Key Issues in Understanding Latin American Labor Markets

Three issues are important in understanding contemporary labor markets in Latin America: the traditional role that unions have played in labor relations in the region, the importance of the informal market in economic production, and the relatively high rate of unemployment facing Latin America today. High unemployment and structural rigidities in the labor market contribute to a large **informal sector,** characterized by low wages and poor working conditions, that reaches levels as high as 60 percent of the labor force in Bolivia. In part the high rate of unemployment can be attributed to a mismatch between skilled and unskilled labor as

the economy has opened to international competition. Labor unions, while protecting the rights of workers, can also contribute to inflexibility and unemployment.
We will consider these issues in turn with an eye to policy suggestions to improve
labor's contributions to global competitiveness.

Labor Policy

Latin American countries have long used labor legislation as a tool of social policy.[1] Minimum wages and measures to protect jobs, such as heavy required severance packages or laws against hiring replacement workers, were seen as political
vehicles for income transfers and the protection of the poor. The unintended result,
however, was labor market rigidity. Labor market distortions in Latin America
include government intervention in setting wages, high costs of dismissal, high
payroll taxes, and the nature of labor–management relations. There is a long tradition of protecting job security. Workers may contest dismissals in court and may
be awarded large severance packages. All these factors reduce the flexibility of
management and make restructuring difficult.

Union activity is concentrated in the urban formal sector. The union movement
in Latin America is often the path to political power, and many government officials are leaders in the union movement. Labor unions along with the military have
historically been among the few interest group power centers with the organizational structure, leadership capacity, and defined objectives to affect policy outcomes.[2] However, labor union influence has varied historically. Beginning in the
1920s, many Latin American governments began enforcing workers' rights. Legislation and public controls to address employment issues and resolve labor conflicts
fit with the populist political paradigm. Governments were directly involved in
collective bargaining, promoting a close alignment between political parties and
labor. Through legislative changes, formal sector employees obtained a number of
guarantees, most important among them job security. Ground was lost in the 1970s
when military governments restricted labor organizing. The return to democracy
in the 1980s was also accompanied by austerity, limiting gains on the labor front.
Trade liberalization in the 1990s has further constrained labor's bargaining power.
Because the number of unions in the public sector tends to be higher than in the
private sector because public firms may be monopolies by statute, privatization has
also contributed to a decrease in union power.[3]

Labor market reforms have not kept pace with the overall reform efforts in
the region. Through 1995, only five countries had undertaken significant reform:
Argentina (1991), Colombia (1990), Guatemala (1990), Panama (1995), and Peru
(1991). Reforms have primarily focused on decreasing the costs of firing and temporarily hiring workers. In most countries in the region, dismissing a worker after
one year carries a severance penalty of more than one month's wage; with ten
years' seniority, the cost rises to between six months' and one year's salary. Temporary hiring practices have traditionally been constrained in the region in the
interest of job security; this interferes with firms' ability to meet cyclical global
demand. Finally, in the absence of strong social legislation, health, social security,

and unemployment compensation schemes have been directly tied to the wage bill. In Argentina, Brazil, Colombia, and Uruguay this tax tops 30 percent of the cost of labor; throughout the rest of the region it ranges between 15 and 30 percent.[4] High social taxes on labor distort whatever advantage abundant labor might confer in the international economy.

Formal sector workers are required to contribute to social security funds, which generally provide workers with pensions, health care, and accident insurance. The difficulties with these funds include their encouragement of early retirement, payments unrelated to individual contributions, and expensive health care packages that exclude the nonworking poor. Pension systems in the region tend to be organized on a pay as you go basis, placing the burden for payments on current enrollees in the system. In Chile a program of mandatory payments into individual accounts with minimum benefits being guaranteed by the government has replaced the pay as you go scheme. Workers may choose among different investment accounts, generating competition in the market. Similar schemes have been adopted in Argentina, Colombia, Mexico, and Peru.[5] Using the market to create the individual incentive to save for retirement may not only take the burden off firms but also raise national savings rates and decrease reliance on capital inflows, a point we made in chapter 7.

Labor relations in Latin America are relatively inflexible. The right to representation is assigned to union officials by the government. For example, in the case of auto workers negotiating with General Motors in Brazil in 1995, when union–management relations broke down, a labor court mediated the outcome. Strikes are permitted as a manner of political expression. Under the old economic model a focus on job creation and solidarity undergirded the socioeconomic order.[6] Labor was an important political player.

Trade union membership in 1995 for South America and Central America combined was 33,472,996. As a basis of comparison, membership in North America was 20,448,500; in Africa and the Middle East combined it was 17,364,491; East Asia and Southeast Asia had 23,930,252 union members; northern, western, and southern Europe combined had 41,449,514 members; and eastern Europe's membership was 13,992,600.[7] Despite relatively high starting points, many Latin American countries show substantial declines in union membership with liberalization. In Argentina, 38.7 percent of wage and salary earners were unionized, reflecting a 42.6 percent fall between 1985 and 1995. Venezuela, with lower membership at 17.1 percent, experienced a smaller decline. Mexico's membership of 42.8 percent was diminished by a −28.2 percent growth rate.

Political opening in Chile after General Pinochet led to a large increase in the number of unions. In 1970, 4,578 unions represented 628,396 workers; those numbers grew to 12,109 unions in 1990 with 661,966 members. While the overall number of unions has increased a great deal in this twenty-year span, the average number of members per union has constantly declined throughout the period, dropping from 132 in 1970 to 55 in 1994. As a result, the rate of growth of unionized workers, once as high as 25.7 percent, has now declined to −3.3 percent.[8]

Mexico provides an interesting example of how political change and economic liberalization are affecting the power of unions. For decades union effectiveness

Increasing labor productivity is a key challenge to compete in global markets. *(Courtesy of David Mangurian and the Inter-American Development Bank.)*

through the Confederation of Mexican Workers (CTM) was tied to the political power of the PRI, the dominant political party in Mexico. As the power of the PRI was challenged by new political parties in the 1990s, space was created for independent breakaway unions. Changes in labor laws have been proposed by upstart labor foundations such as the UNT, or the National Workers Union, to decrease government's control over the unions. New organizations are also benefiting from NAFTA. U.S. and Canadian unions, fearful of being undercut by cheap Mexican labor, have been working to strengthen an independent labor movement in Latin America. International media attention has been called to cases of union bashing in the maquila sector. Oddly, internationalization may work to strengthen the hand of labor in the region.

Globalization may transform the role of unions in Latin America. "Reinventing" the labor movement as an inclusionary, democratic movement that promotes accountability is a challenge for the future.[9] Box 9.1 illustrates a productive approach to labor–management relations in the region. In many countries, contract negotiations have moved from an industry-wide, national level to decentralized collective bargaining at the company level. This allows firms greater flexibility in negotiating contracts that better reflect local conditions and productivity levels. While this of course also decreases the power of the unions to shut down production, greater flexibility has created new employment options economy-wide.[10] To deal effectively with the question of unemployment and poverty tied to informal sector employment, however, unions may no longer be enough. Collective social

Box 9.1.   A Seat at the Table: Union Leaders Urge IDB to Include Workers' Concerns in Reform Programs and Free Trade Negotiations

It was the sort of meeting that presumably never takes place.

At the IDB's Washington, D.C., headquarters last February, senior Bank officials spent a day listening to some of their most legendary critics: labor union leaders from Latin America and the Caribbean . . . including John J. Sweeney, president of the American Federation of Labor–Congress of Industrial Organizations (AFL-CIO), Luis Anderson, president of the Inter-American Regional Workers Organization (ORIT), and top union federation officials from Argentina, Barbados, Brazil, Canada, Chile, the Dominican Republic, Mexico, Venezuela and the United States.

"Much of the mistrust that existed between us before has now disappeared," said ORIT's Anderson. But while he praised the IDB for its willingness to talk with labor leaders, Anderson said most of the region's governments have refused to consult organized labor prior to adopting economic reforms that are promoted by the IDB.

Anderson said this lack of consultation is inexcusable, particularly on issues such as regional integration and trade liberalization, because workers are the first to feel the consequences of these changes. "We've never debated whether or not we agree with economic globalization and integration, because we know it's a reality," Anderson said. "We know that great wealth is being created [thanks to integration], but at the same time we see that poverty is increasing, the number of jobs is decreasing, and the informal sector is growing. So we believe there is a problem in the distribution of the benefits of these reforms."

Anderson and other labor leaders at the meeting said they generally support efforts to open local economies to greater foreign competition, but they warned that governments that fail to address the inequitable distribution of wealth and exclude labor unions from the trade policy debate risk a backlash from voters. . . . As a step in the right direction, Anderson suggested that the IDB promote the creation of a forum for labor consultations as part of negotiations leading to the creation of the Free Trade Area of the Americas (FTAA).

In his remarks at the meeting, IDB President Enrique V. Iglesias agreed that the economic reforms that have swept Latin America in recent years have come at a cost for the regions' workers, and that the problem of unemployment has reached "new dimensions" in many of the region's countries. He also concurred that relations between labor, government, and business have not been as productive as they should, saying there is a need to "improve the quality of the dialogue" between these groups.

Labor participants at the meeting also criticized what they described as a widespread failure to enforce worker rights codified in the various conventions of the International Labor Organization (ILO). The ILO conventions, which most Latin American and Caribbean countries have ratified, set forth a variety of basic workers rights, including the right to organize and bargain collectively, and protections against child labor and on-the-job discrimination based on gender.

Stan Gacek, the AFL-CIO's assistant director for international affairs, said the failure to enforce labor protections stems from a broader refusal by most governments to link social rights to trade policy. He argued that this refusal is difficult to justify when capital rights, such as those protecting intellectual property and trademarks, are explicitly addressed and defended in trade accords. "Governments that violate copyright protections get harsh treatment," Gacek said, "but what about those who violate labor protections?"

On a different note, other union participants at the meeting acknowledged that labor movement leaders have not always kept up with the changing demands of the market. "We recognize that the trade union movement isn't prepared adequately to deal with new technologies and globalization," said Nair Goulart, a Brazilian who is president of

ORIT's Women's Committee. Participants praised an IDB program that paid for selected union leaders to take university courses on labor economics, and they encouraged the IDB to consider additional programs in labor leadership training.

Gustavo Márquez, a labor specialist in the Office of the IDB Chief Economist, said today's union leaders also need to be more understanding of the demands of increasingly specialized and competitive labor markets that require flexible workers to meet evolving production processes. He said many of the labor disputes in Latin America today revolve around outdated work rules that limit the ability of employees' to adapt to these changes. He urged new rules that safeguard worker rights while allowing for greater competitiveness and productivity.

"We have different starting points, different jargon, and a different history," IDB Executive Vice President Nancy Birdsall told participants at the conclusion of the meeting. "But we need more of these meetings because it is clear that we also have a great deal in common. We support open negotiations between business and labor. We support social protections, developing better safety nets and better unemployment insurance arrangements."

Source: Paul Constance, the Inter-American Development Bank homepage, www.iadb.org, 14 June 1998, from *IDB América*, April 1998.

action that includes measures to improve training, productivity, and work organization are important. NGOs have become active participants in reaching down into the informal market to promote labor reform.[11]

Unemployment

Unemployment has become one of the most pressing problems on the Latin American economic agenda. In addition to unemployment generated by the legacy of economic crisis, the relatively young age structure of the population in the region requires substantial new job creation. As shown in table 9.1, the employment problem is compounded by the need not only to find jobs for existing workers but also to accommodate new members of the economically active population (EAP). A growing proportion of workers concentrated in the urban sector further compounds this problem. The industrial sector must create jobs not only faster than the rate of growth of the population but also fast enough to absorb those fleeing rural poverty and land degradation.

Given this challenge, the rate of regional open unemployment of 7.8 percent for 1995 may not look so bad by industrial country standards. Open unemployment refers to those officially counted by governments as actively searching for jobs. Imagine the data difficulties in counting the unemployed in poor countries. Furthermore, most unemployed workers in the region cannot afford the luxury of waiting in line at the unemployment office. With weak unemployment safety nets, people must find whatever work they can to scrape by. White-collar unemployed take blue-collar jobs. You may be surprised at the level of underemployment, for example, if you ever have occasion to debate politics or philosophy with your overeducated Buenos Aires cab driver. Many are subsisting with jobs for which they are extremely overqualified. The informal sector, the topic of our next section,

Table 9.1.   Employment and Wage Data for Latin America

Employment and Wage Data	1980	1985	1990	1995
Population growth rates (annual)	—	2.1	1.9	1.8
Economically active population (EAP) (total annual % growth)	—	3.5	3.1	2.6
Urban EAP (% of total EAP)	66.9	70.0	72.8	75.3
Nonagricultural employment (annual % growth)	—	3.5	4.4	3.0
Rate of open unemployment (% growth)	6.7	10.1	8.0	7.8
Informality (% of total employment)	40.2	47.0	42.1	55.7
Public employment (% of total employment)	15.7	16.6	15.5	13.6
Real wages in manufacturing (index)	100.0	93.1	86.8	96.3
Minimum real wages	100.0	86.4	68.9	70.1

Source: Tokman (1998), table 4.1.

has also claimed large numbers of the unemployed; in 1997 it grew by 4.5 percent. As the number trying to eke out a living in this sector increases, many turn to petty street crime and social violence to survive.

Unemployment is a result of the faster rate of growth of new entrants to the market as compared to new jobs. It has been exacerbated by the severe contraction of state employment under the neoliberal model.[12] Both privatization and the downsizing of central government have released workers. But the fall in public sector employment is not the whole story. Workers in all sectors of the economy may be confronting conditions of "precarious" employment where, compared to past regimes of labor guarantees and state jobs, employment for some has become less remunerative, less regulated by government, and less subject to collective control of workers.[13] An International Labor Organization survey shows that two-thirds of all workers in the region are worried or very worried about losing their jobs.[14] Competition for export assembly in the global arena has decreased worker and community leverage with respect to employment conditions. Economic crises and associated adjustments such as the currency crisis in Mexico have resulted in lower wages and poorer conditions for workers. In table 9.1 we see that 1995 minimum wages adjusted for inflation were 70 percent of their 1980 levels. Imagine if your family income had declined nearly one-third while you grew up. A worsening of formal sector conditions has contributed to the poor progress on poverty reduction in the region.[15]

Women's participation in the labor force has also changed. Long-term forces including technological changes, advances in educational attainment, decreases in fertility, progress in women's rights, shifts in the structure of households, and intensified consumerism have pushed more women into the workplace. But women have also responded to short-term cyclical changes. Labor force participation by women increased from an average of 28 percent in the 1970s to 38 percent in the early 1990s, with variation from 24 percent in Bolivia to 51 percent in El Salvador. The growth of female participation is concentrated at the low end of the income structure, indicating that necessity has pushed women into the workplace.[16] Once at the bottom of the labor market, women tend to stay there. Labor market segmentation, or the stereotyping of jobs suitable for women, has a profound impact on employment potential in the region. A World Bank study found that 60 percent of the earnings differential between men and women in a study of fifteen Latin American countries was attributable to cultural aspects segmenting the market and limiting the suitable jobs for women.[17]

Rates of open unemployment are rising, creating alarming scenarios for public safety. There are approximately 10 million unemployed in Latin America, 6 million of whom are women, and 5.5 million under twenty-five years of age.[18]

Youth unemployment hovers at 20 percent, indicating the difficulties newcomers to the market face finding jobs.[19] As can be seen by looking at table 9.2, from 1990 until 1997 unemployment rates in urban areas increased in twelve out of the seventeen countries. Central American republics, still contending with the legacy of war and the reintegration of ex-combatants at the beginning of the decade, have made some progress. The increase in unemployment in the rest of the region is in part tied to the decrease in the share of public employment without matching private sector growth. In Argentina, for example, the share of public sector employment fell from 19.3 percent to 13.2 percent; in Bolivia, the fall was from 16.5 percent to 11.1 percent.[20] Structural adjustment—changing the shape of the market and the state—has taken its toll on labor.

You may be surprised by the degree of variation in unemployment across the region. Economic integration in Mercosur is complicated by the fact that Argentine unemployment hovers around 15 percent, while Brazilians have rates of about 6

Table 9.2.   Latin America: Urban Unemployment (average annual growth rates in percent)

Country	1990	1991	1992	1993	1994	1995	1996	1997	1998*
Argentina	7.5	6.5	7	9.6	11.5	17.5	17.2	14.9	13.2
Bolivia	7.3	5.8	5.4	5.8	3.1	3.6	3.8	4.4	12.1
Brazil	4.3	4.8	5.8	5.4	5.1	4.6	5.4	5.7	—
Chile	6.5	9.3	7	6.2	7.8	7.4	6.4	6.1	6.1
Colombia	10.5	10.2	10.2	8.6	8.9	8.8	11.2	12.4	15.1
Costa Rica	5.4	6	4.3	4	4.3	5.7	6.6	5.9	5.4
Ecuador	6.1	8.5	8.9	8.9	7.8	7.7	10.4	9.3	—
El Salvador	10	7.9	8.2	8.1	7	7	7.5	7.5	7.2
Guatemala	6.5	4	1.5	2.5	3.3	3.7	3.7	5	5.9
Honduras	7.8	7.4	6	7	4	5.6	6.5	6.4	5.8
Mexico	2.7	2.7	2.8	3.4	3.7	6.2	5.5	3.7	3.3
Nicaragua	11.5	11.5	14.4	17.8	17.1	16.9	16	14.3	12.2
Panama	20	19.3	17.5	15.6	16	16.6	16.7	15.4	15.6
Paraguay	6.6	5.1	5.3	5.1	4.4	5.3	8.2	7.1	—
Peru	8.3	5.9	9.4	9.9	8.8	8.2	8	9.2	9
Uruguay	9.2	8.9	9	8.3	9.2	10.3	11.9	11.5	10
Venezuela	11	9.5	7.8	6.6	8.7	10.3	11.8	11.4	11.2

Source: CEPAL, *Balance Preliminar de la Economía de América Latina y el Caribe,* appendix.
Published each year and available at www.eclac.org, cuadro A-4 (1997 and 1998 editions).
*Forecast.

percent. The variation in employment performance has to do not only with the structure of labor markets, but also with the importance that policy makers placed on employment generation in structural adjustment. Brazil, for example, was able to maintain more expansive growth policies because of its large internal market while Argentina was held to strict external conditionality. Nonetheless, artificially pumping up the economy has costs in terms of fiscal and international balance—issues the Brazilians are struggling with today.

The slowdown associated with the Brazilian and Asian currency crises is likely to hit workers throughout the region hard. With unemployment forecasts as high as 9.5 percent for 1999, women and youth are being forced out of the market. In Peru, for example, with a national unemployment rate of 8 percent, 11.2 percent of women and 13.9 percent of youths are unemployed, despite a youth training program that absorbs much of the younger work force.[21]

Inflexible labor policy is not the only element that needs to be addressed in correcting this problem; strong and stable GDP growth is necessary to improve unemployment.[22] The ECLAC secretariat has estimated that growth rates of 6 percent over a sustained period will be necessary to achieve greater social equity and make sustainable progress toward changing patterns of production. Average growth rates of a moderate 3.1 percent that also exhibit high instability, ranging from 5.3 percent to 0.3 percent in 1994 to 1995, have left most countries short of this goal.[23] Accelerating and steady growth rates are critical to improving in employment performance in the region.

It is important to remember that reducing unemployment involves not only creating jobs for the current work force but also doing so at a faster rate than the increase in the economically active population of a country. Because populations in Latin America are relatively young, with large numbers of new job seekers entering the market each year, the challenge is enormous. The increase in labor force participation rates by women in Latin America from approximately 28 percent in the 1970s to 38 percent in the early 1990s has also put pressure on labor markets. The good news for the future is that as women have entered the work force, population growth rates have fallen from 2 percent a year in the late 1980s to 1.6 percent in the late 1990s. There is, however, wide variation as population rates continue to grow in Central America.[24]

THE RISE OF THE INFORMAL SECTOR

One result of inadequate job growth in the private sector has been the expansion of the informal sector. Survival strategies have sent workers scrambling for subsistence in a sector not covered by insurance, benefits, or regulations. The informal sector acted as the main source of job creation in the 1990s, rising from 51 percent of nonagricultural employment to 57 percent by 1997. Eighty-four out of every 100 new jobs were in the informal sector, while the formal sector employment shrank from 15.3 percent to 13 percent of total employment.[25] Informal sector growth has been strongest in Bolivia, Panama, Paraguay, and Venezuela.[26]

Informality can describe any number of jobs ranging from the street vendor of nail files and the family maid to the small restaurant owner and the corner mechanic. The informal sector has three main areas: microenterprise employment, own-account workers, and domestic service. Microenterprises have been the fastest growing area, at 5.2 percent per year, accounting for 22.5 percent of total employment in the region. Own-account workers have been increasing at 4.4 percent per year, making up 26.5 percent of the region's total working population. Domestic service employment has increased by 3.9 percent, with workers of this sector making up 7.1 percent of the economically active population (EAP). Domestic service and own-account work are the lowest productivity occupations, acting as a drag on overall productivity growth.[27]

The lack of a clear definition for the informal sector makes measurement problematic. Some basic guidelines that characterize informality include a low ratio between capital and labor, small-scale, worker-owned means of production, family-based operations involving children, and the virtual impossibility of accumulation of capital. The list of informal jobs with these characteristics is extensive, including mobile vendors, taxi drivers, small business owners, artisan manufacturers, maids, subcontractors, other services providers, and illegal businesses such as contraband or drug trafficking and professionals who work for themselves.[28] The informal sector is an easy solution for the unemployed because there is little in the way of money, capital, or qualifications needed to become involved. It is also an important source of employment for women and children.

There is overwhelming evidence to suggest that urban poverty and informal employment are closely related. The proportion of working poor in the informal sector varies in each country: Bolivia has 66.2 percent, Brazil 66.4 percent, Costa Rica 63.5 percent, Guatemala 93.3 percent, Honduras 84.9 percent, Panama 87.1 percent, Paraguay 64.7 percent, Uruguay 18.3 percent, and Venezuela 57.4 percent. In Costa Rica in 1982, 75.8 percent of the poorest among the poor were in the informal sector, compared with 53.5 percent of the "not-so-poor" and 31.7 percent of the "nonpoor." In urban Panama in 1983, 67 percent of the urban poor population was in the informal sector.[29]

Informality tends to be associated with unskilled workers. As a large majority of the labor force, the unskilled have difficulty finding formal sector employment. Limited educational opportunity and an unequal social structure constrain workers from investing in their own human capital. With little education, workers land in low-skill jobs—jobs that in a vicious circle are associated with limited on-the-job training opportunities. Furthermore, a low-quality and low-skilled labor force can act as a deterrent to investment if investors need an experienced labor force.

Poverty and inequality in the informal sector appear to be self-perpetuating. The broad income gap between highly skilled workers and those in low-skilled, often informal occupations increased from 40 percent in 1994 to 60 percent in 1996. Skilled labor incomes are increasing while wages for workers outside the modern sector have not experienced growth.[30] As seen in table 9.3, wage differentials between high- and low-productivity workers rose in eight out of ten countries surveyed. Because those at the bottom have even less to invest in their own human capital, they fall further and further behind. Professional and technical wages in Chile, Paraguay, Uruguay, and Venezuela increased sharply; in contrast, wages of

Table 9.3.   Average Incomes and Labor Income Disparities

Country	Year	Professional and Technical Workers	Workers in Low Productivity Sector
Bolivia	1989	7.6	3.4
	1994	7.2	2.3
Brazil	1987	7.7	3.4
	1993	7.5	2.3
Chile	1990	6.6	3.9
	1994	8.4	4.1
Colombia	1990	6.7	3.3
	1994	7.9	2.7
Costa Rica	1990	7.2	3.2
	1994	8.2	3.6
Honduras	1990	6.5	1.5
	1994	4.5	1.4
Mexico	1989	5.5	4.0
	1994	6.3	3.1
Paraguay	1990	3.9	2.4
	1994	6.7	2.0
Uruguay	1990	6.0	2.7
	1994	9.6	3.1
Venezuela	1990	4.2	3.6
	1994	6.3	3.3

Source: Economic Commission for Latin America and the Caribbean, *The Equity Gap: Latin America, the Caribbean, and the Social Summit* (Santiago, Chile: Economic Commission for Latin America and the Caribbean, 1997).

unskilled workers fell in Bolivia and Brazil. In Colombia, Mexico, Paraguay, and Venezuela, where a rise in professional and a drop in unskilled wages occurred, the income gap problem was doubled.

Although it holds limited promise for advancement, the informal sector does serve as a social net for the poor and unskilled and has therefore helped to rescue families from deprivation. Where there are weak social safety nets and limited unemployment insurance, the informal sector is employment of last resort.[31] Beyond poverty and survival, there are other motives for participation in this sector. Sometimes individuals take advantage of profitable opportunities in market niches waiting to be exploited. This may take place by offering tailored services that large enterprises may not find attractive or possible. Also, the informal sector allows businesses to avoid compliance with regulations. Labor legislation in many countries defines not only basic legal rights but also detailed conditions of employment including wages, job security, the number of vacation days, and employer obligations. In Brazil, for example, taxes and labor laws can add up to 70 percent of the base salary. By law, formal sector workers are also entitled to large severance packages. Many businesses therefore remain unregistered or unlicensed to avoid costly compliance with regulations. However, there should be a distinction made between those who are capable of paying the cost of regulations and those who cannot because their incomes are too low. Many nonpoor—who could, for example, be paying taxes—also form part of the informal sector.[32]

The large, untaxed segment of the working population in the informal sector creates challenges for fiscal stabilization. Some, such as analysts within ECLAC, contend that it has widened the wage gap, increased inequality, and lowered average productivity, hampering competitiveness.[33] However, this may be blaming a symptom and not a cause. According to the International Labor Organization, the informal sector arose as a response to the inability of the modern sector to provide sufficient jobs. Urban employment would have to grow more rapidly than the number of new labor market entrants to reduce open unemployment—a daunting objective in the short run. The burden of employment generation therefore falls on the informal sector—not a first best solution.

Given its usefulness in absorbing workers, the challenge is to improve productivity and incomes in the informal sector. There may be hidden opportunities within the informal sector. Job creation was accomplished through micro activity without government subsidy in a hostile policy environment. Informal sector activity is in fact market friendly. It provides a wide array of services cheaply and efficiently. For example, many firms are recyclers, collecting and disposing of garbage in cities in a cost-efficient manner. Also, the bulk of low-income housing is produced in the informal sector. These and other arguments indicate that it may be possible to work with and not against the urban informal sector to promote employment and incomes.[34]

Nonetheless, low productivity drags the rest of the economy down. Because the informal sector is by definition capital poor, this is not surprising. Productivity levels in the formal sector, on the other hand, have been advancing, although the increase in the number of jobs has been slow. Thus, the productivity gap between the two sectors has been increasing.[35] Paralleling the productivity gap, the income gap between the formal and informal sectors has also been increasing.

Chile stands as an exception to the rising trend in informal sector activity, with the largest drop in informal sector activity as a proportion of total employment. Four elements contributed to this decline: rapid growth of the economy; the introduction of private retirement accounts, limiting the burden on the firm for social insurance; increased flexibility in labor legislation; and a strengthening of the legal infrastructure of the state.[36] Consideration of these factors may point to areas of future development in other Latin American countries looking to increase formal sector engagement. We will return in chapter 11 to the problem of the informal sector as it relates to poverty.

> **QUESTION FOR THOUGHT**
>
> How should the employment-informality trade-off be resolved in the region?

INPUT MARKETS: TECHNOLOGY

Enhancements in productivity—increasing the output of workers—are the key to improving material welfare in society. **Labor productivity** in Latin America is be-

BOX 9.2.   THE NEW ENTREPRENEURS: PREPARING THE GROUND FOR SMALL BUSINESS

For Eugenia Kleiman and Martha Gámez of Monterey, Mexico, it began as a whim. "We wanted to build something beautiful, something different," said Kleiman, a former shoe shop owner. So in 1990, she teamed up with Gámez, an interior designer, to create Margen Arteobjeto, a workshop that would make home furnishings from wrought iron.

Using personal savings, the two rented a small garage, hired a craftsman and began displaying their plate holders and lamp stands at regional fairs. Buyers were impressed, and orders began to trickle in. The products also caught the eye of an official from Bancomext, Mexico's export promotion bank, who encouraged the pair to show their wares at trade fairs in the United States. Before long, major department stores were placing bulk orders.

"At first our U.S. customers were hesitant, because they had a bad image of Mexican producers," said Kleiman. "But we made it our business to erase that image through quality and service. Now our U.S. customers say, 'Why should we buy from Southeast Asia when you folks are right here?' "

By late 1996, Margen had grown to some 300 full-time employees operating in three round-the-clock shifts. Annual sales had reached $6 million and are set to top $8 million in 1997, at a time when most of the Mexican economy is still recovering from the effects of the 1995 peso crisis. Most recently, Margen was named one of the four most successful export-oriented companies in Mexico by Bancomext.

THE RIGHT MIX

Margen's story illustrates just how quickly entrepreneurs can germinate when the environment for growth is right. Many economists hoped this environment would emerge naturally from the structural reforms that have reduced the economic role of the state in the region's countries over the last decade. Indeed, privatization programs, financial reforms and trade liberalization have opened whole sectors of the economy to competition, and a new generation of political leaders has embraced the notion that private enterprise should be the engine of growth and development. In some countries most notably Chile these macroeconomic reforms did have the desired effect, stimulating a flowering of start-up companies and new growth among existing small enterprises. But in many other countries, the benefits of reform have accrued primarily to large, well-established corporations, while activity among the small companies has remained stagnant.

Why have these outcomes been so uneven? The principal reason, according to many observers, is that entrepreneurs need much more than a positive macroeconomic environment to take root and thrive. Indeed, a number of less visible factors, including access to credit, access to nonfinancial services such as market research, and the quality of government institutions that regulate business activity, can ultimately have a much bigger impact on entrepreneurs.

The scarcity of bank credit for small borrowers in Latin America has been a perennial problem. "Small businesses justifiably complain about the lack of access to medium- and long-term financing, high interest rates, the difficulty in finding required collateral, excessive red tape, and a general lack of sensitivity shown by banks toward small firms," says Juan Llisterri, an economist in the IDB's Infrastructure and Financial Markets Division.

Kleiman is a case in point. Like many of the region's small entrepreneurs, she simply assumed that commercial banks would not be interested and didn't even bother seeking credit for the first three years after launching Margen. When Kleiman finally did approach a bank, officials seemed more concerned with her gender than with her ability to offer collateral. "The banks didn't think we knew what we were doing because we are women," Kleiman said. Margen's business record eventually persuaded a lender, however, and the company now easily obtains credit.

Although some of the region's commercial banks are in fact beginning to target the small business market segment, the high transaction costs associated with managing multiple small loans still keep most banks from lending to first-time entrepreneurs. As a result, many potential businesses must resort to informal sources of financing at usurious rates that make it difficult to compete.

Even when a start-up enterprise does obtain credit, it often faces additional costs related to official paperwork. In some countries, simply registering a business and obtaining the required government licenses can take months. Moreover, if regulatory institutions are poorly managed and have weak controls, unofficial "service fees" are often necessary to obtain documents and licenses.

While large companies can afford to hire intermediaries to navigate bureaucracies and handle paperwork, entrepreneurs can find these transaction costs prohibitive. In fact, as Peruvian economist Hernando de Soto reported in his landmark study, "The Other Path," many small entrepreneurs claim that the cost of dealing with the government is so high that they must operate illegally (in the informal sector) in order to survive.

But entrepreneurs who opt for informality suffer permanent disadvantages compared to their legal counterparts. They cannot request municipal services or utilities, obtain titles to property, apply for credit, or sign enforceable contracts, to name just a few limitations.

Even for entrepreneurs who do operate in the formal sector, the lack of effective legal protections can be crippling. In countries where law enforcement is weak and the judicial system is hampered by inefficiency and corruption, small companies have little recourse against delinquent customers, broken contracts, or other commercial disputes. Large companies compensate for weak legal protections by forging informal agreements with suppliers and partners based on family contacts and friendships. But these closed, inflexible networks make it difficult for entrepreneurs to break into a market.

MANY INGREDIENTS

A strong, open economy, access to financing, transparent and efficient regulations, and effective legal protections: all these conditions must be present for small entrepreneurs to prosper over the long run.

Source: IDB América, 1997, available at the Inter-American Development Bank homepage, www.iadb.org.

tween one-fourth and one-third of the prevailing U.S. level.[37] Figure 9.1 shows Brazil's labor productivity versus that of the United States, Japan, and Korea. Without productivity enhancement, if a benevolent dictator simply gave everyone a raise, more money would simply be chasing the same quantity of goods. Advances in material life have taken place when technological changes have allowed for the production of more goods with a given set of resources. The three-field crop rotation system and the use of the horse in agriculture to yield an agricultural surplus facilitated the transition from feudalism to capitalism. Eli Whitney and the steam engine promoted the industrial revolution. At the heart of the development challenge is a question of technological change. How can the quality of inputs be improved and the combination of inputs be transformed to raise production? This, by definition, is the role of technology.

Technological change confers advantage on the ones to discover new ways of combining inputs to create outputs. Technology is a commodity bought and sold

Figure 9.1.   Brazilian Labor Productivity versus Select Countries

Select countries index 100 = U.S.

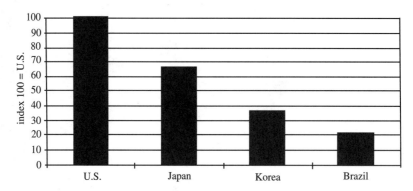

Source: McKinsey Global Institute, *Productivity—The Key to an Accelerated Development Path for Brazil 1998* (São Paulo, Brazil: McKinsey and Company, 1998).

in markets; those nations owning it tend to erect high barriers to its open purchase in the international arena. For a developing country, the challenge is twofold: how to catch up with the dominant technological paradigm and how to carve out a particular niche in the international arena to trade competitively in items produced with new technologies. In table 9.4, we can see how far behind Latin America is compared to other country groupings in science and technology indicators. As a percentage of GDP, Latin America dedicates roughly half as much to research and development as southern Europe, a third of the Asian total, and a fifth of the industrial country level. When countries are ranked according to international competitiveness, Latin America has the worst scores for science and technology; the six most advanced countries in the region rank in the lowest third of the forty-three countries evaluated.[38]

In contrast to industrial countries, the state sector takes the lead in technological development, with nearly 80 percent of expenditures. The private sector in Latin America does not appear to be a dynamic source of technological change. Unlike developed countries, in which businesses themselves account for more than 50 percent of national investment in R&D, in Latin America the private sector finances less than 20 percent.[39] In comparison with developed economies, ECLAC finds a productivity gap in Latin America due to the use of outdated equipment, obsolete production methods, deficient organization of labor, a failure to improve quality, unsystematic marketing techniques, and outdated after-sales services. This gap widened in the postwar era, with the region registering low rates of average productivity in the early 1990s, 30 percent of that of the United States.[40] It is particularly acute for small and medium-sized firms, pointing to a clear need to promote the dissemination of information systems, personnel training, and the outreach of sectoral technology centers to small businesses.[41]

The need for public financing may be explained by market failure. Basic scien-

Table 9.4. Science and Technology Indicators circa 1990

Indicator	Latin America	OECD Countries	East Asian NICS	Southern Europe
Per capita R&D spending (US$)	10	448	23	4
R&D spending (% of GDP)	0.5	2.5	1.4	1
R&D spending (engineers and scientists)	34,858	141,861	50,160	60,647
Engineers and scientists/100,000 economically active population	99	650	115	185
University graduates/100,000 inhabitants	156	592	478	191
R&D expenditure by origin (%)				
Public	78.8	43.1	35.6	46.4
Business	10.5	52.5	61.4	49.5
External funds	3.4	0.4	2.9	3.9
Other	7.3	4.0	0.1	0.2

Source: Fernando Fajnzylber, "Education and Changing Production Patterns with Social Equity," *CEPAL Review* 47 (August 1992): 7–19.

tific knowledge can be considered a public good that the state must provide to promote new activity. With such a low level of basic science and technology infrastructure, it is expensive for firms to span the gap between basic science and industrial applications. With few firms engaging in research and development, there are limited externalities or synergies created by a core of high-tech firms. It would be as if the high-tech corridor in Silicon Valley were distributed one firm at a time across the poorest counties in the poor mountains of Appalachia. Not only would low levels of educational attainment hinder innovation, but the clustering of suppliers and skilled labor would disappear. The challenge clearly has become how to overcome constraints of training and size to improve productivity in the region.

There is also a science and technology gap among countries in the region. Argentina, Brazil, Chile, Mexico, and Venezuela are relatively advanced. Colombia, Costa Rica, and Uruguay have recently generated significant national capacity, but in the rest of the region there is a complete absence of policies and institutions for science and technology development. In technology generation, the number of patents granted to Mexico, Brazil, and Argentina ranged from 3,160 to 663 in 1992; the next highest set of countries in the region—Venezuela, Chile, and Colombia—were awarded between 481 and 248. This stands in stark contrast to Holland, Switzerland, or Taiwan, each granted about 20,000 per year.[42]

Meeting the productivity challenge involves a clearer understanding of the nature of technology. Neoclassical theory tends to see technology as exogenous to the production system, a tradable recipe or input that incurs a short-run cost in production. Technological progress is viewed as continuous and cumulative, in a single-track race for dominance. Neostructuralists view technology differently. Relying in part on the views of Schumpeter, an economist who dedicated much of his work to thinking about technological change, neostructuralists see technology as tacit knowledge not easily transferred, a result of interactive learning and a synergistic process between producers and users. Progress is seen as both continuous and discontinuous, with windows of opportunity for acquisition opening but abruptly shutting at critical junctions in the process of technological change.[43] The policy ramifications of the different views on technology are complex. Can technology be purchased like any input of production to increase output, or are institutional changes required to promote technological absorption into Latin America economic systems?

No matter your theoretical perspective, the problem of catching up with the technological frontier involves the question of technological acquisition. Technology is an asset; it must be procured somewhere. Technology may be acquired through foreign direct investment, through licensing or turnkey plants, or through the promotion of national technological parks. Technological acquisition is often asymmetrical. The seller of a technology naturally has more information about the new product or process than the buyer. In the case of hard technologies (incorporated into machinery and equipment) as well as soft technologies (new management techniques, quality control, industrial relations, and just in time production)—the seller of the technology is really the only agent that knows the nature of the commodity.

In a developing country, the next task is the assimilation of technology. Here our question of institutional change comes into play. Simply installing a modern factory does not result in technological acquisition. Technology can remain a black box poorly understood and unsuitable for adaptation and innovation. Improving productivity in an economy involves both appropriating information about technological systems and assimilating its importance and disseminating its applications beyond the first user. Absorption of technology requires not only a machine but also training a labor force to run it. Sometimes firms are reticent to make such investments in human capital, as well-trained people often leave the firm. Workers themselves, when poor, may not be able to make the educational investments on their own to become productive in the international economy. Financing of technological acquisition is also risky—investments often do not pan out.

Who should invest in a national technological infrastructure? Under the import substitution industrialization regime, investments in technological development were principally made by the state. Publicly funded research and development centers were promoted to support the needs of national businesses to link the domestic supply and demands for science and technology services. The state also intervened with private multinational capital to negotiate positive terms for technology transfers through multinational corporations. A smoothly functioning technological system was an interface between universities and national industry in identifying priority projects for technological investments. That system meets the needs of the final user of technology by effectively organizing research and development facilities in the public and private sectors. Unfortunately, the challenge of technological development was beyond the capabilities of most states, and most nations in Latin America fell further and further behind in the global arena. The private sector has not risen to the challenge. Incentives must be changed to promote technological change in the region.

Given fiscal constraints, states must focus more on structuring incentives for private sector investment in technology rather than directly invest in technology. Tax incentives favorable to R&D and strong laws protecting intellectual property rights are crucial in promoting a business environment conducive to the development of a science and technology infrastructure. Regulatory frameworks to encourage firms to finance and undertake more research and development must be designed. The state can also act as an arbiter of information, disseminating information about best practices. It might also work to promote dynamic cooperation between research communities, universities, and the private sector. Collaboration can maximize the use of scarce resources. The state can work directly to redirect public resources in education to improve the quality of human capital. It can take a leadership role in monitoring and assessing the national stock of technological assets.

Attention should be paid to the gender implications of investments in infrastructure and science and technology education. Gender-aware planning in infrastructure might take the location of housing, workplaces, and nurseries into account; it would pay attention to peak and off-peak transportation networks.[44] Good science and engineering indicators are crucial to informed adjustments in science and technology policy.[45] State promotion of investments in science and technology may help transform the problems of economies of scale and limited time horizons that firms face in allocating resources to technological activity. By adjusting incentives, risk may be minimized for these investments, which tend to have uncertain long-term payoffs.

Latin America has traditionally been plagued by a splintering of capacity in science and technology systems. Businesses, universities, research institutes, and state providers of financing do not interact in a smooth technological system. Jorge Sabato conceived of a smoothly functioning technological system as a triangle in which industry, basic educational institutions, and science and technology centers constantly interact. Latin America has been plagued by gaps among these institutions, such that there is little communication between the private sector and the university or even between state-run research institutes and academic researchers. Clearly, with limited resources in the area, incentives toward public-private partnerships might allow for exploitation of economies of scale in technological innovation and adaptation.

An interesting example of effective investment in human capital to attract high-technology production is the case of Intel in Costa Rica. Intel's 1996 decision to open a microprocessor plant in Costa Rica was a function of an ample supply of well-educated workers across the technical, maintenance, engineering, and management levels. The Intel decision is seen as the culmination of a policy begun in the 1960s to invest in technical education. In 1974 Costa Rica, with International Development Bank assistance, formed the National Council for Scientific and Technological Research (CONICIT) and the Costa Rican Technological Institute (ITCR) to promote technical training. Regional centers of technical training were built in the late 1970s. Inter-American Development Bank funding in part supported the training of researchers, as it did throughout the region. The IDB also set up a technology development fund in Costa Rica (as well as in Argentina,

Brazil, Chile, Colombia, Mexico, and Uruguay). A private Costa Rican Foundation in concert with U.N. and USAID money promoted computer literacy at the elementary level. Costa Rica recently concluded a science and technology program that funded 239 postgraduate fellowships, many of whose recipients are currently teaching in Costa Rican technical institutions. As a small country, Costa Rica decided early on to focus on a limited number of technologies: information systems, environmental sciences, and the agricultural and forestry sectors. It has transformed these narrowly defined investments into international comparative advantage in these fields. It has done a good job of balancing investments at the levels of both basic and higher education. Costa Rica is seen as an example of the gains of smart, modest investments in the technological arena generating long-term rewards.[46]

The Costa Rican case is one example of what can be achieved in a small country. Small and poor countries must be highly selective in targeting research and development dollars. In addition to promoting sectors such as information systems that don't require huge capital investments, countries might consider innovations in agriculture, health, and environmental resource management, in which fields of scientific study may also have social benefits. Over time, however, a clear plan to move up the technological ladder is required such that countries aren't caught forever in a narrow range of low-level technological specialization.[47] Medium-sized and large countries should use the state arm to create incentives for technological innovation in business, facilitate linkages between universities and the private sector, and consolidate or close obsolete institutions. All countries must address the question of financing. Investments in technology are risky and take place over time. Judicious investments in research and development institutions are required, and instruments to reduce risk and encourage investment by private actors must be encouraged to jump-start Latin American technological systems. Multilateral institutions such as the Inter-American Development Bank have in the past contributed to the training of some 20,000 researchers in 100 universities in the region. However, more needs to be done to promote the formation of competent personnel within a healthy regional science and technology infrastructure. In smaller countries, assistance can be directed to laying solid foundations; in larger countries that already possess these institutions, consolidation and modernization can be facilitated.[48]

INFRASTRUCTURE: A CRITICAL COMPLEMENTARY INPUT

In addition to weak technological systems, Latin America faces an infrastructure gap. Underinvestment, particularly during the 1980s and the debt crisis, led to a need for $60 billion annually in injections in telecommunications, roads, and ports.[49] Table 9.5 demonstrates the infrastructure deficit as compared to the United States. In Brazil, one in four phone calls does not go through, and there are nine lines per 100 inhabitants, resulting in a gray market price of $2,500–$7,500 per line for a new installation.[50] It costs $400 to load a container in Santos, the key shipping point outside São Paulo, twice New York rates. These high costs are

Table 9.5.   Infrastructure Deficit

	Telephone Mainlines (per 1,000)	Telephone Faults (per 100 lines)	Population with Access to Water (%)	Water Losses (% of total)	Roads (km per million persons)	Electricity Losses (% of total)
Latin America	69	15	83	34	670	16
East Asia	50	5	45	39	231	11
United States	543	n.a.	n.a.	n.a.	14,172	9

Source: The Financier as presented in *The Economist,* 27 July 1996, p. 55.

manageable. Investments in Chile reduced unit operating costs in ports from 54 to 26 cents per crate and the turnaround time from 129 to 40 hours. In Mexico the poor port facilities led companies located in Monterey to export via Houston and to import via U.S. ports and bring material in over land. There is a clear need for better cargo systems and roads. Inadequate transportation systems are to blame for low competitiveness in the cases of Venezuela, Mexico, and Brazil.[51]

Investments in infrastructure can support economic growth, reduce poverty, and make development environmentally sustainable.[52] In considering reforms in infrastructure, three policy guidelines emerge: infrastructure should be managed like a business, not a bureaucracy; competition should be introduced; and stakeholders should have a strong voice and real responsibility.[53] In infrastructure reform there is a clear need for a public–private partnership. Profit opportunities create incentives for private participation to increase productivity and reduce costs. But incentives from the public sector are critical in reducing risks that make private sector activity alone prohibitive.

Throughout the world, public sector services no longer need to be conceived of as natural monopolies. Revolutions in telecommunications and in provision of electrical and energy services have made a smaller scale possible. Natural monopolies can be opened to the forces of competition, unbundling portions of the service or breaking up service areas geographically. Clearly this must be done with an eye to equity. Profit-oriented telecoms, not surprisingly, are more interested in servicing high-priced business areas rather than low-income neighborhoods or rural sectors. Private activity in one area may need to subsidize access for all.[54]

In the power and gas sector, population concentrations in urban areas make private investment lucrative. Rural inhabitants, however, are more likely to see their service remain under public ownership given the higher costs of servicing remote areas. Telecommunications provide the greatest opportunities for privatization. In transport, possibilities for private road concessions and maintenance are being pursued. In water and waste, public municipalities are accepting bids for lease contracts to private services. However, state activity is critical in providing the technical and financial assistance to the solid waste and wastewater disposal firms.

Public-private partnerships in infrastructure are beginning to provide lessons of how complementary efforts can enhance productivity. In Argentina, with the privatization of the telephone company Entel, phone service requests can now be met in forty-eight hours, as compared to the five- to ten-year waits common in the

1980s. But consumers have new complaints: high prices. One estimate suggests consumers are overpaying by about $1 billion per year—with excess profits going into the coffers of Telecom and Telefonica owners in Italy, Spain, and France. Private monopolies may need regulation or the introduction of competition policies to restrict price gouging.[55] As our discussion of privatization in chapter 6 indicated, competition policies are necessary to minimize monopoly rents.

The private sector alone may not work; the case of Mexican roads is illustrative. In Mexico, 3,600 miles of highways were built from 1988 to 1994 at a cost of $15 billion. These high costs resulted in government bailouts of forty-eight out of the fifty-two concessions granted.[56] Outrageous tolls scared away traffic, making cost recovery problematic. The tolls from Mexico City to Acapulco were a whopping $63! The government stepped in, cutting average tariffs by 60 percent. In part the lesson of Mexican road concessions concerned the short time frame. Given contract periods of between ten and fifteen years, firms were attempting to recover costs too quickly with exorbitant prices. A longer concession period reduces these pressures, making the concessions more profitable.

A more successful outcome of privatization was in the case of Argentine waterworks.[57] In 1992 a consortium led by Lyonaise des Eaux was given a thirty-year contract to run water and sewerage for Buenos Aires. It was able to make post-tax profits of $52 million on $355 million of revenues. The Argentine consortium worked in part because its predecessor, Obras Sanitarias de la Nación (OSN), was hugely inefficient. OSN facilities used to leak half of the water, and the agency was heavily overstaffed. It was therefore relatively easy to make changes. The work force was cut from 7,500 to 4,000. New meters and new pipes were installed. As part of the public-private partnership, the Argentine government financed a retirement scheme for workers, allocating 10 percent of the shares in the company to employees, giving them a stake in the success of the venture.

Brazilians are looking for productivity gains in the privatization of Telebrás, Brazil's huge telecommunications firm. Telebrás was created as a state enterprise in 1972 under the Ministry of Communications. Although its initial stages registered strong growth, as measured by a 16 percent increase in access lines and a 26 percent fall in the congestion rate, the period of the debt crisis brought underinvestment and dismal performance. It was reorganized in the early 1990s, positioning it for privatization in 1998. International bidders were attracted by the unmet potential of the Brazilian market. As the world's fifth most populous nation, Brazil had a two-year waiting list for phones in some areas. The total sale—which was split among eight groups of investors paying more than $19 billion—was roughly 13 percent larger than London's privatization of British Telecom in the early 1990s.[58] Competition will be encouraged, initially regulating prices but then moving to free prices as more firms are established in the market. One benefit of late investments in the industry is the ability to leapfrog over existing technologies to develop a low-cost, high-productivity sector.[59] With investments in infrastructure and associated productivity enhancements in industry and labor productivity, one forecast projects a possible 6 percent per year growth rate, leading to a doubling in GDP per capita over a ten-year period.[60] Productivity—enhancing the performance of labor, infrastructure, and industry—is clearly the key to raising living standards in the region.

OUTPUT MARKETS: THE EMERGING SHAPE OF THE LATIN AMERICAN INDUSTRIAL SECTOR

Macro instability and the contractionary effects of the debt crisis had a profound impact on industrial performance in Latin America. High rates of inflation and associated uncertainly thwarted long-term strategic decision making and investments in the capital stock. Capital formation was stalled by the lack of available finance. Survival depended on financial ingenuity, not investments in plant and equipment. During this period, dramatic changes in information technologies transformed the frontiers of business practice, largely leaving Latin America firms behind. The technological lag in automated production as well as new inventory systems set firms at a competitive disadvantage. Sluggish domestic demand forced a new orientation toward the export sector as opposed to production for the domestic market, but the focus was on agriculture and natural resource–based products. Industries that process raw materials have been more successful than those relying on labor or engineering services. Trade liberalization and associated import competition have had negative effects on textiles, footwear, and the metal and machinery branches.[61] Small and medium-sized enterprises were hard hit, in part because of difficulties in securing bank guarantees critical to exports.[62] Some weathered the crisis by becoming subcontractors to large transnational firms.[63] One study suggests that in the manufacturing sector, the dynamic expected results of liberalization have been muted. At least through the 1980s, manufacturing still suffered from limited competitiveness and a concentration in traditional exports.[64] Insertion into the international economy as a competitive exporter not only involves sound macroeconomic policies and the change toward export orientation but also depends upon institutional change in domestic markets for labor, technology, and infrastructure.

The effect of export-led growth varies by sector. The most efficient of the natural resource processors need few workers. Because they are newly automated, the labor they do use tends to be skilled management and not unskilled line workers.[65] As noted by Gert Rosenthal, head of ECLAC, it would be an irony to return to the primary product production pattern that left Latin America vulnerable to external shocks and commodity price instability.[66] One of the objectives is to move in the direction of what ECLAC calls "changing production patterns"—products with a higher valued added and stronger growth potential. To do so, however, will require changes in labor, technology, and infrastructure.

EXPORT PROCESSING FREE ZONES: GOOD INVESTMENTS OR A WASTE OF MONEY?

The benefits of export processing free zones, EPFZ, sometimes called foreign trade zones or free economic zones, are controversial. EPFZs are designed to attract foreign direct investment into a nation, with intended spillovers to stimulate manufacturing production. Imports of raw materials, equipment, and intermediate production are normally exempted from customs duties, and customized infrastructure such as roads or electricity are usually provided. Special tax incentives or exemption from profit repatriation rules are often offered to lure business to the area, and labor laws are sometimes held in abeyance.

Although these zones have been shown to contribute to employment and the entry of foreign capital, many charge that they operate as enclaves with limited linkages to the broader economy. As such, little technological learning takes place, and the incentive for diversification of production is limited. EPFZ activity tends to be restricted to manufacturing assembly, in a vertically integrated transnational production structure. Jobs are created, but little value is added in production. Because profits are repatriated and taxes forgone, the country may be left with little in the way of foreign contribution to economic activity.[67]

The proliferation of EPFZs in Central America has led to fierce competition to attract foreign capital.[68] One zone in El Salvador, in San Bartolo, includes a wide array of products such as textiles, clothing, shoes, paper bags, cardboard boxes, electronic components, and jewelry. Tax incentives and profit repatriation leave wages as the primary contribution to the economy. However, given the transnationals' preference for inputs from their own subsidiaries, there were few linkages with other industries. Low-skilled employment did little to raise the level of human capital.

Deep in the Brazilian Amazon, one of South America's largest industrial parks—with about 500 corporations, including Toshiba, Philips Electronics, and Xerox—is found alongside traditional river people.[69] Providing environmentally friendly employment for the indigenous population and settlers to the region, the free trade zone gives people an alternative to survival strategies that contribute to deforestation. But the cost to the Brazilian economy is enormous. Imports of components for electronic assembly accounted for $3 billion of Brazil's $8 billion trade deficit in 1997. The government's $2.4 billion annual subsidy to the free trade zone is the equivalent of $50,000 for every job created there—roughly ten times the value of the wage paid to the workers. Local Amazonian firms are irked by the subsidies to multinationals; one ice cream producer is frustrated by the thoughts of how he could expand the sale of exotic Amazonian fruit flavors in the Brazilian ice cream market if he had a small portion of the government incentives to outsiders.

Production in the jungle is subject to regular electricity blackouts and exorbitant freight costs. There isn't much comparative advantage in electronic production in a system defined by biological diversity and fragile ecosystems. TVs produced in the zone are $100 more expensive than those in international markets.

The logic of the Manaus free trade zone traces back to import substitution industrialization. When domestic production was protected behind high tariff walls, assembly in desperately poor Manaus made some sense. People were drawn in from the jungle, decreasing the population that the ecosystem supported and concentrating them in the city. Others were drawn to the region from the overpopulated Northeast. This was consistent with the military's plan to strengthen the northwestern frontier of Brazil.

Reduction of tariff walls under liberalization makes production uneconomical without continuing incentives and tax holidays. Why maintain these subsidies?

High unemployment will prompt a return to the forest; it will also create opportunities for inroads from the Colombian drug cartels to the north. Alternatives are problematic. Under a new development plan called the "Third Cycle," state planners are hoping that Manaus's colonial rubber boom and contemporary electronics-based economy will be followed by an agro-industrial structure that will sustainably develop the region's rich natural base. But politicians with the purse strings may not follow the lead of the planners. It is far easier to attract jobs through the visible entry of a shiny new assembly plant than to engage in the long and difficult process of changing the shape of the Manaus economy.

THE MAQUILA SECTOR IN NICARAGUA

Nicaraguan maquila, production or export processing, expanded quite rapidly in the 1990s, bringing jobs but also hardship.[70] Currently Nicaragua has two free trade zones: Las Mercedes, the larger of the two, and Zona Franca Index, which opened in 1996. Four more have been authorized to open and operate.[71]

The maquila sector's potential in employment generation has made it increasingly more important in Nicaragua. Employment grew in Las Mercedes from 7,000 in 1995 to 13,500 by 1997, and the numbers are certain to grow with the opening of the next free trade zones. In a country whose combined unemployment and underemployment rate is 60 percent, the maquila sector is a key component of the country's economy. For these reasons, the maquila sector has been one of the quickest and the most visible tools used by the Aleman administration in promoting job creation. Many incentives have been offered by the Nicaraguan government to attract investors and expand the sector. These incentives include

- a 100 percent exemption on income tax for the first 10 years of operation
- exemption on sales and capital gains taxes
- tax exemption on the import of raw materials and machinery
- no duties on exports and a U.S. waiver of quotas on textile imports from Nicaragua
- an industrial minimum wage of $.41 an hour
- low rental costs for industrial space.

Those that have taken up the offer include American, European, Nicaraguan, and Asian investors. Las Mercedes has nineteen companies, all differing in size and working conditions. Although some companies do provide adequate conditions for their workers, many have been accused of exploiting workers and providing less than humane working conditions. Garment assembly, the dominant operation within all these companies, tends to be extremely repetitive and tiring work. An individual worker will spend his or her entire day performing the same task. The warehouses have been set up to maximize production, and in some cases, the setup is taken to extremes. Workers are lined up, each with an assigned task such as sewing pockets on a pair of jeans or cutting fabric from patterns. Workers are not allowed to talk to their neighbors, and bathroom schedules are posted on the walls. The workers sit in the same seats for hours at a time without being allowed to stand up. In a country that is known for its hot and humid weather, the production floors lack air conditioning. In addition, many workers have suffered verbal abuse and, in some instances, physical abuse.

The high underemployment rates in Nicaragua give managers and employers the upper hand in the maquila sector because workers have little bargaining power. Afraid to lose their jobs, workers are forced to work under unpleasant conditions. Employers can force workers to work overtime, and they can hire new workers as easily as they can fire uncooperative ones. Employers have indeed used this leverage.

Apart from exploitative working conditions, the maquila sector has little to offer the Nicaraguan economy in the long term. Benefits that can be seen from foreign direct investment, such as technology transfers, do not occur with the maquila sector. Because most raw materials are imported, there are no backward linkages to the economy. The garment industry provides little in the way of human capital investment because the work requires an unskilled labor force. Although the maquila sector has provided employment opportunities for Nicaraguans, it appears to be a short-term solution to problems that require other adjustments within the economy.

Maquila and export zone production illustrate the limited options countries and regions face if the quality of local inputs of labor, technology, and infrastructure does not encourage more sophisticated industrial production. If competitiveness is not achieved through enhancing the quality of inputs, nations are left with the sometimes sad choice of marketing cheap labor.

Emerging Industrial Competitiveness

Despite the many examples of labor-based exports, the terms of competitiveness are changing in the region. Stability on the macro front, a new external orientation, and the stimuli of global competition are transforming the industrial landscape of the region. The emerging productive structure can be characterized by three dimensions: changes in the organization of firms at the firm level, changes in the structure and behavior of markets, and changes in the relative contributions of various activities to each nation's development.[72] Enterprises that are aggressively engaging the global market are integrating within the globalized productive system as subsystem producers. Stronger use of imported as opposed to locally supplied parts (particularly where quality is superior) has created cheaper, more marketable products. Entrepreneurial processes are exhibiting increasing dualism. On one hand, there are a large number of sectors—such as automobiles in Mexico, Brazil, and Argentina; domestic appliances in Chile; ceramic and leather industries

> **QUESTION FOR THOUGHT**
>
> Given the state of labor and technology markets and the existing infrastructure in Latin America, what role do you believe the state should play in promoting industrial competitiveness?

in Uruguay; and textiles and clothing in Colombia and Central America—that are engaged in an intensive process of modernization. However, in other sectors, technological modernization is slow and international competitiveness is declining.

A change in competition policy, or the body of laws and regulations surrounding business practices—including agreements between firms, abuse of market power, monopolization, and mergers and acquisitions—has promoted industrial activity. Emerging competitiveness is as much contingent on human resources and technological capacity as it is on wage costs or natural resources.[73] Linkages and a better flow of information among private agents and between the public and private sectors must be improved to reduce the risks of new investments.[74] The question is how this should proceed. Will this take place spontaneously as more firms are subject to the pressures of the global market? The new political economists would suggest that the market itself is the best way to solve this problem. The neoinstitutionalists would contend that market institutions are underdeveloped and in need of state intervention to provide adequate information to firms. The neostructuralists would suggest that the state assume a more strategic role, guiding business toward developing new areas of comparative advantage.

Key Concepts

Export processing zone	Labor productivity
Informal sector	Maquiladora

Chapter Summary

The Labor Market

- Contemporary labor markets in Latin America are characterized by three main factors: trade unions, the informal sector, and high levels of unemployment. Latin America has historically placed an emphasis on job security, but strict labor legislation has led to market rigidity. Unions have been an important mechanism to achieve certain guarantees for workers. In recent years, union participation has begun to fall after liberalization. Globalization may indeed be changing the role of unions.
- The unemployment rate alone does not give a clear indication of the problems encountered in the labor market in Latin America, such as underemployment. Furthermore, unemployment rates have increased in many countries. The reasons for the increases include privatization and government downsizing under the neoliberal model and an increase in the labor force participation of women. To combat unemployment, the number of jobs

must grow at a faster rate than the increase in the economically active population of a country.

- The informal sector has increased dramatically as a result of inadequate job growth in Latin America. It can be divided into three main categories: microenterprise employment, own-account workers, and domestic service. Its attractiveness to the unemployed, especially the unskilled worker, stems from the minimal requirements of capital, money, and qualifications needed to enter the sector. The informal sector appears to be a solution to the lack of employment generation in the private sector, but it is hardly the best solution. It has led to an increase in income inequality, it is a low-producing sector, and it evades taxation. Yet, it has proved to be a social net and prevented deprivation where the private sector has failed.

Technology

- Compared to the industrialized countries, Latin America is technology poor, but technological innovation is needed to improve the productivity of workers. Therefore, closing the technology gap has become a central issue. Technology must be acquired, perhaps through foreign direct investment, but it must also be accompanied by institutional changes. Due to fiscal constraints, the state can no longer invest as much in research and technology, but it can still play an important role in establishing incentives and regulatory frameworks.

Infrastructure

- The limited investment in infrastructure in the 1980s led to higher costs and a loss of competitiveness. Investment in infrastructure with a well-defined partnership between the public sector and the private sector is needed. The three main guidelines to be kept in mind for reform are the following: infrastructure should be managed like a business, not a bureaucracy; competition should be introduced; and stakeholders should have a strong voice and real responsibility.
- The industrial sector in Latin America has been thwarted by several forces. Though some sectors have managed to modernize, others have remained behind. To improve in competitiveness, Latin America will need reforms in the areas of infrastructure, technology, and improving the flow of information among private agents and between the private sector and the public sector.

Notes

1. Shahid Javed Burki and Sebastian Edwards, *Latin America after Mexico: Quickening the Pace* (Washington, D.C.: World Bank, 1996), 19.

2. Sebastian Edwards and Nora Claudia Lustig, eds., *Labor Markets in Latin America: Combining Social Protection with Market Flexibility* (Washington, D.C.: Brookings Institution, 1997), 32.

3. Ibid., 33–35.

4. Inter-American Development Bank, *Latin America after a Decade of Reforms: Economic and Social Progress 1997 Report* (Washington, D.C: Johns Hopkins University Press/Inter-American Development Bank, 1997).

5. World Bank, *Labor and Economic Reforms in Latin America and the Caribbean: Regional Perspectives on World Development Report* (Washington, D.C.: World Bank, 1995).

6. Victor E. Tokman, "Jobs and Solidarity: Challenges for Post-Adjustment in Latin America," in *Economic and Social Development in the XXI Century*, proceedings of the 1997 Inter-American Bank development conference, ed. Louis Emmerij. Available at www.iadb.org/exr/pub/xxi/sec4.htm.

7. International Labor Organization home page. Available at usa.ilo.org/news.

8. Edwards and Lustig, *Labor Markets in Latin America*, 240, table 8.4.

9. Burki and Edwards, *Latin America after Mexico*, 20.

10. Tokman, "Jobs and Solidarity."

11. Ibid.

12. Richard Tardanico and Rafael Menjívar Larín, "Restructuring, Employment, and Social Inequality: Comparative Urban Latin American Patterns," in *Global Restructuring, Employment, and Social Inequality in Urban Latin America*, ed. Richard Tardanico and Rafael Menjívar Larín (Miami: University of Miami North-South Center Press, 1997).

13. Ibid., 244.

14. "Creating Jobs Is Main Headache," *Latin American Weekly Report,* 5 January 1999, p. 2.

15. Tardanico and Larín, "Restructuring," 252.

16. Ibid., 253.

17. Psacharopoulos and Tzannatos (1992), as presented by Rosemary Thorp, *Progress, Poverty, and Exclusion: An Economic History of Latin America in the 20th Century* (Baltimore: Johns Hopkins University Press/Inter-American Development Bank, 1998), 31.

18. *Latin American Weekly Report*, 26 May 1998, p. 235.

19. R. Ffrench-Davis, comments on Victor E. Tokman, "Jobs and Solidarity: Challenges for Post-Adjustment in Latin America," in *Economic and Social Development in the XXI Century*, proceedings of the 1997 Inter-American Bank development conference, ed. Louis Emmerij. Available at www.iadb.org/exr/pub/xxi/sec4.htm.

20. Inter-American Development Bank, *Latin America after a Decade of Reforms*, 111.

21. "Creating Jobs Is Main Headache," *Latin American Weekly Report*, 5 January 1999, p. 2.

22. Economic Commission for Latin America and the Caribbean, *The Equity Gap: Latin America, the Caribbean, and the Social Summit* (Santiago, Chile: Economic Commission for Latin America and the Caribbean, 1997), 55.

23. Ibid.

24. World Bank, *Labor and Economic Reforms in Latin America and the Caribbean: Regional Perspectives on World Development* (Washington, D.C.: World Bank, 1995).

25. ECLAC, *The Equity Gap*, 60–61.

26. Ibid., 61.

27. Ibid., 66.

28. Vanessa F. Cartaya, "El Confuso mundo del sector informal," in *Nueva Sociedad Marginalidad* 90 (July–August 1987): 81–84.

29. International Labor Organization, headquarters homepage: usa.ilo.org/news.

30. ECLAC, *The Equity Gap*, 70.

31. Jaime Mezzera, "Abundancia como efecto de la escasez. Oferta y demanda en el mercado laboral urbano," *Nueva Sociedad* 90 (1997): 106–117.

32. International Labor Organization home page: usa.ilo.org/news.

33. ECLAC, *The Equity Gap*, 65.

34. International Labor Organization home page: usa.ilo.org/news.

35. ECLAC, *The Equity Gap*, 60.

36. Díaz, cited in Tardanico and Larín, "Restructuring," 249.

37. Tokman, "Jobs and Solidarity."

38. *World Competitiveness Report 1994*, as cited by Román Mayorga, *Closing the Gap*, Inter-American Development Bank Working Paper SOC97–101 (Washington, D.C.: Inter-American Development Bank, 1997), 9.

39. Mayorga, *Closing the Gap*, 15.

40. Economic Commission for Latin America and the Caribbean, *Policies to Improve Linkages with the Global Economy* (Santiago, Chile: Economic Commission for Latin America and the Caribbean, 1995), 149.

41. Mayorga, *Closing the Gap*, 15.

42. Ibid., 9.

43. Hubert Schmitz and José Cassiolato, *Hi-tech for Industrial Development: Lessons from the Brazilian Experience in Electronics and Automation* (London: Routledge, 1992), 9.

44. Caroline Moser, "Gender Planning in the Third World: Meeting Practical and Strategic Gender Needs," *World Development* 17, no. 11 (1989): 1799–1825.

45. Lauritz Holm-Nielsen, Michael Crawford, and Alcyone Saliba, *Institutional and Entrepreneurial Leadership in the Brazilian Science and Technology Sector*, World Bank Discussion Paper no. 325 (Washington, D.C.: World Bank, 1996).

46. Case taken from Paul Constance, "A High Technology Incubator," *IDB América*, 1997. Available at the Inter-American Development Bank homepage at www.iadb.org.

47. Mayorga, *Closing the Gap*, 24.

48. Ibid., 4, 45.

49. World Bank, *Meeting the Infrastructure Challenge in Latin America and the Caribbean* (Washington, D.C.: World Bank, 1995), 10–11, gives data on infrastructure deficits.

50. "Unfinished Business," *The Economist*, 2 March 1996, p. 41.

51. ECLAC, *Policies to Improve Linkages*, 182.

52. World Bank, *World Development Report 1994* (New York: Oxford University Press/World Bank, 1994).

53. Infrastructure report on Latin America and the Caribbean. Information on the energy sector is available at www.eia.doe.gov/emeu/cabs/argentina.html.

54. World Bank, *Economic Growth and Returns to Work* (Washington, D.C.: World Bank, 1995), 17.

55. Juan Manuel Valcarcel, "Calling Someone in Argentina: Dial M for Monopoly," *The Wall Street Journal*, 16 August 1996, p. A11.

56. "Tequila Freeways," *The Economist*, 16 December 1996, p. 66.

57. "Water Works in Buenos Aires," *The Economist*, 24 February 1996, p. 66; Emanuel Idelovitch and Klas Ringskog, *Private Sector Participation in Water Supply and Sanitation in Latin America* (Washington, D.C.: World Bank, 1995).

58. Seth Schiesel, "Brazil Sells Most of State Phone Utility," *New York Times*, 30 July 1998, p. D1.

59. McKinsey Global Institute, *Productivity: The Key to Accelerated Development Path for Brazil 1998*, Telecom case 9 (São Paulo, Brazil: McKinsey and Company, 1998).

60. Ibid.

61. José Miguel Benavente, Gustavo Crespi, Jorge Katz, and Giovanni Stumpo, "Changes in the Industrial Development of Latin America," *CEPAL Review* 60 (December 1996): 62.

62. A firm will typically secure a bank letter of credit to finance goods in transit. The bank loans the firm money while the goods are in transit, before they arrive and are paid for by the importer.

63. Benavente, Crespi, Katz, and Stumpo, "Changes," 63.

64. John Weeks, "The Manufacturing Sector in Latin America and the New Economic Model," in *The New Economic Model in Latin America and Its Impact on Income Distribution and Poverty*, ed. Victor Bulmer-Thomas (New York: St. Martin's, 1996), 271–294.

65. Benavente, Crespi, Katz, and Stumpo, "Changes," 65.

66. Gert Rosenthal, "Development Thinking and Policies: The Way Ahead," *CEPAL Review* 60 (December 1996).

67. Summarized from Teresa S. Weersma-Haworth, "Export Processing Free Zones as Export Strategy," in *Latin America's New Insertion in the World Economy*, ed. Ruud Buitelaar and Pitou Van Dijck (New York: St. Martin's, 1996), 90.

68. Weersma-Haworth, "Export Processing," 90.

69. Aapted from Matt Moffett, "Deep in the Amazon, an Industrial Enclave Fights for Its Survival," *The Wall Street Journal*, 9 July 1998, p. A1.

70. This section was written by Luisa F. Godoy, Colby College graduating class of 1999.

71. From a commercial report done by the Commercial Section of the U.S. Embassy in Managua. Available at www.usia.gov/abtusia/posts/NU1/wwwhei3.html.

72. Economic Commission for Latin America and the Caribbean, *Strengthening Development: The Interplay of Macro and Microeconomics* (Santiago, Chile: Economic Commission for Latin America and the Caribbean, 1996), 37.

73. Ibid., 71.

74. Ibid., 72.

AGRICULTURAL POLICY

Sowing the Seeds of Equitable, Sustainable Growth in Latin America

CHAPTER TEN

Large-scale farms have increased Mexican agricultural exports. *(Courtesy of the Inter-American Development Bank.)*

Due to its unique characteristics, the rural sector presents policy makers with some of the most intractable challenges in development. Agriculture is more than coffee and bananas, wheat or cattle. It is a complex, interrelated set of markets for land, labor, capital, and technology embedded in a socioeconomic web of traditional and corporate farming practices producing for both domestic and international consumption. Successful agriculture must paradoxically meet the need for low-cost national food security as well as provide a sufficient income for rural families. It is increasingly relied upon as an export engine by developing nations in search of comparative advantage, yet it faces relatively high import barriers to agricultural products in the developed world. Agricultural export drives may strain environmental resources, undermining the future productivity of the sector. Agriculture is full of promise yet requires careful tending to maximize the benefits of socially, environmentally, and economically sustainable growth.

In this chapter we will consider the opportunities and constraints in agricultural development in Latin America. We will explore the following questions:

- What are the characteristics of agricultural markets in Latin America? In particular, what are the dimensions of the market for land, labor, capital, and technology? Do agricultural markets behave differently from other markets? How are complementary inputs with respect to infrastructure and transportation provided?
- How have past development strategies shaped agricultural performance in Latin America? What is the legacy of feudal land patterns and/or import substitution industrialization?
- What was the experience with **land reform** to redress some of the inequality in asset distribution in this sector? Was it successful?
- How has the neoliberal model changed agricultural policy? Has it been effective?
- What challenges remain for agriculture in Latin America?

CHANGING PATTERNS OF AGRICULTURAL PRODUCTION IN RURAL LATIN AMERICA

Agriculture in Latin America spans a wide diversity of crops and climates. From the plains of the Argentine pampas to the hilly Guatemalan highlands, from traditional crops such as cattle and coffee to new boom products such as soya and kiwis, the plurality of agricultural systems in the region presents challenges to thinking clearly about agricultural practice. Nonetheless, we can generalize with respect to dominant modes of agricultural production and consider agricultural strategies that will help overcome common constraints of regional production.

Two types of landholdings dominate agriculture in Latin America: relatively small-scale, traditional peasant agriculture and large-scale corporate farming. This pattern of small and large landholdings is a legacy of the colonial latifundia, in which large tracts of land were deeded to Spanish or Portuguese descendants.

Although intermediate-sized producers exist, policy has been driven by this **dualistic structure of production** in agriculture.

The agricultural sector has gone through dramatic changes not only in terms of its relative importance in the economy but also in its internal structure. The latifundia or hacienda system has more or less disappeared, but its large scale has been retained by modern capitalist farming. The nature of agricultural production has changed. Whereas the large oligarchic estates had a certain socioeconomic cohesion, the divide between modern commercial farmers and peasant producers is large. Under the latifundia system, labor for coffee, sugar, and cotton production was tied to the estates through sharecropping, credit, and personal obligations to create a framework of paternalistic relations.[1] With the dissolution of this social structure, although large commercial farms have largely flourished, peasants are marginalized from land, labor, and credit markets.

In some countries, agribusiness has grown rapidly. The primary focus has moved from production for local consumption to nontraditional products for exports. Although manufacturing has assumed increased importance in the export profile of the region, agricultural exports still account for 25 percent of the value of Latin America's exports. Countries of the region have expanded production beyond traditional crops of sugar, cocoa, bananas, and coffee into high-value products such as fruits, vegetables, flowers, nuts, and oils.[2] Brazil has become one of the world's five "food powers" through increasing productivity generated by investments in mechanization. Brazilian farmers have expanded beyond their own borders, planting 33 percent of the soy in Bolivia and Paraguay and owning 4 percent of Uruguay's land.[3]

Mexico's agricultural exports began in the 1960s, promoted by transnational corporations. Strawberry and tomato exports boomed in the 1970s and 1980s, resulting, in conjunction with export of other fruits and vegetables, in more than a doubling of agricultural exports in two decades. Guatemala supplied 80 percent of the snow peas coming into the U.S. market in 1991, roughly double its market share of 1988. Between 1983 and 1993, the share of Central American melons rose from 5 to 58 percent of the U.S. market. Colombia has become known for its cut flowers, becoming the second largest exporter of flowers after the Netherlands. Ecuador has also become a cut flower exporter, increasing global sales fifteenfold from 1985 to 1991.[4] Overall, **nontraditional exports** constitute 15 percent of agricultural exports from Latin America.

Reverse seasons from North America make Latin American production complementary to the U.S. and Canadian markets. As Americans replace meats with more fruits and vegetables, demand has risen year round. Innovations in packaging and refrigerated cargo handling have facilitated long-distance transport. Chilean fruit and wine have become common items on North American tables. Melting Andean snows water rich land in Chile's central zone, supporting new varieties of grapes and pears that are most welcome in northern countries in midwinter. Chilean wines are now winning international competitions. Poor farmlands converted into forest plantations have shown handsome dividends. Agriculture and forestry have contributed to Chile's trade surplus to the tune of more than $2 billion per year.

The transition to nontraditional, high-value exports has been facilitated by development agencies and governments as part of structural adjustment packages. In particular, USAID, the Agency for International Development, has been an active supporter of private incentives in the agricultural sector. The Commonwealth Development Corporation, the World Bank, and the Inter-American Development Bank also provide support for agricultural export growth.[5] Nonetheless, despite efforts to promote nontraditional exports by peasant farmers, the successes are due primarily to large corporate farming. Indeed, the expansion of agricultural exports often has been at a cost to small farmers and the production of subsistence foods for domestic consumption.

Alternative Production: Organic Farming

Organic farming is appealing to small-scale producers in the region because of the minimal use of expensive fertilizers and the high prices organic products obtain in international markets. Yet organic farming is not problem-free. Small farmers still need to find reliable buyers, be able to meet volume and quality requirements, and find affordable and timely transportation to avoid spoilage. They also confront a new kind of nontariff barrier: certification. All organic produce must be certified by an organization such as the Organic Crop Inspectors Association for compliance to strict standards. For an illiterate farmer to provide documentation that a field has been chemical free for at least three years is a daunting task.[6] Farmers must also pay for inspections. Local agricultural organizations help. Cooperatives can help in creating economies of scale in marketing and transportation. In Costa Rica, through a small blackberry farmers' association, APROCAM, berries plucked from mountain bushes at dawn arrive on Miami grocery shelves by that same afternoon. In Guatemala some of the larger farms are selling organic produce directly to supermarket chains such as Fresh Fields. Organic coffees have exhibited more stable (and 20 percent higher) prices due to consumer tastes for designer, chemical-free coffees. In Mexico, a confederation of coffee producer organizations, UNCAFESUR, through an organization called La Selva, is working with small-scale ejido farmers to switch to organic production.[7]

Organic production not only has a stronger market but also is better suited to the needs of the small farmer. It rejects the expensive chemical cocktail of expensive fertilizers in favor of labor-intensive natural composting and weeding by hand.[8] La Selva is working to teach terracing techniques, organic composting, intercropping of bananas to provide shade, and developing nurseries for seedlings. The InterAmerican Foundation, in conjunction with a private foundation and a Dutch coffee broker, supported the transition costs. Although nearly half of the initial harvest was lost to the violence in the Chiapas region, marketing efforts exceeded all expectations, with three North American companies—Aztec Harvests, Ben & Jerry's, and United Airlines—featuring coffee grown by La Selva producers. A potential downside is that the more labor-intensive methods of organic farming have drawn women further into agricultural production, adding to their already burdensome dawn-to-dusk routines. Nonetheless, the additional demand for labor has decreased the degree of migration of males and older children in search of work. Furthermore, organic methods are environmentally sustainable, creating an economic incentive to produce without using inputs that interfere with the ecosystem.[9]

Extralegal Production: Coca

Despite the gains from crop diversification and organic farming, access by peasant farmers to inputs and good land as well as international market conditions limit widespread benefits. Planting coca is easier. As an agricultural crop, coca is versatile and lucrative. It grows in a wide range of conditions, may be harvested from three to six times per year, and can have a gestation period as short as eighteen months. Four-fifths of the coca is grown in the Upper Huallaga Valley of Peru and in the Chapare of Bolivia. Earnings for coca range from ten times that of cacao, to nineteen times that of citrus, to ninety-one times that of rice. There are three markets for coca: traditional, for uses in medicine and folk remedies; licit, for markets controlled by governments for production for cola and pharmaceuticals; and illicit production. Before coca is brought to the illicit market, its leaves are mashed and mixed with chemicals to become paste. The paste is then treated with sulfuric acid and potassium permanganate to form a cocaine base that can range in purity from 90 to 92 percent. It is then transported and cut before reaching the $110 billion international market, double the combined profits of all Fortune 500 companies.

Production is extremely mobile; illegal narcotics have become Latin America's true multinational. The technology is fairly straightforward, low cost, and relatively barrier-free. South American traffickers earn between $5 and $6 billion in the U.S. market. It is also labor-intensive, engaging growers, processors, and distributors in the production chain. The value added at higher levels of production graduates from $500 to $700 for an average kilogram through $160,000 to $240,000 as it hits the street. Although estimates are highly unreliable, some suggest that this illicit trade has a value equal to 10 to 20 percent of Colombia's legal exports, 25 to 30 percent of Peru's, and 50 to 100 percent of Bolivia's. In 1986 Bolivia's president Paz Estenssoro remarked that "cocaine has gained an importance in our economy in direct response to the shrinking of the formal economy; it is perhaps the only wealth in our history that benefits an important sector of the Bolivian population." In 1986 the aggregate value of coca production was 20 percent of farm income; in the Upper Huallaga Valley and Chapare, the proportion hits 90 percent. Peru's Alan García once called cocaine "our only successful multinational." For peasants, coca cultivation can be the margin between subsistence and a decent standard of living.

There are also economic costs to production in imbalanced growth driven by conspicuous consumption, potential inflationary effects from the infusion of money, the displacement of domestic food production as more land is dedicated to coca, and environmental damage, especially through chemical processing. In addition to economic costs, the political price of narco-terrorism, the threat to democratic institutions, and international pressure is relatively high. The governments of the region have tried to promote alternative development by drawing producers toward new crops, but many peasants find the dollar lure of illicit crops irresistible.

PITFALLS OF SUCCESS

As farmers moved into nontraditional and illicit crops and corporate farming has dominated the sector, producers of traditional crops such as wheat, maize, sugar beets, and milk have suffered. In particular, smaller campesino producers have been hurt. Recall the story of the Lehmans from chapter 1, who were squeezed by competitive global tobacco companies. The number of commercial farms has risen by 22 percent, accounting for an additional 30 percent of the land. Smaller producers find it difficult to overcome credit and finance constraints; economies of scale in marketing, packaging, and transport; import regulations and inspections in foreign markets; and production challenges with respect to pest control, soil management, and pesticide use. The result has been a bimodal agricultural sector in which the rich agro-export firms are edging out traditional producers. Many former farmers now find themselves in orchards and packaging plants. Prospects for peasant farmers are dim unless investments in microtechnologies are promoted by the state to bring peasant farmers into small-scale commercial sectors such as the cut flower industry.[10] Transnational corporations command a large proportion of agro-exports. Chiquita (United Brands), Del Monte, and Dole (Standard Fruit) continue to exert substantial influence in Central America, using their base in traditional bananas to capture 25 percent of all nontraditional export production. Three of the four top firms leading the Chilean boom are transnational.[11] Agriculture is big business in Latin America—sometimes to the detriment of the small farmer.

Not surprisingly, corporate farming has transformed relations between peasants and landowners in the region, resulting in a complex structure of agricultural production. With a decline in feudal land forms and a rise in corporate farming, we see several changes with respect to labor. Traditional clientelistic social relations have been replaced by a wage labor system. Capital is increasingly substituted for labor. In table 10.1 we can see that by the mid-1990s, in most countries the percentage of irrigated land has increased, as has the use of fertilizer and farm machinery. In Bolivia, for example, fertilizer consumption has more than tripled, and the number of tractors has increased by more than 25 percent.

At the same time, the share of the labor force in agriculture has fallen from 53 to 47 percent of the population. As machines and fertilizers replace workers, we can see the share of the labor force in agriculture declining in most countries. Table 10.2 groups countries by the magnitude of the shift in the share of labor force employment. Only three countries showed changes of less than 10 percent—Guatemala, Haiti, and Argentina. Imagine the degree of change in the social structure: in the relatively short span of ten years, there is a 25 percent or larger shift in the sector of employment. For anyone who has traveled in Latin America and was amazed at the influx of poor workers from the countryside, perhaps this number is not startling. Landless workers are searching for survival in cities. There is also an increase in the migrant laborers called *volante*—those who fly between the

Table 10.1.   Key Agricultural Inputs

	Arable Land (hectares per capita)		Irrigated Land (% of arable land)		Fertilizer Consumption (hundreds of grams of nutrient per hectare)		Farm Machinery (tractors)	
	1980	1994	1980	1994	1980–1981	1994–1995	1980	1994
Argentina	0.97	0.8	5.8	6.3	42	147	166,700	280,000
Bolivia	0.39	0.33	6.8	4.2	14	45	4,000	5,350
Brazil	0.41	0.32	3.3	5.9	855	933	545,205	735,000
Chile	0.38	0.3	29.6	29.8	314	979	34,380	41,312
Colombia	0.19	0.15	7.7	13.7	601	1,077	28,423	37,000
Costa Rica	0.22	0.16	12.1	23.8	1,453	2,585	5,950	7,000
Dominican Republic	0.25	0.19	11.6	16.9	363	642	2,150	2,350
Ecuador	0.31	0.27	21.1	18.4	295	546	6,198	8,900
El Salvador	0.16	0.13	15.2	16.4	832	1,325	3,300	3,430
Guatemala	0.25	0.19	5	6.5	489	958	4,000	4,300
Haiti	0.17	0.13	7.9	8.2	4	56	175	230
Honduras	0.48	0.35	42.9	28.6	162	281	3,250	4,900
Mexico	0.37	0.27	20.3	24.7	0.37	0.27	115,057	172,000
Nicaragua	0.45	0.31	6.4	6.9	435	244	2,200	2,700
Panama	0.28	0.26	5	4.8	551	481	5,458	5,000
Paraguay	0.55	0.47	3.5	3	36	101	7,300	16,500
Peru	0.2	0.18	33	41.1	336	505	11,900	13,000
Uruguay	0.5	0.41	5.5	10.7	558	828	32,878	33,000
Venezuela	0.25	0.19	3.6	4.9	642	613	38,000	49,000

Source: World Bank, *World Development Indicators, 1997* (Washington, D.C.: World Bank), 147–148.

rural sector and the outskirts of the urban sector as labor demand changes. These are workers without permanent jobs or homes, generally leading lives of misery, contributing to both urban and rural poverty. In Brazil, landless workers suffering from the drought and desperate for survival erupted into violence in 1998, looted stores, and commandeered government buildings in an attempt to call government attention to their plight. Organized by Brazil's landless movement, MST (Movimento Sem Terra), the group has, with the support of churches and international groups, occupied (or invaded) unproductive ranches to pressure for land reform in a country where 2 percent of the richest farmers own 65 percent of the land. Killings by police defending the land have made land reform in Brazil an international human rights issue.

The movement to less labor-intensive means of production has indeed produced gains in output. Table 10.3 shows the gains in agricultural production. From a baseline of 1980, we can see that several countries—Chile, Paraguay, Peru, Brazil, Venezuela, and Costa Rica—have logged relatively rapid growth in the agricultural sector. By 1995 the change in the index of agricultural production in these

Table 10.2. Labor Force Employment in Agriculture

	1980	1990	% Decline in Agriculture's Share
Small shifts in labor force employment			
Guatemala	54	52	3.70
Haiti	71	68	4.23
Argentina	13	12	7.69
Moderate shifts in labor force employment			
Chile	21	19	9.52
Peru	40	36	10.00
Panama	29	26	10.34
Bolivia	53	47	11.32
Paraguay	45	39	13.33
El Salvador	43	36	16.28
Ecuador	40	33	17.50
Uruguay	17	14	17.65
Dramatic shifts in labor force employment			
Venezuela	15	12	20.00
Dominican Republic	32	25	21.88
Mexico	37	28	24.32
Costa Rica	35	26	25.71
Nicaragua	39	28	28.21
Honduras	56	40	28.57
Colombia	39	25	35.90
Brazil	37	23	37.84

Source: World Bank, *World Development Indicators, 1997* (Washington, D.C.: World Bank, 1997), 147–148.

countries exceeded 40 percent, above the 30 percent change in the index of world agricultural production. A second group of countries—Ecuador, Mexico, Colombia, Panama, Uruguay, and Argentina—roughly approximated the change in the world index. Other countries in the region did not fare as well. Not surprisingly, domestic conflict in El Salvador, Nicaragua, Bolivia, Honduras, the Dominican Republic, and Haiti contributed to low growth rates in agriculture. In most cases the conflict itself had roots in highly unequal patterns of land distribution. The outbreak of fighting was the manifestation of social conflict over control of land, a precious commodity. Stability in the region in the latter half of the 1990s should facilitate stronger growth, but more is needed to resolve the underlying unequal conditions of production to generate a sustainable and strong pattern of agricultural growth. Simply improving output without improving the lives of rural residents is not sustainable as a development policy.

But aggregate growth rates don't tell us who the largest regional producers are or how the value of agricultural production fared. Table 10.4 shows that as a percentage of regional output, Brazil, Mexico, and Argentina top the list in agricultural production. Although to some degree this is to be expected, given

Table 10.3.   Agricultural Production Index^a (base period: 1989–1991 = 100)^b

	1980	1995	Change in Index
Rapid growth			
Chile	71	124	53
Paraguay	57	104	47
Peru	77	121	44
Brazil	74	116	42
Venezuela	77	119	42
Costa Rica	72	112	40
Moderate growth			
Ecuador	75	105	30
Mexico	87	112	25
Colombia	76	100	24
Panama	83	106	23
Uruguay	85	108	23
Argentina	89	110	21
Slow growth			
Bolivia	75	92	17
Honduras	87	102	15
Guatemala	89	103	14
Dominican Republic	87	99	12
Stagnation			
Nicaragua	105	107	2
El Salvador	113	113	0
Haiti	103	92	−11
World growth	78.7	109.1	30.4

Source: World Bank, *World Development Indicators, 1997* (Washington, D.C.: World Bank, 1997), 138–141.
^{a}Agricultural production includes all crops and livestock products except fodder crops.
^{b}Index calculations: production quantities of each commodity are weighted by the average international commodity prices in the base period and summed for each year.

endowments of land and population, it is important to remember, because these three countries have become players in global agricultural markets. It should be noted, however, that strong output does not necessarily translate into healthy revenues. Because revenues are determined by both the quantity produced and the price charged, the gains from agricultural production are highly sensitive to price changes. Agricultural prices of Latin America's major commodities, measured in constant dollars, fell to their lowest level of the century during the early 1990s.[12] In part the fall in agricultural prices was driven by a fallacy of composition. As debt-laden countries across the globe adopted the neoliberal focus on agricultural exports, markets were saturated. Excess supply drove prices down. Furthermore, protectionist measures in the developed world limited export opportunities. By one estimate, tariffs and other barriers on agricultural goods worldwide average 40 percent, shrinking market opportunities and contributing to loss of value. Although global farm talks through the World Trade Organization will address high industrialized country tariffs in agriculture, the entrenched interests in industrialized countries make progress difficult.[13]

Revenues and production are also sensitive to the exchange rate. Recall that under import substitution industrialization the overvalued exchange rate biased development against the agricultural sector. Overvalued exchange rates worked against the development of comparative advantage in external markets. Industrial protection distorted the internal terms of trade between the domestic sectors. Very often, agricultural protection of competitive commodities was directly taxed as a means of raising revenue to support industrial expansion. One estimate places indirect taxation through industrial protection and macroeconomic policies at 22 percent of agricultural output. To offset this drain, politically powerful agricultural elites were sometimes able to garner favors in terms of subsidies or infrastructure support—but rarely did these benefits trickle down to the small producers.[14]

Under contemporary macrostabilization schemes such as Argentina's, exports

Table 10.4.   Gross Domestic Product of Agriculture at Constant Market Prices (U.S.$ millions at 1990 prices)

	1980	1985	1990	1995	1995 Share of Latin American Output (%)
Brazil	30,788.4	37,130.8	39,224.4	47,722	43.94
Mexico	16,665.7	18,844.3	18,864.0	19,382.3	17.84
Argentina	8,631.5	9,377.9	9,781.2	11,041.6	10.17
Colombia	4,868.5	5,241.5	6,538.6	7,348.9	6.77
Peru	2,108.4	2,450.5	2,627.3	3,362.9	3.10
Chile	1,443.8	1,699.7	2,500.4	3,206.2	2.95
Venezuela	2,147.4	2,388.2	2,617.6	2,855.5	2.63
Guatemala	1,547.5	1,522.1	1,758.4	2,011.8	1.85
Ecuador	1,064.1	1,213.7	1,610.4	1,859.0	1.71
Paraguay	988.1	1,180	1,462.6	1,649.9	1.52
Dominican Republic	1,076.6	1,181.4	1,115.3	1,292.8	1.19
Uruguay	1,007.9	987.1	1,027.3	1,270.6	1.17
Costa Rica	661.6	716.6	901.3	1,090.1	1.00
Bolivia	677.0	762.1	802.9	961.7	0.89
Honduras	575.8	631.4	751.2	884.5	0.81
El Salvador	947.6	807.1	821.1	884.2	0.81
Nicaragua	712.8	765	663.7	782.5	0.72
Panama	377.2	486.1	503.8	561.5	0.52
Haiti	556.9	527.0	545.2	450.8	0.42
Total	76,847.4	87,912.4	94,116.9	108,618.8	100.00

Source: Economic Commission for Latin America and the Caribbean, *Statistical Yearbook for Latin America and the Caribbean, 1996* (Santiago, Chile: Economic Commission for Latin America and the Caribbean, 1996), 196–197.

are compromised by overvalued exchange rates. A real exchange rate depreciation is important in maintaining agricultural exports. Between exchange rate biases and industrialized country tariffs, agriculture faces significant distortions. But simply getting prices right will not work unless adequate rural infrastructure is available, including irrigation, roads, power, and telecommunications as well as credit, market information, research, extension, and farmer education and health.[15] If the farmer—particularly the small producer—does not have the necessary complementary inputs, production and revenues will not rise. We now turn to look at the structural constraints in agricultural production.

CHARACTERISTICS IMPEDING SUSTAINABLE GROWTH IN THE AGRICULTURAL SECTOR

The rural poor are either landless farm workers in commercial farming areas or small holders in areas of low productivity. They lack adequate access to roads, potable water, electricity, communications, secondary schools, and public health. As a result of tough macroeconomic adjustment strategies, the proportion of destitute in the rural sector rose from 28 to 31 percent. Overall poverty—not the poorest of the poor—claimed more than half of rural inhabitants. In Guatemala and Nicaragua, 85.67 and 76.1 percent of rural inhabitants lived in poverty. Rural poverty has clear connections to environmental degradation. Those without assets find it hard to invest in the land through sustainable agricultural practices. The lack of attention to environmental considerations in the early stages of macroeconomic adjustment further resulted in a high degree of environmental degradation.[16] The intensification of agriculture has also had environmental costs. Attempts to increase agricultural output through intensive application of fertilizer and pesticides have contributed to environmental and human costs. Illiteracy and poor health training among uneducated workers have resulted in the poisoning of workers who spread pesticide by hand and then ate without washing. One investigation showed that 39 percent of pesticide applications were undertaken without protective clothing, and 18 percent of workers admitted to not washing after completing the chore. Mothers in Nicaraguan cotton regions were found to have DDT in breast milk, and some blame agro-chemicals for the region's malaria epidemic.[17] Environmental degradation is a constraint in expanding agricultural output.

Women are the sometimes invisible contributors to agricultural production. Nicaraguan census data report only 5 to 12 percent of women involved in farming, yet an Inter-American Development Bank study found 50 percent of the labor of corn and bean production being carried out by women. Out of their sixteen-hour daily workload, women usually dedicated an average of four hours to farming. The rural woman's day is consumed by food preparation, collection of water and firewood, care of vegetable gardens and domestic animals, clearing and plowing land, weeding, cultivating, milking cows, processing milk and other foods to sell at market, and acting as business managers for the family enterprise.[18] Unlike men, whose crops tend to be seasonal, they work year round to provide food for their families. When men migrate to the cities in search of work, women are left com-

Nontraditional export crops have opened new opportunities for women—but also added to their burden. *(Courtesy of the Inter-American Development Bank.)*

pletely in charge of the farms. The transition to export crops has also opened up new employment opportunities for women. Large agro-industries employ predominantly female labor forces, because women tend to be more readily available to work on a seasonal basis for lower wages.[19] Older daughters in a household take on additional tasks, releasing women for remunerated labor.[20] This naturally calls into question traditional roles in the rural family. Without changes in the social division of labor in the family, women's increased work in the commercial sector is on top of an already long day in the rural home. Sound agricultural policy must take the problems of rural poverty, its environmental dimensions, and its gendered characteristics into account.

Why has agriculture failed to generate an adequate income for most rural inhabitants? A variety of reasons explain failure. Politically, governments have viewed agriculture as a declining sector with falling prices. The rural poor have little political power; urban elites have therefore pursued polices disadvantaging agriculture. Past policies on the part of multilateral organizations have been overly centralized, with top-down integrated rural development schemes ignoring the needs of rural inhabitants. Credit was directed to specific crops and often concentrated in the hands of the rural elites. Frontier settlements contributed to environmental degradation, and many large-scale irrigation projects carried unforeseen environmental costs.[21]

Beyond these policy mistakes, structural characteristics of the agricultural market create challenges for successful policy. The agricultural sector is often characterized by missing or **incomplete markets** for products, labor, and finance, and by high risk, in terms of both crop failure and pricing. Market failures result in inefficient or inequitable outcomes. They often result from inadequate property rights and underpriced or unpriced resources, as well as unwise government regulations and subsidies.

Property rights in the rural sector are often poorly defined, with official records frequently incomplete or nonexistent. A lack of computerization, insufficient staffing, or inappropriate storage facilities may contribute to poor record keeping. Conflicts emerge between nationally registered systems and de facto rights of occupancy by local squatters or customary rights of traditional communities.[22] Indigenous land rights are sometimes mapped but not recognized. Settlers with guns have usurped traditional rights and crudely marked boundaries.[23] Transferability or sale of rights is limited when land records are absent or conflicting, or when a functioning legal system with enforcement capabilities is missing. Secure land titles are often a prerequisite to obtaining credit. Poor judicial and police enforcement may make it difficult to exercise legal claims to land. Uncertainty in retaining property rights over time promotes underinvestment in the land and reduces the incentives to use land efficiently and sustainably. A farmer facing the possibility of eviction is less likely to invest in reforestation or conservation, because there is great uncertainty about reaping the benefits of the investment. For the farmer with tenuous land rights, environmental irresponsibility is economically rational.

Developing countries typically have **segmented credit markets** such that different borrowers are charged different prices. Formal credit markets intermediated by state and private institutions generally charge a low rate of interest that is often government subsidized. But lack of access to collateral to guarantee formal sector loans forces smaller holders to rely on kinship circles, friends, landlords, or professional money lenders, often at higher than market interest rates. Agricultural lending is more difficult than commercial lending. The seasonal nature of agricultural activity yields products only at harvest season. Because the same adverse weather conditions affect all borrowers, diversification is problematic. Several factors complicate lending: a high cost to serving geographically dispersed customers, frequent deficits of collateral, problems in contract enforcement, and a lack of trained and motivated financial personnel in the rural sector.[24] There is an informational constraint as well, because less is usually known about a large number of little farmers. The typically high rates of interest in the informal sector can be traced to the ways these factors affect different groups of farmers. Small producers with uncertain harvests and a lack of collateral are less likely to find formal sector lending than large, mechanized farms. Without credit, the investment in orchards that bear fruit years later, or even in vegetable farming with no returns until the end-of-season harvest, is extremely difficult for the small family farmer.

In addition to credit, the allocation of **water rights** is another important element of incomplete or inefficient agricultural markets. Typically, surface water rights systems accrue based on seniority. Under this system, there is little incentive for those with first rights to conserve water to increase the availability to others. For groundwater, incentives need to be developed to prompt efficient use today and conservation for the future. In the case of surface water in rivers or streams, a market for water rights could be developed. Under this system, if those with prior rights were given a greater number of shares in a water rights systems to head off political opposition, they could trade these shares, also prompting more efficient allocation of this scarce resource.[25]

Agricultural Policy Options

Policy remedies for incomplete markets include securing transferable property rights, creating enforceable contracts, removing subsidies, implementing market-based initiatives as opposed to command and control regulations, adopting green accounting methods and peer monitoring, and co-signing loans to decrease risk. In credit markets, mechanisms have been employed to reduce the risk to lenders of bad loans through relying on local leaders or group lending schemes.[26] Positive incentives such as interest rebates for timely repayment and access to new benefits including longer time horizons may enhance enforcement of repayment. Negative sanctions such as legal proceedings may be useful, but the large number of small producers makes enforcement tough and costly. Local governance structures to promote repayment are more promising, such as cooperative lending. Such nonconventional rural finance can also facilitate the growth of horizontal civic rural institutions, enhancing the sustainability and equity of rural finance.[27]

Policy measures can once again be broken down as neoliberal, new institutionalist, and neostructuralist. Pure marketeers will focus on removing governmental restrictions in the agricultural market, eliminating subsidies, and opening markets to free trade. They would also push to strengthen and clarify contractual property rights. New institutionalists would focus on the high transaction costs imposed by incomplete markets and would revamp agricultural credit systems.

For neostructuralists, policies designed to improve the functioning of the market that don't take into account a socioeconomic understanding of market actors face likely failure. In Latin America, agricultural reform is about more than markets. It involves the power of elites to influence policy outcomes.[28] In a case of imperfect factor markets, in which different-sized farms face different prices for labor, capital, or technology, the strongest—the largest—are most likely to benefit from policy changes. For example, in the macroeconomic changes accompanying neoliberal reforms in the Chamorro government in Nicaragua—a nation that pursued aggressive redistributive land reform—small farmers were shown to fail in tough times, selling between 6 and 13 percent of the land back to large-scale owners or wealthy individuals.[29] Policy must take the market structure into account.

But this doesn't mean that neostructuralists will advocate large size. Although small-scale farmers are more vulnerable to external policy shocks, it is not clear that large farmers are necessarily more productive than small farmers. Evidence suggests that with the exception of plantation crops such as sugar or cotton, or where market imperfections such as access to credit or information about international marketing exist, there are few economies of scale in agriculture for farms larger than a family can operate with its own labor. One historical study contrasted the relatively small landholdings in the United States under the Homesteading Acts, with limits of 160 acres, to large-scale allocations of land in Brazilian agriculture of plots no smaller than 988 acres. It showed that large size forced Brazilian farmers to rely on wage labor, with the resulting inefficiencies in supervising hired labor, as opposed to the incentives for the family farmer to rely on productive family labor.[30] Furthermore, to supplement meager wage earnings on the large Brazilian farm, a system of sharecropping emerged that later introduced its own fears in terms of evictions in the face of possible land invasions or impending land reform. Large landowners evict poor sharecroppers because they are afraid of land invasions from squatters exercising the right of occupancy.

The cost of unequal landholdings may be high. Some evidence suggests that the legacy of unequal landholdings can pose a serious barrier to growth over the long term. One study shows that initial land distribution and associated low primary education for sixteen developing countries explains variation in national growth rates. Other empirical investigations also point to this inverse relationship between land inequality and economic growth.[31] As demonstrated by Southeast Asian nations, small family farmers supplemented by investments in rural infrastructure appear to fare better in terms of long-run growth. In contrast, the unequal land distribution from colonial times in Brazil, Colombia, or Guatemala, as worsened by a policy mix of industrial protection under import substitution industrialization and agricultural taxation, constrained dynamic growth in the agricultural sector.[32]

Experience with Land Reform

For the neostructuralist, unequal landholdings correlate with unequal power and unfair access to resources. Land reform has been used in Latin America to address asset inequality in the rural sector. The land reform movement in Mexico and Bolivia was revolutionary; throughout the rest of the region it was a legislated process. Extensive land reforms were undertaken in Chile, Ecuador, El Salvador, Nicaragua, and Peru—although they have generally failed to reduce the poverty of the peasantry. Several issues inform the process. What is the optimal size of farms? As farms are broken up, will small peasant farmers have access to credit, technology, and new equipment to increase productivity? If the nation does not have idle land, whose land should be taken, and what kind of compensation should be offered? When the easy stage of capturing idle or uncolonized land is over, how will the confiscation affect the credibility of property rights in the economy? Should the process take place quickly to send signals of resolve, or does a slower, more measured program allow for the development of complementary infrastructure? How nations have resolved these questions defined the nature of their land reforms. We will now consider the cases of Mexico, Bolivia, and Chile.

Given high inequality, Mexican agriculture was strongly characterized by the bimodal agricultural production system. In response to high inequality, Mexican land reform was a legacy of the Zapatista agitation in 1917. Based on the constitutional recognition of community rights to land, it created a system of small landholdings called *ejidos*. In practice the ejido was farmed individually, but the land could not be sold. Despite this land reform, some of the best lands remained under the control of wealthy farmers. Today the large farm sector produces 70 percent of all marketable food and nearly half the exports. The ejidos, poorly integrated into the marketplace, suffer from a lack of roads and marketing networks, producing corn and beans for peasant subsistence.[33] Attempts were made by various administrations to assist peasants. During the 1970s, under the Echeverria administration (1970–1976), state marketing agencies bought peasant commodities at subsidized prices to support small-scale agricultural production. President de la Madrid (1982–1988) confronted the problem of land fragmentation without complementary resources, and his successor, President Salinas (1988–1994), called for the modernization of the ejido through privatized joint ventures—without fundamentally altering the campesino way of life.[34] Nevertheless, the primary purpose of the policies was, too often, to support the political arm of government, the PRI (Mexican Revolutionary Party) and not to improve the peasants' lives.

Reduction of subsidies under the neoliberal model, as well as the opening of agricultural markets to imports, has further impoverished the peasantry. The 1994 Chiapas rebellion in Mexico can be seen as evidence of the rural crisis exacerbated by the opening to international markets.[35] An ECLAC study showed approximately 11 percent of ejido agricultural producers in Chiapas to be commercially viable; 58 percent are diversified producers that barely eke out an existence on the land, earning a surplus of about $300 per year, and 31 percent are subsistence farmers on the margins of economic life unable to obtain basic necessities from their efforts.[36] In contrast to the ejido farmers is the commercialized private sector. Large commercial landowners control the most productive assets while Indians and peasants are forced to the margins. Such poverty and inequality is ripe ground for rebellion. Reprivatization of rural institutions of credit and technology and a sharp decline in public investment in the sector have left the Mexican peasantry without access to institutional resources to improve productivity. Small and middle-sized farmers would benefit from the promotion of producer organizations for self-delivery of services and lowering of transactions costs of bringing goods to market. A transition program orchestrated by governmental and nongovernmental organizations and the private sector is necessary to preserve the economic viability of this important sector.[37]

In Bolivia, land reform was designed to address problems of increasing violence in the countryside due to the unbalanced nature of landholdings. Beginning in 1952, 80 percent of land was affected by the redistribution process. Eighty-two percent of farmers—largely poor—holding 1 percent of the land began to invade large estates and claim property. Often the expropriation was spontaneously undertaken by campesinos, without governmental assistance. This later created problems of legal title to the land, and settlement of property rights has taken decades. Furthermore, the process was not accompanied by a program of capital assistance to the peasant farmers. Although the Bolivian reform was a political success, economically it did little to improve the lives of the peasantry. Ironically, a residual of the poorly orchestrated reform process is that cocaine production is easily maintained on a large number of small plots without much in the way of technological assistance.

In Peru, the process of land reform was guided by clear political objectives: to bring social justice to the rural areas, to support an enlargement of the internal market, and to contribute to the capital formation critical for rapid industrialization. The revolutionary military government of General Juan Velasco initiated an ambitious program in 1969 that expropriated between 40 and 50 percent of agricultural land. Land was subject to expropriation if it was between 150 and 200 hectares on the coast and 150 to 330 on the sierra; land could also be subject to expropriation if certain conditions were not met, such as provision of satisfactory living conditions for workers. Workers were also supposed to receive 50 percent of the profit, own 50 percent of the capital, and receive 20 percent of net income.[38] Land was reorganized as CAPs, or agrarian cooperatives. This decision, geared to maintain scale economies and farm cooperatively, did not translate into improving productivity and incomes.[39] The Peruvian land reform experience was state directed as opposed to spontaneously driven by peasant demands. Problems with compensation for expropriated lands bogged down the process, resulting in delays that undermined legitimacy. Later, revolutionary groups such as Sendero Luminoso in the highlands were better able to provide the support peasants needed for survival. As in Mexico and Bolivia, failed Peruvian land reform has had a high political cost.

The Chilean land reform process has been reversed to some degree by the effects of the agro-export boom. Data show that nearly half of the *parceleros,* the small-scale farmers given land under reform measures, completely sold their farms between the late 1970s and 1991, leading to a reconcentration of land in medium to large holdings. Forty-seven percent of parceleros in the fruit boom region became completely landless by 1990, excluding these smaller farmers from the direct benefits of agro-export boom. However, this exclusionary model was somewhat offset by an increase in labor absorption of the boom, providing employment for the landless peasants.[40] The experience in Guatemala demonstrates different results with agro-exports, with small farmers benefiting from the boom in nontraditional exports. The differences between the Chilean and Guatemalan experiences reflect differential impacts of crop choice on small farmers. Small farmers tend to be more risk averse, fearful that the adoption of new technologies or crops could, if unsuccessful, wipe out their livelihood. They tend to face higher prices for inputs and lower prices for outputs than larger farms that are able to take advantage of economies of scale. In particular, they are poorly connected to marketing and transportation networks. Small farmers often have a difficult time gaining access to credit, and they have been able to invest less in their own human capital. These biases against small farmers interact with crop choice. Orchard crops for fruit exports in Chile require multiyear investments; vegetable crops in Guatemala may advantage smaller producers because they are relatively labor intensive. Small-scale farmers did not find themselves in competition with large-scale producers for land or resources.[41] But this is not to say that the land problem is solved in Guatemala. Two percent of landowners hold two-thirds of the country's land.[42]

Several lessons can be distilled from the experience with land reform. First, the easy stages of redistributing unproductive land are over. Land is in short supply, so that redistribution now has a clear economic opportunity cost. The goal of increased production may be harmed because taking land away from large owners may result in less land available for export sectors. Second, land reform has not helped the poorest of the rural poor. Those who were relatively better off were able to take advantage of changes in policy; those on the margins of existence were less adept at working with authorities to transform property rights. Third, land reform works best when accompanied by ample credit and technical assistance. Simply owning land without the complementary inputs does little to raise productivity or incomes. To succeed, land reform therefore requires a comprehensive strategy for rural development. Fourth, policies adopted may have differential effects on small and large landowners. A policy package that reduces biases toward large holders and secures property rights of small peasants may help reduce rural poverty. This package could be supplemented with public investments to develop infrastructure and promote better exchange of information among small farmers to encourage broader-based growth. Picking labor-intensive crops to promote may direct growth toward the small farmer.[43] Fifth, this strategy must incorporate environmental as well as economic dimensions of reform. Environmental deterioration is closely tied to **insecure property rights**, inadequate credit, and poorly designed public infrastructure for water use, waste disposal, or transportation of goods to market.

Agricultural reform is more than land reform. It requires changes in law as well as public and private investments. Public resources for an integrated rural development strategy might come from increased taxation of agricultural land, particularly unproductive land. Higher taxation of larger parcels might encourage private market sales to small-scale producers. Revenues from taxation can be used for public infrastructure as well as financing loans to prospective buyers. Multilateral and bilateral international assistance in agricultural reform can help in project lending for infrastructure, and nongovernmental organizations can facilitate grassroots access to poor farmers to promote extension services well suited to local conditions. Box 10.1 describes a project to increase the income of the rural poor in Guatemala. In one Inter-American Development Bank project in Brazil, rural families are being helped in their efforts to create self-sufficient communities through improving infrastructure, providing social services to settlers, and establishing a set of procedures to transform settlements into economically viable units.[44] Carefully crafted policies with clear results are important to demonstrate the benefits of infrastructure investments as well as gain the confidence of small farmers in new techniques for small-scale production. Concrete achievements will build confidence in the rural reform process. Moving beyond input markets for land or output markets for products, we will now turn to some of the systemic agricultural changes being implemented in the region.

RAISING PRODUCTIVITY: THE KEY TO RAISING RURAL INCOMES

A strategy to spur rural development must take a broad focus, moving beyond the narrow agricultural sector to include the entire rural productive system.[45] The management of natural and human resources, infrastructure development, and social development must be woven into a comprehensive strategy. Past policy mistakes derive in part from a narrow focus. Rather than simply look at irrigation and drainage, questions of resource allocation and comprehensive watershed management must be addressed. Instead of a focus on crop production, forestry, or livestock management, attention must be given to management of natural resources in a sustainable production system. Human capital development, infrastructure, and community-based decision making form the basis of an equitable, sustainable strategy. Stakeholders must be involved in the development and execution of projects.[46]

The greatest challenge in any agricultural strategy is to create equitable pathways to rising farm productivity. Farmers need incentives to produce more with fewer inputs. Cheap food for burgeoning urban populations is often a key policy objective. Yet if the price of foodstuffs falls without a decrease in the costs to the farmer, farm income is likely to suffer. Maintaining rural incomes while supporting urban populations can best be resolved either with an export model that increases the quantity produced through exports or decreases the costs through improvements in technology. But technological change costs money. If the dynamism in the rural sector is going to extend beyond large corporate farms, a system of peasant credit is necessary to support advances in small-scale farming. Technological change is also risky: if a peasant is living on the margins of subsistence, although change might have a large production payoff, it could also fail dismally, and the family would likely starve. Policies to improve productivity for peasant

BOX 10.1. THE RURAL DEVELOPMENT CHALLENGE IN GUATEMALA: A USAID PROGRAM RESPONSE

Guatemala is the largest Central American country in terms of population (10 million) and economic activity (1997 gross domestic product $18 billion), but its largely rural, Mayan population lives in some of the most difficult conditions found in the Central American region. Distribution of land, income, and other wealth is highly skewed toward a small share of Guatemala's Spanish-speaking population. An estimated 75 percent of Guatemalans live in poverty, and the roughly five million Mayans are isolated socially, economically, and politically due to geographic and language barriers. The country's social indicators are among the worst in the hemisphere, and national averages mask even sharper inequalities between ethnic groups and gender. Overall adult literacy is estimated at 48 percent, but literacy among Mayan women is estimated as low as 10 percent. Less than half of rural Guatemalans have access to running water, only a quarter have access to electricity, and less than one in ten have access to modern sanitary facilities. Infant, child, and maternal mortality rates are among the highest in Latin America, despite decreases in recent years. These indicators reflect the country's persistent under-investment in social services and basic rural infrastructure, as well as past practices of political and socioeconomic exclusion of the indigenous population.

To expand economic and social opportunity for the rural poor through programs that will increase incomes, improve the nutritional status of food aid program participants, and improve access to and quality of intercultural bilingual education, USAID—in conjunction with the Guatemalan Ministries of Agriculture, Food and Livestock (MAGA), Public Finance (MOF), and the Economic Planning Secretariat (SEGEPLAN) and with the support of nongovernmental organizations—signed a $16.5 million, five-year agreement to increase productive incomes for the rural poor by expanding access to credit and training and strengthening intermediary organizations. Local and international nongovernmental organizations currently assisting in program implementation are Guatemala's National Coffee Association (ANACAFE), the Banco de Desarrollo Rural, CARE, Catholic Relief Services, and World Share. Earlier, USAID supported the Ministry of Finance and the National Development Bank in the design of a trust fund which is providing credit to micro enterprises and small-scale farmers in rural areas. This fund now provides the Guatemalan government counterpart contribution to the agreement. Sustainability and expansion of activities into the poorest rural areas remains problematic, primarily due to the inability of local organizations to manage credit and to provide direction, leadership, and training to their members. USAID-supported on-the-ground productive activities in formerly conflictive areas have increased income for small coffee producers, with improvements in both the quality and quantity of the product.

The USAID-supported program for increasing the incomes of the rural poor targets on- and off-farm income generation, expanded economic opportunities for micro entrepreneurs and small-scale farmers, and expanded capacity of local organizations and institutions to provide financial and technical assistance services. The delivery network of private voluntary organizations (PVOs) will continue to focus activities on the most marginal rural communities. The nutritional aspects of the program target maternal and child health by increasing the level of understanding of the nutritional and health needs of the family. The program supports small-scale community activities and the development of sustainable agricultural production technologies to encourage income generation and increase food production.

Source: Abstracted from the USAID FY 1999 Congressional Presentation Document for Guatemala. (The CPD is the document the agency transmits to Congress to explain past use of funds and present the coming year's programs. You may find the current CPD at http://www.info.usaid.gov.)

Agricultural extension services promote farmer involvements in sustainable practices.
(Courtesy of the Inter-American Development Bank.)

farmers must acknowledge the risk-averse nature of small-scale producers and provide flexible, extended terms to smooth the potential losses in any one year.

AGRICULTURAL EXTENSION PROGRAMS:
GETTING FARMERS INVOLVED

Simply getting prices right is clearly not enough. **Agricultural extension programs**
must speak to the family and cultural needs of the farmer. Improvements in productivity are driven by encouraging farmers to adopt new agricultural practices.
This has historically been accomplished through agricultural extension programs.
Worldwide, $6 billion was spent in 1988 alone on extension. However, many farm-
ers find agricultural extension programs ineffective. Problems with free extension
services included budget pressures, poorly defined objectives, low motivation, a
lack of accountability to clients, and little interest on the part of farmers in obtaining quality service. Centralized systems are also costly and inefficient delivery
vehicles for services. In an era of fiscal tightening, expensive, centrally directed
extension programs are unsustainable. Demand-driven services operate on the
market concept that extension is an economic input that, if effective, may generate
additional income that farmers would be willing to pay for. Free services may
result in under- or overuse.[47]

As a measure of their effectiveness, when extension services were cut in Nicaragua in December 1995, no one went on strike. Yet when university financial support was cut, strikes were widespread. In part this had to do with an outdated centralized extension system in which information was delivered to peasants and not developed and appropriated by them. Extension can also have a gendered dimension, because in some cultures it is inappropriate for a male outside the household to work closely with a female. Peasant farmers need to be involved in determining the necessary changes in farming practices to solve local problems. A new program shows promise in Nicaragua—a demand-driven accountable extension system through the Agricultural Technology and Land Management Project (ATLMP), financed by the World Bank and the Swiss government. Through a demonstration of a willingness to pay, farmers shape the services of the extension agent. Providers of extension services compete for contracts; because dissatisfied farmers can cease to be clients of extension agents, this creates a stake on the part of the agents to be more attentive to the needs of the farmers.[48] Despite initial objections, through small group meetings with farmers, extension agents overcame the lack of confidence of clients. In a voluntary pilot test, they were convinced that it was to their benefit to pay for services. An NGO provided credit to purchase the extension services. In addition, half the crop increase would go to the extensionist, with half retained by the farmers. The extension agent was to visit the site at least once a week. Although measurement of output was somewhat suspect, with overreporting of historical yields and underreporting of current production, the success of the program was defined by a uniform willingness to sign new contracts for the following season. Similarly, in a Costa Rican project to address the needs of poorer farmers, government vouchers are awarded for extension services to farmers on the basis of farm type.[49] Farmers will trade vouchers for the services of extension agents, building up a corps of private extension agents accountable to local clients. As farmers see the gains from effective extension services, gradually vouchers will be eliminated and private provision of services will take over.

The role of the public sector could best be left in coordination of various extension activities and in ensuring that all farmers have access to some form of extension. Radio programming, for example, can be used to reach less accessible groups. A state role is also critical in dealing with common property and environmental sustainability issues. Public institutions are preferable when benefits are diffuse, when the public policies require change, or when enhanced equity is a central goal. A public–private mix works best when the ability to achieve responsive and flexible management is contingent on political influence. A strictly private provision of services is superior when direct and continuous interaction with users is required.[50] The appropriate mix of state and market is therefore a function of local conditions.

The agricultural sector may be an example where the temptation to employ our neat policy prescriptions of neoliberal, neoinstitutionalist, or neostructuralist may lead to policy failure. It appears that a public–private mix—an approach that encourages the government to supplement the activity of the market—may be superior.

DECENTRALIZATION AND COMMUNITY CONTROL

In part, the difficult challenge of agricultural policy derives from the fact that farmers are not simply workers or owners but are inhabitants in a rural system with different practices from those in urban commercial markets. Agricultural policy—far more so than industrial policy—must be community based. **Demand-driven rural investment funds** (DRIFs) are a new instrument for improving local control of agricultural development. Through DRIFs, central governments transfer funds to local governments and communities to address their own priorities within a carefully constructed set of guidelines. Beneficiaries include neighborhood associations, women's groups, and producer associations or cooperatives. Specific eligibility requirements must be met, including cost limits, and beneficiaries are required to contribute to the project cost either directly or through in-kind work. In Mexico, for example, communities must contribute a minimum of 20 percent of the project costs. Communities decide for themselves what type of technical assistance is required and then receive the funding to pay for it. The Mexican experience with DRIFs has extended to 30,000 subprojects with average costs 30 to 60 percent less than traditional centralized funding mechanisms. The economic sustainability of the projects is also higher, because local groups are vested in the project from the start.[51]

Agricultural policy reform has paralleled broader changes in development policy in the 1990s. The broad elements of reform, as captured by a World Bank directive in 1982, combine the use of markets and prices with strengthening property rights and regulatory institutions to promote productivity increases in the agricultural sector.[52] In part the answer to the new mix between state and market in the agricultural sector depends on the type of good or service being delivered. If the good is a plantation product such as sugar, a new tractor, or new seed, the private sector can probably address the need. If, however, the constraint is in practices such as farm management or marketing, some combination of public and private efforts is most likely to bear fruit. Finally, in areas affected by externalities and uses of common resources, government intervention is critical to provide incentives for cooperative voluntary action. In the agricultural sector the new role for the state is to create enabling environments for private and voluntary action—not to deliver the goods or the technologies, as in the past.[53] Enhancing the voice of farmers in a demand-driven approach may result in a more efficient and equitable agricultural system.

Consistent with neoliberal market approaches, agricultural loans supported by the new strategy with the World Bank are structured to help eliminate price controls, replacing generalized subsidies with targeted interventions. They are geared to develop competitive local markets for inputs and outputs and to reduce state interventions in international trade. In terms of agricultural trade policy, the goals are to replace quantitative restrictions with tariffs and to abolish state marketing boards. Improvements in the legal and regulatory system should include land tenure, export regulations, phytosanitary procedures, and the licensing of commerce. Finally, a stronger emphasis on food security might include targeted spending on food and nutrition programs. For example, Mexico was given a World Bank loan to support trade, price, privatization, and other policy reforms and reduce the government's role in the production, planning, marketing, storage, and processing of agricultural products and inputs. In Honduras support was given to modify the land reform law, improve property rights, permit the development of land markets, and reorient forestry practices toward protection and conservation of the environment.[54]

Overall, the key to a strong agricultural policy is to raise productivity while simultaneously including the poor. In doing so it is essential to triage the really poor, providing emergency relief. From there, working with community organizers to resolve land tenure issues, define emergent farmers, and identify technologies appropriate to local practices and conditions will facilitate rural development. A complementary program between the agricultural and nonagricultural sectors will help stem the migration from the farm to the cities. Providing off-farm activities for those unable to make it in farming will also help reverse the demographic tides toward urbanization. Nonetheless, coordination of an agricultural policy with other

---

BOX 10.2.   STRATEGIC CHECKLIST FOR RURAL DEVELOPMENT

- Macroeconomic and sectoral policies are stable. The foreign exchange, trade, and taxation regimes do not discriminate against agriculture, but are similar for rural and urban sectors.
- The growth of private agriculture is encouraged by minimizing distortions among input and output markets and by market development for agricultural and agro-industrial products, both at home and abroad.
- Public investment and expenditure programs for economic and social infrastructure, health, nutrition, education, and family planning services do not discriminate against rural populations or the rural poor.
- Large farms and large agro-industrial firms do not receive special privileges and are not able to reduce competition in output, input, land, or credit markets.
- The agrarian structure is dominated by efficient and technologically sophisticated family operators, who rely primarily on their own family's labor. The rights and needs of women farmers and wage-laborers are explicitly recognized.
- Access to and security of land and water rights is actively promoted. Restricting land rentals hurts the poor. Where land distribution is highly unequal, land reform is needed. Decentralized, participatory, and market-assisted approaches to land reform can achieve this much faster than expropriations by land reform parastatals.
- Private and public sectors complement each other in generating and disseminating knowledge and technologies. Public sector financing is particularly important for areas of limited interest to the private sector, such as strategic research, smallholder extension, and diffusion of sustainable production systems and techniques.
- Rural development programs mobilize the skill, talents, and labor of the rural population through administrative, fiscal, and management systems that are decentralized and participatory, and through private sector involvement.
- Rural development programs are designed so that the rural poor and other vulnerable groups are fully involved in the identification, design, and implementation of the programs. Otherwise, rural elites will appropriate most of the benefits.

Source: Adapted from World Bank, *Rural Development: From Vision to Action,* Environmentally and Socially Sustainable Development Studies and Monograph Series no. 12 (Washington, D.C.: World Bank), 1997.

aspects of reform may require a super ministry, or a national coordinator with authority over other ministries, and a great deal of political will. Box 10.2 provides a strategic checklist for government rural development policy. Addressing these issues will facilitate a balanced development strategy that provides sustainable resources for a greater portion of the agricultural population in the region.

Key Concepts

Agricultural extension programs
Demand-driven rural investment funds

Dualistic structure of production
Incomplete markets
Insecure property rights

Land reform
Nontraditional exports
Segmented credit markets
Water rights

Chapter Summary

- The agricultural sector in Latin America is characterized by its dualistic nature: corporate farming and small-scale, traditional peasant agriculture. The trend in many Latin American countries has been a shift away from production for local consumption to production for exports. The results have led to an increased marginalization of peasant farmers and their migration from the rural sector into the cities.
- Though some Latin American countries have experienced slow growth in agriculture, many have seen moderate to rapid growth in production. Nevertheless, falling prices, international trade barriers, overvalued exchange rates, and other forms of indirect taxation have placed constraints on the agricultural sector.
- Agriculture has not been able to generate sustainable incomes for the rural majority. Rural poverty contributes to a number of problems such as environmental degradation or harmful use of pesticides. Women's contributions to agricultural production are many times unaccounted for, yet women play a major role in the agricultural sector.
- The failure of the agricultural sector to generate adequate incomes for the rural poor is due to several factors. Previous policies and incomplete markets have been biased against the peasant farmer and in favor of the rural elite. Ambiguity with property rights, common in the region, has led to underinvestment, barriers in obtaining credit, and inefficiency in the use of land. Peasant farmers face more obstacles in obtaining much-needed credit due to their lack of collateral and the nature of agricultural activity. Policies to remedy the problem must use nonconventional forms of allocating credit for the small farmer and address the issue of unequal landholding.

- Historically, many Latin American countries have engaged in land reforms to address the issue of inequality. The experience in the region has shown that land reform has done little to improve the quality of life of the rural peasant. Its failure is due to a lack of complementary policies that will address problems such as the biases disadvantaging the poor relative to the elite, the problem of credit, and environmental sustainability.
- Agricultural policy must be multidimensional. Farm productivity must be raised, but policy needs to take into account the concerns and behavior of the poor, who tend to be risk averse. Polices that consider factors such as migration to urban sectors, infrastructure, credit, and landholding patterns will tend to be more successful in the long run.
- Decentralization through demand-driven rural investment funds has increased local control and participation in agricultural development. Communities must usually meet certain requirements before the funds are distributed. This type of fund allocation allows different groups to set their own priorities and address their own needs.

Notes

1. Johan Bastiaensen, "Non-Conventional Rural Finance and the Crisis of Economic Institutions in Nicaragua," in *Sustainable Agriculture in Central America*, ed. Jan P. de Groot and Ruerd Ruben (New York: St. Martin's, 1997).

2. Lori Ann Thrupp, *Bittersweet Harvests for Global Supermarkets: Challenges in Latin America's Agricultural Export Boom* (Washington, D.C.: World Resources Institute, 1995), 17.

3. James Brooke, "Home, Home on the Range, in Brazil's Heartland," *New York Times*, 26 April 1995.

4. Thrupp, *Bittersweet Harvests*, 18, 58.

5. Ibid., 24.

6. Jim Adriance, "Living with the Land in Central America," *Grassroots Development* 19, no. 1 (1995): 15.

7. Ejidos were created by the Mexican government following the 1910 revolution. The structure adapted a pre-Columbian farming practice of communal landholdings, requiring the Mexican government to cede tracts of land to Mexican peasants. Each ejido comprises between 20 and 2,000 ejidatarios and is governed by a general assembly and an elected administrative council. Although the individual ejidatario cannot sell, mortgage, or rent the land, he may pass it on to his spouse, children, or other relatives. The 1992 agricultural law has worked to privatize ejidos.

8. "Green, as in Greenbacks," *The Economist*, 1 February 1997, p. 42.

9. Ellen Contreras Murphy, "La Selva and the Magnetic Pull of Markets: Organic Coffee-Growing in Mexico," *Grassroots Development* 19, no. 1 (1995): 27–34.

10. "New Farms for Old," *The Economist*, 10 January 1998, p. 30.

11. Thrupp, *Bittersweet Harvests*, 67.

12. John Weeks, "Macroeconomic Adjustment," as noted in "Latin America's Export of Manufactured Goods," a special section of *Economic and Social Progress in Latin America 1992 Report* (Washington, D.C.: Inter-American Development Bank, 1992), 68.

13. "Fifty Years On," *The Economist*, 16 May 1998, p. 22.

14. Maurice Schiff and Alberto Valdes, "The Plundering of Agriculture in Developing Countries," 1994 draft paper, available at the World Bank homepage at www.worldbank.org/html/extpb/PlunderingAgri.html. Also Krueger, Schiff, and Valdes (1991), cited in Hans P. Binswanger and Klaus Deininger, "Explaining Agricultural and Agrarian Policies in Developing Countries," *Journal of Economic Literature* 35 (December 1997): 1958–2005.

15. Jacob Meerman, *Reforming Agriculture: The World Bank Goes to Market* (Washington, D.C.: World Bank, 1997), 38.

16. Michael Redclift, "The Environment and Structural Adjustment: Lessons for Policy Intervention," in *Structural Adjustment and the Agricultural Sector in Latin America and the Caribbean*, ed. John Weeks (New York: St. Martin's, 1995).

17. Andy Thorpe, "Sustainable Agriculture in Latin America," in *Sustainable Agriculture in Central America*, ed. Jan P. de Groot and Ruerd Ruben (New York: St. Martin's, 1997), 42.

18. Inter-American Development Bank, "Invisible Farmers," in *IDB Extra: Investing in Women* (Washington, D.C.: Inter-American Development Bank, 1994).

19. Cristóbal Key, "Rural Development and Agrarian Issues in Contemporary Latin America," in *Structural Adjustment and the Agricultural Sector in Latin America and the Caribbean*, ed. John Weeks (New York: St. Martin's 1995).

20. Elizabeth G. Katz, "Gender and Trade within the Household: Observations from Rural Guatemala," *World Development* 23, no. 2 (1995): 327–342.

21. World Bank, *Rural Development: From Vision to Action*, Environmentally and Socially Sustainable Development Studies and Monographs Series no. 12 (Washington, D.C.: World Bank, 1997), 33.

22. Karla Hoff, "Designing Land Policies: An Overview," in *The Economics of Rural Organization*, ed. Karla Hoff, Avishay Braverman, and Joseph Stiglitz (New York: Oxford University Press/World Bank, 1993), 231.

23. Michael Richards, "Alternative Approaches and Problems in Protected Area Management and Forest Conservation in Honduras," in *Sustainable Agriculture in Central America*, ed. Jan P. de Groot and Ruerd Ruben (New York: St. Martin's, 1997), 147.

24. Avishay Braverman and J. Luis Guasch, "Administrative Failures in Government Credit Programs," in *The Economics of Rural Organization*, ed. Karla Hoff, Avishay Braverman, and Joseph Stiglitz (New York: Oxford University Press/World Bank, 1993), 53.

25. Fared Shah, David Zilberman, and Ujjayant Chakravorty, "Water Rights Doctrines and Technology Adoption," in *The Economics of Rural Organization*, ed. Karla Hoff, Avishay Braverman, and Joseph Stiglitz (New York: Oxford University Press/World Bank, 1993), 478.

26. Bastiaenen, "Non-Conventional Rural Finance," 199.

27. Ibid., 199.

28. Robert L. Paarlberg, "The Politics of Agricultural Resource Abuse," *Environment* 36, no. 8 (October 1994).

29. Jon Jonakin, "The Interaction of Market Failure and Structural Adjustment in Producer Credit and Land Markets: The Case of Nicaragua," *Journal of Economic Issues* 31, no. 2 (June 1997): 355.

30. Binswanger and Elgin (1989), cited in Binswanger and Deininger, "Explaining Agricultural and Agrarian Policies," 1968.

31. Roderick (1994), as described in Carlos Acevedo, Deborah Barry, and Herman Rosa, "El Salvador's Agricultural Sector: Macroeconomic Policy, Agrarian Change and the Environment," *World Development* 23, no. 12 (1995): 2153–2172.

32. Johan van Zyl et al. (1995), cited in Binswanger and Deininger, "Explaining Agricultural and Agrarian Policies," 1964.

33. Michael Foley, "Agenda for Mobilization: The Agrarian Question and Popular Mobilization in Contemporary Mexico," *Latin American Research Review* 26, no. 2 (1991): 66.

34. Ibid., 61.

35. Roger Burbackh and Peter Rosset, "Chiapas and the Crisis of Mexican Agriculture," *Food First Policy Brief*, no. 1 (San Francisco: Institute for Food and Development, 1994).

36. As cited in Burbackh and Rosset, "Chiapas and the Crisis of Mexican Agriculture."

37. Alain de Janvry and Elisabeth Sadoulet, "NAFTA and Mexico's Maize Producers," *World Development* 23, no. 8 (August 1995): 1349–1362.

38. David Lehmann, ed., *Agrarian Reform and Agrarian Reformism: Studies of Peru, Chile, China, and India* (London: Faber & Faber, 1974), 51–59.

39. Michael Carter and Dina Mesbah, "State-Mandated and Market-Mediated Reform in Latin America," in *Including the Poor*, ed. Michael Lipton and Jacques Van der Gaag (Baltimore: Johns Hopkins University Press/World Bank, 1993).

40. Michael Carter and Bradford Barham cite Dina Mesbah in "Level Playing Fields and Laissez Faire: Postliberal Development Strategy in Inegalitarian Agrarian Economies," *World Development* 24, no. 7 (July 1996): 1136.

41. Ibid., 1136–1138.

42. H. Byrnes and B. Spencer, "U.S. Must Aid Guatemala's Shift to Peace," *St. Louis Post-Dispatch*, 20 December 1996.

43. Carter and Barham, "Level Playing Fields," 1144–1148.

44. Nora Lustig and Ruthanne Deutsch, *The Inter-American Development Bank and Poverty Reduction: An Overview* (Washington, D.C.: Inter-American Development Bank, 1998). Available at www.iadb.org.

45. World Bank, *Rural Development: From Vision to Action*, Environmentally and Socially Sustainable Development Studies and Monograph Series no. 12 (Washington, D.C.: World Bank, 1997).

46. Ibid., 17.

47. Gabriel Keynan, Manuel Olin, and Ariel Dinar, "Cofinanced Public Extension in Nicaragua," *World Bank Research Observer* 12, no. 2 (August 1997): 230.

48. Ibid., 226.

49. Ibid., 227.

50. Rogers, as cited in Charles Ameur, *Agricultural Extension: A Step beyond the Next Step*, World Bank Technical Paper no. 247 (Washington, D.C.: World Bank, 1994), 12–13.

51. World Bank, *Rural Development*, 83. Excerpted from box 6.10.

52. Meerman, *Reforming Agriculture*, 2, 40–41.

53. Robert Picciotto and Jock Anderson, "Reconsidering Agricultural Extension," *World Bank Research Observer* 12, no. 2 (August 1997): 254.

54. Meerman, *Reforming Agriculture*, 53.

POVERTY AND INEQUALITY

Addressing the Social Deficit in Latin America

CHAPTER ELEVEN

Housing in Latin America is woefully inadequate. *(Courtesy of the Inter-American Development Bank.)*

The social challenges of poverty and inequality constitute the greatest obstacle to sustained growth in the region. One in three inhabitants of the region—approximately 150 million people—live below the **poverty line.**[1] Poverty constrains human beings from investing in the education and health necessary for productivity. Inequality skews opportunities toward the rich, not those who desperately need it. When people lack the ability to invest in the future, they are forced to deplete natural resources to survive today. Despite this need, programs to address poverty in the region have failed dismally, in part due to the fact that the poor themselves have not been involved in their design or implementation. For poverty programs to do more than simply ward off starvation or malnutrition, the people themselves must be involved. As the president of the World Bank said,

> The lesson is clear: for economic advance, you need social advance—and without social development, economic development cannot take root. For the Bank, this means that we need to make sure that the programs and projects we support have adequate social foundations by designing more participatory country strategies and programs, reflecting discussions not only with governments, but also with community groups, nongovernmental organizations and private businesses, by putting more emphasis on social, cultural and institutional issues, with their interplay with economic issues and in our project and analytical work, and by learning more about how the changing dynamics between public institutions, markets and civil society affect social and economic development.[2]

Discrimination against women and ethnic minorities limits their full potential as economic actors. Poverty exacts a toll on the environment as people lack the assets to invest in their future. Poorly nourished children will not grow up to be productive members of the global work force. Reducing the depth of poverty in the region is key to long-term, sustainable development.

This chapter will focus on the question of development for whom and ask how marginalized groups can more fully participate in the benefits of growth. The following questions will shape our understanding of the issue:

- How do we measure poverty? Is Latin America poor?
- How do we measure inequality in the region? What are trends in inequality?
- How do poverty and inequality define living standards?
- What effects do gender and inequality have on economic well-being in Latin America?
- How did macroeconomic performance affect poverty?
- What are areas for action to reduce poverty and the social deficit in the region?

IS LATIN AMERICA POOR?: A PROFILE OF POVERTY

Is Latin America poor? As measured against the typical North American family, the answer is yes. Compared to the images of starvation from the most destitute countries of the world, Latin Americans are relatively well-off. How is poverty defined? This is a controversial question. Poverty in a major metropolis such as Buenos Aires will differ from that in a small remote village in the Andes. We somewhat arbitrarily define the poor as the portion of the population unable to meet basic needs such as food, health care, education, and shelter. The poverty line is determined as the minimum income needed to purchase socially determined essentials for living.[3]

International comparisons of poverty are complicated by cultural differences in defining human needs, the variety of local goods available at different prices, and divergent government policies including transfer payments, exchange rates, and inflation. Counting the poor is extremely difficult, especially for those without permanent residences. Unlike the people enumerated in data generated by income tax payments, census takers, or those in formal public support programs, the very poor are often nameless. The data should therefore be interpreted with caution. Setting a dollar benchmark is also controversial. The World Bank uses $50 per month as a rule of thumb; ECLAC uses $60, categorizing those making less than $30 per month as living in extreme poverty. Moderate poverty is therefore roughly $2 per day, with those living in extreme poverty subsisting on $1 per day.

Once a poverty line is established, the **headcount ratio** estimates those who fall below it. We can see from the data in table 11.1 that in 1990, 46 percent of Latin Americans lived in poverty, with extreme poverty concentrated in the rural sector.[4] Twenty-two percent of the population live in conditions of extreme poverty. They are not able to meet their nutritional requirements even if they spend everything they have on food. Poverty in the region has risen since the 1970s and has become increasingly urbanized, with 39 percent of city dwellers living in poverty. The urbanization of poverty has made the problem more visible as cosmopolitan residents must face the tragic contradictions of development on street corners, on hillsides, or in rings of shacks and squalor at the city limits.

We should, however, look at trends in poverty line data with some caution. Temporary macroeconomic factors affect the numbers. Recession increased the number of poor in 1980. What we don't know from the headcount numbers is the degree to which this is a temporary phenomenon in which those with income just above the line are pushed below temporarily, or whether chronic poverty with

Table 11.1.   Changes in the Extent of Poverty, 1970–1990

Year	Poverty[a] (thousands and percentage)			Extreme Poverty[b] (thousands and percentage)		
	total	urban	rural	total	urban	rural
1970	119,800 (45)	44,200 (29)	75,600 (67)	63,700 (24)	19,900 (13)	43,800 (40)
1980	135,900 (41)	63,900 (30)	72,000 (60)	62,400 (19)	22,500 (11)	39,900 (33)
1986	170,200 (43)	94,400 (36)	75,800 (60)	81,400 (21)	35,800 (14)	45,600 (36)
1990	195,900 (46)	115,500 (39)	80,400 (61)	93,500 (22)	44,900 (15)	48,600 (27)

[a]Poverty = $60/month.
[b]Extreme poverty = $30/month.
Source: Gert Rosenthal, "On Poverty and Inequality in Latin America," *Journal of Inter-American Studies and World Affairs* 38, no. 2–3 (Summer–Fall 1996): 15.

structural causes has increased in the region. The headcount tells us how many are poor, but not why they find themselves unable to meet basic needs.

Furthermore, although the headcount ratio gives us a sense of the number living in poverty at any point in time, it does not measure the extent of immiseration. A person making $45 and a person making $20 per month would each count as one poor person despite tragically different lives. A second measure of poverty therefore calculates the size of the income shortfall or the amount of money it would take to raise the person to the poverty line. This **income gap** measures the depth of poverty a nation faces. In table 11.2 we can see that in Guatemala, Bolivia, and Honduras, on average, people's income falls short of the poverty line by 39.3, 24.4, and 24.2 percent respectively. This is in contrast to Costa Rica or Chile, where on average the poor are short of the poverty line by 1.3 or 2.8 percent.

Quality of Life

Even with the income gap statistic, we really don't know what $60 can buy in living standards. Measures that count the poor are best complemented by statistics that capture the quality of their lives. The 1997 *Human Development Report* introduced a new measure, the HPI, or human poverty index. The HPI concentrates on three dimensions of poverty: vulnerability to death at an early age, exclusion from global communications as measured by literacy rates, and a decent standard of

Table 11.2. Poverty Gap, 1989

Country	Average % Shortfall from Poverty Line of $60
Guatemala	39.3
Bolivia (urban)	24.4
Honduras (urban)	24.2
Brazil	18.8
El Salvador (urban)	16.9
Panama	14.3
Peru (Lima)	13.3
Ecuador	6.9
Mexico	5.8
Venezuela	4.2
Colombia (urban)	3.3
Chile	2.8
Argentina (Buenos Aires)	2.1
Paraguay (Asunción)	1.8
Uruguay (urban)	1.4
Costa Rica	1.3

Source: George Psacharopoulos, Samuel Morley, Ariel Fiszbein, and Haeduck Lee, *Poverty and Income Distribution in Latin America: The Story of the 1980s* (Washington, D.C.: World Bank, 1997), table 4.3.

living as approximated by the percentage of people with access to health services and safe water and the proportion of malnourished children under five. As a weighted composite of deprivation, the HPI gives us a comparative basis to judge the extent of human poverty. The data for the HPI in Latin America show that Cuba, Chile, and Costa Rica have made significant progress in reducing poverty, with less than 10 percent of the population affected by severe poverty. Colombia, Mexico, Panama, and Uruguay fall into the next cluster, with rates hovering above the 10 percent level. Honduras, Bolivia, Peru, and Paraguay have nearly one quarter of the population falling below this line; Nicaragua, El Salvador, and Guatemala are the worst performers. On the positive side, only Guatemala falls within the bottom half of developing countries as measured by the HPI index.

Life for the Poor in Latin America

The living conditions of the poor constrain their human potential. Poverty and inequality interact to limit the opportunities for the less fortunate. Poverty is a complex, multidimensional phenomenon. How do the realities of their daily lives constrain them from pursuing better options? If you ever have the opportunity to observe life in a poor neighborhood—a *favela* in Brazil, a *villa miseria* in Argentina, or a *callampas* (mushroom) in Chile, where roughly one in four Latin Americans live—you will notice that nearly everyone is working hard to survive. Why aren't these tremendous energies transformed into a better quality of life for people?

Quality of life statistics can give us an appreciation for the standard of living in the region. The U.N. *Human Development Report* calculates the HDI, or human development index, as a composite of life expectancy at birth, educational attainment (measured by adult literacy and school enrollments), and income. The GDI, or gender development index, discounts the HDI for gender inequality in life expectancy, educational attainment, and income, by assigning a penalty for inequality. The greater the gender disparity, the lower the GDI. The GEM, or gender empowerment index, concentrates on economic, political, and professional participation by incorporating variables such as female share of income, access to professional and managerial jobs, and seats in public office. The GEM therefore measures the degree to which opportunities are open to women in society. It should be noted that these indexes also have their drawbacks. Although as composite indexes they take attention away from GDP as a measure of human development, the measures of life expectancy, education, and income do not take the distribution of the population around the average into account, covering considerable variation in performance.[5] We will return to the difficult problem of inequality in Latin America in a moment.

Table 11.3 presents the HDI, GDI, and GEM for Latin American countries. Some interesting results appear. The best performer in terms of the quality of life is Costa Rica, ranking twenty-eighth in the world. The difference between the Costa Rican standard of living and Costa Rica's rank in terms of per capita GDP is a striking thirty-two points. Costa Rica is clearly doing something to improve

Table 11.3.   Indicators of Living Standards in Latin America, 1994

Country	HDI	HDI Rank	Real GDP Per Capita Rank	Real GDP Per Capita Minus HDI Rank	GDI	GDI Rank	GEM	GEM Rank
Costa Rica	0.884	33	60	27	0.763	36	0.474	26
Argentina	0.883	36	39	10	0.768	47	0.415	n/a
Uruguay	0.881	37	53	15	0.802	31	0.361	54
Chile	0.880	30	41	13	0.759	44	0.402	57
Venezuela	0.859	47	40	1	0.765	43	0.391	55
Panama	0.856	45	59	14	0.765	41	0.43	36
Mexico	0.842	50	47	0	0.741	50	0.399	31
Colombia	0.836	51	60	7	0.720	40	0.435	38
Brazil	0.804	68	64	0	0.709	60	0.358	58
Ecuador	0.784	72	72	5	0.641	73	0.375	n/a
Cuba	0.769	86	88	17	0.726	68	0.524	23
Paraguay	0.723	94	90	2	0.628	82	0.343	64
Peru	0.709	89	94	5	0.631	76	0.4	53
Nicaragua	0.611	127	105	10	0.560	106	0.427	n/a
Guatemala	0.591	117	123	− 16	0.481	107	0.39	29
Bolivia	0.588	113	112	− 1	0.519	99	0.344	62
El Salvador	0.579	112	118	3	0.533	97	0.397	44
Honduras	0.578	116	120	7	0.524	103	0.406	51

Source: "Human Development Index," in *Human Development Report, 1997* (New York: Oxford University Press, 1997): 146–148.

the longevity and human capital investments of its people beyond what its gross national product would indicate. In contrast, the standard of living in Mexico and Venezuela appears to fall below their income ranking. As weighted by the degree of inequality between the sexes in access to resources, Uruguay is the best regional performer. Nonetheless, in terms of participation in economic and political life, Cuba and Costa Rica top the list.

Measures such as housing, communications, and basic infrastructure help fill out the picture of poverty in Latin America. Housing in the region is woefully inadequate. Adequate housing is critical to the development of individual capability and to fostering family and community ties. Table 11.4 shows that in more than half of the countries, more than one-third of the housing stock is deficient. ECLAC estimates that between 20 and 30 percent of children in Latin America grow up in conditions of overcrowding, with three or more people per bedroom, a condition closely associated with poor school performance. In Bolivia, Peru, El Salvador, and Nicaragua, 20 percent or more of the dwellings are beyond repair, a threat to health and life. Some rural indigenous workers in Bolivia and in Brazil are kept in a state of virtual slavery as employers charge them more for room and board than they earn. The most extreme housing deprivation is to be homeless. In Brazil, more than 200,000 children are growing up on the streets without the protection a home

Table 11.4.   Houses and Available Housing

Country	Year	Estimated Households	Adequate Dwellings	%	Dwellings Beyond Repair	%	Repairable Dwellings	%
Argentina	1991	9,380,204	6,43,209	75	624,274	7	1,496,212	18
Bolivia	1992	1,614,995	880,172	55	406,979	25	327,844	20
Brazil	1991	35,517,542	19,490,609	56	5,098,394	15	10,145,712	29
Chile	1992	3,365,462	2,394,995	77	364,760	12	361,212	12
Colombia	1985	5,824,857	3,303,051	63	525,127	10	1,423,095	27
Costa Rica	1984	527,299	339,840	68	43,804	9	116,386	23
Cuba	1981	2,350,221	1,698,649	74	335,427	15	256,100	11
Ecuador	1990	2,136,889	1,375,212	68	296,609	15	336,834	17
El Salvador	1992	1,091,728	508,858	49	359,873	34	180,461	17
Guatemala	1989	1,610,994	874,111	55	283,225	18	433,952	27
Honduras	1988	808,222	481,658	63	90,921	12	189,767	25
Mexico	1990	17,394,368	11,382,906	71	1,964,712	12	2,687,615	17
Nicaragua	1991	—	128,545	20	289,994	45	220,992	35
Panama	1990	541,704	365,650	70	86,268	17	72,366	14
Paraguay	1992	873,694	517,578	61	143,080	17	194,889	23
Peru	1993	4,762,779	2,231,469	50	872,221	20	1,323,828	30
Dominican Republic	1981	1,140,798	676,791	59	126,238	11	337,769	30
Uruguay	1985	902,300	685,934	83	40,998	5	104,553	13
Venezuela	1990	3,750,940	2,672,168	76	529,702	15	315,359	9
Region average				63		14		23

Source: Economic Commission for Latin America and the Caribbean, *The Equity Gap: Latin America, the Caribbean, and the Social Summit* (Santiago, Chile; Economic Commission for Latin America and the Caribbean, 1996), 144.

affords. Box 11.1 sadly illustrates life on the streets in Guatemala. The waste of young lives to poverty is a tragic result of slow growth and limited opportunity.

Two measures of literacy and the effect of the media on public consciousness are the number of newspapers sold daily and televisions per 100 people. Table 11.5 gives a sense of the role of the media in shaping people's worldview. It is not surprising that the more affluent nations sell more newspapers. Literacy is correlated with wealth. Furthermore, if a newspaper costs fifty cents, for those making two or three dollars a day, it is quite a luxury. During the periods of macroeconomic crisis in Brazil, even upper-middle-class families would get together in a buying group for *Veja*, the Brazilian equivalent of *Time* magazine. Indeed, if you walk the streets in a Latin American city, you are likely to find people standing around the newspaper kiosk reading the headlines of papers for sale. The number of televisions has exploded in the region, although not quite approaching the industrial country average of one television for every two people. Television transforms culture. Many American TV shows are translated and rebroadcast. The contradiction of walking into a favela, or poor barrio, and seeing an imported sitcom on the lives of the rich and famous is startling. In countries where literacy is not universal, the ability to communicate (or miscommunicate) through the media is a powerful

Box 11.1.   Casa Alianza: An NGO Helping Street Children in Guatemala

More than 5,000 children live on the streets of Guatemala City. Some are as young as seven. Most are addicted to glue or other poisonous solvent-based products. Many resort to petty robbery and prostitution to survive. Each year, scores of children are abused, tortured, or killed by police or other authorities. Some are assaulted by other street children. Others take their own lives out of utter desperation. Most have chosen the streets to escape family abuse. Many number among the 250,000 children who have been orphaned by a brutal thirty-year civil war that has displaced an estimated 1 million people. They are children of "street families" who come to the city in search of a "better" life—and end up hawking cigarettes, candy, and food on street corners. With many mouths to feed, parents abandon their children to their fate.

ABOUT GUATEMALA

With the largest population in Central America, estimated in 1990 to be 9.9 million and growing at a rate of 3.1 percent each year, Guatemala has one of the youngest populations in the world, with 55 percent less than nineteen years old. In Guatemala today, 80 percent of the population lives in poverty; 54 percent of those who live in poverty are children. In 1991, the per capita gross national product was $930 per year; however, many people, especially the indigenous, earn far less. With 40 percent of its population now living in cities, Guatemala's urban population is soaring, with a growth rate of 3.5 percent. The urban growth rate in the United States is 1.2 percent; Canada's is 1.3 percent; Germany's 0.5 percent; and the United Kingdom's 0.2 percent.

More than 40 percent of the total population does not have access to safe drinking water or adequate sanitation, and only 34 percent have access to health services. The mortality rate for children below the age of five is estimated at 76 per 1,000 live births—the second highest in Latin America, after Bolivia. With less than half the population able to read, Guatemala ranks second behind Haiti among countries in the region with the highest illiteracy rates. Only 36 percent of those who enroll in the first grade complete primary school. More than 80 percent never make it to secondary school. Poverty and rapid urbanization are the reasons why Guatemala City's 224,000 children live in shantytowns and 789,000 children live in extreme poverty.

These problems, along with a high rate of family disintegration, have forced 27 percent of Guatemala's children between the ages of ten and seventeen to work to supplement their families' income.

CASA ALIANZA GUATEMALA

Casa Alianza began operating in Guatemala in 1981 as a refuge for children orphaned by the civil war. In 1986, the organization expanded its focus to street children. Currently, about 330 children are in Casa Alianza's residential programs in Guatemala, and street educators and other staff attend to the needs of about 1,000 street children per year.

Here is the story of one of the street children Casa Alianza is helping. Other stories are available at: http://www.casa-alianza.org.

My name is Gabriela. I am thirteen years old. I've been on my own for three years now. I used to beg for money, but now I am working. I am a prostitute. I don't like to say that, because it's not who I am inside. I dream of my village, and the fresh mountain air there, and the smell of the freshly turned earth. But here in "El Hoyo," it smells like a dirty toilet, and the diesel smoke from the buses turns my stomach. I hate this place. I hate the men who I sleep with. All I can do when they touch me is think of something else—of the walks I used to take through the fields with my sister Juliana on Sunday mornings. I think of the good things I loved at home. It makes it all a little easier.

You may wonder why I still do this, even though I hate it. I don't know, really.

Somehow it works. Marta, the lady who owns the bar where the men come for me, she takes care of me. When I have a bad night, she'll let me cry and stroke my head, and give me some warm milk—and then I'm ready to work again. She's the closest thing to a mother I've got now. You see, my father killed my mother the day I left home. He was drunk and was hitting her, like he always did, but she fell backwards and slammed her head, and never got up again. All I could do was scream when I saw her, and run. I was afraid he'd kill me too. I hated it when he drank. But when he was sober, I was his little girl. I remember his big hands, and the smell of cows that stuck on his clothes. He'd give me a big hug with his big hands, and I felt so warm and safe inside. But now, if I saw him, I'd want to chop off those hands for what they did to Mama.

There are a bunch of other girls who work with me. Aida, Mercedes, and Silvia. Aida is eighteen. She showed me how to wear makeup, and how to look at men so they'd want me. She's real good at it. But she has been sick a lot lately. She doesn't want to get up in the morning, always has some kind of problem, she's got so thin, and she's got these marks growing on her face. I'm worried about her. Someone said she might have this bad sickness called AIDS. But she's so sweet. It was always the off-duty soldiers who would like Aida—they would pay her about 10 quetzals (U.S.$2) a time. But if she got sick, I wonder if some of the soldiers did too?

Mercedes is like my sister. We make each other laugh about the men we see. We have nicknames for each of them. You don't want to hear them, though. If Mama were still alive, she'd wash my mouth out with soap if I uttered any of them. Mercedes got pregnant once, which is really bad for work. When any of us girls get pregnant we kick her in the stomach several times. It hurts a lot, but it's a way of getting unpregnant. It didn't work with Mercedes, though, and she got an abortion. It was terrible. She went to a friend of Marta's—they call her La Carnicera, the Butcher—because the girls always bleed so much after they see her. She's not a doctor or anything. She just does it—with a hanger, I think. Some girls have died. But we don't talk about that. La Carnicera helps us. It's not her fault that some girls can't take the pain, I guess. I hope I never have to see her.

Sometimes I wish I could meet a nice boy. I don't like these men. I want a boy to play with. But it's hard here. All of the boys in "El Hoyo" are so dirty and crazy. All they do is sit around and sniff that stupid glue all day, and fight with each other. It makes them so stupid. Sometimes they also "work" the street—like me, selling their bodies so they can buy food and glue. Sometimes terrible things happen to them, too. The police come and they pour the glue over the boys' heads. Oh, it looks so terrible. They even kicked to death one of Francisco's best friends—Nahamán. When the police went to pour the glue on his head, he resisted—and God, it was terrible. You could hear his shrieks from blocks away. Poor Nahamán, he was so sweet. He was my age. I never told anyone, not even Mercedes, but I liked Nahamán. We kissed one night, it was so beautiful—so different from the ugly kisses of the men who come for me. Nahamán. When I say his name now, all I want to do is cry. Why did they have to do that? Why?

Sometimes I dream of another life—the one my grandmother told me about. She was a beautiful, wise woman, and she knew how to make such a beautiful Huipul. Yes, she was an Anciana. To be hugged by her was to know the hug of God for the world. She knew the secrets of all good things. She died before Mama. Thank God. I wish she were here now, to tell me something good—to give me one of her hugs. Everything would be better then, I know.

But I'm here, in El Hoyo, and if I don't get to work soon, I won't have enough money for Marta. I need to pay her, otherwise I'll be out on the street. She takes care of me. Sometimes I wonder if she'd do this to her own daughter, though, if she had one. I wouldn't want this life for mine.

Oh God, I'd love to have a baby of my own someday. But not here, not in El Hoyo. It's not a place for a kid. Oh God, no, it's no place for me, either.

Marta's calling. Okay, okay, Marta, I'm coming. I'm coming, now.

Got to go.

Source: www.casa-alianza.org/children/child.htm

social and political tool. Without widespread literacy, people do not have the opportunity to evaluate competing arguments, and they come to accept pronouncements made on television as truth.

Health statistics not only paint a picture of human misery but also are a proxy for the shortfall in resources for investment in human capital. Poor people find it difficult to purchase health care. It is estimated that 130 million people, or one in three Latin Americans, do not have routine access to health services. Maternal and child health programs are deficient. More than 10 million children under five suffer from malnutrition in Latin America. PAHO, the Pan American Health Organization, evaluated 1,700 lab services and hospitals in eighteen countries and found eighty unsatisfactory.

Education is lacking. Despite strong enrollment rates, repetition and dropout rates are high. Income and educational attainment are clearly correlated. In Guatemala, for example, a poor child is likely to complete only one year of schooling while a wealthy child on average will finish seven. Even in Costa Rica, one of the region's best performers on social indicators, as many as one in three school-age children do not attend school; about 20 percent of those between seven and ten are absent, primarily among the poor and the rural communities. This contrast is maintained in the wealthier countries as well. In Chile, a poor child might complete 6.1 years of schooling while a wealthy one will likely complete 11.6. Both cause and effect are at work here. Wealthy individuals have lower opportunity costs for education, and the higher level of education helps improve their income. For the poor, the additional wages of children are important to family incomes. Because the poor complete fewer years of school, their income is likely to be lower. Education is the greatest explanatory variable in both income inequality and the probability of being poor. Differences in educational attainment account for nearly 25 percent of the total income inequality in the region. Improving education will not only improve the distribution of income but also improve the standard of living of the poor.[6] In chapter 12 we will take up these important issues of health and education in depth.

WHO ARE THE POOR?

Poverty varies by country in the region. Much of the poverty is concentrated in Brazil, Mexico, and Peru. Forty-four percent of the region's poor live in Brazil, which is home to 33 percent of the region's total population. Mexico and Peru account for 11 and 9 percent of the poor respectively; despite their small size, Bolivia, El Salvador, Guatemala, Haiti, Honduras, and Nicaragua together account for an additional 19 percent.[7] Whether you live in the city or the rural sector matters enormously, with rural poverty being twice as high as urban poverty region-

Table 11.5.   Communication Profiles

Country	Copies of Daily Newspapers (per 100 people) 1994	Televisions (per 100 people) 1994	Printing/ Writing Paper Consumed 1994	Main Telephone Lines 1994	International Telephone Calls 1994
Ecuador	n/a	13	6.0	5.9	3.2
Chile	n/a	25	15.9	11.0	4.5
Uruguay	24	52	13.7	18.4	14.6
Venezuela	21	18	12.6	10.8	7.3
Argentina	14	32	17.5	14.1	5.1
Mexico	12	19	11.7	9.3	8.4
Cuba	12	19	1.4	3.2	1.1
Costa Rica	10	22	11.2	13.0	16.7
Panama	9	17	7.2	11.1	13.9
El Salvador	9	23	6.7	4.4	11.1
Peru	7	10	9.0	3.3	2.2
Colombia	6	22	9.8	9.2	3.3
Brazil	5	25	11.6	7.4	1.1
Bolivia	5	14	3.2	3.5	2.2
Paraguay	4	7	6.9	3.1	3.3
Honduras	3	8	3.0	2.4	6.7
Nicaragua	2	15	1.7	2.0	5.2
Guatemala	2	5	4.8	2.4	5.5
Industrial countries	29	50	74.0	40.1	35.1

Source: United Nations Development Program, *Human Development Report* (New York: Oxford University Press for the United Nations Development Program, 1997).

wide. A separate HPI was calculating for the poor Northeast versus the relatively affluent South of Brazil. The Northeast region of Brazil shows an HPI of 46 percent, consistent with some of the worst poverty in Asia, whereas the South and Southeast enjoy relatively low rates at 17 and 14 percent. This disparity has grown in Brazil, leading to the nickname of "Belindia" for Brazil: a country with luxuries similar to Belgium yet the misery of India. Diversity of needs within countries makes policy a difficult political issue.

Women in Latin America have a greater chance of being poor than men, primarily due to the fact that they are segregated in low-income jobs, earning on average 14 percent to 53 percent less.[8] Poverty in the region has therefore become feminized, forcing a rethinking of how to reduce the misery throughout Latin America. In most low-income households, women face a triple burden: they are responsible for the reproductive work of the home, enter the workplace as secondary income earners, and tend to be the central force in community organizing.[9] Box 11.2 discusses the progress on gender equality and its implications for poverty reduction.

Indigenous groups, particularly concentrated in Bolivia, Guatemala, Mexico,

BOX 11.2.   SUSTAINABLE DEVELOPMENT, POVERTY, AND
GENDER IN LATIN AMERICA AND THE CARIBBEAN

Economic participation by women in Latin America and the Caribbean continues to increase and today they make up one third of the work force. Without women's incomes the number of households classified as poor would rise between 10 percent and 20 percent. In 1994, women with jobs contributed between 28 percent and 38 percent of total household income.

These figures are included in the study *Sustainable Development, Poverty and Gender, Latin America and the Caribbean: Working Towards the Year 2000*, prepared by ECLAC as a contribution to the Seventh Session of the Regional Conference on the Integration of Women in Economic and Social Development of Latin America and the Caribbean, held between 19 and 21 of November 1997 at the Commission's headquarters in Santiago, Chile.

The study includes data gathered since 1995 on poverty as it affects women in Latin America and the Caribbean. It describes measures taken to eradicate poverty, to achieve gender equality, and move towards a society which combines greater justice with sustainable development.

While it continues to be an important task to increase awareness of the connections between gender and poverty, the study notes that what is currently needed to accelerate changes are "new perspectives and new tools."

Overcoming poverty among women "is much more than implementing small-scale projects." Rather, public policies must be formulated and national programs implemented to allow for the development of skilled human resources, productive employment programs, changes in school curricula, amendments to existing legislation and inclusion of the gender approach in social security programs.

The study notes that the economic reforms of recent years have had different effects on poor men and on poor women. Income inequality between men and women is explained partly by occupational segmentation. In the early 1990s, women's salaries in Latin America averaged 72 percent of those earned by men. The improvement in the educational level of women brought increased wages, but these incremental changes proved to be higher than those of men only up to the level of secondary qualifications. Postsecondary studies bring greater benefits for men, who occupy higher and better-paid posts.

Rising unemployment rates are harder on women, who remain in the more vulnerable "pockets" of the economy, are victims of wage discrimination and do not have the same opportunities as men for vocational training. In the workplace, girls between ages 10 and 19 account for a significant share of the region's work force. The labor market is segmented into occupations "for" women and poor men. In the 1990s, employment for women was concentrated in small and medium businesses and many jobs involved working at home, which is another precarious form of employment. Because they have so few options, poor women tend to work mainly in the services sector, particularly in domestic service and commerce and, to a lesser extent, in agro industry.

Approximately 16 percent of women work in industry, 46 percent of them in the textile industry and 24 percent in the production of food, tobacco, and beverages. In Chile, Colombia, Costa Rica, and Jamaica, more than 30 percent of small businesses are run by women, who generally have low levels of schooling.

Given the extent of poverty in the region, ECLAC notes there is little point in asking who are the poorest among the poor. Instead, analysts should focus on evaluating which measures are the most effective in eradicating poverty among women.

It is essential to improve information gathering regarding the situation of women. Despite the importance of measuring the participation of women in the economy, no systematic method of classification by sex has yet been worked out, nor has the gender perspective been incorporated into the indicators. Meanwhile, most of the measures adopted to eradicate poverty among women have been geared toward welfare programs; they have not formed an integral part of development policy, and have not been linked to the market or provided with enough capital to stay afloat.

ECLAC argues that it is possible to achieve progress toward the eradication of poverty if adequate growth, estimated at 6 percent, is combined with macroeconomic stability and an increase in employment. Employment in Latin America is not growing enough and it is concentrated in low-quality jobs. Unemployment is on the rise, public sector jobs—many of which are performed by the poor—are declining, small businesses and the informal sector are becoming increasingly important, and social protection measures are being cut back. Measures to reduce poverty among women should form part of a broader framework of policies and programs which are integrated and viable, both financially and institutionally.

However, significant progress has been achieved in the legal status of women in Latin America and the Caribbean in the nineties. During the past four years, eight countries have approved equal opportunity programs for women. In the region as a whole, legislation has been introduced promoting the integration of women in social and economic development.

Among the legal advances achieved, ECLAC emphasizes the constitutional recognition of equality and the elimination of discriminatory norms. Also highlighted is the creation and reinforcement of offices in charge of women's issues at national, provincial, and municipal levels.

New networks of congresswomen, female politicians, and government ministers have emerged and joined those already in place, strengthening their political base by promoting women's issues at decision-making levels. The political and legal fields reflect the greatest progress on the issue of gender equality in Latin America and the Caribbean.

Source: CEPAL News, December 1997.

and Peru, earn approximately 60 percent less than minority populations. In table 11.6 we can see the significantly higher rate of poverty among indigenous groups as opposed to nonindigenous populations. Afro-Latin Americans, most commonly Brazilians of African descent, are 1.9 times as likely to live in poverty as their white counterparts.[10] Some of this may be attributable to colonization patterns. In Brazil and Spanish America in 1825, the early period of independence, roughly one-fifth of the population was white, with black and indigenous people constituting the bulk of the labor force. The white minority controlled agricultural and mining assets, with the rest of the population living on the edge of subsistence. The reverse was true in the United States, where 20 percent of the population was slave or Native American Indians without assets, and distribution was more widely

Table 11.6.   Poverty and Ethnicity (% of population below the poverty line)

Country	Indigenous	Nonindigenous
Bolivia	64.3	48.1
Guatemala	86.6	53.9
Mexico	80.6	17.9
Peru	79.0	49.7

Source: G. Psacharopoulos and H. Patrinos, eds., *Indigenous People and Poverty in Latin America* (Washington, D.C.: World Bank, 1994), 57, 100, 134, 170.

Table 11.7.   Latin America and the Caribbean: Estimates of Landless or Nearly Landless Peasant Families

Country	Peasant Families (%)
Bolivia	85
Brazil	70
Colombia	66
Costa Rica	55
Ecuador	75
El Salvador	80
Guatemala	85
Mexico	60
Peru	75
Dominican Republic	68

Source: Emiliano Ortega, "Evolution of the Rural Dimension in Latin America and the Caribbean," *CEPAL Review* 47 (1992): 124.

spread among white landowners and mine owners. Wealth was therefore hierarchically configured in Latin America from the very start.[11]

While urban poverty is increasing, rural poverty has been prevalent in the region. In table 11.7 we can see that this is in part attributable to the large percentage of rural residents without access to land. In Bolivia and Guatemala, for example, landless peasants reach 85 percent of the rural population.[12] Concentration in land ownership is also skewed. In Brazil, 50 percent of farms are small, covering 2.2 percent of the land. The top 5 percent of farms are large, accounting for 69.2

Table 11.8.   Social Indicators: Bottom and Top 20% of the Population

Country	Access to Public Water Supply Bottom 20%	Access to Public Water Supply Top 20%	Access to Sewage Bottom 20%	Access to Sewage Top 20%	Access to Electricity Bottom 20%	Access to Electricity Top 20%
Honduras	20.1	79.7	n/a	n/a	8.5	80.5
Guatemala	38.5	93.0	48.3	88.8	58.8	98.9
Peru	46.9	86.8	n/a	n/a	16.1	86.1
Brazil	48.3	89.8	26.7	83.8	45.6	95.8
Mexico	50.2	95.0	14.2	83.2	66.2	99.0
Uruguay	53.7	88.8	10.4	62.2	94.5	99.2
Venezuela	79.4	98.0	n/a	n/a	89.4	99.7
Paraguay	81.5	96.9	n/a	n/a	92.6	98.8
Colombia	84.8	89.9	52.6	87.4	n/a	n/a
Argentina	89.2	99.4	n/a	n/a	99.0	99.9
Bolivia	94.0	99.7	87.3	99.4	98.6	99.7

Source: George Psacharopoulos, Samuel Morley, Ariel Fiszbein, and Haeduck Lee, *Poverty and Income Distribution in Latin America: The Story of the 1980s* (Washington, D.C.: World Bank, 1997), annex 15.

percent of the land.[13] In Brazil, the pressure on the part of the landless for reform has become violent. Squatters have invaded farms and ranches, united in the Movimento Sem Terra (MST), or the movement of the landless.[14] We remember many of the causes of rural impoverishment from our discussion in chapter 10 of the deficiencies of the rural sector.

THE QUESTION OF INEQUALITY

Differences by region, gender, and ethnicity give rise to another critical issue: inequality. Inequality is a defining characteristic of the pattern of development in Latin America. Compared to other regions, Latin America contains the most unequal income distribution in the world.[15] The wealthiest 20 percent of the population in Latin America have an average income ten times higher than that of the poorest 20 percent, compared to 6.7 times in other low-middle-income countries.[16] When we look at average incomes such as GNP per capita, we don't get a sense of the national range of incomes. Brazil, for example, has a GNP per capita of $2,930 per year or $244 per month, yet nearly 40 percent of its population lives under the poverty line of $60 per day. This is due to a highly unequal income distribution in which the top 20 percent of the population makes about thirty times the income of the bottom 20 percent. In the United States that ratio is closer to 8:1.[17] In table 11.8 we can see how the poverty profile, as described by access to water, sewage, and electricity, dramatically varies by income level.

To understand the quality of life, it is therefore important to measure the degree of income inequality in a country using the **Gini coefficient**. The Gini coefficient measures the difference between a hypothetical population with all income divided equally and the actual distribution in an economy. In figure 11.1, we can see that the 45 degree line represents the hypothetical situation of perfect equality. If the population is divided into quintiles from lowest to highest, in a perfectly equal society the first 20 percent of the population would hold 20 percent of the income, the next 20 percent for a cumulative 40 percent would hold another 20 percent for a cumulative 40 percent, and so on. However, societies are not equal. The **Lorenz curve** measures the actual distribution. As shown in the Lorenz curve for Latin America in figure 11.1, the first 20 percent of the population only held 2.5 percent of the income, the first 40 percent a cumulative 8.6 percent. The bottom 60 percent accounted for 19.6 percent of income, with the top 20 percent holding nearly two-thirds of the total. Indeed, the top 10 percent holds almost half of the regional pie.

The Gini coefficient is equal to the area between the line of perfect equality and the Lorenz curve, labeled "a," and the whole triangle or a + b. If a society were perfectly equal, the area "a" would be empty, because the distribution would be the same as the line of perfect equality, and a/(a + b) would therefore be zero. If a society were perfectly unequal, one person would hold all the wealth, so that the area "a" would take up the whole triangle, or a/(a + b) would equal one.

The average Gini for the region is .49, fifteen points higher than in either the industrialized countries or the countries of Southeast Asia.[18] Table 11.9 shows

Figure 11.1.   Latin America: Income Distribution, 1995

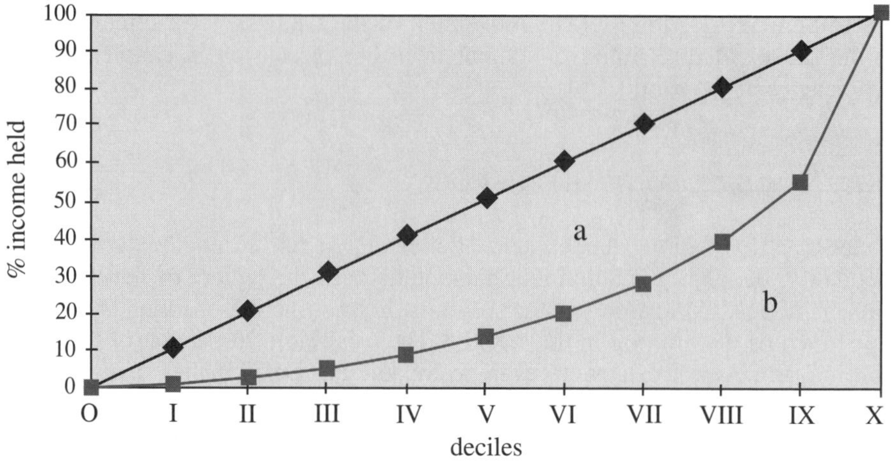

Source: Juan Luis Londoxo and Miguel Szekely, *Persistent Poverty and Excess Inequality: Latin America, 1970–1995,* Office of the Chief Economist, Inter-American Development Bank Working Paper no. 357 (Washington, D.C.: Inter-American Development Bank, 1997).

the distribution of income for Latin American countries as found in the *World Development Report.* Sorted by the share of income held by the top 10 percent of the population, Brazil, Honduras, and Guatemala have the highest degree of inequality; the top 10 percent of the population holds more than 45 percent of national wealth. No Latin American country reaches the level of the United States, Germany, or Japan, at less than 25 percent.

What Causes Inequality in Latin America?

What factors have shaped the high degree of inequality in the Latin American region? Inequality tends to be driven by the allocation of endowments and by the distribution of natural resources and human capital in society. As we remember from chapter 2, initial endowments based on patterns of colonization in the region were highly unequal. In contrast to the values of individualism, materialism, and scientific inquiry that characterized northern European colonialists, Spanish and Portuguese culture tended to transmit values of tradition, order, and spirituality.[19]

Nonetheless, one cannot forever blame the Spanish and the Portuguese for the woes of the region. Policy making in the almost 200 years since independence has continued to favor wealthy elites over the poor. The 15 percent excess of inequality in Latin America versus the rest of the world can be decomposed into different sources. Because scarce capital attracts high returns, the owners of capital have had a premium paid to them that accounts for 1 percent of this excess inequality. Inequality in the distribution in natural resources explains another 5 percent, but the bulk of the excess inequality is driven by underdevelopment of human capital.[20]

Table 11.9.   Income Distribution: Percentage Share of Income or Consumption

	Year	Lowest 20 Percent	Second quintile	Third quintile	Fourth quintile	Highest 20 Percent	Highest 10 Percent
High inequality							
Brazil	1989[d, e]	2.1	4.9	8.9	16.8	67.5	51.3
Honduras	1989[d, e]	2.7	6.0	10.2	17.6	63.5	47.9
Guatemala	1989[d, e]	2.1	5.8	10.5	18.6	63.0	46.6
Moderate to high inequality							
Panama	1989[d, e]	2	6.3	11.6	20.3	59.8	42.1
Nicaragua	1993[b, c]	4.2	8	12.6	19.9	55.3	39.8
Dominican Republic	1989[d, e]	4.2	7.9	12.5	19.7	55.6	39.6
Colombia	1991[d, e]	3.6	7.6	12.6	20.4	55.8	39.5
Costa Rica	1989[d, e]	4.0	9.1	14.3	21.9	50.8	39.5
Mexico	1984[d, e]	4.1	7.8	12.3	19.9	55.9	39.5
Moderate inequality							
Peru	1985–1986[b, c]	4.9	9.2	13.7	21.0	51.4	35.4
Argentina	1970[f, g]	4.4	9.7	14.1	21.5	50.3	35.2
Chile	1992[d, e]	3.3	6.9	11.2	18.3	60.4	34.8
Venezuela	1989[d, e]	4.8	9.5	14.4	21.9	49.5	33.2
Jamaica	1990[b, c]	6	9.9	14.5	21.3	48.4	32.6
Trinidad and Tobago	1975–1976[f, g]	4.2	9.1	13.9	22.8	50	31.8
Bolivia	1990–1994[b, c]	5.6	9.7	14.5	22	48.2	31.7
El Salvador	1976–1977[f, g]	5.5	10	14.8	22.4	4.3	29.5
Industrial comparison countries							
United States	1985[f, g]	4.7	11.0	17.4	25.0	41.9	25.0
Germany[a]	1988[f, g]	7.0	11.8	17.1	23.9	40.3	24.4
Japan	1979[f, g]	8.7	13.2	17.5	23.1	37.5	22.4

Source: World Bank, *World Development Report* (Washington, D.C.: World Bank, various years).
[a]Distribution data refer to the Federal Republic of Germany.
[b]Refers to expenditure shares by fractiles of persons.
[c]Ranked by per capita expenditure.
[d]Refers to income shares by fractiles of persons.
[e]Ranked by per capita income.
[f]Refers to income shares by fractiles of households.
[g]Ranked by household income.

In particular, growth in the number of years of education has been slower in Latin America than in the rest of the world. Table 11.10 shows that today Latin America has an average of 5.2 years of education, almost 2 less than expected for its level of development and 4 less than countries of East Asia. To lower inequality, countries must focus on building educational opportunities, a topic we will concentrate on below and in the following chapter.

**Table 11.10.   Gaps in Human Development for Latin America
and the Caribbean, 1995**

	Actual *(%)*	*Expected*[a] *(%)*
Education		
Fourth grade completed	66.0	82
Average years of schooling	5.2	7
Health		
Infant mortality	47.0	39
Life expectancy	69.5	72

Source: Inter-American Development Bank, *Economic and Social Progress in Latin America 1996
Report* (Washington, D.C.: Johns Hopkins University Press, 1996), 242.
[a]Expected is calculated relative to the international average for the Latin American income average.

Trends in Poverty and Inequality

Inequality in Latin America not only is high but also has worsened. The Gini
coefficient for Latin America at the end of the 1980s was .50, compared with the
.39 for non-Latin countries. Time series data for Brazil are shown in Box 11.3.
What is happening to increase inequality in the region? Some suggest that contrary
to expectation, poverty and inequality have not declined significantly with economic stabilization in the region.[21] Increasing economic polarization is illustrated
by changes at the extremes in the income distribution. In 1970, the richest 1 percent of the population made 363 times the amount of the poorest 1 percent. After
falling to a multiple of 237 prior to the debt crisis, by 1995 this ratio had climbed
to 417. The reason for the increase in inequality appears to be that the poor have
not benefited from growth as much as the rich.[22] One study, suggesting that Latin
America suffers from excess inequality, estimated Gini coefficients based on levels
of development. That is, it asked the question of what levels of inequality are
"usually" present at different levels of economic growth. Based on these estimates, Latin America has an "excess inequality" of between 11.4 and 14.7 points
on the Gini coefficient. With the regional Gini of .49, this results in a Gini coefficient 25 percent higher than its forecast given GDP per capita.

The slow progress on poverty reduction in the region appears tied to inequality. If inequality were not in excess of international levels commensurate with
similar GDPs—that is, if excess inequality were eliminated—poverty in Latin
America would have been reduced by half. Indeed, if Latin America had an income
distribution similar to other comparable nations, it would be the developing region
with the lowest poverty rates.[23] Chile remains an exception to this story, having
experienced an increase in inequality in the 1980s and a decline in the 1990s.
Poverty in Latin America can be seen as largely a distributive problem. As we will
come back to in the conclusion to this chapter, policy programs should therefore
be targeted less at an insufficiency of resources and more squarely at improving
the access of the poor to the assets in the economy.

Box 11.3.   Inequality in Brazil

Table 11.A shows the evolution of income distribution in Brazil. The Gini coefficient for Brazil is high compared to those of South and East Asia, at .35 and .39 respectively. It is also significantly higher than the average in the early 1990s for Argentina, Bolivia, Chile, Colombia, Costa Rica, Mexico, and Panama of .42. The Gini coefficient increased over the period from 1959 to 1989, from .51 to .63. This is a dramatic change in a coefficient that normally does not show strong variation. Economic stabilization after the Real plan appears to have moderated the growth in inequality, indicating the positive effect of economic stability on the poor. Poverty rates also declined as a result of the fall in prices. Interestingly, the Gini coefficient in Brazil rose during periods of strong economic growth as well as during anemic performance. Although stabilization in the 1990s has helped the poor, income inequality remains high by international standards. Macroeconomic stabilization can only go so far in reducing inequality; changes in the distribution of assets such as land or opportunities in education are prerequisites for more fundamental change.[25]

Table 11.A.   Income Distribution in Brazil

Year	Gini
1959	.51
1962	.54
1965	.52
1968	.52
1971	.58
1976	.58
1979	.59
1989	.63
1990	.62
1991	.58
1992	.58
1993	.60
1994	.62
1995	.59

Source: Kirk S. Bowman, "Should the Kuznets Effect be Relied on to Induce Equalizing Growth?" *World Development* 25, no. 1 (1997): 127–143; and Benedict Clements, "The Real Plan, Poverty, and Income Distribution in Brazil," *Finance & Development* (September 1997), from charts 2 and 3.

In addition to the effect of equality on poverty, economists have long wondered about the relationship between overall growth rates and equality. This is slightly different from changes in poverty. A nation could grow rapidly, with the absolute conditions of the poor not changing but the relative distance between the poor and the rich increasing. Alternatively, growth could improve the position of the poor with respect to the rich, or it could leave the lives at the extremes untouched and encourage the expansion of a middle class. What happens to the relative positions of income groups as countries grow? In turn, how do different levels of inequality affect the possibilities for growth?

The puzzling relationship between economic growth and inequality, discussed below, has led economists to test the relationship between economic growth and inequality. In pathbreaking work in the 1950s, Nobel Prize winner Simon Kuznets hypothesized that inequality follows a U-shaped path as economic growth expands. Called the Kuznets curve, it shows inequality increasing as countries begin to grow rapidly. As the country continues to develop, however, inequality should decline as more people begin to benefit from the growth process.

The empirical evidence regarding the Kuznets curve is contradictory. Although some studies confirm the pattern, others indicate that inequality does not necessarily have to increase before it lessens. Indeed, some economists argue that the causality might run in the other direction: increasing equality could help to spur growth. If more people had money, they would spend it. Improving income distribution could work to increase domestic demand for goods and services, providing a consumer-led expansion for growth. Furthermore, greater access to assets could improve investment in complementary resources. With greater equality, the poor might find it easier to borrow to invest in human capital. That is, if income were more equally distributed, one might see a stronger demand for investments in human capital such as health and education, improving economic performance. In contrast, unequal income distribution weakens the accumulation of physical and human capital, acting as a drag on productivity growth, the key to economic change.[24] Improving equality would therefore be growth enhancing.

The inequality and growth puzzle is difficult to resolve empirically because of data limitations. Good census surveys are time-consuming and costly. They are even more problematic in developing countries than in industrial countries. Furthermore, limited observations of slow-moving inequality data versus frequent and volatile macroeconomic growth rates make estimates difficult. Cross-country comparative studies run into trouble because of the different institutional characteristics of economies and different data collection techniques over time. Nevertheless, despite these difficulties, interesting work has emerged. Recent studies at the World Bank indicate that inequality as measured by the Gini coefficient has been relatively stable over periods that include divergent macroeconomic patterns. In a study of eighty-eight cases in which a country's GDP per capita grew for a decade, inequality increased in forty-five countries and decreased in forty-three.[26] This calls into question the Kuznets proposition that growth will initially lead to an increase in inequality. It also raises questions about the ability of growth to reduce inequality. However, it is important to remember that magnitudes of growth rates and time matter. As one Bolivian economist put it, "You don't eradicate centuries of structural inequalities with 4 percent growth rates."[27] Policy conditioning the kind of growth and how it is distributed is apparently an important variable.

Some have suggested that economic liberalization has worked against improving inequality because opening to international markets favors lower wages. However, liberalization may also introduce more capital to combine with labor, can limit monopoly power, might reduce the bias against agriculture, and can exert greater pressure for efficiency and technical change.[28] The empirical evidence is mixed, with the work leading us to conclude that the relationship between growth and equality may not be a direct one. Growth may enhance equality or, if the rewards from growth are unevenly distributed, it may increase inequality. More research needs to be done in this area.

What research appears to be telling us, however, is that if social or ethical concerns direct policy makers toward improving inequality, this does not necessarily have to come at the price of economic growth. Indeed, poor growth records may have inhibited improvements in equality. Some studies show that high levels of inequality are statistically linked to weak macroeconomic performance.[29] Growth-dampening political conflict and populist redistributive cycles may be propelled by inequality. Bolivia, for example, has gone through more than 250 rebellions and military coups in its 150-year history. Unequal income distribution may also limit the market size and interfere with human capital accumulation.[30] Political opening with more genuine democratic participation may create incentives toward equity enhancing policies. High incomes have been maintained by the special privilege and protection enjoyed by economic elites in the region; as the poor exercise greater voting power, there may be political incentives to design policies to improve economic opportunities for the poor.[31]

Sadly, throughout the 1980s, poverty and inequality worsened. Whereas from 1970 to 1980 poverty declined in the region, a legacy of the debt crisis was a worsening of poverty rates. Indeed, the IDB estimates that if Latin America's macroeconomic stability had mirrored that of industrial countries, an estimated 7 percent of the region's population, or 25 percent of the poor, would have been lifted out of poverty.[32] Another study traces a rough one to one trade-off between growth in GDP per capita and the annual decrease in poverty. For example, from 1987 to 1994, Chile experienced a healthy annual 5.5 percent increase in real growth in GDP per capita, and it reduced poverty by about 5 percent a year; Brazil only lodged a 0.5 percent increase in per capital GDP, and poverty increased 2 percent on an annual basis.[33] Depending on the country, another study found a 1 percent increase in growth to be associated with a 1.5 to 4 percent decline in poverty. Although these estimates vary—in part due to how poverty itself is measured in each study—we can be confident of one thing: growth helps reduce poverty, although not as much as we might hope.

The increase of poverty in the 1980s can be attributed to a number of factors. The economic crisis hit the poor hard because they are less able to protect themselves from inflation. Although the wealthy are able to use financial instruments to cushion the inflationary effects, the poor found themselves worse off as prices rose while wages stagnated. Real wages, those adjusted for inflation, fell in most countries. Opportunities for productive employment declined as a result of low and negative growth rates. Stabilization packages calling for reductions in government spending resulted in significant cuts in social safety nets. In table 11.11 we can see the legacy of the debt crisis in per capita spending on education and health, which fell on average nearly 3 and 6 percent regionally.

Although growth in the 1990s reversed the trend toward increasing poverty, significant progress in reducing the number of the region's poor has not been made. A puzzle of the recovery in the 1990s has been the relatively weak effect of growth on reducing poverty. Why hasn't the economic engine been stronger? One of the lessons has been that the economic slowdown clearly hurt the poor, but that growth does not automatically ensure that the poor will become better off. Growth

**Table 11.11. Average Annual Percentage Growth Rate of Spending on
Education and Health**

Country	Pre Debt Crisis PC Education	Post Debt Crisis Education	Pre Debt Crisis Health	Post Debt Crisis Health
Argentina	6.4	−1.4	3.5	9.7
Brazil	0.7	17.8	6.8	−6.8
Chile	−1.4	−4.8	−0.8	−5.7
Ecuador	11.5	−7.5	24.8	−15
Mexico	11.8	−11.4	7.1	−12
Peru	−1.4	−8.3	2.3	−5.3
Venezuela	4.3	−5.1	−0.6	−6.3
Seven-country average	4.56	−2.96	6.16	−5.91

Source: Alain de Janvry and Elizabeth Sadoulet, "Rural Development in Latin America: Relinking Poverty Reduction to Growth," in *Including the Poor,* ed. Michael Lipton and Jacques van der Gaag (Washington, D.C.: World Bank, 1993).
Note: Argentine data are for 1970–1981 and 1981–1987; Brazilian for 1970–1982, 1982–1986; Chilean 1970–1981, 1981–1985; Ecuadorian 1970–1981, 1981–1986; Mexican 1971–1981, 1981–1985; Peruvian 1971–1981, 1981–1985; and Venezuelan 1971–1981, 1981–1986.

must be accompanied by a social strategy favoring human capital investment to promote the productivity of the poor.

A complementary explanation is that the kind of growth that has taken place in the 1990s has not been of a labor-intensive character. This is somewhat surprising. The international trade theory we studied in chapter 8 would lead us to believe that as Latin American countries lowered tariffs and opened up to the international market, they would export those goods that use relatively intensively the region's most abundant factor: unskilled labor. Instead, we see that trade liberalization has tended to benefit skilled labor. The gap between skilled and unskilled workers has risen, leaving the poor further behind. Explanations for why this has happened include the fact that liberalization may have cheapened the price of capital, making it more attractive as a complement to skilled labor. A second consideration is the position of unskilled Latin American labor in the world economy. It may be cheap by North American standards but still relatively expensive compared to the labor supply in India or China. Institutional rigidities protecting workers in Latin American labor markets, discussed in chapter 9, may also have worked to slow the absorption of poor, informal workers into the skilled sector.

This interaction between relatively rapid growth and anemic poverty rates in the 1990s leads us to an important conclusion: Growth is a necessary but not sufficient condition for poverty alleviation. Growth is critical to reducing poverty in the region, but if changes are not made to enhance the ability of the poor to participate in the growth process and its rewards, poverty and inequality will remain a sad fact of life in Latin America.

Areas for Action:
Enhancing the Assets of the Poor

Reducing poverty and inequality remains the central development challenge for the region. Three categories of the poor can be identified: those unable to provide for themselves, such as the elderly or children; those able to work but whose incomes are low and irregular; and those forced into poverty through temporary shocks such as structural adjustment or agricultural disaster. In addition to long-term assistance for groups such as the handicapped, poverty reduction programs include short-term emergency programs to address the consequences of stabilization and long-term investments in basic education, health services, job training, and credit facilities to reduce the vulnerability of the poor to short-term shocks and improve access to opportunity in the economy. Poverty reduction in Latin America is a tough but not insurmountable challenge.

Change that is sustainable over time usually involves changes in institutions. In both the short and the long terms, the poor must be brought into the process of change so that they become actors in transforming their lives and not passive victims receiving assistance. Short-term measures are critical in alleviating human suffering, but it is the long-term structural changes that create opportunities to transform the lives of the poor. Direct transfers to the poor are best when they are simultaneously asset building. For example, scholarships for the children of poor families may help supplement family incomes and also entice kids to stay in school. Compensation for visits to health posts can help balance the family budget while encouraging preventive health care.

Social Investment Funds

One mechanism to address the short-term effects of macroeconomic instability has been **social investment funds (SIFs).** Social investment funds are targeted toward emergency employment programs including building or repairing roads, bridges, and schools; social assistance programs such as food aid; and improving productivity through credit, microenterprise development, and worker training. SIFs were characteristically independent of the national bureaucracy, reporting directly to the president. The emergency nature of the funds in the 1980s has evolved into their use as parallel institutions for the delivery of social services. Because they enjoy broad administrative, technical, and financial autonomy, they are able to respond to local demand more quickly and effectively. The main source of financing comes from foreign grants and donations and national public contributions. Their transparency creates public confidence because there is little doubt how the funds are used.[34] Effects are rapid and demonstrable. Resources are distributed in response to requests from local groups, enhancing the role of NGOs as mediators.[35] Funds are best directed at projects sustainable beyond the terms of the grant.

A model social investment fund in Bolivia through the World Bank facilitated the process of decentralization by assisting local authorities and communities in managing investment resources as well as building and maintaining social infrastructure. The Bolivian social investment fund was focused on four areas: economic infrastructure, social infrastructure, social assistance, and credit schemes. In its inception it was targeted at employment generation; it then turned to social assistance and infrastructure creation. In the least, it contributed to the political sustainability of the adjustment process.[36] Reaching between 3.5 and 4 million people, the fund has supported the building or refurbishing of health and educational facilities and rural water supplies. Health indicators as measured by number of severe diseases among children have decreased, vaccinations and birth control dissemination have increased, and teaching performance and school attendance have improved.[37]

Public works programs may have multiple benefits: improve the infrastructure in a community, change local institutions, and create employment for residents. Improving infrastructure, including the region's woefully inadequate housing stock, is designed to enhance the physical and emotional well-being of the poor. In the rural sector the timing of public works projects should be in the agricultural off season. In both the rural and urban cases, setting the wage below the minimum wage helps to attract the poorest into the program. Public works programs in Chile during the 1980s, for example, set the wage for public works jobs at 70 percent of the national minimum, so that people already employed did not leave their jobs for attractive public works projects. Work projects located close to low-income communities help to decrease transportation costs—a significant factor for a poor person. Programs can be designed to encourage the participation of women by paying attention to child care and schoolday issues, and the involvement of local NGOs can help to increase the accountability of the programs to the public and reduce the likelihood of corruption.[38]

Social investment funds also have their drawbacks. Unfortunately, because the most indigent are the least politically able to organize, social investment funds do little to help the poorest of the poor. The funds tend to help the new poor, that is, those made temporarily poor through tough economic adjustment policies, as opposed to dealing with the tough issues of helping the chronically poor.[39] A lack of coordination with state bodies has also led to duplication of services. The reliance on foreign finance introduces year-to-year uncertainty. In the case of the Honduran social investment fund created by UNDP in 1990, the bulk of the spending was directed toward short-term infrastructure, with little reaching the marginalized poor. Nonetheless, policies can be especially targeted to the poor. In the initial stages of combating Chile's 18 percent open unemployment in its early introduction of the neoliberal model, a minimum employment program (PEM) and an occupations program for heads of households (POJH) employed close to 11 percent of the country's labor force, in hopes of holding off political opposition to tough economic measures.[40] The employment, however, was often dead end and did little to improve human capital investment. Under the democratic governments, a new approach was taken. The Chilean Solidarity and Social Investment Funds (FOSIS) has been more successful in combating poverty because of its focus on the long-term, structural causes of poverty. Its priorities included credit, marketing and training of small businesses and small farmers, youth job training, and building self-help capacity in poor communities.[41] Institutionally independent of the state planning ministry, FOSIS is by design flexible and open to local participation. It is therefore able to respond to the heterogeneous and decentralized nature of poverty in Chile. Fostering grassroots participation, it works closely with Chile's relatively well-articulated network of NGOs to reach the poorest of the poor. Nonetheless, it faces the same difficulty as social investment funds in other countries: the most destitute are the least well organized to demand government services.[42]

Involving the Poor

To promote sustainable programs, the poor must be involved in the process of planning and implementing poverty-alleviation efforts. They should be thought of as clients rather than recipients, reinforcing the view that they can take action against their human suffering. In addition, programs should be integrated into the broader economy instead of creating enclaves of the poor. The example of infrastructure development in Rio de Janeiro serves to illustrate these points. Rio de Janeiro has embarked on an ambitious project to upgrade its favelas, or slum areas. Rather than relocate residents to planned, affordable urban housing with the unintended side effect of destroying the social fabric of a community, the city is working with residents to upgrade the standard of living within the poor communities. The city inaugurated its efforts with a competition for proposals from prominent and budding architects for community designs. The mayor's office then took these proposals to the Inter-American Development Bank, which loaned it $300 million for the projects. Two key aspects defined the favela projects. First, the favelas were to be integrated into the surrounding communities and not reinforced as poverty enclaves. For example, in one of the most famous favelas in Rio, Serinha (the home of the samba), housing and workshop space for samba artists, costume areas, after-hours samba instruction facilities, an area for the macumba religious cere-

---

BOX 11.4. THE CASE OF COSTA RICA

Costa Rica is a case where policy initiatives to reduce inequality led to a decrease not only in the inequality of income allocation but also in the rates of poverty. In 1960 Brazil and Costa Rica had similar levels of inequality; by 1989 the Gini coefficient for Brazil was .6331 and that for Costa Rica .4604. Brazil had 40.9 percent of its population in poverty, and Costa Rica had 3.4 percent. What were the ingredients of the success in Costa Rica? The foundation of Costa Rican social policy was state intervention following the 1948 civil war. In part the ability of the state to use resources to promote equality was due to the weakened position of the coffee oligarchy in the postwar period. In addition, the military was disbanded, and defense spending was redirected to education and social policies. By 1976, 30 percent of the Costa Rican budget was spent on education versus 7 percent worldwide. As defense spending was slashed from 25 percent of the national budget in the late 1940s to 2 percent in 1958, federal spending on health and social services more than doubled from 20 percent in 1938 to 45 percent in 1958.[43] Costa Rica also benefited from a land reform in 1961, redistributing land assets. Investments in social services combined with asset distribution have contributed to the nation's standout performance on poverty reduction in the region.

mony, a cultural center and arena stage, and a tramway to bring visitors into the favela were planned alongside a water pumping station, day care facilities, and tanks of potable water.

The second concept is community engagement. Favela residents have been involved in planning changes and must ultimately approve plans before construction begins. The city pays for the improvements in common services, and residents are responsible for improving their own houses. Through another World Bank loan, Rio de Janeiro is using digital technology to remap the entire city, including favelas. This is critical to homeowners because previously the squatter settlers had no legal right to the land their homes were on, decreasing the incentive for permanent improvements. Streets will be named and houses numbered so residents can apply for titles, and perhaps the 1 million residents of the favelas will be able to receive mail. With titles they can also use their homes as collateral for lending. Of course, a less welcome aspect of the improvement will be that the tax agency will also know where to call![44]

The Role of the Market in Poverty Reduction

One approach toward poverty reduction is to build on the entrepreneurial energies within the **informal sector**, improving productivity and therefore income. We remember from chapter 9 that the poor tend to be concentrated in the informal sector,

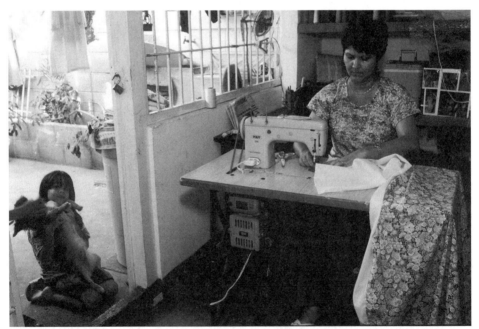

Microentrepreneurs, such as this Venezuelan woman, help sustain families; without additional capital, improvement is unlikely. *(Courtesy of the Inter-American Development Bank.)*

without access to social security and health services. In Latin America, somewhere between 18 and 57 percent of the population works in the informal sector. As shown in table 11.12, even countries such as Argentina, with a small informal sector as a percentage of its economically active population, have a large urban informal sector. The informal sector is a catchall term for individuals and small firms or microenterprises operating in open, unregulated markets outside the tax base, using local resources and labor-intensive technologies. The objective of activity in the informal sector is basically to guarantee subsistence of the family group.[45] Jobs in the informal sector are often characterized by low productivity (with little associated capital investment) and instability. They are a means of survival without social safety nets. Women are disproportionately represented in the informal sector, in food services, domestic washing and cleaning, tourism, petty trading, dressmaking, companionship, and sex. This may be attributed to the difficulties women face in accessing formal education and credit, as well as technical training.[46] Women tend to be pushed into the informal sector to earn money for family survival.

In Brazil, Chile, and Costa Rica it is estimated that between 72 and 76 percent of the informal sector employees are women, concentrated in domestic service.[50] The informal sector allows women greater flexibility in terms of hours of employ-

Table 11.12. Informal Sector Size

	% of Economically Active Population 1980	% Urban Economically Active Population around 1990
Large informal sectors		
Paraguay	57	50
Ecuador	53	—
Peru	52	—
Guatemala	47	54
Honduras	47	30
Medium informal sectors		
Brazil	38	46
Mexico	37	36
Panama	37	39
Colombia	35	—
Smaller informal sectors		
Venezuela	27	33
Chile	23	30
Costa Rica	22	22
Uruguay	21	35
Argentina	18	40

Source: Guillermo Rosenbluth, *CEPAL Review* 52 (April 1994): 155–175; Juan Pablo Pérez Sáinz and Rafael Manjívar Larín, *Informalidad urbana en Centroamérica: entre la acumulación y la subsistencia* (FLACSO: Editorial Nueva Sociedad, 1991).

ment and child care as well as lower entry barriers. Unfortunately, these jobs are also characterized by low remuneration, with between 75 and 80 percent of those employed in the informal sector earning less than the poverty level. Labor legislation, social security, and minimum wage laws are not enforceable in the informal sector. Labor, benefits, payments into social security funds, and vacations can add as much as 20 percent to the firm's labor bill.

The impetus behind the informal sector is the urban labor surplus created in part by unemployed rural migrants. During the economic crisis of the 1980s, the size of the informal sector increased by more than 30 percent.[47] Neoliberals argue that this surplus is exacerbated by excessive government regulation in the labor market, creating rigidities in hiring. High tax rates may also encourage black markets in goods. Neostructuralists contend that the surplus labor is created by technology-intensive production in the formal sector patterned after the industrialized world. Because firms don't use appropriate labor-intensive technologies, arguably fewer workers are hired.

Some characterize the informal sector as an illegal sector because business are not registered for health and safety inspections, do not pay taxes, and are not bound by labor legislation. Nonetheless, some studies identify up to 50 percent of so-called illegal firms as having some sort of official licensing or tax obligation.[48] In practice, a continuum of legality can be observed in the structure of firms that can be tied to timing or a balancing of costs. Even if a firm wants to be legal, the time involved in filing the appropriate registrations can be up to one year. There are also registration costs and compliance costs to meet health and safety standards. For example, for a sandwich maker to comply with health regulations including a net to keep insects out, a spring to close a door, and ceramic tiles on the wall and floor, the investment would be $500, possibly more than the entrepreneur could afford.[49] This firm by necessity will remain outside the formal sector.

The addition of capital and technology to the entrepreneurial and survival instincts of the hard-working poor may improve the position of the marginalized. This of course involves investment—a critical constraint in enterprise expansion. Small loans are often not profitable for banks because of their high transactions and monitoring costs as well as low repayment rates. NGOs and, increasingly, the public sector have begun to attend to this need through microfinance or microcredit. A microenterprise is defined as a sole proprietorship with fewer than ten employees that lacks the collateral and traditional creditworthiness to borrow money from traditional banks. They account for the employment of 120 million people in the Latin American region. Microfinance organizations attempt to substitute the traditional financing requirements—collateral and a credit history—with terms appropriate to their businesses and social context. Solidarity groups—where members of the group share responsibility for repayment of the loan—have been an effective mechanism for self-monitoring and maintaining high repayment rates. Globally, more than $1 billion a year is lent to 8 million people in poor countries.[51] BancoSol has been particularly effective in microlending. Beginning as a microlender, it has now grown to serve 70,000 clients, more than one-third of Bolivia's banking customers. With an average loan size of $828, its return on equity was 30 percent in the 1997–1998 period. Other microenterprise lenders have also found

Box 11.5. The New Entrepreneurs: A Microlending Giant—Bolivia's BancoSol Shows Small Loans Are Profitable

When Domitila Yupanqui arrived in the Bolivian capital of La Paz, she hoped merely to survive.

One of thousands of Bolivians who emigrated to the city after several state-owned mines in the province of Oruro were closed in the 1980s, Yupanqui had few contacts and no prospects.

"When we first moved to La Paz, we rented a single room," Yupanqui recalls. "I used to sell candy on the street. I would sit there, thinking about my children and their future, and feel very sad."

That was before Yupanqui heard about a bank that offered small, short-term loans without requiring collateral. Intrigued, she inquired at the nearest branch of BancoSol and to her surprise was immediately treated as a potential customer. Told that she would need to form a small cooperative of fellow borrowers in order to qualify for a loan, Yupanqui recruited members for a group that called itself "The Cornfields."

Yupanqui used her first BancoSol loan to buy canned food. Since her vending stall was close to a public school, she used her second loan for school supplies. She continued to diversify, and by the time she had qualified for a fifth loan Yupanqui was able to rent a small storefront and begin selling electrical appliances.

Today Yupanqui owns three stores and is paying to send two of her children to college, in a striking example of the effect that BancoSol has had on thousands of Bolivian microentrepreneurs.

BancoSol began life in 1992 as the successor to the nonprofit Foundation for the Promotion and Development of Microenterprises (PRODEM). From its inception in 1985, PRODEM used the "solidarity group" concept, in which four to eight borrowers come together to receive and repay loans as a group, cross-guaranteeing each other's loans. Initial loans were usually for less than $100 for three months, but as borrowers established a good record, the amounts were gradually allowed to increase. PRODEM also offered training sessions on credit handling for microentrepreneurs.

PRODEM proved immensely popular with street vendors, shoemakers, bakers, tailors, and other small entrepreneurs in Bolivia who had never had access to credit. Eager to qualify for new loans, the cooperative borrowing groups showed extraordinary repayment discipline, with overall default rates as good as or better than the average for commercial banks. By 1991 PRODEM had 116 employees, eight branches, more than 20,000 clients and a loan portfolio in excess of $4 million.

PRODEM grew so fast that its status as a nonprofit began to constrain its ability to expand, since it could not legally raise capital. With the help of three leading Bolivian banks and in collaboration with Acción International, a U.S.-based micro credit promotion agency, Canada's Calmeadow Foundation, and the Inter-American Investment Corporation (IIC), PRODEM decided to convert itself into a fully regulated commercial bank. The IIC pledged to purchase 24 percent of the shares of the future Banco Solidario S.A. (BancoSol), a move that was instrumental in attracting other equity investors, according to BancoSol general manager Hermann Krutzfeldt.

Finally, in February 1992, BancoSol opened its doors as the first private commercial bank in Latin America specializing in microentrepreneurs. While retaining its basic solidarity group approach, BancoSol expanded its offerings to include larger loans for fixed capital, construction, and home building and a variety of interest-bearing savings accounts.

Traditional banking theory holds that low-income groups have very little saving power, but savings accounts have turned out to be one of BancoSol's most popular features. The bank did away with traditional requirements for opening an account, such

(continued)

(continued)

as literacy and a minimum deposit level. As a result, the average BancoSol client has $120 in the bank, the equivalent of around one-eighth of annual per capita GDP. "Savings is as important a service as credit in this market," said Krutzfeldt. "Our services allow people to earn interest on their money instead of placing it under a mattress."

BancoSol turned a profit in its first year of operations, and by 1996 profits had soared to $1.1 million on revenues of $14.6 million. Total assets during the same period grew from $11 million to $59 million. Employment has tripled, from 147 to 480, and the bank now operates 33 branches. Today BancoSol is Bolivia's largest bank in terms of customers: its 71,000 clients account for 34 percent of the borrowers in Bolivia's financial system. Past due loans represent just 2.6 percent of the bank's portfolio, and the average loan has grown to $661. And perhaps most significantly, 70 percent of BancoSol's customers are women who, like Domitila Yupanqui, are giving a new face to entrepreneurship in Latin America.

Despite successes, questions with respect to the effects of microenterprise lending can be raised. One study suggests that many microentrepreneurs are borrowing simply to keep their heads above water, and not finding enough spare cash to invest in growth. The study points to difficulties in monitoring loans, indicating little quality control. It also questions the cultural indoctrination that accompanies some of the training sessions for microentrepreneurs, noting that it often ignores indigenous and traditional values.

Source: Excerpted from *IDB America* and Stephanie Small, Colby College graduating class of 1998, unpublished manuscript.

success, in large part because the small borrowers are surprisingly more likely to repay loans, with a past due rate on loans of just 2.6 percent.[52]

In 1978 the IDB approved the allocation of $5 million for a program to assist small enterprises with concessional funds. Individual projects were limited to $500,000. A year later the bank authorized continuation of the program indefinitely without the $5 million ceiling. Over the period 1993 through 2001, the bank hopes to have committed nearly $1 billion to programs supporting microlending. Under this program the IDB does not collect its usual fee to cover administrative costs and does not require that repayment comply with maintenance of value obligations (in other words, payments or repayments in local currency when it has depreciated need not be compensated with additional local currency). Credit terms are at market rates. The first showcase was Manos del Uruguay.[53] The IFC, the International Finance Corporation, the private sector arm of the World Bank, launched Porfund, a $35 million fund to invest in microbanks in Latin America and the Caribbean. The private sector is also in on the microcredit game. Citibank, for example, provides loans to the nonprofit Acción, headed by a former Wall Street broker. A key element of Acción's philosophy is that success is measured by projects that become self-sustaining over time. Acción provides technical assistance through a local banking intermediary, but the ideas are generated by the borrower and the collateral is in the group's peer pressure to repay. Interestingly, after success in Latin America, Acción is trying microcredit programs in the United States.[54]

Studies of the effects of microcredit lending on the intended beneficiaries, the poor, have only begun to appear. Loan impacts appear to be small for the very poor, because they tend to use loans to finance consumption rather than investment; the not-so-poor are better able to transform loans into productive business investments.[55] Moreover, it is important to remember that microcredit lending is not enough. Complementary measures, particularly in infrastructure, health, and education, are necessary to address the problem of poverty. It doesn't matter if a woman has the money to invest in a sewing machine if she cannot market her goods or if the possibilities aren't open for her child to become more than a seamstress.

The question of poverty alleviation in Latin America isn't the amount of resources but how to mobilize them. A collaborative program between the public and private sectors can increase resources from the state while avoiding some of the political problems that have plagued official small-scale development projects. Corporate philanthropy and social responsibility are not well-developed traditions in the region. Deriving from the U.S. experience, in which 67 percent of consumers will choose a product associated with a socially responsible cause, American Express launched a successful campaign against hunger in Brazil, raising $150 million while simultaneously increasing profits. Meetings are being convened around the region to discuss possible cooperation with CEOs of top corporations. The Kellogg Foundation has instituted a series of traveling seminars around the region and to the United States for Latin American corporate executives to learn how the nonprofit world is organized. The opening up of international trade has created enormous wealth in the region; creating incentives to channel some portion of this wealth to the poor can help redress the social deficit in the region. A nonprofit treaty called the double taxation treaty accompanied the NAFTA treaty to remove the legal barriers to the flow of philanthropic resources between the United States and Mexico. The Inter-American Foundation, an independent but federally funded organ of the U.S. government, has partnered with various nongovernmental organizations in the North and the South to promote socially responsible programming to bridge the uneasy coexistence of wealth and poverty in the region.[56] Public–private partnerships may help provide resources and entrepreneurial energies to assist in poverty alleviation.

THE MANAGEMENT OF POVERTY PROGRAMS: THE ROLE OF THE STATE

Combating poverty in Latin America is very much tied up in the broader question of the role of the state in the economy. The neoliberal approach advocates minimizing the role of the state in meeting the needs of the poor. For the neoliberal, the market should provide the mechanism to improve the standard of living. Neostructuralists, in contrast, argue that the problem of persistent poverty can not be addressed without a proactive role for the state. Although neostructuralists understand the tight fiscal constraints of contemporary policy making in the region, they contend that investment in people is critical to enhancing long-term growth potential. Nonetheless, the debate on the role of the state versus the role of the market in reducing poverty is not as starkly divided as views on privatization or the role of foreign investment. All agree that the problem of persistent poverty and the social deficit in Latin America must be addressed to promote sustainable growth. The debate centers on how much state participation is optimal in achieving this objective.

One approach to decrease the role of social welfare bureaucracies is that of **decentralization**. Decentralization moves state activity from the national to the local level. The premise behind decentralization is that local control will decrease costs and increase the effectiveness of each dollar spent on local services. In principle local authorities are in better touch with the needs of their constituencies, and can therefore make better choices in programming. There are four elements to decentralization: deconcentration, delegation, devolution, and privatization. Deconcentration shifts workloads from central ministries to federally paid employees located outside national capitals. Delegation involves the transfer of authority from the central government, whereas devolution genuinely transfers authority. Privatization turns the administration of social programs over to nongovernmental or private sector agencies.[57] In most cases of decentralization, financing flows through block grants from the central government to equalize revenue across regions. However, decentralization may also include revenue and expenditure decision making.[58]

Although the goal of hard-line neoliberals might be to take the federal government out of social assistance, some evidence suggests the need for a central government role in building capacity in local institutions to deliver quality services. Linkage between local and national levels is also important in setting and enforcing national standards and regulations. Administrators in remote areas may not have had the training necessary to manage a variety of social assistance programs; the federal government is important in developing professional local capacity. Although most now agree that huge bureaucracies in state capitals are not the most efficient way to deliver social services, a role for central government in allocation, training, and oversight is warranted.

Streamlining State Spending: Targeting

Another mechanism to increase the efficiency of social expenditures is called **targeting**. Rather than broad national food subsidies for milk or tortillas, targeting involves identifying eligible recipients to direct expenditures toward those who need them most.[59] For example, in Ecuador subsidies for electricity and gas together account for 2 percent of GDP, although only 17 percent of the electricity subsidy and 23 percent of the cooking gas subsidy reach the poor. Removing this subsidy and targeting the resources so that all the funds benefit the poor would be a more effective poverty reduction strategy, although it may not be as politically popular with the other roughly 80 percent of beneficiaries! Although this might sound like common sense, it is not always as easy as it sounds.

Targeted dollars should be spent in response to local demand. Communities might mobilize around a soup kitchen, a day care center, or improvements in water collection. In rural Argentina poor small-scale farmers are being introduced to sustainable agro-forestry practices. In a marginal neighborhood in Bogota, Colombia, funds are targeted at investments in water, sewage, and flood control. An urban transport project in Bogota will assist 630,000 low-income residents with access to public transportation to get to work. In rural Peru investments in secondary and primary roads connecting the poorest communities to national markets are designed to reduce rural poverty. Local contributions—perhaps in the form of voluntary labor contributions to building a day care center—can hold the cost down. A project in Argentina is aimed at women and children in twenty poor municipalities to improve reproductive health and supplemental feeding programs while simultaneously focusing on domestic violence prevention and the early detection of high-risk families. In Honduras a project is targeted at the modernization of the land administration system to reduce conflict among small-scale farmers and improve methods of community forestry. In rural Mexico, banking offices in remote locations are being experimented with to increase access for ethnic communities and other disadvantaged groups. Targeting redirects the money broadly spent on social welfare and public subsidies to poor communities.

Nonetheless, although spending directed to where the people themselves want it has a certain democratic appeal, it may leave others out. The poorest of the poor most often don't have street addresses, nor are they part of an organized neighborhood or church community. In addition, some have suggested that targeting imposes an additional burden on women as providers of community-based programs in poor neighborhoods. State oversight and mechanisms of accountability at the local level are necessary to ensure high-quality programs.

Despite these difficulties, Mexico has identified an innovative mechanism for targeting food subsidies. Needy families are given a smart credit card with a food account to replace public tortilla subsidies that also benefited the rich. Families must self-identify by coming into the local health clinic for preventive health care. While they are there for visits they get their food account renewed. Parents who keep their kids in school are given an extra bonus, creating incentives for education. The government is able to identify those who need services the most and not spend money on generalized public assistance programs. These benefits are part of an overall poverty reduction strategy in Mexico called PRONASOL, later reorganized to give states more power under the name Alianza para el Bienestar. It is defined by three complementary strategies: first, the provision of welfare benefits such as food credits, housing, and sanitation targeted to the poor; second, production programs of rural credit and loans for infrastructure development to raise the investment potential of the poor; and third, regional development programs in road and education infrastructure to improve the social capital of the poorest regions.[60] It is an attempt to meet the short-term needs of the poor while also transforming the structural conditions of poverty.

A Lean State Machine: Effective Selectivity

Investment in the social sector will not spontaneously take place through the market. Although the private sector must be incorporated as a partner in social change, investments will be led by the state. Given the budgetary limitations, however, hard choices must be made. Some structuralists who hold that the state must assume an active role in the improvement of the quality of life in the region offer the concept of **effective selectivity** as a criterion for state intervention. The goal is to identify where the benefits of spending would be greatest and to pursue projects with the highest rates of social return. They see the state holding a twofold role: in the short run minimizing the impact of structural change on the poor, and in the long run investing in human resource development. It is their contention that central government spending in the social sector in Latin America is not out of control but rather inefficient. Social spending in Latin America is relatively low. Table 11.13 groups countries into high, moderate, and low regional spenders. Even the high social spenders such as Costa Rica do not approach the 23.6 percent of GDP that the United States spends—much less the 33.6 percent of GDP that Germany or the 35 percent of GDP that France spends.[61] This is particularly striking when it is noted that defense expenditures (included in central government expenditures, or CGE) for the region are under 2 percent of GDP, leaving most of the spending in the social and economic arena. We remember from chapter 6 that in part this derives from the limited ability of the Latin American state to raise revenues. Reduction of poverty will require a strengthening of the revenue raising capabilities of the state so that it can become an effective actor. Combined with mechanisms to improve the delivery of services, selective interventions by the state may reduce the suffering of the poor in the region.

In large part improving social services in the region entails improving program quality and assessing the distributional impacts of development strategies. For example, in the health arena investments in basic health care would make a big difference in the lives of children. Many public health systems exclude the poor in that they pay benefits only to working contributors. Improving the quality of teachers would change educational outcomes. Students from families in the upper two quintiles receive 75 percent of the educational subsidies because these support higher education in the region. We will take a closer look at sectoral improvements in health and education in the next chapters.

INTEGRATING GROWTH AND EQUITY

Improving the standard of living of the poor in Latin America must, like the Mexican program, go beyond temporary food assistance. Attacking the roots of poverty involves changes in the overall pattern of development. ECLAC advocates an **integrated approach** to poverty reduction. It proceeds from the premise that growth policies have a distributional impact and that social policies affect growth. A strategy for growth with greater equity must therefore include both dimensions in economic and social policy making. Changing production patterns to compete in a globally integrated economy should involve considerations of equity. As we saw in chapter 9, sources of competitiveness for participating in the global economy will require improvements in the quality of the labor force, enhancing the returns to human capital. Otherwise the poor will not benefit from growth. This should include job retraining as well as investments in education, health, and housing to improve the productivity of labor.

Table 11.13. Social Expenditures in Latin American Countries (average)

Country	Real per Capita Social Expenditure (in 1987 dollars)		Social Expenditure/ GDP		Social Expenditure/ Total Public Expenditure	
	1990–1991	1994–1995	1990–1991	1994–1995	1990–1991	1994–1995
High social expenditure	333.6	424.9	15.2	17.2	52.7	60.4
Uruguay	463.2	624.9	18.9	23.6	63.0	75.1
Costa Rica	334.0	388.6	19.8	20.8	45.5	44.3
Panama	349.9	466.5	17.1	20.0	37.5	44.2
Argentina	548.5	703.8	17.1	18.3	58.0	66.0
Chile	259.1	318.3	13.1	13.4	60.3	63.3
Mexico	156.4	247.3	8.4	13.1	53.3	71.8
Brazil	224.0	224.8	11.6	11.2	51.0	57.8
Moderate social expenditure	99.1	126.6	9.0	10.9	35.5	47.4
Colombia	107.2	164.2	8.2	11.6	33.9	54.0
Nicaragua	97.4	86.4	10.8	10.6	36.2	48.8
Ecuador	92.7	129.3	7.8	10.4	36.5	39.5
Venezuela	215.6	n/a	8.5	n/a	32.1	n/a
Low social expenditure	42.3	54.3	4.8	5.9	31.0	33.2
Honduras	72.2	69.6	7.8	7.6	33.1	29.1
Paraguay	25.9	66.7	2.6	6.6	33.2	43.2
Bolivia	34.4	49.5	4.6	6.3	36.0	32.0
El Salvador	50.1	53.7	5.5	5.3	23.6	25.0
Guatemala	28.7	32.2	3.3	3.7	29.8	36.4
Dominican Republic	36.3	n/a	4.7	n/a	36.6	n/a
Peru	20.6	n/a	2.1	n/a	n/a	n/a
Regional average	189.6	241.7	10.4	12.2	42.1	48.7

Source: Economic Commission for Latin America and the Caribbean, *The Equity Gap: Latin America, the Caribbean, and the Social Summit* (Santiago, Chile: Economic Commission for Latin America and the Caribbean, 1996), 96.

ECLAC is focusing on the positive synergies between human capital invest-ments, economic growth, and improvements in income distribution and standards of living. Macroeconomic reforms in the fiscal and monetary realm should be complemented by social sector investments for long-term stable growth.[62] In par-ticular greater attention must be paid to the informal sector, technological modern-ization, the promotion of microenterprises, and rural development facilitated by improved access to land and credit. Complementary reforms in education, health, housing, and social security are needed. Programs to promote social cohesion such as programs for families and children at risk, compensatory or transfer policies for those for whom employment can't help, programs to strengthen community life, and instruments to protect communities from violence and drug trafficking are also critical to provide the underpinning for stable, long-run growth with equity.[63] Poverty reduction is therefore built into a re-visioning of the development strategy.

Key Concepts

Decentralization	Income gap	Poverty line
Effective selectivity	Informal sector	Social investment funds
Gini coefficient	Integrated approach	Targeting
Headcount ratio	Lorenz curve	

Chapter Summary

Defining Poverty

- Poverty is clearly prevalent in Latin America, but it is difficult to establish a precise definition of poverty itself. Different measures have been developed, such as the Human Poverty Index, but these measures still do not give a complete picture of the problems associated with poverty in the region.

Poverty, Income Inequality, and Growth

- Poverty needs to be looked at in conjunction with income inequality. Indicators such as the Gini coefficient and the Lorenz curve help give a quantitative and visual perspective on the income gap between the rich and the poor.
- The relationship between income and inequality is unclear. Simon Kuznets theorized that as a country grows, the gap between the rich and poor will initially widen, but eventually that gap will narrow. Recent studies show that this relationship is not direct and that other factors need to be considered.
- Latin America has the most unequal income distribution in the world, with Brazil, Honduras, and Guatemala taking the sad lead. The causes of inequality lie mainly in policies that have favored the rich, especially policies that neglect the importance of investment for human capital.

The Characteristics of Poverty

- Various indicators such as the Human Development Index, the Gender Development Index, and the Gender Empowerment Index help in understanding the levels of living standards within a region. It is also helpful to look at level of housing, literacy, access to popular forms of communication, health, and education.
- Women and indigenous groups have a greater chance of being poor. Poverty is characteristic of the women in the region and indigenous groups that have been marginalized by Latin American societies.
- The informal sector created by a labor surplus plays a large role in Latin

American economies. This type of economic activity is many times considered illegal and consists, in the majority, of female laborers.

Addressing Poverty Reduction

- One approach to poverty reduction has been through microenterprise lending. This form of finance allocation organization targets smaller businesses unable to receive credit through traditional means.
- During the 1980s, poverty and inequality increased in Latin America. Although the wealthy were able to protect themselves from the effects of the debt crisis, the poorer groups suffered from inflation and the effects of stabilization programs.

Notes

1. *Latin American Weekly Report*, 26 May 1998, p. 235, citing study by Lustig and Deutsch.

2. James D. Wolfensohn, remarks to the Board of Governors of the World Bank Group, 1 October 1986 (LEXIS-NEXIS database).

3. D. L. Blackwood and R. G. Lynch, "The Measurement of Inequality and Poverty," *World Development* 22, no. 4 (1994): 567–578.

4. An Inter-American Development Bank study by Nora Lustig and Ruthanne Deutsch, *The Inter-American Development Bank and Poverty Reduction: An Overview* (Washington, D.C.: Inter-American Development Bank, 1998), numbers one in three Latin Americans living in poverty, suggesting that poverty has fallen in the region.

5. Frances Stewart, *Adjustment and Poverty: Options and Choices* (London: Routledge, 1995), 17.

6. George Psacharopoulos et al., *Poverty and Income Distribution in Latin America: The Story of the 1980s*, World Bank Technical Paper no. 351 (Washington, D.C.: World Bank, 1997), 116.

7. Ibid.

8. Ann Helwege, "Poverty in Latin America: Back to the Abyss?" *Journal of Inter-American Studies and World Affairs* 37, no. 3 (Fall 1995): 99.

9. Caroline Moser, "Gender Planning in the Third World: Meeting Practical and Strategic Gender Needs," *World Development* 17, no. 11 (1989): 1799–1825.

10. Helwege, "Poverty in Latin America," 99.

11. Joseph Ramos, "Poverty and Inequality in Latin America: A Neostructuralist Perspective," *Journal of Inter-American Studies and World Affairs* 38, no. 2 (Summer–Fall 1996).

12. Emiliano Ortega, "Evolution of the Rural Dimension in Latin America and the Caribbean," *CEPAL Review* 47 (August 1992): 124.

13. Food and Agriculture Organization of the United Nations, *The State of Food and Agriculture* (Rome: Food and Agriculture Organization of the United Nations, 1994).

14. "Land for the Landless," *The Economist,* 13 April 1996, p. 38.

15. Diana Tussie, *The Inter-American Development Bank*, vol. 4 of *The Multilateral Development Banks* (Ottawa: North-South Institute, 1995), 80.

16. Nora Lustig, *Coping with Austerity* (Washington, D.C.: Brookings Institution, 1995), 2, 31.

17. Data taken from the World Bank, *World Development Report 1995* (New York: Oxford University Press, 1995).

18. Juan Luis Londoño and Miguel Székely, "Distributional Surprises after a Decade of Reforms: Latin America in the Nineties," paper prepared for the annual meeting of the Inter-American Development Bank, Barcelona, March 1997, p. 3.

19. John Sheahan and Enrique Iglesias, "Kinds and Causes of Inequality in Latin America," in *Beyond Trade-Offs: Market Reform and Equitable Growth in Latin America*, ed. Nancy Birdsall, Carol Graham, and Richard Sabot (Washington, D.C.: Brookings Institution Press/Inter-American Development Bank, 1998), 39.

20. Based on a regression of the Gini coefficient to natural resources, level of physical and human capital, land ownership, and educational assets. Londoño and Székely, "Distributional Surprises," 10.

21. Juan Luis Londoño and Miguel Székely, *Persistent Poverty and Excess Inequality: Latin America, 1970–1995*, Office of the Chief Economist, Inter-American Development Bank Working Paper no. 357 (Washington, D.C.: Inter-American Development Bank, 1997).

22. Data for 1985 and 1990 showed the steady climb, at 285 and 361 respectively. Londoño and Székely, *Persistent Poverty*, 34.

23. Ibid.

24. Inter-American Development Bank, *Facing Up to Inequality in Latin America: Economic and Social Progress in Latin America, 1998–1999 Report* (Washington, D.C.: Johns Hopkins University Press/Inter-American Development Bank, 1998), 21.

25. Benedict Clements, "The Real Plan, Poverty, and Income Distribution in Brazil," *Finance and Development*, September 1997, p. 46.

26. Deininger and Squire study as reported in "Slicing the Cake: What Is the Relationship between Inequality and Economic Growth?" *The Economist*, 19 October 1996, p. 2.

27. Carlos F. Toranzo Roca, as quoted by Clifford Kraus, "When Even an Economic Miracle Isn't Enough," *New York Times*, 12 July 1998, p. 3.

28. Sheahan and Iglesias, "Kinds and Causes of Inequality," 48.

29. See, for example, Dani Rodrick, *King Kong Meets Godzilla: The World Bank and the East Asian Miracle*, CEPR Discussion Paper no. 944 (London: Centre for Economic Policy Research, 1994).

30. Michael Carter and Bradford Barham, "Level Playing Fields and Laissez Faire: Postliberal Development Strategy in Inegalitarian Agrarian Economies," *World Development* 24, no. 7 (July 1996): 1133.

31. Sheahan and Iglesias, "Kinds and Causes of Inequality," 52.

32. Inter-American Development Bank, *1995 Report: Overcoming Volatility* (Washington, D.C.: Johns Hopkins University Press/Inter-American Development Bank, 1995), 190. Morely estimated an elasticity of poverty to growth of -2; that is, had the annual growth rates been 1 percent higher during the 1980s, the number of people below the poverty line would have been lower by some 20 percent.

33. McKinsey Global Institute, *Productivity—The Key to an Accelerated Development Path for Brazil 1998* (São Paulo, Brazil: McKinsey and Company, 1998), 45.

34. Inter-American Development Bank, *Latin America after a Decade of Reforms: Economic and Social Progress, 1997 Report* (Washington, D.C: Johns Hopkins University Press/Inter-American Development Bank, 1997), 186.

35. Karin Stahl, "Anti-Poverty Programs: Making Structural Adjustment More Palat-

able," *NACLA Report on the Americas* 29, no. 6 (May-June 1995): 32.

36. Frances Stewart, *Adjustment and Poverty: Options and Choices* (London: Routledge, 1995), 115.

37. *Poverty Reduction and the World Bank: Progress in Fiscal 1996 and 1997* (Washington, D.C.: World Bank, 1998). Available at www.worldbank.org.

38. These factors were highlighted in *Poverty Reduction and the World Bank*, 26.

39. Stewart, *Adjustment and Poverty*, 214.

40. Carol Graham, *Safety Nets, Politics, and the Poor: Transitions to Market Economies* (Washington, D.C.: Brookings Institution, 1994), 33. Chapter 2 describes the employment programs in detail.

41. Stahl, "Anti-Poverty Programs," 32.

42. Graham, *Safety Nets*, 1994.

43. "Urban Renaissance," *IDB Extra*, 1997, 134.

44. "Urban Renaissance," *IDB Extra*, 1997.

45. Marinte Guerguil, "Some Thoughts on the Definition of the Informal Sector," *CEPAL Review* 35 (August 1988): 60.

46. Kate Young, *Planning Development with Women: Making a World of Difference* (New York: St. Martin's, 1993), 85–90.

47. Victor Tokman, "Policies for a Heterogeneous Informal Sector," *World Development* 17, no. 7 (1989): 1067–1076.

48. Studies presented in Victor Tokman, *Beyond Regulation: The Informal Economy in Latin America* (Boulder, Colo.: Lynne Rienner, 1992).

49. Tokman, *Beyond Regulation*, 10.

50. Tokman, "Policies," 1071.

51. "From Sandals to Suits," *The Economist*, 1 February 1997, p. 75.

52. "Making Money from Microcredit," *IDB America*, June 1998, p. 13.

53. Tussie, *The Inter-American Development Bank*, 100.

54. Skip Kaltenheuser, "Fitting Microcredit into a Macro Picture," *Christian Science Monitor*, 5 February 1997, p. 19. More information on microcredit is available at www.microcreditsummit.org.

55. Paul Moseley and David Hulme, "Microenterprise Finance: Is There a Conflict between Growth and Poverty Alleviation?" *World Development* 26, no. 5 (1988): 783–790.

56. Stephen G. Vetter, "The Business of Grassroots Development," *Grassroots Development* 19, no. 2 (1885): 2–12.

57. Taryn Rounds Parry, "Achieving Balance in Decentralization: A Case Study of Education Decentralization in Chile," *World Development* 25, no. 2 (1997): 212.

58. Ibid.

59. Margaret E. Grosh, *Administering Targeted Social Programs in Latin America* (Washington, D.C.: World Bank, 1994).

60. Humberto Pánuco-Laguette and Miguel Székely, "Income Distribution and Poverty in Mexico," in *The New Economic Model in Latin America and Its Impact on Income Distribution and Poverty*, ed. Victor Bulmer-Thomas (New York: St. Martin's, 1996), 207. The reorganization took place June 14, 1995. Laura Randall, ed., *Changing Structure of Mexico: Political, Social and Economic Prospects* (Armonk, N.Y.: M. E. Sharpe, 1996).

61. World Bank, *World Development Report 1995* (New York: Oxford University Press for the World Bank), table 10.

62. Economic Commission for Latin America and the Caribbean, *The Equity Gap: Latin America, the Caribbean, and the Social Summit* (Santiago, Chile: Economic Commission for Latin America and the Caribbean, 1997).

63. Gert Rosenthal, "On Poverty and Inequality in Latin America," *Journal of Inter-American Studies and World Affairs* 38, no. 2–3 (Summer–Fall 1996): 15.

CHAPTER TWELVE

HEALTH POLICY

Investing in People's Future

Hard choices sometimes need to be made between hospital-based urban health care and rural needs. *(Courtesy of Willie Heinz and the Inter-American Development Bank.)*

Addressing poverty and improving human capital in Latin America rest on progress in health and educational systems in the region. As the World Health Organization (WHO) argues, the promotion of health is the process of enabling people to increase their control over improvements in their environment to reach a state of complete physical, mental, and social well-being. Beyond disease reduction, health promotion is critical not only to maintaining a decent quality of life but also to achieving human and social potential. Education is the key to transforming demographic trends and increasing human capital in the region. Education reform will determine Latin America's competitiveness in the global economy as well as the character of democratic political life and a more just economic distribution within each nation. Without a healthy, well-educated citizenry, Latin America will be left behind.

Our next two chapters consider the health and educational deficits in the region and identify strategies for reform. Chapter 12 begins by analyzing the good news and the bad news in the regional health profile. The good news is that substantial progress has been made as measured by health indicators. The bad news is that improvement was stalled by the economic crisis of the 1980s and the new fiscal realities of the region. Smaller public sectors leave less to invest in health and education. Given financial constraints, we then consider ways of organizing health care delivery systems that may be able to do more with less. Efficient and effective delivery of health services is the key to the future well-being of the nearly 507 million residents of the region. Education has faced similar challenges. Chapter 13 will show that although literacy rates in the region measure signs of progress, high rates of repetition and unequal access to education limit the gains from education to society. Innovation in educational policy is critical for Latin American countries to compete in the global arena in the twenty-first century.

Key questions for exploration in this chapter include the following:

- What is the health profile for Latin America? What health conditions most threaten lives in the region?
- How do health needs of women and indigenous groups differ from those of the broader population?
- How do health delivery systems differ in the rural and the urban sectors? Are centrally located urban hospitals a better health investment than rural community health providers?
- How should health care be financed? What is the best balance between government spending and the role of private insurers?

A PROFILE OF HEALTH IN THE REGION

Health must be seen as integrally linked into the human, social, political, and economic development of a country. The opportunities for human development condition the national health profile. Health systems develop in a social context and are further shaped by the political environment. Without political will to provide health services as a basic human right, even the wealthiest of countries will have significant health deficits among the poor. The level of economic develop-

Figure 12.1.   Intersectoral Cooperation: The Health-Development Framework

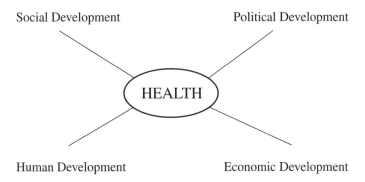

Source: Rosalia Rodriguez-García and Ann Goldman, eds., *The Health-Development Link* (Washington, D.C.: PAHO, 1994), 38.

ment in part determines the social resources available for health care as well as individuals' ability to invest in their own well-being. A poor person has little control over the external environment of open sewage, polluted water and air, or safety from violence. A poor country has limited resources to provide health services and transform the social infrastructure into one that provides basic human needs for all. Avoidable mortality—deaths that could be prevented by improvements in basic health conditions—hover in the 45 percent range in the region. A startling 1.5 million persons under the age of sixty-five are dying each year from avoidable causes.

Health priorities for Latin America include health and the environment (including water supply and sewage disposal); food and nutrition issues; maternal and child health; control and elimination of preventable diseases, with particular attention to lifestyles and risk factors; worker health; substance abuse; AIDS; population control; mental health; and violence. AIDS has now spread to all countries in Latin America, with the risk of transmission highest among the poor. It is estimated that at least 1.3 million adults, or one in 1,000, is infected with HIV. Fifty-two percent of reported AIDS cases in Latin America and the Caribbean are in Brazil, with between 560,000 and 850,000 persons infected, giving Brazil the dubious distinction of ranking second to the United States in terms of AIDS cases in the hemisphere. Transmission is primarily sexual; in Mexico a man having sex with another man faces a one in three chance that the partner is HIV positive. The epidemic is concentrated among the poor. Drug injectors are another group at risk. In Mexico between 3 and 11 percent of IV drug users are infected; in Brazil and Argentina the rate reaches nearly 50 percent. The epidemic has spread to include women, who now account for one-fourth of all reported AIDS cases.[1] In Santos, a city outside São Paulo, a condom social marketing strategy is generating positive results. Supported by USAID and the Ministry of Health, the program aims to use marketing to change social behavior and encourage responsible sexual practices. Box 12.1 further describes social marketing.[2]

BOX 12.1. SOCIAL MARKETING

Social marketing uses commercial marketing techniques to influence social behaviors. Playing to the market, it creates important information about the demand for a given product. People appear to value things they must pay for, even if the payment is very modest. Paying customers demand more from services, making providers more attentive to clients. Advertising campaigns can be used to change the tastes of the target audience to promote socially beneficial choices for society. If marketing can sell Pepsi, why not prophylactics?

Social marketing began in the 1970s as public health professionals realized that programs needed to be attentive to the needs and desires of recipient communities. This technique has since been successfully used in international health programs, especially in the areas of contraceptive distribution and oral rehydration therapy (ORT) for infants. Social marketers follow the four Ps: product, price, place (distribution), and promotion. Products can be tangible items such as condoms or rehydration salts, or services (medical exams and education) and practices (breast feeding). Prices for these products and services are very low, often below production costs, to service the needs of the poor. These low prices are made possible through heavy subsidization. Most programs are funded by organizations such as the U.S. Agency for International Development (USAID), with as much as 80 percent of the costs covered. These programs, which are often run by private providers, work with or alongside government-run programs to promote social health to a broad portion of the general public.

One example of a successful program in Latin America is in Mexico, which has in recent years had a surplus of doctors. Start-up funding has allowed these unemployed doctors to set up health clinics in previously underserved communities. The Fundacion Mexicana para la Planeacion Familiar (MEXFAM), with support from USAID and the International Planned Parenthood Federation, has helped 175 doctors set up clinics in the past ten years. These clinics provide family planning and child health services in small towns and poor urban areas. With subsidies from MEXFAM, after two years the doctor is able to buy the office and medical equipment from MEXFAM for half of its original setup cost. MEXFAM continues to provide contraceptives and training after the two-year period.

Source: Weinreich Communications, *The Social Marketing Place,* http://www.members.aol.com/weinreich/whatis.html; and Population Reports, Johns Hopkins University Population Information 19, no. 4 (November 1991): 14.

Violence, especially domestic violence, has risen to become one of the most serious health problems in urban areas of the region. The leading cause of death in Colombia, for example, is homicide.[3] The explosion of violence sweeping the continent has complex causes. In Colombia and El Salvador it may be linked to historical conflicts over land. Rapid urbanization in the context of huge disparities between rich and poor may exacerbate social violence. Traditional values practiced in the countryside are lost on the new generation of tough urban youth often lured by alcohol and drugs. Rising unemployment associated with globalization may also be a contributing factor. As police capabilities are overwhelmed and judicial systems choked, repression and brutality are more common than prevention and reform. Such violence exacts a high human and economic cost. One World Bank economist estimated that the net accumulation of human capital was cut in half because of the increase in crime and violence since the mid-1980s.[4]

Nonetheless, progress has been made in overall health in the region. Over the period 1960 through 1990 (table 12.1) we can see a dramatic improvement in health in the Latin American region. Life expectancy, a general proxy for health, has improved by more than ten years. Death by diseases most often associated with poverty and deficient living standards—infectious, nutritional, and birth-related diseases—declined significantly from 7.6 deaths per thousand to 2.1 in 1990. The region is going through an **epidemiological transition**, reflecting new causes of death associated with the ills of modern living, which include noninfectious disease such as heart failure and cancer. Accidents and violence as measured by intentional and unintentional lesions are expected to increase. Health systems are easily overwhelmed by confronting traditional and emerging health concerns simultaneously. Health becomes a battle on two fronts: continuing to address the basic health deficit and making progress on new threats such as AIDs, violence, and cardiocare.

There is of course a great deal of diversity in health performance in the region. As can be seen in table 12.2, life expectancy ranges from a low of sixty years in Bolivia to a high of seventy-six in Cuba. Nicaragua and Bolivia are the worst performers on child mortality, although Chile, Cuba, and Colombia have achieved low child mortality rates. Cuba scores high across the board in the number of doctors and hospital beds per 1,000 in the population and the nurse-to-doctor ratio, although Nicaragua and Bolivia are again dismally low. In countries with either the political will or the money, significant strides have been made in creating health systems to treat these diseases. Countries such as Cuba and Costa Rica have gone through an epidemiological transition and have health profiles similar to developed countries. The least developed countries, like Bolivia, have truncated transitions and suffer primarily from infectious diseases, such as malaria, and diseases of deficiency, such as malnutrition. The middle- and high-income countries, such as Ecuador and Brazil, which have begun their epidemiological transition, suffer from an accumulation of both the infectious and deficiency diseases found in the LDCs and, as a result of the demographic transition toward a more urbanized and aging society, also have high levels of emerging, chronic, and degenerative diseases.[5] This situation is known as an **epidemiological backlog**. This double health burden puts a strain on social welfare budgets. These systems must solve the problems of poorer countries while also being challenged by the health concerns of the wealthier world. Table 12.3 classifies countries by disease type, underscoring the prevalence of deficiency and infectious diseases in poor countries.

Table 12.1. Mortality by General Causes in Latin America, 1960–2020

	1960	1970	1980	1990	2000	2010	2020
Life Expectancy at Birth in Years	57.1	61.2	65.4	68.7	71.1	73.2	75
Mortality by Cause (rates per 1,000)							
Infectious, nutritional, and birth-related diseases	7.6	5	2.9	2.1	1.9	1.5	1.2
Non-infectious diseases	4.9	4.7	4.5	3.8	5	6.4	8.1
Intentional and unintentional lesions	0.8	0.8	0.9	0.9	1.1	1.3	1.4

Source: Rafael Lozano, *Cambios en el Perfil Epidemiológico en América Latina: desigualdades, alcances, y retos* (presented at LASA 1997, Guadalajara, Mexico, April 17–19, 1997), 15.

Table 12.2. Health Statistics by Country

Country	Life Expectancy at Birth		Child Mortality Rate per 1,000 Live Births			Doctors per 1,000 Population	Nurse-to-Doctor Ratio	Hospital Beds per 1,000 Population
	1960	*1990*	*1960*	*1975*	*1990*	*1988–92*	*1988–92*	*1985–1990*
Nicaragua	50	62	191	149	106	0.6	0.5	1.8
Honduras	49	67	203	126	62	0.32	1	1.1
Bolivia	43	60	251	205	125	0.48	0.7	1.3
Guatemala	49	64	205	152	84	0.44	2.5	1.7
Ecuador	53	70	174	120	42	1.04	0.3	1.7
Peru	45	65	233	157	73	1.03	0.9	1.5
El Salvador	51	69	188	146	52	0.64	1.5	1.5
Colombia	58	73	132	88	21	0.87	0.6	1.5
Paraguay	64	70	92	70	37	0.62	1.7	1
Chile	55	73	155	68	20	0.46	0.8	3.3
Venezuela	67	72	78	59	26	1.55	0.5	2.9
Argentina	67	72	73	56	26	2.99	0.2	4.8
Uruguay	71	74	55	58	23	2.9	0.2	4.6
Brazil	52	66	179	110	69	1.46	0.1	3.5
Mexico	56	70	148	95	38	0.54	0.8	1.3
Cuba	71	76	49	34	12	3.75	1.7	5
Established Market (EME)	70	76	36	21	11	2.52	2.1	8.3

Source: World Bank, *World Development Report 1993* (New York: Oxford University Press, 1993).

Countrywide data should, however, be interpreted with caution. If you are an affluent Mexican, for example, chances of your baby dying in infancy are 13.4 per 1,000 live births; if you are poor the odds escalate to a tragic 109.76. Rural Peruvian babies are about three times as likely to die as those in Lima. Malnutrition in Ecuador among children under five ranges from 8 to 42.6 percent, depending on the socioeconomic district. A rural inhabitant in Brazil can expect to live twenty fewer years than a wealthy cousin in the city.[6] Divergent rural and urban standards of living result in widely different health profiles. Health ministries must therefore make tough choices about where to invest the nation's health resources. Should investments be made in cities to confront new challenges to health with technologically sophisticated systems? Or should resources be placed in the poorest rural sectors to address traditional threats of disease?

GENDER, ETHNICITY, AND HEALTH

Maternal malnutrition is a leading cause of both maternal and infant mortality. Without adequate prenatal care, an infant will not receive important nutrients for

Table 12.3.   Diseases of the Americas: The Epidemiological Transition

	Poorest Latin American Countries: Bolivia	*Middle Income Latin American Countries: Ecuador*	*High Income Latin American Countries: Brazil*	*Latin American Countries with a Strong Safety Net: Costa Rica/Cuba*	*Developed Countries: USA/Canada*
Deficiency					
Malnutrition	X				
Intestinal Disease	X				
Infectious					
Chagas	X				
Malaria	X	X			
TB	X	X	X		
Respiratory Infections		X	X		
Parasitic					
Influenza				X	X
Pneumonia				X	X
Emerging					
Malaria			X		
Parasitic		X	X		
Cancer					X
Heart Disease				X	
Chronic					
TB					
Tumors					
Malignant Tumors				X	
Pulmonary Infections					X
Degenerative					
Tumors					
Malignant Tumors					
Cerebrovascular				X	
Cancer					X
Congenital					
Heart Disease		X	X		
Diabetics		X	X		
Congenital Anomalies				X	
Heart Attacks					
Birth Defects					X
Environmental					
Accidents		X	X	X	X
Homicides					X
Tumors			X		
Parasitic					

Source: PAHO (1989 and 1993) data and the Ministry of Health, Ecuador.

growth. Breast-feeding by well-nourished mothers transfers needed antibodies to their children to fight viral and bacterial infections such as diarrhea and pneumonia, rashes, and allergies. In urban areas, many women, however, have been substituting more "modern" infant feeding practices for breast-feeding, leading to a decline in infant health.

An important element in health care is a woman's ability to control her own fertility. A Save the Children/Bolivian mothercare project found that women identified their most urgent health problem as having too many children.[7] As women have entered the marketplace in increasing numbers, the opportunity cost of children has risen. As some market women note, customers want to be waited on quickly and not be distracted by crying babies.[8] Use of contraceptives ranges from 60 percent in Brazil to less than 30 percent in Guatemala; demand (including unmet needs) is between 50 and 80 percent.[9] The most widely used method of contraception in the region has been female sterilization. Family planning, however, remains somewhat controversial, given both religious preferences and the position of some multilateral donor agencies. For some indigenous women, the thought of (mostly male) doctors poking inside them prevents them from seeking medical advice on family planning methods. Traditional men sometimes fear that contraception will encourage promiscuous behavior among their wives and daughters. Tragically, unwanted pregnancies are often terminated with self-induced abortions that threaten the lives of the mother or leave deformities in the child should it be born. Some alliance between ethnomedicine (traditional healers) and biomedical practitioners might help alleviate the difficulties in providing health care to indigenous women. Biomedical practitioners need to better understand the role of patient attitudes and responses in improving the delivery of health services in traditional areas. Husbands need to be included in educational efforts at family planning to dispel widely held myths concerning the negative effects of family planning.

The health and nutritional levels of indigenous communities in Latin America are well below national averages. Viral diseases, including influenza, measles, dengue, and respiratory infections, frequently become epidemics under poor sanitary conditions in indigenous communities. Activities such as mining and oil exploration exact high costs in terms of the health of otherwise isolated indigenous groups. In addition to disrupting the environment, workers introduce diseases for which indigenous communities have not developed immunities. In the Amazon Basin countries, the most important challenges to the health of indigenous communities come from the overexploitation of resources. Cultural differences between health care dispensed in hospitals and traditional practices promoted by healers and midwives in indigenous communities also create a health services gap, particularly in practices such as childbirth, which are highly sensitive to custom and tradition. In Guatemala, for example, the maternal mortality rate in the indigenous population is 83 percent higher than the national rate. To be effective, health delivery systems must be sensitive to cultural practices. The 1993 Pan American Health Organization (PAHO) workshop on Indigenous Peoples and Health held in Winnipeg, Canada, set out guidelines for health promotion, advocating community participation, preservation of habitat and traditional lifestyles, evaluation and monitoring of the health status and living conditions of indigenous peoples, and formulation of na-tional health policies to address the problems of indigenous communities. None-theless, as the communiqué initiating the meeting characterized, the health of indigenous peoples is "perhaps the most technically complex and difficult health issue of the day."[10] Interim evaluation of progress on indigenous health care im-provements indicates the need for supplemental funding for NGOs to reach indige-nous populations, improvement of the database on indigenous health concerns, better preparation of health care workers in multicultural communities to attend to the needs and be respectful of the traditional practices of indigenous peoples, and improved dissemination of program efforts to illustrate best case practices for other countries.[11] Policy measures will require patience and perseverance for success.

THE IMPORTANCE OF PRIMARY HEALTH CARE

The first step in improving health indicators and the well-being of citizens is uni-versal access to basic health services. Primary health care (PHC) is the essence of the "Health for All by the Year 2000" (**HFA2000**) strategy adopted at the 1978 Alma Alta joint World Health Organization(WHO)–UNICEF conference and en-dorsed by the WHO Assembly in 1981. The landmark document outlined program-matic health objectives as part of a new model for health care based on comprehensive **primary health care**. These included water, sanitation, food supply, nutrition, mother and child care (MCC), family planning, immunization, control of local diseases, essential drugs, and education. Health for All encourages culturally sensitive plans that employ appropriate treatment and technology. Health should be integrated into national development plans to improve the social and economic development of the community. Education and active participation are seen as the keys to the promotive, preventive, curative, and rehabilitative services of PHC. The primary health care approach is aimed at mobilizing individuals and commu-nities to improve health systems to provide fair and equitable delivery of needed services. The issue of inequality is particularly important in Latin America; PAHO sees overcoming inequality as the major constraint in meeting the goal of universal access to basic health services for the inhabitants of the region.[12]

The strategies for achieving HFA2000 and the subsequent emphasis on PHC are based on three pillars: participation, equity, and intersectoral cooperation. Pri-mary health care emphasizes social justice, a broadly defined concept of health that includes lifestyle and environmental components, intersectoral integration, and community participation. PHC employs a holistic approach, embracing the individual's relationship with community and family. Participation is central to the implementation of effective health plans. It can be viewed as the first step toward the decentralization of local health systems.[14] Equity is threefold: between the first and third worlds, rural and urban areas, and genders. The call for equity is grounded in the fundamental right to health care. Intersectoral cooperation[15] refers to the need to link health and development plans, as seen in PAHO's "health in development" and WHO's "health as a conditionality for economic development" strategies.

Home health agents bring basic services—and hope—to the very poor. *(Courtesy of David Mangurian and the Inter-American Development Bank.)*

Investing in primary health care can at times involve tough choices. In Brazil, the Institute Materno–Infantil de Pernambuco (IMIP) faced such a tough trade-off. IMIP, a winner of a UNICEF award for a child-friendly hospital, had to decide whether to maintain its pediatric intensive care unit or engage in community outreach. With 95 percent of its financing coming from the Brazilian Ministry of Health, it had to match costs to average revenues set by the government. The intensive care unit cost more than the government was willing to pay. Furthermore, the children sent to the unit from all over northeastern Brazil were so sick and malnourished that the mortality rate remained high despite the expensive interventions. A more cost-effective strategy to saving children's lives was pursued: close the intensive care unit and expand the network of small community health posts in slum neighborhoods of the major city of Recife. Indeed, infant mortality declined from 147 to 101 per 1,000 live births in those neighborhoods.[15] Box 12.2 demonstrates another case of effective delivery of preventive health services in Brazil. Local control and local initiative can work to reverse the devastating effects of neglect on children and families in poor rural regions.

> **QUESTION FOR THOUGHT**
>
> Given limited funding, how would you propose that the health care dollar be spent in Latin America? Does focus on primary health care leave Latin America further behind or a step ahead?

Most countries have some elements of PHC in their Ministry of Health (MOH) health care delivery systems and have decreased emphasis on the medicalization of health as well as the engineering model, which saw the body as a machine and good health a question of getting it tuned correctly. However, due primarily to budgetary and political reasons, selective primary health care programs, as opposed to comprehensive PHC programs, have been implemented. Weaker versions, limited to growth monitoring, oral rehydration, breast-feeding, immunization, family planning, food production, and female education, have been the norm. The poor have had an increasing burden of paying for health services out of pocket. With budget cuts, many health posts can no longer provide basic services. In Ecuador, for example, spending on health has come to absorb between 12 to 17 percent of the family budget. Those unable to afford private sector service are left without critically needed curative care and rarely invest in preventive care.[16] Public and private international donor agencies, led in part by WHO and PAHO, can facilitate a broader adoption of PHC programs through partnerships with state and local governments to bridge the fiscal gap.

HEALTH CARE SYSTEMS IN LATIN AMERICA

In addition to choices about the level of sophistication of health care, improvements in health require changes in systems of delivery. The health status of the people of Latin America is affected not only by extant diseases and each country's socioeconomic status but also by institutions and systems established to provide health services for the populations and the environments in which these institutions

BOX 12.2. PREVENTIVE HEALTH CARE IN CEARÁ: REVERSING A HEALTH NIGHTMARE

Prior to decentralization of health care, Ceará, Brazil, had some of the worst health indicators in the region. Fewer than a third of the state's municipal districts had a nurse; most people had never seen a doctor. Infant mortality was twice the Brazilian average, and only one in four children had been vaccinated against measles or polio. A new preventive health care system, called the Health Agent System (Programa de Agentes de Saúde, PAS), radically transformed the health profile of the state. Infant deaths declined 36 percent, vaccination coverage is nearly complete, and each of the districts has a nurse and a public health program. The program cost was about $1.50 per person served—markedly lower than the $80 per capita cost of Brazil's existing health care system. How was this minor medical miracle—with such tangible gains to so many Brazilians—accomplished?

Starting PAS as an employment-generating program in the drought-stricken Northeast in 1987, the state committed to funding it permanently in 1989. The program supported a small army of public health agents who went from house to house (sometimes, in more distant areas, traveling by bicycle, donkey, or canoe) to teach families good health practices. Agents were paid more than teachers or the wage paid to male agricultural labor, although this sometimes did not amount to the national minimum wage. In an area in which nonagricultural opportunities were rare, the jobs were seen as highly prestigious positions. The work was rewarded by warm public support, as the effects were demonstrable to the community. Standards were high. Unlike many government jobs, these were without tenure, and the community (especially those not selected as agents) was told to report lax behavior on the part of the extensionists. People were told to expect a visit once a month to their homes, and for health agents to be a part of the communities in which they worked. Nurse supervisors brought in to train agents and administer the program were, through their success, accorded more control, respect, and admiration than they had received in poorly run city hospitals. Administratively, the program was efficient and cost-effective.

At first agents confronted mistrust from rural inhabitants unaccustomed to government programs and comfortable with traditional medicines and faith healers. Agents used curative tasks such as oral rehydration techniques for a baby seemingly near death to convince mothers of the benefits of modern medicine. With the baby playing happily a few hours after nearly dying, the mother was more amenable to hearing about the benefits of breast-feeding, hygienic food preparation, and water filtration systems. Agents developed a bond of trust with often lonely and overburdened mothers, sometimes helping with cooking or child care. The decentralization of services and the empowerment of 7,300 never before salaried rural women through training and extension services have truly transformed the health profile in Ceará.

Source: This box is based on the study by Judith Tendler, *Good Government in the Tropics* (Baltimore: Johns Hopkins University Press, 1997), 21–45.

operate. The challenges to Latin American health care delivery systems are numerous and require a redefinition of the traditional health care system. Old or accumulated challenges include insufficient coverage of the population, poor technical quality, inadequate patient referral, and deficient management of institutions. New challenges to health delivery systems are composed of cost escalation, financial insecurity, and dealing with technological expansion in light of their opportunity costs in terms of primary health care.

Rural health care poses particular challenges for 25 percent of the hemisphere's population. In some rural areas, health care can be a four- to eight-hour bus ride or a one- to two-hour walk away. Between 50 and 80 percent of all health expenditures go to hospitals located near urban centers. Inaccessible health facilities make prenatal and other types of preventive primary health care particularly problematic. Shifting from hospital-based to community-based health systems can help direct resources toward the needs of the local population rather than urban patterns of demand. Although a hospital has the advantage of being a physically distinct unit in which health services can be coordinated under one roof, it can also be a center of power and influence that drains resources from community health systems. Major resources

> **QUESTION FOR THOUGHT**
>
> Go to the PAHO website at www.paho.org or to the Center for International Health Information site at www.cihi.com. Select two countries, one a relatively poor country (perhaps Guatemala) and the other a relatively affluent country (such as Chile). How do the specific health problems and risks differ? How are health services organized? What do you see as the health priorities for each country?

may be tied up in plant, equipment, and services that come at an opportunity cost to meeting people's primary health care needs. Unless the hospital is integrated into a community health care system, when patients are discharged they may find little continuity of care and suffer from a fragmentation of health services.[17] Health care must extend into the community.

How health care is provided varies across the region. Although each Latin American country has a unique mixture of social security facilities, private practitioners, and government ministries responsible for health, generalizations can be made. Health care systems have two service factors: finance and delivery of service. Financing refers to how, and by whom, services are paid for. Delivery refers to the actual provision of services. Each factor can be provided either by the public or by the private sector. For example, financing could be public, through universal health insurance, but rely on the services of private practitioners. Alternatively, some financing—especially for the poor—might be public, with a mix of public hospitals and private providers. In Cuba, both financing and provision are public. The Costa Rican model is also largely public, with its nearly universal state coverage, although private sector services are available. Paraguay and Argentina are closer to the U.S. model, which is a mixture of private health insurance that includes out of pocket expenditures and public resources. The United States is a pure example of this model. In Brazil, public financing is nearly universal and the services are contracted out.

Moving from financing to delivery of health services, the most common structure in Latin America is a mixed system. Three main health sectors in Latin America are present: the Social Security Institutes (SSI)[18] (*cajas de seguro social*) for formal sector employees, the private sector for those who can afford private insurance and those who are uninsured and choose to seek private services, and the Ministry of Health (MOH) for the poor. The formal sector finances and provides health care services to its employees. The MOH is responsible for the coordination of health care service delivery for approximately 70 percent of the population but has only approximately 40 percent of the financing.

Figure 12.2 illustrates the breakdown of health coverage for Bolivia in 1992. The Ministry of Social Provision and Public Health orchestrates curative and preventive care through 101 general and regional hospitals, 418 health centers, and 910 rural health outreach posts. Although it is officially responsible for covering 75 percent of the population, it reaches only about 38 percent. The Bolivian Social Security Institute covers formal sector employees with pension, sickness and maternity, work injuries, and family allowance programs. The Social Security Institute operates its own health facilities in the urban areas and frequently uses private contractors for users outside the cities. Private health providers cover about 5 percent of the population, with another 4–5 percent receiving health care through the 500 nongovernmental organizations at work in Bolivia. Foreign donations and foreign loans compose roughly 22.5 percent of the public health budget, with user fees covering 9.4 percent and central government budget and transfers making up the balance. USAID provided over 5 percent of the total central government financing in 1991, with other funds coming from the World Bank and the United Nations Development Program.[19]

Figure 12.2.   Bolivian Health Care Coverage, 1992

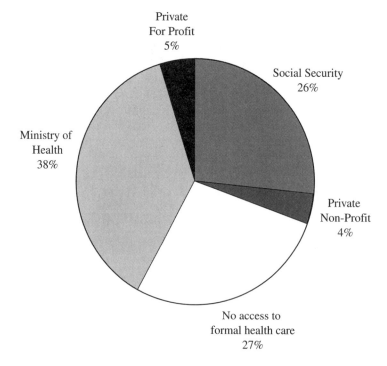

Source: Center for International Health Information, *Country Health Profile/Bolivia, December 1996.* Available on-line at www.cihi.com.

There are numerous problems with this common Latin American health care model. Because many institutions provide similar services to different client bases, there is unnecessary duplication of services, especially of costly high-tech items. Services are concentrated in urban areas. There are concerns of quality, especially for the lower classes who utilize the resource-poor MOH facilities. Health care reflects broader social patterns in the region, defined by a high degree of class inequality. Better use of health resources will require a restructuring of the delivery systems in the region while tackling tough issues of social inequality.

REFORMING HEALTH SERVICE DELIVERY: THE CHALLENGE TO POLICY

Health care policy is determined by a number of critical choices a nation faces. How much should people pay for health care? How should the trade-off between high-quality, sophisticated treatment and increased access to basic health and nutrition be resolved? Should health services be provided by the public or the private sector? How should governments resolve the tension between hospital-based urban care and comprehensive rural coverage? What kind of health insurance schemes will meet society's goals? Policies to improve health care in Latin America include improving the choices households face, transforming the pattern of public spending on health, and changing the structure of the health care market.

Households are constrained by income and education in the choices they make about health care. Governments should consider pursuing policies that improve choices, particularly among the poor. This includes expanded investments in the link between education and health, particularly for girls. Girls in the region play important roles in the care of younger siblings. An example of public education is a radio program in Bolivia directed toward eight- to thirteen-year-old children providing lessons on food preparation, sanitation, diarrhea prevention and oral hydration, cholera, and immunizations to improve family health practices. Women are an important target group. The pattern of public spending might be oriented toward the financing of public health interventions and community health services that deliver the greatest improvements in health care per dollar spent, rather than expensive investments in tertiary care for the wealthy. The use of health promoters—members of the community trained and practicing under a doctor's supervision—can extend the medical reach. Promoters engage in preventive medicine and health education, as well as carrying small medical kits to deal with wounds, infections, and simple medical problems such as diarrhea. As members of the community themselves, health promoters have the trust of their clients, travel to remote areas, and often help bridge the gap between modern medicine and traditional healing practices.

The direction of health policy should in part be shaped by the local demand for health care. The perceived need for medical care—generally determined by medical experts—may diverge from the demand for health care based on a community's assessment of its own health conditions and socioeconomic circumstances. Demand for health care might be influenced by cultural norms and traditional medical practices, income, and prices that include not only monetary fees paid for services but also the travel time and forgone income to seek care.[21] Perception of illness also varies across cultures. If an illness becomes a way of life for a community, fewer members might seek treatment than in a community in which the same disease is rare. Tourists, for example, rarely forget their malaria shots and pills or their diarrhea remedies; inhabitants in some tropic communities may simply find these diseases part of the natural cycle of life—and sometimes death. Education and literacy also condition the demand for health care. Sadly, what people don't know can kill them. Estimating local demand for health services is important to direct funds away from underutilized services and toward unmet needs. A process of health education at the community level can facilitate grassroots participation in the determination of the demand for health.

PAYING THE BILL FOR HEALTH

Who should pay for health services? Traditionally, health services in Latin American have been controlled by central governments. Consistent with the changes of the neoliberal model, in Latin America there has been a move to limit governmental responsibility for health. There are three variants to this reform: privatization, decentralization, and contracting. Privatization has been especially popular in reference to the Social Security Institutes, as seen in Chile. Decentralization involves the devolution of previously centralized responsibilities to the local level. In Chile, responsibility for health care was brought down to the municipal level; the budget for primary health care and 50 percent of the health staff were transferred from the national health service to local governments. Chilean workers, with a mandatory 7 percent deduction from their paychecks, were given a choice of enrolling in either public or private health insurance plans.[21] To overcome limited Ministry of Health budgets and improve equity, participation, and intersectoral cooperation, Colombia's decentralized contracting system appears to be a viable model for reforming Latin American health care systems. Multinational companies such as Aetna and Cigna are entering the Latin American market as partners to local providers of private health insurance. In Argentina, international investors are funding the development of Excell Corporation, the booming HMO insurance enterprise of Juan Navarro, the entrepreneur we met in Chapter 1 of this text. Argentina's move to market-based providers has been facilitated by a $350 million loan from the World Bank to restructure health care debt in the interest of improving competitiveness in the sector. Box 12.3 discusses reforms in Mexican health care in greater depth.

In addition to the question of who should pay for health services, the question of "how much" arises. Given fiscal constraints, some evidence suggests that even the poor can and should pay for at least a part of services rendered. The very poor can be given vouchers to cover expenses, but payment for service sets up greater accountability at the local level. In some areas user fees have been introduced to stretch scarce public resources in the health field. Some research indicates that even the poor are willing to pay for health services, if the introduction of fees is accompanied by an improvement in quality.[22] In cases such as El Salvador, where user fees have been instituted, evidence suggests that cost was an inconsequential factor in determining why rural residents did not seek health care.[23] The additional income can be used to increase the stock and variety of effective drug treatments.

In contrast to tax-funded "free" health services from the central government, payment at the local level establishes a direct relationship between quality of services delivered and fair compensation. It may encourage cost savings and more efficient delivery of health services.

Nevertheless, some third world medical experts are wary of user fees, especially in very poor areas where barter practices and lack of cash income limits

> **QUESTION FOR THOUGHT**
>
> The following table gives data on spending on health care in selected countries in the Western Hemisphere. Given the social and economic priorities we have addressed thus far in this text, is Latin America investing enough in health care?

the ability to pay for health services. User fees can also be seen as a form of regressive tax by which the poor pay proportionately more of their income for health than the rich. Box 12.4 illustrates a public–private initiative in Guatemala where fincas owners and workers share costs. Unfortunately, there may be few alternatives. With a fixed budget for public health, governments must make tough choices about the allocation of resources. Market-oriented reforms may be needed as a key element of system overhauls. Cost-effectiveness is a criteria that guides many decisions in the health care field.

The market, however, is not enough. Some services (e.g., aerial spraying to reduce dengue carrying mosquitoes) would simply not take place without government. The market alone is not sufficient as an allocator of health services. Without proper state guidance and oversight, the market alone often fails to provide equity and, in many cases, does not yield the expected improvements in efficiency. Even insurance magnate Navarro himself notes the need for market regulation in managed care to provide a framework for prices and services.[24] The market for health services involves a complicated array of interconnected markets, including health care professionals, pharmaceuticals, medical equipment, and education. Market failures in health delivery bedevil sophisticated industrial economies.[25] Marketization of health care may also lead to a fragmentation of services.[26] In Chile, for example, as funding chased the quantity of services offered, quality suffered. Decentralization negatively affected the excellent preventive care that had traditionally characterized the Chilean system, in which funding was targeted to curative as opposed to preventive purposes.[28] Furthermore, as workers were given a choice between private and public plans, the healthier participants were drawn to the private sector; those unable to get coverage from risk-averse private insurers were left on the public rolls. Finally, marketization is unlikely to work for those most severely affected by the health crisis in Latin America: the poor, particularly the indigenous, outside the market economy.

The challenge for policy in Latin America is to achieve a workable balance between private sector participation and public sector control to address critical health challenges in the region. It is unlikely that the state or the private sector

BOX 12.3.   REFORM OF MEXICAN HEALTH CARE

While the overall health of the Mexican people has improved significantly, including an increase in life expectancy from 62 to 70 years from 1980 to 1994, compared with industrial economies there is considerable room for improvement. Modern health problems of Mexico's NAFTA neighbors coexist with the epidemiological characteristics of low-income countries. Mexicans still face problems of infectious diseases, malnutrition, and concerns related to insufficient mother and infant care, while simultaneously confronting the needs of a more urbanized and aging population. Challenges to the Mexican health system include extending coverage, particularly in rural areas; reducing disparities in health status among regions; responding to the needs of a more urban and higher-income group; and preparing for the coming needs of an elderly population. Systemic reform is crucial to meeting divergent challenges.

Mexico's health system is segmented into various social security schemes covering insured workers in the formal sector, public health services provided by the Ministry of Health, and a private sector that is largely unregulated. Those falling in the public sector are a heterogeneous group including rural inhabitants and those in marginal urban zones. Some in the social security sector overlap, also using private sector services; provision for the poor is clearly separated from that for the working class and the rich. In reality some 10 million Mexicans have access to little or no health care. Coordination between the different segments of the system is typically low, resulting in a duplication of services. There have been few systemic incentives to improve efficiency or extend coverage.

Improving equity in health services is a goal of the Mexican government. Deficiencies in infrastructure, lack of trained health professionals, long waiting times, large distances to services, lack of medication at clinics, and poor supervision are common complaints. Deficient public health services force the poor to spend meager savings on vital care. As a proportion of their income, the bottom 40 percent of the population spends 5 percent, as opposed to 3 percent in the upper half of the income distribution. Mexico allocates between 5.0 and 6.5 percent of GDP on health care, an amount within the normal range given its income level.[27] The problem in Mexico is not necessarily the level of spending but rather the large unmet needs and regional disparities in the health system.

The Mexican health system may exhibit tendencies from the worst of two options in health care, relying on elements of the public integrated model and the private contract model. Much of the population falls under the national health system, and the social insurance schemes are subject to the quasi-monopoly power of providers, with no effective consumer choice. Because the provider of services is also the regulator, supervision and quality control are erratic. The private sector of the market must attend to those dissatisfied with public services.

Table 12.A.   Health Care Spending

	Per Capita	% of GDP
U.S.	$4,403	14.1
Argentina	675	7.3
Chile	364	6.2
Uruguay	318	5.7
Venezuela	293	6.5
Brazil	288	5.8
Mexico	171	3.8

Source: The Wall Street Journal, 6 August 1998.

Systemic reforms aim to increase public access, make service provision more efficient, and contain future cost escalation. One element of the reform is to bring informal sector workers with prepayment abilities—those in small firms and family businesses—into the social security scheme. A voluntary affiliation scheme will allow unaffiliated individuals to buy into the social security plan. The plan allows for user choice of primary physicians. Regional decentralization is also being pursued to better meet local health demands. It is designed to reduce duplication of services at the national and local levels while addressing equity through a formula for funding that accounts for health needs, poverty, and financial capacity of state governments. Nonetheless, experience shows that decentralization should be phased in gradually to avoid a deterioration of services in poorer regions. Ensuring that local providers meet national standards will be the responsibility of the National Health Council (Consejo Nacional de Salud, CNS) and the Ministry of Health. A program targeted to those in extreme poverty financed by federal transfers is focused on twelve primary health services selected for their cost-efficient nature. This program benefited some 6 million people by 1997. The federal government will maintain the normative, coordination, planning, and evaluation functions under the new health plan.

The ambitious reform of the health care sector embarked upon by the Mexican government creates the potential for better delivery of health services to millions of Mexicans. In the new health model, preventive strategies dominate over curative approaches, covering the life cycle from reproductive health through aging. Success, however, will depend on the political will to overcome resistance to vested interests in the old, inefficient system of delivery.

Source: The Reform of the Mexican Health Care System, OECD Economic Surveys: Mexico (Paris: Organization for Economic Cooperation and Development, 1998).

alone will be able to meet what are seen as the ten common and urgent health problems faced by health institutions in the Americas:[29]

- health and the environment (including water supply and sewage disposal)
- childhood and nutrition
- maternal and child health
- control and elimination of preventable diseases, paying particular attention to lifestyles and risk factors
- workers' health
- substance abuse
- AIDS
- population control
- mental health
- violence

Partnerships among governments, multilateral lending agencies, and the nongovernmental community represent the key to health sector reform. It is important to keep in mind that health care policies must be designed not only for nations but also for multiethnic communities within nations that may have differing health needs. Participation of communities with different traditional practices is critical in the design of health care policies.

BOX 12.4.   PRIVATE PROVISION OF RURAL HEALTH SERVICES: GUATESALUD

Integration of health services into a network of health-related public agencies such as agricultural extension, education, employment, and public works may reduce costs, decrease duplication of services, and improve delivery systems. Guatesalud, the Guatemalan Association for the Promotion of Rural Health, is a nonprofit agency that works with the private sector to provide a kind of "peasants HMO" for agricultural workers. Begun in 1989, Guatesalud operates on payments from both the owners of farms (or fincas) and the workers themselves. The finca owner commits to establishing a clinic, stocking the initial inventory of medicines, and paying for the training of a local part-time health worker called a health promoter. The finca owner pays a flat fee to Guatesalud each month as well as the salary of the health promoter; users pay for recurrent costs and the twice-monthly doctor's visits. Doctors meet with patients, provide ongoing training to the promoter, and replenish the stock of medicines. Medicines are sold to clients above cost but at about half the price from a pharmacy. The finca owner pockets the profits on the medicines and the doctor's fees. Among Guatesalud's 400,000 clients are workers on coffee, banana, and sugar cane farms. The service has been effective in dealing with treatment of diarrheal illnesses, respiratory infections, tuberculosis, cholera, and malaria, as well as providing improving water quality control and sanitation and enhancing health education, especially in family planning, child immunization, deworming, and vitamin A supplements for children under five.

Source: Private Initiatives for Primary Health Care, a project funded by USAID. Information available at www.jsi.com/intl.init.

Key Concepts

Epidemiological backlog	Epidemiological transition	HFA2000 Primary health care

Chapter Summary

Health Care

- Health is an essential component of human development. In Latin America, there was an improvement in health indicators from 1960 through 1990. However, each Latin American country still faces critical health matters.
- The World Health Organization has promoted a comprehensive primary health care plan known as the HFA2000 that would include participation, equity, and intersectoral cooperation. However, budget constraints force government to make tough choices when investing in primary health care.
- One of the major determinants of health performance in Latin America is the lack of adequate institutions and systems under which health care programs

operate. Though each country has its own system of delivering health care, the most common is a mixed delivery system made up of Social Security Institutes for formal sector employees, the private sector, and a Ministry of Health for the poor.

- Policies to improve health care in Latin America must include improving the choices available to households, changing the patterns of public financing to include local demand for health care, and finding a balance between the public and private sectors' roles in health care.

Notes

M. Holly Peirce, Ph.D. (Colby College graduating class of 1990), collaborated in the conceptualization and the writing of this chapter.

1. World Health Organization, *Report on the Global HIV/AIDS Epidemic, June 1998* (Geneva: UNAIDS, 1998). Available at www.who.int/emc-hiv.

2. USAID Congressional Presentation Document (CPD), Brazil, US FY 1999. Available at www.info.usaid/pubs/cp99/br.htm. U.S. agencies must present past program achievements and new fiscal years objectives to Congress in the spring of each fiscal year to justify its annual budget. An agency's CPD is a good source of information on U.S. policy.

3. Pan American Health Organization, *Strategic and Programmatic Orientations, 1995–1998*, presented at the Inter-American Meeting, Washington, D.C., 25–27 April 1995. Available at www.paho.org.

4. Robert L. Ayres, *Crime and Violence as Development Issues in Latin America* (Washington, D.C.: World Bank, 1998).

5. Emerging diseases are new diseases such as Lyme's disease; chronic diseases develop slowly and persist over a period of time and are generally related to lifestyle; and degenerative diseases involve decay of the structure or function of tissue.

6. Pan American Health Organization, *Strategic and Programmatic Orientations, 1995–1998*.

7. Barbara Kwast, "Reeducation of Maternal and Peri-natal Mortality in Rural and Peri-urban Settings: What Works?" *European Journal of Obstetrics and Gynecology and Reproductive Biology* 609 (1996): 49.

8. Sidney Choque Schuler and Ruth Choque Schuler, "Misinformation, Mistrust, and Mistreatment: Family Planning among Bolivian Market Women," *Studies in Family Planning* 25 (1994): 214.

9. Miriam Krawczyk, "Women in the Region: Major Changes," *CEPAL Review* 49 (April 1993).

10. Pan American Health Organization, *PAHO Resolution V: Health of Indigenous Peoples,* series HSS/SILOS, 34 (Washington, D.C.: Pan American Health Organization, 1993). Available at www.paho.org.

11. Anonymous, "Health of Indigenous Peoples," *Pan American Journal of Public Health* 2, no. 25 (1997): 357–362.

12. Visit PAHO's website at www.paho.org to read more about PAHO's goals and strategic plans.

13. Pan American Health Organization, *Implementation of the Global Strategy: Health for All by the Year 2000,* vol. 3 (Washington, D.C.: PAHO, 1993), 10.

14. Also referred to as multisectoral cooperation or collaboration and the health-development link.

15. "Cost Information and Management Decision in a Brazilian Hospital," *World Development Report* (1993): 60.

16. World Bank, *Poverty Reduction and the World Bank: Progress in Fiscal 1996 and 1997*. Available at www.worldbank.org.

17. World Health Organization, *Integration of Health Care Delivery: Report of a WHO Study Group*, WHO Technical Report Series 861 (Geneva: WHO, 1996), table 5, "The Role of the Hospital in the District Health System."

18. It is important to remember that in most cases we are talking about more than one Social Security Institute. Often each public sector will have its own insurance fund and facilities, leading to unnecessary duplication within the sector, not to mention across sectors.

19. Center for International Health Information, *Country Health Profile/Bolivia* (Arlington: Center for International Health Information, December 1996). Available at www. cihi.com.

20. Catherine Overholt and Margaret Saunders, *Policy Choices and Practical Problems in Health Economics: Cases from Latin America and the Caribbean*, Economic Development Resources Series (Washington, D.C.: World Bank, 1996).

21. For an overview of the evolution of the Chilean health care system, see Jorge Jimenez de la Jara and Thomas J. Bossert, "Chile's Health Sector Reform: Lessons from Four Reform Periods," in *Health Sector Reform in Developing Countries: Making Health Development Sustainable*, ed. Peter Berman (Cambridge: Harvard University Press, 1995), 199–214.

22. Harold Alderman and Victor Lavy, "Household Responses to Public Health Services: Cost and Quality Tradeoffs," *World Bank Research Observer* 11, no. 1 (February 1996): 3–22.

23. Ricardo Britan and Keith McInnes, *The Demand for Health Care in Latin America*, Economic Development Institute Seminar Paper no. 46 (Washington, D.C.: World Bank, 1993).

24. David Swafford, "A Healthy Trend: Health Care Reform in Latin America," *Latin Finance* 83 (December 1996).

25. William C. Hsiao, "Marketization—The Illusory Magic Pill," *Health Economics* 3 (1994): 351–357.

26. World Health Organization, *Integration of Health Care Delivery*.

27. Pan American Health Organization, "Mexico," in *Health in the Americas*, vol. 2 (Washington, D.C.: Pan American Health Organization, 1998), 370.

28. World Health Organization, *Integration of Health Care Delivery*.

29. Adapted from Yvette M. Delph, "Health Priorities in Developing Countries," *Journal of Law, Medicine, & Ethics* 21, no. 1 (1993): 18.

EDUCATION POLICY

The Source of Equitable, Sustainable Growth

Education of indigenous children presents special challenges of language and culture. *(Courtesy of the Inter-American Development Bank.)*

Education is seen as the key to promoting equitable, sustainable growth in Latin America. Education raises the level of human capital, enhancing a nation's productivity. Reducing poverty rests upon upgrading basic skills as well as increasing the number of technologically sophisticated workers in the economy. A more informed citizenry is better able to participate in democratic decision making, demanding that government be accountable to the people. A better-educated populace will make more informed decisions about health and family planning, and it can participate more fully in environmentally sustainable development practices.

Few dispute the promise of education in enhancing the quality of life in Latin America, yet the record is dismal by nearly any standard. Although there have been gains in universal access, quality suffers. Segments of the population are excluded from higher education by a primary and secondary school system that encourages repetition and dropping out rather than excellence. Public primary education has been emaciated as dollars are funneled into public university systems. Teachers are poorly trained and managed. Poor statistics provide little guidance or incentive for reform.

This chapter discusses the discouraging state of education in the region and assesses efforts and prospects for reform. Questions we will explore include the following:

- What is the current evidence on educational performance in Latin America?
- What are the causes of the **educational deficit** in the region?
- What is the role of the market in educational reform?
- What other structural reforms are necessary to improve educational performance in the region?

THE RECORD: EDUCATIONAL ACHIEVEMENTS AND DEFICITS

Education in Latin America has made great strides in recent decades, increasing access to segments of the population that previously had no formal schooling. As shown in table 13.1, literacy rose on average from 74 to 87 percent from 1970 through 1994, although the lows of about 56 percent in Guatemala and about 70 percent in El Salvador and Honduras are cause for great concern. Table 13.2 shows that enrollments in preschool programs rose from 2 percent in 1960 to 17 percent in 1990. Enrollment rates at the primary school level grew by nearly 50 percent, placing 90 nearly percent of age-eligible starters in the classroom. Two-thirds of secondary-age children are now in the classroom, as opposed to just over one-third in 1960. Opportunities for higher education have been extended to four times as many students of the 1990s as compared to the 1960s. The diversification of the postsecondary educational network has expanded to include polytechnic training institutes, traditional universities, and new universities (public and private). Through the explosion of the Internet as well as international exchanges, universities have become linked to their international counterparts, spurring internal reorganization of faculties and upgrading of degrees and skill bases. Region-wide networks of private research centers such as FLACSO, or the Facultad Latinoamericana de Ciencias Sociales, entirely separate from the universities, have also flourished, producing an important body of scholarship on Latin America, in part through funding from international donor agencies such as the Ford Foundation.[1]

But these successes are not nearly enough in today's global economy. Education in Latin America is deficient. Compared to other regions of the world, the 4.2 years of schooling Latin American children receive is roughly half that of their counterparts in the United States, Japan, and Germany and two-thirds of those in the Asian newly industrialized countries, or NICs.[2] Half the students in Latin America never complete sixth grade.[3] A large proportion of the region's population between the ages of twenty and twenty-four has fewer than ten years of schooling—the level considered necessary to lead to employment generating acceptable levels of well-being. More than three-quarters of those from poor households will leave home without education sufficient to meet the demands of modern society.[4] Despite the fact that one out of ten persons in the continent is estimated to have some form of a disability, little attention is paid to their educational needs. Rural migrant workers' children are rarely incorporated into educational systems. There is a radical separation between the region's educational systems and its growing development needs in competitive, open democracies.

Table 13.1.   Adult Literacy Rate

Country	Adult Literacy Rate (%)	
	1970	1994
Chile	89	95
Costa Rica	88	95
Argentina	93	96
Uruguay	93	97
Panama	81	91
Venezuela	75	91
Mexico	74	89
Colombia	78	91
Brazil	66	83
Ecuador	72	90
Cuba	87	95
Peru	71	88
Paraguay	80	92
Guyana	n/a	n/a
El Salvador	57	71
Bolivia	57	83
Honduras	53	72
Guatemala	44	56
Nicaragua	n/a	n/a
Latin America average	74	87

Source: United Nations Development Program, *Human Development Report, 1997* (New York: Oxford University Press, 1997), 146–148.

Table 13.2.   Net Enrollment Rates by Level of Education

Level of Education	1960	1970	1980	1990	1992
Preschool (ages 0–5)	2.4	3.3	7.8	16.7	17.4
Primary (ages 6–11)	57.7	71.0	82.9	87.1	87.5
Secondary (ages 12–17)	36.3	49.8	62.9	66.2	68.0
Tertiary (ages 18–23)	5.7	11.6	24.1	26.9	25.4

Source: Jeffrey Puryear, Inter-American Dialogue homepage at www.preal.cl.
Note: Net enrollment rate = number of students (regardless of age) divided by population of same age group.

Performance varies widely by country. Table 13.3 provides a regional score-card for educational performance. Cuba, Uruguay, Guyana, and Costa Rica rank in the top twenty of global developing country performers as measured by the **educational performance index** (EPI) of Oxfam, an international NGO. This index captures the extent of educational deprivation by incorporating measures of enroll-ment, gender equity, and completion rates. Bolivia, the Dominican Republic, Nica-ragua, Honduras, Colombia, El Salvador, and Guatemala don't even make it into the group of the global top fifty, finding themselves in the company of countries such as Vietnam, Nigeria, and India. What is perhaps most intriguing about this index is the lack of correlation between per capita income ranks and the EPI index. Colombia, for example, has an EPI rank of 68, but its per capita income rank is 23. This negative difference indicates that despite having a relatively high level of wealth for a developing country, it has fallen behind in educational performance. This might be contrasted to Nicaragua—also a poor performer by the educational index, but doing relatively better than its per capita income level would indicate, with a positive difference of 12. This divergence between income levels and educa-tional performance suggests that educational outcomes are driven by more than simply money. How educational systems are organized, the quality of inputs, and the political will behind reform efforts influence how many students stay in school and for how long.

The weak relationship between income and educational outcomes indicates that *how* money is spent is as important as *how much* is spent. On average Latin American nations spend 4 percent of GNP on education, but spending is dispropor-tionately concentrated at the university level. In contrast to the Asian NICs, which allocate 1.5 percent of GNP for primary education, Latin American nations spend 1.1 percent of GNP on primary schooling. If a goal is global competitiveness, Latin America must devise a way for educational outcomes to exceed expenditures. With other budget items claiming public resources, 4 percent of GNP translates into approximately $143 per capita. In contrast, developed countries, with higher GDPs, are spending approximately $1,089 per student.

Public spending on education fell during the lost decade of the 1980s in twelve of the eighteen countries in the region.[5] The structural adjustment policies of the period forced ministries to cut back on spending—including investments in educa-tion. Nicaragua spends five times as much paying debts as it does teaching its

Table 13.3.   Educational Performance Index

Country	EPI Rank among LDCs	Per Capita Income Rank/LDCs	Difference
Cuba	5	50	45
Uruguay	10	20	10
Guyana	16	53	37
Costa Rica	18	25	7
Mexico	21	18	−3
Chile	24	13	−11
Panam	31	24	−7
Venezuela	35	17	−18
Paraguay	37	46	9
Argentina	41	15	−26
Ecuador	46	34	−12
Brazil	48	32	−16
Peru	50	44	−6
Bolivia	54	56	2
Dominican Republic	58	38	−20
Nicaragua	59	71	12
Honduras	62	63	1
Colombia	68	23	−45
El Salvador	69	58	−11
Guatemala	88	48	−40

Source: Oxfam, *Education Now,* available at www.oxfam.org.

children. Despite the goal of improving competitiveness, structural adjustment has also had negative effects on teacher salaries and class size in some countries. Mexico's teachers in 1993 made 40 percent of their 1981 salaries; those in El Salvador fell to 32 percent of the 1980 level by 1992. Chile, Colombia, and Uruguay run counter to this trend, increasing teacher salaries to attract competent professionals.[6] Short-term budget balancing measures will have long-term consequences in terms of the future productivity in the region. Redressing the educational deficit is critical to new political and economic opportunities.

UNEQUAL EDUCATION

Rather than promoting opportunity and class mobility, education has perpetuated inequality in Latin America. Primary and secondary schooling continue to be segregated by class. The poorest 20 percent of the population are allocated 16 percent of total public spending on education while the richest 20 percent receive a share of 24 percent.[7] At the Santiago Summit of the Americas, the region's leaders characterized education's split personality, noting that "students from the region's top private schools perform at levels comparable to schools in industrialized countries. Public school students, in contrast, perform dismally by any standard. Latin America's future will be bleak until all its children are provided real opportunities for decent education."[8] Public funds have flowed disproportionately to the upper class, reflecting elite political power. Wealthy Latin Americans wanted world-class universities. Private producers could not meet this need, because university systems require costly investments in faculties, libraries, and laboratories. In response to powerful constituents' demands, governments chose to expand secondary and higher education, leaving little left over for the primary level. The best universities in the region are public (and often free)—but it takes a high-priced private education to pass the matriculation tests for admission.

Neglected, primary education in Latin America is plagued by a high rate of **grade repetition.** Of the 9 million six- or seven-year-olds entering first grade in the region, approximately 4 million fail the first time around. In total, 29 percent of all primary students repeat their grade annually. As shown in table 13.4, a startling 1 percent of Brazilians reach the sixth grade without repeating. Latin America spends U.S.$2.5 billion—or nearly one-third of total public expenditure on primary education in the region—teaching repeaters. High repetition, especially in the lowest grades, is mainly an indicator of inadequate learning, prompted in large part by the low quality of inputs into the system.[9] Reducing repetition rates would release resources for new educational opportunities.

With primary school enrollments exploding from 50 percent of age-eligible children to nearly 90 percent from 1960 to 1990, facilities were overrun with students.[10] Latin America has the highest proportion of workers in developing economies with some primary education but is second to sub-Saharan Africa with the lowest number of workers with some secondary education.[11] Nearly all children in South America start school, but by the fifth year 40 percent of the poor have dropped out while 93 percent of the rich remain in school. The figures for Central America are more dismal, with nearly two-thirds of students leaving by fifth grade.[12] In many cases schools are operating two or three shifts daily, leaving fewer

Table 13.4.   Repeaters

Country	% of First Grade Repeaters, 1990	% Graduating from Sixth Grade without Repeating, 1989
Argentina	29.8	17
Brazil	53.0	1
Chile	19.6	41
Colombia	33.9	26
Costa Rica	23.4	31
Dominican Republic	49.8	3
Guatemala	35.9	9
Mexico	29.3	23
Nicaragua	54.8	n/a
Peru	30.0	21
Venezuela	19.7	14

Source: Jeffrey M. Puryear, "Education in Latin America: Problems and Challenges," Partnership for Educational Revitalization in the Americas [PREAL], 7 May 1997. www.preal.cl.

than three and a half hours per day in the classroom. Students in Latin America score poorly on internationally standardized tests. Academic performance is below that of industrial and East Asian countries. Only those students who have benefited from elite private schools are on par with international levels.[13] Teaching materials are poor (when they even exist), and some teachers haven't even graduated from high school themselves. Rural students are most deprived, with unprepared teachers, scarce resources, and limitations on the number of grades offered.[14] Teachers are woefully underpaid, resulting in frequent strikes as well as low morale.[15] Low salaries make it more difficult to recruit young talent into education, depressing future educational opportunity.

Malnutrition, poor health, and easily remedied problems such as a need for eyeglasses limit poor children's educational success. The poor attend inadequate public schools at the primary and secondary levels while the wealthy place their children in better-equipped private schools.[16] Many of the poor can't afford school at all, because even public schools have associated private costs. With the direct cost of education for books and transportation amounting to 4 percent of a family's income per child, as well as the accompanying opportunity costs of lost income from the child, many poor children become poor adults without the means to invest in their own human capital. Expanding educational access at the primary level is a concrete achievement in the region over the past thirty years; inequality remains entrenched, however, in the way students advance throughout the system.

The highly stratified educational system is an impediment to social mobility. The effects of educational inequality are compounded by the time the students get into the work force; better educated (and wealthier) workers make ten times the amount of their poorer counterparts. The high degree of income inequality we studied in chapter 11 is perpetuated by unequal educational opportunities. Because the wealthy benefit from access to a strong public university and the poor generally lack the sophistication, information, and power necessary to influence policy, the social demand for education reform is weak.[17]

There is also a gender gap in education in the region; in some countries women receive less formal education than men. There is a relationship between low levels of female education and overall health levels. An increase of between one and three years of a mother's schooling can reduce infant mortality by 15 percent; the comparable rate for men is 6 percent. In Peru, it was shown that an addition of six years of schooling cut infant mortality by a dramatic 75 percent. In addition to having better income-earning capabilities, women with education make greater use of prenatal health services and are generally healthier themselves.[18] Evidence suggests that for countries of similar labor force and capital stock, if the

> **QUESTION FOR THOUGHT**
>
> Links for educational resources for the Americas can be found at www.americas-edu.org, a homepage sponsored by the Inter-American Development Bank in cooperation with private sector and university initiatives. Identify two educational initiatives addressed at the primary school level. How do these programs contribute to reducing the country's educational deficit? What problems or limitations can you observe in the program?

Box 13.1.   Will She Make It? Guatemala Finds New Ways to Keep Girls in School

by Christina MacCulloch

In a cramped two-room house in Villa Nueva, a working-class district south of Guatemala City, seven-year-old Gabriela González Hernández is getting ready for her first day of school. Although she probably does not consider herself a child of privilege, Gabriela is already part of an elite, because slightly less than half of all Guatemalan girls do not enroll in elementary school at all. If she perseveres in her studies, Gabriela could join an even more select group: the one out of eight Guatemalan girls who complete sixth grade.

Gabriela's chances are relatively good. Her mother is herself an elementary school graduate, and her father completed high school. Though their home has but a zinc roof, bare cement floors and no running water, Gabriela's parents are determined to keep her in school because they are convinced that education represents her best chance to escape poverty. Gabriela is also lucky because she lives near a city that offers relatively good access to roads, schools and income-generating work for her parents.

But for girls in Guatemala's rural areas, the outlook is much bleaker. Simply walking to and from a distant school each day can challenge a young girl's endurance and threaten her safety. In households where both parents must do full-time agricultural work, school can seem like a questionable luxury. Most girls end up staying home to care for younger siblings, cook and help wherever else they are needed. The pressures are such that even among girls in rural Guatemala who do enroll in first grade, 66 percent drop out before reaching third grade. And when families feel they can afford to send a child to school, they generally send a boy. In 1991, some 500,000 girls between 7 and 15 were estimated to be missing school in Guatemala, compared to only 300,000 boys. Overall, 60 percent of Guatemalan women are illiterate, and 80 percent of these are from the country's rural indigenous regions, according to official figures compiled early this decade.

Guatemala is hardly alone in this respect. Mayra Buvinic, chief of the IDB's Social Development Division, cites global literacy statistics showing that in 1990, there were only 74 literate women for every 100 literate men worldwide. "The same studies estimated that globally there were 77 million girls between the ages of 6 and 11 who were not attending school, compared to 52 million boys, and that does not take into account repetition, absenteeism and dropout rates that make the gap even wider," says Buvinic.

Although the bias against educating girls has complex social and cultural roots, it is almost universally exacerbated by poverty. The nations of Latin America and the Caribbean are a case in point. In the region's most developed countries and in its largest cities, the education gender gap is either small or nonexistent. But among the tens of millions of Latin Americans who live in acute poverty, even in the richest countries, the problem is pronounced.

HIDDEN COSTS

Societies pay a high price for the failure to educate girls. While investing in boys' education is obviously beneficial, there is evidence that the same investment in female education yields higher returns for society as a whole. Why? Because although both men and women who went to school are more likely to earn better wages and improve a country's productivity, education tends to affect aspects of women's lives that don't apply to men.

Educated women are more likely to obtain prenatal, delivery and postnatal care, which leads to lower rates of infant and maternal mortality. Indeed, a World Bank study of 25 countries found that an increase of one to three years in a mother's schooling reduced infant mortality in the first year of life by 15 percent. Among fathers, the same increase in schooling resulted in only a six percent reduction in infant mortality rates.

Likewise, better-educated women in almost all societies wait longer before they get married and tend to have fewer children—two factors that lower the risk of birth-related health problems for both infants and mothers.

The children of women with as little as three to six years of formal education tend to be better nourished, and they are more likely to enroll and stay in school than the children of uneducated mothers. Educated women also tend to be more active and effective participants in local government, particularly in issues involving social services. In short, because of their multiple roles in the marketplace, the community, and the home, educated women can have a higher impact than educated men on the development and well-being of their societies.

NATIONAL CONCERN, LOCAL APPROACHES

In Guatemala, concern about girls' limited access to education has led to a unique effort to confront the problem head-on. Starting in 1991, a diverse group of educators, researchers, business leaders, civic groups, and donor organizations formed what would later become the National Association for Girls' Education. The association immediately began working with the Ministry of Education to develop a girls' education strategy within the ministry's broader program to strengthen elementary education.

In 1992, with support from the United States Agency for International Development and local foundations, the association commissioned a detailed diagnostic study that for the first time showed the extent of the shortfall in girls' education in Guatemala. The study identified the regions and municipalities where the problem was most severe and proposed a plan of action that included outlines of 37 potential projects.

Soon thereafter, the Ministry of Education launched the Girls' Education Program, a multifaceted effort to develop and test practical ways of increasing enrollment and retention of girls through the sixth grade. The program included projects in four broad areas: technical assistance for the Ministry of Education, the National Association for Girls' Education and individual schools working to implement girls' education programs; training for government officials, teachers and parents; conducting original research on the problem of girls' education; and developing motivational books and other didactic materials in Mayan languages for use by rural schoolgirls (see below).

From the outset, the program's organizers realized that a successful intervention would require coordinating the activities of students, parents, teachers, community leaders and high-level government officials who supported the effort. To find effective approaches, the program launched a pilot "Educate Girls Project," that tested different combinations of initiatives such as training teachers, offering scholarships to individual students, forming parents committees and providing supplementary curricula to schools. The project also hired indigenous women to work as education aides to provide special support to schoolgirls and their families.

The pilot project yielded a number of lessons. For example, project leaders discovered that although teachers were generally receptive to new ideas, they needed training on the theory and practice of reaching girls in the classroom, as well as appropriate teaching aids and materials.

Gabriela Núñez, a sociologist who coordinated the pilot project, believes the training sessions were important because they boosted teachers' sense of their importance in the process. "We found it was crucial to reinforce teachers' assessments of their own value as people, because only with a positive self-image can they transmit a sense of self-worth and recognition to their girl students," she says.

The pilot project also found that even modest scholarship grants, amounting to the equivalent of around five U.S. dollars per month, were a very cost-effective way of encouraging attendance because they helped compensate for the loss of a girl's labor around the house. Although scholarships were also found to improve long-term retention,

(continued)

(continued)

project officials concluded that financial support would have to be complemented by a variety of other strategies to encourage girls to return to school year after year.

Núñez argues that efforts to improve educational opportunities for girls invariably benefit boys as well. "When boys see girls becoming more active in class and in school organizations, they get more involved themselves, because they don't want to be left out." Likewise, parent committees formed as part of the pilot project increased the parents' engagement in the education of all their children, regardless of gender.

Although it is hard to quantify the success of Guatemala's girls' education efforts to date, one fundamental accomplishment is clear. "The need to improve girls' access to education is now understood and considered a priority among policymakers at the national level," says Isabel Nieves, lead author of the Guatemalan diagnostic study and now a social development specialist at the IDB.

This new awareness became evident during the drafting of the 1996 Peace Accords that brought an end to Guatemala's civil war. The accords included specific mandates to end gender inequalities in education, a goal that was also specifically addressed in the Guatemalan government's 2000 action plan. Indeed, that plan set an ambitious target of 80 percent primary school enrollment for girls by the year 2000 as part of educational reform programs.

Now, the IDB is supporting that program through a $15 million loan approved last year for Guatemala's Ministry of Education. The funds will be used to pay for training teachers and supplying schools with bilingual and Spanish-language materials, implementing programs to reduce first grade repetition, consolidating community participation and replicating successful innovations from the Girls' Education Program.

"The IDB support is arriving at a crucial time," says Nieves. "These funds are allowing the Guatemalan government to mainstream many of the lessons learned during the girls' education pilot project into its overall educational reform program."

The IDB is supporting innovative girls' education efforts in other countries as well. In Bolivia, where illiteracy among women averages 67 percent and girls spend only 60 percent as much time in school as boys, a recent educational reform program partly financed by the Bank set out specifically to reduce dropout rates among girls. The program included a variety of incentives, including scholarships and day care centers where girls could drop off younger siblings in order to attend classes.

In Mexico, an IDB-funded program to assist up to three million children in extreme poverty is testing a different approach to easing the child-care duties of school-age children: letting them bring their younger siblings into the classroom. Though it is too early to judge the effectiveness of this concept, the aim is both to keep girls in school and to offer a more stimulating environment to preschool children.

The ultimate success of these kinds of programs depends, of course, on the perseverance of girls like Gabriela González Hernández and the commitment of parents, teachers and community leaders. But as the progress achieved in Guatemala illustrates, governments can help to create an environment where perseverance and commitment can bear fruit in the lives of individual girls.

Reproduced from *IDB América*, April 1998, p. 4–7.

ratio of female to male at given levels of education falls below 0.75, GDP growth is likely to be 25 percent lower. Investment in girls' education clearly has public returns. Nonetheless, in terms of income forgone and relatively low levels of economic opportunity, the private costs of education are high. Girls are needed in the home and on the farm to help in chores and supervise younger siblings. Many families simply cannot afford the indirect costs of schooling.[19]

THE INDIGENOUS AND EDUCATION

The gravity of the educational deficit is greater for the indigenous in Latin America. The direct and indirect costs of education to the poor—the clothes, shoes, books, transportation, or perhaps room and board in the nearest large village for middle or high school as well as the forgone earnings of the child—are compounded by a frequent inability to speak Spanish. Ten percent of Mexicans do not speak Spanish. In Guatemala, 60 percent of the indigenous people have no education.[20] On average, the number of years of schooling for indigenous Guatemalan males is 1.8 years and females 0.9 years as opposed to their nonindigenous counterparts with 4.5 and 4 years each. A social-demographic survey in Guatemala in 1989 reported 9 percent of nonindigenous and 21 percent of indigenous children as being employed.

Particularly for those in the agricultural sector, the opportunity costs of children's labor is high. In Bolivia, the incidence of no schooling for monolingual indigenous is 77.9 percent, bilingual indigenous 11 percent, and nonindigenous 2.8 percent, indicating that basic education is not equitably distributed over different ethnic groups.[21] In Peru the difference between indigenous and nonindigenous education levels is narrowing to approximately 20 percent. Nevertheless, when analyzed by gender, indigenous females continue to receive less than half the education of their nonindigenous counterparts, perhaps reflecting the difficult investment decisions families face with respect to education. Given scarce resources, the indigenous poor may choose to invest in their male children who have a greater probability of remaining in the labor market than in their sisters for whom the cultural perception is that she will return to the home.[22]

> **QUESTION FOR THOUGHT**
>
> Recall the discussion in chapter 11 on the indigenous and poverty. Can you think of ways to promote education among the indigenous populations? Are there other complementary programs in addition to education to improve the welfare of indigenous communities in Latin America?

More education, however, is not the simple answer. Education in the indigenous communities may also have unintended cultural effects. Educational programs may work to obliterate the distinctive languages and customs of the indigenous. Participation of indigenous leaders is critical to ensure the transfer of traditional customs and practices as part of the child's educational experience. Bilingual education can facilitate this process of preserving cultural practices. Change should be respectful of local cultures but open up opportunities for the indigenous poor. Educational policy must be informed by the needs of the target group.

WHAT ARE THE CAUSES OF THE EDUCATIONAL DEFICIT IN LATIN AMERICA?

The educational deficit in Latin America is the result of ineffective demand by poor families and deficient quantity and quality of the supply offered by school

BOX 13.2.   BOLIVIA: GETTING KIDS BACK IN SCHOOL

Samuel Ardaya Rivera, 13, knows first hand how hard it is to attend school when you're dirt poor. The little he makes washing auto windshields on the streets of Santa Cruz, Bolivia, goes to help with home expenses and pay for school supplies, according to the newspaper *El Mundo.* Life is a struggle, and for many children like Rivera, school is an unaffordable luxury. Helping to get working children off the streets and into the classroom, and at the same time strengthen parental involvement in their children's education, is the aim of a new project being carried out by nongovernmental groups in Santa Cruz as well as the cities of La Paz, El Alto and Cochabamba. Financed with the help of a $2.65 million IDB grant, the program is benefiting 1,900 children from extremely poor families—21 percent of the total number of working children in those cities—with after-school tutoring, school supplies, clothing, snacks and meals. In Santa Cruz, each of the three institutions carrying out the program has contracted eight tutors. Their main job is to help the children keep on top of their school work as well as engage them in recreational, artistic, cultural and science activities. The program has resulted in a significant decline in school dropout and repetition rates. In fact, a year into the program, 90 percent of the 1,900 participating children completed the school year. An important side effect of the tutoring is strengthening the children's self-esteem, which in many cases has been damaged by their work experience and family situation.

Reproduced from *IDB América*, November 1997, p. 14. Available on-line at www.iadb.org/English/projects/projects.html.

systems. With clear positive returns to education, why don't families elect to invest in more years of schooling? In addition to the direct costs of clothing, books, and other supplies, unfortunately, for many families, the opportunity costs of education are high. In many parts of the region, children's income is an important contribution to the family's survival. School calendars often do not accommodate children's work schedules, particularly around harvest times in the agricultural sector. In the urban sector, one estimate places children's participation in the informal sector between 20 and 30 percent of family income.[23] When survival is at stake, education appears to be a luxury. The demand for education must be seen in the context of the price of day-to-day living.

The supply of a quality education has also deteriorated. The lost decade of the 1980s took its toll on education in Latin America. The goals of eliminating illiteracy, extending basic education from eight to ten years, and improving the quality of basic education in the "Mexico Declaration" signed by the region's education ministers were stalled by the lack of available resources. Although per capita expenditures on education increased from 1975 to 1980 by 4.29 percent, they decreased by 6.14 percent between 1980 and 1985.[24] The rate of growth of students receiving preschool education fell from 10.6 percent for the 1970–1980 period to 4.7 percent for 1985–1988. Likewise, the rate of growth of primary education was more than halved from 4 percent prior to the crisis to 1.5 percent in the late 1980s.[25] The economic slowdown stalled progress on education.

In addition to constrained choices families make about the economic opportunity costs of education and falling expenditures, the management of educational systems in Latin America has led to inferior outcomes. Education has traditionally been managed by central governments insulated from local demands. Teachers have normally been employed by state governments rather than municipalities or individual schools. In Venezuela, for example, the Ministry of Education is the country's largest employer. Bureaucratic educational machines become overly involved in their own interests to the detriment of the student. Often geographically distant and powerless, families have little effective involvement in educational policy at the ministerial or school level.[26]

With policy efforts focused on expanding access to schools, quality suffered enormously. This was acutely felt in the qualifications and training of teachers in the region. National systems of pay, put in place by powerful teachers' unions, leave principals little recourse in local-level administration. Political and administrative obstacles impede much-needed reform. Teachers' unions have resisted **decentralization** and enhanced parental choice. Salaries absorb more than 90 percent of the total educational budget in fifteen of twenty-one countries for which data was available.[27] Politicians fear the loss of control over patronage jobs they can offer, and university students and their families have been able to defend their subsidies for higher education. Politicians would rather channel funds to a new building than contend with reforms in teacher training and performance. As a leading analyst of education in Latin America noted, "You don't see primary-school students protesting in the streets, like university students do."[28] Teachers and elites present a formidable coalition of interests for a poor community to come up against. This intersection of weak demand and inferior supply comes at a high cost to the development of human capital in the region.

BENEFITS OF EDUCATIONAL REFORM

The political roadblocks explain poor outcomes and sluggish reform in education in Latin America. Globalization may, however, be creating a new set of conditions. International competitiveness demands a highly skilled, educated work force. The educational deficit in Latin America has a high social cost. As noted in a recent Inter-American Development Bank report, education is by far the main factor in determining whether a working individual is poor.[29] There is a strong correlation between national investment in education and economic growth. A better educated work force will be more productive and competitive in the global economy. As noted by Alejandro Foxley, former Chilean minister of the economy and OAS coordinator on education issues for the OAS, "The issue of a well trained labor force is critical to maintaining a path of economic development that is sustainable."[30] Education strongly influences farmer productivity, encourages a reduction in fertility, and results in improved health and nutrition.

No country has made significant economic progress without a strong educational infrastructure. A recent study of economic returns by education level in fourteen Latin American and Caribbean countries showed that the social rate of return of primary education averaged over 17 percent—a high rate of return for any social investment.[31] It has been estimated that an increase of one year in Latin America's average educational level of the work force over current trends would increase long-term economic growth by 1 percent on average in the next decade. An additional year increases productivity by 0.8 percent annually. Evidence from Honduras, Guatemala, and El Salvador shows that an additional year of education translates into a 5 to 10 percent increase in informal sector earnings. Another study in the case of Brazil dramatically shows an additional year of education adding between 5 and 20 percent to real output.[32] In a world in which competitiveness is increasingly defined by technology, well-skilled work forces are critical to managing growth. Increasing the educational attainment in the region, with its associated gains in productivity, would bring the region in line with East Asian levels.[33] Education is estimated to account for 40 percent of the divergence in growth rates between Latin America and East Asia.[34] Women with a secondary education are three times as likely to attend political meetings. Global interests have created new incentives for elites to demand better public education systems. The new coalition of interests driven by global competition may have broken the logjam on educational policy change. The million dollar question is how should this be done?

STATE AND MARKET IN THE REFORM EFFORT

Educational policy reform, like other areas of social investment, must address the question of the role of the state versus the role of the market. Given scarce resources, what should be the level of state spending for education? Is there a complementary role for the private sector? What direction should investments in education take?

Does education fit the neoliberal prescription for market-based policies? The case against the reliance on the market and for the public provision of education rests on several arguments: education creates **externalities**, is considered a **merit good**, has long lead and lag times, has equity implications, may suffer from principal/agent problems, and exhibits scale economies that allow for decreasing costs.[35] Let's consider this list in turn. Improving literacy creates externalities in lowering the transaction costs between individuals in society. Instructions at work can be written, not only spoken; social and environmental campaigns can take place in the print media. Literacy may contribute to improving the health profile and fertility control because health education is often disseminated in print. With positive externalities, one person's welfare is enhanced by increasing the educational status of another. Essentially, this position argues that the social rate of return to education, particularly at the primary level, exceeds the individual's investment.

Education is also considered a merit good. The direct benefits of education may be worth more to individuals than they themselves are aware. Purchasers of education may estimate the benefits in terms of a better job, for example, but may not be able to anticipate the effects on family health and nutrition. As a result, they might demand less education than the whole family's return on the investment would indicate. Given long gestation times, the signals for increasing educational investments may be slow to reach the buyers.

Equity concerns inform the educational investment debate. The poor are unable to invest in education, particularly if credit markets do not reach down the economic ladder for student loans. Finally, a principal/agent problem plagues decisions about individual investments in education. The parents act as the agent of the child. The returns to education are primarily in the child's future; the cost comes to the parents today. Underinvestment in education may therefore be a rational response to immediate family needs as weighed against uncertain future returns. Principal/agent problems may be magnified in the case of girls' education or the enrollment of indigenous children. Given traditional norms, parents may choose to underinvest on behalf of their children. On the supply side of the equation, with economies of scale in higher education—the libraries, scientific equipment, and computer facilities necessary—the provision of higher education may be economically feasible only through the visible hand of the state.

In counterpoint to these arguments for the public provision of education, neoliberals point to the need for private sector participation. Advocating a much reduced role for the state, they point to the benefits of market allocation of education. Governments, they contend, have failed to provide quality public education. Resource constraints, coupled with systematic misallocation of funds, point toward the market solution. Policy prescriptions offered by neoclassical economists include the adoption of user fees, student loans, and the encouragement of private schooling. Particularly at the higher levels of education, parents should become responsible for educational expenses, with scholarships offered to students without the means to pay. Student loans, as opposed to outright subsidies, could facilitate educational opportunity. Private education is seen as more cost-effective and quality conscious, with the saving generated redirected toward deficient primary school education.

> **QUESTION FOR THOUGHT**
>
> Should educational reform in Latin America be market driven?

STAGE ONE OF EDUCATIONAL REFORM IN LATIN AMERICA

Educational reform has been motivated by three factors: competitiveness, finance, and equity.[36] Changing demand for labor driven by globalization has created an impetus for better training to compete in world markets. Given the constraints of less government spending, education spending in Latin America has been redirected from the university and secondary levels to focus on primary education. Secondary and higher education have increasingly become privatized or financed through user fees. With equity as a goal, education is seen as an instrument to improve social mobility. Equity-driven reforms tend to focus on acquiring basic literacy skills, increasing school supplies in the poorest areas, and reaching groups such as women and the indigenous populations that have lagged behind in educational performance. To improve equity considerations, the state must assume a central role. Given the goal of increasing competitiveness under fiscal constraints, the private sector has been increasingly involved.

To improve equity, educational reform must attend to the constraints on the most disadvantaged. In particular, the high opportunity costs of sending children to school must be addressed. The Colombian Escuela Nueva program offers an innovative approach to formal education. Working from the assumption that children in rural areas need flexible schedules to accommodate agricultural work, it operates under a multigrade, independently paced framework. Using problem solving rather than rote learning, semiprogrammed modules allow students to work alone when necessary to catch up with the class. Because the modules are relevant to the problems students are facing at home, academic learning is reinforced by practical application.[37] Pilot studies indicate that Escuela Nueva students have performed better and stayed in school longer than students attending traditional institutions.[38]

As an example of how the private sector might assist, financed by a small private international organization, Mayan girls in Guatemala are offered a small scholarship—$6 per month—to provide pencils, notebooks, and shoes as well as cover some of the money the girls may have provided to the family. A small but inspiring result of this program was the achievement of two girls in a small mountain village entering the fifth grade: the first ever in the community to do so.[39] A discussion of educational efforts in Guatemala is presented in box 13.1.

Community involvement in educational reform is critical. One of the trends in educational reform in the region has been decentralization of educational policy to the local level. This doesn't necessarily mean less government but rather a different combination of levels of government. Local input and control can reduce educational inefficiency. If decisions are made at the local level, greater responsiveness to local needs should result. In Chile under the Pinochet military government, educational reform moved decision making from a central bureaucracy to the municipalities. The central government continued to finance education and provide technical support, but there was greater autonomy at the local level in how to spend the money. Municipalities had the power to hire and fire teachers. Schools were encouraged to compete for funds, and allocations were based on student attendance under a school choice program.[40] Pegging grant payments to pupil days in school improved attendance records, and competition to attract students improved the quality of teaching.

Nonetheless, the market-driven spirit of the reforms was biased against poor communities with fewer resources and institutional capacities. After democratization, spending on education was increased to 3.2 percent of GDP, a 54 percent increase over the previous government. The P900 emergency program introduced in 1990 targeted teacher training and resources in Chile's 900 lowest achieving schools. The MECE program, funded in part by the Chilean government ($73 million) and in part by the World Bank ($170 million), is designed to improve the physical and educational conditions of primary schools. Through a competitive application process, schools could be awarded project funds from the central government to enhance computer learning. Teachers were empowered to make changes in their own classrooms. The program has been successful in enhancing the textbooks and teaching materials available to schools and encouraging innovative teaching methods and community involvement—the critical goals of the program.[41]

Chile has also experimented with the use of vouchers in the school systems.

People can spend educational vouchers in public municipal or private subsidized schools. The demand registered by users is supposed to create a quasi-market in which the buyers of the good, education, can direct educational outcomes. School districts can also ask parents for contributions to costs. The results, however, have been problematic in light of the goal of greater equity. Markets for education developed only in large towns and in less poor neighborhoods in which private subsidized schools were able to turn a profit. Municipal schools in less advantaged areas found it difficult to raise funds, contributing to budget pressures.[42] Poorly educated parents appeared more concerned with things like school appearance, whereas wealthier families demanded qualitative changes in curriculum. Many low-income families were not able to take advantage of access to schools in more affluent areas; the costs of transportation, uniforms, and the commuting time away from home or market work precluded participation.[43] The market may be a useful tool under certain socioeconomic circumstances, but it may have a high price in terms of equity under unequal conditions.

Brazil provides an example of what can be accomplished with strong political will that engages educational stakeholders and draws upon the interests of the public sector to improve a highly unequal and ineffective educational system. Since 1934 universal primary education has been the law for children ages seven to fourteen, yet Brazil has one of the highest illiteracy rates in the region. National adult literacy stood at 20 percent in the 1990s, with levels twice as bad in the poor Northeast. During the 1970s, the government invested lavishly in education, expanding on educational infrastructure. Schools popped up everywhere, but without funding for books, supplies, and teacher training, educational outcomes were dismal. Most of the spending went to universities.

Brazil was a striking outlier in terms of the weakness of its primary school system. The educational attainment of upper-income compared to lower-income children was highly divergent. The issue is not the amount of money being spent. From 1980 to 1988 expenditure on education as a proportion of GNP doubled, and it also increased as a percentage of total federal government expenditure, from 6.1 to 8.2 percent. Despite these real increases in total expenditure, resources directed to primary education were reduced by 39 percent between 1986 and 1989, whereas those to higher education increased 59 percent over the period. The Brazilian education system is asymmetric. Rich students go to private primary and secondary schools and then attend free public universities. The poor attend public primary and secondary schools. Poorly prepared, they can only get into private universities—which suffer from a lack of funding.[44] In 1996 the Brazilian Congress approved an amendment that mandated 25 percent of state and municipal revenues be spent on education, with at least 60 percent of the total money to be allocated to raising teachers salaries. But funding to federal universities, which receive 80 percent of all federal spending, was preserved, as Congress was unwilling to touch such middle-class entitlements.[45] Because of unequal distribution of educational opportunity, Brazil has spending levels in education comparable to middle-income countries and educational outcomes similar to those in very poor countries. The problem is not a lack of resources but uneven distribution of educational spending.

The results of the skewed spending on education in Brazil are startling. The average worker in the São Paulo area has only a fourth-grade education. As shown in figure 13.1, less than 20 percent of the population has some high school, in contrast to more than 40 percent in Chile and Mexico, 65 percent in Japan, and 90 percent in the United States. In the poorest regions in the Northeast, public school teachers earn less than $50 a month—drawing in the least talented in the society, many without secondary education themselves.[46]

Despite the difficulties in educational policies, some progress has been made. Figure 13.2 shows the gains in education since the 1970s. It also highlights, however, the unequal distribution by gender, region, and race. The educational deficit in the face of global competitiveness was enormous. Radical changes in educational policy were implemented under the Cardoso administration. Under the astute political leadership of education minister Paulo Renato de Souza, responsibility for education was decentralized to the local level. Financing was devolved to the local level as well, where the demand for education could address local school board needs. A new role was set for the central government: establishing standards and assessing progress. Efforts are being made at computerization, installing 100,000 computers in the schools. Textbook distribution increased 83 percent over 1995, and there was an increase in school lunch programs as well as improvements in the TV school system for distance learning. One innovative program pays children to stay in school. In a suburb of Brasilia, 24,000 children draw one minimum

Figure 13.1. Percentage of Population with Some High School

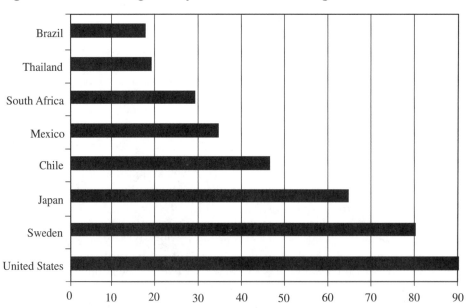

Source: Unesco, *Statistical Yearbook 1998* (Paris: UNESCO Publishing & Bernan Press, 1998), 1-44-1-S4.

Figure 13.2.   Average Years of Schooling in Brazil, 1970 versus 1990

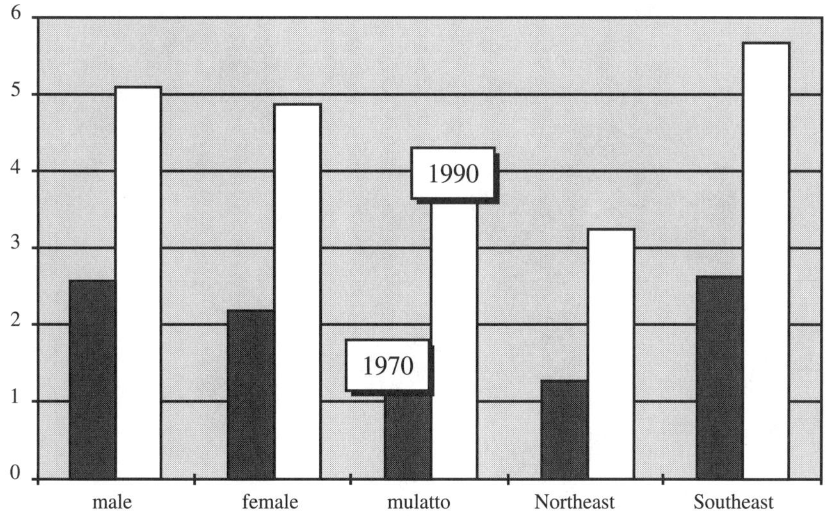

Source: Amaury de Souza, "Education in Brazil," paper presented at IDB Conference, November 1997.

wage of $110. A deposit is made each year that the student stays in school and can be touched only after four successful years of schooling. Enrollments are up and dropouts rare. The historical repeat rate in this district was 17 percent; it has now fallen to 8 percent.

In the Brazilian state of Minas Gerais, decentralization has improved efficiency and educational outcomes. The philosophy is that the school belongs to the community. Before decentralization, if a rural school wanted to buy a few new chairs, it would have to send a requisition to the state capital. Now local schools receive four quarterly payments for supplies and educational materials. School boards were formed to make personnel decisions, and competency exams for teachers were instituted. To overcome problems of patronage, principals are elected by the community among prequalified candidates using secret ballots.[47] The state has seen dramatic improvements in student scores: math scores have doubled, primary school graduation rates increased 47 percent, and repeaters fell from 29 to 17 percent.[48] Surprisingly, participation has been strongest among poor communities.

The overall results of educational reform have been dramatic. Illiteracy is down 15 percent, and test scores are rising. National teacher standards are improving, with nine out of ten teachers attaining a high school education or better. Nonetheless high repetition rates continue to plague the system.

What lessons can be drawn from educational reform in Brazil?[49] First, there was strong leadership from the top that was complemented by action from the bottom. Programs engaged stakeholders, bringing parents and the private sector together in the battle to keep kids in school. The leadership created a shared per-

Improving school materials and classroom conditions can promote better educational outcomes. *(Courtesy of David Mangurian and the Inter-American Development Bank.)*

spective on what needed to be done to reach common goals and engaged various levels of society to make it possible. The central government function performed well in producing and disseminating information while the local level had enough leeway for innovation and local experimentation. Much remains to be done in Brazil, but the educational future looks brighter.

THE PROCESS OF DECENTRALIZATION

As demonstrated in the Brazilian case, decentralization of education works best when it is supported by the following factors: political will at all levels of government; explicit guidelines delineating which functions of the educational system will be decentralized or provided by the private sector; an implementation timetable and strategy with clear operational guidelines; continuous training for educational administrators provided at the local level; development of performance indicators to measure outcomes; and adequate financial, human, and physical resources to sustain the process.[50] Incentives should be built into the system to encourage good management and discourage corruption at the local administrative level. Clear lines of responsibility should be defined to encourage accountability for poor standards and failed systems. Decentralization is a process that will take time to alter the rules of financing and delivery systems; it must be carefully monitored for efficiency and effectiveness. Decentralization may confront political obstacles, as centralized ministries lose power. Some countries might choose to decentralize particular components of the education system, rather than instituting a frontal attack. Decentralization that takes place too quickly could simply transfer the inefficiencies from central bureaucracies to the local level.[51]

Decentralization does not mean the abdication of responsibility for education at the national level. PREAL, the Partnership for Educational Revitalization in the Americas, recommends in its task force report, *The Future at Stake*, that governments establish clear standards for education, introduce national tests, and use results to revise programs and reallocate resources. Local governments should have the authority to run schools, but central administration of funds, standards, equity assurances, and monitoring of results is crucial. Better measures of assessment of educational outcomes must be developed to evaluate new directions in policy. Without effective assessment of outcomes, it is difficult to set clear goals. The few assessments that exist focus on inputs such as spending and the number of teachers rather than indicators of educational performance.[52] Assessment data should be disseminated to the local level to direct resources to the greatest need.[53] In Chile, for example, assessments were used to target schools at greatest educational risk. High- and medium-risk schools were eligible to apply for additional resources for reform.

PUBLIC–PRIVATE PARTNERSHIPS

As businesses have worried about global competitiveness, the private sector has also assumed a role in education in the region. In Brazil, employees of Rigesa, a Brazilian subsidiary of Westvaco, a New York–based paper company and a blue jeans factory owned by a large Brazilian textile manufacturer, sponsor basic literacy classes after hours. A major Brazilian Bank, Bradesco, finances roughly fifty primary and secondary classes around the nation. The need to operate more sophisticated equipment drives the company programs.[54] A São Paulo cosmetics firm called Natura donated more than $3 million to train public school teachers. In Venezuela, a widow of a wealthy industrialist funded a school adjacent to the factory she owned to improve her workers' children's education. Another Venezuela-based firm, the Cisneros Group, is working with IBM and Microsoft in a project to use its Direct TV satellite to beam programs for teachers into 120 school across the region.[55] Microsoft is working with the Inter-American Development Bank in a program called Informatics 2000 to promote computer skills at the elementary and high school levels. To meet the skills gap to compete in the global economy, Mexico's private sector has taken steps by creating a National Commission of Normalization of Job Skills. Patterned on a Japanese program, it provides workers with a certification of job skill or knowledge level, regardless of how or where the skills were obtained.

Public sector provision of early childhood programs may be complemented by private sector initiatives. Partnerships of governments, NGOs, and communities should be encouraged. Informal programs such as the *hogares comunitarios* in Colombia have much lower salary and investment costs than formal programs. Public financing of preschool should start with the most deprived children in the urban and rural slums, and governments should resist middle-class pressures for general support of preschooling until the needs of the poor are met.[56] In Mexico, under the National Solidarity Program, PRONASOL, a poverty reduction program, the residents complemented state investments by providing half the funds and the labor for the building and refurbishing of schools. Local businesses contributed materials. Schoolchildren voted on which classmates were most deserving of funds to help their families while the children attended school.[57] Community participation matters in improving educational outcomes. Nonetheless, there is a long way to go in private participation in social efforts. With different sets of tax laws in the region, there is a limited tradition of corporate philanthropy in Latin America.

MULTILATERAL EFFORTS

As we discussed in chapter 8 in the section on the Free Trade Agreement of the Americas, at the 1994 Miami summit heads of Latin American governments ratified their commitment to guarantee universal access to **quality primary education by the year 2010**, a 100 percent primary school completion rate, and a rate of 75 percent inscription in secondary schools.[58] At the 1998 Santiago summit, heads of state from the region defined education and the so-called second generation of reforms as critical to strengthening Latin America's fragile political and economic system. Vulnerable groups, including women, indigenous people, geographically dispersed and migrant populations, urban marginalized communities, and the illiterate population over twenty-five, will be targeted through compensatory programs, preschool education, certificates of on-the-job training, and distance learning programs.[59]

Multilateral funding commitments make the achievement of these goals possible. The World Bank has identified lending to facilitate educational reform as a top priority, with financing for primary education increasing from an average of U.S.$20 million per year in 1985–1990 to an expected U.S.$500 million per year in 1991–1995.[60] Lending through the Inter-American Development Bank increased from $150 million in 1989 to $500 million in 1993.[61] The IDB has provided training for nearly 20 percent of the region's primary and secondary teachers through education loans. As a result of the summit, the World Bank and the Inter-American Development Bank committed U.S.$8.2 billion over a three-year period to jumpstart the process.[62] For the ILO (International Labor Organization), the focus is on equality of access. The ILO advocates setting basic education and vocational training as priority areas. UNESCO's goals center on enhancing the role of national partners and developing strategies for national capacity in education planning, budgeting, and educational administration.[63]

New technologies offer new opportunities for education that both national governments and multilateral agencies are exploiting. The Internet brings a wide range of materials into even the most remote classroom. Students in rural classrooms can read the more than 1,000 national and international newspapers on the Internet. Wiring schools, even in remote areas, vastly enhances educational resources—and students often find it fun. Satellite classrooms and videotapes can work around the limitations of teacher training. In Brazil, Telecurso 2000 offers a basic high school equivalency program by television for young adults, with lessons broadcast at different times of day to accommodate work schedules. The workbook to accompany the course can be purchased at newsstands. Brazil is now moving to Internet-based courses to complement televised distance learning opportunities.

Nonetheless, technical solutions must be carefully evaluated for cost-effectiveness. Putting computers in classrooms is an expensive venture. Appropriate software must also be procured. If teachers are not adequately trained in the use of computers, their potential is wasted. Simply providing the hardware and software without clear plans to integrate computers into the classrooms increases the likelihood of failure.

EDUCATION AS SOCIAL CHANGE

Educational reform should not be limited to the walls of the classroom. In developing countries, adult learners play a large role in the educational challenge. Those who support education as a vehicle for **social change** argue that education should be used to empower the poor to participate in defining their own needs and transforming their physical world. Brazilian sociologist Paulo Freire, in his pathbreaking *Pedagogy of the Oppressed*, provided a methodology by which community-based groups, through the identification of common symbols, would become "consciencitized" to the causes of their poverty and empowered through education to change their situation. Freire rejects the "banking concept" of education, in which students are stocked with facts but rarely enter into a dialogue with instructors that is useful in transforming social reality.[64] Instead, through a process of community-based culture circles, Freire advocates the communal problematizing of local conditions and using education as a means of change and empowerment.

Ivan Illich, an Austrian-born social critic, in the 1960s and 1970s made Cuernavaca, Mexico, his home. He argued for "deschooling," or the breakup of the formal (and expensive) educational system in favor of creating mechanisms at the local level to transform the lives of the poor.[65] Nonformal education based on mass media, the distribution of printed materials, and group sessions animated by a local contact may cost a third or a fifth of the unit cost in primary education.[66] Adult education is a central element of the goal of Universal Access to Education for 2010 adopted by the Miami summit. Simply reforming the school will leave generations of the economically active population without the skills to compete in the global environment. Adult education and empowerment will contribute to human capital development in the region.

Key Concepts

Decentralization
Educational deficit
Educational
   performance index

Equity concerns
Externalities
Grade repetition
Merit good

Quality primary
   education by the
   year 2010
Social change

Chapter Summary

- In comparison to other regions in the world, Latin America is deficient in the area of education.
- Primary education is segregated by class, where the rich not only benefit from private schooling but also are allotted a greater share of public expenditures on education. Furthermore, schools suffer from high grade repetition rates due to inadequate learning, incurring higher costs to reteach those students.
- Indigenous groups and women benefit least from the already inadequate schooling. Indigenous groups are hindered by language and cultural barriers and the opportunity cost of labor forgone in attending school. Families with girls often underinvest in education because of high opportunity costs. Improving educational opportunities for women can reduce infant mortality and contribute to economic growth.
- Causes of the educational deficit include the importance of children as income earners. The opportunity costs of attending school are high. The debt crisis of the 1980s also took its toll on education, decreasing government expenditures in that area of human capital investment.
- Education will produce a more productive work force and positively affect real output. Educational programs that address the opportunity costs of attending school and involve the community in decision making will prove to be the most effective in improving education in the region. In addition, the participation of international organizations and NGOs, along with the respective governments, will also prove to be beneficial.
- Education does not have to be limited to younger students and the classroom. Many believe that social change can come about by using nontraditional methods of education to empower and educate certain marginalized groups. The private sector also has a role in closing the educational deficit in the region.

Notes

1. Statistics from Jeffrey M. Puryear, "Education in Latin America: Problems and Challenges," Partnership for Educational Revitalization in the Americas [PREAL], 7 May

1997. Presented to the Council of Foreign Relations, 27 February 1996, for the Latin America program study group, "Educational Reform in Latin America," New York. Available on-line at www.preal.cl/index-i.htm. Key FLACSO into your favorite search engine to get a sense of the broad range of activity in the region.

2. Laurence Wolff, Ernesto Schiefelbeing, and Jorge Valenzuela, *Improving the Quality of Primary Education in Latin America and the Caribbean: Toward the 21st Century* (Washington, D.C: World Bank, 1994), 12.

3. Partnership for Educational Revitalization in the Americas [PREAL], *The Future at Stake: Report of the Task Force on Education, Equity and Economic Competitiveness in Latin America and the Caribbean* (Santiago, Chile, and Washington, D.C.: PREAL, in conjunction with the Inter-American Dialogue and CINDE, 1998). Available on-line at www.preal.cl/index-i.htm.

4. Lance Taylor and Ute Piper, *Reconciling Economic Reform and Sustainable Human Development: Social Consequences of Neo-Liberalism*, United Nations Development Programme Discussion Paper Series (New York: United Nations Development Programme, 1996), 73.

5. Fernando Reimers, "Educación para todos en América Latina en el siglo XXIL. Los desafíos de la establzación, el ajuste y los mandatos de Jomtien," paper presented at UNESCO workshop, Peru, December 1990. Described in Carlos Alberto Torres and Adriana Puiggrós, "The State and Public Education in Latin America," *Comparative Education Review* 39, no. 1 (1995): 10.

6. "A Teacher's Lot," *The IDB*, May 1996, p. 9.

7. Amaury de Souza, "Redressing Inequalities: Brazil's Social Agenda at Century's End," in *Brazil under Cardoso*, ed. Susan Kaufman Purcell and Riordan Roett (Boulder, Colo.: Lynne Rienner, 1997), 71.

8. Peter Bate, "Education: The Gordian Knot," *IDB Today*. On-line edition available at www.iadb.org.

9. Wolff et al., *Improving the Quality of Primary Education*, 2.

10. Puryear, "Education in Latin America."

11. Inter-American Development Bank, *Facing Up to Inequality in Latin America: Economic and Social Progress in Latin America, 1998–1999 Report* (Baltimore: Johns Hopkins University Press/Inter-American Development Bank, 1998), 51.

12. Bate, "Education."

13. Inter-American Development Bank, *Facing Up to Inequality*, 53.

14. PREAL, *Future at Stake*, 7.

15. Wolff et al., *Improving the Quality of Primary Education*, 5.

16. Torres and Puiggrós, "The State and Public Education," 1.

17. Puryear, "Education in Latin America."

18. Inter-American Development Bank, *Women in the Americas: Bridging the Gap* (Baltimore: Johns Hopkins University Press, 1995).

19. M. Anne Hill and Elizabeth M. King, "Women's Education in Developing Countries: An Overview," in *Women's Education in Developing Countries: Barriers, Benefits, and Policies*, ed. M. Anne Hill and Elizabeth M. King (Baltimore: Johns Hopkins University Press, 1993), 19.

20. Diane Steele, "Guatemala," in *Indigenous People and Poverty in Latin America*, ed. George Psacharopoulos and Harry Anthony Patrinos (Washington, D.C.: World Bank, 1994), 104.

21. Bill Wood and Harry Anthony Patrinos, "Urban Bolivia," in *Indigenous People and Poverty in Latin America*, ed. George Psacharopoulos and Harry Anthony Patrinos (Washington, D.C.: World Bank, 1994), 63.

22. Donna Macisaac, "Peru," in *Indigenous People and Poverty in Latin America*, ed. George Psacharopoulos and Harry Anthony Patrinos (Washington, D.C.: World Bank, 1994), 170.

23. William Myers, ed., *Protecting Working Children* (London: Zed, 1991); and Anthony Dewees and Steven Klees, "Social Movements and the Transformation of National Policy: Street and Working Children in Brazil," *Comparative Education Review* 39, no. 1 (1995).

24. Fernando Reimers, "The Impact of Economic Stabilization and Adjustment on Education in Latin America," *Comparative Education* 35, no. 2 (May 1991): 322.

25. Fernando Fajnzylber, "Education and Changing Production Patterns with Social Equity," *CEPAL Review* 47 (August 1992): 8.

26. Puryear, "Education in Latin America."

27. Inter-American Development Bank, *Facing Up to Inequality in Latin America*, 129.

28. Katherine Ellison, "Latin Summit's Focus: Education of Kids," *Miami Herald*, April 13, 1998, p. A1. Available on-line at www.alca-cupula.org.

29. A. Fiszbein and G. Psacharopoulos, *Income Inequality in Latin America: The Story of the Eighties*, Technical Department for Latin America Working Paper (Washington, D.C.: World Bank, 1995), as cited in Inter-American Development Bank, *IDB Annual Report: Making Social Services Work* (Washington, D.C.: Inter-American Development Bank, 1996), 245.

30. "Skills Gap May Be Biggest Trade Barrier," *Journal of Commerce*, April 20, 1998. On-line edition. Available at www.alca-cupula.org.

31. Wolff et al., *Improving the Quality of Primary Education*, 1.

32. Lawrence J. Lau, Dean T. Jamison, Shucheng Liu, and Steven Rivkin, "Education and Economic Growth: Some Cross-Sectional Evidence," in *Education in Brazil*, ed. Nancy Birdsall and Richard H. Sabot (Washington, D.C.: Inter-American Development Bank, 1996), 83–116. The large variation, between 5 and 20 percent, is a function of the existing educational infrastructure. If initial levels are low, large returns accrue after four years. The authors estimate that after this jump, the relationship will smooth out, with each year adding 5 percent in output.

33. Eduardo Lora and Felipe Barrera, "A Decade of Structural Reform in Latin America: Growth, Productivity, and Investment Are Not What They Used to Be," document for discussion at the Inter-American Development Bank Barcelona seminar, "Latin America after a Decade of Reform: What Next?" 16 March 1997.

34. PREAL, *Future at Stake*, 10.

35. Christopher Colclough, "Education and the Market: Which Parts of the Neoliberal Solution Are Correct?" *World Development* 24, no. 4 (1996): 589–610.

36. Martin Carnoy, "Structural Adjustment and the Changing Face of Education," *International Labor Review* 134, no. 6 (1995): 653–673.

37. Rosemary T. Bellew and Elizabeth M. King, "Educating Women: Lessons from Experience," in *Women's Education in Developing Countries: Barriers, Benefits and Policies*, ed. Elizabeth M. King and Rosemary Bellew (Baltimore: Johns Hopkins University Press, 1993), 305.

38. George Psacharopoulos, Carlos Rojas, and Eduardo Velez, "Achieving Evaluation of Colombia's Escuela Nueva: Is Multigrade the Answer?" *Comparative Education Review* 37, no. 3 (1993).

39. Molly Moore, "Mayan Girls Make Fifth Grade History," *The Washington Post*, 20 June 1996, p. A19.

40. Taryn Rounds Parry, "Achieving Balance in Decentralization: A Case Study of Education Decentralization in Chile," *World Development* 25, no. 2 (February 1997): 211–225. For a review of the Pinochet period, see Tarsicio Castañeda, "Combating Poverty," in *Reforms in Education* (San Francisco: International Center for Economic Growth, 1992).

41. Alan Engell, "Improving the Quality and Equity of Education in Chile: The Programa 900 Escuelas and the MECE-Basica," in *Implementing Policy Innovation in Latin America: Politics, Economics and Techniques*, ed. Antonio Silva (Washington, D.C.: Inter-American Development Bank, 1996), 94–117.

42. Emmanuel de Kadt, "Thematic Lessons from the Case Studies," in *The Public-Private Mix in Social Services*, ed. Elaine Zuckerman and Emanuel de Kadt (Washington, D.C.: Inter-American Development Bank, 1997), 131–143.

43. Carol Graham, *Private Markets for Public Goods: Raising the Stakes for Economic Reform* (Washington, D.C.: Brookings Institution Press, 1998), 45.

44. Eduardo Amedeo, José Márcio Camargo, Antônio Emílio S. Marques, and Cândido Gomes, "Fiscal Crisis and Asymmetries in the Education System in Brazil," in *Coping with Crisis: Austerity, Adjustment, and Human Resources*, ed. Joel Samoa (New York: UNESCO/ILO, 1994), 48.

45. De Souza, "Redressing Inequalities," 76.

46. Diana Jean Schemo, "The ABC's of Doing Business in Brazil," *New York Times*, 16 July 1998, p. D7.

47. PREAL, *Future at Stake*, 12.

48. Mary Anastasia O'Grady, "A Brazilian State Shows How to Reform Schools," *The Wall Street Journal*, 16 August 1997, p. A17.

49. Summarized from presentation of Juan Carlos Navarro, IDB conference, Washington, D.C., 12 November 1997.

50. Juan Prawda, "Educational Decentralization in Latin America: Lessons Learned," *International Journal of Educational Development* 13, no. 3 (1993): 253–264.

51. Council on Foreign Relations, "Reforming Education in America," study group on reforming education in Latin America, "The Second Wave of Reform," directed by Allison L.C. de Cerreño, New York, February-October 1996.

52. PREAL, *Future at Stake*, 11.

53. For a review of educational assessment instruments, see Laurence Wolff, "Educational Assessments in Latin America: Current Progress and Future Challenges," *Partnership for Educational Revitalization in the Americas*, June 1998, p. 11. On-line publication available at www.preal.cl/index-i.htm.

54. Schemo, "The ABC's," D7.

55. Ellison, "Latin Summit's Focus."

56. Wolff et al., *Improving the Quality of Primary Education*, 8.

57. David E. Lorey, "Education and the Challenges of Mexican Development," *Challenge* 38, no. 2 (March-April 1995): 52.

58. Summit of the Americas Information Network Education. Available on-line at www.summit-americas.org.

59. *Action Plan for Universal and Quality Basic Education by the Year 2000*, Summit of the Americas. Available on-line at www.summit-americas.org.

60. Wolff et al., *Improving the Quality of Primary Education*, 1.

61. Gert Rosenthal, "On Poverty and Inequality in Latin America," *Journal of Inter-American Studies and World Affairs* 38, no. 2–3 (Summer-Fall 1996): 15.

62. "The Summiteers Go to School," *The Economist*, 25 April 1998, pp. 37–38.

63. Lucila Jallade, Eddy Lee, and Joel Samoff, "International Cooperation," in *Coping*

with Crisis: Austerity, Adjustment, and Human Resources, ed. Joel Samoff (New York: UNESCO/ILO, 1994), 254–266.

64. Paulo Freire, *Pedagogy of the Oppressed* (New York: Seabury, 1970).

65. John A. Britton, ed., *Molding the Hearts and Minds: Education, Communications, and Social Change in Latin America* (Wilmington, Del.: Scholarly Resources, 1994), xxiv. For more on social change, see Carlos A. Torres, *Education and Social Change in Latin America* (Albert Park, Australia: James Nicolas, 1997).

66. Wolff et al., *Improving the Quality of Primary Education*, 4.

ENVIRONMENTAL CHALLENGES

Internalizing the Costs of Development

CHAPTER FOURTEEN

Automobiles are a major source of urban pollution. *(Courtesy of the Inter-American Development Bank.)*

Understanding environmental issues in Latin America is very much about understanding the broader pattern of development that has shaped the region. The environment is inextricably linked with past economic performance and social conditions, as well as local and global policy choices. In the context of our understanding of the history of the region, the import substitution model, the challenge of the debt crisis, and the transformations of the neoliberal model, we now turn our focus specifically to the environment.

The following questions inform our discussion:

- How do countries, grappling with problems of economic growth and stability, and burdened by poverty, address environmental concerns?
- Is there a trade-off between a brighter economic future for the millions of impoverished in Latin America and the health of the environment?
- How should countries weigh the pressing needs of present generations versus a clean environment for the future?

Such environmental concerns have challenged and transformed the core of development economics. Traditional economic models neglected to account for externalities in the growth process or the finite nature of natural resources. Today development economics is being redefined by the concept of **sustainable development**. A simple definition of sustainable development offered by the World Commission on Environment and Development is that current generations should "meet their needs without compromising the ability of future generations to meet their own needs."[1] This vision has inspired local, national, and international organizations to work to define a development model that balances economic growth with environmental sensibility. The 1992 United Nations Conference on the Environment and Development held in Rio de Janeiro was a turning point for the region and the world in re-visioning the development process.

But implementation of a development strategy that weighs the needs of current generations against the requirements of the future is complicated in practice. Difficult policy questions arise:

- How should competing needs of the present and the future, the economy and the environment, be prioritized?
- How can we think systematically about the complex interrelationships between social, economic, and ecosystems in the region?
- What are the elements of an economically sound and politically viable environmental policy?

After exploring the concept of sustainable development in greater detail, we will consider its application in the region. Latin America is geographically diverse, ranging from deserts to rain forests, mountains to plains, from the most rural settlements to the densely populated and extensive megacities. Each area itself contains a huge variety of plants, animals (including humans), and minerals. The complexity of social and ecosystems adds to the complexity of environmental management in Latin America. Priorities in environmental management vary from country to country, as does the institutional capacity to meet the challenge of sustainable development. This chapter will describe the diverse environmental concerns Latin America faces in terms of human standards of living as well as ecological conditions. It will then turn to consider the best policy mix to meet the standard of sustainable development in the region.

JUST WHAT IS SUSTAINABLE DEVELOPMENT?

The challenge set by the 1987 Brundtland Report of the World Commission on Environment and Development, which defined environmentally sustainable development as meeting the needs of the current generation without compromising the ability of future generations, is—perhaps like all great ideas—a deceivingly simple concept. Meeting the needs of a current generation involves integrating economic, social, environmental, and political concerns.[2] Sustainable development promotes the efficient use of resources in the service of a stable growth path. The growth pattern, however, is very much shaped by social conditions. Without attention to poverty and inequality, the basic needs of the current generation are not met. The Brundtland Report notes that a "world in which poverty is endemic will always be prone to ecological and other catastrophes."[3] All people, including marginalized groups, must be vested in the development process. How can people living in absolute poverty support the hard choices that sometimes must be made to postpone present consumption to favor future sustainability? Postponing consumption while living on the margins of existence threatens survival. Without participation of all segments of the population, a social consensus cannot be achieved to balance present and future needs.

For development to be sustainable, economic and social changes must be set against the capabilities of the physical environment to support human activity. Achieving sustainability is therefore a delicate balancing act between a growing population and the ability of the physical environment to absorb the waste of human activity.[4] Technical fixes are one way out of this bind. The capacity of the physical environment to support human life can be transformed by technological changes allowing people to do more with less. However, betting future sustainability on potential technological change is fraught with uncertainty. We might hope that new (and cheap) technologies are developed to provide energy, recycle solid and hazardous wastes, purify sewage and industrial wastes before they hit the sea, and reduce emission from motor vehicles, but can we count on it?

Sound environmental policy involves hard choices. Who makes them? Identifying whose needs are met in the present and the future involves political decisions—decisions in Latin America that historically have been made by elites. As can be seen in figure 14.1, economic, environmental, political, and social factors influence policy at the local, national, and international levels. The priorities at each level might be in conflict. Although global concerns for biodiversity or greenhouse effects might dominate the agenda of the more industrialized nations, the interaction of poverty and the environment is likely to be of greater concern at the local and national levels.

Figure 14.1.   The Complexity of Environmental Decision Making

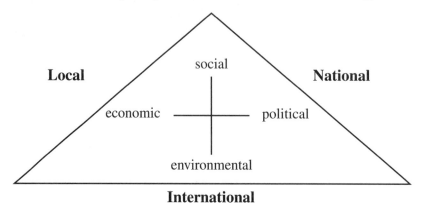

When the problems of current generations are so pressing, it is tough (especially for elected officials) to postpone meeting today's needs in favor of the future. Furthermore, it is difficult for governments to even assess the well-being of present generations. How do we measure environmental quality? Is it measured by homes with sewer connections, clean air, the number of endangered species, or the acreage in protected national parks?[5] An accurate measure of environmental quality involves much better data collection and estimation of current and future resource stocks.[6] Better data would permit a more consistent estimation of the present value of future resource use. This tough calculation of society's willingness to pay today for future access to a sustainable environment is at the core of strong policy recommendations.

To assess the bundle of social and environmental capital that one generation should pass on to the next, some environmental economists promote the concept of a **safe minimum standard.**[7] The safe minimum is seen as a social compact that, in the face of high ecological uncertainty, provides a basis for sustainable growth. Of course the differing priorities of the industrialized North and the developing South make such a compact on global issues precarious. To a large degree, natural capital or biodiversity finds its home in the South, whereas social capital, including scientific and technical knowledge to preserve natural capital, is largely lodged in the North. Different valuations placed on the need to employ natural capital today versus desires to preserve ecological diversity for the future suggest that the North, having already depleted much of its natural stocks, will have to compensate the South to preserve biodiversity. But how much, and on whose terms?

The Global Environmental Facility (GEF) was formed after the Rio meetings to address financial and technological transfers. Following the conference, the concept of sustainable development found expression in five basic agreements: The Rio Declaration, which articulated political principles for re-visioning development models; **Agenda 21,** a comprehensive agenda for action; the Convention on Biological Diversity; the Convention on Climate Change; and the Declaration of Principles on the Management, Conservation, and Sustainable Development of

Forests. The success of such multilateral as well as bilateral efforts will certainly be a function of local, national, and international capacity building in institutions to operationalize the simple yet rich concept of sustainable development.

Sustainable development is not a concept that can easily be applied to guide the development process. It is complicated by problems of measurement, the uncertainty of future technological change, and political will on local, national, and international levels to make and pay for hard choices. Yet for all its limitations, it is an extremely useful policy principle. Meeting the needs of the present for a better life without compromising the stock of assets available to future generations is an important criterion that can be applied to policies addressing industry, infrastructure development, or poverty. How to bring this principle into the policy arena in a way that minimizes the economic costs and maximizes the environmental benefits will be addressed at the end of the chapter. But before we design policy, we must first better understand the nature of the environmental problem in the Latin American region.

ENVIRONMENTAL PRIORITIES IN LATIN AMERICA

What is the most pressing environmental problem in Latin America? In fact this is not a very good question. There is a broad array of environmental issues in the region that vary in importance based upon who you are, where you live, and what economic resources are available to you. The priority list depends on whether you are rich or poor, urban or rural. A middle-class resident of Santiago, Chile, is likely to complain most about air quality, while someone living in a shack along the Tiete River in São Paulo might be most affected by problems of water sanitation. A rubber tapper might ally with an international rain forest activist in arguing that tropical deforestation is the most pressing issue, but for very different reasons. Problems in maintaining fishing stocks off the coast of Argentina might seem a long way from the concerns of the Indians in Peru's Altiplano. As Latin America is diverse, so are its environmental concerns.

THE POOR: AGENTS AND VICTIMS OF ENVIRONMENTAL DESTRUCTION

Throughout Latin America—urban or rural, tropical or polar—it is clear that sustainable development is not possible without making progress toward alleviating poverty. The poor are both agents and victims of an unsafe environment. Lacking resources to invest in cleaner water or waste removal, or the assets necessary in agriculture to reinvest in soil quality, the poor promote environmental degradation. But they are also the worst victims of unhealthy water and air quality, and they are often financially unable to flee the worst zones of pollution.

Poverty, and its associated social and economic conditions of malnutrition, underdeveloped human capital, disease, and lack of savings, is linked to environmental damage. Loss of biodiversity, deforestation and desertification, soil erosion and nutrient depletion, and water pollution are in part caused by resource con-straints of land scarcity, receding fuel wood and water supply, reduced agricultural productivity, and unhygienic sanitation.[8] Unable to postpone present consumption or invest in the future, the poor scrape to survive. They use whatever resources are available, and most often they do not have accessible solid waste and wastewater services.

Poverty can be exacerbated by population growth. If the economic pie is not growing, more inhabitants leave fewer people with the ability to sustain themselves today and invest in their futures. Population growth increases the demand for goods and services, as well as introducing more pollutants into the waste stream. The 1994 U.N. International Conference on Population and Development (ICPD) held in Cairo, Egypt, made explicit the links between population, development, and the environment and called for changes in unsustainable consumption and production patterns through legislative, economic, and administrative measures.[9] In Latin America the population grew 2.4 percent from 1970 to 1980 and approxi-mately 2 percent from 1980 until 1995. Over the lost decade of the 1980s, as gross domestic product rose only 1.1 percent, population growth rates far outpaced the economy, leaving little for environmental progress.

THE PROBLEMS OF THE URBAN ENVIRONMENT

Population growth rates outpaced the economy in the 1980s, but as the region has recovered in the 1990s, the environmental dividend has been far from evident. Why? In part this is due to the fact that population growth has taken place dispro-portionately in the urban sector. In 1965, 55.9 percent of the population in South America lived in cities; by 1995 this number reached 78 percent. This is higher than the U.S. ratio of 76.2 percent. Comparable rates of **urbanization** of 87.5 per-cent in Argentina, 78.7 percent in Brazil, 92.9 percent in Venezuela, 90.3 percent in Uruguay, and 85.9 percent in Chile challenge the folkloric picture of a peasant in a small village or an Indian in the rain forest that many hold as typical of Latin America. It is estimated that by 2025 Latin America will have the highest rate of urbanization in the world at approximately 85 percent.[10] The rate of transformation of these urban centers has overwhelmed the capacity of municipalities to provide clean air and water or rapid and reasonable transportation and telecommunications infrastructure to their inhabitants.

Urbanization in Latin America is compressed in a few megacities. In the United States 41.7 percent of urban dwellers live in forty-three cities with at least 750,000 inhabitants; in Argentina 42.7 percent of urban dwellers are spread over only three large cities. Forty percent of all Chileans live in Santiago, 25 percent living below the poverty line. Four cities in Latin America make the global top ten list of megacities: Mexico City, São Paulo, Rio de Janeiro, and Buenos Aires. By the year 2000, São Paulo and Mexico City are projected to have populations of 22,558,000 and 16,190,000 respectively, putting them in the top six megacities with Shanghai, Bombay, Tokyo, and New York.[11] As anyone who has lived in or visited New York or Los Angeles knows, the air, water, and transport problems of

This Colombian recycling project contributes to urban clean-up and generates jobs.
(Courtesy of Willie Heinz and the Inter-American Development Bank.)

the city overpower even the best of intentions. Imagine trying to solve the same set of problems with even fewer financial resources available.

The size of urban cities makes environmental problems extraordinarily complex. Less than half the Brazilian urban population has garbage collection. Only 3 percent of the waste is properly disposed of, 63 percent is thrown into streams and rivers, and 34 percent is left in unmanaged open spaces.[12] Lima, Peru, is home for approximately 7 million of the country's inhabitants living in what the government euphemistically refers to as "emergency dwellings." The lack of running water, electricity, and sanitation make perfect conditions for the spread of infectious disease such as cholera.[13] Guatemala City collects only 65 percent of its municipal waste; the rest is disposed of in unofficial locations. In most slums—the many barrios and favelas of the region—garbage collection is nonexistent, seen as outside formal sector services or inaccessible through narrow, unpaved streets.[14] Ironies abound. Although Mexico can store 10 percent less garbage than it produces, 36,000 tons of toxic waste a year are imported from the United States.[15] Of course, if Latin Americans produced as much garbage as those who live in the United States, the result would simply be unbearable. For example, each person in Quito, Ecuador, produces about 281 kilograms of solid waste a year. In São Paulo per capita solid waste generation stands at 352 kilograms—low compared to the average resident in Washington, D.C., who produces 1,246 kilograms of solid waste.[16]

The costs of urban environmental problems are enormous. The World Bank estimates that the welfare costs of illness and death due to dirty air and water in the region are between $1 billion and $3 billion. Brazilians calculate that 70 percent of all hospital admissions are due to diseases related to lack of sanitation. The leading source of death among children under five in most Latin American countries is traceable to water-transmitted diseases.[17] One study estimated that the cost of water pollution in Mexico in terms of the incidence of diarrheal diseases and premature death was U.S.$3.6 billion—nearly 2 percent of total Mexican GDP in 1988.[18] The cost to Peru of the cholera epidemic was a $1 billion, more than three times what Peru invested in water supply and sanitation during the entire 1980s. The urban environmental challenge in Latin America is a pressing health issue with overwhelming economic and human costs.[19]

It has been estimated that more than 80 million dwellers, or 27 percent of the urban population and 19 percent of the total population, are exposed to air pollution levels exceeding World Health Organization (WHO) guidelines.[20] In the cities, a larger percentage of the population live in the open air, with greater exposure to toxic pollutants.[21] A primary cause of poor air quality is motor vehicles. Concentrated in a few large cities, they account for 80 to 99 percent of carbon monoxide emissions.[22] Half the Mexican fleet operates in Mexico City, and one quarter of Brazilian cars are registered in São Paulo. More than in industrialized countries, motor vehicles are a significant source of airborne toxic pollutants because cars are in poor condition and lower-quality fuels are used. It could get worst. Imagine the damage if instead of 67.9 cars per 1,000 residents in Latin America and the Caribbean, the 561 per 1,000 rate of the United States were matched.[23]

Geographic characteristics compound the environmental problems of some cities. Mexico City sits in a basin surrounded by mountains. Ventilation is poor, and during winter, thermal inversions occur up to twenty-five days per month. More than 30,000 industries and 12,000 service facilities are located in the valley, and 2.5 million motor vehicles—buses, minibuses, taxis, trucks, vans, private cars—operate in the area. WHO guidelines are exceeded regularly, especially during the morning rush hour when low temperature, atmospheric stability (inversion), and heavy traffic occur simultaneously.[24] Sadly, one should not be surprised by the 1988 study that showed more than 25 percent of newborns with toxins in their blood at levels high enough to impair neurological and motor-physical development.[25]

Water quality is problematic in both the rural and the urban areas. In Latin America, less than 2 percent of sewage receives treatment, contributing to the spread of typhoid and cholera.[26] Roughly one in five urban dwellers in the region has no sanitary services.[27] In 1990 São Paulo was a city of approximately 18 million people with only 16 percent of households connected to municipal sewage treatment plants.[28] Most widespread contamination of water is from disease-bearing human waste, but in the rural areas agro-industrial effluent, especially fertilizer use, is particularly damaging. Toxic chemical buildup in rivers, including lead and mercury, lowers oxygen levels and also threatens fish and aquatic culture. Rapid urban growth will add more than 140 million to the region's inadequate urban infrastructure.[29]

THE ENERGY PROBLEM

Migration to the cities also pressures the efficient provision of energy to the population. Energy consumption packs a double environmental whammy. Not only is raw energy a scarce natural resource, but the consumption of energy also generates significant externalities. Table 14.1 dramatically portrays both the rapid rate of growth in demand for energy resources and the North-South imbalance in per capita energy consumption. The growth in energy consumption has been strong over the period 1970–1995. We can see from the data that in countries such as Paraguay, El Salvador, Ecuador, and Bolivia per person energy consumption has increased more than 100 percent; the second group, including Mexico, Brazil, and Costa Rica, has increased rates in line with the Japanese, whereas Nicaragua has limited increases in per capita energy consumption to under 15 percent and Venezuela and Uruguay have actually decreased consumption.

Low rates of growth of energy consumption are not unambiguously a good thing. They may simply reflect a low level of economic development. The use of energy will naturally increase as a country is growing. Growth may result in electrical access for more homes, more appliances for the middle class, and greater industrial requirements. The World Bank projects increased demand for energy in less developed countries due to growth of populations and per capita incomes, migration to urban areas (substitution of energy for fuel wood), and increasing use of energy-intensive products (such as fertilizers, petrochemicals, cements, vehicles, appliances, and motors), as well as poor energy efficiency in the developing world.[30] Higher growth rates of energy consumption are expected at higher income

Table 14.1.   Energy Consumption per Capita (kilograms of oil equivalent)

Country	1970	1995	% Change 1970–1995	% of U.S. per Capita Consumption (1995)
Paraguay	114	308	170	3.90
El Salvador	157	410	161	5.19
Ecuador	216	553	156	7.00
Bolivia	183	396	116	5.01
Brazil	410	772	88	9.77
Mexico	786	1,456	85	18.42
Costa Rica	378	584	54	7.39
Japan	2,654	3,964	49	50.15
Germany	3,077	4,156	35	52.57
Colombia	490	655	34	8.29
Argentina	1,208	1,525	26	19.29
Honduras	191	236	24	2.99
Chile	867	1,065	23	13.47
Guatemala	170	206	21	2.61
Nicaragua	253	265	5	3.35
United States	7,665	7,905	3	100.00
United Kingdom	3,847	3,786	−2	47.89
Venezuela	2,206	2,158	−2	27.30
Uruguay	797	639	−20	8.08

Source: The World Bank, *World Development Report 1993* (New York: Oxford University Press/World Bank, 1993), 246–247; The World Bank, *World Development Report 1998/9* (New York: Oxford University Press/World Bank, 1999), 224–225.

levels. Some of the lower energy consumption rates over the period 1970–1991 can sadly be attributed to severe economic contraction or the dislocation of energy supplies in the Central American war. This is not the case with Chile. Despite strong rates of growth throughout the period, Chileans were able to maintain relatively low rates of per capita energy consumption. The puzzle in this positive story may be resolved by a growth strategy that is accompanied by greater attention to energy efficiency.

Energy planning for efficient use of resources is clearly indicated—perhaps most for the United States! The last column in table 14.1 indicates the percentage of energy a person in each country uses as a proportion of the individual energy use in the United States. On a per person basis, a Brazilian uses approximately 9.77 percent of the electricity of someone living in the United States. Imagine if the Brazilians' appetite for energy continued to grow to emulate their northern neighbors. The demands on the Brazilian balance of payments, not to mention global resources, would be enormous. Conversely, imagine if those living in the United States were able to conserve even a portion of the apparent excess consumption of energy.

In the developing world there are important opportunities for enhancing energy efficiency. Energy sectors in developing countries have been characterized by pricing below costs; concentrated, often state-held enterprises; companies acting as a direct extension of government, with little distinction between ownership, regulation, and management; high information costs; weak management expertise; and the need for a more transparent regulatory process.[31] Pricing energy to market cost, promoting efficiency at the enterprise level, and increasing transparency in regulatory agencies should, as in Chile, encourage economic growth while holding down energy consumption and costs. NGOs such as Enersol promote grassroots introduction of renewable energy technologies. Encouraging the use of solar-electric systems through financing and technical assistance, Enersol helps local organizations install energy systems that are economically and environmentally sustainable over time.[32]

Some countries in the region are energy exporters. The development patterns of Mexico, Ecuador, and Venezuela have clearly been shaped by their oil sectors. As shown in table 14.2, in 1994 Venezuela produced approximately 944 million barrels of oil and Mexico 1.02 billion. Measured by known reserves, Mexico ranks eighth in the world and Venezuela, a member of OPEC, fifth. Together they account for more than a tenth of the world's reserves of oil.

Although the oil sectors have traditionally been under the arm of state control, foreign participation has recently increased.[33] Oil production can have devastating environmental costs. One analyst estimates that since oil production began in Ecuador in 1972, the trans-Andean pipeline has spilled one and a half times the oil spilled in the *Exxon Valdez* disaster and discharged 4.3 million gallons of toxic

Table 14.2.   Estimates of Petroleum Reserves and Crude Oil Production

	Estimated Reserves 1995 (thousands of barrels)	*% of World Reserves*	*Crude Oil Production 1994 (thousands of barrels)*	*% of World Crude Oil Production*
North America, total	81,136,250	7.28	4,099,589	18.11
Canada	8,630,750	0.77	639,543	2.83
Cuba	273,500	0.02	10,950	0.05
Mexico	49,775,000	4.47	1,017,620	4.50
United States	22,457,000	2.01	2,431,476	10.74
South America, total	81,717,100	7.33	1,855,450	8.20
Argentina	2,194,700	0.20	243,328	1.08
Bolivia	128,000	0.01	9,382	0.04
Brazil	4,200,000	0.38	252,945	1.12
Chile	123,000	0.01	4,491	0.02
Columbia	5,000,000	0.45	164,250	0.73
Ecuador	3,000,000	0.27	135,050	0.60
Peru	1,215,000	0.11	48,016	0.21
Trinidad and Tobago	560,000	0.05	48,009	0.21
Venezuela	64,878,000	5.82	944,438	4.17
Others	418,400	0.04	5,541	0.02

Source: DeGolyer & MacNaughton, *Twentieth Century Petroleum Statistics 1995.*

waste daily. There has been an increase in skin and intestinal disease, headaches, and fever, with contaminants in drinking water reaching 1,000 times the safety standards set by the U.S. EPA. This is not to mention the cultural conflict of oil versus indigenous people in the region.[34] Box 14.1 discusses the oil and environment dilemma in Ecuador.

Given problems with the high cost and environmental problems of oil consumption and production, increasingly countries have turned to harness the enormous hydroelectric power in the region. But both the consumption and production of energy have environmental costs. A strategy to minimize costs is critical to sustainable development.

DEFORESTATION OF TROPICAL RAIN FORESTS

Among issues relating to the natural environment, perhaps the most well known and visible problem is the deforestation of the rain forests. A tropical rain forest is defined as an evergreen or partially evergreen forest located in an area that receives no less than four inches of precipitation per month for two out of three years. The mean annual temperature exceeds twenty-four degrees C with no frost.[35] The Amazon rain forest covers 7 percent of the Earth, has 15 to 20 percent of the unsalted water on the planet, and is home to more than half the world's biological wealth.[36] In addition rain forests take CO_2 out the atmosphere and are a source of food and medicines as well as recreation.[37]

> **QUESTION FOR THOUGHT**
>
> Many of the environmental problems in Latin America have both domestic and international causes and consequences. Land deforestation, for example, is driven by internal land use forces but also by global demand for forest products. Halting deforestation could have global benefits to reduce the pressures on global warming. How much should citizens of North America be willing to pay to help reduce environmental pressures in the South? Would you be willing to pay a global environmental tax? How much?

The approximately 7 million square kilometers of the Amazon territory cover eight sovereign states with 42,000 kilometers of highways, river networks, and airports.[38] Its expanse houses a great heterogeneity of climates, geological formations, soils, flora, fauna, and cultural history. Between 5 and 30 million existing species are estimated to inhabit the Amazon, of which 750,000 insects, 40,000 vertebrates, 250,000 plants, and 360,000 microbiota have been identified. Of these, more than 2,000 species of plants have been found as useful for medicinal and nutritive properties and as producers of oils, greases, waxes, varnishes, aromas, tannins, saponin, latex, rubber, condiments, and toxins.

The Amazon River, longer than the Nile, is the most powerful river in the world. Not surprisingly, there is considerable hydroenergy potential. Its many rivers, lakes, lagoons, and swamps contain varieties of mammals, birds, reptiles, fish, and invertebrates. It is estimated that the Amazon River supports 2,500 to 3,000 fish species, ten times the number found in the great Mississippi.[39] Although there is some dispute as to whether the Amazon is truly the lungs of the earth, it carries approximately one-sixth of the fresh water flowing into the seas from all the rivers of the world.[40]

The Amazon's roughly 20 million human inhabitants are likewise diverse—the Indians, rubber tappers, woodland societies engaged in logging and mining, and riverbank people, all with rich cultural traditions. Between 1 and 1.25 million indigenous people of approximately 400 ethnic groups remain after the ravages

BOX 14.1.   WHO IS RESPONSIBLE FOR OIL SPILLS IN THE ECUADORIAN RAIN FOREST?

As Latin America proceeds with the privatization of natural resource development, crucial questions emerge with respect to responsibility for ensuring environmentally safe and sustainable practices.

Ecuadorians in Shushufindi fear the black slime that forms in pools in their backyards and schools. Florinda Balla's cows have died from drinking the sludge thick with arsenic and other toxic wastes. Crops have been lost, and rivers used for drinking, bathing, and fishing have been contaminated by spills and poor extraction practices. The soil is contaminated, its salty crust crumbling when poked with a stick. Trees are defoliated, branches brittle. Roughly 17 million barrels of oil were spilled as 17 billion were extracted from Ecuador's rich petroleum reserves.

Residents are trying to make Texaco accountable for the damage to their ecosystem. The U.S.-based company began operations in Ecuador in 1964 but became a minority partner after the contract 1977 with Petroecuador, the state-owned company. Lawyers for the community group allege that although Texaco was not the lead company, all extraction technologies were under the supervision of the U.S. firm. The case is being filed in U.S. court, for more than a billion dollars in damages and cleanup costs, because the maximum fine for environmental damage in Ecuador is $12,500.

Texaco vehemently denies wrongdoing, claiming that it met all environmental and health regulations at the time, consistent with prevailing international practice. Furthermore, it signed a cleanup agreement with the Ecuadorian government in 1995, although activists charge that treatment has not taken place. Texaco pledged more than $1 million for reforestation, new schools, and medical dispensaries, but improvements have not yet materialized. Other pools with oil spills are not covered by the agreement.

Environmental officials in Ecuador contextualize the damage as a legacy of a pre-environmentally conscious age, and Petroecuador's involvement as following Texaco's instructions.

Texaco, which pulled out of Ecuador in 1990, argues that the responsibility for the remaining problems falls in the government's lap. Policy mistakes, including drawing settlers into the region to strengthen its border with Peru, remain the burden of the government.

The losers appear to be the people of Shushufindi, in the Oriente rain forest. Although Ecuador depends on oil and related products for 44 percent of its national budget, less than 3 percent returns to the region. In the town, fewer than 0.2 percent of the homes have tap water. Oil has done little to alleviate their poverty and immiseration.

How should Ecuador balance the need for foreign investment to develop its natural resources with its obligation to protect the environment? What options do Ecuadorians have when they believe their government is not acting in their best interest? Should environmental standards differ for U.S. citizens and Ecuadorians? Should responsibility for meeting international standards be imposed retroactively in a country?

Adapted from Diana Jean Schemo, "Ecuadorians Want Texaco to Clear Toxic Residue," *New York Times*, 31 January 1998. Available at LatinoLink at www.latinolink.com.

of disease and displacement of centuries of colonization. Twenty percent of the Amazonian population is dedicated to farming, and 50 to 60 percent live in one of the cities or urban zones. Some of the cities have suffered a more than fiftyfold increase in population since 1940, overwhelming the local infrastructure.[41] The basin contains rich oil reserves as well as bauxite, gold, manganese, copper, and iron. Garimpeiros, or gold miners, roughly 30 percent of the basin's population, have attracted a good deal of environmental and social attention for the questions they raise about poverty and wealth and their conflicts with the indigenous peoples and the environment.

Despite its importance, it should be remembered that the Amazon is not the only forest area under threat in the region. The fastest rates of deforestation are occurring in Central America; between 2 and 3 percent of forests in Costa Rica, El Salvador, Honduras, and Paraguay are deforested annually.[42] In contrast to the Amazon basin, where larger commercial interests dominate, land degradation in Central America is tied to the desire to obtain property rights under uncertain economic conditions.

Causes of deforestation throughout the region include the conversion of land to agriculture (approximately 64 percent of deforestation), commercial logging (18 percent), firewood gathering (10 percent), and cattle ranching (8 percent).[43] Inadequate property rights in other agricultural zones and government incentives to colonize land contribute to the destructive human activity in the rain forest region. For example, in Brazil during the late 1960s and early 1970s, government regional development programs provided incentives to ranchers and other farmers to move into Amazonia. In addition, mining projects such as the Grande Carajas Program accelerated deforestation.[44] It is important to note that the primary agricultural or mining activity is not the only cause of destruction in the region. Secondary destruction results from road construction and the equipment necessary to sustain distant settlements.

Clearing forested land for agriculture is the main driving force behind deforestation. However, in most cases agricultural use of these lands is not sustainable due to the generally nutrient poor soils. The results include erosion and water pollution (especially through pesticide use), leaving behind nonproductive land and a depleted resource base. The costs of deforestation are not limited to plant life. Of the 6–9 million Indians once calling the Amazon home, only remnants of their tribes remain. The twentieth century saw ninety tribes go out of existence.[45]

With the signature of the Amazon Cooperation Treaty in 1978 the countries of the region began coordination of development strategies to promote rational and sustainable use of resources. In addition to national and regional organizations, local and international nongovernmental groups are also active in the region. The good news is that the rate of deforestation has declined from a peak of 22 percent (average annual rate) between 1978 and 1988 to 11.1 percent in 1990–1991. The sad fact is that despite substantial progress, the area destroyed each year is still half the size of the state of Massachusetts.[46]

Forests are not the only ecosystem suffering under the weight of population pressures. Coastal habitats, one of the richest sources of marine biodiversity and a vital source of food supply, are threatened by the so-called progress of develop-

Table 14.3.   Percentage Change of Forests in Latin America

| | Total Forest | | Rain Forests | | |
Country	1990 (thousands of hectares)	% Annual Change 1981–1990	1990 (thousands of hectares)	% Annual Change 1981–1990	% of Total Forest That Is Rain Forest
Bolivia	49,317	−1.10	0	0.00	0
Brazil	561,107	−0.60	291,597	−0.30	52
Colombia	54,064	−0.60	47,455	−0.40	88
Costa Rica	1,428	−2.60	625	−2.60	44
Ecuador	11,967	−1.70	7,150	−1.70	60
El Salvador	123	−2.00	33	−2.00	27
Guatemala	4,225	−1.60	2,542	−1.60	60
Honduras	4,605	−2.00	1.286	−2.00	28
Mexico	48,586	−1.20	2,441	−1.00	5
Nicaragua	6,013	−1.70	3,712	−1.70	62
Panama	3,117	−1.70	1,802	−1.60	58
Paraguay	12,859	−2.40	0	0.00	0
Peru	67,906	−0.40	40,358	−0.30	59
Venezuela	45,690	−1.20	19,602	−0.70	43
Latin America	918,115	−0.70	450,162	−0.40	49

Source: Derived from World Resources Institute, *World Resources 1994–95* (New York: Basic Books, 1995), 309.

ment. In South America 50 percent of the coastlines are under moderate or high potential threat.[47] Coastal development, overfishing, increased waste disposal, industrial pollution, oil spills, and population density have led to dramatic changes in habitat. As shown in table 14.4, increased consumption of fertilizers has pressured rural water supplies. Environmental concerns in Latin America are clearly broad. From city sewage to mangrove swamps, from air pollution alerts to the felling of trees, questions of sustainability abound. Without change in current practice, future generations will not be as well-off.

POLICY FORMULATION: WHAT CAN BE DONE ABOUT ENVIRONMENTAL PROBLEMS IN THE REGION?

Given the wide range of problems as well as limited resources, what would constitute good environmental policy in Latin America? How can different groups with widely varied interests be brought together in the service of environmental sustainability? Who should pay for a cleaner environment in the region?

Environmental goodwill has been part of the political platform of Latin American governments in the 1990s. Yet progress has sometimes been frustratingly slow. Why do policies fail? Policy failures, certainly not limited to the Latin American region, may be attributed to undervaluation of forest resources, inadequate understanding of affected groups, difficulty in analyzing policy impacts, administrative

BOX 14.2.   CHICO MENDES

On December 24, 1988, the *New York Times* reported the murder of Francisco "Chico" Alves Mendes. At the time of his death, he was the president of the Xapuri Rural Workers' Union and a committed spokesperson for the defense of the Amazon rain forest in Xapuri Acre in northwest Brazil. Chico Mendes became a martyr in the plight to prevent the deforestation of the Amazon forest.

Since the eighteenth century and through World War II, the Amazon was a major source of rubber. It is the home to a species of trees from the genus *Havea*, which produces the best rubber in the world. Ninety-five percent of world rubber production comes from these trees, of which there are an estimated 300 million scattered throughout the Amazon and Orinoco River basins.

Until the 1960s, the rubber industry was based on rubber estates operating in a system of debt bondage. Rubber tappers, who were kept illiterate and innumerate, were obliged to sell their product at artificially low prices to the estate owners. Hence, as a son of a rubber tapper, Chico Mendes first went to school in the forest, where he learned the basic plant–animal relationships and the unique method of extracting rubber from Havea trees. It was not until the age of twenty that he began to read and write.

In the 1960s, the Brazilian government began to promote the settlement and development of Acre by opening the BR-364 road. Incentives were given to cattle ranchers, and estate owners were bought out. The result was the eviction of many rubber tappers and a constant harassment of those who remained. Very often, the tappers were forced to labor for the cattle ranchers, engaging in clear-cutting and slash-and-burn techniques to adapt the land for cattle grazing. Western Brazil became like the American west of the nineteenth century, lawless and without order. Arguments of manifest destiny were used to justify the taking over of the land and the exploitation of its inhabitants.

To protect the rubber tappers and their lifestyle, the Rural Workers Union was founded in the mid-1970s. As the clear-cutting intensified and the evictions increased, the Union actively began to stop the destruction of the forest. It assembled tappers and their families as human walls to prevent clear-cutting by cattle ranchers. This classic form of passive resistance was called an *empate*, frequently translated as a stalemate or draw. The empates became so successful by 1979 that the ranchers arranged for the murder of the union's founder, Wilson Pinheiro, leaving Chico with the leadership.

In 1985, the National Rubber Tappers Congress assembled in Brasilia to work out alternative development proposals for the protection of the Amazon and the rubber tappers. Chico wanted to justify the empates by providing an alternative development strategy for the forest. He came up with the idea of "Extractive Reserves." In the same manner that the Indians' traditional habitat and living style were protected, Chico proposed the creation of reserves to preserve the rain forests and continue rubber tapping.

Chico's proposal was the weapon that international environmental groups needed to persuade the Brazilian government to slow down the burning of the Amazon. These groups realized that the government might approve because it was not simply another U.S. proposal, but instead was a native initiative undertaken by grassroots groups who wanted to preserve their habitat. Thus, Chico was taken to testify before the Inter-American Development Bank's board of directors. He also met informally with members of the U.S. Senate Appropriations Committee to obtain funds for the protection of the rain forests in Acre. In 1987, Chico was awarded the Global 500 Prize from the United Nations and the medal from the Society for a Better World for his fight to preserve Amazonia.

In 1988, the first extractive reserve was put in place in Acre. This reserve fell on the land claimed by a prominent cattle rancher who previously had many encounters with the Union's empates. On 22 December 1988, the embittered son of this cattle rancher assassinated Chico Mendes in the doorway of his home. His death did not quiet the Union but strengthened it by attracting more international attention. Chico Mendes's legacy is the expansion of extractive reserves in Brazil to protect the rain forest and the lifestyle of rubber tappers.

REFERENCES

Mendes, Chico. *Fight for the Forest*. London: Latin American Bureau, 1990.
Shoumatoff, Alex. *The World Is Burning*. Boston: Little, Brown, 1990.
More on Chico Mendes and the Amazon is available at the Environmental Defense Fund website at www.edf.org/programs/international/chico/chicotimeline.html.

corruption, and operational difficulties.[48] Ineffective policies, or policies that don't achieve their objectives, most often result from a poor match between ends and means. The policy goal may have been too broad given available resources or institutional capacity. Inefficient policies are policies that could have been achieved at a lower cost.

Environmental policies have to make good economic sense to continue over time. Other policy failures have occurred because the goal was unidimensional, focusing on the environment to the exclusion of the economy or the social base. Environmental policies must consider the linkages between social, environmental, and economic objectives for success. Intersectoral linkages are also critical. As demonstrated in table 14.5, infrastructure, mining, energy, trade, monetary, fiscal, and agricultural policies are linked. In analyzing potential policy outcomes, these complex linkages must be taken into account. Such environmental accounting is extremely tough but vitally important. Although it is difficult to assign monetary value to natural resources, estimate the effects on a variety of social groups, predict direct and indirect linkages, and account for administrative and operational weaknesses, not doing so will further compromise achievements in the environmental arena.

The design of policies can be broken down into three types: **direct government investment**, **market-based incentives** (MBI), and **command and control (CAC) mea-**

Table 14.4.   Consumption of Fertilizers

Country	1970	1980	1990	% Growth 1970–1980	% Growth 1980–1990
Argentina	87,030	115,560	165,500	33	43
Bolivia	1,550	2,970	5,170	92	74
Brazil	1,001,920	4,200,520	3,164,100	319	−25
Chile	129,490	132,740	295,480	3	123
Costa Rica	49,370	73,500	108,600	49	48
Mexico	537,720	1,237,920	1,798,600	130	45
Nicaragua	25,880	54,200	40,020	109	−26
Peru	84,300	118,130	125,160	40	6

Source: Derived from Economic Commission for Latin America and the Caribbean, *Statistical Yearbook of Latin America and the Caribbean* (Santiago, Chile: Economic Commission for Latin America and the Caribbean, various years).

Table 14.5. Examples of Policy Linkages

Movement Policy/Practice	Potential Effects on Management and Conservation of Forest Resources
• Settlement policies	• Deforestation, forest degradation.
• Transport infrastructure policies	• Increase in prices of forests resources. • Increase in competitive uses of land and conversion to nonforest uses.
• Mining development policies	• Better access and increased competitive uses of land can create effects similar to those caused by expansion of transportation infrastructure.
• Trade policies	• Industrial protectionism policies that lead to industrial processing inefficiency may increase due to the growth of monopolistic forces. Effects on forest resources would depend on the degree of industrial integration and the degree of competition in forest raw materials markets. • Log bans may produce two opposite effects: a) decrease prices of forest resources and profitability of forest management and encourage competitive uses of lands, thus inducing deforestation; b) reduce exploitation of forest resources, particularly in common lands.
• Land delimitation, demarcation, and titling	• Increase in land tenure security may stimulate propensity to invest in forest resources management and conservation. • High interest rate policies discourage long-term investments in forest management and conservation.
• Monetary and credit policies	• Subsidized livestock and/or agricultural credit promote deforestation by increasing profitability of competitive land uses.
• Fiscal policies	• Changes in the propensity to invest in forest management and conservation and in competitive uses of land: alternative fuel subsidies may reduce the demand for firewood; higher taxes on logging would reduce forest harvesting, etc.
• Exchange policies	• Changes in investments in forestry activities that are directly or indirectly related to international trade. Exchange rate devaluation would increase profitability of timber exports.
• Policies that assign land ownership based on proof of land use	• Incentives to deforest to prove land use. • On the other hand, secure land titles may induce investment in resource management and conservation.
• Agricultural/livestock policies	• Policies that stimulate cattle-ranching and agricultural activities, such as subsidized credit or ag-

Movement Policy/Practice	Potential Effects on Management and Conservation of Forest Resources
	ricultural price support and price guarantees, stimulate competitive uses of forest land and therefore deforestation.
• Energy policies	• Increased supply of alternative fuels and reduced firewood use.
	• Loss of forest resources due to flooding associated with hydroelectric works. Displacement of population may induce further deforestation.
	• Changes in transportation costs and therefore changes in access to remote forest resources may increase their value and induce forest investment and deforestation (see transport infrastructure policies above).
	• Environmental charges (such as payment for the protection of watersheds supplying hydroelectric dams) can generate additional funds for forest resources management and conservation.

Source: Hernán Curtés-Salás, Ronnie de Camino, and Arnoldo Contreras, *Readings of the Workshop on Government Policy Reform for Forestry Conservation and Development in Latin America* (San José, Costa Rica: Inter-American Institute for Cooperation on Agriculture, 1995).

sures. The government may invest directly in infrastructure projects such as waste treatment plants or sewage lines to improve environmental quality. Market-based incentives encourage or discourage certain behaviors. For example, taxes have been used effectively to reduce industrial wastewater in Brazil by almost half, and gasoline taxes can reduce the consumption of energy. Regulations, or command and control measures, are most effective when the risk to public health is severe and when the number of polluters is relatively limited.[49] When the regulatory arm is used, it is important that legislation is matched by institutional capacity for enforcement. Lofty environmental goals without the ability to implement and enforce regulations only contribute to a lack of credibility in government. A practical, pragmatic policy mix of government investment, CAC, and MBI gradually implemented will better serve long-run environmental interests.

The focus of environmental policy might differ in the rural and the urban sectors. Rural priorities include fuel plantations; tree nurseries; sapling distribution; fuel wood quasi-self-sufficiency; southern carbon sink forests fully paid for by the North; alternative small-scale energy systems such as solar, wind, and biogas; intensification of food production through terraces, fish ponds, and small livestock; perennial crops; wood processing from plantation forests; and improved water supply with wells and low-technology pumps, as well as social organizations and collective action by the poor to improve resource management. In the urban sector, low-technology sanitation, drinking water loss reduction for slums, promotion of cleaner slum fuels (methanol versus charcoal), solar stove and cooker efficiencies, garbage and biogas/methane digesters, garbage prevention, promotion of slum cooperatives and "fair price" shops, health, hygiene, breast-feeding, and family planning education campaigns, and pro bono medical aid for vaccines and oral rehydration, supported by social organization by the urban poor, are possible policy measures.[50]

How should this long list of policy options be prioritized? **Cost-effectiveness** is an important criterion to evaluate alternative policies. For example, water-related illness and death, the largest health impact of urban pollution, can be addressed at a reasonable cost. In contrast, although sewage and sanitation services are often demanded, they may have to be postponed until more vital needs are met. As the technology is available, solid waste problems may be solved by additional resources—but this might come at an opportunity cost to more pressing needs. Cost matters for policies to be sustainable over time. Governments might have the greenest of intentions, but without long-term financing, little of enduring value will be accomplished.

Market-based initiatives have the advantage of limiting fiscal impacts on cash-strapped governments. For example, in Argentina a competitive thirty-year concession for the provision of water services was awarded to the private firm Aguas Argentinas. It has expanded the water network to 600,000 new residents, eliminated shortages, and increased potable water production by 26 percent. Reductions in the work force and better collection policies have transformed the financial performance from losses that strained state budgets to profits for the private provider of services. But market magic did not take place spontaneously. This successful transition to private provision of services was facilitated over a two-year period by a World Bank loan that supported repairs and rehabilitation of the water system as well as a portion of the voluntary retirement program.[51]

Addressing the problem of air pollution involves a mix of regulatory and market policies. Mexico City has a contingency program restricting vehicles and activity of highly polluting industries, including PEMEX refineries, on bad air days. This long-run strategy to substitute low- for high-polluting industries will, however, take time. Using outdated technology, domestically assembled automobiles in Latin America are half as fuel efficient as best practice in the United States and Japan. The Volkswagen Beetle is still in production in Mexico and Brazil. Only Brazil has succeeded in eliminating lead in gas.[52] Based on Latin American experience, the most cost-effective programs include inspection and maintenance programs to comply with emissions standards; the use of reformulated and alternative fuels (with fuels modified to accommodate seasonal geographical variations); traffic management, including bus policy regulations and liberalization, route restructuring, rationalization of truck and bus sizes, traffic signal improvements, area traffic bans, car pooling, and bikeways; road construction (paving decreases dust) and creating HOV lanes; fuel pricing; and a vehicle emissions tax.[53]

The Chileans used an innovative mix of regulation and market incentives to reduce air pollution levels in Santiago that were reaching critically unhealthy levels about once a week. Ironically, part of the problem had originated in an effort to make transportation more competitive. When bus routes were deregulated, thousands of cheap, old—and polluting—buses were imported. In 1991, 2,600 buses

Ecotourism, well managed, can provide local income and contribute to sustainability.
(Courtesy of David Mangurian and the Inter-American Development Bank.)

with pre-1972 engines, or 20 percent of the fleet, were banned. More stringent emission standards for new buses and limits on the kinds of buses permitted on downtown routes were implemented. The market came into play through the auction of bus transit rights in the city center. Routes were awarded based on fares to be charged and the type of buses to be operated. In this way private firms could make money through the exclusive right to operate in the downtown area, pollution was to be reduced by regulating the kinds of buses in the downtown area, and low fares would favor the use of public transportation. The result was a reduction in the number of winter days with critical pollution levels by approximately one-third. Although the number of buses permitted in the downtown area was limited, fleets needed fewer vehicles because each bus could make more round trips with reduced congestion. Average fares were reduced by 10 percent, and the auction yielded revenues to finance improvements in dust-reducing paved roads.[54]

Policies to promote sustainability of small farming in the Amazon likewise involve a mix of the market, direct investment, and regulation. Zoning and promoting settlements only where land is sufficiently productive, taxing capital gains to reduce speculative land sales, a stumpage tax on deforestation, the diffusion of appropriate technology, improving market and storage systems to help small farmers, and credit and other institutions have been found to promote good farming frontiers and to help farmers stay where they are without pressuring virgin areas.[55] Environmental policy requires a partnership between the public and the private sectors.

A critical step toward good environmental policy is incorporating **environmental assessments** (EA) into development policy making. Environmental problems are most often the byproduct of the development process. Encouraging environmental accounting before the damage is done will promote the goal of future sustainability. There are three steps in conducting an environmental assessment: data collection, the identification of the problem, and a CBA or cost-benefit analysis. Data collection is useful in establishing priorities for rational decision making in the environmental area. It is important when identifying the problem that both direct and indirect costs and benefits are included. For example, in assessing the Carajas project in Brazil, the Brazilian mining firm CVRD did a good job of working with FUNAI, the Brazilian Indian Protection Agency, to identify the direct effects on Indian lands. What was not accounted for, however, were the indirect costs. New roads led to squatter settlements that encroached on Indian property and brought new disease into the region. These indirect costs were the greatest source of environmental damage.

EA is not cheap and is not always simple. It may be difficult to forecast the benefits of a project. How can one estimate all the benefits of a virgin forest or cleaner air? One approach that attempts to address this problem is called the **contingent valuation** method. A survey is undertaken, asking people's willingness to pay for a given policy. In São Paulo, for example, it was found that people were three times as willing to pay for sewage than for a park.[56] Contingent valuation helps policy planners assess and measure the benefits of a given environmental project.

An alternative method to a CBA would be a CEA, or a cost-effectiveness analysis. A CEA approach gets around the problem of estimating willingness to pay for future programs by simply ranking projects on a basis of many environmental indicators rather than estimating a dollar benefit. This qualitative assessment, combined with environmental and conventional costs, is a useful, less expensive tool for decision makers. Difficulties in identifying full costs and benefits should not prevent policy makers from insisting on the best possible estimates of environmental impacts. Limited information is better than none at all in accounting for the environment.

Selecting the appropriate combination of policy instruments is a function of the institutional capacity of each country.[57] Policies are not implemented in a vacuum. Different instruments place different demands on the public sector to define a problem, design an instrument, and impose unpopular policies. It is important that agencies develop the technical skills for monitoring ambient conditions and the activities of regulated parties. Accurate data and record keeping are an important basis for the formulation of policy and midcourse corrections. The legal system must be sufficiently sophisticated to cover the forms of pollution discharge, renewable resource damage, and overharvesting that might be the target of policy. Institutions must be financially and technologically capable of turning laws into enforceable rules, with skilled people to monitor compliance. The political will must be available to impose costs on sometimes powerful agents. The residue of import substitution industrialization and the latifundia agricultural system is a legacy of powerful, concentrated firms in both the industrial and agricultural sectors.

Is the government willing to take on these dominant interests in exchange for returns that are likely to be diffuse and to spread into the future? Is the government capable of monitoring the urban and rural informal sector participants contributing to environmental degradation? Strong and independent media are necessary both to present information to the citizenry on environmental costs and to act as a watchdog against corrupt government and business practices. The institutional capacity of government and public institutions in the face of commercial and agricultural interests is a binding constraint on good environmental policy. The use of market-based instruments, for example, is limited by the degree to which efficient market transactions have permeated all levels of economic activity. Countries may need to begin with simpler mechanisms and gradually phase in more complicated mixtures of incentives and tax-based instruments as the institutional capacity to enforce and monitor develops.

WHO SHOULD PAY FOR A CLEAN ENVIRONMENT?

The biggest constraint on good environmental policy in Latin America is financial. As countries are struggling to reduce government budgets, it is difficult to legislate new programs of environmental action. Because the benefits of a clean environment accrue not only to Latin Americans, but also to the global community, this raises the question: Who should pay for environmental progress in the region?

Global financing must be used to strengthen local institutions. To improve the environment in Latin America one must change the behaviors of people—people who live in rural communities, towns, and cities. Environmental action, to be sustainable, must empower localities and provide incentives for change. Box 14.3 demonstrates a win-win example of international environmental policy in reducing greenhouse emissions.

As table 14.6 illustrates, environmental policy making involves a wide range of local, national, and international actors, often with conflicting priorities. Addressing local problems will begin to contribute to global solutions. Where such local actions benefit global concerns (such as biodiversity), the developed world should pay. This ought not be perceived as aid but a responsible policy of paying for environmental change demanded.[58] The responsibilities for sustainable development should be shared by North and South, as will share in the gains.

Given budget constraints of most governments of the Latin American and Caribbean regions, there are limited resources for conservation projects with more global than local significance. The Global Environmental Facility was a three-year experiment set up in 1991 with funds from three sources: a core of $800 million pledged by twenty-four countries, concessional financing of $300 million, and $200 million from the interim trust of the Montreal Protocol. This financial mechanism was replenished with more than $2 billion in 1994 to offer grants and concessional funds in four focal areas: climate change, biological diversity, international waters, and stratospheric ozone. Institutionally, GEF projects are managed through the U.N. Development Program (UNDP), which provides technical assistance for the GEF; the U.N. Environmental Program (UNEP), which provides the secretar-

Box 14.3.   North-South Trade in Greenhouse Gases

Latin American countries could play a key role in the global efforts to mitigate "greenhouse gas" emissions, stem global warming, and contribute to their own long-term economic growth by moving ahead on a Clean Development Mechanism (CDM) initiative, according to Christiana Figueres, executive director of the Washington-based Center for Sustainable Development in the Americas.

The CDM, scheduled to start operations in the year 2000, was endorsed by the G-77 group of developing countries at the Third Conference of the Parties to the Framework Convention on Climate Change held in December 1997 in Kyoto, Japan, which Figueres attended as a Costa Rican delegate. As conceived by its original sponsors, Brazil and Costa Rica, the CDM would serve as an international mechanism to transact "decarbonization services" between industrialized countries that produce most of the carbon dioxide and developing nations that can help to greatly reduce those noxious emissions.

Latin America could furnish such services in several ways. It could cut its own emissions of greenhouse gases by resorting to renewable energy generation or improving its energy efficiency, or it could "sequester" carbon by improving land use methods. Through photosynthesis, one hectare of new forest "sinks," or retains, an average of one ton of carbon a year, equivalent to 3.67 tons of carbon dioxide.

Costa Rica has already received offers from industrialized countries to buy two million of the sixteen million tons of carbon reduction it has certified, Figueres told IDB staffers at a briefing held at the Bank in January 1998. Prices range from $15 to $20 a ton. At the same time, the creation of a market for decarbonization services would offer an economic incentive for developing countries to opt for environmentally friendly technologies and land use methods, Figueres added.

Under the protocol adopted in Kyoto, industrialized countries are legally bound to reduce carbon emissions to 5.2 percent below their 1990 levels by the 2008–2012 period. Developing nations, which generate far less greenhouse gases, agreed to no such commitments. Because most rich countries will not be able to fully comply with their national or regional targets within the agreed timetable, the CDM would allow their industries to offset excess emissions by purchasing decarbonization services from developing nations. The challenge for Latin American nations—which are neighbors of the world's largest source of greenhouse gases, the United States—will be to ensure that all the procedures of the CDM are ready to go by the end of the century, Figueres said.

The fourth conference of parties to the climate change convention held in Argentina in November 1998 adopted the Buenos Aires Action Plan, which established deadlines for financial mechanisms to assist the developing world to respond to climate change, development, and transfer of technologies. The agreement broke a deadlock in debate on achieving a common understanding between G-77 countries (plus China) and the industrialized world. Argentina broke ranks with other developing countries, voluntarily adopting binding commitments to abate greenhouse gas emissions. Negotiations of the division of global responsibilities will continue at future annual conferences; updates may be found on-line at www.unfccc.de.

Source: Peter Bate at the Inter-American Development Bank. Available at www.iadb.org; "COP-r Adopts Buenos Aires Plan of Action," *Linkages,* a multimedia resource for environment and development policy makers developed by the *Earth Negotiations Bulletin,* as found on-line at www.llsd.ca.

iat; and the World Bank, which is responsible for implementation.[59] Countries are eligible for GEF funds if they are eligible to borrow from the World Bank or receive technical assistance grants from UNDP; they may apply through one of these implementing agencies.

The most ambitious GEF biodiversity project in Latin America draws nine

Table 14.6.   Table of Actors

Local organizations: Includes grassroots organizations (GROs) as well as other membership organizations such as burial societies and kinship groups.

Grassroots organizations (GROs): Third World membership organizations that work to improve and develop their own communities. Consist of three types:

1. Local development associations (LDAs): Work on development issues that concern the entire community.
   Examples: Village councils, neighborhood associations.
2. Interest associations: More limited in membership with focus on specific issues.
   Examples: Women's groups, water users' associations.
3. Community-based enterprises: Distinguishable from other for-profit organizations by broad-based ownership and participation in wider community development activities. Include pre-cooperatives and cooperatives.
   Example: Yanesha Tribe (Palcazú Valley, Peru): Formed the Yanesha Forestry Cooperative in 1985 to manage sustainable forests. Clear-cut long, narrow strips of land (30–40m wide), instead of huge tracts of land, to aid the natural regeneration of the forest's native species by mimicking small-scale natural disturbances. Net returns were estimated at $3,500 per hectare.[60]

National/regional organizations

Grassroots support organizations (GRSOs):   Nationally or regionally based development assistance organizations, usually composed of paid professionals working with GROs in communities other than their own.

   Example: Acción Ecología (Ecuador): Radical group building social support to solve ecological problems, which are seen as a reflection of deeper social and political injustices.[61]

Government ministries

   Example: Ministry of Environment and Natural Resources (MARNR) (Venezuela): As a result of the enacting of the Organic Law of 1976 by the Venezuelan Congress, MARNR was created in 1977, making Venezuela the first country in Latin America to create a Ministry of Environment. Created as multipurpose environment management agency to establish regulations, policies, and enforcement for natural resource protection and technological hazards.[62]

International organizations

International nongovernmental organizations (INGOs): Organizations carrying out development assistance whose central headquarters are not based in the countries where they work.

   Example: The Nature Conservancy in 1989 was involved in a debt-for-nature swap with the Costa Rican government. The Nature Conservancy bought Costa Rica's $5.6 million debt from the American Express Bank for only $784,000. In exchange, Costa Rica issued bonds totaling $1.7 million plus interest to be used to finance tropical forest preservation and other conservation measures involving $355,000 acres of land.

Multilateral agencies

World Bank: After decades of ignoring the environment, with the creation of the Environment Department in 1987, the World Bank began to require environmental assessment in its development projects.[63]

(continued)

(continued)

> *Global Environmental Facility (GEF):* Created by the World Bank in 1990 as a "pilot program to obtain practical experience in promoting and adopting environmentally sound technologies and in strengthening country-specific policy and institutional frameworks to support prudent environmental management." Four objectives are
> 1. To limit the increase in greenhouse gases.
> 2. To preserve areas of rich ecological diversity.
> 3. To protect international waters.
> 4. To halt the destruction of the ozone layer.

Central American countries together in an effort to consolidate the Mesoamerican biological corridor, a proposed network of protected areas and their buffer zones. In another effort, the GEF Honduras Protected Areas project is working with indigenous communities, particularly focused on the role of women's groups. Its goal is to address the link between natural resource management and women's double workload in the home and in the market. Table 14.7 describes a GEF program in Bolivia. In Argentina a GEF grant is supporting rural electrification through photovoltaics, wind power, and minihydroelectric schemes as sustainable sources of energy. A Brazilian program has invested $40 million through the GEF to pioneer the commercialization of electricity-generating technology that uses wood chips from plantation forests for fuel.[64] The GEF attempts to meet the enormous environmental needs of the developing world with financing from the global community in pursuit of the common goal of sustainable economic practices.

Sustainability will become a way of life only if it reaches all levels of society. On a hemispheric basis the Summit Conference on Sustainable Development, held in Santa Cruz, Bolivia, in 1996, set out a series of principles and initiatives for hemispheric cooperation on environmental issues. With the support of the presidents of the region, an inter-American seminar on public participation in sustainable development has been instituted under the auspices of the Organization of American States to promote greater participation by civil society in development planning and environmental issues. Particular attention has been paid to the environmental concerns of the indigenous and means of empowering NGOs. This project stems from the view that environmental change will be sustainable only when it is embraced by all members of society. The strategy is to promote exchange of experience and information between government representatives and groups in civil society, develop legal and institutional mechanism for participatory decision making, and develop training programs to improve technical and administrative capacities. This process is supported by a grant from the UNEP/GEF and USAID.[65] The pilot program is using three environmentally sensitive sites as "laboratories": the Scotts Head Marine Reserve in Dominica, an area of tropic forests around the Gulf of Honduras, and Peru's Bahia de Ferrol.

QUESTION FOR THOUGHT

How would a neoliberal, a new institutionalist, and a neostructuralist promote sustainable environmental development in the region?

Table 14.7. Bolivia: Rural Electrification Program

Program for Rural Electrification with Renewable Energy Using the Popular Participation Law and implemented by the United Nations Development Program

Dates	October 1997–October 2001
GEF Allocation	US$4,445,719
Cofinancing (total)	US$4,056,250
	US$100,000 (UNDP)
	US$711,700 (user contributions)
	US$603,750 (private sector)
	US$1,390,800 (Popular Participation Law)
	US$1,000,000 (government of Bolivia)
	US$250,000 (government of Bolivia, in kind)
Total financing	US$8,501,969

Environmental Problem
- Widespread use of diesel generators in rural areas for electricity, producing greenhouse gases

Project goals
- Promote widespread adoption of renewable energy in rural areas

Background

Most of Bolivia's population lives in remote rural areas, which have the fewest resources. Only about 25 percent of the rural population has access to electricity. Power generation in small communities typically has come from small diesel generators, which, in burning diesel fuel, emit greenhouse gases.

Although the government is solidly committed to rural electrification, several barriers prevent it from reaching its goal of 78 percent electrification by 2001. Grid extension is the chief means for those areas within reach of the national grid. Given Bolivia's rugged terrain and decentralized population, this is not an economic option for much of the country. Bolivia, however, has a rich endowment of energy resources, including fuelwood, bagasse, animal waste, hydroelectric, fossil fuels (oil and gas), and abundant solar and wind resources. If all rural Bolivians outside the reach of the national electrical grid were provided electricity from renewable sources, the potential savings in carbon dioxide emissions would come to nearly 665,000 tons over twenty years.

This project is intended to remove barriers to widespread adoption of renewable energy, for example, small hydropower and photovoltaics, in rural Bolivia. The government of Bolivia requested GEF assistance for the project, which is being implemented by Bolivia's National Secretariat of Energy. Under Bolivia's new Popular Participation Law, passed in 1994, 20 percent of national government revenues are now passed on to municipal governments, helping communities to garner resources for development. Part of the project's funding will come from municipalities that wish to invest in rural electrification efforts.

The project offers several new approaches to Bolivian experience: (a) a new approach to the capture and management of national funding to finance renewable rural electrification, (b) development of local public-private sector companies to assume responsibility for operating local systems, (c) employment of community-level small hydro systems and independent photovoltaic systems, (d) demonstration of financial and economic advantages of using renewable energy–based electricity supply over extending a grid to rural areas, and (e)

(continued)

(continued)

linkage of investments in power systems with investments in social and economic development.

Activities: The project has six components
- Evaluation of institutional options for implementing renewable-based rural electricity companies
- Removal of barriers to the efficient and effective operation of the financial sector for renewable energy–based electrification projects
- Training to strengthen local electricity companies
- Development and installation of pilot renewable energy facilities
- Development of standards and certification procedures
- Program management, supervision, and monitoring

Benefits
- Avoid production of nearly 21,100 metric tons of carbon dioxide in twenty-five years
- Serve as a model for replication elsewhere in Bolivia, leading to further decreases in greenhouse gases

Global institutions must work with national environmental agencies to protect the environment. Care must be taken to respect national sovereignty. Some Brazilians, particularly in the military, find the insistent zeal of international environmentalists a threat to national autonomy. They maintain that Brazilians have as much right as the settlers of the wild west to claim natural resources in the service of growth. Long-run change in the service of sustainable development must take local attitudes and institutions into account or it will certainly fail over time.

Key Concepts

Agenda 21	Direct government	Safe minimum standard
Command and control	investment	Sustainable
measures	Environmental	development
Contingent valuation	assessments	Urbanization
Cost-effectiveness	Market-based incentives	

Chapter Summary

Sustainable Development

- A sustainable development model, or being able to meet the needs of present generations without compromising the needs of future generations, requires the recognition of economic, social, environmental, and political concerns. The application of such a model can prove to be a complex process in a region as diverse as Latin America, with difficulties in measurement, the uncertainty of future technological change, and the political will on local, national, and international levels.

Environmental Problems in Latin America

- Poverty contributes to environmental degradation. Individuals must use current resources as they struggle to survive. However, the poor also suffer when they are financially unable to protect themselves from the same degradation.
- Population growth and its subsequent urbanization rates compound problems in many Latin American cities. Garbage collection is insufficient, especially in poor areas; garbage is thrown in open streets or nearby rivers and streams. Air pollution is becoming an increasing problem with carbon monoxide emissions from the increase in the number of vehicles within the cities, many of which are in poor condition. Unreliable water is common due to inadequate sewage systems.
- Excessive consumption of energy can be environmentally unsustainable, because energy is a scarce resource and it produces externalities. Given that low energy consumption can be an indicator of low economic growth, plans must be made for sustainable future increases. One important solution is pricing energy at market cost to promote efficiency and limit consumption.
- One well-known environmental concern is the alarming rate of deforestation of rain forests in the region. Some of the common reasons for deforestation include conversion of land to agriculture, firewood gathering, commercial logging, and cattle ranching as populations increase and seek to find a livelihood.

Environmental Policy

- The most effective type of environmental policies are those that combine direct government investment, market-based incentives (MBI), and command and control (CAC) measures. Considerations of environmental policy must recognize the differences between rural and urban problems. Governments must use cost-effectiveness to evaluate alternative policies and make choices as to the country's most pressing needs. Finally, when formulating development policies, environmental assessments (EA) will analyze the environmental costs and benefits of projects and programs before they are begun.
- Environmental policies can be costly. The question then arises of who should pay for such policies. Cooperation between local, national, and international governments and organizations will facilitate achieving the goal of sustain-

able development. Environmental degradation affects not only the region but the external environment as well.

N o t e s

1. World Commission on Environment and Development, *Our Common Future* (Oxford: Oxford University Press, 1987), 43.

2. Adapted from Mohan Munainghe and Wilfrido Cruz, *Economy Wide Policies and the Environment: Lessons from Experience* (Washington, D.C.: World Bank, 1995).

3. World Commission on Environment and Development, *Our Common Future*, 8.

4. Dennis Pirages, "Sustainability as an Evolving Process," *Futures* 26, no. 2 (1994): 197–205.

5. John M. Antle and Gregg Heidebrink, "Environment and Development: Theory and International Evidence," *Economic Development and Cultural Change* 43, no. 3 (April 1995): 604.

6. Jerry Taylor, "The Challenge of Sustainable Development," *Regulation* 17, no. 1 (1994): 35–50.

7. Michael A. Toman, "Economics and 'Sustainability': Balancing Trade-offs and Imperatives," *Land Economics* 70, no. 4 (November 1994): 399–413.

8. Robert Goodland and Herman Daly, *Poverty Alleviation Is Essential for Environmental Sustainability,* World Bank, Environment Department, Divisional Working Paper no. 1993-42 (Washington, D.C.: World Bank, 1993).

9. Alene H. Gelbard, *An Action Plan for Population, Development, and the Environment: Woodrow Wilson Center Spring 1996 Report* (Washington, D.C.: Woodrow Wilson Center, 1996).

10. World Resources Institute, *World Resources, 1996–7* (New York: Oxford University Press, 1997), 3.

11. Data from World Resources Institute, *World Resources 1994–5* (New York: Oxford University Press, 1995).

12. Porus Olpadwala and William Goldsmith, "The Sustainability of Privilege: Reflection on the Environment, The Third World City and Poverty," *World Development* 20, no. 4 (1992): 633.

13. "Latin America Struggles to Find Solutions to Megacity Woes," *Agence France Press,* 2 June 1992. Available on-line in the LEXIS-NEXIS database.

14. World Resources Institute, *World Resources, 1996–7*, 23.

15. Diego Cevallos, "Environment-Mexico: Toxic Waste, A Dirty Problem," Inter Press Service, 11 August 1995. Available on-line in the LEXIS-NEXIS database.

16. World Resources Institute, *World Resources, 1996–7*, 70.

17. John Dixon, *The Urban Environmental Challenge in Latin America*, LATEN Dissemination Note no. 4, World Bank Latin America Technical Department, Environment Division (Washington, D.C.: World Bank, 1993), 8.

18. Margolis, cited by Dixon, *The Urban Environmental Challenge*, 9.

19. Dixon, *The Urban Environmental Challenge*, 19.

20. Asif Faiz, Surhid Gautam, and Emaad Burki, "Air Pollution from Motor Vehicles: ˥ ˋes and Options for Latin American Countries," *The Science of the Total Environment* (1995): 303–310.

21. World Bank, *Energy Efficiency and Conservation in the Developing World: The World Bank's Role* (Washington, D.C.: World Bank, 1993), 66

22. Faiz, Gautam, and Burki, "Air Pollution," 303–310.

23. World Resources Institute, *World Resources, 1996–7*, 82.

24. "Mexico City: A Topographical Error," *Environment* 36, no. 2 (1994): 25–26.

25. World Resources Institute, *World Resources, 1996–7*, 47.

26. World Bank, *World Development Report, 1992* (New York: Oxford University Press/World Bank), 47.

27. Dixon, *The Urban Environmental Challenge*, 19.

28. Olpadwala and Goldsmith, "Sustainability of Privilege," 631.

29. Dixon, *The Urban Environmental Challenge*.

30. World Bank, *Energy Efficiency*.

31. Ibid., 38.

32. Visit Enersol's website at www.enersol.org to learn about some of its projects. Following Hurricane Mitch, for example, Ernersol worked to install ultraviolet water disinfection systems to provide clean water.

33. "Energy in Latin America: Even Oil Is Growing Less Sacred," *The Economist*, 1 June 1996, p. 63.

34. Judith Kimerling, cited by Suzana Sawyer, "Indigenous Initiatives and Petroleum Politics in the Ecuadorian Amazon," *Cultural Survival*, Spring 1996, p. 27.

35. John Vandermeer and Ivette Perfecto, *Breakfast of Biodiversity: The Truth about Rain Forest Destruction* (Oakland, Calif.: Institute for Food and Development Policy, 1995), 19.

36. Commission on Development and Environment for Amazonia, *Amazonia without Myths* (Washington, D.C.: Inter-American Development Bank, 1992), xii.

37. Vandermeer and Perfecto, *Breakfast*, 3.

38. The countries and the percentage held of the Amazon are as follows: Bolivia (11.20 percent), Brazil (67.79 percent), Colombia (5.52 percent), Ecuador (1.67 percent), Guyana (0.08 percent), Peru (13.02 percent), and Venezuela (0.72 percent). Suriname and the territory of French Guiana are considered to be part of the "greater Amazon," not countries of the hydrographic watershed. Commission on Development and Environment for Amazonia, *Amazonia without Myths*.

39. Goulding in Bradley Bennett, "Plants and People of the Amazonian Rainforests: The Role of Ethnobotany in Sustainable Development," *BioScience* 42, no. 8 (1992): 599.

40. Commission on Development and Environment for Amazonia, *Amazonia without Myths*, 6.

41. Ibid., 37.

42. Ramón López, *Policy Instruments and Financing Mechanisms for the Sustainable Use of Forests in Latin America*, no. ENV-16 (Washington, D.C.: Inter-American Development Bank, 1996), 1.

43. First appeared in Brian Johnson, *The Great Fire of Borneo: Report of a Visit to Kalimantan-Timur a Year Later, May 1994* (London: World Wildlife Fund, 1991); also see Carlos Alberto Primo Braga, "Tropical Forests and Trade Policy: The Case of Indonesia and Brazil," in *International Trade and the Environment*, ed. Patrick Low (Washington, D.C.: World Bank, 1992), 177.

44. Braga, "Tropical Forests," 178.

45. Commission on Development and Environment for Amazonia, *Amazonia without Myths*.

46. Phillip Fearnside, "Deforestation in Brazilian Amazonia: The Effect of Population and Land Tenure," *Ambio* 22, no. 8 (December 1993): 542.

47. World Resources Institute, *World Resources, 1996–7*, 250.

48. Hernán Cortés-Salas, Ronnie de Camino, and Arnoldo Contreras, *Readings of the Workshop on Government Policy Reform for Forestry Conservation and Development in Latin America*, June 1–3, 1994 (Washington, D.C.: Inter-American Institute for Cooperation on Agriculture, 1995).

49. World Bank, *Environment and Development in Latin America and the Caribbean: The Role of the World Bank* (Washington, D.C.: World Bank), 21.

50. Goodland and Daly, *Poverty Alleviation*, 28.

51. World Bank, *Privatization Principles and Practice*, IFC Lessons of Experience Series (Washington, D.C.: World Bank, 1995), 44.

52. Faiz, Gantam, and Burki, "Air Pollution," 303–310.

53. Ibid.

54. World Bank, *Environment and Development*.

55. Anna Luíza Ozório de Almeida and João S. Campari, *Sustainable Settlement in the Brazilian Amazon* (Oxford: Oxford University Press, 1995), 75–80.

56. World Bank, *Environment and Development*.

57. The argument for this paragraph is distilled from Clifford S. Russell and Philip T. Powell, *Choosing Environmental Policy Tools: Theoretical Cautions and Practical Considerations*, no. ENV-102 (Washington, D.C.: Inter-American Development Bank, June 1996).

58. World Bank, *Environment and Development*.

59. More on the GEF is available at www.gefweb.com.

60. Gary S. Hartshorn, "Natural Forest Management by the Yanesha Forestry Cooperative in Peruvian Amazonia," in *Alternatives to Deforestation: Steps toward Sustainable Use of the Amazon Rain Forest*, ed. Anthony B. Anderson (New York: Columbia University Press, 1990), 128–138.

61. Susan E. A. Hall, "Conoco's Green Strategy," Harvard Business School Case #9-394-001, 4 October 1993.

62. Allen T. White, "Venezuela's Organic Law: Regulating Pollution in an Industrializing Country," *Environment* 33, no. 7 (September 1991): 16.

63. Peter S. Thatcher, "The Role of the United Nations," in *The International Politics of the Environment: Actors, Interests, and Institutions*, ed. Andrew Hurrell and Benedict Kingsbury (Oxford, U.K.: Clarendon, 1992), 183–211.

64. Mohamed T. El-Ashry, *Statement to the Fourth Session of the Conference of the Parties to the United National Framework Convention on Climate Change*, Buenos Aires, 11 November 1998 (Washington, D.C.: Global Environment Facility, 1998). El-Ashry is CEO and chair of the Global Environment Facility.

65. More about this initiative is available at www.ispnet or ispnet@oas.org.

CHAPTER FIFTEEN

LESSONS LEARNED

Cycles in Latin American Development

The devastation of Hurricane Mitch underscored the fragility of life, especially for the poor. *(Courtesy of David Mangurian and the Inter-American Development Bank.)*

Nearing his seventy-second birthday, Colombian Nobel laureate Gabriel García Marquez bought a newspaper company, *El Cambio*. He jokingly noted that after his 1982 Nobel Prize, no one would employ him as a journalist because he was too expensive. His reentry into journalism has promoted a greater spirit of open press in his native country, a critical component of accountable government policy. Unfortunately, the magical realism of his novels find stark parallels in contemporary life in Latin America, giving him much to write about. As he said in a *New York Times* interview describing his political activism as a writer, his engagement in critical issues is driven by the fact that "underdevelopment is total, integral, it affects every part of our lives."[1] Life has imitated art in Latin America.

Many of the political obstacles to underdevelopment that concerned Marquez at the time of his award have changed. Most importantly, the region has gone from one dominated by repressive military regions to one of open democracy. The economic model has radically been altered from state-centered import substitution industrialization to a market-driven approach. But political and economic openness have not yet transformed the devastating landscape of underdevelopment in the region. The cycle of poverty and oppression in Marquez's literature and his contemporary world remain a sad reminder of unresolved developmental challenges.

As an example of the cycles of poverty, consider the challenges facing Honduras and Ecuador as they move into the twenty-first century. Honduras, along with its Central American neighbors, was ravaged by Hurricane Mitch late in 1998. Decades of development were turned back by this powerful storm. Schools and hospitals were decimated, and the loss of life was staggering. Swelling rivers washed away homes, farms, and factories. Honduras lost export crops such as bananas, coffee, shrimp, and melons; its small farms have no arable soil left to grow sources of domestic sustenance, including rice and corn.

Honduras was terribly unlucky to be in the path of Mitch, but its own development path had made it more vulnerable to the destruction of the storm. Its fragile ecosystem, weakened from overfarming, overlogging, and overpopulation, left little resistance to wind and water. As noted by Edwin Mateo Molina, a Honduran sociologist specializing in environmental issues for the Inter-American Development Bank, "Everyone realizes that the damage was magnified by the misuse of resources. It will happen again, and will be even worse unless we look for a way to use the land in a more responsible manner."[2]

In Ecuador the damage has come from political forces as much as from those of nature. With three heads of state in two years, political instability has exacerbated the economic crisis and natural disaster. "Everything in the politics of this country is about short-term management," said Fernando Carrion, director of the Ecuador branch of FLACSO, the Latin American Faculty for Social Sciences, a regional research and analysis group. "But our real problems are structural, long-term problems, and we are no closer to a solution to any of those."[3] The inflation rate is one of the highest in the region at 40 percent, and the country suffered a megadevaluation to align external prices. Ecuador is saddled with debt incurred by previous profligate administrations, and the collapse of oil prices and the devasta- of El Niño have undermined the ability to pay. Nearly $1 billion was spent g out poorly managed banks. A sweeping austerity package brought Ecuadorans to the streets as they found their bank accounts frozen, the price of gasoline doubled, and new taxes levied to balance fiscal accounts.

The news is not, however, all bad. After a decade of economic reform, Latin America is more squarely following a sustainable development path. Decentralization has placed more power in the hands of local governments. Women and indigenous groups have achieved greater recognition in the design of development strategies, although many tangible gains will accrue only over time. Environmental projects have sprung up throughout the region to support sustainable practices. Macroeconomies are better balanced, and the region is integrating through bilateral and regional accords. Cycles have persisted, but Latin America may have reversed some of the practices promoting downward cycles and replaced them with new directions in its unfolding development story.

CHALLENGES FOR DEVELOPMENT POLICY IN LATIN AMERICA REVISITED

In thinking about the progress and the prospects of development in Latin America, we will find it useful to recall the five critical issues for development policy in Latin America introduced in chapter 1:

- How can a balance be achieved between internal and external constraints on development?
- How can change be promoted even as stability is encouraged?
- Which interests should economic policy serve—the needs of the poor or the investment requirements of the industrialists?
- What role should the state play in promoting a development agenda? What are the appropriate roles for the market?
- How should the needs of people today be addressed while leaving future generations as well-off?

We noted that it is important to understand how economies have resolved these issues to avoid negative historical cycles. What have we learned from our study of Latin American economic development with respect to how these issues have been dealt with across the different periods of development? What lessons can we bring to bear on understanding whether the future of economic development in the region will reflect the cycles of the past?

THE ECONOMIC LABORATORY OF LATIN AMERICA

Latin America has been a virtual economic laboratory to analyze imbalances across the domestic and international sectors. Our study of import substitution industrialization showed that an internal focus was implemented because of the dissatisfaction with the primary product export model in the late 1880s and early 1900s. Despite comparable starts, it appeared that the region was falling behind relative to Europe and North America. The surprising progress of Latin America as it was isolated during World War II from the international economy led analysts to believe that international capitalism was a cause of the underdevelopment of the region. According to the dependency theorists, powerful industrial countries were draining Latin America of its wealth. Alliances between elites in the center and the periphery perpetuated a model that privileged a few but immiserized the masses. Patterns of asset distribution in large latifundia or estate production determined by colonial decree were reproduced in industrial circles. Internal dynamism was lacking, with weak linkages between the export-oriented agricultural sector and the fragile and thin industrial sector. Technological prowess was building in the North, to the exclusion of the South. The perception was that the international economy was strangling dynamic domestic development.

To move beyond dependent development, import substitution industrialization constructed the state as the defined change agent. Employing planning tools and the aggressive arm of state-led firms, governments opened new sectors to industrial activity. A focus on linkages and breaking down bottlenecks of production led the state to target key sectors. High tariffs kept multinational firms at bay, unless special technological licensing agreements or local production were negotiated to provide critical inputs of production. Monetary policy was essentially passive, with central banking authorities accommodating the expansionist thrust of the model. An initial euphoria surrounded the ability to promote development in the region. The ambitious plan to build Brasilia, moving it inland as a heartland capital to integrate diverse regions, was a symbol of the unbounded power of state energy. New light and heavy manufacturing sectors developed to meet the needs of domestic consumers. The labor movement strengthened, as unions promoted workers' rights. Public utilities were expanded, providing electricity and telephone services throughout the region. Ambitious projects such as the trans-Amazonian highway and the Itaipu Dam were begun with financing from capital markets bullish on Latin America. Latin American nations were transforming their economic landscape.

Unraveling Import Substitution Industrialization

But signs of disequilibrium began to surface. Balance of payments accounts were pressured by the need to import costly intermediate machinery for final goods production. As import bills surged, the exchange rate bias worked against exports. The state's attempt to do too much too fast resulted in an inflationary tendency in the economy. Rapid change meant frequent supply shortages, and state-led megaprojects required high levels of public finance. Powerful firms and powerful unions passed cost increases around. It was not a total coincidence that as the economies began to twist and crack, militaries around the region were called to govern by industrial elites to maintain order and progress. Stability was threatened by an uneven and unbalanced development process.

Given highly unequal income distributions and a model that had promoted a urban privileged class, it was risky to begin tinkering too much with the internal and external balance. Rapid structural change made the management of economic outcomes unpredictable. Populist policies to buy off labor and business without strong regard for external constraints dominated the region. Corruption was encouraged by the ability of agents within the state to control economic property rights. Many abused privileges for personal gain in protected state jobs. Quotas on foreign exchange or technology import licenses led to under the table payments to grease the economic wheels. Sadly but predictably, the poor were largely neglected, the rural sector was nearly abandoned, and the environment was devastated.

International price shocks dislodged the inward-looking system of import substitution industrialization. Global interest rate hikes to restrain worldwide inflation also triggered a massive debt crisis across the region. Countries faced default in adjusting to high real interest rates after the artificial luxury of low to negative rates over several years. External constraints became overwhelming when the price of international capital rose. Consumption or investment imports could no longer be cheaply financed. Countries could no longer support living beyond their means. A radical reorientation of the development model was required.

NEOLIBERAL REFORMS

Import substitution industrialization was replaced by variants of the neoliberal model throughout the region. The state itself was delegitimized as the economic guardian. Instead, markets became the primary allocators of resources. State spending was slashed to maintain fiscal balance, and state firms were privatized to promote profit and efficiency as the way to provide goods and services in the market. Privatization created enormous profit potential, which enticed international capital back to the region. Tariff walls came tumbling down, exposing firms to competition in the international market. Openness to international competition rooted out inefficiencies in production, and formerly protected firms scrambled to find new market niches. Nontraditional exports penetrated new markets. Agriculture and agro-industries got a boost from international demand. Cheaper imports from the global market provided consumers with new choices of goods at lower prices. Multinational firms established local production to meet the needs of consumers with real purchasing power for the first time in years. As countries looked outward and a democratic revolution swept the hemisphere, subregional integration efforts gained momentum. The external sector was again seen as the engine of development.

Latin American nations once again became darlings of international capital. With inflation in retreat throughout the region and democratic governments installed in all nations save Cuba, stability encouraged investor confidence. Money flowed back to the region, this time through bond and stock markets rather than commercial bank lending. Foreign direct investment blossomed because multinationals were enthusiastic about long-term development prospects. Not every country, however, benefited equally. Larger countries attracted the bulk of capital while smaller and poorer economies struggled. Nonetheless, the experiences of countries such as Costa Rica demonstrate that small countries that have invested in technology and work force development can indeed succeed.

The Compelling Social and Environmental Agenda

Opening to the external economy also exposed weaknesses in the domestic political economy. Global attention to environmental and social issues promoted by new actors on the global stage, the nongovernmental organizations, directed some attention to issues of sustainable development and labor standards. Protests on the negative social and environmental effects of IMF- and World Bank–type conditionality packages led to a rethinking of the sustainability of short-term stabilization measures. Short-term export targets for the release of funds resulted in further deforestation; sweatshops started to spring up throughout the region as multinationals took advantage of cheaper, often female labor. In response to international outcries, new units were set up in multilateral organizations to safeguard environmental concerns and promote the interests of the least advantaged in society. Greater attention was paid to issues of gender and ethnicity in development. Recognition of the economic and social contributions of women and indigenous peoples began to inform decision making. But institutional change is slow and incomplete, and the intermediate environmental and social costs have been high.

There was an extraordinary degree of financial dislocation in the process of rapid transformation from closed to open economies. Some governments have been better able to manage this process than others. Mistakes such as the Mexican management of the 1994 peso overvaluation were made, with devastating financial costs. Brazil appears to have weathered its 1998–1999 crisis after a bungled devaluation, fiscal imprudence, and political infighting that shook market confidence. Changing policies and outcomes have challenged the ability of governments to maintain credibility with their citizens and with international investors. Pleasing one has sometimes come at a cost to another. Labor market reform hasn't moved quickly for fear of upsetting domestic labor coalitions. Privatization may have taken place too rapidly, allowing some firms to be sold for less than market value. Appropriate regulatory measures were not always in place to protect consumer and environmental interests in the face of newly privatized monopolies. Finance ministers have had to manage not only money supplies but also extensive public relations efforts with the major brokerage houses around the world. Increasing transparency and credibility in policy making has been critical to maintaining confidence in Latin American markets.

Addressing the Social Deficit

At the same time that the economies have grappled with both the costs and the 'fits of globalization, the Latin American state has had to figure out how to ore with less. The accumulated social and environmental deficits are huge impediments to sustained future growth. Radical structural change shook up the system, energizing productive potential. Realizing this potential in the long run, however, is a function of enhancing investments in human capital. Health and education systems must be revamped. Latin America must contend with its epidemiological backlog, eradicating traditional diseases linked to poor living conditions and inadequate nutrition as well as making headway against the ills of modern society such as violence, AIDS, and heart disease. Quality improvements in the supply of educational services, including better teacher training, appropriate texts, and computer-based learning, are critical to compete in the global economy. Environmental decision making must be systematically incorporated at the local level because people themselves demand it. The complex host of environmental problems borne of insufficient infrastructure and unmanaged economic expansion must be reconciled with communities' needs today and for the future.

Yet governments are not able to spend their way out of these challenges; the money just isn't there. Instead, with diligent attention to the fiscal bottom line, states are attempting to create incentives for the market to pull some weight in the social arena. Public–private partnerships to improve delivery of health and educational services are being employed to reinvigorate moribund systems. Decentralization of social services allows for more local ownership of projects. Local governments are partnering with businesses in communities that have a vested interest in the development of better-educated, healthier work forces and cleaner work environments. Nonetheless, the market is not a substitute for good policy or hard choices, particularly in the areas of public goods provision. It can complement good governance, but it cannot replace it.

THE BALANCING ACT OF THE STATE

In balancing between global demands and local needs, the tricky policy issue is deciding just how much government is enough. We have devoted a great deal of attention in this text to discussing the positions of neoliberals, new institutionalists, and neostructuralists. The latter two groups might argue that the pendulum may have swung too far toward the market, in the light of the weakness of market institutions in guaranteeing property rights, overseeing competition policy, and promoting social welfare. Although public–private partnerships are useful to attend to unmet needs, the invisible hand of the market may not work its magic when economic agents are unable to make rational, self-interested decisions because they simply don't have the minimal level of social assets to invest in themselves. States must be vigilant in their attempts to promote incentives for the formation of a domestic economy oriented not necessarily toward short-term consumption but rather to long-term investments in social and environmental systems. Incentives must be structured to change time horizons to preserve choices in the future.

However noble this task may be, its feasibility may be legitimately questioned. Orientation to the international arena drives countries to focus on short-term macroeconomic performance variables: prices, exchange rates, and fiscal and current account balances. The room to maneuver is extremely limited. Once international investors get a sniff of disequilibrium or social discontent, they quickly shift to another, more stable investment. One of the downsides of the broadening of the stock market to include a large number of smaller players is that the day trader or the middle America investors' circle is unlikely to have a profound understanding of the complexity and the diversity of Latin American economies. An increase in the current account can mean many things, some of which threaten stable growth (such as luxury consumption) and others that may promote change (business investment). Sorting out the causes of imbalances and placing them in a historical context requires information unavailable to many small investors.

Development is not a process of harmonious equilibrium. Much like people, economies may grow in fits and starts, taking new and unintended directions. Yet the costs today of short-term disequilibrium are loss of investor confidence and instantaneous capital flight. We may have arrived at a kind of MTV international economy with an attention span that is limited to sixty-second sound bites. Economic policy makers have to learn tools of international marketing to sell information about the national product in the global marketplace. The message must be clear and consistent. But the message won't be a pleasant one unless the problems of inequality and poverty are resolved. Unfortunately, short-term policy making doesn't encourage the necessary social investments to reverse the plight of the poor, reduce inequality, and promote sustainable development. Latin America is precariously poised with one foot in the fast-moving international arena and the other stuck in a complicated web of unequal social relations that act as a drag on productivity and change.

MULTILATERAL SUPPORT

As the world has become more tightly integrated and the ability to make economic mistakes has become more circumscribed, there may be a stronger role warranted for multilateral institutions. In the wake of the Asian, Russian, and Brazilian currency crises, there have been calls for a re-visioning of the International Monetary Fund to become more than an institution of last resort. Multilateral development banks such as the World Bank and the Inter-American Development Bank can also play important roles in promoting systematic attention to investments in the social and environmental agendas. The Global Environmental Fund is an innovative financial mechanism to transfer funds from North to South and share responsibility for global sustainability. Nongovernmental organizations are key not only in raising awareness of issues but also as local conduits between bi- or multilateral organizations and the local community.

As a consumer of goods produced in the international economy, you too have a role in articulating your social preferences. Public attention is directed not only to governments; the international media and the Internet provide important devices to articulate demands for socially and environmentally sound production. In the least, it is hoped that by reading this book you have become more aware of the problems facing people in other parts of the world, better able to interpret and contextualize the enormous challenges of development, and better prepared, should you so choose, to participate in this arena as a more informed manager, policy maker, activist, or consumer in the international economy.

REVISITING OUR FIVE ISSUES

To summarize, we can perhaps conclude that because development is a continuous but not smooth process, the five factors we have considered will be found in constant tension. As firms expand when markets are incomplete, they are likely to require imported components. Consumers, facing strong employment prospects in expanding markets, euphorically accelerate purchases with a consumption boom. With relatively weak domestic macroeconomic tools to fine-tune the economy, external disequilibrium mounts, pressuring the exchange rate. Capital flees, creating an external crisis that is resolved by painful domestic austerity.

Economic change can be disruptive, challenging stability. It can also threaten ruling elites, if formulated to attend to the marginalized masses. Ironically, if policy does not include those most needy of government attention to raise living, health, and education standards to a level consistent with human dignity and self-empowerment, the development prospects will confront a human capital deficit that is unsustainable in the modern global economy. State intervention in promoting human development is circumscribed by the domestic constraints of financing as well as by the role of the state as an institutional actor. Recent changes in Latin America have shifted this debate to ask what is the appropriate role of state participation at various levels of governance. Centrally funded and monitored local action plans can reduce inefficiency and benefit from local entrepreneurial partnerships. As decentralization plays out, however, it would not be surprising to see a swing back in the activity of the state in certain arenas. As priorities in environmental management shift from locally based sewage and sanitation to industrial pollutants that are not bounded by municipalities, the locus of action might shift as well. Changing development problems require dynamic solutions.

STAGES OF ADJUSTMENT

The resolution of the key issues of internal and external balance, development for whom, confidence and stability in the face of change, the role of the state, and future sustainability has varied with the different stages countries have passed through in their economic adjustment processes. Development, as we defined it in our first chapter, is a process of meeting the basic human needs of the population while enhancing options for how economic resources will be allocated today and in the future to increase the choices citizens have in their daily lives. As we have investigated issues of stabilization, adjustment, and growth, we can identify three contemporary stages that countries have passed through on this development journey. The first stage, immediately following the debt crisis, was characterized by often **severe stabilization** measures designed to bring macrofundamentals into line. Macroeconomic stabilization efforts were shaped by the financial constraints of the debt crisis as well as the historical legacy of asset distribution and policy making that constrained policy options. Restraining internal spending to achieve external balance became the dominant concern. Without external finance, countries no longer had the option of pursuing expansionary, inward-looking development strategies. Yet the earlier experience with export orientation left lingering doubts as to the social and environmental effects of active participation in the global economy.

But these questions were of necessity tabled. At the time of the crisis, macroeconomic considerations were primary. In the second phase, **structural transformation** was initiated. The shape of the economy changed with respect to the relative balance of internal and external orientation as well as the roles of the state and the market. Trade reforms, financial liberalization, integration, and privatization have changed the economic rules of the game in the region. The international market has been placed at the center of the development process. International capital flows, both short-term portfolio as well as long-term foreign direct investment, have become important arbiters of international growth. Liberalization of trade and the accompanying process of economic integration have become the drivers of change. State ownership in the economy has been severely curtailed, with local and multinational firms providing not only traditionally traded products but also many of the services, such as transportation and power, that had been the purview of public utilities. The goal of international competitiveness has prompted countries to think differently about labor relations, the generation of technology, and the provision of infrastructure. The agricultural sector has been infused with market-based policies, including the use of profit incentives for the provision of extension services and water. The structure of economies across the region has been radically altered over the past decade.

Having readjusted the orientation of the economy and the roles of key actors, the challenge of stage three is a long-term process of **capacity building** of human capital, improving productivity, and promoting sound use of natural resources, including land.[4] In short, stage three seeks to enlarge the options each society faces in allocating scarce resources, as well as to promote economically and environmentally sustainable development. These are no easy tasks. These reforms profoundly shape the ways people interact within institutions. **Institutions** are the rules that shape the behavior of organizations and individuals. **Formal rules**, such as constitutions, laws, and regulations, or **informal rules**, such as values and norms, condition and are conditioned by the process of economic change.[5] Old or brittle institutions may collapse under the weight of new economic challenges. The private sector, for example, has demanded changes in the quality and efficiency of financial and public services and judicial reform as it now perceives competitiveness to hinge on strong social, financial, and legal institutions. Institutional reform may also promote changes in the way economic agents behave. Increased transparency in judicial systems, for example, will encourage accountability in business dealings and foster international confidence in economic transactions. Institutional reform poses significant political and technical challenges. Losers in the political systems must somehow be convinced that the long-run gains are worth the cost. It is clear that new models of institutional reform are difficult to implement in economies struggling with a range of unresolved social and economic issues. Nonethe-

Capacity building at the local level can promote more equitable and efficient use of resources. *(Courtesy of the Inter-American Development Bank.)*

less, the resolve of the regional presidents at the Santiago summit in 1998 heralds an optimistic commitment to a new institutional structure in the region.

As governments move away from crisis management and radical economic restructuring toward the hard, slow process of deepening market institutions and their political environment, they must simultaneously balance issues of credibility and fairness in reform. Given the globalization of international capital, markets must be assured that macrofundamentals remain in place. Confidence is the name of the game.

At the same time, economic actors are beginning to sort out the welfare implications of the radical structural changes of economies. When economies were in crisis, people were willing to make sacrifices. There seemed to be little choice but to reform. As tariff walls came down, international capital found new opportunities, and private capital began to provide the water, telecommunications, and productive services of the region. There have been winners and losers. As growth has accelerated in some sectors, others have felt left behind. As different sectors of society have the opportunity to sort out the effects of reform, new claims will likely be made on the political and economic systems of the region. In many countries these systems are newly democratized, with evolving practices.

Changes in the economy necessarily call into question the perceived fairness of the results for citizens of the region. Balancing competing demands in newly consolidating democracies is a tricky act. Several questions define policy approaches to emerging concerns:

- As Latin America continues to move forward in the consolidation of economic and political reform, what are likely to be the pressure points constraining the evolution of a model of sustainable economic development?
- How can policy makers balance the need for confidence and credibility against the sometimes dislocating process of promoting dynamic growth?
- How can political momentum be maintained if outcomes are moderate at best, or at worst, when crisis rocks the hard-won gains of stabilization? Will economic frustrations burst the seams of democratic society?
- Can Latin American nations define a social compact on the responsibilities of the state and the market to resolve the deep inequalities in the region, or are the social divisions simply too great?
- Can the enthusiasm for outward-looking development be maintained, and the landscape of integration be practically and pragmatically defined beyond this first, relatively easy state of integration? Can and should the commitment to a free trade area be realized? What will the costs be if it is not?
- Can the fledgling environmental movement in the region be sustained through an era of thin financing? Can a kind of cost-effective environmentalism be promoted in Latin America that will be supplemented by the energies of public–private partnerships?

The first stage of reform was crisis driven. Emergency measures were taken to address short-term goals of inflation stabilization and external balance. There was little choice but to take a deep breath and move ahead with macroeconomic stabilization as economies had spun out of control. Stage two has largely changed the structure of the game. The private sector now controls a larger portion of the economy, and internationalized production and finance regimes shape outcomes. But changes in the rules with respect to who plays in the international arena are more easily implemented than the long-term qualitative changes necessary in social systems of health and education or information. It is simpler to pass a law reflecting lower tariff rates, open the doors to international capital, or put a state enterprise on the auction block than to engage in the painfully slow process of building institutions to promote social fairness. We know less about changes in social systems and how to gauge results. Reforms in health care, education, and environmental management are less clear-cut, and the results take longer to materialize. Yet without this third stage of capacity building and institutional deepening, Latin America is doomed to repeat the cycle of unstable growth that has characterized its economic performance for centuries.

Key Concepts

Capacity building	Institutions	Structural
Formal rules	Severe stabilization	transformation
Informal rules		

Chapter   Summary

- Latin America has confronted persistent cycles of development, calling into question the resolution of internal and external constraints, the problem of stability in the face of change, the target of economic policy, the role of the state, and the tension between current needs and sustainable future development.
- The periods of primary product exports, import substitution development, and the neoliberal model have addressed these issues differently. The economic contradictions of one period cause the pendulum to swing to a different combination of openness and role of the state in another.
- In analyzing periods of adjustment, we can identify three stages: severe adjustment, structural transformation, and institutional capacity building. The ability of Latin American countries to create positively reinforcing cycles of development hinges on progress in capacity building to create stronger institutions in support of a more equitable growth process.

Notes

1. Marlise Simons, "A Talk with Gabriel Garcia Marquez," *New York Times*, 5 December 1982, sec. 7, p. 7. Available at www.nytimes.com/books/97/06/15/reviews/marquez-talk.html and in the LEXIS-NEXIS database.

2. Dudley Althaus, "Deforestation Contributed to Tragedy by Mitch in Honduras, Experts Claim," *Houston Chronicle*, 30 December 1998, A. 1, as found in the LEXIS-NEXIS database.

3. Larry Rohter, "Ecuadoran President Imposes Sweeping Austerity Measures," *New York Times*, 21 March 1999, as found at latinolink.com.

4. Alejandro Foxley uses these three stages in his preface to Victor Bulmer Thomas, ed., *The New Economic Model in Latin America and Its Impact on Income Distribution and Poverty* (New York: St Martin's, 1996).

5. World Bank, *Beyond the Washington Consensus: Institutions Matter*, Regional Brief (Washington, D.C.: World Bank, 1998). Available at www.worldbank.org.

Appendix A

A Sampling of Institutional Actors in Latin American Economic Policy

As we move forward in our study of the region, it is useful to have a guide to the key governmental and nongovernmental actors in the region. What follows is a sampling of both multilateral and U.S.-based organizations. You are encouraged to visit their websites (at which much of this information was garnered) for further exploration. This is a sampling, not a comprehensive list, to give you an idea of the multilateral, U.S. governmental, and nongovernmental policy makers in the region.

REGIONAL MULTILATERAL ORGANIZATIONS

Inter-American Development Bank (IDB or BIAD)

Headquarters: Washington, D.C.
www.iadb.org

The IDB, the largest regional multilateral institution, was established in 1959 to accelerate social and economic change in the region. Its membership is composed of forty-six nations, including twenty-six Latin American and Caribbean countries, the United States, Canada, and eighteen nonregional countries. Its mission is to raise funds in financial markets for development in Latin American and Caribbean member countries, to supplement private investment where private capital is not available, and to provide technical assistance for the preparation, financing, and implementation of projects. Its first loan was made in 1961 to improve the water and sewerage system of Arequipa, Peru. In 1994 the Multilateral Investment Fund (MIF) was created to assist investment reforms and promote private development throughout the region. In 1996 the bank approved $6.7 billion in loans.

United Nations Economic Commission for Latin America and the Caribbean (ECLAC or CEPAL)

Headquarters: Santiago de Chile
www.eclac.cl

The Economic Commission for Latin America (ECLA) was established by the U.N. Economic and Social Council in 1948 and was redesignated the Economic Commission for Latin America and the Caribbean in 1984. It disseminates economic and social information. It has little decision-making power but provides a second opinion for governments' economic and social policy. The functions established by its mandate are to promote economic and social development through regional and subregional cooperation; to gather, organize, interpret, and disseminate economic and social development information; to provide advisory services to governments; to plan and advocate development assistance activities; to organize intergovernmental conferences, seminars, workshops, and expert group meetings; and to help bring a regional perspective to global problems. ECLAC's influence is best known for the ISI strategy and the dependency theories of its first secretary-general, Raúl Prebisch. Today, the commission has adopted a more centrist approach.

The Organization of American States (OAS)

Headquarters: Washington, D.C.
www.oas.org

The OAS is the oldest regional organization in the world, finding its roots in the first International Conference of American States, held in Washington, D.C., in 1890. The OAS charter was signed in 1948. Its members include all thirty-five states of the Americas. The function of the organization is to strengthen the peace and security of the region; to ensure the peaceful settlement of disputes among member states; to promote and consolidate representative democracy; to provide common action on part of a member state in the case of aggression; to seek the solution to economic, juridical, and political problems that may arise among the states; and to promote through cooperative action the economic, social, and cultural development of member states. In the Miami summit of 1994, the leaders of the hemisphere's democratic nations agreed to establish a free trade area of the Americas by 2005; the OAS is providing institutional support in this effort. The OAS's most important roles have been to promote the pacific settlements of disputes among and within member states and to actively participate in democratization.

Pan American Health Organization (PAHO)

Headquarters: Washington, D.C.
www.paho.org

PAHO is an international health association that provides a forum for the consolidation and cooperation of health efforts by countries within the Americas region. Together, the thirty-five member countries work to promote physical and mental health, lengthen life, and fight diseases within their countries. PAHO dates back to the 1902 establishment of the International Sanitary Bureau. Since then its name has been changed several times. It operates under a budget consisting of member quotas and other outside extra budgetary funds.

GLOBAL MULTILATERAL ORGANIZATIONS

International Labor Organization (ILO)

Headquarters: Geneva, Switzerland
www.un.org/Depts/ilowbo/

The ILO is an independent agency in the U.N. system with a mandate to improve working conditions, create employment, and promote human rights around the world. It has 173 member countries, of which 70 percent are LDCs. It is the only U.N. agency in which the private sector works actively with government in decision making. Its activities involve setting international labor standards, carrying out technical assistance and training programs, and providing information on products and services.

International Bank of Reconstruction and Development (IBRD or The World Bank)

Headquarters: Washington, D.C.
www.worldbank.org

The World Bank, a product of the 1944 Bretton Woods Conference, provides capital, technical assistance, and policy advice to developing countries. Like the IDB, it raises funds from capital markets to help finance development where private capital is not available. All of its monetary assistance comes in the form of loans. There are two forms of loans. The first type is for countries able to pay near-market interest rates. Money for these loans comes from private investors who purchase World Bank bonds. The second type of lending is for the poorest countries and is issued by the International Development Association, a World Bank affiliate. Money for these loans does not come from capital markets, but rather from thirty donor countries. There is no interest on these loans except for a 0.75 percent administrative charge, and they have thirty-five- to forty-year terms. In addition to providing loans, the bank has become one of the most important sources of development information and publications.

International Monetary Fund (IMF)

Headquarters: Washington, D.C.
www.imf.org

The IMF, a result of the 1944 Bretton Woods Conference, was formally established in 1945 as an institution dedicated to the supervision of international monetary systems. It works to coordinate efforts and to encourage cooperation among its 181 voluntary member countries in the creation of economic policies. Acting as a forum for international monetary exchange, the IMF oversees transactions between countries to ensure that they occur smoothly and quickly. Additionally, through often very large loans, the IMF provides access to the different international capitals made available through their quota subscriptions, or membership fees.

United Nations Development Programme (UNDP)

Headquarters: New York
www.undp.org

The UNDP is a network of 134 country offices that administers service to 174 countries and territories. Working together, the UNDP network countries work to create and develop sustainable development, through sound governance and market development. Priorities are placed on poverty elimination, job creation, the advancement of women, and environmental regeneration.

U.S.-BASED GOVERNMENTAL AND QUASI-GOVERNMENTAL ORGANIZATIONS

Inter-American Foundation (IAF)

Headquarters: Washington, D.C.
www.iaf.gov

The IAF is a public–private bipartisan U.S. agency supporting programs in Latin America that promote grassroots development, self-reliance, and popular empowerment. It responds to the request for grants by indigenous nongovernmental organizations that provide assistance to peasant cooperatives, small enterprises, trade unions, women's collectives, human rights organizations, and cultural groups. Established in 1969, it was created as a small organization with no overseas staff to reduce costs and maximize program returns. It is viewed by many as a risk taker and groundbreaker for development assistance with its focus on supporting innovative and experimental programs. Between 1972 and 1996, the IAF approved more than 4,000 grants totaling $450 million to support more than 3,500 organizations.

United States Agency for International Development (USAID)

Headquarters: Washington, D.C.
www.info.usaid.gov

USAID is an independent government agency established by President John F. Kennedy in 1961 to respond to the threat of communism and help poorer nations. In the post–cold war era its mission is to ensure U.S. national security by promoting economic, political, environmental, and social development of developing nations. USAID views underdevelopment as a major threat to global stability. It aids participatory development with the aim of building indigenous capacity, enhancing participation, and encouraging transparency, decentralization, and the empowerment of communities and individuals. USAID is formally part of the U.S. Department of State.

NGO AND ADVOCACY GROUPS

Inter-American Dialogue

www.iadialog.org

Started in 1982, the Inter-American Dialogue is a distinguished U.S. center for policy analysis, study, and commentary on Western Hemispheric affairs. Membership consists of 100 leading citizens throughout the Americas who together seek to promote economic and political cooperation and communication through informed policy issue debate. The Dialogue is noted for its influence in shaping the agenda of inter-American relations.

Latin American Working Group

igc.org/lawg

A coalition of activist groups that dedicates its efforts to lobbying the U.S. Congress on Latin American issues. Since 1983 LAWG has worked to craft common policies through public education.

Woodrow Wilson Center—The Americas Program

wwics.si.edu

The Woodrow Wilson Center Latin American Program was established in 1977 to encourage academic-style research and discussion on inter-American issues facing the region as well as specifically Latin American topics. The center provides the opportunity for research and writing on issues of concern to Washington policy makers.

Center for Strategic and International Studies (CSIS)

www.csis.org

The Center for Strategic and International Studies, founded in 1962, is a prominent institution dedicated to effective analysis and recommendations of policies worldwide. The Americas Program focuses efforts on Latin American policy impact as well as U.S. and Canadian influences throughout the Americas. Policy study is considered from a variety of viewpoints covering such prominent Latin American issues as market integration, threats of narcotics trafficking, and political and economic reform.

Washington Office on Latin America (WOLA)

www.wola.org

The Washington Office on Latin America is an advocacy group with particular interests in human rights and counternarcotics policy. Funded in 1974, it facilitates dialogue between governmental and nongovernmental actors and monitors the impact of their policies and programs.

ACCION International

www.accion.org

ACCION International, established in 1961, is a nonprofit organization dedicated to providing microentrepreneurs with critical access to working capital in the form of credit and training. Through short-term loans, "solidarity group" lending, and technical business support, self-employed poor throughout Latin America are able expand their businesses, which indirectly leads to the creation of more jobs. ACCION works with affiliates in fourteen countries, and in 1998, ACCION disbursed nearly $577 million in loans, with about 447,000 small business recipients receiving an average of nearly $1,300 per loan.

Council of the Americas

www.counciloftheamericas.org

Founded in 1965 under the leadership of David Rockefeller and other businesspeople, the Council for the Americas encourages free markets and private enterprise throughout the Americas according to the belief that these policies encourage economic growth. The council acts in strategic ways through the advocacy of public discourse as well as through collaboration with private sector organizations in hopes of achieving economic prosperity. Membership consists of more than 240 firms that share an interest in Latin American investment.

SUMMIT OF THE AMERICAS, DECLARATION OF PRINCIPLES

Partnership for Development and Prosperity: Democracy, Free Trade, and Sustainable Development in the Americas

The elected Heads of State and Government of the Americas are committed to advance the prosperity, democratic values and institutions, and security of our Hemisphere. For the first time in history, the Americas are a community of democratic societies. Although faced with differing development challenges, the Americas are united in pursuing prosperity through open markets, hemispheric integration, and sustainable development. We are determined to consolidate and advance closer bonds of cooperation and to transform our aspirations into concrete realities.

We reiterate our firm adherence to the principles of international law and the purposes and principles enshrined in the United Nations Charter and in the Charter of the Organization of American States (OAS), including the principles of the sovereign equality of states, non-intervention, self-determination, and the peaceful resolution of disputes. We recognize the heterogeneity and diversity of our resources and cultures, just as we are convinced that we can advance our shared interests and values by building strong partnerships.

TO PRESERVE AND STRENGTHEN THE COMMUNITY OF DEMOCRACIES OF THE AMERICAS

The Charter of the OAS establishes that representative democracy is indispensable for the stability, peace and development of the region. It is the sole political system which guarantees respect for human rights and the rule of law; it safeguards cultural diversity, pluralism, respect for the rights of minorities, and peace within and among nations. Democracy is based, among other fundamentals, on free and transparent elections and includes the right of all citizens to participate in government. Democracy and development reinforce one another.

We reaffirm our commitment to preserve and strengthen our democratic systems for the benefit of all people of the Hemisphere. We will work through the appropriate bodies of the OAS to strengthen democratic institutions and promote and defend constitutional democratic rule, in accordance with the OAS Charter. We endorse OAS efforts to enhance peace and the democratic, social, and economic stability of the region.

We recognize that our people earnestly seek greater responsiveness and efficiency from our respective governments. Democracy is strengthened by the modernization of the state, including reforms that streamline operations, reduce and simplify government rules and procedures, and make democratic institutions more transparent and accountable. Deeming it essential that justice should be accessible in an efficient and expeditious way to all sectors of society, we affirm that an independent judiciary is a critical element of an effective legal system and lasting democracy. Our ultimate goal is to better meet the needs of the population, especially the needs of women and the most vulnerable groups, including indigenous people, the disabled, children, the aged, and minorities.

Effective democracy requires a comprehensive attack on corruption as a factor of social disintegration and distortion of the economic system that undermines the legitimacy of political institutions.

Recognizing the pernicious effects of organized crime and illegal narcotics on our economies, ethical values, public health, and the social fabric, we will join the battle against the consumption, production, trafficking and distribution of illegal drugs, as well as against money laundering and the illicit trafficking in arms and chemical precursors. We will also cooperate to create viable alternative development strategies in those countries in which illicit crops are grown. Cooperation should be extended to international and national programs aimed at curbing the production, use and trafficking of illicit drugs and the rehabilitation of addicts.

We condemn terrorism in all its forms, and we will, using all legal means, combat terrorist acts anywhere in the Americas with unity and vigor.

Recognizing the important contribution of individuals and associations in effective democratic government and in the enhancement of cooperation among the people of the Hemisphere, we will facilitate fuller participation of our people in political, economic and social activity, in accordance with national legislation.

To Promote Prosperity Through Economic Integration and Free Trade

Our continued economic progress depends on sound economic policies, sustainable development, and dynamic private sectors. A key to prosperity is trade without barriers, without subsidies, without unfair practices, and with an increasing stream of productive investments. Eliminating impediments to market access for goods and services among our countries will foster our economic growth. A growing world economy will also enhance our domestic prosperity. Free trade and increased economic integration are key factors for raising standards of living, improving the working conditions of people in the Americas and better protecting the environment.

We, therefore, resolve to begin immediately to construct the "Free Trade Area of the Americas" (FTAA), in which barriers to trade and investment will be progressively eliminated. We further resolve to conclude the negotiation of the "Free Trade Area of the Americas" no later than 2005, and agree that concrete progress toward the attainment of this objective will be made by the end of this century. We recognize the progress that already has been realized through the unilateral undertakings of each of our nations and the sub-regional trade arrangements in our Hemisphere. We will build on existing sub-regional and bilateral arrangements in order to broaden and deepen hemispheric economic integration and to bring the agreements together.

Aware that investment is the main engine for growth in the Hemisphere, we will encourage such investment by cooperating to build more open, transparent and integrated markets. In this regard, we are committed to create strengthened mechanisms that promote and protect the flow of productive investment in the Hemisphere, and to promote the development and progressive integration of capital markets.

To advance economic integration and free trade, we will work, with cooperation and financing from the private sector and international financial institutions, to create a hemispheric infrastructure. This process requires a cooperative effort in fields such as telecommunications, energy and transportation, which will permit the efficient movement of the goods, services, capital, information and technology that are the foundations of prosperity.

We recognize that despite the substantial progress in dealing with debt problems in the Hemisphere, high foreign debt burdens still hinder the development of some of our countries.

We recognize that economic integration and the creation of a free trade area will be complex endeavors, particularly in view of the wide differences in the levels of development and size of economies existing in our Hemisphere. We will remain cognizant of these differences as we work toward economic integration in the Hemisphere. We look to our own resources, ingenuity, and individual capacities as well as to the international community to help us achieve our goals.

TO ERADICATE POVERTY AND DISCRIMINATION IN OUR HEMISPHERE

It is politically intolerable and morally unacceptable that some segments of our populations are marginalized and do not share fully in the benefits of growth. With an aim of attaining greater social justice for all our people, we pledge to work individually and collectively to improve access to quality education and primary health care and to eradicate extreme poverty and illiteracy. The fruits of democratic stability and economic growth must be accessible to all, without discrimination by race, gender, national origin or religious affiliation.

In observance of the International Decade of the World's Indigenous People, we will focus our energies on improving the exercise of democratic rights and the access to social services by indigenous people and their communities.

Aware that widely shared prosperity contributes to hemispheric stability, lasting peace and democracy, we acknowledge our common interest in creating employment opportunities that improve the incomes, wages and working conditions of all our people. We will invest in people so that individuals throughout the Hemisphere have the opportunity to realize their full potential.

Strengthening the role of women in all aspects of political, social and economic life in our countries is essential to reduce poverty and social inequalities and to enhance democracy and sustainable development.

TO GUARANTEE SUSTAINABLE DEVELOPMENT AND CONSERVE OUR NATURAL ENVIRONMENT FOR FUTURE GENERATIONS

Social progress and economic prosperity can be sustained only if our people live in a healthy environment and our ecosystems and natural resources are managed carefully and responsibly. To advance and implement the commitments made at the 1992 United Nations Conference on Environment and Development, held in Rio de Janeiro, and the 1994 Global Conference on the Sustainable Development of Small Island Developing States, held in Barbados, we will create cooperative partnerships to strengthen our capacity to prevent and control pollution, to protect ecosystems and use our biological resources on a sustainable basis, and to encourage clean, efficient and sustainable energy production and use. To benefit future generations through environmental conservation, including the rational use of our ecosystems, natural resources and biological heritage, we will continue to pursue technological, financial and other forms of cooperation.

We will advance our social well-being and economic prosperity in ways that are fully cognizant of our impact on the environment. We agree to support the Central American Alliance for Sustainable Development, which seeks to strengthen those democracies by promoting regional economic and social prosperity and sound environmental management. In this context, we support the convening of other regional meetings on sustainable development.

Our Declaration constitutes a comprehensive and mutually reinforcing set of commitments for concrete results. In accord with the appended Plan of Action, and recognizing our different national capabilities and our different legal systems, we pledge to implement them without delay.

We call upon the OAS and the Inter-American Development Bank to assist countries in implementing our pledges, drawing significantly upon the Pan American Health Organization and the United Nations Economic Commission for Latin America and the Caribbean as well as sub-regional organizations for integration.

To give continuity to efforts fostering national political involvement, we will convene specific high-level meetings to address, among others, topics such as trade and commerce, capital markets, labor, energy, education, transportation, telecommunications, counter-narcotics and other anti-crime initiatives, sustainable development, health, and science and technology.

To assure public engagement and commitment, we invite the cooperation and participation of the private sector, labor, political parties, academic institutions and other non-governmental actors and organizations in both our national and regional efforts, thus strengthening the partnership between governments and society.

Our thirty-four nations share a fervent commitment to democratic practices, economic integration, and social justice. Our people are better able than ever to express their aspirations and to learn from one another. The conditions for hemispheric cooperation are propitious. Therefore, on behalf of all our people, in whose name we affix our signatures to this Declaration, we seize this historic opportunity to create a Partnership for Development and Prosperity in the Americas.

Note

This document is available on the World Wide Web at www.cidi.oas.org/summit/miamidec.htm.

Glossary

Absorption: Absorption is domestic consumption of goods both produced at home and imported from abroad. The IMF promoted the absorption approach, or the reduction of domestic utilization of resources to release them for export to earn hard currency to finance a country's debt.

Agenda 21: A comprehensive agenda for environmental action established at the 1992 United Nations Conference on the Environment and Development held in Rio de Janeiro.

Agricultural extension programs: Programs to introduce new agricultural practices to peasant farming communities.

Andean Community: Signed in 1960, the Andean Community treaty allowed for free commerce among Bolivia, Ecuador, Colombia, Venezuela, and Peru, with a common external tariff.

Austral plan: Argentina's Austral plan, named after the new currency put in place in 1985, was designed to combat inflation. The Austral plan was labeled as heterodox but also included some orthodox measures. To attack the inertial component of inflation, the administration declared a price freeze in June of 1985, froze wages, and implemented exchange rate controls. These measures were taken to convince the population that prices would not increase, but the plan fell apart after people lost confidence in the ability of the government to manage the economy.

Backward linkage: As industry A grows, demand for inputs to produce industry A's product will increase. This increase in demand can spur investment in a new industry B that will produce inputs for industry A. Central to the thought of A. O. Hirschman, investing in industries with strong backward linkages on the supply chain should promote growth.

Bresser plan: A follow-on to the Cruzado plan, the Brazilian use of heterodox policy to combat inflation in 1987. Wages were frozen, mini-devaluations were used to manage the exchange rate, and interest rates were targeted above the rate of inflation. Citizens were deputized as price inspectors. Despite initial success, shortages and external balance problems caused by excess consumer spending reignited inflation once again.

Caciques: Spanish word for the landlords of large agricultural estates prevalent in the Latin American colonial period.

Capacity building: Refers to investments in human capital, improvements in productivity and system design, and greater efficiency in the use of resources within economic, political, and social institutions.

461

Capital controls: Mechanisms such as licensing of foreign exchange used to limit imports or reduce capital flight, or taxation on short-term foreign investments to reduce the volatility of short-term capital flows.

Capital flight: Large outflows of domestic capital into safer or more stable foreign banks and foreign stock markets to protect the value of that capital. This phenomenon is associated with countries suffering from severe inflation or the likelihood of devaluation. Individuals opt to invest abroad when they lose confidence in their country's currency.

Central American Common Market: Formed early in the 1960s, this attempt at integration among Central American countries to take advantage of economies of scale in production was set back in the 1970s and 1980s by political strife. The 1990s saw new commitment to strengthening the legal and institutional framework, joint actions to reduce debt, and cooperation on sectoral issues.

Chicago school: This free market school of thought, a precursor to the neoliberal model, advocated a hands-off role for the state. Adherents believe that the market and open international trade are the main engines behind development.

Collor plan: Economic policy engineered by Brazil's president, Fernando Collor de Mello in 1990 to address inertial inflation through orthodox and heterodox measures. Assets were frozen and a 30-day price freeze instituted. These measures initially restrained inflation, but pressures such as increasing oil prices and shortages of goods, in addition to a lack of credibility in the government, caused an acceleration in inflation soon afterward.

Command and control measures: Government regulations and penalties used to reduce environmental pollution.

Commodity lottery: A term used by Victor Bulmer-Thomas that describes the export-oriented pattern of the late 1800s, when most Latin American countries were dependent on one export good, such as nitrates in Chile, coffee in Brazil, and tin in Bolivia.

Common market: A form of integration in which countries coordinate policy-making measures in such areas as agriculture and the social sector, along with establishing a common external tariff.

Conditionality: A term associated with the prerequisites necessary for disbursal of IMF funds to developing countries. Countries seeking loans from the IMF must first implement tough stabilization policies such as a decrease in fiscal spending, tight monetary policy, and strict trade policies. Conditionality is strongly debated because it forces a government to contract its economy and imposes social costs.

Contingent valuation: A form of environmental assessment that asks people to assign a value to their willingness to pay to preserve a natural resource.

Convertibility plan: Introduced in 1991 in Argentina, this policy to combat inflation tied the Argentine peso to the U.S. dollar and used a currency board to constrain monetary policy by law. The money supply could not increase unless there was a parallel increase in dollar reserves. Inflation was almost eliminated, but at a high cost in terms of recession and unemployment.

Cost-effectiveness: A criterion used to decide among competing priorities, especially in the environmental arena. Programs with broad impact and low cost are more desirable than programs of limited scope and high cost.

Cost-push elements: Certain conditions or external shocks such as food shortages or increasing oil prices that will fuel inflation through the interaction with powerful labor organizations or a concentrated industry structure. Rising costs are seen as pushing up prices.

Cruzado plan: Based on a structural diagnosis of inflation, the first Cruzado plan in Brazil, in 1986, focused on the inertial component of inflation and implemented heterodox measures by freezing prices, wages, and exchange rates. Brazilians were deputized as "fiscais," or price inspectors, to police the price freeze in supermarkets and shopping malls. Indexation of contracts with less than one year's duration was prohibited. A new currency, the cruzado, was created at a value of 1,000 cruzeiros. After a devaluation, the cruzado was fixed at 13.84 cruzados to the dollar. A neglect of tough fiscal adjustments combined with passive monetary policy that accommodated domestic deficits resulted in the re-eruption of inflation.

Customs union: A form of regional trade integration in which a common external tariff is established for the group.

Debt trap: When long-term projects are financed through short-term debt issues, countries may find themselves paying more in interest and principal than they are receiving in new money. Initially, the borrower is able to finance the project as well as pay the principal and interest with new lending each year. With each coming year, new lending available for investment dwindles because some of the money from new loans is used to pay the principal and interest on previous loans. The debt trap sets in when the new lending is not enough to pay for the principal and interest and the project is not yet generating significant returns to make up the difference.

Debt-for-equity swap: A win-win method used by firms, banks, and indebted countries to reduce exposure to the debt crisis. A firm wishing to invest in a particular country would buy the country's debt at a discount from a bank through the secondary market. Owing the firm and not the bank, the country could pay the firm in local currency, as opposed to dollars, which the firm then used to buy local supplies and pay workers. Banks got risky loans off their books, countries were released from the need to earn hard currency to service the debt, and firms were repaid the full value of the loan bought at a discount. The plan was limited, however, by inflationary risk and the demand for equity investments.

Debt-for-nature swap: An environmental twist on debt-for-equity swaps, in which international organizations buy a country's discounted debt from the secondary market. Debts are reduced or canceled in exchange for a country establishing nature preserves or otherwise protecting the environment. A financial commitment to long-term management of the parks, sometimes through a trust fund, was an important element of success.

Decentralization: A devolution of governmental responsibilities from centralized bureaucracies to state and local levels. The ability to raise revenues is sometimes also moved to the local level, although systems of fiscal accountability need to be tightened to improve internal balance.

Declining terms of trade: Terms of trade are the price of exports relative to the price of imports, mathematically expressed as P_x/P_m, an index of export prices divided by an index of import prices. Declining terms of trade are reflected in a decrease in the ratio, meaning that the price of imports is increasing relative to the price of exports. Under these conditions, countries must export increasing amounts of their own goods (often agricultural goods or commodities) to pay for imports (more likely to be machinery and high-tech items).

Demand-driven rural investment funds (DRIFs): The allocation of central government funds to local governments or communities to promote local control of agricultural development. Certain eligibility requirements must be met, and beneficiaries must contribute to the cost of the projects, often through volunteer labor.

Dependency theory: Despite different emphases by scholars, the central theme behind dependency is the proposition that a country does not develop because of its natural endowments; its growth is constrained by centers of power in the international system. Industrialized countries (the center) advance at the expense of the third world (the periphery), causing underdevelopment in the region through exploitation of cheap labor and extraction of resources. Underdevelopment was seen as linked to the relationship between the elite of Latin America and the center in their search for short-term profits as opposed to long-term growth.

Development: The process of meeting the basic needs of the population and enhancing options for how economic resources will be allocated today and in the future to increase the choices citizens have in their daily lives.

Direct government investment: In addition to command and control measures and market-based initiatives, this is a third policy option available to states to promote sound environmental practices. Governments might choose to invest in infrastructure such as sanitation or water projects to promote a cleaner environment.

Dualism: The simultaneous existence of modern and traditional economies, usually characterized by an expanding industrial sector and a large self-subsistence agricultural sector. Dualistic models tend to benefit the elite and marginalize the poor.

Dualistic structure of production: a bimodal pattern of agricultural production in which large corporate farming practices crowd out peasant farming, lowering employment and the production of basic foodstuffs in favor of lucrative export crops.

Dutch disease: Named after Holland's experience with natural gas, the term describes a country's inclination to concentrate its financial resources into a few profitable sectors. This behavior was prevalent throughout Latin American history with investments in oil and sugar, and it contributed to the unbalanced development of the region as other important sectors were ignored.

Economic populism: Economic populism is patterned after the behavior of many charismatic Latin American leaders, such as Juan Perón in Argentina, whose programs were symbolically designed to attend to the needs of the poor. Industry was pacified with large subsidies. The welfare of future generations is sacrificed for the welfare of current generations through excessive current spending to satisfy pressure groups. In a desire to increase the standard of living today, this kind of behavior ignores external balance of payments constraints and large fiscal deficits, conditions that make inflation nearly inevitable.

Economic union: A group of countries that have moved beyond a common market to embrace common sectoral policies. Common monetary policies and a common currency constitute an additional step toward an economic community. Mercosur is therefore an economic union, whereas the European Community has moved a step beyond.

Educational deficit: The gap between Latin America and the rest of the world in educational attainment and years of schooling. The 4.2 years of schooling Latin American children receive is roughly half of counterparts in the United States, Japan, and Germany, and two-thirds those in the Asian newly industrialized countries.

Educational performance index: Measure developed by the international NGO Oxfam using weighted values of school enrollment, gender equity, and completion rates.

Effective rate of protection: The nominal tariff adjusted for the tariff on intermediate goods. If the garment industry faced a 10% tariff and the sewing machines to make clothing faced a 5% tariff, the effective rate of protection (adjusted for the importance of the machine in production) would be 15%.

Effective selectivity: A policy approach advocated by the neostructuralists that promotes prioritizing and allocating limited government funds to areas that will produce the highest social returns.

Ejidos: Land that had been held communally for centuries before the introduction of private property. This is the predominant form of peasant landholding in Mexico.

Empowerment: The full participation of beneficiaries in their own development process.

Enclaves: Industries, in isolation from the rest of the economy, that fail to spur domestic investment, employment, and income.

Encomienda: Land received by conquistadors or other Spanish settlers from the Spanish Crown that was accompanied by the deeding of Indian labor to work this land.

Engel's law: When the increase in the demand for agricultural goods is slower than an increase in income (that is, there is a low income elasticity of demand), exporters of agricultural goods lose ground to producers of manufactured goods. When a low income elasticity for agricultural products exists, this means that if individuals experience an increase in their income, they will not increase their consumption of food or commodities by the same proportion. There is, for example, only so much coffee or sugar one will consume, no matter the increase in income. Engel's Law was used by economists such as Raúl Prebisch to explain why the developing world, which tends to export agricultural commodities, experiences declining terms of trade.

Environmental assessment: An impact statement identifying the likely environmental effects of a development policy. Most new development projects today require environments assessments prior to approval.

Epidemiological backlog: The simultaneous health challenge of addressing traditional diseases (such as cholera or dysentery tied to inadequate infrastructure and malnutrition) and the diseases of modern society (such as cancer and heart disease).

Epidemiological transition: The transition from a focus on fighting traditional diseases such as cholera to a focus on more modern concerns such as heart disease.

Equity: The access to equal opportunities within a nation. Although growth may increase inequality, models of growth with equity attempt to promote a more equal distribution of income. Equity also refers to ownership of capital—a very different use of the same term.

Equity investments: The purchase of stock by foreigners.

Expenditure switching: Changes in the prices of products, most often through an exchange rate adjustment, that make imports more expensive and exports cheaper. The higher price of imports switches people away from them, helping to balance trade.

Export pessimism: A term associated with the Prebisch-Singer thesis, stating that exports alone cannot be the engine of growth because of the effect of declining terms of trade.

Extreme poverty: Although levels vary by the local cost of living, those subsisting on roughly less than $1 a day are considered to be living in extreme poverty. Moderate poverty is roughly $2 per day, or between $50 (World Bank benchmark) and $60 a month (ECLAC level).

Externalities: A cost or a benefit that results from an activity or transaction that is imposed on parties outside the transaction. Pollution is a negative externality of production; reducing the spread of disease is a positive externality of education.

Factor price equalization: As a country opens up to trade, the demand for its products, made with its most abundant (and cheap) factor, should in theory over time result in an increase in the price of this factor to world levels. Global factor prices should therefore become more uniform.

Fazenda: Large feudal estates, similar to the hacienda in Spanish America, during the colonial period in Brazil.

Fiscal austerity measures: Policy initiatives such as decreasing government spending, privatization, increasing tax revenues, and reducing subsidies to relieve pressure on domestic budgets. The IMF often recommends fiscal austerity measures.

Fiscal covenant: A term coined by ECLAC to reflect a socioeconomic agreement between a government and civil society. This fiscal covenant incorporates consolidation of the ongoing fiscal adjustment, increases in the productivity of public management, transparency of fiscal activity, promotion of social equity, and development of democratic institutions.

Foreign direct investment: Describes the investment by foreigners through ownership of equity shares or setting up production facilities within a country. The most common type of foreign direct investor is the multinational corporation.

Formal rules: The constitutions, laws, and written regulations that structure economic activity and guarantee property rights.

Forward linkage: The production of a good that is complementary to another industry may spur the development of that new sector; such development is called a forward linkage. As opposed to a backward linkage, which calls for the production of critical inputs, a forward linkage moves ahead in the production chain. Roadside restaurants might be a forward linkage to automobile production, whereas tires would be considered a backward linkage.

Free trade area: A form of regional integration in which trade restrictions are abolished between participating countries, but each country maintains an independent trade policy and separate tariff rates with the rest of the world.

Gender Development Index (GDI): The GDI discounts the Human Development Index for gender inequality in life expectancy, educational attainment, and income, by assigning a penalty for inequality. The greater the gender disparity, the lower the GDI.

Gender Empowerment Index (GEM): The GEM concentrates on economic, political, and professional participation by incorporating variables such as female share of income, access to professional and managerial jobs, and seats in public office. The GEM therefore measures the degree to which society's opportunities are open to women.

Gini coefficient: A measure of income inequality that gauges the difference between a hypothetical society where income is perfectly equal and the actual income distribution. It is derived from the Lorenz curve. The higher the Gini coefficient, the more extensive is income inequality.

Golden age of primary product exports: The period in Latin American history from the late 1800s to the early 1900s, when primary product exports boomed and contributed to the economic growth of the region.

Grade repetition: A pervasive problem of educational systems in Latin America. Nearly one third of all school children repeat their grades annually, primarily because of poor educational inputs.

Growth: A simultaneous gradual increase in quantities such as GDP, population, saving, and wealth. If the benefits of growth are not widely shared, it may not be considered development.

Headcount ratio: The proportion within a country's population falling below the poverty line.

Heckscher-Olin theorem: A key theoretical construct in international trade that suggests that a country should trade that good which uses relatively intensively that country's most abundant factor.

Heterodox policies: Monetary and fiscal policies grounded in the belief that one of the primary components of inflation is the inertia built into an economic chain, with wages increased in anticipation of future price increases, making inflation a self-fulfilling prophecy. Heterodox policies attempt to combat inflation by neutralizing expectations through price and wage freezes.

HFA2000: A program promoted by the World Health Organization mobilizing efforts to provide basic health services for all by the year 2000.

Human Development Index (HDI): The United Nations Human Development Report calculates the HDI as a composite of life expectancy at birth, educational attainment (measured by adult literacy and school enrollments), and income.

Illiquidity: A condition in which cash flow does not match financial obligations. As opposed to insolvency, when an economic entity cannot and will not ever likely meet its obligations, illiquidity may be a temporary condition in which revenues do not cover costs of debt service. In the first stage of the debt crisis, countries were thought to have temporary liquidity problems; it was later seen that fundamental restructuring and debt relief were called for.

Import substitution industrialization (ISI): ISI was the dominant economic policy in Latin America during the 1950s, 1960s, and 1970s as a response to dependency and structuralist theories. It represented a shift away from the outward orientation of export promotion, to an inward-looking orientation. ISI was designed to replace imports with domestic production under the guiding hand of the state. Governments used activist industrial, fiscal, and monetary policy to achieve growth.

Income gap: A measure of poverty that captures the difference between actual incomes and incomes at the officially designated poverty line.

Incomplete markets: Markets in developing countries may be incomplete in the sense that they do not efficiently convey price signals to buyers or sellers. This may be due to lack of information, a limited number of participants, or the market infrastructure. When markets do not adjust smoothly, transactions costs rise and economic activity is compromised. Neostructuralists and new institutionalists suggest a role for the state in supplementing economic activity where markets are incomplete.

Indexation: Under a system of indexation, countries will revise wages and financial prices upward by taking into account expected as well as past inflation. When indexation occurs, countries have embraced inflation and it becomes a part of daily life. Because incomes are protected, the inflation is less painful.

Inertial inflation: Implies that inflation is not driven solely by an increase in the money supply, but by expectations as well. As individuals anticipate inflation, they will demand higher wages or set prices accordingly, which will push prices upward.

Inflationary expectations: The expectations of a society, based on past experience, of future rates of inflation. When they anticipate future price increases, economic actors demand higher wages or set prices higher to cover the inflation they expect in the future, making the expectations a self-fulfilling prophecy. Inflationary expectations are a large part of inertial inflation.

Informal rules: Values and norms that condition and are conditioned by the process of economic change.

Informal sector: Small-scale business operations such as selling goods on street corners or providing cleaning services in homes. The informal sector operates outside the official, taxed economy. It is characterized by a low capital-labor ratio, family-intensive production, and worker-owned means of production. The informal sector can be divided into three areas: microenterprise employment, own-account workers, and domestic service.

Insecure property rights: When owners of property are not sure of their rights to use or dispose of their property. When institutions guaranteeing land titles are inefficient or nonexistent, farmers may underinvest in developing property because there is a good chance that the returns from efforts will be appropriated by another. Insecure property rights are an important cause of environmental damage, because economic actors may exploit land and natural resources now if they assume that they will not, or may not, continue to have access to these inputs in the future.

Institutionalist tradition: A vision of development policy that accords a strong role for nonmarket institutions. Institutionalists assume that markets are not perfect, that people are not purely rational, self-interested maximizers, and that economic power rather than efficiency will shape outcomes. For institutionalists, access to and control over technology is an important ingredient of dynamic (or sluggish) growth.

Institutions: Rules that shape the behavior or organizations and individuals engaged in economic activity.

Integrated approach: Addressing poverty by means of growth policy and social policy, as suggested by the Economic Commission for Latin America and the Caribbean (ECLAC).

Involuntary lending: During the debt crisis, involuntary lending described the process of rolling over the principal and interest payments due on a loan into new (usually more expensive) loans to give countries breathing room to meet their financial obligations. It was believed that after their economies became more productive through the tough measures required by the IMF, these countries would then be able to pay off their debt. Banks preferred to package the interest and principal due into a new loan because it kept the loan in the "performing" category rather than having a past-due amount trigger a classification of this asset as nonperforming and therefore worth less.

Kuznets curve: A graphical, U-shaped representation that illustrates income inequality initially increasing with economic growth, but later decreasing after economic growth has reached a certain level. At first economies may be equal but poor; equality may fall during rapid growth, but as economies mature, equality should rise again.

Labor productivity: A measure of output produced by workers. The productivity of workers, conditioned by their education, health, and access to complementary inputs such as machinery and technology, is an important ingredient of growth. If productivity is rising faster than prices and population, a society will have more goods to distribute and welfare should improve.

Land reform: Given unequal patterns of landholdings created by colonial patronage, some governments have attempted to redistribute land. These movements have been revolutionary at times, taking tracts of land from the rich and giving them to the poor, as well as progressive, where only land that has been idle or unproductive is reassigned to those who might use it more intensively.

Latifundia: Feudal estates in Spanish Latin America, which stood in great contrast to the small parcels of land (known as minifundias) used by peasant farmers. The latifundia also served as a form of political, social, and economic organization and later contributed to a pattern of concentrated landholdings and power.

Lorenz curve: A graphical representation of income distribution. The population is sorted by income, usually deciles, and the percentage of income that each portion of the population holds is plotted. For example, in the Lorenz curve for Latin America, the first 20% of the population holds 2.5% of the income, and the first 40% a cumulative 8.6%. Altogether, the bottom 60% accounts for 19.6% of income, with the top 20% holding nearly two-thirds of the total.

Mandamiento: A system by which communities, most often indigenous, were forced to provide workers for harvest when there were labor shortages, often under brutal working conditions.

Market-based incentives: In addition to command and control measures and direct government investment, one of three types of tools used in environmental policy.

Instruments such as tax incentives are used to encourage market investments in such areas as recycling and use of solar power as a means of promoting sustainable development. The premise behind market-based initiatives is that if someone can profit from doing environmental good, the policy is more likely to endure over time.

Market failure: Neoclassical economic theorists believe that when left on its own, the market will promote economic growth. When the market fails to promote growth, primarily because of information constraints or ineffective price signals, this is known as market failure.

Mercosur: The South American common market comprising Argentina, Brazil, Uruguay, and Paraguay as well as associate members Chile and Bolivia.

Merit good: Investment in public goods such as education and health that have benefits for society in general.

Microcredit: Banking services that reach down to the small-scale entrepreneur. Collateral for loans is often provided by an investment circle that guarantees repayment of members. Microlending makes investment over time possible for the poor, but some question whether, because of the amounts involved and the repayment structure, microcredit makes a significant difference in people's lives.

Minifundia: The small parcels of land used for subsistence farming by Latin American peasants during the colonial period and whose remnants can still be seen today.

Moderate poverty: A standard of living corresponding to income of about $50–60 dollars a month, or $2 a day. Roughly 40% of the population of Latin America lives in moderate poverty.

NAFTA: The North American Free Trade Agreement was signed by the United States, Canada, and Mexico in 1994. It sought to reduce tariffs within a 10-year period, increase trade in the region, promote cross-border investment, and introduce environmental and labor standards across the region.

Neoclassical tradition: Belief among some economists that rational, self-interested maximizers, if left alone by governments to operate within markets, will generate the greatest quantity of goods for society.

Neostructuralists: Adherents of this school of economic thought do not believe that the market alone will spur development; the state should intervene in those areas where there has been market failure. Concentration of economic power in both the domestic and international arenas requires selective intervention to promote equitable development. The principal difference between structuralists and neostructuralists is that the latter place a greater emphasis on outward-looking export development as opposed to the inward-looking policies that defined import substitution industrialization.

New institutional economics: New institutionalists argue that culture matters in defining the ways the economy provides for society. New institutionalists claim that certain institutional arrangements are necessary to reduce transaction costs that arise in imperfect markets. The arrangements may include improving property rights, providing effective and impartial judicial systems, and instituting transparent regulatory frameworks.

New political economy: The new political economy grounds its assumptions in the material self-interest and rational calculus of economic actors. Intervention by the state will serve only to interfere with market signals and the allocation of resources. The state should, therefore, play a minimal role in the market.

Nontraditional export promotion: Policies such as agricultural extension training or preferential credit to promote goods that are not in the traditional export profile. By diversifying exports, countries are able to capture new markets and be less dependent on price swings in traditional commodities.

Olivera-Tanzi effect: The process by which inflation erodes the true value of tax receipts because of the time lag between assessment of tax liability and actual collection.

Open regionalism: Promoted by ECLAC, this policy encourages the formation of regional and subregional trading units without excluding trade initiatives with other parts of the world.

Orthodox theory of inflation: For the orthodox theorist, inflation is a monetary phenomenon: Too much money chasing too few goods increases the overall price level. This phenomenon is usually the result of governments trying to finance their budget deficits in one of three ways: raising money domestically, borrowing from abroad, and/or seignorage (printing money). To reduce inflation, the orthodox economists would attack not only the increase in the money supply but also large budget deficits. For the orthodox school, letting the markets work and limiting government intervention is the key to reducing inflation. The purpose behind tight monetary policy and a decrease in expenditures is to reduce aggregate demand that would otherwise lead to higher prices and not higher output.

Overvalued exchange rates: Under a fixed exchange rate system, a rate is overvalued when inflation has eroded the true value of the money but a new par or official rate has not been established. For example, if inflation in country A is 25% a year higher than in country B and their currencies are fixed in terms of each other, the country experiencing inflation will have a currency that is 25% overvalued at the end of one year. Overvaluation of a currency is not sustainable because it encourages imports and discourages exports. If it is not corrected by contracting the economy, people will expect a devaluation, or adjustment in the currency price. As reserves to pay for the current account imbalance are drawn down, people will begin to vote with their feet, moving capital to currencies without the risk of devaluation.

Pact for Economic Solidarity: Also known as *El Pacto*, this was an agreement between the Mexican state, business, and labor to limit price increases as a way to combat inflation.

Planning model: A vision of development policy that accords a strong role to a nation's government to jump start economic change.

Portfolio bonds: Short-term financial instruments held in emerging market portfolios that make a country vulnerable to quick movements of international capital flows.

Portfolio investors: Refers to certain types of investor, such as mutual funds or insurance companies, that generally invest with a short-term outlook.

Poverty line: The minimum income required to purchase the goods necessary for subsistence. Although this varies by location, $2 per day is the global benchmark for moderate poverty and $1 a day for extreme poverty.

Preferential trade agreements: Trade agreements such as free trade arrangements or customs unions that promote economic activity within a region by favoring trading partners within that region over those outside it.

Primary health care: Health care that promotes basic sanitation and nutrition practices to increase people's control over improvements in their environment so as to maintain a decent quality of life and achieve human and social potential.

Productivity: A measure of output in relation to inputs. Rising productivity is a key to economic growth.

Provisioning: A response by banks to the debt crisis whereby they would set aside profits (before dividend payments) against risky loans so as to reduce their exposure to debt.

Purchasing power parity: A good sold in two markets should sell for the same price, adjusted for the exchange rate, in both locations. If it does not, this suggests that one currency is overvalued.

Quality primary education by the year 2010: The goal of 100% primary school completion rates and 75% secondary inscription rates agreed to by the Presidents of the region at the 1994 Miami summit; action items to promote this goal were elaborated at the 1998 Santiago summit, including targeting vulnerable groups through compensatory programs, preschool education, and distance learning.

Real plan: Introduced by Brazilian President Henrique Fernando Cardoso when he was minister of the economy, the Real plan redenominated wages, prices, taxes, and the exchange rate in a new accounting unit called the urv. Later, a new currency, the real, was introduced. Contractionary monetary policies were undertaken. Unlike many previous attempts, the Real plan proved to be successful, neutralizing inflationary expectations and curbing inflation.

Regional integration: Regional integration is the matching of economic and other policies within a region. The simplest form of integration is a free trade area (FTA) covering goods, with lower (or no) tariffs on goods exchanged within the region. The next level would include an FTA with services and perhaps regulations in other areas such as the environment or social concerns. A customs union deepens the commitment with a common external tariff. A common market permits the movement of factors of production among member countries, and an economic union expands on this to cede sovereignty over commercial, fiscal, and monetary policy to a supranational authority. Regional integration may make the liberalization process politically palatable through playing on sentiments of reciprocity of neighbor markets, and it may improve the confidence of investors because policies of openness have been locked in by treaty.

Repartida: Monopoly control over mines and land in the New World was accorded through the encomienda system, which gave land rights to colonists, with a share of the output or repartida owed in return back to the home country.

Returned value: Revenue earned through exports that is retained by a country.

Safe minimum standard: The highest level of pollution that a society can safely tolerate with the reasonable expectation that future generations will not be made worse off by the choice.

Secondary market: A market for a financial instrument that separates the initial debt issuer from the eventual lender. During the debt crisis, many banks were pessimistic about the ability of Latin American countries to repay loans. In particular, small and medium-sized banks wanted to unload risky loans and offered them for resale below their face value in the secondary market. Larger banks (with a greater likelihood of being repaid) or multinational corporations interested in operating in a foreign market might choose to assume this credit risk at a discounted price. The larger bank or firm might, for example, pay 50 cents for a piece of paper saying that the borrowing country owed it a dollar. The greater the risk of default, the lower the secondary market price. Buyers of the debt could earn a substantial profit if a Latin American country paid off its debt in full, or in any proportion higher than what the debt was bought for.

Segmented credit markets: Different groups of borrowers are assigned different prices for loans, and barriers between the groups prevent arbitrage from evening out the spread in interest rates. These barriers might be geographic distances or may be cultural or social differences that keep one group—perhaps poor minority women—separated from another portion of the population.

Seignorage: An increase in the money supply by the mere printing of more currency, usually for the purpose of financing government spending. A government can profit from such an operation because it results in inflation. The government then is able to repay its debts in currency that is worth less than the currency that was borrowed. The result of monetary expansion might be short-run expansion of output, but eventually the increase in money will mean only an increase in prices.

Severe stabilization: The first and often very painful stage of macroeconomic adjustment designed to bring macroeconomic fundamentals into line.

Short-term money: This includes the "hot" capital flow of portfolio bonds and stocks that may be moved from country to country in an internationally linked global financial system with the stroke of a keyboard.

Social investment funds: Targeted emergency aid for poverty reduction.

Stolper-Samuelson effect: As the price of the more abundant (and cheaper) factor rises after an opening of trade, the owners of this factor—in the case of the developing countries, labor—will accrue the largest gain. Trade should therefore make owners of the cheapest factor better off.

Structural adjustment programs: Often supported by the World Bank and the IMF, these programs are designed to address internal and external balance by decreasing domestic expenditure, enhancing revenue collection, promoting exports, and limiting luxury imports. These programs changed the shape or structure of economies from the inward-oriented import substitution model to an externally oriented export promotion program, simultaneously privatizing state industries, decreasing government expenditures, and encouraging inflows of foreign capital.

Structural transformation: The second stage of economic adjustment designed to change the shape of the economy, particularly with respect to decreasing the active role of the state and increasing the economy's orientation to the international market.

Structuralists: Drawing on the work of the Economic Commission for Latin America (ECLA) under Raúl Prebisch, structuralists begin from the assumption that the underlying structure of developing economies differs from that of more industrialized nations. Macro policy for structuralists rests on the premise that relatively concentrated industrial elites can pass on price increases, resulting in inertial inflation. Structuralists tend to downplay the importance of fiscal balance in favor of an activist state policy to redress production bottlenecks. Structuralists and their intellectual descendants, the neostructuralists, have little faith in the ability of the market to generate spontaneous or equitable growth. Borrowing from dependency analysts, structuralists believe that the position of countries in the international system, especially their access to technology, limits possibilities for autonomous growth. Although neostructuralists appreciate the benefits of international trade and finance, they caution that states should intervene to mitigate the social and environmental costs of openness.

Sustainable development: Development strategies that will meet today's needs without sacrificing the ability of future generations to meet their own needs.

Targeting: A method of allocating social expenditures by identifying and distributing funds to those most in need. Targeted policies have often replaced general programs such as subsidies on tortillas or milk that could not distinguish between the needy and the well-off. An example of a targeted policy would be a food debit card that is replenished when a mother brings a child to a clinic for preventive child care.

Technological change: The key to economic development, technological change allows for new combinations of capital and labor to create more efficient production.

Tesobono: A dollar-denominated treasury bond offered by the Mexican government during the Mexican financial crisis. The bonds were structured to convince investors to keep their capital in Mexico by eliminating exchange risk. After a series of political events that deepened the crisis and scared capital away, the tesobono led to a further depletion of dollar reserves because the Mexican government had to cover its dollar-based obligations.

Theory of comparative advantage: This theory states that to maximize global output, each country should apply its resources to producing those goods that it can produce relatively most efficiently.

Trade creation: A benefit of economic integration whereby a trade agreement leads to an increase in overall trade. An integration agreement has positive effects if trade creation exceeds trade diversion.

Trade diversion: An effect of economic integration, when trade with a more efficient global producer is discontinued in favor of products from a regional trading partner.

Transnational corporations: Transnational corporations, also known as multinational corporations (MNCs) and transnational enterprises (TNEs), are firms with central offices located in one country but with operations abroad. Transnational corporations are the primary form of foreign direct investment. TNCs bring capital, expertise, and jobs but also may thwart the growth of local industries and have been accused of exploiting low-wage workers.

Urbanization: The growth of large cities. The high levels of urban living in Latin America, with rates in Argentina, Brazil, Venezuela, Uruguay, and Chile higher than that of the United States, create enormous environmental difficulties.

Value added tax (VAT): A consumption tax levied on the value added at each stage of production. The advantage of the VAT over other tax instruments is its self-regulating mechanism: Each producer requires a receipt from its supplier to demonstrate that taxes already have been paid on the earlier levels of production.

Velocity of money: The amount of national output supported by the money supply; mathematically, it is expressed as GDP/M, or gross domestic product divided by the money supply. Velocity is higher when a small stock of money supports a higher level of output. The higher the velocity, the larger the effect of any increase in the money supply.

Water rights: a critical element in agricultural policy. Access to water rights, if accrued on the basis of seniority or local power, often interferes with the efficient allocation of resources in an agricultural community.

BIBLIOGRAPHY

Acevedo, Carlos, Deborah Barry, and Herman Rosa. "El Salvador's Agricultural Sector: Macroeconomic Policy, Agrarian Change and the Environment." *World Development* 23, no. 12 (1995).

Action Plan for Universal and Quality Basic Education by the Year 2000, Summit of the Americas. Available on-line at www.summit-americas.org.

Adelman, Irma, and Cynthia Taft Morris. "Development History and Its Implications for Development Theory." *World Development* 25, no. 6 (June 1997): 841–840.

Adriance, Jim. "Living with the Land in Central America." *Grassroots Development* 19, no. 1 (1995).

Agarwala, A. N., and S. P. Singh, eds. *The Economics of Underdevelopment*. New York: Oxford University Press, 1963.

Alderman, Harold, and Victor Lavy. "Household Responses to Public Health Services: Cost and Quality Tradeoffs." *World Bank Research Observer* 11, no. 1 (February 1996): 3–22.

Althaus, Dudley. "Deforestation Contributed to Tragedy by Mitch in Honduras, Experts Claim." *Houston Chronicle*. 30 December 1998, p. A1, as found in the LEXIS-NEXIS database.

Amedeo, Eduardo José Márcio Camargo, Antônio Emílio S. Marques, and Cândido Gomes. "Fiscal Crisis and Asymmetries in the Education System in Brazil." In *Coping with Crisis: Austerity, Adjustment, and Human Resources*, edited by Joel Samoff. New York: UNESCO/ILO, 1994.

Ameur, Charles. *Agricultural Extension: A Step beyond the Next Step*. World Bank Technical Paper no. 247. Washington, D.C.: World Bank, 1994.

Anayiotos, George, and Jaime de Piniés. "The Secondary Market and the International Debt Problem." *World Development* 18, no. 2 (1990): 1655–1660.

Aninat, Eduardo, and Christian Larraín. "Capital Flows: Lessons from the Chilean Experience." *CEPAL Review* 60 (December 1996).

Anonymous. "Health of Indigenous Peoples." *Pan American Journal of Public Health* 2, no. 25 (1997): 357–362.

Antle, John M., and Gregg Heidebrink. "Environment and Development: Theory and International Evidence." *Economic Development and Cultural Change* 43, no. 3 (April 1995).

Argentina Business: The Portable Encyclopedia for Doing Business with Argentina. San Rafael, Calif.: World Trade Press, 1995.

Arriagada, Irma. "Unequal Participation by Women in the Working World." *CEPAL Review* 40 (April 1990): 83–98.

"Auto Industry Delivers Vote of Confidence in Brazil and Mercosur." *Latin American Weekly Report*. 3 February 1998.

Ayres, Robert L. *Crime and Violence as Development Issues in Latin America*. Washington, D.C.: World Bank, 1998.

Baer, Werner. "Changing Paradigms: Changing Interpretations of the Public Sector in Latin America's Economies." *Public Choice* 88 (1996): 365–379.

Baer, Werner. "Latin America and Europe in the Nineteenth Century: The Impact of an

Unequal Relationship." In *Development and Underdevelopment in America*, edited by Walther Bernecker and Hans Werner Tobler. New York: Walter de Gruyter, 1993.

Baer, Werner, and Melissa Birch, eds. *Privatization in Latin America*. Westport, Conn.: Praeger, 1994.

Baer, Werner, and Annibal V. Villela. "Privatization and the Changing Role of the State in Brazil." In *Privatization in Latin America*, edited by Werner Baer and Melissa Birch. Westport, Conn.: Praeger, 1994.

Baran, Paul A. "On the Political Economy of Backwardness." *Manchester School* 20, no. 1 (1952). Reprinted in *The Economics of Underdevelopment*, edited by A. N. Agarwala and S. P. Singh (New York: Oxford University Press, 1963), and in *Political Economy of Development and Underdevelopment*, edited by Charles K. Wilber (New York: Random House, 1973).

Bastianensen, Johan. "Non-Conventional Rural Finance and the Crisis of Economic Institutions in Nicaragua." In *Sustainable Agriculture in Central America*, edited by Jan P. de Groot and Ruerd Ruben. New York: St. Martin's, 1997.

Bate, Peter. "Education: The Gordian Knot." *IDB Today*. On-line edition available at www.iadb.org.

Bauer, P., and B. Yamey. *The Economics of Underdeveloped Countries*. New York: Cambridge University Press, 1967.

Bellew, Rosemary T., and Elizabeth M. King. "Educating Women: Lessons from Experience." In *Women's Education in Developing Countries: Barriers, Benefits and Policies*, edited by Elizabeth M. King and Rosemary Bellew. Baltimore: Johns Hopkins University Press, 1993.

Bellos, Alex. "Ronaldo's Fame Hasn't Hit Home." *Minneapolis Star Tribune*. 10 July 1998, p. C6.

Benavente, José Miguel, Gustavo Crespi, Jorge Katz, and Giovanni Stumpo. "Changes in the Industrial Development of Latin America." *CEPAL Review* 60 (December 1996).

Bennett, Bradley. "Plants and People of the Amazonian Rainforests: The Role of Ethnobotany in Sustainable Development." *BioScience* 42, no. 8 (1992).

Berstein, Aaron. "Sweatshop Reform: How to Solve the Standoff." *Business Week*. 3 May 1999.

Bernstein, H., ed. *Underdevelopment and Development*. Harmondsworth, U.K.: Penguin, 1973.

Bhagwati, Jagdish. "The FTAA Is *Not* Free Trade." In *Trade: Towards Open Regionalism*, proceedings of the 1997 World Bank Conference on Development in Latin America and the Caribbean. Washington, D.C.: World Bank, 1998.

Biersteker, Thomas J. *Dealing with Debt*. Boulder, Colo.: Westview, 1993.

Biersteker, Thomas J. *Distortion or Development? Contending Perspectives on the Multinational Corporation*. Cambridge, Mass.: MIT Press, 1978.

Binswanger, Hans P., and Klaus Deininger. "Explaining Agricultural and Agrarian Policies in Developing Countries." *Journal of Economic Literature* 35 (December 1997).

Birdsall, Nancy, and Carlos Lozada. "Recurring Themes in Latin American Economic Thought: From Prebisch to the Market and Back." In *Securing Stability and Growth in Latin America*, edited by Ricardo Hausmann and Helmut Reisen. Paris: OECD Publications, 1996.

Bitran, Eduardo, and Pablo Serra. "Regulation of Privatized Utilities: The Chilean Experience." *World Development* 26, no. 6 (1998): 945–962.

Blackwood, D. L., and R. G. Lynch. "The Measurement of Inequality and Poverty." *World Development* 22, no. 4 (1994): 567–578.

Blomström, Magnus, and Ari Kokko. *Regional Integration and Foreign Direct Investment*.

National Bureau of Economic Research Working Paper no. 6019. Cambridge, Mass.: National Bureau of Economic Research, 1997.

Blomström, Magnus, and Edward N. Wolff. "Multinational Corporations and Productivity Convergence in Mexico." In *Convergence of Productivity: Cross-National Studies and Historical Evidence*, edited by William Baumol, Richard R. Nelson, and Edward N. Wolff. New York: Oxford University Press, 1994.

Bloomberg Latin America. "Argentine Markets Climb after IMF, Banks Move to Shore Up Confidence." Retrieved from the World Wide Web, 14 July 1999, at www.quote.bloomberg.com.

Blumenstein, Rebecca. "GM to Build a Low-Priced Car in Brazil." *The Wall Street Journal.* 19 March 1997.

"Bolivia: Getting Kids Back in School." *IDB América* (November 1997): 14. Available online at www.iadb.org/English/projects/projects.html.

Bonior, David. "I Told You So." *New York Times.* 13 July 1997.

Borenstein, E., J. De Gregorio, and J. W. Lee. "How Does Foreign Investment Affect Economic Growth?" *Journal of International Economics* 45 (1998): 115–135.

Bowman, Kirk S. "Should the Kuznets Effect Be Relied on to Induce Equalizing Growth?" *World Development* 25, no. 1 (1997): 127–143.

Bradford, Colin, Jr. "Future Policy Directions and Relevance." In *The Legacy of Raúl Prebisch*, edited by Enrique V. Iglesias. Washington, D.C.: Inter-American Development Bank, 1994.

Braga, Carlos Alberto Primo. "Tropical Forests and Trade Policy: The Case of Indonesia and Brazil." In *International Trade and the Environment*, edited by Patrick Low. Washington, D.C.: World Bank, 1992.

Brainard, S. Lael, and David Riker. *Are U.S. Multinationals Exporting U.S. Jobs?* National Bureau of Economic Research Working Paper no. 5958. Cambridge, Mass.: National Bureau of Economic Research, 1997.

Braverman, Avishay, and J. Luis Guasch. "Administrative Failures in Government Credit Programs." In *The Economics of Rural Organization*, edited by Karla Hoff, Avishay Braverman, and Joseph Stiglitz. New York: Oxford University Press/World Bank, 1993.

"Brazil: Domestic Debt Dynamics and Implications." *ING Barings Emerging Markets Weekly Report.* 5 March 1999, p. 1–3.

"Brazil's Affluent Are Hurt by Crisis." *Washington Post.* 25 January 1999.

"Brazil's Iron King." *Financial Times.* 29 June 1998.

"Brazil's Neighbors Are Very Nervous." *Business Week.* 17 November 1997.

Britan, Ricardo, and Keith McInnes. *The Demand for Health Care in Latin America.* Economic Development Institute Seminar Paper no. 46. Washington, D.C.: World Bank, 1993.

Britton, John A., ed. *Molding the Hearts and Minds: Education, Communications and Social Change in Latin America.* Wilmington, Del.: Scholarly Resources, 1994.

Brooke, James. "Home, Home on the Range, in Brazil's Heartland." *New York Times.* 26 April 1995.

Bruton, Henry. "Import Substitution." In *Handbook of Development Economics*, vol. 2, 3d ed., edited by Hollis Chenery and T. N. Srivivasan. New York: Elsevier, 1996.

Bruton, Henry. "A Reconsideration of Import Substitution." *Journal of Economic Literature* 36 (June 1998).

Bulmer-Thomas, Victor. *The Economic History of Latin America since Independence.* New York: Cambridge University Press, 1994.

Burbackh, Roger, and Peter Rosset. "Chiapas and the Crisis of Mexican Agriculture." *Food First Policy Brief*, no. 1. San Francisco: Institute for Food and Development, 1994.

Burki, Shahid Javed, and Sebastian Edwards. *Dismantling the Populist State*. Washington, D.C.: World Bank, 1996.

Burki, Shahid Javed, and Sebastian Edwards. *Latin America after Mexico: Quickening the Pace*. Washington, D.C.: World Bank, 1996.

Burns, Bradford E., ed. *Latin America: Conflict and Creation: A Historical Reader*. Englewood Cliffs, N.J.: Prentice Hall, 1992.

Byrnes, H., and B. Spencer. "U.S. Must Aid Guatemala's Shift to Peace." *St. Louis Post-Dispatch*. 20 December 1996.

Caldwell, Laura. "Swapping Debt to Preserve Nature." *Christian Science Monitor*. 11 September 1990.

Camdessus, Michel. "The Private Sector in a Strengthened Global Financial System." Remarks at the International Monetary Conference, Philadelphia, 8 June 1999. Available on-line at www.imf.org/external/speeches.

"CANTV in 1994." *Harvard Business School Case Studies*. 28 February 1996.

Cardoso, Fernando Henrique. Interview on the occasion of the second anniversary of the Real plan, as reported in FBIS-LAT-96-129 (Foreign Broadcast Information Services, Latin America), 3 July 1996. Originally appeared on the Rede Globo website, 1 July 1996.

Carnoy, Martin. "Structural Adjustment and the Changing Face of Education." *International Labor Review* 134, no. 6 (1995): 653–673.

Carter, Michael, and Dina Mesbah. "State-Mandated and Market-Mediated Reform in Latin America." In *Including the Poor*, edited by Michael Lipton and Jacques van der Gaag. Baltimore: Johns Hopkins University Press/World Bank, 1993.

Carter, Michael, and Bradford Barham. "Level Playing Fields and Laissez Faire: Postliberal Development Strategy in Inegalitarian Agrarian Economies." *World Development* 24, no. 7 (July 1996).

Cartaya, Vanessa F. "El Confuso mundo del sector informal." *Nueva Sociedad* 90 (July–August 1987): 81–84.

Castañeda, Tarsicio. "Combating Poverty." In *Reforms in Education*. San Francisco: International Center for Economic Growth, 1992.

Caves, Richard E. *Multinational Enterprise and Economic Analysis*. 2d ed. Cambridge: Cambridge University Press, 1996.

Center for International Health Information. *Country Health Profile/Bolivia*. Arlington: Center for International Health Information, December 1996. Available on-line at www.cihi.com.

Central Intelligence Agency. *The World Fact Book*. Available on-line at www.odci.gov/cia.

Cevallos, Diego. "Environment-Mexico: Toxic Waste, a Dirty Problem." Inter Press Service. 11 August 1995. Available on the LEXIS-NEXIS database.

Chipman, Andre. "U.S., Latin-American Oil Companies Build Alliance as Mideast Clout Fades." *The Wall Street Journal*. 9 March 1998.

Choque Schulter, Sidney, and Ruth Choque Schulter. "Misinformation, Mistrust, and Mistreatment: Family Planning among Bolivian Market Women." *Studies in Family Planning* 25 (1994).

Clements, Benedict. "The Real Plan, Poverty, and Income Distribution in Brazil." *Finance and Development* (September 1997).

Coatsworth, John. "Notes on the Comparative Economic History of Latin America and the United States." In *Development and Underdevelopment in America*, edited by Walther Bernecker and Hans Werner Tobler. New York: Walter de Gruyter, 1993.

Coes, Donald V. *Macroeconomic Crises, Policies, and Growth in Brazil, 1964–90*. Washington, D.C.: World Bank, 1995.

Colclough, Christopher. "Education and the Market: Which Parts of the Neoliberal Solution Are Correct?" *World Development* 24, no. 4 (1996): 589–610.

Commission Economica Para America Latina. *Indicadores Económicos*. Santiago, Chile: Commission Economica Para America Latina, 1997.

Commission on Development and Environment for Amazonia. *Amazonia without Myths*. Washington, D.C.: Inter-American Development Bank, 1992.

Conger, Lucy. "A Fourth Way? The Latin American Alternative to Neoliberalism." *Current History*. November 1998.

Constance, Paul. "A High Technology Incubator." *IDB América*. 1997. Available at the Inter-American Development Bank homepage at www.iadb.org.

Constance, Paul. "A Seat at the Table: Union Leaders Urge IDB to Include Workers' Concerns in Reform Programs and Free Trade Negotiations." *IDB América*. April 1998. Available at the Inter-American Development Bank homepage at www.iadb.org.

Contreras Murphy, Ellen. "La Selva and the Magnetic Pull of Markets: Organic Coffee-Growing in Mexico." *Grassroots Development* 19, no. 1 (1995): 27–34.

Corbo, Vittorio. "Economic Policies and Performance in Latin America." In *Economic Development: Handbook of Comparative Economic Policies*, edited by Enzo Grilli and Dominick Salvatore. Westport, Conn.: Greenwood, 1994.

Cortés-Salas, Hernán, Ronnie de Camino, and Arnoldo Contreras. *Readings of the Workshop on Government Policy Reform for Forestry Conservation and Development in Latin America*, 1–3 June 1994. Washington, D.C.: Inter-American Institute for Cooperation on Agriculture, 1995.

"Cost-Cutting Takes a Private Road." *Euromoney*. September 1996.

"Cost Information and Management Decision in a Brazilian Hospital." In *World Development Report 1993*. New York: Oxford University Press/World Bank, 1993.

Council on Foreign Relations. "Reforming Education in America." Study group on reforming education in Latin America, "The Second Wave of Reform," February–October 1996.

"Creating Jobs Is Main Headache." *Latin American Weekly Report*. 5 January 1999.

Cuddington, John T. *Capital Flight: Estimates, Issues, and Explanations*. Princeton Studies in International Finance no. 58. Princeton, N.J.: Princeton University Press, 1986.

de Janvry, Alain, and Elisabeth Sadoulet. "NAFTA and Mexico's Maize Producers." *World Development* 23, no. 8 (August 1995): 1349–1362.

de Janvry, Alain, and Elisabeth Sadoulet. "Rural Development in Latin America: Relinking Poverty Reduction to Growth." In *Including the Poor*, edited by Michael Lipton and Jacques van der Gaag. Washington, D.C.: World Bank, 1993.

de Souza, Amaury. "Redressing Inequalities: Brazil's Social Agenda at Century's End." In *Brazil under Cardoso*, edited by Susan Kaufman Purcell and Riordan Roett. Boulder, Colo.: Lynne Rienner, 1997.

"Declaration and Action Plan for Latin American Economic Recovery." *UN Chronicle* 21, no. 3 (March 1984): 13–17.

della Paolera, Gerardo, and Alan Taylor. *Finance and Development in an Emerging Market: Argentina in the Interwar Period*. National Bureau of Economic Research Working Paper Series no. 6236. Cambridge, Mass.: National Bureau of Economic Research, 1997.

Delovitch, Emanuel, and Klas Ringskog. *Private Sector Participation in Water Supply and Sanitation in Latin America*. Washington, D.C.: World Bank, 1995.

Delph, Yvette M. "Health Priorities in Developing Countries." *Journal of Law, Medicine & Ethics* 21, no. 1 (1993).

Devlin, Robert, Ricardo Ffrench-Davis, and Stephany Griffith-Jones. "Surges in Capital

Flows and Development: An Overview of Policy Issues." In *Coping with Capital Surges*, edited by Ricardo Ffrench-Davis and Stephany Griffith-Jones. Boulder, Colo.: Lynne Rienner, 1995.

Dewees, Anthony, and Steven Klees. "Social Movements and the Transformation of National Policy: Street and Working Children in Brazil." *Comparative Education Review* 39, no. 1 (1995).

Díaz Alejandro, Carlos. "International Markets for LCDs: The Old and the New." *American Economic Review* (May): 254–269.

Dietz, James L., and James H. Street, eds. *Latin America's Economic Development: Institutionalist and Structuralist Perspectives*. Boulder, Colo.: Lynne Rienner, 1987.

Dixon, John. *The Urban Environmental Challenge in Latin America*. LATEN Dissemination Note no. 4, World Bank Latin America Technical Department. Environment Division. Washington, D.C.: World Bank, 1993.

Dornbusch, Rudiger. *Stabilization, Debt, and Reform: Policy Analysis for Developing Countries*. Englewood Cliffs, N.J.: Prentice-Hall, 1993.

Dornbusch, Rudiger, and Sebastian Edwards. "The Political Economy of Latin America." In *The Macroeconomics of Populism in Latin America* (a National Bureau of Economic Research conference report), edited by Rudiger Dornbusch and Sebastian Edwards. Chicago: University of Chicago Press, 1991.

Dos Santos, Theodoro. "La crisis de la teoría del desarollo y las relaciones de dependencia en América Latina." *Boletin de CESO* 3 (1968). English translation in H. Bernstein, ed., *Underdevelopment and Development*. Harmondsworth, U.K.: Penguin, 1973.

Echavarría, Juan José. "Trade Flow in the Andean Countries: Unilateral Liberalization or Regional Preferences." In *Trade: Towards Open Regionalism*, proceedings of the 1997 World Bank Conference on Development in Latin America and the Caribbean. Washington, D.C.: World Bank, 1998.

Economic Commission for Latin American and the Caribbean. Communique on the international financial crises. 15 September 1998. Available on-line at www.cepal.org.english/coverpage/financialcrisis.htm.

Economic Commission for Latin America and the Caribbean. *Economic Survey of Latin America and the Caribbean*. Santiago, Chile: Economic Commission for Latin America and the Caribbean, various years.

Economic Commission for Latin America and the Caribbean. *The Equity Gap: Latin America, the Caribbean, and the Social Summit*. Santiago, Chile: Economic Commission for Latin America and the Caribbean, 1997.

Economic Commission for Latin America and the Caribbean. *The Fiscal Covenant: Strengths, Weaknesses, Challenges*. Santiago, Chile: Economic Commission for Latin America and the Caribbean, 1997.

Economic Commission for Latin America and the Caribbean. *Foreign Investment and the Caribbean: 1997 Report* (English summary). Available on-line at www.eclac.cl/english/Publications/invest/summary.html.

Economic Commission for Latin America and the Caribbean. *Indicadores Económicos*. Santiago, Chile: Economic Commission for Latin America and the Caribbean, 1997.

Economic Commission for Latin America and the Caribbean. *Preliminary Overview of the Economies of Latin America and the Caribbean*. Santiago, Chile: Economic Commission for Latin America and the Caribbean, 1998.

Economic Commission for Latin America and the Caribbean. *Statistical Yearbook for Latin American and the Caribbean, 1996*. Santiago, Chile: Economic Commission for Latin America and the Caribbean, 1996.

Economic Commission for Latin America and the Caribbean. *Panorama de la insercion internactional de América Latina y el Caribe, 1996.* Santiago, Chile: Economic Commission for Latin America and the Caribbean, 1996.

Economic Commission for Latin America and the Caribbean. *Policies to Improve Linkages with the Global Economy.* Santiago, Chile: Economic Commission for Latin America and the Caribbean, 1995.

Economic Commission for Latin America and the Caribbean. *Strengthening Development: The Interplay of Macro and Microeconomics.* Santiago, Chile: Economic Commission for Latin America and the Caribbean, 1996.

Edwards, Sebastian. *Capital Flows into Latin America: A Stop-Go Story?* National Bureau of Economic Research Working Paper no. 6441. Cambridge, Mass.: National Bureau of Economic Research, 1998. Available on-line at www.nber.org/papers/w6441.

Edwards, Sebastian. *Crisis and Reform in Latin America: From Despair to Hope.* New York: Oxford University Press, 1995.

Edwards, Sebastian. "The Mexican Peso Crisis: How Much Did We Know? When Did We Know It?" *World Economy* 21, no. 1 (1998).

Edwards, Sebastian. "The Political Economy of Inflation and Stabilization in Developing Countries." *Economic Development and Cultural Change* 42, no. 2 (January 1994): 235–266.

Edwards, Sebastian, and Daniel Lederman. *The Political Economy of Unilateral Trade Liberalization: The Case of Chile.* National Bureau of Economic Research Working Paper no. 6510. Cambridge, Mass.: National Bureau of Economic Research, 1998. Available on-line at www.nber.org/papers/w6510.

Edwards, Sebastian, and Nora Claudia Lustig, eds. *Labor Markets in Latin America: Combining Social Protection with Market Flexibility.* Washington, D.C.: Brookings Institution, 1997.

El-Ashry, Mohamed T. *Statement to the Fourth Session of the Conference of the Parties to the United Nations Framework Convention on Climate Change,* Buenos Aires, 11 November 1998. Washington, D.C.: Global Environment Facility, 1998.

"Energy in Latin America: Even Oil Is Growing Less Sacred." *The Economist.* 1 June 1996.

Engell, Alan. "Improving the Quality and Equity of Education in Chile: The Programa 900 Escuelas and the MECE-Basica." In *Implementing Policy Innovation in Latin America: Politics, Economics and Techniques,* edited by Antonio Silva. Washington, D.C.: Inter-American Development Bank, 1996.

Ellison, Katherine. "Latin Summit's Focus: Education of Kids." *Miami Herald.* 13 April 1998, p. A1. Available on-line at www.alca-cupula.org.

Employment Policy Foundation. "Open Trade: The 'Fast Track' to Higher Living Standards." *Contemporary Issues in Employment and Workplace Policy* 111, no. 10 (October 1997). Internet publication available at http://epfnet.org.

Energy Information Administration. *Petroleum Supply Annual, 1995.* Washington, D.C.: U.S. Department of Energy, 1995.

Evans, Peter. *Dependent Development.* Princeton, N.J.: Princeton University Press, 1979.

Evans, Peter. "The Eclipse of the State: Reflection on Stateness in an Era of Globalization." *World Politics* 50 (October 1997).

Faiz, Asif, Surhid Gautam, and Emaad Burki. "Air Pollution from Motor Vehicles: Issues and Options for Latin American Countries." *The Science of the Total Environment* 169 (1995): 303–310.

Fajnzylber, Fernando. "Education and Changing Production Patterns with Social Equality." *CEPAL Review* 47 (August 1992).

Farber, Daniel. *Environment under Fire.* New York: Monthly Review Press, 1993.

Fanelli, José María, and José Luis Machinea. "Capital Movements in Argentina." In *Coping with Capital Surges: The Return of Finance to Latin America*, edited by Ricardo Ffrench-Davis and Stephany Griffith-Jones. Boulder, Colo.: Lynne Rienner, 1995.

Fanelli, José María, and Roberto Frenkel. "Macropolicies for the Transition from Stabilization to Growth." In *New Directions in Development Economics: Growth, Environmental Concerns, and Government in the 1990s*, edited by Mats Lundahl and Benno J. Ndulu. London: Routledge, 1996.

Fearnside, Phillip. "Deforestation in Brazilian Amazonia: The Effect of Population and Land Tenure." *Ambio* 22, no. 8 (December 1993).

"Fifty Years On." *The Economist*. 16 May 1998, p. 22.

Fischer, Stanley. "Reforming World Finance." *The Economist*. 3–9 October 1998. Reproduced at www.imf.org.

Fiszbein, A., and G. Psacharopoulos. *Income Inequality in Latin America: The Story of the Eighties*. Technical Department for Latin America working paper. Washington, D.C.: World Bank, 1995.

Foley, Michael. "Agenda for Mobilization: The Agrarian Question and Popular Mobilization in Contemporary Mexico." *Latin American Research Review* 26, no. 2 (1991): 39–74.

Food and Agriculture Organization of the United Nations. *The State of Food and Agriculture*. Rome: Food and Agriculture Organization of the United Nations.

Foxley, Alejandro. "Preface." In *The New Economic Model in Latin America and Its Impact on Income Distribution and Poverty*, edited by Victor Bulmer-Thomas. New York: St. Martin's, 1996.

Ffrench-Davis, Ricardo. Comment on L. Allan Winters, "Assessing Regional Integration." In *Trade: Towards Open Regionalism*, proceedings of the 1997 World Bank Conference on Development in Latin America and the Caribbean. Washington, D.C.: World Bank, 1998.

Ffrench-Davis, Ricardo. "Policy Implications of the Tequila Effect." *Challenge*. March-April 1998.

Ffrench-Davis, Ricardo, Manuel Agosin, and Andras Uthoff. "Capital Movements, Export Strategy and Macroeconomic Stability in Chile." In *Coping with Capital Surges: The Return of Finance to Latin America*, edited by Ricardo Ffrench-Davis and Stephany Griffith-Jones. Boulder, Colo.: Lynne Rienner, 1995.

Frank, Andre Gundar. *Capitalism and Underdevelopment in Latin America*. New York: Monthly Review Press, 1967.

Freire, Paulo. *Pedagogy of the Oppressed*. New York: Seabury, 1970.

Friedland, Jonathan. "Their Success Earns Chileans a New Title: Ugly Pan-Americans." *The Wall Street Journal*. 3 October 1996.

"From Sandals to Suits." *The Economist*. 1 February 1997.

Furtado, C. *Development and Underdevelopment*, translated by Ricardo W. Agruar and Eric Charles Drysdale. Berkeley: University of California Press, 1965.

Galal, Ahmed, Leroy Jones, Pankaj Tandon, and Ingo Vogelsang. "Divestiture: Questions and Answers." In *Welfare Consequences of Selling Public Enterprises*. Washington, D.C.: World Bank, 1994.

Gavin, Michael. "Surviving Economic Surgery." *The IDB*. December 1996, p. 4–5.

Gavin, Michael, Ricardo Hausmann, Roberto Perotti, and Ernesto Talvi. *Managing Fiscal Policy in Latin America and the Caribbean: Volatility, Procyclicality, and Limited Creditworthiness*. Inter-American Development Bank, Office of the Chief Economist Working Paper no. 326. Washington, D.C.: Inter-American Development Bank, 1996.

Gelbard, Alene H. *An Action Plan for Population, Development, and the Environment:*

Woodrow Wilson Center Spring 1996 Report. Washington, D.C.: Woodrow Wilson Center, 1996.

Gereffi, Gary, and Peter Evans. "Transnational Corporations, Dependent Development, and State Policy in the Semiperiphery." *Latin American Research Review* 16, no. 3 (1981): 31–64.

Goodland, Robert, and Herman Daly. *Poverty Alleviation Is Essential for Environmental Sustainability*. World Bank, Environment Department, Divisional Working Paper 1993-42. Washington, D.C.: World Bank, 1993.

Goulet, Denis. *The Cruel Choice: A New Concept in the Theory of Development*. New York: Atheneum, 1971.

"Green, as in Greenbacks." *The Economist*. 1 February 1997.

Graham, Carol. *Private Markets for Public Goods: Raising the Stakes for Economic Reform*. Washington, D.C.: Brookings Institution Press, 1998.

Graham, Carol. *Safety Nets, Politics, and the Poor: Transitions to Market Economies*. Washington, D.C.: Brookings Institution, 1994.

Griffith-Jones, Stephany. "The Mexican Peso Crisis." *CEPAL Review* 60 (December 1996).

Grilli, Enzo, and Dominick Salvatore, eds. *Economic Development: Handbook of Comparative Economic Policies*. Westport, Conn.: Greenwood, 1994.

Grosh, Margaret E. *Administering Targeted Social Programs in Latin America*. Washington, D.C.: World Bank, 1994.

Guerguil, Marinte. "Some Thoughts on the Definition of the Informal Sector." *CEPAL Review* 35 (August 1988).

Gunnarsson, C., and M. Lundahl. "The Good, the Bad, and the Wobbly." In *New Directions in Development Economics: Growth, Environmental Concerns, and Government in the 1990s*, edited by Mats Lundahl and Benno J. Ndulu. London: Routledge, 1996.

Haass, Richard N., and Robert E. Litan. "Globalization and Its Discontents." *Foreign Affairs* 77, no. 3 (1998).

Hall, Susan E. A. "Conoco's Green Strategy." Harvard Business School Case #9-394-001. 4 October 1993.

Hanson, Simon. *Economic Development in Latin America*. Washington, D.C.: Inter-American Affairs Press, 1951.

Harriss-White, Barbara. "Maps and Landscapes of Grain Markets in South Asia." In *The New Institutional Economics and Third World Development*, edited by John Harriss, Janet Hunter, and Colin M. Lewis. London: Routledge, 1996.

Hartshorn, Gary S. "Natural Forest Management by the Yanesha Forestry Cooperative in Peruvian Amazonia." In *Alternatives to Deforestation: Steps toward Sustainable Use of the Amazon Rain Forest*, edited by Anthony B. Anderson. New York: Columbia University Press, 1990.

Hausmann, Ricardo, and Ernesto Stein. "Searching for the Right Budgetary Institution for a Volatile Region." In *Securing Stability and Growth in Latin America*, edited by Ricardo Hausmann and Helmut Reisen. Paris: OECD Publications, 1996.

Hausmann, Ricardo, and Helmut Reisen, eds. *Securing Stability and Growth in Latin America*. Paris: OECD Publications, 1996.

Helleiner, Gerald K. "Toward a New Development Strategy." In *The Legacy of Raúl Prebisch*, edited by Enrique V. Iglesias. Washington, D.C.: Inter-American Development Bank, 1994.

Helwege, Ann. "Poverty and Inequality in Latin America and the Caribbean." *CEPAL Review* 47 (August 1992).

Helwege, Ann. "Poverty in Latin America: Back to the Abyss?" *Journal of Inter-American Studies and World Affairs* 37, no. 3 (Fall 1995).

Henriot, Peter J. "Development Alternatives: Problems, Strategies, Values." In *The Political Economy of Development and Underdevelopment*, edited by Charles K. Wilber. 2d ed. New York: Random House, 1979.

Higgins, B. *Economic Development: Problems, Principles, and Policies*. New York: W. W. Norton, 1968.

Hikino, Takashi, and Alice Amsden. "Staying Behind, Stumbling Back, Sneaking Up, Soaring Ahead: Late Industrialization in Historical Perspective." In *Convergence of Productivity: Cross-National Studies and Historical Evidence*, edited by William Baumol, Richard R. Nelson, and Edward N. Wolff. New York: Oxford University Press, 1994.

Hill, M. Anne, and Elizabeth M. King. "Women's Education in Developing Countries: An Overview." In *Women's Education in Developing Countries: Barriers, Benefits, and Policies*, edited by M. Anne Hill and Elizabeth M. King. Baltimore: Johns Hopkins University Press, 1993.

Hirata, Helena, and John Humphrey. "Workers' Response to Job Loss: Female and Male Industrial Workers in Brazil." *World Development* 19, no. 6 (1991): 671–682.

Hoff, Karla. "Designing Land Policies: An Overview." In *The Economics of Rural Organization*, edited by Karla Hoff, Avishay Braverman, and Joseph Stiglitz. New York: Oxford University Press/World Bank, 1993.

Hoff, Karla, Avishay Braverman, and Joseph Stiglitz, eds. *The Economics of Rural Organization*. New York: Oxford University Press/World Bank, 1993.

Hoff, Karla, Avishay Braverman, and Joseph Stiglitz. "Introduction." In *The Economics of Rural Organization*, edited by Karla Hoff, Avishay Braverman, and Joseph Stiglitz. New York: Oxford University Press/World Bank, 1993.

Holm-Nielsen, Lauritz, Michael Crawford, and Alcyone Saliba. *Institutional and Entrepreneurial Leadership in the Brazilian Science and Technology Sector*. World Bank Discussion Paper no. 325. Washington, D.C.: World Bank, 1996.

Hsiao, William C. "Marketization—The Illusory Magic Pill." *Health Economics* 3 (1994): 351–357.

"Human Development Index." In *Human Development Report, 1997*, edited by United Nations Development Program. New York: Oxford University Press, 1997.

Idelovitch, Emanuel, and Klas Ringskog. *Private Sector Participation in Water Supply and Sanitation in Latin America*. Washington, D.C.: World Bank, 1995.

Iglesias, Enrique V., ed. *The Legacy of Raúl Prebisch*. Washington, D.C.: Inter-American Development Bank, 1994.

Iglesias, Enrique V. "The Search for a New Economic Consensus in Latin America." In *The Legacy of Raúl Prebisch*, edited by Enrique V. Iglesias. Washington, D.C.: Inter-American Development Bank, 1994.

"In the Gap and Sweatshop Labor in El Salvador." *NACLA Report on the Americas* 29, no. 4 (January–February 1996): 37.

Inter-American Development Bank. *Economic and Social Progress in Latin America 1995 Report: Overcoming Volatility*. Washington, D.C.: Inter-American Development Bank, 1995.

Inter-American Development Bank. *Economic and Social Progress in Latin America 1996 Report: Making Social Services Work*. Washington, D.C.: Inter-American Development Bank, 1996.

Inter-American Development Bank. *Facing Up to Inequality in Latin America: Economic and Social Progress in Latin America, 1998–1999 Report*. Washington, D.C.: Johns Hopkins University Press/Inter-American Development Bank, 1998.

Inter-American Development Bank. *Intra-Hemispheric Exports by Integration Group*. 12 July 1997. Available on-line at www.iadb.org/statistics/notaest.htm.

Inter-American Development Bank. "Invisible Farmers." In *IDB Extra: Investing in Women*. Washington, D.C.: Inter-American Development Bank, 1994.

Inter-American Development Bank. *Latin America after a Decade of Reforms: Economic and Social Progress 1997 Report*. Washington, D.C: Johns Hopkins University Press/ Inter-American Development Bank, 1997.

Inter-American Development Bank. *Women in the Americas: Bridging the Gap*. Baltimore: Johns Hopkins University Press, 1995.

International Monetary Fund. *International Financial Statistics, 1997*. Washington, D.C.: International Monetary Fund, 1997.

International Trade Administration, U.S. Department of Commerce. *U.S. Foreign Trade Highlights, 1995*. Washington, D.C.: U.S. Department of Commerce, 1995.

"Involving the Private Sector and Preventing Financial Crises." *IMF Survey* 28, no. 12 (21 June 1999).

"It's Time to Bite the Bullet." *Euromoney*. September 1996.

Jallade, Lucila, Eddy Lee, and Joel Samoff. "International Cooperation." In *Coping with Crisis: Austerity, Adjustment, and Human Resources*, edited by Joel Samoff. New York: UNESCO/ILO, 1994.

Jameson, Kenneth P. "The Financial Sector in Latin American Restructuring." In *Privatization in Latin America*, edited by Werner Baer and Melissa Birch. Westport, Conn.: Praeger, 1994.

Jenkins, Rhys. "Car Manufacture in East Asia and Latin America." *Cambridge Journal of Economics*. October 1995, pp. 625–646.

Jenkins, Rhys. *Transnational Corporations and Industrial Transformation in Latin America*. New York: St. Martin's, 1984.

Jenkins, Rhys. *Transnational Corporations and the Latin American Automobile Industry*. Pittsburgh: University of Pittsburgh Press, 1987.

Jimenez de la Jara, Jorge, and Thomas J. Bossert. "Chile's Health Sector Reform: Lessons from Four Reform Periods." In *Health Sector Reform in Developing Countries: Making Health Development Sustainable*, edited by Peter Berman. Cambridge: Harvard University Press, 1995.

Johnson, Brian. *The Great Fire of Borneo: Report of a Visit to Kalimantan-Timur a Year Later, May 1994*. London: World Wildlife Fund, 1991.

Jonakin, Jon. "The Interaction of Market Failure and Structural Adjustment in Producer Credit and Land Markets: The Case of Nicaragua." *Journal of Economic Issues* 31, no. 2 (June 1997).

Kadt, Emmanuel de. "Thematic Lessons from the Case Studies." In *The Public-Private Mix in Social Services*, edited by Elaine Zuckerman and Emanuel de Kadt. Washington, D.C.: Inter-American Development Bank, 1997.

Kaltenheuser, Skip. "Fitting Microcredit into a Macro Picture." *Christian Science Monitor*. 5 February 1997.

Kapstein, Ethan. "Global Rules for Global Finance." *Current History*. November 1998.

Kate, Adriaan ten, and Robert Bruce Wallace. "Nominal and Effective Protection by Sector." In *Protection and Economic Development in Mexico*, edited by Adriaan ten Kate and Robert Bruce Wallace. Hampshire, U.K.: Gower, 1980.

Katz, Elizabeth G. "Gender and Trade within the Household: Observations from Rural Guatemala." *World Development* 23, no. 2 (1995): 327–342.

Katz, Ian. "Snapping up South America." *Business Week*. 18 January 1999.

Keen, Benjamin. *Latin American Civilization*. 3d ed. Boston: Houghton Mifflin, 1974.

Key, Cristóbal. "Rural Development and Agrarian Issues in Contemporary Latin America."

In *Structural Adjustment and the Agricultural Sector in Latin America and the Carib-bean*, edited by John Weeks. New York: St. Martin's, 1995.

"The Key Points of the FTAA Agenda." *Latin American Weekly Report*, WR-97-20, 1997.

Keynan, Gabriel, Manuel Olin, and Ariel Dinar. "Cofinanced Public Extension in Nicaragua." *World Bank Research Observer* 12, no. 2 (August 1997).

Knight, Alan. "Populism and Neo-Populism in Latin America, Especially Mexico." *Journal of Latin American Studies* 30 (1998): 223–248.

Kraus, Clifford. "Argentina to Hasten End of a Phone Monopoly." *New York Times*. 11 March 1998.

Kraus, Clifford. "When Even an Economic Miracle Isn't Enough." *New York Times*. 12 July 1998.

Krawczyk, Miriam. "Women in the Region: Major Changes." *CEPAL Review* 49 (April 1993).

Kronish, Rich, and Kenneth S. Mericle. "The Development of the Latin American Motor Vehicle Industry, 1900–1980: A Class Analysis." In *The Political Economy of the Latin American Motor Vehicle Industry,* ed. Rich Kronish and Kenneth S. Mericle. Cambridge: MIT Press, 1984.

Krugman, Paul R., and Maurice Obstfeld. *International Economics: Theory and Policy.* 3d ed. New York: HarperCollins, 1994.

Kuttner, Robert. "What Sank Asia? Money Sloshing Around the World." *Business Week.* 27 July 1998.

Kuznets, Simon. "Modern Economic Growth: Findings and Reflections." *American Economic Review* 63, no. 3 (June 1973).

Kwast, Barbara. "Reeducation of Maternal and Peri-natal Mortality in Rural and Peri-urban Settings: What Works?" *European Journal of Obstetrics and Gynecology and Reproductive Biology* 609 (1996).

Lamb, James J. "The Third World and the Development Debate." *IDOC-North America.* January–February 1973.

"Land for the Landless." *The Economist.* 13 April 1996.

Larner, Monica, and Ian Katz. "It's Ronaldo's World." *Business Week.* 22 June 1998, p. 204.

"Latin America Struggles to Find Solutions to Megacity Woes." *Agence France Press.* 2 June 1992. Available on the LEXIS-NEXIS database.

Latin America Weekly Report. 26 May 1998.

"Latin America's Car Industry Revving Up." *The Economist.* 27 April 1996.

"Latin America's Export of Manufactured Goods." Special section of *Economic and Social Progress in Latin America 1992 Report.* Washington, D.C.: Inter-American Development Bank, 1992.

Lau, Lawrence J., Dean T. Jamison, Shucheng Liu, and Steven Rivkin. "Education and Economic Growth: Some Cross-Sectional Evidence." In *Education in Brazil*, edited by Nancy Birdsall and Richard H. Sabat. Washington, D.C.: Inter-American Development Bank, 1996.

Lehmann, David, ed. *Agrarian Reform and Agrarian Reformism: Studies of Peru, Chile, China, and India.* London: Faber & Faber, 1974.

Lepziger, Danny, Claudio Frischtak, Homi J. Kharas, and John F. Normand. "Mercosur: Integration and Industrial Policy." *World Economy* 20, no. 5 (1997).

Lewis, Colin M. "Industry in Latin America." In *Dependency and Development*, edited by Fernando Henrique Cardoso and Enzo Faletto, translated by Marjory Mattinglly Urquidi. Berkeley and Los Angeles: University of California Press, 1979.

Lewis, Paul. "Latin Americans Say Russian Default Is Hurting Their Economies." *New York Times*. 6 October 1998, p. A13. On-line edition.

Lizano, Eduardo, and José M. Salazar-Xirinach. "Central American Common Market and Hemispheric Free Trade." In *Integrating the Hemisphere, 1997: The Inter-American Dialogue*, edited by Ana Julia Jatar and Sidney Weintraub. Santafé de Bogotá, Colombia: Tercer Mundo, 1997.

Londoño, Juan Luis, and Miguel Székely. "Distributional Surprises after a Decade of Reforms: Latin America in the Nineties." Paper prepared for the annual meetings of the Inter-American Development Bank, Barcelona, March 1997.

Londoño, Juan Luis, and Miguel Székely. *Persistent Poverty and Excess Inequality: Latin America, 1970–1995*. Office of the Chief Economist, Inter-American Development Bank Working Paper no. 357. Washington, D.C.: Inter-American Development Bank, 1997.

López, Ramón. *Policy Instruments and Financing Mechanisms for the Sustainable Use of Forests in Latin America*. No. ENV-16. Washington, D.C.: Inter-American Development Bank, 1996.

Lora, Eduardo, and Felipe Barrera. "A Decade of Structural Reform in Latin America: Growth, Productivity, and Investment Are Not What They Used to Be." Document for discussion in the Inter-American Development Bank Barcelona seminar, "Latin America after a Decade of Reform: What Next?" 16 March 1997.

Lorey, David E. "Education and the Challenges of Mexican Development." *Challenge* 38, no. 2 (March–April 1995): 51–55.

Lustig, Nora. *Coping with Austerity*. Washington, D.C.: Brookings Institution, 1995.

Lustig, Nora, and Ruthanne Deutsch. *The Inter-American Development Bank and Poverty Reduction: An Overview*. Washington, D.C.: Inter-American Development Bank, 1998. Available on-line at www.iadb.org.

MacCulloch, Christina. "Will She Make It? Guatemala Finds New Ways to Keep Girls in School." *IDB América*. April 1998, p. 4–7.

Macisaac, Donna. "Peru." In *Indigenous People and Poverty in Latin America*, edited by George Psacharopoulos and Harry Anthony Patrinos. Washington, D.C.: World Bank, 1994.

Maddison, Angus. "Economic and Social Conditions in Latin America, 1913–1950." In *Long Term Trends in Latin American Economic Development*, edited by Miguel Urrutia. Washington, D.C.: Inter-American Development Bank/Johns Hopkins University Press, 1991.

Maddison, Angus. *Monitoring the World Economy, 1820–1992*. Washington, D.C.: OECD Publications and Information Center, 1995.

Mahon, James E., Jr. "Was Latin America Too Rich to Prosper? Structural and Political Obstacles to Export-Led Industrial Growth." *Journal of Development Studies* 28, no. 2 (1992).

"Making Money from Microcredit." *IDB América*. June 1998.

Mandel-Campbell, Andrea. "I Bet the Ranch, and I Won—Absolutely." *Business Week*. 22 June 1998, p. 64–65.

Mangurian, David. "Against the Odds: How a Seemingly Hopeless Energy Project Became a Model for Investors." *IDB América*. March 1998. Available on-line at www.iadb.org.

Margolis, Mac. "Hat in Hand." *Newsweek*. 12 October 1998.

Martinussen, John. *Society, State, and Market: A Guide to Competing Theories of Development*. London: Zed, 1997.

Mayer-Serra, Carlos Elizondo. "Tax Reform under the Salinas Administration." In *The*

Changing Structure of Mexico, edited by Laura Randall. Armonk, N.Y.: M. E. Sharpe, 1996.

Mayorga, Román. *Closing the Gap*. Inter-American Development Bank Working Paper SOC97–101. Washington, D.C.: Inter-American Development Bank, 1997.

McLarty, Thomas F. "Hemispheric Free Trade Is Still a National Priority." *The Wall Street Journal*. 26 May 1995.

McKinsey Global Institute. *Productivity: The Key to an Accelerated Development Path for Brazil 1998*. São Paulo: McKinsey and Company, 1998.

Meerman, Jacob. *Reforming Agriculture: The World Bank Goes to Market*. Washington, D.C.: World Bank, 1997.

Meier, Gerald M. *Leading Issues in Economic Development*. 6th ed. Oxford: Oxford University Press, 1995.

Meier, Gerald M., and Dudley Seers. *Pioneers in Development*. Oxford: Oxford University Press, 1984.

Meller, Patricio. "IMF and World Bank Roles in the Latin America Foreign Debt Problem." In *The Latin American Development Debate: Neostructuralism, Neomonetarism and Adjustment Processes*, edited by Patricio Meller. Boulder, Colo.: Westview, 1991.

Mendez, Chico. *Fight for the Forest*. London: Latin American Bureau, 1990.

"Mercosur Survey." *The Economist*. 12 October 1996.

"Mexico City: A Topographical Error." *Environment* 36, no. 2 (1994): 25–26.

"Mexico Domestic Sales Rise Sharply." *Reuters Financial Service*. 4 June 1997. Available on-line on the LEXIS-NEXIS database.

Mezzera, Jaime. "Abundancia como efecto de la escasez. Oferta y demanda en el mercado laboral urbano." *Nueva Sociedad* 90 (1997): 106–117.

Mishkin, Frederick. "Understanding Financial Crises: A Developing Country Perspective." In *The Annual World Bank Conference Report on Development Economics, 1996*. Washington, D.C.: World Bank, 1997.

Moffett, Matt. "Deep in the Amazon, an Industrial Enclave Fights for Its Survival." *The Wall Street Journal*. 9 July 1998.

Molano, Walter. *Financial Reverberations: The Latin American Banking System during the Mid-1990s*. Working paper, SBC Warburg, April 1997.

Moore, Mick. "Toward a Useful Consensus." In *The Bank, the State, and Development: Dissecting the World Development Report, 1997. IDS Bulletin* 29, no. 2, special issue (1998).

Moore, Molly. "Mayan Girls Make Fifth Grade History." *The Washington Post*. 20 June 1996.

Morales, Juan Antonio, and Jeffrey Sachs. "Bolivia's Economic Crisis." In *Developing Country Debt and the World Economy*, edited by Jeffrey Sachs. Chicago: University of Chicago Press, 1989.

Morandé, Felipe G. "Savings in Chile: What Went Right?" *Journal of Development Economics* 57, no. 1 (1998).

Mosbacher, Robert, chairman, Council of the Americas. "Trade Expansion within the Americas: A U.S. Business Perspective." Remarks at the Chile–United States Issues Round Table, Crown Plaza Hotel, Santiago, Chile, 17 April 1998. Available at http://207.87.5.23/sr.html; accessed 12 July 1999.

Moseley, Paul, and David Hulme. "Microenterprise Finance: Is There a Conflict between Growth and Poverty Alleviation?" *World Development* 26, no. 5 (1988): 783–790.

Moser, Caroline. "Gender Planning in the Third World: Meeting Practical and Strategic Gender Needs." *World Development* 17, no. 11 (1989): 1799–1825.

Munainghe, Mohran, and Wilfrido Cruz. *Economy Wide Policies and the Environment: Lessons from Experience.* Washington, D.C.: World Bank, 1995.

Myers, William, ed. *Protecting Working Children.* London: Zed, 1991.

"NAFTA: Where's That Giant Sucking Sound?" *Business Week.* 7 July 1997, p. 45.

Nasar, Sylvia. "The Cure That Can Sometimes Kill the Patient." *New York Times.* 19 July 1998.

Nazmi, Nader. *Economic Policy and Stabilization in Latin America.* New York: M. E. Sharpe, 1996.

"The New Entrepreneurs: Preparing the Ground for Small Business." *IDB América.* 1997. Available on-line at the Inter-American Development Bank homepage at www.iadb.org.

"New Farms for Old." *The Economist.* 10 January 1998.

"A New Risk of Default." *Euromoney.* September 1996.

Newfarmer, Richard S. *Profits, Progress, and Poverty.* South Bend, Ind.: University of Notre Dame Press, 1984.

North, Douglas C. "The New Institutional Economics and Third World Development." In *The New Institutional Economics and Third World Development,* edited by John Harriss, Janet Hunter, and Colin M. Lewis. London: Routledge, 1995.

Ocampo, José Antonio. "Towards a Global Solution." *ECLAC Notes* no. 1 (November 1998).

"Of Cranes, Aid, and Unintended Consequences." *The Economist.* 5 October 1996.

O'Grady, Mary Anastasia. "A Brazilian State Shows How to Reform Schools." *The Wall Street Journal.* 16 August 1997.

Olpadwala, Porus, and William Goldsmith. "The Sustainability of Privilege: Reflection on the Environment, The Third World City and Poverty." *World Development* 20, no. 4 (1992).

Ortega, Emiliano. "Evolution of the Rural Dimension in Latin America and the Caribbean." *CEPAL Review* 47 (August 1992).

Overholt, Catherine, and Margaret Saunders. *Policy Choices and Practical Problems in Health Economics: Cases from Latin America and the Caribbean.* Economic Development Institute Resources Series. Washington, D.C.: World Bank, 1996.

Ozório de Almeida, Anna Luíza, and João S. Campari. *Sustainable Settlement in the Brazilian Amazon.* Oxford: Oxford University Press, 1995.

Paarlberg, Robert L. "The Politics of Agricultural Resource Abuse." *Environment* 36, no. 8 (October 1994).

Palma, Gabriel. "Dependency: A Formal Theory of Underdevelopment or a Methodology for the Analysis of Concrete Situations of Underdevelopment?" *World Development* 6, no. 7–8 (July–August 1979): 881–924.

Palmer, Ingrid. "Public Finance from a Gender Perspective." *World Development* 23, no. 11 (1995).

Pan American Health Organization. *Implementation of the Global Strategy Health for All by the Year 2000,* vol. 3. Washington, D.C.: Pan American Health Organization, 1993.

Pan American Health Organization. "Mexico." In *Health in the Americas,* vol. 2. Washington, D.C.: Pan American Health Organization, 1998.

Pan American Health Organization. *PAHO Resolution V: Health of Indigenous Peoples.* Series HSS/SILOS, 34. Washington, D.C.: Pan American Health Organization, 1993. Available on-line at www.paho.org.

Pan American Health Organization. *Strategic and Programmatic Orientations, 1995–1998.* Presented at the Inter-American Meeting, Washington, D.C., 25–27 April 1995. Available on-line at www.paho.org.

Panagariya, Arvind. "The Free Trade Area of the Americas: Good for Latin America?" *World Economy* 19, no. 5 (1996).

Pánuco-Laguette, Humberto, and Miguel Székely. "Income Distribution and Poverty in Mexico." In *The New Economic Model in Latin America and Its Impact on Income Distribution and Poverty*, edited by Victor Bulmer-Thomas. New York: St. Martin's, 1996.

Parry, Taryn Rounds. "Achieving Balance in Decentralization: A Case Study of Education Decentralization in Chile." *World Development* 25, no. 2 (1997).

Partnership for Educational Revitalization in the Americas. *The Future at Stake: Report of the Task Force on Education, Equity and Economic Competitiveness in Latin America and the Caribbean*. Santiago, Chile: PREAL, in conjunction with the Inter-American Dialogue and CINDE, 1998. Available on-line at www.preal.cl/index-i.htm.

Patterson, Allen. "Debt for Nature Swaps and the Need for Alternatives." *Environment* 21 (December 1990): 5–32.

Peach, James T., and Richard Adkisson. "Enabling Myths and Mexico's Economic Crises (1976–1996)." *Journal of Economic Issues* 31, no. 2 (June 1997).

Perry, Guillermo, and Ana Maria Herrera. *Public Finance, Stabilization, and Structural Reform in Latin America*. Washington, D.C.: Johns Hopkins University Press/Inter-American Development Bank, 1994.

Phillip, Michael. "South American Trade Pact Is under Fire." *The Wall Street Journal*. 23 October 1996.

Picciotto, Robert. *Putting Institutional Economics to Work: From Participation to Governance*. World Bank Discussion Papers, no. 304. Washington, D.C.: World Bank, 1995.

Picciotto, Robert, and Jock Anderson. "Reconsidering Agricultural Extension." *World Bank Research Observer* 12, no. 2 (August 1997).

Poverty Reduction and the World Bank: Progress in Fiscal 1996 and 1997. Washington, D.C.: World Bank, 1998. Available on-line at www.worldbank.org.

Pirages, Dennis. "Sustainability as an Evolving Process." *Futures* 26, no. 2 (1994): 197–205.

Pleskovic, Boris, and Joseph E. Stiglitz, eds. *Annual World Bank Confrence on Development Economics, 1997*. Washington, D.C.: World Bank, 1998.

Prawda, Juan. "Educational Decentralization in Latin America: Lessons Learned." *International Journal of Educational Development* 13, no. 3 (1993): 253–264.

"Privatization." *Euromoney*. September 1996.

Psacharopoulos, George, et al. *Poverty and Income Distribution in Latin America: The Story of the 1980s*. World Bank Technical Paper no. 351. Washington, D.C.: World Bank, 1997.

Psacharopoulos, G., and H. Patrinos, eds. *Indigenous People and Poverty in Latin America*. Washington, D.C.: World Bank, 1994.

Psacharopoulos, George, Carlos Rojas, and Eduardo Velez. "Achieving Evaluation of Colombia's Escuela Nueva: Is Multigrade the Answer?" *Comparative Education Review* 37, no. 3 (1993).

Puryear, Jeffrey M. "Education in Latin America: Problems and Challenges." Presented to the Council of Foreign Relations, 24 February 1996, for the Latin American Program Study Group, "Educational Reform in Latin America," New York. Available on-line at www.preal.cl/index-i.htm.

Rajapatirana, Sarath. *Trade Policies in Latin America and the Caribbean: Priorities, Progress, and Prospects*. San Francisco: International Center for Economic Growth, 1997.

Ramos, Joseph. "Poverty and Inequality in Latin America: A Neostructuralist Perspective." *Journal of Inter-American Studies and World Affairs* 38, no. 2–3 (Summer–Fall 1996).

Randall, Laura, ed. *Changing Structure of Mexico: Political, Social and Economic Prospects*. Armonk, N.Y.: M. E. Sharpe, 1996.

Redclift, Michael. "The Environment and Structural Adjustment: Lessons for Policy Intervention." In *Structural Adjustment and the Agricultural Sector in Latin America and the Caribbean*, edited by John Weeks. New York: St. Martin's, 1995.

The Reform of the Mexican Health Care System. OECD Economic Surveys: Mexico. Paris: Organization for Economic Cooperation and Development, 1998.

Reimers, Fernando. "Educación para todos en América Latina en el Siglo XXIL. Los defafíos de la establización, el ajuste y los mandatos de Jomtien." Paper presented at UNESCO workshop, Peru, December 1990.

Reimers, Fernando. "The Impact of Economic Stabilization and Adjustment on Education in Latin America." *Comparative Education* 35, no. 2 (May 1991).

Richards, Michael. "Alternative Approaches and Problems in Protected Area Management and Forest Conservation in Honduras." In *Sustainable Agriculture in Central America*, edited by Jan P. de Groot and Ruerd Ruben. New York: St. Martin's, 1997.

Rodrick, Dani. *King Kong Meets Godzilla: The World Bank and the East Asian Miracle*. CEPR Discussion Paper no. 944. London: Centre for Economic Policy Research, 1994.

Rodrick, Dani. "Why Do More Open Economies Have Bigger Governments?" *Journal of Political Economy* 16, no. 5 (1998).

Rodriguez-Garcia, Rosalia, and Ann Goldman, eds. *The Health-Development Link*. Washington, D.C.: Pan American Health Organization, 1994.

Rodríguez-Mendoz, Miguel. "The Andean Group's Integration Strategy." In *Integrating the Hemisphere, 1997: The Inter-American Dialogue*, edited by Ana Julia Jatar and Sidney Weintraub. Santafé de Bogotá, Colombia: Tercer Mundo, 1997.

Rohter, Larry. "Crisis Whipsaws Brazilian Workers." *New York Times*. 16 January 1999. On-line edition.

Rohter, Larry. "Ecuadoran President Imposes Sweeping Austerity Measures." *New York Times*. 21 March 1999. Available on-line at latinolink.com.

Rojas-Suarez, Liliana, and Steven R. Weisbrod. "Building Stability in Latin American Financial Markets." In *Securing Stability and Growth in Latin America*, edited by Ricardo Hausmann and Helmut Reisen. Paris: OECD Publications, 1996.

Roldán, Jorge. Interview. *IDB Extra*. 14 June 1998. On-line edition.

Rosenthal, Gert. "Development Thinking and Policies: The Way Ahead." *CEPAL Review* 60 (December 1996).

Rosenthal, Gert. "On Poverty and Inequality in Latin America." *Journal of Inter-American Studies and World Affairs* 38, no. 2–3 (Summer–Fall 1996).

Russell, Clifford S., and Philip T. Powell. *Choosing Environmental Policy Tools: Theoretical Cautions and Practical Considerations*. No. ENV-102. Washington, D.C.: Inter-American Development Bank, June 1996.

Ryan, John. "The Shrinking Forest." *NACLA Report on the Americas* 25, no. 2 (September 1991).

Sachs, Wolfgang, ed. *The Development Dictionary: A Guide to Knowledge as Power*. London: Zed, 1992.

Sachs, Jeffrey, and Alvaro Zini. "Brazilian Inflation and the Plano Real." *World Economy* 19, no. 1 (January 1996).

Sáinz, Pérez, and Menjívar Larein. *Gender in the Urban Informal Sector*.

Sánchez, M., R. Corona, L. F. Herrera, and O. Ochoa. "A Comparison of Privatization Experiences: Chile, Mexico, Colombia, and Argentina." In *Privatization in Latin America*, edited by M. Sánchez and R. Corona. Baltimore: Johns Hopkins University Press, 1994.

Sawyer, Suzana. "Indigenous Initiatives and Petroleum Politics in the Ecuadorian Amazon." *Cultural Survival*. Spring 1996.

Schemo, Diana Jean. "The ABC's of Doing Business in Brazil." *New York Times*. 16 July 1998. On-line edition.

Schemo, Diana Jean. "Brazil Farmers Feel Squeezed by Tobacco Companies." *New York Times*. 6 April 1998. On-line edition.

Schemo, Diana Jean. "Brazilians Fret as Economic Threat Moves Closer." *New York Times*. 20 September 1998. On-line edition.

Schemo, Diana Jean. "Ecuadorians Want Texaco to Clear Toxic Residue." *New York Times*. 31 January 1998. Available on-line at LatinoLink, www.latinolink.com.

Schemo, Diana Jean. "A Latin Bloc Asks U.S. and Europe to Ease Trade Barriers." *New York Times*. 23 February 1999. On-line edition.

Schiesel, Seth. "Brazil Sells Most of State Phone Utility." *New York Times*. 30 July 1998, p. D1.

Schiff, Maurice, and Alberto Valdes. "The Plundering of Agriculture in Developing Countries." 1994 draft paper, available at the World Bank homepage at www.worldbank.org/html/extpb/PlunderingAgri.html.

Schmitz, Hubert, and José Cassiolato. *Hi-tech for Industrial Development: Lessons from the Brazilian Experience in Electronics and Automation*. London: Routledge, 1992.

Schott, Jeffrey J. "NAFTA: An Interim Report." In *Trade: Towards Open Regionalism*, proceedings of the 1997 World Bank Conference on Development in Latin America and the Caribbean. Washington, D.C.: World Bank, 1998.

Sedelnik, Lisa. "CANTV: Inside the IPO." *Latin Finance* 83 (1997): 43–46.

Seers, Dudley. "What Are We Trying to Measure?" *Journal of Development Studies*. April 1972.

Sen, Amartya. "The Concept of Development." In *Handbook of Development Economics*, vol. 1. Netherlands: North-Holland, 1988.

Shah, Fared, David Zilberman, and Ujjayant Chakravorty. "Water Rights Doctrines and Technology Adoption." In *The Economics of Rural Organization*, edited by Karla Hoff, Avishay Braverman, and Joseph Stiglitz. New York: Oxford University Press/World Bank, 1993.

Shapiro, Helen. *Engines of Growth: The State and Transnational Auto Companies in Brazil*. Cambridge: Cambridge University Press, 1994.

Shapiro, Helen. *Mexico: Escaping the Debt Crisis*. Harvard Business School case. Boston: Harvard Business School, 1991.

Sheahan, John, and Enrique Iglesias. "Kinds and Causes of Inequality in Latin America." In *Beyond Trade-Offs: Market Reform and Equitable Growth in Latin America*, edited by Nancy Birdsall, Carol Graham, and Richard Sabot. Washington, D.C.: Brookings Institution Press/Inter-American Development Bank, 1998.

Shoumatoff, Alex. *The World Is Burning*. Boston: Little, Brown, 1990.

Simons, Marlise. "A Talk with Gabriel Garcia Marquez." *New York Times*. 5 December 1982, sec. 7, p. 7. Available at www.nytimes.com/books/97/06/15/reviews/marquez-talk.html and in the LEXIS-NEXIS database.

Sims, Calvin. "Peruvians Climb onto the Web." *New York Times*. 1996. 27 May 1996. Available on-line at latinolink.com/life/0528/per.html.

"Skills Gap May Be Biggest Trade Barrier." *Journal of Commerce*. April 20, 1998. On-line edition. Available at www.alca-cupula.org.

"Slicing the Cake: What Is the Relationship between Inequality and Economic Growth?" *The Economist*. 19 October 1996.

"Some Mutual Funds Go Back Full Throttle to Emerging Markets." *The Wall Street Journal.* 12 November 1996.

Sprout, Ronald V. A. "The Ideas of Prebisch." *CEPAL Review* 46 (April 1992).

"The Sputtering Spark from South America's Car Industry." *The Economist.* 15 April 1995.

Stahl, Karin. "Anti-poverty Programs: Making Structural Adjustment More Palatable." *NACLA Report on the Americas* 29, no. 6 (May–June 1995).

Steele, Diane. "Guatemala." In *Indigenous People and Poverty in Latin America*, edited by George Psacharopoulos and Harry Anthony Patrinos. Washington, D.C.: World Bank, 1994.

Stein, Ernesto, Ernesto Talvi, and Alejandro Grisanti. *Institutional Arrangements and Fiscal Performance: The Latin American Experience.* National Bureau of Economic Research Working Paper no. 6358. Cambridge, Mass.: National Bureau of Economic Research, 1998.

Stewart, Frances. *Adjustment and Poverty: Options and Choices.* London: Routledge, 1995.

Stiglitz, Joseph E. "The Role of Government in Economic Development." In *Annual World Bank Conference on Development Economics 1996.* Washington, D.C.: World Bank, 1997.

Streeten, Paul. "A Basic Needs Approach to Economic Development." In *Directions in Economic Development*, edited by Kenneth P. Jameson and Charles K. Wilber. Notre Dame, Ind.: University of Notre Dame Press, 1979.

Streeten, Paul. "From Growth to Basic Needs." In *Latin America's Economic Development: Institutionalist and Structuralist Perspectives*, edited by James L. Dietz and James H. Street. Boulder, Colo.: Lynne Rienner, 1987.

Sturzenegger, Federico A. "Description of a Populist Experience: Argentina, 1973–1976." In *The Macroeconomics of Populism in Latin America*, edited by Rudiger Dornbusch and Sebastian Edwards. Chicago: University of Chicago Press, 1991.

"The Summiteers Go to School." *The Economist.* 25 April 1998, p. 37–38.

Sunkel, Osvaldo. *Development from Within: Toward a Neostructuralist Approach for Latin America.* Boulder, Colo.: Lynne Rienner, 1993.

Swafford, David. "A Healthy Trend: Health Care Reform in Latin America." *Latin Finance* 83 (December 1996).

Sylos Labini, Paolo. "The Classical Roots of Development Theory." In *Economic Development: Handbook of Comparative Economic Policies*, edited by Enzo Grilli and Dominick Salvatore. Westport, Conn.: Greenwood, 1994.

Tanzi, Vito. "Fiscal Federalism and Decentralization: A Review of Some Efficiency and Macroeconomic Aspects." Presented at the World Bank Conference on Development Economics, World Bank, May 1995. (As summarized by the *Economist*, 3 June 1995)

Tardanico, Richard, and Rafael Menjívar Larín. "Restructuring, Employment, and Social Inequality: Comparative Urban Latin American Patterns." In *Global Restructuring, Employment, and Social Inequality in Urban Latin America*, edited by Richard Tardanico and Rafael Menjívar Larín. Miami: University of Miami North-South Center Press, 1997.

Taylor, Lance, and Ute Piper. *Reconciling Economic Reform and Sustainable Human Development: Social Consequences of Neo-Liberalism.* United Nations Development Programme Discussion Paper Series. New York: United Nations Development Programme, 1996.

Taylor, Alan M. *Argentina and the World Capital Market: Saving, Investment and International Capital Mobility in the Twentieth Century.* National Bureau of Economic Research Working Paper no. 6302. Cambridge, Mass.: National Bureau of Economic Research, 1997.

Taylor, Alan M. "On the Costs of Inward-Looking Development: Price Distortions, Growth, and Divergence in Latin America." *Journal of Economic History* 58, no. 1 (March 1998).

Taylor, Jerry. "The Challenge of Sustainable Development." *Regulation* 17, no. 1 (1994): 35–50.

"A Teacher's Lot." *The IDB*. May 1996.

"Telebras Sold for US$19.1b." *Latin American Weekly Report*. 4 August 1998.

Templeman, John. "Is Europe Elbowing the U.S. Out of South America?" *Business Week*. 4 August 1997, p. 56.

Tendler, Judith. *Good Government in the Tropics*. Baltimore: Johns Hopkins University Press, 1997.

"Tequila Freeways." *The Economist*. 16 December 1996.

Thatcher, Peter S. "The Role of the United Nations." In *The International Politics of the Environment: Actors, Interests, and Institutions*, edited by Andrew Hurrell and Benedict Kingsbury. Oxford, U.K.: Clarendon, 1992.

Thorp, Rosemary. "Import Substitution: A Good Idea in Principle." In *Latin America and the World Economy: Dependency and Beyond*, edited by Richard J. Salvucci. Lexington, Mass.: Heath, 1996.

Thorp, Rosemary. *Progress, Poverty, and Exclusion: An Economic History of Latin America in the 20th Century*. Baltimore: Johns Hopkins University Press/Inter-American Development Bank, 1998.

Thorpe, Andy. "Sustainable Agriculture in Latin America." In *Sustainable Agriculture in Central America*, edited by Jan P. de Groot and Ruerd Ruben. New York: St. Martin's, 1997.

Thrupp, Lori Ann. *Bittersweet Harvests for Global Supermarkets: Challenges in Latin America's Agricultural Export Boom*. Washington, D.C.: World Resources Institute, 1995.

"Til Debt Do Us Part." *The Economist*. 28 February 1987.

Todaro, Michael P. *Economic Development*. 5th ed. White Plains, N.Y.: Longman, 1994.

Tokman, Viktor. *Beyond Regulation: The Informal Economy in Latin America*. Boulder, Colo.: Lynne Rienner, 1992.

Tokman, Victor E. "Jobs and Solidarity: Challenges for Post-Adjustment in Latin America." In *Economic and Social Development in the XXI Century*, proceedings of the 1997 Inter-American Bank development conference, ed. Louis Emmerij. Available on-line at www.iadb.org/exr/pub/xxi/sec4.htm, 1998.

Tokman, Victor. "Policies for a Heterogeneous Informal Sector." *World Development* 17, no. 7 (1989): 1067–1076.

Toman, Michael A. "Economics and 'Sustainability': Balancing the Trade-offs and Imperatives." *Land Economics* 70, no. 4 (November 1994): 399–413.

Torres, Carlos A. *Education and Social Change in Latin America*. Albert Park, Australia: James Nicolas, 1997.

Torres, Carlos Alberto, and Adriana Puiggrós. "The State and Public Education in Latin America." *Comparative Education Review* 39, no. 1 (1995).

Trebat, Thomas. *Brazil's State-Owned Enterprises: A Case Study of the State as Entrepreneur*. New York: Cambridge University Press, 1983.

Tullio, G., and M. Ronci. "Brazilian Inflation from 1980 to 1993: Causes, Consequences and Dynamics." *Journal of Latin American Studies* 28 (October 1996): 635–666.

Tussie, Diana. *The Inter-American Development Bank*. Vol. 4 of *The Multilateral Development Banks*. Ottawa: North-South Institute, 1995.

Twomey, Michael J. *Multinational Corporations and the North American Free Trade Agreement*. Westport, Conn.: Praeger, 1993.

"Unfinished Business." *The Economist*. 2 March 1996.

United Nations. *World Investment Report 1994*. New York: United Nations, 1994.

United Nations Development Program. *Human Development Report, 1997*. New York: Oxford University Press, 1997.

U.S. Department of State. *1996 Country Reports on Economic Policy and Trade Practices*. January 1997. Available on-line at www.state.gov/www/issues/trade_reports/latin_america99/costarica96.html and www.state.gov/www/issues/economic/trade_reports/latin_america96/panama96.html.

Valcarel, Juan Manuel. "Calling Someone in Argentina: Dial M for Monopoly." *The Wall Street Journal*. 16 August 1996.

Van der Hoeven, Rolph, and Gyorgy Sziraczi. *Lesson from Privatization*. Geneva: International Labour Office, 1997.

Vandermeer, John, and Ivette Perfecto. *Breakfast of Biodiversity: The Truth about Rain Forest Destruction*. Oakland, Calif.: Institute for Food and Development Policy, 1995.

Vera-Vassallo, Alejandro C. "Foreign Investment and Competitive Development in Latin America and the Caribbean." *CEPAL Review* 60 (December 1996).

Verhovek, Sam Howe. "Pollution Problems Fester South of the Border." *New York Times*. 4 July 1998. On-line edition.

Vetter, Stephen G. "The Business of Grassroots Development." *Grassroots Development* 19, no. 2 (1995): 2–12.

Vogel, Thomas T., Jr. "Venezuela Privatization Proves Paltry." *The Wall Street Journal*. 17 July 1996.

Wade, Robert. "The Asian Crisis and the Global Economy: Causes, Consequences and Cure." *Current History*. November 1998.

Wallace, Robert Bruce. "Policies of Protection in Mexico." In *Protection and Economic Development in Mexico*, edited by Adriaan ten Kate and Robert Bruce Wallace. Hampshire, U.K.: Gower, 1980.

Warburg Dillon Read. "The Impact of the Asian Crisis on Latin America." Fax newsletter. 14 July 1998, p. 2.

Warburg Dillon Read. *The Latin American Adviser*. Fax newsletter. February 1998.

Warburg Dillon Read. *The Latin American Adviser*. Fax newsletter. 9 July 1998.

Warts, Tom. "Protection and Private Foreign Investment." In *Protection and Economic Development in Mexico*, edited by Adriaan ten Kate and Robert Bruce Wallace. Hampshire, U.K.: Gower, 1980.

"Water Works in Buenos Aires." *The Economist*. 24 February 1996.

Weeks, John. "Macroeconomic Adjustment." As noted in *Economic and Social Progress in Latin America 1992 Report*, special section, "Latin America's Export of Manufactured Goods." Washington, D.C.: Inter-American Development Bank, 1992.

Weeks, John. "The Manufacturing Sector in Latin America and the New Economic Model." In *The New Economic Model in Latin America and Its Impact on Income Distribution and Poverty*, edited by Victor Bulmer-Thomas. New York: St. Martin's, 1996.

Weersma-Haworth, Teresa S. "Export Processing Free Zones as Export Strategy." In *Latin America's New Insertion in the World Economy*, edited by Ruud Buitelaar and Pitou Van Dijck. New York: St. Martin's, 1996.

Weinberg, Bill. *War on the Land: Ecology and Politics in Central America*. Atlantic Highlands, N.J.: Zed, 1991.

Weintraub, Sidney. "In the Debate about NAFTA, Just the Facts, Please." *The Wall Street Journal*. 20 June 1997. p. A19.

Welch, John. "The New Face of Latin America: Financial Flows, Markets, and Institutions in the 1990s." *Journal of Latin American Studies* 25 (1993): 1–24.

White, Allen T. "Venezuela's Organic Law: Regulating Pollution in an Industrializing Country." *Environment* 33, no. 7 (September 1991).

Wilber, Charles K., *The Political Economy of Development and Underdevelopment*. New York: Random House, 1973.

Wilber, Charles K. and Steven Francis. "The Methodological Basis of Hirschman's Development Economics: Pattern Modeling vs. General Laws." *World Development* 14, no. 2, special issue (February 1986): 181–191.

Winters, L. Allan. "Assessing Regional Integration." In *Trade: Towards Open Regionalism*, proceedings of the 1997 World Bank Conference on Development in Latin America and the Caribbean. Washington, D.C.: World Bank, 1998.

Wolfensohn, James D. Remarks to the Board of Governors of the World Bank Group, 1 October 1996. Available on-line in the LEXIS-NEXIS database.

Wolff, Laurence. "Educational Assessments in Latin America: Current Progress and Future Challenges." *Partnership for Educational Revitalization in the Americas*. June 1998. On-line publication, available at www.preal.cl/index-i.htm.

Wolff, Laurence, Ernesto Schiefelbeing, and Jorge Valenzuela. *Improving the Quality of Primary Education in Latin America and the Caribbean: Toward the 21st Century*. Washington, D.C.: World Bank, 1994.

Wood, Bill, and Harry Anthony Patrinos. "Urban Bolivia." In *Indigenous People and Poverty in Latin America*, edited by George Psacharopoulus and Harry Anthony Patrinos. Washington, D.C.: World Bank, 1994.

Woodruff, David, Ian Katz, and Keith Naughton. "VW's Factory of the Future." *Business Week*. 7 October 1996.

World Bank. *Beyond the Washington Consensus: Institutions Matter*. Regional Brief. Washington, D.C.: World Bank, 1998. Available on-line at www.worldbank.org.

World Bank. *Economic Growth and Returns to Work*. Washington, D.C.: World Bank, 1995.

World Bank. *Energy Efficiency and Conservation in the Developing World: The World Bank's Role*. Washington, D.C.: World Bank, 1993.

World Bank. *Environment and Development in Latin America and the Caribbean: The Role of the World Bank*. Washington, D.C.: World Bank.

World Bank. *Global Development Finance*. Washington, D.C.: World Bank, 1997.

World Bank. *Global Development Finance 1998*. Washington, D.C.: World Bank, 1998.

World Bank. *Global Development Finance 1999*. Washington, D.C.: World Bank, 1999.

World Bank. *Labor and Economic Reforms in Latin America and the Caribbean: Regional Perspectives on World Development Report*. Washington, D.C.: World Bank, 1995.

World Bank. *Meeting the Infrastructure Challenge in Latin America and the Caribbean*. Washington, D.C.: World Bank, 1995.

World Bank. *Other Financial Mechanisms: Debt-for-Nature Swaps and Social Funds*. Available on-line at www-esd.worldbank.org/html/esd/env/publicat/edp/edp1116.htm.

World Bank. *Privatization Principles and Practice*. IFC Lessons of Experience Series. Washington, D.C.: World Bank, 1995.

World Bank. *Rural Development: From Vision to Action*. Environmentally and Socially Sustainable Development Studies and Monographs Series no. 12. Washington, D.C.: World Bank, 1997.

World Bank. *Trade: Towards Open Regionalism*, proceedings of the 1997 World Bank Conference on Development in Latin America and the Caribbean. Washington, D.C.: World Bank, 1998.

World Bank. *World Debt Tables*. Washington, D.C.: World Bank, various years.

World Bank. *World Development Indicators, 1997*. Washington, D.C.: World Bank, 1997.

World Bank. *World Development Report 1988/9*. New York: Oxford University Press/World Bank, 1989.

World Bank. *World Development Report 1992*. New York: Oxford University Press/World Bank, 1992.

World Bank. *World Development Report 1994*. New York: Oxford University Press/World Bank, 1994.

World Bank. *World Development Report 1995*. New York: Oxford University Press/World Bank, 1995.

World Commission on Environment and Development, *Our Common Future*. Oxford: Oxford University Press, 1987.

World Health Organization. *Integration of Health Care Delivery: Report of a WHO Study Group*. WHO Technical Report Series 861. Geneva: World Health Organization, 1996.

World Health Organization. *Report on the Global HIV/AIDS Epidemic, June 1998*. Geneva: UNAIDS, 1998. Available on-line at www.who.int/emc-hiv.

World Resources Institute. *World Resources: A Guide to the Global Environment 1996–7*. New York: Oxford University Press, 1997.

World Resources Institute. *World Resources, 1994–5*. New York: Oxford University Press, 1995.

Wrobel, Paulo. "A Free Trade Area of the Americas in 2005?" *International Affairs* 74, no. 3 (1998).

Yeager, Timothy. "Encomienda or Slavery? The Spanish Crown's Choice of Labor Organization in Sixteenth Century Spanish America." *Journal of Economic History* 55, no. 4 (December 1995).

Young, Kate. *Planning Development with Women: Making a World of Difference*. New York: St. Martin's, 1993.

Zimbalist, Andrew. "Costa Rica." In *Struggle Against Dependence: Nontraditional Export Growth in Central America and the Caribbean*, edited by Eva Paus. Boulder, Colo.: Westview, 1988.

Zuckerman, Laurence. "In South America Car Makers See One Big Showroom." *New York Times*. 25 April 1997.

Index

Page references followed by *f, t,* b, or n indicate figures, tables, boxes, or endnotes, respectively.
References in *italics* indicate maps and photos.

absorption, 92–94, 461
  market capacity, 177–79
Acción, 340
Acción Ecología, 425t
Acción International, 339b, 453
Adelman, Irma, 18b, 24
adjustment stages, 441–44
adult literacy, 374–75, 375t
advantage, comparative, 212–13
advocacy groups, 451–53
Aetna, 366
AFL-CIO. *See* American Federation of Labor-Congress of Industrial Organizations
Africa, 31–32b, 240f, 240–41, 243t, 254
African slaves, 35
Afro-Latin Americans, 323
Agenda 21, 404, 461
Agenda Venezuela, 163b–164b
agricultural extension programs, *303,* 303–4, 461
agricultural policy, 283–310
  effects on management and conservation of forest resources, 417–19, 418t–419t
  options, 296–97
  summary, 307–8
agricultural production
  dualistic structure of, 285
  index, 289–90, 291t
  patterns of, 284–88
Agricultural Technology and Land Management Project (ATLMP), 304
agriculture, 288–93
  characteristics impeding sustainable growth, 293–301
  exports, 285
  gross domestic product of, 290–92, 292t
  key inputs, 288, 289t
  labor force employment, 288–89, 290t
  loans, 305–6
Aguas Argentinas, 420
Aguaytía project, 186b–188b
AIDS, 353
ALADI. *See* Asociación Latinoamericana de Integración
Alejandro, Carlos Díaz, 214
Alianza para el Bienestar, 343
Allueca, Jorge E., 95b
Alma Alta, 359
alternative production, 286–87

Amazon
  deforestation of, 412–15, 416b–417b
  extractive reserves, 416b
  holdings, 431n38
  oil spills in, 413b
Amazon Cooperation Treaty, 414
American Express, 341
American Express Bank, 425t
American Federation of Labor-Congress of Industrial Organizations (AFL-CIO), 230, 256b–257b
Americas Business Forums, 245t
ANACAFE. *See* National Coffee Association
Andean Community, 239, 461
Andean Group, 238, 238t
Andean Pact, 73
Andean Trade Preference Act, 234t
Anderson, Luis, 256b
Aninat, Eduardo, 200
Antigua and Barbados, 236t
APROCAM, 286
Ardaya Rivera, Samuel, 384b
Argentina
  agriculture, 288–92, 289t–292t
  and Asian economic crisis, 201
  Austral plan, 128–29, 461
  automobile industry, 68, 70, 72
  balance of goods, 242t
  Brady deal, 102, 104t
  Buenos Aires, 406
  capital flight from, 89, 89t
  Chilean investment in, 198
  communications, 7, 9t, 317–20, 321t
  convertibility plan, 129, 133b–134b, 462
  current account balance, 215, 215t
  debt and development patterns, 84–86, 85t
  debt crisis, 105, 116–18
  education spending growth, 331, 332t
  educational performance index, 376, 377t
  energy consumption, 409–10, 410t
  environmental policy, 420
  exchange rate indexes, 87b–88b, 87t
  exchange rate performance, 224, 224t
  exports, 37–38, 39f, 40t, 218t, 218–19, 219t, 221, 223t, 238–39, 242t
  fertilizer consumption, 415, 417t
  fiscal surplus/deficit, 114t, 114–15
  foreign direct investment, 181, 182t
  foreign investment in, 42–44, 43t

foreign shares of industries, 62, 62t
GDP growth per capita, 64, 66t
grade repetition, 378, 378t
growth, 30, 31t, 134
health care spending, 331, 332t, 367t
health care system, 363, 366
health statistics, 355, 356t
housing, 316–17, 317t
imports, 71, 218t, 218–19, 219t, 242t
income distribution, 325–26, 327t
industrial competitiveness, 276–77
inflation, 112, 112t, 129f, 129–32
informal sector, 337, 337t
infrastructure, 237, 271–72
labor and social relations, 35
labor management relations, 256b–257b
labor market reform, 253
labor policy, 253
literacy, 374–75, 375t
living standards, 315–16, 316t
market capitalization, 178–79, 179t
Mercosur membership, 233
money supply growth, 114–15, 115t
petroleum reserves and crude oil production,
    411, 411t
poverty gap, 314, 314t
price stabilization, 128–31
privatization, 157–59, 158t, 160, 162
quality of life, 7, 7t, 9–10
savings, 202
science and technology, 267
secondary market price spreads on debt, 94–
    96, 96t
social expenditures, 344, 345t
social indicators, 324t, 325
state spending, 342
tariffs, 59, 217t, 217–18
technology development, 269–70
technology generation, 266
telephone service, 271–72
urban unemployment, 259t, 259–60
urbanization, 406
U.S. oil imports from, 241, 243t
wages, 97, 102f
waterworks, 272
arrears, 91b
ASEAN, 240–41, 243t
Asia, 31–32b, 202, 240f, 240–41. See also East
    Asia
Asian economic crisis, 199–201, 205–6
Asian tigers, 199
Asociación Latinoamericana de Integración
    (ALADI), 233
ATLMP. See Agricultural Technology and Land
    Management Project
AT&T, 163b
austerity, 72–73
austerity measures, 72–73
Austral plan, 128–29, 461
Australia, 240f, 240–41
automobile industry, 68–74, 231, 401

austerity, 72–73
contracting market, 71–72
domestic boom, 72–73
early, 69–70
market forces, 72–73
promotion of, 69
role in industrialization, 69
state role in, 70–71
Aztec Harvests, 286

backward linkage, 41, 56, 461
backwardness, 52–53
Bahamas, 157–59, 158t, 236t
Bahía de Ferrol (Peru), 426
Baker plan, 97–102
balance of goods, 242t
balance of payments, 226, 226t
Baltodano, Emilio, 225b
Banco de Desarrollo Rural, 302b
Banco Mercantil, 163b
Banco Solidario S.A. (BancoSol), 339b–340b
Bancomext, 264b–265b
Bank for International Settlements (BIS), 197,
    203
Bank of America, 90–91, 92t
Bank of Boston, 99
Bankers Trust, 2, 90–91, 92t
banking
    domestic, 190–92
    exposure to highly indebted countries, 90–91,
        92t
    privatization of, 162–65
banking concept of education, 395
Baran, Paul Alexander, 18b, 52
Barbados
    CARICOM-Venezuela Free Trade Agree-
        ment, 236t
    exports of basic products from, 221, 223t
    labor management relations, 256b–257b
    privatization, 157–59, 158t
Bauer, P., 12b
BEFIEX (Special Fiscal Benefits for Exports)
    (Brazil), 66, 71
Belize
    CARICOM-Colombia Free Trade Agreement,
        236t
    CARICOM-Venezuela Free Trade Agree-
        ment, 236t
    exports of basic products from, 221, 223t
    privatization, 157–59, 158t
Ben & Jerry's, 286
benevolent social guardians, 169n32
Benson, Wilfred, 10
BIAD. See Inter-American Development Bank
biological holocaust, 35
Birdsall, Nancy, 257b
BIS. See Bank for International Settlements
BNDES. See State National Development Bank
Bolívar, Simón, 239
Bolívar Program, 225b

Bolivia
agriculture, 288–92, 289t–292t
Amazon holdings, 431n38
Andean Trade Preference Act, 234t
Brady deal, 102, 104t
Chilean investment in, 198
coca production, 287–88
communications, 7, 9t, 317–20, 321t
current account balance, 215, 215t
debt-for-nature swaps, 98b
diseases of, 355, 357t
education of indigenous in, 383
educational performance index, 376, 377t
educational reform, 382b, 384b
energy consumption, 409–10, 410t
exchange rate performance, 224, 224t
exports, 37, 38t, 218t, 218–19, 219t, 221,
    223t
fertilizer consumption, 415, 417t
fiscal surplus/deficit, 114t, 114–15
forest change in, 414, 415t
GDP per capita, 64, 66t
health care coverage, 364, 364f
health statistics, 355, 356t
housing, 316–17, 317t
human poverty index, 315
imports, 218t, 218–19, 219t
income distribution, 325–26, 327t
inequality in, 331
inflation, 112, 112t
inflation reduction, 132
informal sector growth, 260
labor force, 258, 288–89, 290t
labor market, 252
land reform, 298–99
landless or nearly landless peasant families,
    324, 324t
literacy, 374–75, 375t
living standards, 315–16, 316t
Mercosur membership, 237
monetarist applications, 126–28
money supply growth rates, 114–15, 115t
New Economic Policy, 128, 133b–134b
petroleum reserves and crude oil production,
    411, 411t
poverty, 261, 314, 314t, 320–24, 323t
privatization, 157–59, 158t
quality of life indicators, 7, 7t, 9–10
rural electrification program, 426, 427t–428t
social expenditures, 344, 345t
social indicators, 324t, 325
social investment fund, 333–34
tariffs, 217t, 217–18
taxes, 116
urban unemployment, 259t, 259–60
various indicators, 126–28, 127t
wage differentials, 261–62, 262t
bonds, portfolio, 178
Border Environment Cooperation Commission,
    232
Bradesco, 393

Brady deals, 102, 104t
Brady plan, 1989, 101–2
Brahma, 2, 238–39
Brandão, B. F., 44–45
Brazil
agricultural policy, 297
agriculture, 288–92, 289t–292t
Amazon holdings, 431n38
and Asian economic crisis, 199–201
automobile industry, 68, 70–72
balance of goods, 242t
as Belindia, 321
Brady deal, 102, 104t
Bresser plan, 123–24, 461
capital flight from, 89, 89t
carbon dioxide emissions, 7
Ceará, 362b
Clean Development Mechanism (CDM) ini-
    tiative, 424b
Collor plan, 124, 462
communications, 7, 9t, 10, 317–20, 321t
Cruzado plan, 122–23, 133b–134b, 463
current account balance, 215, 215t
debt and development patterns, 84–86, 85t
debt crisis, 94, 105–6, 438
diseases of, 355, 357t
education, 376, 377t, 390–91, 391t
education spending growth, 331, 332t
educational reform, 389–92
energy consumption, 409–10, 410t
environment, 35, 44–45
environmental policy, 419–20
exchange rate performance, 224, 224t
export processing free zones, 274
exports, 37–38, 38t, 39f, 218t, 218–19, 219t,
    221, 223t, 242t
fertilizer consumption, 415, 417t
fiscal surplus/deficit, 114t, 114–15
as food power, 285
foreign investment, 42–44, 43t, 181, 182t
foreign shares of industries, 62, 62t
forest change in, 414, 415t
GDP growth, 64, 66t
geographic distribution of exports, 38, 40t
grade repetition, 378, 378t
growth, 7, 30, 31t, 134
health, 353, 355–56, 356t
health care spending, 331, 332t, 367t
health care system, 363
high school education, 390, 390t
housing, 316–17, 317t
imports, 64–65, 71, 218t, 218–19, 219t, 242t
income distribution, 325–26, 327t, 329b, 329t
industrial competitiveness, 276–77
inequality in, 329b
inflation, 112, 112t, 122, 123f
inflation reduction, 132
inflation stabilization, 122–26
informal sector, 337, 337t, 337–38
infrastructure, 237, 270–72
labor policy, 253

labor productivity, 263–65, 266*f*
labor relations, 35, 256b–257b
land reform, 301
landless or nearly landless peasant families, 324*t*, 324–25
literacy, 374–75, 375*t*
living standards, 315–16, 316*t*
macroeconomic indicators, 124–25, 125*t*
Manaus, 274–75
market capitalization, 178–79, 179*t*
Mercosur membership, 233
Minas Gerais, 35, 391
money supply growth rates, 114–15, 115*t*
national interest rates, 114–15, 116*t*
National Monetary Council, 117–18
petroleum reserves and crude oil production, 411, 411*t*
poverty, 261, 314, 314*t*, 320–21, 323–24, 331
poverty alleviation, 341
preventive health, 362b
privatization, 157–59, 158*t*, 161–62
quality of life indicators, 7, 7*t*, 9–10
racial composition, 35, 36*t*
real exchange rate indexes, 87b–88b, 87*t*
Real plan, 124–25, 133b–134b, 238, 472
and Russian ruble collapse, 200
savings, 202
science and technology, 267
secondary market price spreads on debt, 94–96, 96*t*
social expenditures, 344, 345*t*
social indicators, 324*t*, 325
social relations, 35
Special Fiscal Benefits for Exports (BE-FIEX), 66, 71
state enterprise share in economy, 58, 59*t*
stock market, 181b
summer plan, 124
tariffs, 59, 217*t*, 217–18
technology development, 269–70
technology generation, 266
telecommunications, 270–71
Third Cycle, 275
trade role, 7
trade with Argentina, 238–39
transnational corporations, 64
urban environmental problems, 408
urban unemployment, 259*t*, 259–60
urbanization, 7, 406
velocity of money, 120
wages, 97, 102*f*, 261–62, 262*t*
Bresser plan, 123–24, 461
British American Tobacco, 184*t*
Brown University, 2
Brundtland Report (World Commission on Environment and Development), 403
Buenos Aires Action Plan, 424b
Bulmer-Thomas, Victor, 462
Bunge & Born, 184*t*
Business Forums of the Americas, 242–44, 245*t*
Fifth, 245*t*
First, 245*t*
Fourth, 245*t*
Second, 245*t*
Third, 245*t*

CAC measures. *See* command and control measures
caciques, 34, 461
CACM. *See* Central American Common Market
cajas de seguro social. See Social Security Institutes
Caldera, Rafael, 163b
callampas, 314
Calmeadow Foundation, 339b
Camarones del Pacífico (CAMPA), 225b
Camdessus, Michel, 203
CAMPA. *See* Camarones del Pacífico
Canada
carbon dioxide emissions, 7
communications indicators, 7, 9*t*, 10
diseases of, 355, 357*t*
exports, imports, and balance of goods, 242*t*
labor management relations, 256b–257b
per capita growth rates, 7, 30, 31*t*
performance of, 31, 32b
petroleum reserves and crude oil production, 411, 411*t*
racial composition, 35, 36*t*
trade role, 7
urbanization, 7
U.S. oil imports from, 241, 243*t*
CANTV (Compañía Anónima Nacional Teléfonos de Venezuela), 163b–164b
CAP (Compañía de Acero), 159
capacity building, 442, *443*
capital
financial, 30–32, 33*t*, 46, 47*t*
foreign, 41–44, *173*
capital controls, 190, 461
capital flight, 86–90, 88b, 190
definition of, 462
foreign investment vs., 89
from selected countries, 89, 89*t*
capital flows
behavior of, 174–76
international, 190–92
to Latin America, 176–79
net private, *177,* 177–78
new, 188–90
new international, 173–209, 191b
regulating inflows, 205
summary, 204–5
capital mobility, 121b, 201–4, 206
capitalization, market, 178–79, 179*t*
Carajas project, 422
Cardoso, Fernando Henrique, 53, 200, 472
CARE, 302b
Cargill, 184*t*
Caribbean, *xix*
aggregate net resource flows and net transfers, 97, 99*f*

debt indicators, 89–90, 90t, 102–5, 105t
exports, 221, 222t–223t
gross national product, 97, 100f
health priorities, 353
human development gaps, 326–27, 328t
index of real effective exchange rate of exports, 224, 224t
landless or nearly landless peasant families, 324, 324t
stock markets, 180b
sustainable development, poverty, and gender, 322b–323b
CARICOM-Colombia Free Trade Agreement, 236t
CARICOM-Venezuela Free Trade Agreement, 236t
Carrefour Supermarkets, 184t
Cartagena Consensus Group, 94
Casa Alianza, 318b–319b
Catholic Church, 44
Catholic Relief Services, 302b
CBA. See cost-benefit analysis
CDM. See Clean Development Mechanism
CEA. See cost-effectiveness analysis
CEC. See Commission for Environmental Cooperation
Celadon Trucking, 231
Center for Strategic and International Studies (CSIS), 452
Central America. See also specific countries
   balance of goods, 242t
   Colombia-Central America Free Trade Agreement, 236t
   environment, 44
   export processing free zones, 272
   exports, 37, 242t, 285
   imports, 242t
   industrial competitiveness, 276–77
   Mexico-Central America Free Trade Agreement, 235t
   stock markets, 180b
   trade union membership, 254
   Venezuela-Central America Free Trade Agreement, 236t
Central American Common Market (CACM), 21, 239–40, 462
   exports from, 238, 239t
central bank discount rates, 114–15, 116t
CEPAL (Comisión Económica para América Latina). See Economic Commission for Latin America
Chase Manhattan, 90–91, 92t
Chemical, 90–91, 92t
Chicago school, 25, 219, 462
Chile
   agriculture, 288–92, 289t–292t
   and Asian economic crisis, 199–200
   automobile industry, 70
   communications, 7, 9t, 10, 317–20, 321t
   current account balance, 215, 215t
   debt crisis, 190

debt-for-equity swaps, 96
economic participation by women, 322b
education, 317, 376, 377t
education spending, 331, 332t, 377
educational reform, 388–89
energy consumption, 409–10, 410t
energy problems, 411
environmental policy, 420–21
exchange rate performance, 224, 224t
exports, 37–38, 38t, 39f, 218t, 218–19, 219t, 221, 223t, 285
fertilizer consumption, 415, 417t
fiscal surplus/deficit, 114t, 114–15
foreign investment, 42–44, 43t, 181, 182t
foreign shares of industries, 62, 62t
GDP per capita, 64, 66t
geographic distribution of exports, 38, 40t
grade repetition, 378, 378t
growth, 30, 31t, 135
health care spending, 331, 332t, 367t
health care system, 369
health statistics, 355, 356t
high school education, 390, 390t
housing, 316–17, 317t
human poverty index, 315
imports, 218t, 218–19, 219t
income distribution, 325–26, 327t
industrial competitiveness, 276–77
inequality, 328
inflation, 112, 112t
informal sector, 337, 337t, 337–38
infrastructure, 237, 271
labor management relations, 256b–257b
labor policy, 253
land reform, 298–300
literacy, 374–75, 375t
living standards, 315–16, 316t
market capitalization, 178–79, 179t
Mercosur, 234
money supply growth rates, 114–15, 115t
P900 program, 388
petroleum reserves and crude oil production, 411, 411t
Pinochet model, 25
poverty, 314, 314t, 331
privatization, 157–59, 158t, 159–60, 162
public works programs, 334
quality of life indicators, 7, 7t, 9–10
real exchange rate indexes, 87b–88b, 87t
regulating capital inflows, 205
regulating global inflows, 198–99
savings rates, 202
science and technology, 267
secondary market price spreads on debt, 94–96, 96t
social expenditures, 344, 345t
Solidarity and Social Investment Funds (FOSIS), 334–35
stock market, 181b
tariffs, 59, 217t, 217–18
technology development, 269–70

technology generation, 266
trade liberalization, 219–21
trade union membership, 254
urban unemployment, 259t, 259–60
urbanization, 406
wages, 97, 102f, 261–62, 262t
Chile-Mexico Free Trade Agreement, 234t
Chile-Venezuela Free Trade Agreement, 234t
CHILGENER, 159
China
    exports, imports, and balance of goods, 241,
        242t
    investment in Latin America, 42, 43t
Chiquita, 288
Chrysler, 72, 184t
Cigna, 366
Cisneros Group, 393
Citibank, 105–6, 340
Citicorp, 90–91, 92t, 99
Clean Development Mechanism (CDM) initia-
    tive, 424b
Clinton, William, 197
CNN, 182
coastal habitats, 414–15
coca, 287–88
Coca-Cola, 181, 184t
cocaine, 287
Codelco, 159
coffee prices, 40
Cold War, 10
Collor plan, 124, 462
Colombia
    agricultural policy options, 297
    agriculture, 288–92, 289t–292t
    Amazon holdings, 431n38
    Andean Trade Preference Act, 234t
    balance of goods, 242t
    CARICOM-Colombia Free Trade Agreement,
        236t
    coca production, 287
    communications, 7, 9t, 317–20, 321t
    current account balance, 215, 215t
    economic participation by women, 322b
    education spending, 377
    educational performance index, 376, 377t
    educational reform, 388
    energy consumption, 409–10, 410t
    Escuela Nueva, 388
    exchange rate performance, 224, 224t
    exports, 37, 38t, 218t, 218–19, 219t, 221,
        223t, 242t, 285
    fiscal surplus/deficit, 114t, 114–15
    foreign investment, 42–44, 43t, 181, 182t
    foreign shares of industries, 62, 62t
    forest change in, 414, 415t
    GDP per capita, 64, 66t
    geographic distribution of exports, 38, 40t
    grade repetition, 378, 378t
    health care system, 366
    health statistics, 355, 356t
    hogares comunitarios, 394

housing, 316–17, 317t
human poverty index, 315
imports, 218t, 218–19, 219t, 242t
income distribution, 325–26, 327t
industrial competitiveness, 276–77
inflation, 112, 112t
informal sector size, 337, 337t
interest rates, 114–15, 116t
labor market reform, 253
labor policy, 253
landless or nearly landless peasant families,
    324, 324t
literacy, 374–75, 375t
living standards, 315–16, 316t
market capitalization, 178–79, 179t
money supply growth rates, 114–15, 115t
petroleum reserves and crude oil production,
    411, 411t
poverty gap, 314, 314t
privatization, 157–59, 158t
quality of life indicators, 7, 7t, 9–10
science and technology, 267
secondary market price spreads on debt, 94–
    96, 96t
social expenditures, 344, 345t
social indicators, 324t, 325
state spending, 342–43
tariffs, 59, 217t, 217–18
technology development, 269–70
technology generation, 266
urban unemployment, 259t, 259–60
U.S. oil imports from, 241, 243t
violence, 354
wage differentials, 261–62, 262t
Colombia-Central America Free Trade Agree-
    ment, 236t
Colombia-Venezuela Free Trade Agreement,
    234t
Colosio, Luis Donaldo, 195
COMIBOL, 128
Comisión Económica para América Latina
    (CEPAL). See Economic Commission for
    Latin America
command and control policies, 417–19, 462
Commission for Environmental Cooperation
    (CEC), 232–33
commodity exports, 37, 38t, 38–40
commodity lottery, 37, 462
common market, 226–27, 462
Common Market Group, 237
communications
    indicators, 7, 9t, 10
    profiles, 317–20, 321t
    telecommunications, 271–72
community-based enterprises, 425t
community control, 305–7
community engagement, 336
community integration, 335
Compania Nacional de Espanola, 163b
Compania Vale do Rio Doce (CVRD), 159, 161,
    422

comparative advantage
  theory of, 212–13, 474
comparative growth
  patterns, 30
  rates, 32b
competitiveness
  industrial, 251–81
conditionality, 93, 462
condom social marketing, 353
Confederation of Mexican Workers (CTM), 255
confidence, lack of, 89
CONICIT. *See* National Council for Scientific
  and Technological Research
consumption
  energy, 409–10, 410*t*
  fertilizer, 415, 417*t*
  percentage share of, 325–26, 327*t*
contagion effect, 199–201
Continental Illinois, 90–91, 92*t*
contingent valuation, 422, 462
Contreras, Jessy, 3
Convention on Biological Diversity, 404
Convention on Climate Change, 404
convertibility plan, 129, 133b–134b, 462
Coopers and Lybrand, 161
CORFO. *See* Corporación de Fomento de la Producción
"The Cornfields," 339b
Corporación de Fomento de la Producción
  (CORFO), 61, 159
corporations. *See also specific corporations*
  multinational, 181–88
  transnational, 62, 475
Costa Rica
  agriculture, 288–92, 289*t*–292*t*, 304
  Brady deal, 102, 104*t*
  Clean Development Mechanism (CDM) ini-
    tiative, 424b
  Colombia-Central America Free Trade Agree-
    ment, 236*t*
  communications, 7, 9*t*, 10, 317–20, 321*t*
  current account balance, 215, 215*t*
  debt reduction, 101
  debt-for-nature swaps, 97–98b
  diseases of, 355, 357*t*
  economic participation by women, 322b
  education, 317, 376, 377*t*
  energy consumption, 409–10, 410*t*
  exchange rate performance, 224, 224*t*
  exports, 37, 38*t*, 218*t*, 218–19, 219*t*, 221,
    223*t*
  fertilizer consumption, 415, 417*t*
  fiscal surplus/deficit, 114*t*, 114–15
  forest change in, 414, 415*t*
  GDP per capita, 64, 66*t*
  grade repetition, 378, 378*t*
  health care system, 363
  housing, 316–17, 317*t*
  human poverty index, 315
  imports, 218*t*, 218–19, 219*t*
  income distribution, 325–26, 327*t*
  inflation, 112, 112*t*
  informal sector, 337*t*, 337–38
  interest rates, 114–15, 116*t*
  landless or nearly landless peasant families,
    324, 324*t*
  literacy, 374–75, 375*t*
  living standards, 315–16, 316*t*
  Mexico-Central America Free Trade Agree-
    ment, 235*t*
  money supply growth rates, 114–15, 115*t*
  National Council for Scientific and Techno-
    logical Research (CONICIT), 268
  organic farming, 286
  poverty, 261, 314, 314*t*
  privatization, 157–59, 158*t*
  quality of life indicators, 7, 7*t*, 9–10
  science and technology, 267
  social expenditures, 344, 345*t*
  social policy initiatives, 335b
  stock market, 180b
  tariffs, 217*t*, 217–18
  technical education, 268
  technology development, 269–70
  urban unemployment, 259*t*, 259–60
  Venezuela-Central America Free Trade
    Agreement, 236*t*
  wage differentials, 261–62, 262*t*
  working poor, 261
Costa Rica-Mexico Free Trade Agreement, 235*t*
Costa Rican Foundation, 270
Costa Rican Technological Institute (ITCR), 269
cost-benefit analysis, 422
cost-effectiveness, 420
cost-effectiveness analysis, 422
cost-push elements, 117, 463
costs
  of debt adjustment, 100–101
  of development, 401–32
  of education, 380b–381b
  environmental policy, 423–28
Council of the Americas, 453
covenants, fiscal, 144
Credibanco, 180b–181b
credit markets, segmented, 295–96, 473
credit policies, 417–19, 418*t*
crude oil production, 411, 411*t*
Cruzado plan, 122–23, 133b–134b, 463
CSIS. *See* Center for Strategic and International
  Studies
CTC, 159
CTM. *See* Confederation of Mexican Workers
Cuba, 36
  communication profile, 317–20, 321*t*
  diseases of, 355, 357*t*
  educational performance index, 376, 377*t*
  foreign investment, 42, 43*t*
  geographic distribution of exports, 38, 40*t*
  health care system, 363
  health statistics, 355, 356*t*
  housing, 316–17, 317*t*
  human poverty index, 315

literacy, 374–75, 375t
living standards, 315–16, 316t
petroleum reserves and crude oil production,
    411, 411t
single commodity exports, 37, 38t
current account balance, 215, 215t
current account sustainability, 194
customs union, 226–27, 463
CVRD (Compania Vale do Rio Doce), 159, 161,
    422

da Silva, Luis Ignacio ("Lula"), 200
debt, 80–97
    accumulation of, 107–8
    adjustment to
        social and environmental costs of, 100–101
        timing and, 120–22
    bank exposure to highly indebted countries,
        90–91, 92t
    and development patterns, 84–86, 85t
    external, 80–81, 81f
        long-term, 91b
    indicators, 89–90, 90t, 102–5, 105t
    reduction of, 101–2
    secondary market price spreads on, 94–96,
        96t
    servicing, 118
debt crisis, 71–72, 79, 79–109, 111
    absorption approach to, 92–94
    Baker plan for, 97–102
    effects of, 116–18
    IMF approach to, 91–92
    lessons of, 106–7
    market reaction to, 94–97
    responses to, 108
    summary, 108
debt service, 91b
debt trap, 81, 82t, 463
debt-for-equity swaps, 96, 463
debt-for-nature swaps, 97, 463
debt-led growth, 71–72
decentralization, 146, 305–7, 342, 385
    definition of, 463
    elements of, 342
    process of, 392–93
Declaration and Action Plan for Latin American
    Economic Recovery, 94–95b
Declaration of Principles on the Management,
    Conservation, and Sustainable Develop-
    ment of Forests, 404–5
Declaration of Quinto, 94–95b
declining terms of trade, 40, 54b, 464
default, sovereign, 91b
deficit
    financing, 113–15
    infrastructure, 270–71, 271t
deforestation
    Chico Mendes, 416b–417b
    of tropical rain forests, 412–15
Del Monte, 288
demand-driven rural investment funds, 305, 464

dependency theory, 24, 52–55
    definition of, 464
    summary, 74–75
deschooling, 395
development, 1–28
    cycles in, 433–45
    debt and, 84–86, 85t
    definition of, 26, 464
    economic, 5–21, 20t
        characteristics of, 5–13
        definition of, 10–13, 12b–14b
        exchange rate policy and, 61b
        foundation for, 80–97
        growth vs., 11–15
        pioneers in, 17b–19b
    Gender Development Index, 314, 467
    health-development framework, 353t
    human, 326–27, 328t
    Human Development Index, 314, 467
    internalizing costs of, 401–32
    lessons for, 67–68
    measures of, 15–16
    rural, 302b, 306b
    sustainable, 13b, 322b–323b, 402–5, 428–29,
        474
    technology, 268
    theoretical approaches to state activity in,
        147–51
development policy, 21, 53–55
    challenges, 435
    summary, 27
development theory, 16–21, 26
Díaz, Porfirio, 185b
direct foreign investment, 159, 181, 182t, 185b
    in Peru, 186b–188b
direct government investment, 417–19, 464
Direct TV, 393
disbursements, 91b
diseases
    of Americas, 355, 357t
    emerging, 371n5
Dole, 288
domestic banking, 190–92
domestic monetary autonomy, 121b
Dominican Republic
    agriculture, 288–92, 289t–292t
    Brady deal, 102, 104t
    CARICOM-Colombia Free Trade Agreement,
        236t
    CARICOM-Venezuela Free Trade Agree-
        ment, 236t
    current account balance, 215, 215t
    educational performance index, 376, 377t
    GDP per capita, 64, 66t
    grade repetition, 378, 378t
    housing, 316–17, 317t
    income distribution, 325–26, 327t
    labor management relations, 256b–257b
    landless or nearly landless peasant families,
        324, 324t
    privatization, 157–59, 158t

single commodity exports, 37, 38t
social expenditures, 344, 345t
Dos Santos, Theotonio, 12b
double taxation treaty, 341
DRIFs. *See* demand-driven rural investment
    funds
dualism, 15, 285, 464
Dutch disease, 39, 464

EAs. *See* environmental assessments
East Asia, 243t
    communications indicators, 7, 9t
    infrastructure deficit, 270–71, 271t
    science and technology indicators, 265–66,
        267t
    trade union membership, 254
    U.S. trade, 240–41, 243t
Eastern Europe
    exports, imports, and balance of goods, 242t
    performance of, 31–32b
    trade, 240–41, 243t
ECLA. *See* Economic Commission for Latin
    America
ECLAC. *See* Economic Commission for Latin
    America and the Carribbean
economic change, 30–34
    conceptualizing, 1–28
Economic Commission for Latin America
    (ECLA), 53–56, 75n3
Economic Commission for Latin America and
    the Carribbean (ECLAC or CEPAL), 52,
    144, 202, 448–49
    changing production patterns, 273
    integrated approach, 344–45, 469
    open regionalism, 228
economic development
    comparative indicators of, 19, 20t
    definition of, 5–21
    pioneers in, 17b–19b
economic integration, 73
economic policy, 22–23
economic populism, 57, 83, 464–65
economic union, 226–27, 465
economics
    Latin American laboratory, 435–36
    new institutional, 149
economy
    extractive, 34–35, 48–49
    new political, 147
    participation by women, 322b–323b
    of scale, 73
ecotourism, *421*
Ecuador
    agriculture, 288–92, 289t–292t
    Amazon holdings, 431n38
    Andean Community, 239
    Andean Trade Preference Act, 234t
    Brady deal, 102, 104t
    carbon dioxide emissions, 7
    communications, 7, 9t, 317–20, 321t
    current account balance, 215, 215t

debt-for-nature swaps, 98b
development cycles, 434
diseases of, 355, 357t
education spending growth, 331, 332t
educational performance index, 376, 377t
energy consumption, 409–10, 410t
exchange rate performance, 224, 224t
exports, 218t, 218–19, 219t, 221, 223t, 285
fiscal surplus/deficit, 114t, 114–15
forest change in, 414, 415t
GDP per capita, 64, 66t
growth rate, 7
health spending growth, 331, 332t
health statistics, 355–56, 356t
housing, 316–17, 317t
imports, 218t, 218–19, 219t
inflation, 112, 112t
informal sector size, 337, 337t
interest rates, 114–15, 116t
land reform, 298
landless or nearly landless peasant families,
    324, 324t
literacy, 374–75, 375t
living standards, 315–16, 316t
market capitalization, 178–79, 179t
money supply growth rates, 114–15, 115t
oil spills, 411–12, 413b
petroleum reserves and crude oil production,
    411, 411t
poverty gap, 314, 314t
privatization, 157–59, 158t
quality of life indicators, 7, 7t, 9–10
secondary market price spreads on debt, 94–
    96, 96t
social expenditures, 344, 345t
state spending, 342
tariffs, 217t, 217–18
trade role, 7
transnational corporations, 64
urban environmental problems, 408
urban unemployment, 259t, 259–60
urbanization, 7
U.S. oil imports from, 241, 243t
Eddie Bauer, 3–4
"Educate Girls Project," 381b
education, 320, 373–400
    access to, 380b–382b
    achievements, 374–77
    banking concept of, 395
    in Brazil, 390–91, 391t
    costs, 380b–381b
    decentralization process, 392–93
    enrollment rates, 374–75, 376t
    Escuela Nueva, 388
    for girls, 380b–382b
    grade repetition, 378, 378t
    high school, 390, 390t
    of indigenous children, *373, 383*
    local approaches, 381b
    public-private partnerships, 393–94
    quality primary guarantee, 394

as social change, 395
  spending, 331, 332*t*, 376–77
  technical, 268
  unequal, 377–82
educational deficit, 374–77
  causes of, 383–85
  definition of, 465
educational performance index, 376, 377*t*
educational reform, *392*
  benefits of, 385–86
  Bolivian, 382b, 384b
  Mexican, 382b
  multilateral efforts, 394–95
  stage one, 387–92
  state and market in, 386–87
  Universal Access to Education for 2010, 395
effective rate of protection, 465
effective selectivity, 343–44, 465
ejidos, 44, 298, 308n7, 465
El Cambio, 434
El Niño, 244
El Pacto. See Pact for Economic Solidarity
El Salvador
  agriculture, 288–92, 289*t*–292*t*
  Colombia-Central America Free Trade Agreement, 236*t*
  communications, 7, 9*t*, 317–20, 321*t*
  current account balance, 215, 215*t*
  education spending, 377
  educational performance index, 376, 377*t*
  educational reform, 386
  energy consumption, 409–10, 410*t*
  exchange rate performance, 224, 224*t*
  export processing free zones, 272
  exports, 37, 38*t*, 218*t*, 218–19, 219*t*, 221, 223*t*
  fiscal surplus/deficit, 114*t*, 114–15
  forest change in, 414, 415*t*
  GDP per capita, 64, 66*t*
  health care, 367
  health statistics, 355, 356*t*
  housing, 316–17, 317*t*
  human poverty index, 315
  imports, 218*t*, 218–19, 219*t*
  income distribution, 325–26, 327*t*
  inflation, 112, 112*t*
  labor force participation by women, 258
  land reform, 298
  landless or nearly landless peasant families, 324, 324*t*
  literacy, 374–75, 375*t*
  living standards, 315–16, 316*t*
  Mexico-Central America Free Trade Agreement, 235*t*
  money supply growth rates, 114–15, 115*t*
  Nueva Ocotepeque Agreement, 236*t*
  poverty, 314, 314*t*, 320–21
  quality of life indicators, 7, 7*t*, 9–10
  San Bartolo, 274
  social expenditures, 344, 345*t*
  tariffs, 217*t*, 217–18
  urban unemployment, 259*t*, 259–60
  Venezuela-Central America Free Trade Agreement, 236*t*
  violence, 354
El Salvador-Guatemala Free Trade Agreement, 234*t*
Electricidad de Caracas, 163b
electrification, 426, 427*t*–428*t*
EMBRATEL, 162
emergency dwellings, 408
emergency social funds, 128
employment, 35–36, 257–58, 258*t*
  unemployment, 257–60
  urban unemployment, 97, 101*f,* 259*t*, 259–60
empowerment, 16, 465
  Gender Empowerment Index, 314, 467
enclaves, 38, 465
encomienda, 34, 465
Endesa Spain, 184*t*
energy consumption, 409–10, 410*t*
energy policies, 418, 419*t*
energy problem, 409–12
energy projects, 186b–188b
ENERSIS, 159
Engel's Law, 40, 465
Entel, 271–72
enterprises, state-owned, 57–58
entrepreneurs, new, 180b–181b, 264b–265b, 339b–340b
environment
  costs of debt adjustment to, 100–101
  deforestation of, 412–15, 416b–417b
  destruction of, 405–6
environmental agenda, 438
environmental assessments, 422, 465
environmental challenges, 401–32
environmental decision making, 403, 404*f*
environmental dimension, 23, 44–45
environmental policy
  actors, 425*t*–426*t*
  costs, 423–28
  design types, 417–19
  formulation of, 415–23
  linkages, 417–19, 418*t*–419*t*
  priorities, 405
  summary, 429–30
environmental problems
  in Latin America, 429
  urban, 406–9
EPFZs. *See* export processing free zones
EPI. *See* educational performance index
epidemiological backlog, 355, 466
epidemiological transition, 355, 357*t*, 466
equitable sustainable growth, 283–310
equity, 2, 386–87
  debt-for-equity swaps, 96
  definition of, 466
equity investments, 178, 466
Escuela Nueva (Colombia), 388
ESFs. *See* emergency social funds
Estenssoro, Victor Paz, 128

ethnicity
    and health, 356–59
    and poverty, 321–24, 323*t*
EU. *See* European Union
Europe. *See also* Eastern Europe
    trade union membership, 254
    U.S. trade, 240*f*, 240–41
European Union (EU), 237–38, 242*t*
Excell Corporation, 366
exchange rate policy
    and development, 61b
    and forest resources, 417–19, 418*t*
    and new international capital flows, 191b
exchange rates
    fixed, 121b
    overvaluation of, 60, 87b–88b, 471–72
    performance of, 224, 224*t*
    real, 194–95, 195*f*
    real effective, of exports, index of, 224, 224*t*
    real indexes, 87b–88b, 87*t*
expenditure switching, 466
export enclave, 38
export infrastructures, *229*
export pessimism, 40, 466
export processing free zones, 273–75
export promotion, 71
    nontraditional, 471
export subsidies, 60b
exports, 218–19, 219*t*
    according to categories, 221, 222*t*
    agricultural, 285
    geographic distribution of, 38, 40*t*
    growth rates, 218*t*, 218–19
    index of real effective exchange rate of, 224,
        224*t*
    nontraditional, *211*, 285, *294*
    primary product, golden age of, 37, 467
    by selected countries and geographic areas,
        242*t*
    single commodity, 37, 38*t*, 38–40
    from trade areas, 238, 238*t*
    unsustainable, *118*
external debt
    long-term, 91b
    total disbursed, 80–81, 81*f*
external financing
    limits of, 79–109
external shocks, 83–84, 86–90
externalities, 386
extractive economy
rewards of, 34–35
summary, 48–49
    extractive reserves, 416b
    extralegal production, 287–88
    extreme poverty, 466
    Exxon, 184*t*

factor price equalization, 213, 466
Facultad Latinoamericana de Ciencias Sociales
    (FLACSO), 375
fair price shops, 420

Faletto, Enzo, 53
farming. *See also* agriculture
    involvement of farmers, *303,* 303–4
    large-scale farms, *283*
    organic, 286–87
favelas, 314, 335
fazenda, 36, 466
FDI. *See* foreign direct investment
Fei, John, 18b
Fernandez, Roque, 129–30
fertilizer consumption, 415, 417*t*
Fiat, 62, 72–73
Fiat Spa, 184*t*
financial capital
    early characteristics, 46, 47*t*
    and growth patterns, 30–32, 33*t*
financial sector reform, 201–4
financing
    deficit, 113–15
    external, 79–109
Finland, 242*t*
First Chicago, 90–91, 92*t*
fiscais, 123, 463
fiscal austerity measures, 72–73, 466
fiscal covenant, 144, 466
fiscal policy, 65b, 417–19, 418*t*
fiscal surplus/deficit, overall, 114*t*, 114–15
Fischer, Stanley, 203
FLACSO (Facultad Latinoamericana de Cien-
    cias Sociales), 375
flexible manufacturing, 69
Ford, 62, 69, 72–73, 184*t*, 375
Fordism, 69
foreign capital, 41–44, *173*
foreign direct investment, 159, 174
    definition of, 466
    in Mexico, 185b
    net, 181, 182*t*
    in Peru, 186b–188b
foreign exchange controls, 60b
foreign investment
    vs. capital flight, 89
    in Latin America, 42, 42*t*
    per capita, 42, 43*t*
foreign investment/GDP, 42–44, 43*t*
foreign shares of industries, 62, 62*t*
foreign trade zones. *See* export processing free
    zones
forests
    change of, 414, 415*t*
    unsustainable exports of products of, *118*
forward linkage, 41, 56, 466–67
FOSIS. *See* Solidarity and Social Investment
    Funds
Foundation for the Promotion and Development
    of Microenterprises (PRODEM), 339b
France
    carbon dioxide emissions, 7
    exports, imports, and balance of goods, 242*t*
    growth rate, 7
    imports from Latin America, 38, 40*t*

investment in Latin America, 42, 42*t*
market capitalization, 178–79, 179*t*
merchandise exports to GDP, 37–38, 39*f*
privatization, 160
trade role, 7
urbanization, 7
Frank, Andre Gundar, 52
free economic zones. *See* export processing free
    zones
free trade, 246
    theoretical benefits of, 212–14
    theory of, 247
Free Trade Agreement of the Americas (FTAA),
    241–42, 244–46
free trade agreements, 233, 234*t*–236*t*, 240–46.
    See also specific agreements
Free Trade Area of the Americas (FTAA),
    256b–257b, 457
free trade areas, 226–27, 467
free trade zones, 273–75
Freire, Paulo, 395
French Guiana, 431n38
Fresh Fields, 286
Friedman, Milton, 25, 113, 147
FTAA. *See* Free Trade Agreement of the Ameri-
    cas; Free Trade Area of the Americas
FUNAI (Indian Protection Agency), 422
Fundación Mexicana para la Planeación Famil-
    iar (MEXFAM), 354b
Furtado, Celso, 12b

Gabriela (child), 318b–319b
Gacek, Stan, 256b
Gámez, Martha, 264b–265b
Gap, 3–4
GATT. *See* General Agreement on Tariffs and
    Trade
GDI. *See* Gender Development Index
GDP. *See* gross domestic product
GE, 2
GEF. *See* Global Environmental Facility
GEM. *See* Gender Empowerment Index
gender
    and health, 356–59
    keeping girls in school, 380b–382b
    poverty and, 322b–323b
Gender Development Index, 314, 467
Gender Empowerment Index, 314, 467
General Agreement on Tariffs and Trade
    (GATT), 185b, 230, 242
General Motors (GM), 2, 62, 72–73, 184*t*, 254
Germany
    energy consumption, 409–10, 410*t*
    exports, imports, and balance of goods, 242*t*
    imports from Latin America, 38, 40*t*
    income distribution, 325–26, 327*t*
    investment in Latin America, 42, 42*t*
    merchandise exports to GDP, 37–38, 39*f*
Gifford, Kathy Lee, 182–83
Gini coefficient, 325, 467

girls
    access to education, 380b–382b
    "Educate Girls Project" (Guatemala), 381b
    education costs, 380b–381b
Girls' Education Program (Guatemala), 381b–
    382b
Global Environmental Facility (GEF), 404, 423,
    426*t*
Global Environmental Fund, 440
global multilateral organizations, 449–51
GM. *See* General Motors
GM do Brasil, 62
golden age of primary product exports, 37, 467
González Hernández, Gabriela, 380b
goods
    composition of, 221
Goulart, Nair, 256b–257b
Goulet, Denis, 12b
government investment, direct, 417–19, 464
government services market, 144
governmental organizations
    U.S.-based, 451
grade repetition, 378, 378*t*
Grande Carajas Program, 414
grassroots organizations, 425*t*
grassroots support organizations, 425*t*
Great Britain, 42, 42*t*
Great Depression, 45
greenhouse gases, 424b
Grenada, 236*t*
GROs. *See* grassroots organizations
gross domestic product (GDP)
    foreign investment/GDP, 42–44, 43*t*
    merchandise exports to, 37–38, 39*f*
    percentage growth per capita, 64, 66*t*
Group of Three, 235*t*
growth
    comparative, 30, 32b
    debt-led, 71
    definition of, 12b–14b, 14, 467
    vs. development, 11–15
    early patterns, 46, 47*t*
    factors shaping, 32, 33*t*
    GDP per capita, 64, 66*t*
    income inequality and, 346
    as measure of development, 15–16
    patterns, 48
    per capita rates, 30, 31*t*
    poverty and, 346
    from stabilization to, 132–35
    sustainable, 293–301
    unequal and unstable, 29–50
GRSOs. *See* grassroots support organizations
grupos, 190
Guatemala, 318b
    agricultural policy options, 297
    agriculture, 288–92, 289*t*–292*t*
    Casa Alianza, 318b–319b
    Colombia-Central America Free Trade Agree-
        ment, 236*t*
    communications, 7, 9*t*, 317–20, 321*t*

current account balance, 215, 215*t*
"Educate Girls Project," 381b
education, 317, 376, 377*t*, 383
educational reform, 386, 388
El Salvador-Guatemala Free Trade Agreement, 234*t*
energy consumption, 409–10, 410*t*
exchange rate performance, 224, 224*t*
exports, 37, 38*t*, 218*t*, 218–19, 219*t*, 221, 223*t*, 285
fiscal surplus/deficit, 114*t*, 114–15
forest change in, 414, 415*t*
GDP per capita, 64, 66*t*
Girls' Education Program, 381b–382b
girls in school, 380b–382b
grade repetition, 378, 378*t*
health statistics, 355, 356*t*
housing, 316–17, 317*t*
human poverty index, 315
imports, 218*t*, 218–19, 219*t*
income distribution, 325–26, 327*t*
inflation, 112, 112*t*
informal sector size, 337, 337*t*
interest rates, 114–15, 116*t*
labor market reform, 253
landless or nearly landless peasant families, 324, 324*t*
literacy, 374–75, 375*t*
living standards, 315–16, 316*t*
Mexico-Central America Free Trade Agreement, 235*t*
money supply growth rates, 114–15, 115*t*
Nueva Ocotepeque Agreement, 236*t*
organic farming, 286
poverty, 261, 293, 314, 314*t*, 320–24, 323*t*
privatization, 157–59, 158*t*
quality of life indicators, 7, 7*t*, 9–10
rural development, 302b
social expenditures, 344, 345*t*
social indicators, 324*t*, 325
stock market, 180b
tariffs, 217*t*, 217–18
urban environmental problems, 408
urban unemployment, 259*t*, 259–60
U.S. oil imports from, 241, 243*t*
Venezuela-Central America Free Trade Agreement, 236*t*
Guatemalan Association for the Promotion of Rural Health (Guatesalud), 370b
Guatesalud, 370b
Gulf of Honduras, 426
Guyana
    Amazon holdings, 431n38
    educational performance index, 376, 377*t*
    fiscal surplus/deficit, 114*t*, 114–15
    inflation, 112, 112*t*
    interest rates, 114–15, 116*t*
    literacy, 374–75, 375*t*
    money supply growth rates, 114–15, 115*t*
    privatization, 157–59, 158*t*

Haiti
    agriculture, 288–92, 289*t*–292*t*
    poverty, 320–21
    privatization, 157–59, 158*t*
    single commodity exports, 37, 38*t*
HDI. *See* Human Development Index
headcount ratio, 313, 467
Health Agent System (Programa de Agentes de Saúde, PAS), 362b
health care, 320, 351–72
    Bolivian coverage, 364, 364*f*
    development framework, 353*t*
    ethnicity, gender, and, 356–59
    home services, *360*
    Mexican reform, 368b–369b
    paying for, 366–69
    policy challenge, 365–66
    preventive, 362b
    primary, 359–61, 472
    problems faced by institutions, 369
    reforming service delivery, 365–66
    regional profile, 352–56
    rural services, *351,* 370b
    spending, 331, 332*t*, 367*t*
    statistics, 355, 356*t*
    summary, 370–71
    systems of, 361–65
"Health for All by the Year 2000" (HFA2000) strategy, 359, 467
Heckscher-Ohlin theorem, 213
hemispheric free trade agreements, 240–46
Henriot, Peter J.A., 13b
heterodox policies, 117, 122–26, 467
HFA2000, 359, 467
Higgins, B., 12b
Hirschman, Albert Otto, 17b
historical legacies, 29–50
    land distribution, *29*
    lessons from, 46–47
    per capita growth rates, 30, 31*t*
hogares comunitarios, 394
Holland, 266
home health agents, *360*
Honda, 72
Honduras
    agriculture, 288–92, 289*t*–292*t*, 306
    Colombia-Central America Free Trade Agreement, 236*t*
    communications, 7, 9*t*, 10, 317–20, 321*t*
    current account balance, 215, 215*t*
    development cycles, 434
    educational performance index, 376, 377*t*
    educational reform, 386
    energy consumption, 409–10, 410*t*
    exchange rate performance, 224, 224*t*
    exports, 37, 38*t*, 218*t*, 218–19, 219*t*, 221, 223*t*
    fiscal surplus/deficit, 114*t*, 114–15
    forest change in, 414, 415*t*
    GDP per capita, 64, 66*t*
    health statistics, 355, 356*t*

housing, 316–17, 317*t*
human poverty index, 315
imports, 218*t*, 218–19, 219*t*
income distribution, 325–26, 327*t*
inflation, 112, 112*t*
informal sector size, 337, 337*t*
interest rates, 114–15, 116*t*
literacy, 374–75, 375*t*
living standards, 315–16, 316*t*
Mexico-Central America Free Trade Agreement, 235*t*
money supply growth rates, 114–15, 115*t*
Nueva Ocotepeque Agreement, 236*t*
poverty, 261, 314, 314*t*, 320–21
privatization, 157–59, 158*t*
quality of life indicators, 7, 7*t*, 9–10
social expenditures, 344, 345*t*
social indicators, 324*t*, 325
state spending, 343
stock market, 180b
tariffs, 217*t*, 217–18
urban unemployment, 259*t*, 259–60
Venezuela-Central America Free Trade Agreement, 236*t*
wage differentials, 261–62, 262*t*
Honduras Protected Areas project, 426
Hong Kong, 242*t*
hospital-based urban health care, *351*
"hot" money, 178
housing, *8, 311,* 316–17, 317*t*
emergency dwellings, 408
HPI. *See* human poverty index
human development gaps, 326–27, 328*t*
Human Development Index, 314, 467
Human Development Report (UN), 16
human needs, basic, 15–16
human poverty index, 314–15
Hurricane Mitch, *433,* 434

IAF. *See* Inter-American Foundation
IBM, 184*t*, 393
IBRD. *See* International Bank of Reconstruction and Development
IDB. *See* Inter-American Development Bank
IFC. *See* International Finance Corporation
Iglesias, Enrique, 228, 241
IIC. *See* Inter-American Investent Corporation
illegal narcotics, 287
Illich, Ivan, 395
illiquidity, 91, 467–68
ILO. *See* International Labor Organization
IMF. *See* International Monetary Fund
IMIP. *See* Institute Materno–Infantil de Pernambuco
import licensing, 60b
imports, 218–19, 219*t*
growth rates, 218*t*, 218–19
by selected countries and geographic areas, 242*t*
import-substitution industrialization, *51,* 51–78, 436–37

automobile industry case, 68–74
crisis of, 65–67
definition of, 468
fiscal and monetary policy, 65b
industrial policy, 65b
international instruments, 65b
lessons from, 67–68
performance of, 64–65, 66*t*
from structuralism to, 55–57
summary, 75
toolbox, 57–64, 65b
Incas, 35
incentives
industrial, 60b
market-based, 417–19, 470
income
average, 261–62, 262*t*
distribution, 325–26, 326*f*, 327*t*
distribution in Brazil, 329b, 329*t*
inequality, 346
labor disparities, 261–62, 262*t*
percentage share of, 325–26, 327*t*
rural, 301–3
income gap, 314, 314*t*, 468
incomplete markets, 295, 468
inconsistent trinity, 120–21
independence, 36–38
index of real effective exchange rate of exports, 224, 224*t*
indexation, 119, 468
India, 42, 43*t*
Indian lands, 44
Indian Protection Agency (FUNAI), 422
Indians, 34
indigenous peoples
education of, *373, 383*
groups below poverty line, 321–24, 323*t*
Proposed American Declaration on the Rights of Indigenous Peoples, 244
Indochina, 42, 43*t*
Indonesia
economic crisis, 199
exports, imports, and balance of goods, 242*t*
investment in Latin America, 42, 43*t*
industrial competitiveness
emerging, 276–77
international, 251–81
industrial countries. *See also specific countries*
communication profile, 317–20, 321*t*
industrial linkages, weak, 41–44
industrial policy, 65b
active, 57–58
tools of, 61–64
industrial sector, 273
industrialization
automobile industry role in, 69
foreign shares of, 62, 62*t*
import-substitution, *51,* 51–77, 436–37, 468
incentives, 60b
inequality, 325–32
areas for action, 333–41

in Brazil, 329b
causes of, 326–27
in education, 377–82
excess, 328
income, 346
trends in, 328–32
inertial inflation, 118, 468
inflation, 112, 112*t*
Argentine, 129*f*, 129–31
equation for, 113
heterodox approaches to stabilization of, 122–26
inertial, 118, 468
Mexican, 129*f*, 131
monetarist theory of, 136
orthodox theory of, 471
reduction of, 131–32
structuralist theory of, 136–38
theories of, 113–18
inflationary expectations, 119, 468
informal rules, 442
informal sector, 252, 336–38
definition of, 468
rise of, 260–63
size, 337, 337*t*
Informatics 2000, 393
infrastructure, 270–72
improving, 251, 251–81
intellectual, 225b
summary, 278
infrastructure deficit, 270–71, 271*t*
INGOs. *See* international nongovernmental organizations
input markets, 263–70
inputs, 30–34
insecure property rights, 300, 468–69
Institute Materno–Infantil de Pernambuco (IMIP), 361
institutional economics, new, 149, 471
institutionalist tradition, 24–25, 469
institutions, 439
integrated approach, 344–45, 469
integration
community, 335
deep, 227
economic, 73
regional, 472–73
regional agreements, 233, 234*t*–236*t*
regional arrangements, 227
summary, 247–48
trade, 226–28, 246
INTEL, 105
Intel, 269–70
intellectual infrastructure, 225b
Inter-American Commission on Women, 245
Inter-American Development Bank (IDB or BIAD), 301, 335, 340, 448
educational reform funding, 394
emergency social fund, 128
Informatics 2000, 393
technology development funds, 269–70

Inter-American Dialogue, 451–52
Inter-American Foundation (IAF), 286, 341, 451
Inter-American Investment Corporation (IIC), 180b–181b, 225b, 339b
Inter-American Program, 244
Inter-American Regional Workers Organization (ORIT), 256b–257b
Inter-American Strategy for Public Participation, 244
interest associations, 425*t*
interest rates
national, 114–15, 116*t*
real, 83–84, 84*t*
International Bank of Reconstruction and Development (IBRD) (World Bank), 146, 193, 364, 366, 424, 450
agricultural loans, 305–6
Agricultural Technology and Land Management Project (ATLMP), 304
Baker plan, 97–99
educational reform, 388, 394
emergency social fund, 128
Environment Department, 425*t*
social investment funds, 333–34
international capital flows
and domestic banking, 190–92
new, 173–209, 191b
International Development Bank, 269
International Finance Corporation (IFC), 340
international industrial competitiveness, 251–81
International Labor Organization (ILO), 256b, 394, 449–50
International Monetary Fund (IMF), 91–94, 197, 203, 450
Baker plan, 97–99
international organizations, 425*t*–426*t*. *See also specific organizations*
nongovernmental, 425*t*
International Planned Parenthood Federation, 354b
Internet, 10, 182, 374
investment
demand-driven rural funds, 305, 464
direct government, 417–19, 464
equity, 178, 466
foreign, 42*t*, 42–44, 43*t*
foreign direct, 159, 174, 181, 182*t*, 185b–188b, 466
long-term, 181–88
social funds, 333–35
investors
portfolio, 472
search for, 187b–188b
involuntary lending, 91b, 93, 469
Isabella, 34
ISI. *See* import-substitution industrialization
Italy, 160, 242*t*
ITCR. *See* Costa Rican Technological Institute

Jamaica
CARICOM-Colombia Free Trade Agreement, 236*t*

CARICOM-Venezuela Free Trade Agreement, 236t
economic participation by women, 322b
exports of basic products from, 221, 223t
income distribution, 325–26, 327t
privatization, 157–59, 158t
Japan
    automobile industry in Latin America, 71
    Brady plan, 1989, 101
    energy consumption, 409–10, 410t
    exports, imports, and balance of goods, 242t
    high school education, 390, 390t
    income distribution, 325–26, 327t
    labor productivity, 263–65, 266f
J.C. Penney, 3–4
J.P. Morgan, 193
"just in time" production, 70

Kellogg Foundation, 341
Keynes, John Maynard, 113
"king sugar," 39–40
Kleiman, Eugenia, 264b–265b
K-mart, 183
knife production, 63
Korea
    economic crisis, 199
    exports, imports, and balance of goods, 242t
    investment in Latin America, 42, 43t
    labor productivity, 263–65, 266f
Krueger, Anne, 18b
Kuznets, Simon, 13b
Kuznets curve, 330, 469

La Selva, 286
labor, 35–36. See also employment
    productive approach to management relations, 256b–257b
    quality improvement, 251–81
labor force
    employment in agriculture, 288–89, 290t
    participation by women, 258
labor income disparities, 261–62, 262t
labor market(s)
    key issues, 252–57
    summary, 277–78
labor movement, 255
labor policy, 253–57
labor productivity, 255, 263–65, 266f, 469
labor resources
    early characteristics, 46, 47t
    and growth patterns, 30–32, 33t
LAIA. See Latin American Integration Association
Lamb, James J., 13b
land
    Agricultural Technology and Land Management Project (ATLMP), 304
    early characteristics, 46, 47t
    and growth patterns, 30–32, 33t
    historical patterns of distribution, 29
land policies, 417–19, 418t

land reform, 284, 298–301, 469
landless peasant families, 324t, 324–25
Las Mercedes free trade zone, 275–76
latifundia, 36, 469
Latin America, 1–2. See also specific countries
    agriculture, 284–88
    automobile industry, 68–74
    balance of payments, 226t, 226–27
    capital flows, 176–79, 188–90, 204–5
    central government expenditures, 151–52, 152f
    communications indicators, 7, 9t
    current account balance, 215, 215t
    debt crisis, 79, 79–109
    debt indicators, 89–90, 90t, 102–5, 105t
    development, 1–28, 433–45
    diseases of, 355, 357t
    economic change, 1–28
    economic laboratory of, 435–36
    educational deficit, 383–85
    environment, 405, 429
    equitable sustainable growth, 283–310
    ethnicity, 321–24
    exports, 38, 40t, 218t, 218–19, 219t, 221, 222t–223t
    external debt, 80–81, 81f
    fiscal surplus/deficit, 114t, 114–15
    foreign investment in, 42, 42t, 181, 182t
    forest change in, 414, 415t
    gender, 322b–323b
    gross national product, 97, 100f
    growth, 46, 47t, 132–35, 135t
    health, 352–56
    health care systems, 361–65
    human development gaps, 326–27, 328t
    imports, 218t, 218–19, 219t
    income, 37, 325–26, 326f, 327t
    index of real effective exchange rate of exports, 224, 224t
    industrial sector, 273
    inequality in, 326–27
    inflation, 112, 112t
    infrastructure deficit, 270–71, 271t
    labor markets, 252–57
    landless or nearly landless peasant families, 324t, 324–25
    liberalization record, 217–21
    literacy, 374–75, 375t
    living standards, 315–16, 316t
    long-term project lending, 81, 82t
    money supply growth rates, 114–15, 115t
    mortality by general causes, 354–55, 355t
    multinationals in, 181–82, 184t
    national interest rates, 114–15, 116t
    performance, 31–32b
    poverty, 312–24, 313t, 322b–323b
    privatization, 157–59, 158t
    public sector, 167
    racial composition, 35
    resource flows and transfers, 97, 99f
    return to markets, 173–209

science and technology indicators, 265–66, 267*t*

secondary market price spreads on debt, 94–96, 96*t*

social deficit, 135–36, 311–49

social expenditures, 344, 345*t*

state role in, 143–44

stock markets, 180b–181b

sustainable development, 322b–323b

tariffs, 217*t*, 217–18

trade performance, 220*t*

urban unemployment, 97, 101*f*, 259*t*, 259–60

U.S. trade, 240–41, 242*t*–243*t*

Latin American Integration Association (LAIA), 233

Latin American Working Group, 452

LAWG. *See* Latin American Working Group

LDAs. *See* local development associations

Lehman, Blasio and Claire, 4

Lehman, Ismail, 4

lending

bilateral loans, 91b

concerted, 91b

involuntary, 91b, 93, 469

loan default, 91b

long-term project, 81, 82*t*

microcredit, 340–41

microenterprise, 338–40

small loans, 339b–340b

targeted, 61–64

Lewis, W. Arthur, 10, 12b, 17b

liberalization

critique of, 214–15

implementation of, 216–17

rationale for, 215–16

record in Latin America, 217–21

of trade, *211,* 273

LIBOR (London Interbank Offer Rate), 91b

licensing, import, 60b

light manufacturing, *63*

linkage, forward, 466–67

literacy, 374–75, 375*t*

livestock policies, 417–19, 418*t*–419*t*

living standards, 315–16, 316*t*

loans. *See* lending

local development associations, 425*t*

local organizations, 425*t*

long-term external debt, 91b

long-term investment, 181–88

Lorenz curve, 325, 469–70

Lovejoy, Thomas, 98b

Lucas, Robert, 11

Lyonaise des Eaux, 272

macroeconomic balance, 21–22

macroeconomic policy trilemma, 120–21, 121b

Madueno, Manuel Molla, 3

Malaya, 42, 43*t*

Malaysia, 199

Manaus free trade zone, 274–75

Manchuria. *See* China

mandamiento, 44, 470

Mandarin International maquiladora factory, 3–4

Manos del Uruguay, 340

Manufacturers Hanover, 90–91, 92*t*

manufacturing, flexible, 70

Maple Gas Corp., 186b–188b

Maquila program, 185b

maquila sector (Nicaragua), 275–76

maquiladoras, 3–4, 230

Margen Arteobjeto, 264b–265b

market(s), 177–79

absorptive capacity of, 177–79

capitalization of, 178–79, 179*t*

characteristics of, 177–79

and debt crisis, 94–97

in educational reform, 386–87

effective, 148b

failure of, 56, 470

for government services, 144

incomplete, 295, 468

input, 263–70

labor, 277–78

political, 144

in poverty reduction, 336–41

return to, 173–209

secondary, 94

state and, 23–26

market-based incentives, 417–19, 470

marketing, social, 353–54b

MARNR. *See* Ministry of Environment and Natural Resources

Márquez, Gabriel García, 434

Márquez, Gustavo, 257b

Mastercard, 2

Maxus Energy Corporation, 160

Mayans, 35, 302b, 388

MBIs. *See* market-based incentives

MCC. *See* Mercosur Commerce Commission

MCI, 162

MECE program, 388

Meetings of Ministers of Trade, 245*t*

megacities, 406

Meier, Gerald M., 13b

Mendes, Francisco "Chico" Alves, 416b–417b

merchandise exports, 37–38, 39*f*

Mercosur. *See* South American Common Market

Mercosur Commerce Commission (MCC), 237

merit good, 386

Merrill Lynch, 161

MEXFAM. *See* Fundación Mexicana para la Planeación Familiar

Mexican peso crisis, 130*f,* 192–97, 228, 438

summary, 205

tequila effect of, 194–95, 195*f,* 202

Mexican Revolutionary Party (PRI), 193–94, 298

Mexicanization, 185b

Mexico

agriculture, *283, 285*–86, 288–92, 289*t*–292*t*, 306

automobile industry, 68, 70–73
balance of goods, 242t
Brady deals, 102, 104t
capital flight from, 89, 89t
carbon dioxide emissions, 7
Chile-Mexico Free Trade Agreement, 234t
communications, 7, 9t, 317–20, 321t
Costa Rica-Mexico Free Trade Agreement, 235t
current account balance, 215, 215t
current account deficit, 193, 194f, 194–95, 195f
debt, 84–86, 85t
debt crisis, 90–91, 102, 103b, 190
demand-driven rural investment funds, 305
development, 19, 20t, 84–86, 85t
education, 376, 377t, 383
education spending, 331, 332t, 377
educational reform, 382b, 384
ejidos, 44, 298, 308n7, 465
energy consumption, 409–10, 410t
environmental policy, 420
exchange rate, 87b–88b, 87t, 194–95, 195f, 224, 224t
exports, 218t, 218–19, 219t, 221, 223t, 242t, 283
fertilizer consumption, 415, 417t
fiscal surplus/deficit, 114t, 114–15
foreign investment, 42–44, 43t, 62, 62t, 181, 182t, 185b
foreign production, 183–85
forest change, 414, 415t
GDP per capita, 64, 66t
geographic distribution of exports, 38, 40t
grade repetition, 378, 378t
growth rates, 7, 30, 31t
health, 353, 355–56, 356t
health care reform, 368b–369b
health care spending, 331, 332t, 367t
high school education, 390, 390t
housing, 316–17, 317t
human poverty index, 315
imports, 71, 218t, 218–19, 219t, 242t
income distribution, 325–26, 327t
industrial competitiveness, 276–77
inflation, 112, 112t, 129f, 131–32
informal sector size, 337, 337t
infrastructure, 271
labor management relations, 256b–257b
labor policy, 253
land reform, 298–99
landless or nearly landless peasant families, 324, 324t
Law of New and Necessary Industries, 62
light manufacturing, 63
literacy, 374–75, 375t
living standards, 315–16, 316t
maquiladora program, 230
market capitalization, 178–79, 179t
Mexico City, 406
money supply growth rates, 114–15, 115t

National Commission of Normalization of Job Skills, 393
National Solidarity Program (PRONASOL), 394
North American Free Trade Agreement (NAFTA), 228–33
Pact for Economic Solidarity (El Pacto), 131, 133b–134b, 472
petroleum reserves and crude oil production, 411, 411t
poverty, 314, 314t, 320–24, 323t
privatization, 157–59, 158t, 160–61, 164
quality of life indicators, 7, 7t, 9–10
roads, 270
savings, 202
science and technology, 267
secondary market price spreads on debt, 94–96, 96t
social deficit, 135
social expenditures, 344, 345t
social indicators, 324t, 325
state spending, 343
tariffs, 59–60, 217t, 217–18
technology development, 269–70
technology generation, 266
trade role, 7
trade unions, 254–55
transnational corporations, 62–64
urban environmental problems, 408
urban unemployment, 259t, 259–60
urbanization, 7
U.S. oil imports from, 241, 243t
U.S. trade, 231t, 231–32
wages, 97, 102f, 261–62, 262t
Mexico Declaration, 384
Mexico-Central America Free Trade Agreement, 235t
Meza, Jorge, 186b
microcredit, 340–41, 470
microenterprise, 336, 338–40
microlending, 339b–340b
Microsoft, 393
Middle East, 240f, 240–41, 254
minifundia, 36, 470
mining, 41, 44–45, 414
    Carajas project, 422
    development policies, 417–19, 418t
ministerials, 242–44, 245t
Ministry of Health (MOH), 363–64
Mobil Oil, 186b
MOH. See Ministry of Health
monetarist theory of inflation, 113–18
    early applications, 126–28
    summary, 136
monetary autonomy, domestic, 121b
monetary correction, 119
monetary policy, 65b
    effects on management and conservation of forest resources, 417–19, 418t
    passive, 61–64

money
  "hot," 178
  short-term, 189
  velocity of, 119–20, 475
money supply growth, 114–15, 115*t*
Monserrat, 236*t*
Montreal Protocol, 423
moratorium, 91b
Morgan Guarantee, 90–91, 92*t*
Morris, Cynthia Taft, 18b, 24
mortality, 354–55, 355*t*
Movimento Sem Terra (MST), 289, 325
multilateral agencies, 425*t*–426*t*. *See also spe-*
    cific agencies
Multilateral Investment Fund, 180b, 225b
multilateral organizations. *See also specific or-*
    ganizations
  global, 449–51
  regional, 448–49
multilateral support, 440–41
multinational activity, 61–64
multinational corporations. *See* transnational
    corporations
multinational organizations. *See also specific*
    organizations
  in Latin America, 181–82, 184*t*
  in Peru, 186b–188b
multinational production, 183b

NADBank (North American Development
    Bank), 233
NAFTA. *See* North American Free Trade Agree-
    ment
NAFTA production, 231
narcotics, illegal, 287
National Coffee Association (ANACAFE) (Gua-
    temala), 302b
National Council for Scientific and Technologi-
    cal Research (CONICIT), 269
National Councils for Sustainable Development,
    244
national interest rates, 114–15, 116*t*
National Workers Union (UNT), 255
national/regional organizations, 425*t*. *See also*
    specific organizations
Natura, 393
natural resources, 34–35
  debt-for-nature swaps, 97
  early characteristics, 46, 47*t*
  and growth patterns, 30–32, 33*t*
Nature Conservancy, 425*t*
Navarro, Juan, 2
needs, basic human, 15–16
neoclassical theory, 267
neoclassical tradition, 470
neoliberalism, 73–74, 338, 437–38
neostructuralists, 267–68, 338, 470–71
Nestlé, 184*t*
New Economic Policy (Bolivia), 128
NGOs. *See* nongovernmental organizations

Nicaragua
  agricultural policy, 297
  Agricultural Technology and Land Manage-
    ment Project (ATLMP), 304
  agriculture, 288–92, 289*t*–292*t*, 304
  Colombia-Central America Free Trade Agree-
    ment, 236*t*
  communications, 7, 9*t*, 317–20, 321*t*
  current account balance, 215, 215*t*
  education spending, 376–77
  educational performance index, 376, 377*t*
  energy consumption, 409–10, 410*t*
  exchange rate performance, 224, 224*t*
  exports, 37, 38*t*, 218*t*, 218–19, 219*t*, 221,
    223*t*
  fertilizer consumption, 415, 417*t*
  fiscal surplus/deficit, 114*t*, 114–15
  forest change in, 414, 415*t*
  GDP per capita, 64, 66*t*
  grade repetition, 378, 378*t*
  health statistics, 355, 356*t*
  housing, 316–17, 317*t*
  human poverty index, 315
  imports, 218*t*, 218–19, 219*t*
  income distribution, 325–26, 327*t*
  inflation, 112, 112*t*
  interest rates, 114–15, 116*t*
  land reform, 298
  Las Mercedes, 275–76
  literacy, 374–75, 375*t*
  living standards, 315–16, 316*t*
  maquila sector, 275–76
  Mexico-Central America Free Trade Agree-
    ment, 235*t*
  money supply growth rates, 114–15, 115*t*
  poverty, 293, 320–21
  privatization, 157–59, 158*t*
  quality of life indicators, 7, 7*t*, 9–10
  social expenditures, 344, 345*t*
  tariffs, 217*t*, 217–18
  urban unemployment, 259*t*, 259–60
  Venezuela-Central America Free Trade
    Agreement, 236*t*
  Zona Franca Index, 275
NIE. *See* new institutional economics
Nigeria, 241, 242*t*–243*t*
Nike, 2, 181
nongovernmental organizations, 451–53. *See*
    also specific organizations
  international, 425*t*
nontraditional export promotion, 471
nontraditional exports, *211,* 285, *294*
North America, *xvii. See also specific countries*
  exports, imports, and balance of goods, 242*t*
  per capita income, 37
  petroleum reserves and crude oil production,
    411, 411*t*
  trade union membership, 254
North American Development Bank (NAD-
    Bank), 233
North American Free Trade Agreement

(NAFTA), 73, 185b, 192, 221, 228–33, 234t
Border Environment Cooperation Commission, 232
Commission for Environmenal Cooperation (CEC), 232–33
definition of, 470
double taxation treaty, 341
exports from, 238, 238t
as iterative process, 233
Transitional Adjustment Assistance, 231
North-South trade, 424b
Nueva Ocotepeque Agreement, 236t
Nurske, Ragnar, 17b

OAS. *See* Organization of American States
Obras Sanitarias de la Nación (OSN), 272
Oceania, 31–32b
OECD countries, 151–52, 152f, 265–66, 267t
oil
    crude, 411, 411t
    spills in Ecuador, 411–12, 413b
    U.S. imports from Latin America, 241, 243t
Olivera-Tanzi effect, 116, 471
OPEC countries, 242t
open regionalism, 228, 233, 471
Organic Crop Inspectors Association, 286
organic farming, 286–87
Organization of American States (OAS), 244, 449
organizations. *See also specific organizations*
    global multilateral, 449–51
    grassroots, 425t
    local, 425t
    multinational, 181–82, 184t, 186b–188b
    national/regional, 425t
    quasi-governmental, 451
    regional multilateral, 448–49
    U.S.-based governmental, 451
Oriente rain forest, 413b
ORIT. *See* Inter-American Regional Workers Organization
orthodox paradigm, 13b
orthodox theory of inflation, 471
OSN. *See* Obras Sanitarias de la Nacion
output markets, 273
outputs, 30–34
overvalued exchange rates, 60, 471–72
Oxfam, 376, 377t

P900 program, 388
Pacific countries, 7, 9t
Pacific Rim Countries, 242t
Pact for Economic Solidarity *(El Pacto)* (Mexico), 131, 133b–134b, 472
PAHO. *See* Pan American Health Organization
Pan American Health Organization (PAHO), 244, 358–59, 361, 449
Panama
    agriculture, 288–92, 289t–292t
    Brady deal, 102, 104t

Colombia-Central America Free Trade Agreement, 236t
communications, 7, 9t, 317–20, 321t
current account balance, 215, 215t
debt crisis, 105
educational performance index, 376, 377t
exports, 37, 38t, 218t, 218–19, 219t, 221, 223t
fiscal surplus/deficit, 114t, 114–15
forest change in, 414, 415t
GDP per capita, 64, 66t
housing, 316–17, 317t
human poverty index, 315
imports, 218t, 218–19, 219t
income distribution, 325–26, 327t
inflation, 112, 112t
informal sector, 260, 337, 337t
labor market reform, 253
literacy, 374–75, 375t
living standards, 315–16, 316t
market capitalization, 178–79, 179t
money supply growth rates, 114–15, 115t
poverty, 261, 314, 314t
privatization, 157–59, 158t
quality of life indicators, 7, 7t, 9–10
social expenditures, 344, 345t
tariffs, 217t, 217–18
urban unemployment, 259t, 259–60
Venezuela-Central America Free Trade Agreement, 236t
Paraguay
    agriculture, 288–92, 289t–292t
    communications, 7, 9t, 317–20, 321t
    current account balance, 215, 215t
    educational performance index, 376, 377t
    energy consumption, 409–10, 410t
    exchange rate performance, 224, 224t
    exports, 218t, 218–19, 219t, 221, 223t, 229
    fiscal surplus/deficit, 114t, 114–15
    forest change in, 414, 415t
    GDP per capita, 64, 66t
    health care system, 363
    health statistics, 355, 356t
    housing, 316–17, 317t
    human poverty index, 315
    imports, 218t, 218–19, 219t
    inflation, 112, 112t
    informal sector, 260, 337, 337t
    interest rates, 114–15, 116t
    literacy, 374–75, 375t
    living standards, 315–16, 316t
    money supply growth rates, 114–15, 115t
    poverty, 261, 314, 314t
    privatization, 157–59, 158t
    quality of life indicators, 7, 7t, 9–10
    social expenditures, 344, 345t
    social indicators, 324t, 325
    tariffs, 217t, 217–18
    transnational corporations, 64
    Treaty of Asunción, 237

urban unemployment, 259t, 259–60
wage differentials, 261–62, 262t
Parmalat, 2
partnerships
    promoting, 23–26
    public-private, 393–94
PAS. *See* Programa de Agentes de Saúde
peasant families, 324t, 324–25
PEMEX, 420
PepsiCo., 184t
Pérez, Carlos Andrés, 163b
Perón, Eva, 83
Perón, Juan, 56, 83
Peru, *3*
    agriculture, 288–92, 289t–292t
    Aguaytía project, 186b–188b
    Amazon holdings, 431n38
    Andean Trade Preference Act, 234t
    Brady deal, 102, 104t
    Chilean investment in, 198
    coca production, 287–88
    communications, 7, 9t, 317–20, 321t
    current account balance, 215, 215t
    debt crisis, 94
    education spending growth, 331, 332t
    educational performance index, 376, 377t
    exchange rate performance, 224, 224t
    exports, 37–38, 39f, 218t, 218–19, 219t, 221, 223t
    fertilizer consumption, 415, 417t
    fiscal surplus/deficit, 114t, 114–15
    foreign investment, 42–44, 43t, 62, 62t, 186b–188b
    forest change in, 414, 415t
    GDP per capita, 64, 66t
    geographic distribution of exports, 38, 40t
    grade repetition, 378, 378t
    growth rates, 30, 31t
    guano economy, 40
    health spending growth, 331, 332t
    health statistics, 355–56, 356t
    housing, 316–17, 317t
    human poverty index, 315
    imports, 218t, 218–19, 219t
    income distribution, 325–26, 327t
    inflation, 112, 112t
    informal sector size, 337, 337t
    infrastructure, 234
    interest rates, 114–15, 116t
    labor market reform, 253
    labor policy, 253
    land reform, 298–99
    landless or nearly landless peasant families, 324, 324t
    literacy, 374–75, 375t
    living standards, 315–16, 316t
    market capitalization, 178–79, 179t
    Mercosur, 234
    money supply growth rates, 114–15, 115t
    multinational involvement in, 186b–188b
    petroleum reserves and crude oil production, 411, 411t
    poverty, 314, 314t, 320–24, 323t
    privatization, 157–59, 158t
    quality of life indicators, 7, 7t, 9–10
    secondary market price spreads on debt, 94–96, 96t
    social expenditures, 344, 345t
    social indicators, 324t, 325
    state spending, 343
    tariffs, 217t, 217–18
    urban environmental problems, 408
    urban unemployment, 259t, 259–60
    U.S. oil imports from, 241, 243t
    wages, 97, 102f
Peruvian Scientific Fund, 3
peso crisis, 130f, 192–97, 202, 205, 228, 438
pessimism
    excessive, 143
    export, 40, 466
petrochemicals, *51*
Petroecuador, 413b
petroleum reserves, 411, 411t
PHC. *See* primary health care
Philip Morris, 4
Philippines, 199
Philips Electronics, 274
Philips Morris Companies, 184t
Pinochet model, 25
planning model, 24, 472
Polanyi, Karl, 145
policy environment, 30–32, 33t
    early characteristics, 46, 47t
policy linkages, 417–19, 418t–419t
political change, 36–38
political economy, new, 147, 471
political market, 144
pollution
    safe minimum standard, 473
    urban, *401*
poor population, 320–21
    agents and victims of environmental destruction, 405–6
    enhancing assets of, 333–41
    involvement of, 335–36
    working, 261
population
    Amazonian, 413–14
    poor, 320–21
populism, economic, 57, 83, 464–65
Porfund, 340
portfolio bonds, 178
portfolio investors, 472
Portillo, Lopez, 103b
Portuguese, 35
poverty, *2*, 293, 311–49
    characteristics of, 320–21, 346–47
    cycles of, 434
    defining, 346
    and environmental destruction, 405–6
    and ethnicity, 321–24, 323t

extent of, 313, 313*t*
extreme, 466
and gender, 322b–323b
and growth, 346
human poverty index, 314–15
life of, 314–20
moderate, 470
population, 320–24
profile of, 312–20
trends in, 328–32
poverty gap, 314, 314*t*
poverty line, 312, 472
poverty programs, 341–42
poverty reduction
    addressing, 347
    areas for action, 333–41
    market in, 336–41
Prebisch, Raúl, 17b–18b, 52–53, 54b, 56, 67
Prebisch-Singer thesis, 17b–18b
preferential trade agreements, 472
preventive health, 362b
PRI (Mexican Revolutionary Party), 193–94,
    298
price stabilization, 111–39
    Austral plan, 128–29
    Bresser plan, 123–24
    Collor plan, 124
    convertibility plan, 129, 133b–134b
    Cruzado plan, 122–23, 133b–134b
    heterodox approaches to, 122–26
    lessons for, 131–32
    monetarist applications, 126–28
    price of, 135–36
    Real plan, 124–25, 133b–134b
    taxes and, 115–16
    variations of, 133b–134b
prices
    factor price equalization, 213
    secondary market spreads, 94–96, 96*t*
    sugar, 39–40
primary education, 394
primary health care, 359–61, 472
primary product exports, golden age of, 37, 467
Princeton University, 2
private capital flows, net, *177,* 177–78
privatization, 271–72
    banking sector, 162–65
    gains from, 165
    of Latin American countries, 157–59, 158*t*
    mechanics of, 155–57
    participation in, 157–59
    promise of, 154–55
    of public utilities, *141*
    record, 159–62
    of rural health services, 370b
    summary, 167–68
PRODEM. *See* Foundation for the Promotion
    and Development of Microenterprises
product exports, primary, 37, 467
production
    alternative, 286–87

changing patterns of, 273
    dualistic structure of, 285
    extralegal, 287–88
productivity, 272
    definition of, 472
    labor, 263–64, 469
    raising, 301–3
professional wages, 261–62, 262*t*
Programa de Agentes de Saúde (PAS), 362b
projects
    long-term lending for, 81, 82*t*
    mismatched returns, 82–83
PRONASOL, 343
property rights, insecure, 300, 468–69
Proposed American Declaration on the Rights
    of Indigenous Peoples, 244
protection
    effective rate of, 465
    protectionism
    as tool, 58–61
    tools of, 60b
provisioning, 94, 472
PTAs. *See* preferential trade agreements
public sector, *141,* 167
public works programs, 334
public-private partnerships, 393–94
Puerto Rico, 36
purchasing power parity, 472

quality of labor, 251–81
quality of life, 314–15
    indicators, 7, 7*t,* 9–10
quality primary education guarantee, 394
quasi-governmental organizations, 451
Quinto Declaration, 94–95b
quotas, 60b

racial compositions, 35, 36*t*
rain forest
    deforestation of, 412–15, 416b–417b
    extractive reserves, 416b
    oil spills in, 413b
Ranis, Gustav, 18b
real effective exchange rate of exports, index of,
    224, 224*t*
real exchange rate, Mexican, 194–95, 195*f*
real exchange rate indexes, 87b–88b, 87*t*
real interest rates, 83–84, 84*t*
Real plan, 124–25, 133b–134b, 238, 472
real wages, 97, 102*f*
recycling, *407*
regional balance of payments, 226, 226*t*
regional integration, 472–73
regional integration agreements, 233, 234*t*–236*t*
regional integration arrangements, 227
regional multilateral organizations, 448–49
regional organizations, 425*t*
regional stock markets, *173*
regional trading agreements, 239–40
regional trading arrangements, 226–28
regionalism, open, 228, 233, 471

relative returns, 176
Renault, 72
repartida, 34, 473
reserves, extractive, 416b
resource flows, net, 174–75, 175*f*
returned value, 473
returns
    mismatched projects and, 82–83
    relative, 176
RIAs. *See* regional integration arrangements
Ricardo, David, 212–13
Rio de Janeiro, 335–36, 406
Rio Declaration, 404
roads, *251,* 272
Robinson, Sherman, 18b
Rockefeller, David, 453
Roldán, Jorge, 180b–181b
Ronaldo, 2–3
Roosen, Gustavo, 164b
Rosenstein-Rodan, Paul, 10, 17b
Rostow, Walt W., 17b
Royal Dutch Shell, 184*t*
rules
    formal, 442
    informal, 442
rural agricultural production patterns, 284–88
rural development
    Bolivian electrification program, 426, 427*t*–428*t*
    in Guatemala, 302b
    strategic checklist for, 306b
rural health care, *351*
    private provision of services, 370b
rural incomes, 301–3
rural investment funds, demand-driven, 305, 464
Russia, 205–6, 242*t*
Russian ruble collapse, 200

Sábato, Jorge, 269
safe minimum standard, 404, 473
San Bartolo free trade zone, 274
San Marcos Free Trade Zone, 3–4
São Paulo, 406
Saudi Arabia, 241, 242*t*–243*t*
Save the Children/Bolivian mothercare, 358
school. *See* education
Schumpeter, Joseph, 11, 267–68
science and technology. *See also* technology
    gap, 267
    indicators, 265–66, 267*t*
Scotts Head Marine Reserve, 426
secondary market, 94, 473
    price spreads on Latin American debt, 94–96, 96*t*
Seers, Dudley, 12b–12b
segmented credit markets, 295–96, 473
seignorage, 114, 473
selectivity, effective, 343–44, 465
Sen, Amartya, 14b
Serinha, 335

service fees, 265b
settlement policies, 417–19, 418*t*
short-term money, 189
SIFs. *See* social investment funds
Singapore, 242*t*
single commodity exports, 37, 38*t,* 38–40
small business, 225b
    ground preparation for, 264b–265b
small loans, 339b–340b
Smith, Adam, 25
social agenda, 438
social deficit, 135–36, 311–49, 438–39
social expenditures, 343–44, 345*t*
social guardians, benevolent, 169n32
social indicators, 324*t,* 325
social investment funds, 333–35
    definition of, 473
    emergency, 128
    Solidarity and Social Investment Funds (FOSIS), 334–35
social marketing, 354b
    condom, 353
social policy, 335b
social relations, 35–36
Social Security Institutes (SSI) *(cajas de seguro social),* 363, 366, 372n18
SOEs. *See* state-owned enterprises
Solidarity and Social Investment Funds (FOSIS), 334–35
solidarity group concept, 339b
SOMISA, 157–59
Soros, George, 202
South Africa, 390, 390*t*
South America, *xvii, xviii. See also specific countries*
    exports, imports, and balance of goods, 242*t*
    petroleum reserves and crude oil production, 411, 411*t*
    trade union membership, 254
South American Common Market (Mercosur), 21, 73, 160, 226, 233–39, 470. *See also specific member countries*
    Common Market Group, 237
    exports from, 238, 238*t*
    Forum, 237
    Parliamentary Commission, 237
South Korea, 200
Southeast Asia, 151–52, 152*f,* 254
Southern Europe, 31–32b
sovereign default, 91b
Spain, 19, 20*t,* 160, 178–79, 179*t*
Spanish America, 35, 36*t*
Special Fiscal Benefits for Exports (BEFIEX) (Brazil), 66, 71
spending
    education, 331, 332*t,* 376–77
    expenditure switching, 466
    health, 331, 332*t,* 367*t*
    social expenditures, 343–44, 345*t*
    state, 342–43
    streamlining, 342–43

SSI. *See* Social Security Institutes
St. Kitts and Nevis, 236t
St. Lucia, 236t
St. Vincent and the Grenadines, 236t
stability, 22
stabilization, severe, 441
Standard Fruit, 288
standards
  of living, 335
  safe minimum, 404
state
  as benevolent social guardian, 169n32
  desirable and sustainable activity, 141–71
  in educational reform, 386–87
  and market, 23–26
  in poverty management, 341–42
  role of, 141–71, 343–44, 439–40
  shape of, 144–47
  size and structure of, 151–53
  theoretical approaches to activity, 147–51
  theoretical framework for intervention by, 167
state enterprises
  in Brazilian economy, 58, 59t
  reasons for, 58
  role of, 57–58
State National Development Bank (BNDES) (Brazil), 61, 161–62
state spending
  selectivity, 343–44
  streamlining, 342–43
  targeting, 342–43
Stiglitz, Joseph E., 14b, 145b
stock markets
  new entrepreneurs in, 180b–181b
  regional, *173*
Stolper-Samuelson effect, 213, 473
strategic diversification, 89
street families, 318b
Streeten, Paul, 13b
structural adjustment, 99
structural adjustment programs, 474
structural transformation, 442
structuralist school, 53–55, 74–75
structuralist theory of inflation, 136–38
structuralists, 55–57, 113–18, 474
subsidies, export, 60b
sugar prices, 39–40
Summit of the Americas, 241, 245t
  Declaration of Principles, 244, 455–59
  Second, 244, 245t
  Third, 245t
support organizations, grassroots, 425t
Suriname
  Amazon holdings, 431n38
  fiscal surplus/deficit, 114t, 114–15
  inflation, 112, 112t
  money supply growth, 114–15, 115t
  privatization, 157–59, 158t
sustainability, current account, 194
sustainable development, 402

definition of, 13b, 403–5, 474
  and gender, 322b–323b
  summary, 428–29
sustainable development agreements, 404–5
sustainable growth
  in agricultural sector, 293–301
  equitable, 283–310
  sustainable state activity, 141–71
Sweden, 390, 390t
Sweeney, John J., 256b
Switzerland, 266

Taiwan, 242t, 266
takeoff, 18b
targeted lending, 61–64
targeting, 342–43, 474
tariffs, 60b
  average, 217t, 217–18
  high, 58–61
taxes, 153–54
  double taxation treaty, 341
  price stabilization and, 115–16
  Tobin tax, 204
  value added tax, 153, 475
technical education, 268
technical wages, 261–62, 262t
Technit, 159
technological change, 11, 474
technology, 263–70
  Agricultural Technology and Land Management Project (ATLMP), 304
  development of, 269–70
  early characteristics, 46, 47t
  generation of, 266
  and growth patterns, 30–32, 33t
  improving, 251–81
  indicators, 265–66, 267t
  summary, 278
Telebrás, 162, 272
Telecom, 272
telecommunications, 271–72
Telecurso 2000, 395
Telefónica, 3, 162, 272
Telefónica de España, 184t
Teléfonos de México, 161
Telesp, 162
tequila effect, 194–95, 195f, 202
terms of trade
  declining, 54b, 464
terms of trade, declining, 40
tesobonos, 196, 474
Texaco, 413b
Thailand, 199, 390, 390t
theory of comparative advantage, 212–13, 474
theory of free trade, 247
theory of trade integration, 226–28
Third Cycle, 275
timing, 22
Tobin tax, 204
Tordesillas, treaty of, 35
Toshiba, 274

tourism, *421*
Toyota, 72
Toyotaism, 69
trade
    declining terms of, 40, 54b, 464
    free, 212–14, 246–47
    gains from, 215–16
    in greenhouse gases, 424b
    hemispheric agreements, 240–46
    imbalances, 226
    Latin American performance, 220*t*
    liberalization of, *211,* 273
    preferential agreements, 227, 472
    regional agreements, 239–40
    regional arrangements, 226–28
trade areas
    exports from, 238, 238*t*
trade creation, 239, 475
trade diversion, 239, 475
trade integration, 246
    categories of, 226
    theory of, 226–28
trade policy
    contemporary, 211–50
    effects on management and conservation of
        forest resources, 417–19, 418*t*
trade union membership, 254
transformation, structural, 442
transitional economies, 10
transnational corporations, 62, 181–88, 475. *See
    also specific corporations*
transnational enterprises. *See* transnational cor-
    porations
transport infrastructure policies, 417–19, 418*t*
Travelers Insurance, 2
Treaty of Asunción, 236
trilemma, 120–21, 121b
Trinidad and Tobago
    CARICOM-Colombia Free Trade Agreement,
        236*t*
    CARICOM-Venezuela Free Trade Agree-
        ment, 236*t*
    exports of basic products from, 221, 223*t*
    income distribution, 325–26, 327*t*
    petroleum reserves and crude oil production,
        411, 411*t*
    privatization, 157–59, 158*t*
tropical rain forests, 412–15
Truman, Harry S, 10

UNCAFESUR, 286
underdevelopment, 10, 12b–14b
UNDP. *See* United Nations Development Pro-
    gramme
unemployment, 257–60
    urban, 97, 101*f,* 259*t,* 259–60
unequal education, 377–82
UNESCO, 394
UNICEF, 359
Unilever, 184*t*
United Airlines, 286

United Brands, 288
United Fruit Company, 21, 38
United Kingdom
    balance of goods, 242*t*
    energy consumption, 409–10, 410*t*
    exports, 37–38, 39*f,* 242*t*
    imports, 38, 40*t,* 242*t*
    market capitalization, 178–79, 179*t*
United Nations, 270
United Nations Development Programme
    (UNDP), 364, 423, 450–51
United Nations Environmental Program
    (UNEP), 423
United States
    Andean Trade Preference Act, 234*t*
    1989 Brady plan, 101
    carbon dioxide emissions, 7
    communications indicators, 7, 9*t,* 10
    diseases of, 355, 357*t*
    economic development indicators, 19, 20*t*
    energy consumption, 409–10, 410*t*
    governmental organizations, 451
    growth rates, 7, 30, 31*t*
    health care spending, 367*t*
    health care system, 363
    high school education, 390, 390*t*
    imports from Latin America, 38, 40*t,* 241,
        242*t*
    income distribution, 325–26, 327*t*
    infrastructure deficit, 270–71, 271*t*
    interest rates, 83–84, 84*t*
    investment in Latin America, 42, 42*t*
    labor management relations, 256b–257b
    labor productivity, 263–65, 266*f*
    market capitalization, 178–79, 179*t*
    and Mexican peso crisis, 197
    Mexican trade, 231*t,* 231–32
    North American Free Trade Agreement
        (NAFTA), 228–33
    participation in privatization, 160
    performance of, 31–32b
    poverty and ethnicity, 323–24
    quality of life indicators, 7, 7*t,* 9–10
    racial composition, 35, 36*t*
    trade, 7, 240*f,* 240–41, 243*t*
    urbanization, 7, 406
United States Agency for International Develop-
    ment (USAID), 270, 286, 302b, 354b,
    364, 451
United States–Mexico Border XXI Program,
    232
Universal Access to Education for 2010, 395
UNT. *See* National Workers Union
urban environmental problems, 406–9
urban health care, *351*
urban pollution, *401*
urban unemployment, 97, 101*f,* 259*t,* 259–60
urbanization, 406
Uruguay
    agriculture, 288–92, 289*t*–292*t*
    Brady deal, 102, 104*t*

communication profile, 317–20, 321*t*
current account balance, 215, 215*t*
education spending, 377
educational performance index, 376, 377*t*
energy consumption, 409–10, 410*t*
exchange rate performance, 224, 224*t*
exports, 218*t*, 218–19, 219*t*, 221, 223*t*
fiscal surplus/deficit, 114*t*, 114–15
foreign investment, 42–44, 43*t*
GDP per capita, 64, 66*t*
geographic distribution of exports, 38, 40*t*
health care spending, 367*t*
health statistics, 355, 356*t*
housing, 316–17, 317*t*
human poverty index, 315
imports, 218*t*, 218–19, 219*t*
industrial competitiveness, 276–77
inflation, 112, 112*t*
informal sector size, 337, 337*t*
interest rates, 114–15, 116*t*
labor policy, 253
literacy, 374–75, 375*t*
living standards, 315–16, 316*t*
money supply growth rates, 114–15, 115*t*
poverty, 261, 314, 314*t*
privatization, 157–59, 158*t*
science and technology, 267
social expenditures, 344, 345*t*
social indicators, 324*t*, 325
tariffs, 59, 217*t*, 217–18
technology development, 269–70
Treaty of Asunción, 237
urban unemployment, 259*t*, 259–60
urbanization, 406
wage differentials, 261–62, 262*t*
U.S. Fisher-Price Corporation, 231
USAID. *See* United States Agency for International Development
USIMAS, 159

Valderrama, César, 186b–188b
value, returned, 473
value added tax, 153, 475
Vargas, Getulio, 56
VAT. *See* value added tax
velocity of money, 119–20, 475
Venezuela
   agriculture, 288–92, 289*t*–292*t*
   Amazon holdings, 431n38
   and Asian economic crisis, 200
   automobile industry, 73
   balance of goods, 242*t*
   Brady deal, 102, 104*t*
   capital flight from, 89, 89*t*
   CARICOM-Venezuela Free Trade Agreement, 236*t*
   Chile-Venezuela Free Trade Agreement, 234*t*
   Colombia-Venezuela Free Trade Agreement, 234*t*
   communications, 7, 9*t*, 10, 317–20, 321*t*
   current account balance, 215, 215*t*
   education, 376, 377*t*, 385
   education spending growth, 331, 332*t*
   energy consumption, 409–10, 410*t*
   exchange rate performance, 224, 224*t*
   exports, 37–38, 38*t*, 40*t*, 218*t*, 218–19, 219*t*, 221, 223*t*, 242*t*
   fiscal surplus/deficit, 114*t*, 114–15
   foreign investment, 42–44, 43*t*, 62, 62*t*, 181, 182*t*
   forest change in, 414, 415*t*
   GDP per capita, 64, 66*t*
   grade repetition, 378, 378*t*
   health spending, 331, 332*t*, 367*t*
   health statistics, 355, 356*t*
   housing, 316–17, 317*t*
   imports, 218*t*, 218–19, 219*t*, 242*t*
   income distribution, 325–26, 327*t*
   inflation, 112, 112*t*
   informal sector, 260, 337, 337*t*
   infrastructure, 271
   interest rates, 114–15, 116*t*
   labor management relations, 256b–257b
   literacy, 374–75, 375*t*
   living standards, 315–16, 316*t*
   microentrepreneurs, *336*
   mining, *41*
   Ministry of Environment and Natural Resources (MARNR), 425*t*
   money supply growth rates, 114–15, 115*t*
   petroleum reserves and crude oil production, 411, 411*t*
   poverty, 261, 314, 314*t*
   privatization, 157–59, 158*t*
   quality of life indicators, 7, 7*t*, 9–10
   real exchange rate indexes, 87b–88b, 87*t*
   science and technology, 267
   secondary market price spreads on debt, 94–96, 96*t*
   social expenditures, 344, 345*t*
   social indicators, 324*t*, 325
   tariffs, 217*t*, 217–18
   technology generation, 266
   trade union membership, 254
   urban unemployment, 259*t*, 259–60
   urbanization, 406
   U.S. oil imports from, 241, 243*t*
   wage differentials, 261–62, 262*t*
   during World War I, 45
Venezuela Free Trade Agreement, 235*t*
Venezuela-Central America Free Trade Agreement, 236*t*
vice ministerials, 242–44, 245*t*
vicious circles, 119–20
Viera, Judith Yanira, 3–4
villa miseria, 314
violence, 354
volante, 288–89
Volcker, Paul, 86–88
Volkswagen, 62, 72–73, 184*t*, 420
VW. *See* Volkswagen

wages, 258, 258*t*
 differentials, 261–62, 262*t*
 real, 97, 102*f*
Wal-Mart, 184*t*
Washington Office on Latin America (WOLA),
  452
water rights, 296
Webster's Dictionary, 12b
Wells Fargo, 90–91, 92*t*
Western Europe, 31–32b, 240–41, 243*t*
Western Hemisphere Free Trade Agreement,
  241
Western Hemisphere Trade Ministerials, 245*t*
Western Hemisphere Vice Ministerials, 245*t*
Wilber, Charles K., 12b
WOLA. *See* Washington Office on Latin
  America
women
 economic participation by, 322b–323b
 education of, 380b–382b
 health of, 356–59
 Inter-American Commission on Women, 245
 labor force participation by, 258
 in poverty, 322b–323b

Woodrow Wilson Center–The Americas Pro-
  gram, 452
working poor, 261
The World Bank. *See* International Bank or Re-
  construction and Development
World Commission on Environment and Devel-
  opment, 13b, 403
World Health Organization (WHO), 359, 361,
  467
World Share, 302b
World Trade Organization, 292
World War I, 45–46
World Wide Web, *3*

Xerox, 274

Yamey, B., 12b
Yanesha Forestry Cooperative, 425*t*
Yanesha Tribe, 425*t*
YPF, 160
Yupanquí, Domitila, 339b

Zedillo Ponce de Leon, Ernesto, 195–96
Zeroméxico, 161
Zona Franca Index, 275

About the Author

Patrice Franko is associate professor of economics and international studies at Colby College (Waterville, Maine) where she teaches international finance, Latin American economic policy, and microeconomics. She was a Pew Faculty Fellow in International Affairs and an American Association for the Advancement of Science Fellow in International Security Affairs. She has served as a consultant for the National Academy of Sciences, the Center for Hemispheric Studies at the National Defense University, and the Office of Inter-American Affairs, the Pentagon. She also holds a position as an adjunct fellow at the Center for Strategic and International Studies in Washington, D.C., in the Americas Program.

A specialist on economics and security relations in South America, she has authored *The Brazilian Defense Industry* (Westview Press, 1992) and numerous journal articles. She lives in Rome, Maine, with her husband, L. Sandy Maisel.